Cisco® Routers for IP Networking

Black Book

Innokenty Rudenko
and
Tsunami Computing

President and CEO
Keith Weiskamp

Publisher
Steve Sayre

Acquisitions Editor
Charlotte Carpentier

Marketing Specialist
Tracy Schofield

Project Editor
Dan Young

Technical Reviewer
David Stabenaw

Production Coordinator
Laura Wellander

Cover Designer
Jody Winkler

Layout Designer
April Nielsen

CD-ROM Developer
Michelle McConnell

The Coriolis Group, LLC
14455 N. Hayden Road
Suite 220
Scottsdale, Arizona 85260

(480) 483-0192
FAX (480) 483-0193
www.coriolis.com

Library of Congress Cataloging-in-Publication Data
Rudenko, Innokenty.
   Cisco routers for IP networking black book / by Innokenty Rudenko.
      p. cm.
   Includes index.
   ISBN 1-57610-610-1
   1. Routers (Computer networks)   2. TCP/IP (Computer network protocol)   3. Computer networks--Management.   I. Title.
TK5105.543. R83   2000
004.6'2--dc21   00-029055
                                                                      CIP

Printed in the United States of America
10 9 8 7 6 5 4 3 2 1

The Coriolis Group, LLC • 14455 North Hayden Road, Suite 220 • Scottsdale, Arizona 85260

Dear Reader:

Coriolis Technology Press was founded to create a very elite group of books: the ones you keep closest to your machine. Sure, everyone would like to have the Library of Congress at arm's reach, but in the real world, you have to choose the books you rely on every day *very* carefully.

To win a place for our books on that coveted shelf beside your PC, we guarantee several important qualities in every book we publish. These qualities are:

- *Technical accuracy*—It's no good if it doesn't work. Every Coriolis Technology Press book is reviewed by technical experts in the topic field, and is sent through several editing and proofreading passes in order to create the piece of work you now hold in your hands.

- *Innovative editorial design*—We've put years of research and refinement into the ways we present information in our books. Our books' editorial approach is uniquely designed to reflect the way people learn new technologies and search for solutions to technology problems.

- *Practical focus*—We put only pertinent information into our books and avoid any fluff. Every fact included between these two covers must serve the mission of the book as a whole.

- *Accessibility*—The information in a book is worthless unless you can find it quickly when you need it. We put a lot of effort into our indexes, and heavily cross-reference our chapters, to make it easy for you to move right to the information you need.

Here at The Coriolis Group we have been publishing and packaging books, technical journals, and training materials since 1989. We're programmers and authors ourselves, and we take an ongoing active role in defining what we publish and how we publish it. We have put a lot of thought into our books; please write to us at **ctp@coriolis.com** and let us know what you think. We hope that you're happy with the book in your hands, and that in the future, when you reach for software development and networking information, you'll turn to one of our books first.

Keith Weiskamp
President and CEO

Jeff Duntemann
VP and Editorial Director

Look for these related books from The Coriolis Group:

Cisco Routers for IP Routing
by Innokenty Rudenko

Cisco Switching Black Book
by Sean Odom and Hanson Nottingham

CCIE Routing and Switching Exam Cram
by Henry Benjamin and Tom Thomas

CCNA Routing and Switching Exam Cram, Second Edition
by Jason Waters

CCNP Routing Exam Cram
by Eric McMasters, Brian Morgan, and Mike Shroyer

Also recently published by Coriolis Technology Press:

Windows 2000 TCP/IP Black Book
by Ian McLean

XHMTL Black Book
by Steven Holzner

To Adelya and Steve

About the Author

Innokenty Rudenko has a Master's degree in Computer Science. He is a CCIE #3805 and MCSE. His primary area of specialization is computer networks based on Cisco routers and switches.

Tsunami Computing is a consulting company providing Fortune 500 companies with IT solutions ranging from Network Design and Implementation to Database and E-Commerce System Development. Tsunami Computing's list of satisfied customers includes Deutsche Bank, Chase Manhattan Bank, JP Morgan, Lazard Freres, Merrill Lynch, and ORACLE Corporation. Company's corporate Web site is **www.hugewave.com**.

Acknowledgments

There are many people whom I would like to thank for contributing to this book.

I would like to thank the Coriolis team, who made this book possible. Special thanks to Dan Young, my project editor, Tom Gillen, the copyeditor of the book. I would like to thank David Stabenaw, who was the technical reviewer for my book—he managed to catch some barely visible yet critical errors, discrepancies, and typos. Many thanks to Stephanie Wall, the acquisitions editor; Laura Wellander, the production coordinator; Bonnie Trenga, the proofreader; Tracy Schofield, the marketing specialist; Jody Winkler, the cover designer; Michelle McConnell, the CD-ROM developer; April Nielsen, the layout designer; and Janet Perlman, the indexer.

Special thanks to Boris Guzman, Alex Meved, Kris Acharya, Pat Coen, and Marina Oliynyk who made a few excellent reviews on the key parts of the book.

Many thanks to Alex Zinin for his absolutely invaluable input on many essential aspects of OSPF.

I would like to show my appreciation to Roger Hampar for the equipment that he courteously lent me; this equipment was necessary to conduct some important research, which was necessary to complete the book.

I would like to thank Stuart Paulsen, Ian Preston, Antoine Shagoury, Tony Coppola, Binoy Barman-Roy, Gary Esposito, Nelson Gyi, Nabeel Madry, Wentao Zhang, Tomas Lee, Andrew Chang, Howard Poznansky, Cornelius Hull, Anuj Kumar, George Young, Mike Andrascik, Ronnie Sun, Albert Mui, Julie Yip, Will Dutton, Bill Hammill, Dmitri Tcherevik, Sergey Ignatiev, Andrew Sveshnikoff, Valery Tsyplenkov, and all those I have missed in this list for their insight and inspiration.

In addition, I would like to express my gratitude to a person whom I unfortunately barely know but for whom I have a lot of professional and personal respect—Radia Perlman, for her excellent book *Interconnections*. This was the book that made me become seriously interested in networking and this is the book that I highly recommend to anyone who wants to achieve a clear and deep understanding of networking algorithms, concepts, and technologies.

And the last but not the least, I want to thank my dear wife Adelya, to whom I dedicate this book, for her love, support and patience with me while I was writing this book.

—*Innokenty Rudenko*

Contents at a Glance

Chapter 1   Internet Protocol (IP)   1

Chapter 2   Transparent and Source-Route Bridging   89

Chapter 3   Static Routing   179

Chapter 4   Routing Information Protocol (RIP)   213

Chapter 5   Interior Gateway Routing Protocol (IGRP)   315

Chapter 6   Enhanced Interior Gateway Routing Protocol (EIGRP)   357

Chapter 7   Open Shortest Path First (OSPF) Protocol   423

Chapter 8   Controlling Routing Information   535

Chapter 9   Special Cases of Routing   639

Appendix A   Connecting Two Cisco Routers Back-to-Back   711

Appendix B   Configuring Cisco Routers for Frame Relay Switching   715

Appendix C   Using RSH and RCP with Cisco Routers   721

Appendix D   Using **ping** with Timestamps   731

Appendix E   Performing Summarization in RIP Version 2 by Means of Prefix Lists   733

Appendix F   Configuring IS-IS   741

Table of Contents

Introduction xvii

Chapter 1
Internet Protocol (IP) 1

In Depth

The Need for a Communication Model   2
Multilayer Communication Model   5
OSI/RM   15
The Internet Communication Model   17
What Is the Maximum Size of a PDU?   19
The Internet Protocol Suite   20
The Internet Documentation   20
The Anatomy of Internet Protocol   22
IP Datagram Format   26
IP Addressing   34
Unicast IP Routing Model   46
Internet Control Message Protocol   61
Link Layer Addressing Considerations   65
Final Notes   67

Immediate Solutions

Configuring IP Addressing on an Interface   70
Configuring a Frame Relay Interface   70
Performing Frame Relay Configuration on an Interface   71
Performing Frame Relay Configuration on a Subinterface   73
Understanding and Configuring a Loopback Interface   76
Understanding and Configuring a Tunnel Interface   77
Configuring IP Unnumbered   79
Configuring and Understanding ProxyARP   80
Using Access Lists to Filter Traffic   81
Using Standard Access Lists   81
Using Extended Access Lists   84
Using Named Access Lists   87

Chapter 2
Transparent and Source-Route Bridging.. **89**

In Depth

The Concept of Bridging   90
Why Do We Discuss Bridging?   91
MAC Addresses   92
Transparent Bridging   94
Source-Route Bridging   112

Immediate Solutions

Configuring Transparent Bridging   126
  Using a Single Bridge Group on a Single Router   126
  Using Multiple Bridge Groups   129
  Configuring Mixed-Media Transparent Bridging   131
  Bridging over HDLC   132
  Bridging over Frame Relay   134
  Configuring CRB   137
  Configuring IRB   139
  Tuning the Spanning Tree Parameters   140
Configuring Source-Route Bridging   147
  Configuring Source-Route Bridging for Two Interfaces   147
  Configuring Source-Route Bridging Using a Virtual Ring   149
  Understanding the **multiring ip** Command   150
  Configuring RSRB   151
  Configuring Spanning Explorers   167
Configuring Source-Route Translational Bridging   176

Chapter 3
Static Routing.. **179**

In Depth

Immediate Solutions

Understanding the **ip routing** Command   181
Using Connected Interfaces to Perform Basic Routing   181
Understanding the Administrative Distance of Connected Routes   182
Configuring Basic Static Routing   183
Changing the Administrative Distances of Static Routes   186
Using an Output Interface Instead of a Next-Hop Router in Static Routes   191
Configuring Classless Routing   195
Understanding the Longest Match Concept   198
Configuring a Default Route   200
Configuring Individual Host Routes   202
Configuring Equal-Cost Load Balancing Using Static Routing   203
Configuring Unequal-Cost Load Balancing Using Static Routing   208

Chapter 4
Routing Information Protocol (RIP) 213

In Depth

Distance-Vector Algorithm   214
Routing Table Maintenance Rules Revisited   224
Classful and Classless Routing Protocols   225
Details of RIP   228

Immediate Solutions

Understanding the Output of the **show ip route** Command   238
Modifying the Network Prefix Format   240
Understanding Candidate Default Routes and Gateways of Last Resort   242
Performing Basic RIP Configuration   249
Understanding How RIP Processes Routing Updates   252
Understanding the Relation between the Routing Table Contents and RIP
   Routing Updates   257
Understanding RIP Auto-Summarization   259
Using Individual Host Addresses   261
Configuring RIP to Originate a Default Route   264
Understanding How RIP Handles Secondary IP Addresses   265
Understanding How RIP Handles IP Unnumbered   272
Making RIP Passive on an Interface   280
Using Unicast Routing Updates with RIP   282
Changing the Administrative Distance of RIP Routing Updates   287
Performing Equal-Cost Load Balancing with RIP   294
Changing RIP Metrics   297
Adjusting RIP Timers   299
Using RIP in the Presence of NBMA Networks   300
Configuring RIP Version 2   303
Disabling RIP Version 2 Auto-Summarization   305
Understanding How RIP Versions 1 and 2 Can Be Used Together   312

Chapter 5
Interior Gateway Routing Protocol (IGRP) 315

In Depth

IGRP   316

Immediate Solutions

Performing Basic IGRP Configuration   328
Understanding How IGRP Processes Routing Updates   331
Understanding How IGRP Handles Secondary IP Addresses   335
Understanding and Changing IGRP Metrics   341
Performing Equal- and Unequal-Cost Load Balancing with IGRP   344

Configuring IGRP to Originate a Default Route   349
Adjusting IGRP Timers   356
Modifying the IGRP Metric Weights   356

Chapter 6
Enhanced Interior Gateway Routing Protocol (EIGRP) 357

In Depth
Diffusing Update Algorithm (DUAL)   358
Protocol Overview   368
EIGRP Metrics   368
DUAL in IP EIGRP   369
EIGRP Transport Protocols and Their PDUs   369

Immediate Solutions
Performing Basic EIGRP Configuration   385
Understanding the **show ip eigrp topology** Command   391
Understanding the **show ip eigrp neighbors** Command   392
Understanding the Output of the **show ip eigrp interfaces** Command   393
Using the Extended **network** Command of IOS 12.0(X)T   394
Understanding Basic DUAL Operation   399
Understanding How EIGRP Handles Secondary IP Addresses   408
Disabling EIGRP on an Interface   412
Understanding How EIGRP Works across NBMA Networks   412
Configuring Route Summarization with EIGRP   416
Modifying the Active Time   422

Chapter 7
Open Shortest Path First (OSPF) Protocol 423

In Depth
How Deep Is This "In Depth" Section?   427
Dijkstra's Shortest-Path Algorithm   428
OSPF   431

Immediate Solutions
Performing Basic OSPF Configuration—Single Area   477
Using the **router-id** Command to Change the OSPF Router ID   483
Understanding the **show ip ospf interface** Command   484
Understanding the **show ip ospf neighbor** Command   485
Displaying the OSPF Link-State Database   486
Modifying OSPF Interface Costs   491
Using OSPF Router Priorities   492
Understanding How OSPF Handles IP Unnumbered   494
Understanding the **neighbor** Command   495

Performing Equal-Cost Load Balancing with OSPF   497
Configuring OSPF with Multiple Areas   497
Configuring OSPF to Originate the Default Gateway Route   506
Understanding the **show ip ospf border-routers** Command   507
Configuring OSPF Stub Areas   508
Understanding How OSPF Handles Secondary IP Addresses   510
Using Virtual Links to Connect Remote Areas   511
Using Virtual Links to Restore a Partitioned Backbone   517
Configuring OSPF over NBMA Networks   522
    Configuring OSPF over Fully Meshed NBMA Networks   523
    Configuring OSPF over Non-Fully Meshed NBMA Networks   526

Chapter 8
Controlling Routing Information 535

In Depth

Redistribution   536
Filtering Routing Information   553

Immediate Solutions

Understanding the Interoperation of Routing Protocols without Redistribution   556
Understanding and Using Redistribution of Routing Information   563
    Configuring Basic Redistribution   563
    Understanding Summarization when Redistributing into RIP and IGRP   568
    Understanding and Configuring Redistribution Metrics   572
    Using and Understanding One-Way Redistribution   573
    Understanding the Automatic Redistribution of Pseudo-Connected Routes into
      IGRP and RIP   578
    Understanding Redistribution into EIGRP   581
    Understanding and Using Redistribution between EIGRP and IGRP   586
    Understanding the Specifics of Redistribution into OSPF   591
Filtering Routing Information   607
    Filtering Routing Updates Using Access Lists   607
    Filtering Routing Updates Using Prefix Lists   612
    Filtering Routing Information during Redistribution   617
    Filtering Routing Information during Redistribution Using Route Maps   619
Understanding Routing Loops   623
    Understanding Routing Loops Emerging from a Single Redistribution Point   623
    Understanding Routing Loops Emerging from Multiple Redistribution Points   629
    Understanding Routing Loops Emerging from Redistribution and Disabled
      Split-Horizon Rule   633

Chapter 9
Special Cases of Routing **639**

In Depth

Policy-Based Routing   640
NAT   642
HSRP   645

Immediate Solutions

Configuring Policy-Based Routing   657
  Using Policy-Based Routing for Routing over a Dedicated Link   658
  Using Application-Sensitive Policy-Based Routing   664
  Using Policy-Based Routing in Migration Scenarios   667
Configuring NAT   672
  Configuring Static Translation of Inside IP Addresses   672
  Configuring Dynamic Translation of Inside IP Addresses   677
  Configuring NAT with Overloading Global Inside IP Addresses   687
  Configuring NAT to Translate between Overlapping Address Spaces   689
  Configuring NAT for TCP Load Balancing   692
Configuring HSRP   696
  Configuring Basic HSRP   696
  Using MHSRP for Load Balancing   702
  Using HSRP in Backup Scenarios   706

Appendix A
Connecting Two Cisco Routers Back-to-Back **711**

Appendix B
Configuring Cisco Routers for Frame Relay Switching **715**

AppendixC
Using RSH and RCP with Cisco Routers **721**

Appendix D
Using ping with Timestamps **731**

Appendix E
Performing Summarization in RIP Version 2 by Means of Prefix Lists **733**

Appendix F
Configuring IS-IS **741**

Glossary **759**

Index **765**

Introduction

Thank you for buying *Cisco Routers for IP Networking Black Book.*

Is This Book for You?

Cisco Routers For IP Networking was written with the intermediate or advanced user in mind. Among the topics that are covered, are:

- OSI/RM and Internet communication models.

- IP addressing, IP routing algorithms (classful and classless), and routing table maintenance rules, including the explanation of the use of metric, administrative distances, and load-balancing.

- The interoperation between IP with the Link layer technologies (which, in the OSI/RM terminology are called *Data Link layer* technologies).

- Static and connected routes.

- The distance-vector algorithm and two routing protocols based on it: IGRP and RIP, including RIP version 2.

- The diffusing update algorithm (DUAL) and EIGRP, the routing protocol based on DUAL.

- The paradigm of link-state routing protocols and the details of the most popular link-state routing protocol—OSPF. (One of the appendices also explains how to configure IS-IS; however, no deep explanation of IS-IS is provided.)

- Redistribution and filtering of routing information. The topics include access lists, prefix lists, and route-maps.

- Policy-based routing, network address translation (NAT), and HSRP.

How to Use This Book

The chapters in the book are tied to each other only loosely, so you can read most of them independently. When an explanation in some chapter requires understanding of something that was covered in another chapter, a reference is typically made to the exact section in the previous or following chapter.

I suggest that you read Chapter 1, especially the section regarding the IP routing algorithms and the rules for routing table maintenance. What I noticed is that this is often a poorly or incompletely understood subject. The consequences of not understanding the topics, however, can significantly impair the reader's ability to understand the other important routing concepts, which are largely based on these subjects. I hope I was able to present the IP routing algorithms and routing table maintenance rules in a compact yet understandable form. I also provide several examples that demonstrate how the algorithms work and how the rules apply.

The *Black Book* Philosophy

Written by experienced professionals, The Coriolis Group's *Black Books* provide immediate solutions to global programming and administrative challenges, helping you to complete specific tasks, especially those that are critical and not well documented in other books. The *Black Book*'s unique two-part chapter format—thorough technical overviews followed by practical immediate solutions—is structured to help you use your knowledge, solve problems, and quickly master complex technical issues to become an expert. By dividing complex topics into easily manageable components, our format helps you quickly find what you're looking for, and with the diagrams and configurations you need to make it happen.

I welcome your feedback on this book. You can either email The Coriolis Group at **ctp@coriolis.com** or email me directly at **irudenko@home.com**. I do want to hear your feedback, good or bad, and whatever else you want to write to me.

Chapter 1

Internet Protocol (IP)

If you need an immediate solution to:	See page:
Configuring IP Addressing on an Interface	70
Configuring a Frame Relay Interface	70
Understanding and Configuring a Loopback Interface	76
Understanding and Configuring a Tunnel Interface	77
Configuring IP Unnumbered	79
Configuring and Understanding ProxyARP	80
Using Access Lists to Filter Traffic	81

In Depth

The primary focus of this chapter is internet protocol (IP), which includes subjects such as the internet communication model, IP functions, the structure of IP packets, and so on.

If you are familiar with IP and related topics, you can use this chapter as a reference. However, you should read the sections "The Internet Documentation," "Terminology," "Final Notes," and "Listings" because they explain how the references are made, the terminology that is used throughout the book, the notation of router commands, and what to expect from the listings.

However familiar you are with IP, I also suggest you review the section Unicast "IP Routing Model" because it explains my understanding of how IP routing works. It may or may not coincide with yours; hence, it's important to find that out as soon as possible. After all, the book is about routers and routing.

The Need for a Communication Model

Let's ask ourselves a question: What do we expect from a network? The answer will probably be rather simple: We expect transparent communication among the devices connected to the network, where transparent means that no user intervention is required to establish and maintain communication. For example, in Figure 1.1, we would expect host H to communicate with server S using, let's say, Telnet or file transfer protocol (FTP) in such a way that the user does not notice the presence of the network (although it's obvious that the network is what makes the communication possible).

Let's now go a bit deeper and ask ourselves another question: How do we implement the network component of the hosts and the network so that it provides for a transparent communication on the user level? (By *network component*, we mean all network-related hardware and software.) This time, the answer may not be as simple.

One way to implement a network component is to make it a single-piece "thing." For example, we might come up with a piece of hardware—called a *network adapter*—that the application software (Telnet or FTP in our case) would have to use directly to pass the data via the network. For example, a Telnet client

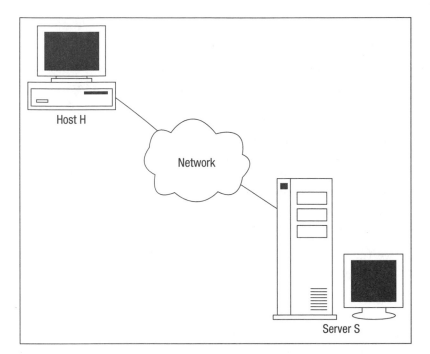

Figure 1.1   The network interconnects host H and server S.

application on host H would have to format the data that it intends to transmit to server S in the way that is acceptable for the network adapter; then it would need to submit the formatted data to the adapter and command it to send the data across the network. At the same time, the Telnet client application would somehow need to handle incoming data, which may arrive unsynchronized with the transmission of outgoing data. The task becomes even more complicated if the network consists of multiple devices. In this case, the Telnet client application would also need to figure out which next-hop device to use and how to let this device know what the final destination of the data is.

This approach, however, has a few shortcomings, one of the most obvious of which is that the design of the Telnet client application is too complex. The application needs to do a lot of tasks, such as formatting data, communicating with the network adapter, handling the asynchronous arrival of incoming data, and so on. A consequent shortcoming of this approach is that it's not very flexible. All these things would need to be repeated in every other network-related application.

In addition, we assumed that we were going to use Telnet or FTP, both well-known Internet "tools." If, however, the single-piece approach were the reality, most likely we would have numerous proprietary Telnets and FTPs that were created by different vendors and were completely incompatible with each other.

Although this list of shortcomings is by no means complete, it is already obvious that taking a single-piece approach would be a big mistake.

The problems we've just outlined fall into several categories that are more or less independent. For example, formatting data in order to make it "understandable" by different implementations by different vendors falls into a category of data-presentation issues. Establishing and maintaining the connection between the end devices—including retransmitting corrupted data, sorting out-of-sequence pieces of data, and so on—clearly belongs to a category that handles end-to-end communication. Determining which next-hop device must be used to forward the data towards the final destination falls into a category that comprises issues relating to the routing of data across networks. Communicating with the network hardware belongs to a category that covers hardware communication.

It's easy to notice that each category has a unique functionality. In other words, the issues handled by one category do not appear in any other category.

It's also easy to notice that, although each category is unique, the categories clearly depend on each other. For example, the category that handles end-to-end communication needs to pass the data between the ends. Of course, the ends are separated by the network, which can consist of multiple devices interconnected with multiple links. Therefore, the end-to-end communication category must rely on the functionality of the category that deals with routing data across the network.

However, if some category relies on the functionality of another category, the opposite is generally not true. In our example, the category that concerns routing data across the network does not depend in any way on the end-to-end communication category. This allows us to conclude that the categories exist in a certain order, or hierarchy. We can say that the higher-order categories rely on lower-order categories to deliver their functionalities.

In the networking world, the categories we've just discussed are known as *layers*. Now we can reiterate that layers represent a certain functionality that has to be delivered in order to perform communication of data across a network. The relative order in which the layers exist is called a *layer stack*. The nature of a stack dictates that a layer must rely on a *single* lower adjacent layer in order to deliver its own functionality.

Finally, the layers and their relative stacking order form what's known as a *multilayer communication model*, which we thoroughly examine in the next section.

A generic multilayer communication model has been taken as a foundation for several real-world communication models. In upcoming sections, we're going to study two of these real-world communication models: the open systems interconnection reference model (OSI/RM) and the internet communication model.

Multilayer Communication Model

The primary purpose of a communication model is to define a framework that helps create a communication system, which provides for the transparent exchange of user data between the devices connected to the network. I specifically use the term *user data* because, in addition to the user data, some auxiliary data can be exchanged between the devices constituting the network. However, a communication system exists to exchange only user data.

Obviously, the primary purpose of a *multilayer* communication model is the same. In addition, however, we believe that the *multilayer structure* of this model simplifies creating communication systems, making them more interoperable, manageable, and maintainable. In the "Conclusion" section later in this chapter, we'll consider what specific benefits a multilayer approach gives us. But first, we should comprehensively define a generic multilayer communication model and its operation.

We already defined a layer as a bearer of a certain functionality that must be delivered in the process of communicating data across a network. We also said that the layers exist in a stacking order; that is, each layer, except for the lowest one, depends on a single lower adjacent layer to deliver its own functionality. The lowest layer delivers its functionality within itself.

An implementation of a layer is called an *entity* of that layer. Entities belonging to the same layer and capable of communicating with each other are called *peer entities*. Notice that entities that cannot communicate with each other are not peers even if they reside on the same layer. When entities communicate, they do it by means of exchanging special messages called *packets*.

The set of rules that the peer entities use to exchange packets with each other is called a *protocol*. A protocol defines the following conceptual items:

- The formats of packets that the entities can exchange. The packets defined by a certain protocol are called *protocol data units (PDUs)*. (PDUs are distinguished from packets by an emphasis on their affiliation with a specific protocol.)
- The interpretation of information carried in the PDUs.
- The rules that control the exchange of PDUs.

It is convenient to think of a protocol as a language that the peer entities use to communicate with each other. The analogy is quite precise: PDUs are similar to words, which we interpret and understand. Also, when constructing sentences, we obey certain rules (grammar), and when speaking, we obey certain rules, such as expecting an answer when we ask a question.

For convenience, a PDU is said to be transmitted using a protocol when it is passed between peer entities that use this protocol. Likewise, a PDU is created by a protocol when it is created by an entity that uses the protocol.

The functionality of a layer to which peer entities belong translates into specific functions (or *services*) that peer entity perform. The transition from the functionality of a layer to peer entity services is easy if we think of the functionality of a layer as what we want the layer to do for us, and if we similarly think of a set of services as a way to make this happen. Likewise, peer entities are the implementation of a layer.

As the stacking order of a multilayer model suggests, peer entities communicate with each other using the services provided by the peer entities that belong to the lower adjacent layer. The interface through which the services are made available for the higher adjacent layer entities is called a *service(s) access point (SAP)*.

Where do peer entities reside? They reside on so-called *end systems*. From the perspective of the multilayer communication model, end systems are objects 1) that provide the environment for peer entities to operate in, and 2) between which communication on a given layer takes place.

NOTE: *The definition of an end system presented above is a bit "networkcentric." It may seem as if end systems exist only to provide an environment for network entities, but this is not always true. A typical example of end systems is hosts, such as workstations and servers; it is obvious that in this case, network entities exist only to provide hosts with the ability to interoperate. Nevertheless, for purely theoretical purposes (like discussing a generic multilayer communication model), this definition should suffice.*

Now, as we've defined all of the components of a generic multilayer communication model, let's have a look at Figure 1.2, which depicts the process of passing PDUs between two peer entities.

In Figure 1.2, we have two end systems, X and Y, which host an implementation of a multilayer communication model. Of all layers available in the model, only two adjacent layers are shown: *n* and *n-1*. In addition, Figure 1.2 shows two entities A belonging to layer *n* and two entities B belonging to layer *n-1*. Entities A use protocol A to communicate with each other. In a like manner, entities B use protocol B.

When entity A on end system X sends PDUs to its counterpart entity on end system Y, it uses the services provided by entity B of the lower adjacent layer. The horizontal arrow (dark dashes) shows the destination of the PDUs; the two white vertical arrows show how the PDUs are transmitted via the lower-layer entities.

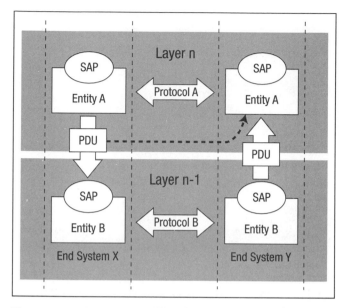

Figure 1.2   The PDUs destined for the counterpart layer *n* peer entity A are sent to
the SAP of layer *n-1* entity B.

I mentioned at the beginning of this section that multiple entities could belong to
the same layer and yet not be peers. This essentially means that several groups of
peer entities can belong to the same layer. To clarify what this means, let's have a
look at Figure 1.3.

In Figure 1.3, two entities A and C on end system X use a single SAP of entity B to
communicate with entities A and C, which reside on end systems Y and Z, respectively. Notice that, this time, the vertical arrows are shown double-headed to reflect that the respective SAP is used to both receive and send PDUs. (Previously,
the arrow was single-headed to show the direction in which the PDU was sent; it
did not mean that the SAP was only for sending.)

Figure 1.3 does not show, however, that entities A, B, and C use protocols A, B,
and C, respectively. What's interesting is that protocols A and C operate on layer
n, whereas protocol B operates on layer *n-1*. In other words, PDUs created by
different protocols are passed using a single protocol of the lower adjacent layer.

This process of a multilayer communication model—allowing PDUs that were
created by non-peer entities belonging to the same layer to be passed through a
single SAP of an entity belonging to the lower adjacent layer—is called *multiplexing*. Likewise, the reversed process—passing PDUs of different protocols to
the appropriate destination entities on the higher adjacent layer—is called
demultiplexing.

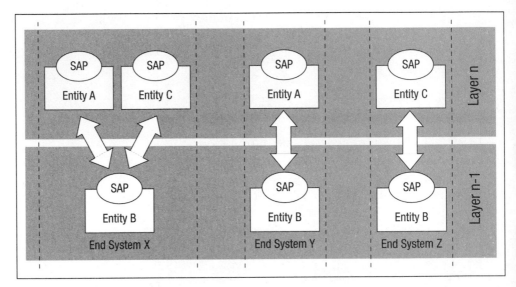

Figure 1.3 Two entities (A and C) on end system X use a single SAP of entity B to communicate with entity A on end system Y and entity C on end system Z.

Returning to Figure 1.2, we may ask how entities B deliver PDUs created by entities A, or, in general, how the lower adjacent layer entities deliver PDUs created by the higher adjacent layer entities. This question and the details behind multiplexing/demultiplexing bring us to the next section, which explains what's carried inside PDUs.

What's inside PDUs?

First, we should expect PDUs to carry the protocol-specific information that allows the protocol to operate. By definition, all packets created by peer entities are the PDUs of the respective protocol; thus, PDUs are the only way for peer entities to exchange protocol-specific information and to sustain the operation of the protocol itself.

Second, we should expect PDUs at some layer to carry the user data traffic. After all, this is the main purpose of communication, providing for the exchange of data between end systems.

Third, in cases in which the higher adjacent layer entities request transmission of their PDUs, we should expect PDUs exchanged by the lower adjacent layer entities to carry sufficient information to reproduce the higher-layer PDUs.

Those were our expectations. Let's now consider how a multilayer communication model addresses these expectations.

A PDU in the scope of a multilayer communication model consists of two parts: the *header*, which conveys the protocol-specific information, and the *payload*, an optional part that carries information that the protocol is requested to transmit between end systems.

Obviously, the presence of a header in a PDU addresses our first expectation—exchanging protocol-specific information.

A protocol is requested to transmit information between end systems in two cases. First, a user application seeking to transmit its data makes a direct call to the SAP of an entity utilizing the protocol. In this case, the user data is included and carried in the payload part of PDUs (satisfying our second expectation). Second, a higher adjacent layer protocol requests the lower adjacent layer protocol to transmit its PDUs. This is performed by including the whole higher-layer PDU into the payload part of a lower-layer PDU, which is an intrinsic feature of a multilayer communication model and is called *encapsulation*. The higher-layer PDU is said to be *encapsulated* into the lower-layer PDU. Once the encapsulated PDU arrives at its destination end system, it is extracted and passed to the destination entity intact, which fulfills our third expectation.

Notice that emphasis was put on the fact that the encapsulated PDU arrives at *its* destination end system. This implies that the lower-layer protocol can have a different perception of what an end system is. To better understand what this means, let's have a look at Figure 1.4.

Figure 1.4 shows three end systems (X, Y, and Z), three layers (*n*, *n-1*, and *n-2*), and four protocols (A, B, C, and D) with corresponding entities. Protocol A operates on layer *n*, protocol B operates on layer *n-1*, and protocols C and D operate on layer *n-2*. End systems X and Z have all three layers present; however, end system Y has only two (*n-1* and *n-2*). On layer *n*, end systems X and Z have a single entity A. On layer *n-1*, all three end systems have a single entity B. But layer *n-2* is represented differently on all three end systems. End system X has entity C, end system Y has two entities C and D, and end system Z has entity D.

Suppose entity A on end system X needs to communicate with its peer on end system Z. To do that, it creates a PDU (let's call it PDU_A) and requests underlying entity B to pass PDU_A to end system Z. Entity B encapsulates PDU_A into its own PDU (PDU_B), and now it should pass PDU_B to entity C for further delivery. Somehow, entity B is aware that end system Z does not have the corresponding entity C. Instead, end system Z has only entity D (which obviously uses protocol D), which entity C on end system X cannot understand. Nevertheless, entity B knows that there is end system Y, which has both entity C and entity D and hence can be used to make a transition to end system Z. Thus, entity B passes PDU_B to entity C

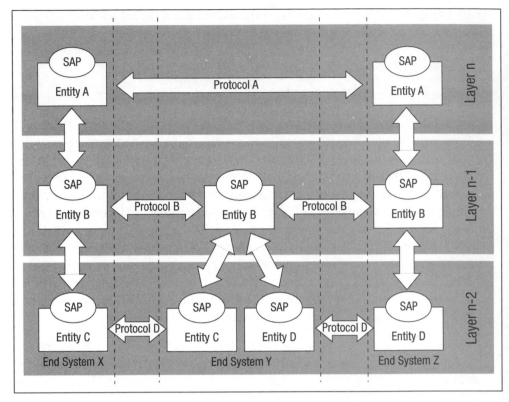

Figure 1.4   The end systems of layer *n* are different from the end systems of layer *n-1*.

and instructs it to send PDU_B to end system Y. Entity C encapsulates PDU_B into PDU_C and, using the underlying layers (if any), transmits PDU_C to end system Y. At end system Y, PDU_B is extracted from PDU_C and passed to entity B. Entity B at end system Y, upon receipt of PDU_B, passes it down to entity D, which encapsulates it into PDU_D and transmits it to end system Z, where it gets delivered to entity A.

Notice that, in the process described, end system Y is not an end system from entity A's perspective (entity A is not implemented on end system Y). Nevertheless, entity B not only perceives end system Y as an end system, but also uses it as an intermediate stop when serving entity A's request to perform a transmission of a PDU to end system Z.

In the course of the above explanation, I mentioned that "*somehow*, entity B is aware that end system Z does not have the corresponding entity C." The obvious question is how "somehow"? Interestingly enough, this question is not answered within the scope of a generic multilayer communication model. Instead, this question must be answered when we implement the corresponding entities, in our case entities B. For example, the protocol used by entities B may include functionality necessary to make entities B aware of such obstacles.

Getting back to the concept of encapsulation, let's look at Figure 1.5., which demonstrates the way the lower-layer header is attached to an encapsulated PDU.

To finalize our overview of generic multilayer communication models, we need to examine how multiplexing and demultiplexing work. Multiplexing seems to be easy: Higher-layer entities can be easily made to know which lower-layer entities are available for transmitting their PDUs and how to access the lower-layer entities' SAPs. After all, they all reside on the same end system. Demultiplexing, though, presents a problem. An ambiguity arises when a PDU is to be passed to a layer with multiple nonpeer entities. Let's use Figure 1.3 as an example. If entity C residing on end system Z decides to send a PDU to its counterpart on end system X, it passes it to underlying entity B. Entity B encapsulates this PDU in its own PDU and, using underlying layers (if any), gets it delivered to its counterpart entity B at end system X. When entity B at end system X extracts the original PDU, it will somehow need to guess that the PDU is destined for entity C and not for entity A.

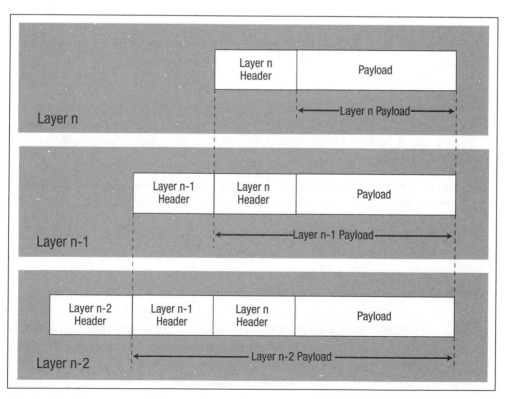

Figure 1.5   The process of encapsulating higher-layer PDUs into lower-layer PDUs.

Therefore, the question is: How does the entity on the lower layer choose the correct destination entity on the upper adjacent layer? Obviously, it can't look into the content of the payload in an attempt to determine its destination, because the payload carries a PDU of another protocol, and the information contained in that PDU can be interpreted by only the entities that use this protocol. The only other place left is the header. The content of the header is under full control of the lower-layer entity and thus can be used to "label" the destination of the payload. And this is indeed how demultiplexing is performed in a multilayer communication model.

The label carried in the header of a PDU that signifies the destination of the payload is called the *demultiplexing key*.

Identification

So far, we have assumed that entities on all layers know how to identify their destination peers when making PDU transmission requests. We have also discussed how the demultiplexing key helps identify the destination entity when multiple entities exist on the higher adjacent layer. This, however, does not yet answer the question about how to identify the end system on which the destination entities run.

The concept of end-system identification is otherwise known as *addressing*. An ID of an end system is called an *address*. I will refer to the set of rules that govern how addresses are represented and administered as the *addressing scheme*.

Although the existence of addressing clearly stems from the nature of a multilayer communication model, addressing itself does not belong to a multilayer communication model. Why addressing is indeed a difficult concept to embed into a multilayer communication model becomes clear from the following problems :

- Should there be a separate addressing scheme on each layer, or must all layers adhere to a single addressing scheme? A unified addressing scheme for all layers leads to a major inflexibility of the model. On the other hand, too big of a diversity leads to a high degree of inconsistancy between the entities of different layers, which in turn, may become a major headache in making the entities work together.

- If each layer implements its own addressing scheme, then how are these schemes mapped onto each other when entities make communication requests to the lower-layer entities? The higher-layer entity obviously can't use the destination address defined on its layer to make a request because the lower- layer entity won't understand this address as it belongs to a different layer. Likewise, the higher-layer entity can't use the lower-layer destination address it doesn't know anything about it. In addition, the latter becomes even a bigger problem because, as we know, the destination end system may differ on the lower layer.

- A single scheme for the whole layer causes inflexibility in terms of protocol design—different protocols are forced to use the same addressing scheme. Should there be a separate identification scheme for each protocol?

- Should the demultiplexing key be considered a part of the end-system identification or not?

In reality, addressing is made a part of individual protocols. As we just saw, making the concept of addressing a part of a communication model, whether generic or particular, would bring havoc in the clear concept of multilayer communication.

A Generic Multilayer Communication Model Finalized

A few open issues must be clarified before we conclude the discussion of a generic multilayer communication model.

A generic multilayer communication model does not prescribe how many layers there must be. Depending on the circumstances, different multilayer communication models can have a different number of layers. Nevertheless, there is always a topmost layer, which is usually the only layer that can accept user data for transmission between end systems.

A generic multilayer communication model does not require peer entities to reside on different end systems. Two or more peer entities can reside on a single end system and communicate. It is unclear, however, how deep down into the layer stack the PDUs exchanged by these peer entities should travel. This issue is left up to individual multilayer communication models.

The description of a generic multilayer communication model does not explicitly indicate that end systems are necessarily interconnected via a communication network in the usual understanding of this term. This flexibility of a generic communication system allows building communication systems that do not use a network as a means to communicate. The discussion of these systems, however, is beyond the scope of this book.

Conclusion

The beauty of the theory on which a generic multilayer communication model is based would be useless and meaningless unless the model and its components described real network elements and their interoperation. Fortunately, the mapping between the generic components and real-world network elements is surprisingly simple.

An end system is essentially a network node, of which there are two types: *end nodes* and *intermediate nodes*. Examples of end nodes are workstations and servers; examples of intermediate nodes are bridges and routers.An entity is a hardware or software module such as a network interface card (NIC), a NIC driver, a protocol module, and so on.

It was mentioned that the payload is an optional part of a PDU. In other words, peer entities can exchange PDUs that do not carry any payload. Those PDUs can serve some protocol-specific purposes, such as opening a connection, closing one, synchronization, and so on. What's interesting though is that entities aren't required to provide transmission services for entities of the upper adjacent layers. Obviously, if there is an upper adjacent layer, there must be at least one entity on the lower adjacent layer that serves the transmission requests of the upper-layer entities. However, there still can be entities on the lower layer that do not serve the transmission requests.

The entities that do not provide transmission services for entities of the upper adjacent layers perform auxiliary functions associated with the management and maintenance of end systems. Examples of such entities are routing protocol modules and address resolution protocol modules.

Let's now review the benefits that the multilayer approach gives us.

Interoperability

The central and most important concept of a multilayer communication model is that of a protocol, the set of rules that control the way peer entities—software and hardware network modules—operate. Therefore, a well-defined protocol achieves interoperability of the modules. Protocol specifications often become standards, which guarantees the highest level of interoperability.

Standard-based software and hardware manufactured by different vendors can seamlessly interoperate, thereby allowing the user to choose the best components.

Clear Concept

A multilayer communication model presents a clear concept of a network communication operation. Each layer has a unique functionality that is essential for the network to operate. The functions of modules are not difficult to define, because they have to sustain the functionality of the layer to which the modules belong. In addition, the functionality of a layer also limits the number of functions each module performs, thereby simplifying development of the modules.

Modularity

Modularity also facilitates the development of network components. Because each module operates independently, it can be optimized to perform its functions without compromising the integrity of the whole communication system.

Flexibility

Multiple modules can use the delivery service of a single lower-layer module, thereby providing flexibility in terms of hosting multiple communication systems within a single end system. Examples are a server that runs a Web and email servers, and a multiprotocol router that routes multiple protocols using the same network interfaces.

Another degree of flexibility is achieved by allowing a single module to use the delivery services of multiple lower-layer modules. Examples are a Lotus Notes server that uses Transmission Control Protocol (TCP) and Internetwork packet Exchange (IPX) for communication with the clients, a file server that has multiple NICs, and a router that uses multiple network interfaces to route upper-layer traffic.

OSI/RM

OSI/RM is a real-world multilayer communication model. It is probably the most well-known multilayer communication model and, as such, is definitely worth our attention. In addition, OSI/RM provides rather comprehensive coverage of networking technology in the form of the layer functionalities.

Nevertheless, we won't delve too deeply into OSI/RM because IP and related protocols are not based on it. Instead, IP and related protocols are based on an alternative model, the internet communication model, which we'll consider in upcoming sections. However, we will need to know something about OSI/RM for Chapter 2. We can't rely on the internet communication model because bridging (the subject of Chapter 2) is based on technologies that lie beyond the scope of Internet development activities; hence, those technologies are not sufficiently addressed in the internet communication model. On the contrary, the comprehensiveness of OSI/RM and further developments of the OSI/RM framework provide all necessary functionality to cover the issues related to bridging.

OSI/RM defines seven layers. The functional description of the OSI/RM layers is shown below, in ascending order.

Physical Layer

The functionality of the physical-layer covers transmission of bits of information across physical media. The physical-layer specifications define the pinouts and shapes of the connectors, encoding bits of information with electrical signals (or light in the case of fiberoptic media), bit-level synchronization, lengths of the cables, and so on. The physical layer is the only layer that does not add a header to the upper-layer PDUs.

Data Link Layer

The data link layer is responsible for transferring data across a link. A link is the physical medium and hardware necessary to send and receive data to and from the medium. The functions of the data link layer include error detection using checksums, hardware-level addressing in the cases when multiple network devices are attached to a single shared medium, and coordinating access to shared medium.

In addition to a header, the data link layer protocols often append a so-called *trailer* right after the payload, which carries an upper-layer PDU. PDUs on the data link layer are most often called *frames*, a term that will be used throughout this book to refer to data link layer PDUs.

Network Layer

The network layer is concerned primarily with forwarding data through the network, which can consist of multiple devices interconnected with various types of media. The main functions of the network layer include forwarding PDUs between adjacent network devices and maintaining destination-reachability information. These two functions are called *routing*. In addition, the secondary functions of the network layer include basic error and congestion control.

The network layer is the first layer that hides the diversity of various data link layer technologies and represents interdevice transmission services via a unified interface.

An important feature of the network layer is that end systems on that layer must be interconnected via a single physical medium. This type of communication is often referred to as *hop-to-hop*.

Transport Layer

The transport layer is responsible for reliable communication between network devices, congestion control, error detection, retransmission of lost or corrupted data, and the reordering of out-of-sequence data. An important feature of the transport layer is that it is the first layer of OSI/RM that provides *end-to-end* connectivity. This means that, regardless of how many intermediate nodes exist in the network, the communicating devices are always end systems from the perspective of the transport layer.

The transport layer defines two types of communication—*connectionless* and *connection-oriented*. Connectionless communication means that every PDU exchanged is sent independently and carries enough information to be delivered to the destination. Connection-oriented communication requires connection establishment and termination and does not assume that every PDU contains all essential delivery information. Instead, PDUs can carry only a connection identifier, which, in the case of an established connection, is sufficient to forward PDUs towards a destination.

Session Layer

The session layer's functionality comprises the management and control of data flow between communicating devices. For example, using the session layer functions, network-based applications can define synchronization points; request full or half duplex transmission; and start, interrupt, stop, and rerun network-related activities.

Presentation Layer

The presentation layer deals with data-representation issues, such as bit and byte order, compression, encryption, and the formats of network-related data structures.

Application Layer

The application layer incorporates the functionalities of all network-based applications. The application layer does not introduce any specific requirements.

The only assumption that exists with regard to the application layer is that the network-based applications can be standard or proprietary. Examples of standard applications are ISO network applications such as File Transfer Access and Management (FTAM) and Virtual Terminal (VT).

The Internet Communication Model

The term *internet communication model* is not used in the Internet documents, such as Requests for Comments (RFCs), which describe or refer to the communication model on which IP and related protocols are based. Instead, these documents simply state that the architecture of the Internet uses the layers described in the following sections as the foundation. Some authors use other terms, such as the TCP/IP model or Department of Defense (DoD) model, when they describe the model. There is a single RFC that comprehensively describes the philosophy of the model and functionality of each layer. This RFC is RFC 871, "A perspective on the ARPANET reference model." It is dated September 1982; back then, ARPANET still existed and was a primary test bed for the emerging Internet technologies. Since then, however, many things, including ARPANET, have changed, so now the term *ARPANET reference model* does not sound appropriate. For that reason, I decided I'd call the communication model the internet communication model because this term 1) points out the model's affiliation with the *internet* technologies, and 2) emphasizes the *communication* nature of the model.

The internet communication model is simple. It has only four layers, whose functional description is shown below in ascending order.

Link Layer

The link layer covers the transmission of information across individual links. The link layer is similar to the combined data link and physical layers of OSI/RM. The difference lies in that the technologies covered by the data link and physical layers of OSI/RM are out of the scope of the Internet standardization activities. Therefore, the Internet uses the existing data link and physical layer standards whenever possible. Consequently, the link layer of the internet communication model is not intended to replace the data link and physical layers of OSI/RM.

The link layer of the internet communication model is primarily concerned with the interaction between the internet protocol (the only protocol existing on the Internet layer that provides a PDU delivery service for the upper -layer protocols) and the technologies that fall into the link layer category.

When it comes to the technologies operating on the physical and data link layers of OSI/RM (such as bridging, Ethernet, and so forth), I will use the OSI/RM terminology because it was specifically developed to cover all these issues.

Internet Layer

The internet layer is responsible for routing data across the network. The end systems in the scope of the Internet layer must be directly reachable; in other words, the operation of the Internet layer protocol is hop-to-hop. (The Internet layer's functionality is very similar to that of the network layer of OSI/RM.)

The interesting feature of the Internet layer is that it has only one protocol, which provides a PDU delivery service to the transport layer. This is IP.

Transport Layer

The transport layer is responsible for reliable end-to-end transmission of data. The common functions of the transport layer protocols are error detection, retransmission of lost and corrupted data, reordering of out-of-sequence data chunks, and congestion control.

The transport layer is similar to the transport layer of OSI/RM. Like the transport layer of OSI/RM, the transport layer of the internet communication model defines connection-oriented and connectionless communication.

Currently, the transport layer has two protocols—TCP and User Datagram Protocol (UDP). TCP is a connection-oriented protocol, while UDP is a connectionless protocol. The list of protocols available on the transport layer of the internet communication model can be expanded in the future.

Application Layer

The application layer of the internet communication model combines the functionalities of the application and presentation layers of OSI/RM.

The application layer protocols fall into two categories:

- *User protocols*—Provide services directly to users. Examples of such protocols are Telnet, FTP, Hypertext Transfer Protocol (HTTP), and Simple Mail Transfer Protocol (SMTP).

- *Support protocols*—Are used for system management and maintenance. Examples of such protocols are Trivial File Transder Protocol (TFTP), Bookstrap Protocol (BOOTP), and Domain Name System (DNS).

What Is the Maximum Size of a PDU?

None of the communication models, whether generic or real world, gives any prescription with regard to the size of PDUs on any layer. The sizing issue lies beyond the scope of the multilayer communication models.

Nevertheless, the sizing issue exists and is primarily caused by real-world constraints, such as errors. For example, information is transmitted through a copper wire as electrical signals, whose form encodes the bits representing the information. The form of the signals can be changed by some external interference, such as magnetic fields. In this case, the received and decoded information will be different from the information that was sent. In other words, the information is received with errors.

Errors need to be detected. If errors are found, the information must be resent. Typically, errors are detected by including so-called *cyclic redundancy check* (CRC) information in the header of PDUs carrying the information. CRC information is a number, usually 32 bits long, that is calculated by performing certain arithmetic operations over the whole chunk of data. The calculation is performed in such a way that, if some part of the data is changed, there is a very small probability that the resulting CRC of the changed data would coincide with the CRC of the original data. CRC information is generated by the sender and is verified by the receiver by recalculating the CRC of the received data and comparing it with the CRC in the PDU's header. Obviously, the larger a PDU, the longer the retransmission will take should an error occur.

NOTE: *The technologies operating on the OSI/RM data link layer often insert CRC information into the trailer of their PDUs.*

I'm sure many other constraints would cause poor communication performance should the PDU be too large. In any case, it makes sense to limit the maximum size of a PDU to a certain value. This value can't be too small either: Too small a value results in poor performance because of the overhead associated with a high header-size-to-payload ratio.

The maximum size of the PDU is expressed as the maximum size of the payload the PDU can carry. This value is called a *maximum transfer unit (MTN) size.*

NOTE: *Some sources indicate that MTU stands for maximum transmission unit.*

On which layer should the MTU size be introduced? As we remember, the lowest layer that still performs encapsulation and therefore has its own PDUs is the data link layer. The lower physical layer is responsible for only transmission of data bits; it does not define any additional encapsulation. Hence, the data link layer has the most acute need for the MTU. All upper layers will have to adhere to the MTU size of the data link layer.

Different data link layer technologies have different MTU sizes. For example, Ethernet has an MTU size of 1,500 bytes, whereas FDDI's MTU size is 4,470 bytes.

The Internet Protocol Suite

The protocols defined within the framework of the internet communication model are called the *Internet Protocol suite* or *TCP/IP protocol suite*, by the names of the two most popular and important Internet-related protocols. Sometimes *suite* is replaced with *stack*, as in "the TCP/IP protocol stack." All these terms are equivalent and interchangeable. Figure 1.6 shows the relation between the Internet Protocol suite and the internet communication model.

Notice that the link layer entities are shown as shaded boxes, denoting that these entities are not really defined by the link layer. As was mentioned earlier, the Internet uses existing standards whenever possible.

The Internet Documentation

The rest of this chapter (and most of this book) is based on an often-undervalued source of information, the RFCs, the "native" Internet documentation. The information set forth in RFCs covers many TCP/IP- and Internet-related subjects. It's perhaps needless to mention that all Internet-related standards, including IP, TCP, UDP, and so on, are always first published as RFCs.Another good thing about RFCs is that they are free. You can download them from many Web sites and pay nothing. For example, you may want to check **www.rfc-editor.org**.

RFCs, usually presenting no vendor-specific information, often help readers understand quite vendor-specific issues much better than the vendor's own documentation

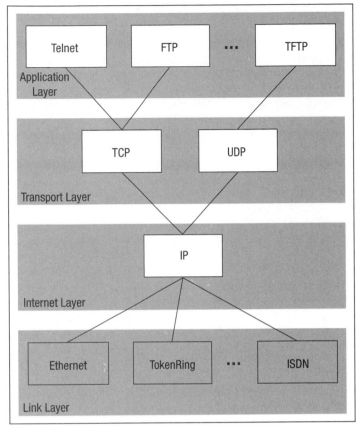

Figure 1.6   Internet protocol suite.

allows. For example, RFC 1812, "Requirements for IP Version 4 Routers," provides an exceptional description of how a router must perform routing table lookup. On the contrary, the Cisco documentation gives you quite a vague explanation of the issue.

Sometimes, RFCs overtly describe vendor-specific issues. For example, Hot Standby Router Protocol (HSRP) is a Cisco proprietary protocol. Nevertheless, it is explained in full details in RFC 2281, "Cisco Hot Standby Router Protocol (HSRP)."

Throughout this book, I will keep referencing RFCs that cover the corresponding subjects. I will stick to the notation I used in this section: I will call an RFC by its number followed by its title (for example, RFC 791, "Internet Protocol"). However, subsequent references to an RFC that has already been mentioned will include only its number.

The Anatomy of Internet Protocol

The Internet protocol is the key and most important element of the Internet protocol suite. This is the only protocol on the Internet layer, which provides a PDU delivery service for the transport layer protocols.

The PDUs of IP are called *datagrams*. The datagram delivery service provided by IP is characterized by three important features:

- *The service is connectionless*—Every datagram is delivered independently of the datagrams that have already been sent and that will be sent.

- *The service is unreliable*—There is no guarantee that a datagram will be delivered.

- *The service is best-effort*—An earnest attempt is made to deliver a datagram. Nevertheless, the datagram can be discarded because of low resources or failures of underlying technologies.

IP Hosts and Routers

The internet communication model and the Internet protocol suite define two types of end systems: *hosts* and *routers*. A host is an end network node, meaning a host cannot forward traffic. A host can receive only traffic whose final destination is the host itself. On the contrary, a router is an intermediate network node. The router's primary function is to receive traffic and forward it towards the final destination.

NOTE: *In the early days of IP, IP routers were called* gateways. *An example of the document that uses the term* gateway *is RFC 791. Now this term is used to refer to certain intermediate devices that operate on the application and transport layers of the internet communication model. This term, however, is not limited to the internet communication model.*

The most important function defined on the Internet layer is routing. Therefore, routers primarily operate on the Internet layer, and they don't have to implement the application and transport layers in order to route. Nevertheless, the modules operating on the transport and application layers are in most cases present on routers, although only for management and maintenance purposes.

The scheme shown in Figure 1.7 depicts the process of transmitting a piece of data between hosts H1 and H2 through router R. The figure shows the interaction of modules on all four layers as the data travels from one module to another.

Figure 1.7 demonstrates why the transport and application layers are not required on router R to forward data between hosts H1 and H2. The Internet protocol module on router R receives the data via link protocol A and immediately sends it further via link protocol B.

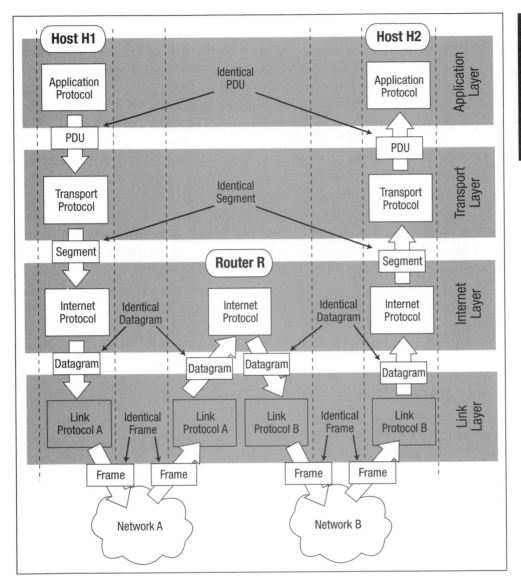

Figure 1.7   Interaction of protocol stacks on IP hosts and routers.

It is convenient to think that the Internet protocol hides the diversity of the underlying link layer technologies and presents the network to the transport layer protocols as a single-piece object.

Not every network requires routers to operate. If the hosts are interconnected via the same medium (as shown in Figure 1.8), there is no need to exchange IP datagrams via the IP module of a router. Because the hosts have the same data link layer modules (link protocol A modules) and are interconnected via a single medium, they can exchange datagrams directly.

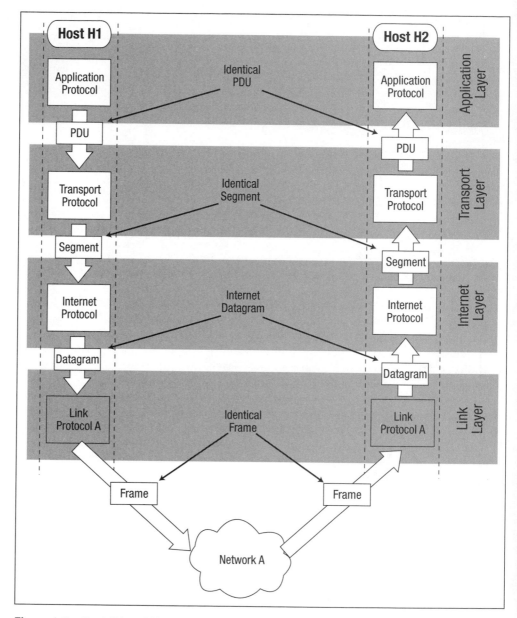

Figure 1.8   Host H1 and H2 are interconnected via the same medium and therefore do not need a router to communicate.

NOTE: *The fact that two hosts have the same data link modules does not guarantee that they don't need a router to communicate. If such hosts are separated by multiple media interconnected with one or more routers, there is no way the hosts can avoid interactions with a router.*

The type of network shown in Figure 1.8 is commonly called a *segment*. Another term frequently used to refer to such networks is *layer 2 networks*, by the order number of the data link layer in OSI/RM. Likewise, segments interconnected with routers are called *layer 3 networks*. In this book, however, I will use the term *segment*.

A Need for Fragmentation

Earlier in this chapter, we discussed that various data link layer technologies have different MTU sizes. Therefore, a network can be comprised of segments with different MTU sizes. The routers that interconnect segments can come across an issue when they have to transmit a datagram that originates from a segment with a large MTU size through a network with a smaller MTU size. Figure 1.9 shows an example of this type of situation.

This issue is resolved by a process called *fragmentation*. The router, which has to transmit a datagram through a segment with an MTU size smaller than the size of the datagram, breaks the datagram into pieces called *fragments* that fit the MTU size of the segment. Fragments are also known as *IP datagrams*. Most fields of the header of the original datagram are copied into the headers of the fragments. The payload of the original datagram is divided into pieces whose size is equal to or smaller than the MTU size, less the size of the header of the corresponding fragment.

The fragments are reassembled into the original datagram only at the destination (and not the intermediate routers). This is because fragments may not necessarily traverse the same path; hence, they may not arrive at the router that could try to reassemble the original datagram.

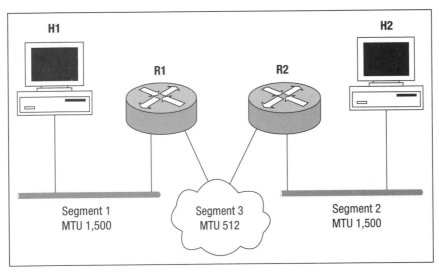

Figure 1.9   The small MTU size of segment 3 makes IP datagrams exchanged by hosts H1 and H2 fragmented by routers R1 and R2.

Bit and Octet Order in IP

What bit order does IP use? Likewise, what octet order in multioctet words does IP use? These are two important questions, because the communication devices based on IP must be interoperable and, at the same time, can be made by different vendors. Obviously, an agreement must be reached on these questions.

Bits in octets and octets in multioctet words can be ordered in two ways. The first is to put the most-significant bits in octets and octets in multioctet words first. This order is known as *big-endian*. The other way is to put the least-significant bits in octets and octets in multioctet words first. This order is know as *little-endian*.

IP uses big-endian order, so the most-significant bits in octets and octets in multioctet words are placed and transmitted first.

IP Datagram Format

The format of the IP datagram header is shown in Figure 1.10. The units of the ruler at the top of Figure 1.10 are bits, and the ruler is 32-bits long. The header is shown as a set of 32-bit words stacked in the transmission order (the first field shown is transmitted first). Following is a description of all individual fields constituting the IP datagram header.

Version

The Version field has 4 bits and contains the IP version number. (The current version is 4.)

IP Header Length

The IP Header Length (IHL) field is the size of the datagram header expressed in 32-bit words. The last field, Options, is optional (what a surprise), which makes the size of the datagram header variable. This in turn justifies the need for the IHL field.

The Options field is rarely used, however; hence, the majority of IP datagrams don't have this field. The size of a header without the Options field is 20 bytes, which makes the IHL value equal to 5 (0101 in binary).

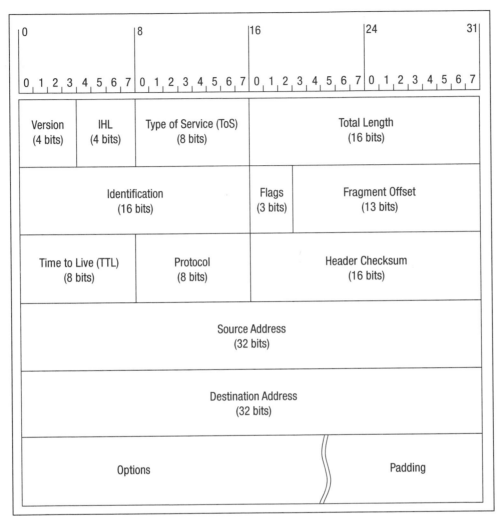

Figure 1.10   The format of the IP datagram header.

ToS Octet

The ToS octet consists of the three fields shown in Figure 1.11. The Precedence field is the first subfield and indicates the importance of the datagram: The higher the value of the Precedence field, the more important the datagram is. This field is 3 bits long; hence, there can be eight different values of precedence, all of which are shown in Table 1.1.

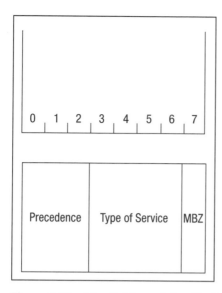

Figure 1.11   The fields contained in the ToS octet.

Table 1.1   Precedence values.

Decimal	Binary	Description
7	111	Network Control
6	110	Internetwork Control
5	101	CRITIC/ECP
4	100	Flash Override
3	011	Flash
2	010	Immediate
1	001	Priority
0	000	Routine (Normal)

The Type of Service field, often referenced as *ToS*, is 4 bits long and can contain the values shown in Table 1.2. The values in the first column are shown using binary numerals. Originally, the ToS field was represented as individual subfields of 1 bit each, which explains why it is more convenient to represent the values of the modern ToS field in binary numerals. The ToS field indicates the desired characteristics of the path along which the datagram should be sent.

Table 1.2   Interpretation of possible ToS values.

ToS Value	Requested ToS
1000	Minimize delay
0100	Maximize throughput
0010	Maximize reliability
0001	Minimize monetary cost
0000	Normal service

Conceptually, ToS is an attractive idea. If a router has more than one path to the destination, it can choose the one that satisfies the requested characteristics. For example, if you use Telnet to communicate with a remote host, you expect a quick response from the host. Therefore, you may need to set the value of the ToS field to 1000 (binary) in the headers of the datagrams carrying the Telnet session. Doing so would force the connection to be carried over a path with a low delay. On the contrary, if you want to download a large file from an FTP server, you don't care about the response time, but you do care about how quickly the file is downloaded. In this case, you may require setting the ToS field to 0100 (binary),which would request a higher throughput for the FTP session.

Unfortunately, the ToS is not guaranteed. The routers are not required to meet the requested ToS, because, in many cases, they cannot know what characteristics a certain path has.

The last field is 1 bit long. It is called MBZ, which stands for "must be zero." This field is reserved. Currently, the originators of IP datagrams are required to clear this field. The routers must not change this field. If the datagram has to be fragmented, the field must be copied into the headers of the fragments.

Total Length

The Total Length field is the size of the datagram measured in octets—that is, 8-bit bytes. This field is 16 bits long, which theoretically allows creating datagrams up to 65,535 octets long. The size of the real datagrams should not be larger than the MTU size of the segments over which the datagrams are sent.

In addition, all hosts and routers are required to accept datagrams with a size of 576 octets or fewer.

Identification, Flags, and Fragment Offset

The Identification, Flags, and Fragment Offset fields are used to facilitate the datagram fragmentation and reassembly processes.The Identification field has 16 bits and is used to specify which original datagram the arriving fragments constitute. Each time the source host creates a datagram, it uses a unique number for the datagram Identification field. When a router decides that it needs to fragment a datagram, it copies most of the fields from the header of the datagram to the headers of the fragments. The Identification field is also copied, thereby providing the destination host with a way of recognizing the fragments as parts of the original datagram.

The Flags field has 3 bits, which are interpreted independently as follows:

* Bit 0 is reserved.

* Bit 1 is called *DF bit*, which stands for "don't fragment." When cleared, it indicates that the datagram can be fragmented. When set, it indicates that the datagram cannot be fragmented.

* Bit 2 is called *MF bit*, which stands for "more fragments." When set, it indicates that this is not the last fragment of the original datagram. When cleared, it indicates that this is the last fragment. If a datagram was not fragmented, this bit must be cleared.

The Fragment Offset field has 13 bits and specifies which part of the original datagram payload the fragment carries. The number that it represents is the offset of the fragment payload measured in units of eight octets from the beginning of the original datagram payload.

Fragmentation

Let's now see how the process of fragmentation works, using Figure 1.9 as an example of a network comprising segments with different MTU sizes. Suppose host H1 sends host H2 a datagram whose size is equal to the MTU size of segment 1 (1500 bytes). The datagram first arrives to router R1, which has to send it further through segment 3. The MTU size of segment 3 is only 512 bytes; hence, router R1 must fragment the datagram. The way it does it is shown in Figure 1.12.

Figure 1.12 shows two shaded areas that depict the state of the datagram and fragments at segments 1 and 3. The first shaded area shows the condition of the datagram as it arrives from segment 1. The second shaded area shows the fragments produced by router R1 and sent to segment 3. Figure 1.12 shows the fields of the datagram's and segments' headers which, are essential for the fragmentation process. In addition, Figure 1.12 shows the sizes of the headers and payloads of the datagram and fragments before and after fragmentation.

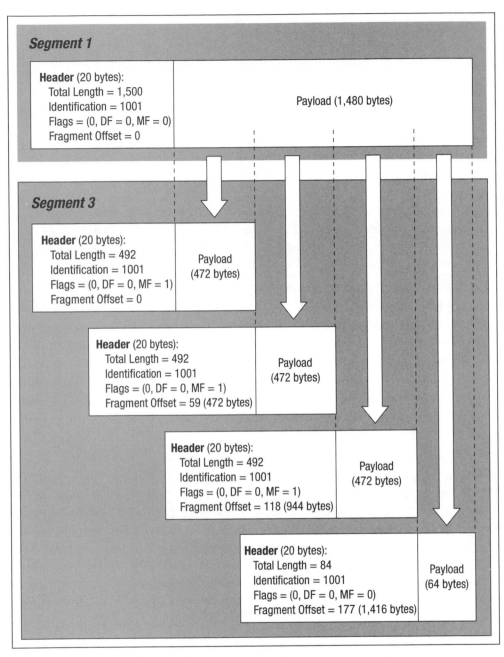

Figure 1.12   The process of fragmenting a large datagram.

Several interesting observations can be made by looking at Figure 1.12:

- The last fragment is much smaller then the first three. This should happen pretty often, because it's unlikely that a datagram can be broken into fragments all of which precisely fit the MTU size of the segment that they have to traverse.

- Even the first three segments do not use the MTU size of segment 3 completely. The MTU size of segment 3 is 512 bytes, although the size of the first three fragments is only 492 bytes. This happens because the Fragment Offset field is measured in units of 8 bytes. Therefore, the payloads of all of the fragments except for the last one must be divisible by 8.

- The total size of all of the fragments is 1560 bytes, whereas the size of the original datagram is 1500. The extra 60 bytes are the headers of the fragments, making the overhead associated with transmission of auxiliary information (such as IP datagram headers) worse.

- In our case, the fragments eventually arrive at segment 2, whose MTU size is, again, 1500. This higher MTU size is not going to be utilized, however: The fragments are not reassembled into the original datagram by the intermediate routers.

- There's an added overhead in terms of CPU processing at the destination host associated with the reassembly process. Unlike multiple small datagrams, fragments must be reassembled into the original datagram, and only after that the payload can be extracted. The reassembly process causes extra memory buffer allocation and consumes additional CPU cycles.

Obviously, fragmentation does not facilitate the efficiency of the transmission. Thus, it must be avoided whenever possible. Hosts are encouraged to take into consideration the smallest MTU size of the path to the destination and create datagrams that fit it. A few techniques have been proposed that facilitate discovery of the smallest MTU size. These techniques, however, lie beyond the scope of this book. It's worth mentioning, though, that these techniques are usually employed on firewalls and Internet proxy servers that connect large networks to the Internet.

Routers and hosts have different requirements in terms of fragmentation and reassembly. Routers *must* be able to perform fragmentation when necessary; the hosts *don't have* to perform fragmentation, although both hosts and routers *must* be able to perform reassembly of the datagrams that are destined for them.

Time To Live

The Time To Live (TTL) field reflects how long the datagram can exist before the intermediate routers drop it as expired. The phrase *Time To Live* is a bit misleading because it is not really expressed in units of time, such as seconds. Routers calculate the TTL field as follows:

1. When a router receives a datagram, it decrements the value of TTL by 1.

2. If the value is 0, the router drops the datagram; otherwise, it forwards the datagram either to the next-hop router or to the final destination.

3. If the router is forced to store the datagram in its memory for more than one second, it decrements the value of the TTL field by 1 for each additional second. This means that when the first second elapses, the router makes the TTL equal 2; when the second second elapses, it makes the TTL equal 3; and so on.

The primary purpose of the TTL field is to avoid network congestion in routing loops. Let's imagine a datagram that has been sent along a route, which eventually brings it back. If TTL did not exist, the datagram would end up being forwarded an unlimited number of times.

NOTE: *In the case of datagrams sent to a multicast IP address, the* TTL *is called the* datagram scope.

Protocol

The Protocol field is used to identify the protocols that should receive the payload of the datagram. In terms of a multilayer communication model, the Protocol field is a demultiplexing key. The Protocol field is 8 bits; hence, it is possible to have 255 different protocols using the IP datagram delivery service. Table 1.3 shows some Protocol field values and the protocols that they represent. Interestingly enough, the protocols that use IP do not necessarily have to be on the transport layer. Some auxiliary protocols—such as Internet Control Message Protocol (ICMP or IGMP)—reside on the internet layer but use IP as the transport.

Table 1.3 **Some protocols and their corresponding numbers.**

Protocol Number (Hexadecimal)	Protocol Number (Decimal)	Protocol Name
6	6	Transmission Control Protocol (TCP)
11	17	User Datagram Protocol (UDP)
1	1	Internet Control Message Protocol (ICMP)
9	9	Cisco Interior Gateway Routing Protocol (IGRP)

(continued)

Table 1.3   Some protocols and their corresponding numbers (continued).

Protocol Number (Hexadecimal)	Protocol Number (Decimal)	Protocol Name
58	88	Cisco Extended Interior Gateway Routing Protocol (EIGRP)
59	89	Open Shortest Path First (OSPF)
4	4	IP in IP encapsulation
2F	47	General Routing Encapsulation (GRE)

Header Checksum

This 16-bit field contains the header checksum. The checksum is calculated only for the header of a datagram and not for the payload. If the payload arrives corrupted, the IP module will not detect it. The transport layer protocol—whose PDU is carried as the payload of an IP datagram—has to have its own verification methods for data integrity. Should the payload arrive corrupted, it is the responsibility of the transport layer protocol to request retransmission if it considers it necessary.

Source and Destination Addresses

The source and destination addresses represent the IP addresses of the host that sent the datagram and the host that is to receive the datagram. The structure of IP addresses is thoroughly examined in the "IP Addressing" section later in this chapter.

Options and Padding

Options are fields that can be used for debugging purposes. Because these fields are usually not particularly helpful, they are rarely used.

The Padding field is used to adjust the options on a 32-bit boundary. The unused space between the last octet of the last option and the 32-bit boundary is filled with zeros.

IP Addressing

IP addressing is cumbersome, yet it is not the fault of its authors. When the Internet protocol suite was devised, nobody thought that it would become so widely used. IP addressing in its original form was quite adequate for the purposes it was supposed to serve. However, when the popularity of the Internet started to grow, IP addressing quickly manifested its limitations. Since then, it's been continuously "improved" to accommodate the avalanche of new requirements. The limitations of original IP addressing and its subsequent modifications of it are a primary reason why IP routing is so complex.

IP addressing evolved in two major stages. The first stage can be called "classical IP addressing," which includes the very first original IP addressing and its subsequent modifications, and the other stage is called "classless IP addressing." The outcomes of these two stages are explained in the following two sections.

Generic Information about IP Addressing

As you learned in the "IP Datagram Format" section, the IP address is a number that is 32 bits long. IP addresses are of two types: *unicast* and *multicast*. Unicast IP addresses are used to identify the network interfaces of hosts and routers, and multicast IP addresses are used to identify a group of hosts that wishes to receive a certain type of IP traffic.

A unicast IP address is subdivided into two parts: the network part, called a *network ID*, and the host part, called a *host ID*. The network ID of an IP address identifies the segment on which the host resides, and the host ID identifies the network interface that connects the host to the segment. All hosts connected to the same segment are supposed to have an identical network ID of their IP addresses assigned on the corresponding interfaces. The host ID of those IP addresses must be unique for each host.

An unfortunate feature of a unicast IP address is that it does not identify a host. It identifies a network interface of a host. If a host has multiple network interfaces, then each interface must have a different IP address. The host itself has no IP-relevant identity.

Theoretically, IP addresses could be represented in the binary notation as a set of 32 ones and zeroes. Obviously, such a notation wouldn't be particularly readable by humans, as the figures produced would be too long (and binary is not natural for human beings).

Instead, a special notation called *dotted decimal notation* became widely accepted. Dotted decimal notation represents IP addresses as four decimal numbers separated by periods. Each decimal number represents 8 bits of an IP address. The first number represents bits 0 through 7, the second bits 8 through 16, and so on. For example, the IP address represented in binary notation as **00001010110000000011100000100101** in dotted decimal notation looks like **10.192.56.37**.

Classical or "Classful" IP Addressing

Classical IP addressing deterministically divides the whole IP address space into a total of five so-called *network classes*: A, B, C, D, and E. Each network class defines a certain non-overlapping range of IP addresses, where *non-overlapping* means that every IP address belongs to exactly one network class.

Network classes A, B, and C define unicast IP addresses and dictate how many bits of the address belong to the network ID and how many to the host ID. Network class D defines multicast IP addresses (or, as they are now called, *multicast groups*). Network class E defines a group of experimental IP addresses.

The class of an IP address is determined by the combination of the first several bits of the first octet of the IP addresses. Figure 1.13 shows the relation between the combinations of bits and the IP network classes.

The original justification behind network classes A, B, and C was to define separate IP address ranges for physical networks with different numbers of hosts. The number of bits allocated for the host ID clearly defines the maximum number of hosts that can reside on the segment with the corresponding network ID. Because the number of bits in the host ID comes at the expense of bits left for the network ID, the number of networks that allow a high number of hosts is smaller than the number of networks with fewer hosts.

Classical IP addressing takes some addresses out of the "classified" address space and makes them special-purpose IP addresses, as shown here:

- The network ID whose bits are all 0s denotes *this network*. An IP address with the network of ID whose bits are all 0s can be used only as a source IP address.

- The IP address whose bits are all 0s, or 0.0.0.0 in dotted decimal notation, is interpreted as *this host* on *this network*. 0.0.0.0 can be used only as a source IP address. This IP address and any IP address with the network ID whose bits are all 0s are intended for hosts that don't know which network they reside on and possibly don't know their host IDs. Such hosts can temporarily use these IP address until they find out their regular IP addresses.

- The IP address whose bits are all 1s, or 255.255.255.255 in dotted decimal notation, is called a *local broadcast address*. The local broadcast address can be used as a destination IP address only. It addresses all hosts on a segment.

- The IP address whose host ID bits are all 1s is called a *directed broadcast address*. A directed broadcast address can appear as a destination IP address only. It addresses all hosts on the segment whose network ID is equal to the network ID of the directed broadcast address.

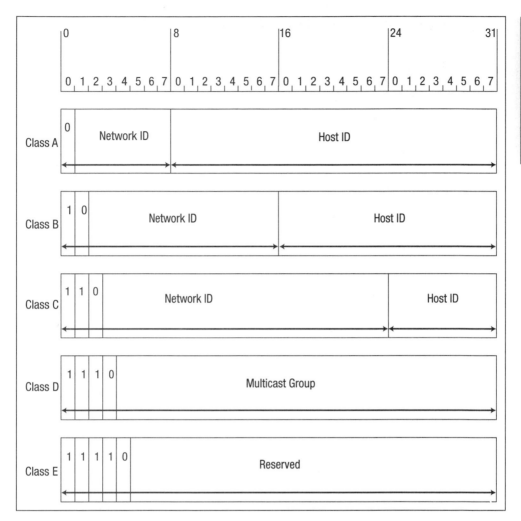

Figure 1.13   The IP network classes.

- The IP address whose host ID bits are all 0s is called a *network address*. A network address is used to denote a segment. It can be used neither as a source nor as a destination IP address.

- Any IP address whose first octet is equal to 127 is called a *loopback address*. This address always addresses the host itself. It can be used internally only; no datagram carrying this address either as a destination or source IP address can ever appear outside the host. Usually, this address is used for testing purposes, such as debugging a network-based application when no network is present.

Keeping all these special-purpose IP addresses in mind, let's see how many networks and hosts network classes A, B, and C allocate:

- Class A yields 2^7- 2, or 126, network addresses, each of which allows up to 2^{24}-2, or 16,777,214, hosts. Class A defines the range of network addresses 1.0.0.0 through 126.0.0.0.

- Class B yields 2^{14}-1, or 16,383, network addresses, each of which allows to 2^{16}-2, or 65,534, hosts. Class B defines the range of networks 128.0.0.0 through 191.255.0.0.

- Class C yields 2^{21}-1, or 2,097,151, network addresses, each of which allows up to 2^8-2 or 254, hosts. Class C defines the range of networks 192.0.0.0 through 223.255.255.0.

For the purposes of further discussion, I will call the described addressing scheme *pure classful IP addressing*. Additionally, the term *class X IP address*, where *X* can be A through E, will be used to denote an IP address that belongs to the corresponding class. Likewise, the term *class X network address* will be used to denote a network address belonging to the corresponding class.

One of the most obvious shortcomings of pure classful IP addressing is that only class C produces a reasonable number of hosts (254). The number of hosts that can be accommodated on class A and B networks looks absurd, especially when you keep in mind that a network address is supposed to be assigned to a single segment.

Subnetting

A modification of pure classful IP addressing called *subnetting* was invented to address the issues associated with the fixed (and, in most cases, inadequate) number of hosts defined by network classes A, B, and C. Subnetting allows the host ID to be subdivided into two parts—a *subnet ID* and a *host ID*. A subnet ID identifies a segment, and the new host ID (as before) identifies an interface of a host connected to the segment. Subnetting also redefines the meaning of the network ID. This time, a network ID identifies a group of networks under the same administrative authority.

Subnetting is performed by specifying a so-called *subnet mask* in addition to an IP address. A subnet mask is 32-bit value whose set bits signify that the corresponding bits in the IP address constitute the subnet ID and whose cleared bits signify that the corresponding bits in the IP address constitute the host ID. The notation commonly used to specify subnet masks is also dotted decimal notation.

NOTE: *A subnet mask is not a part of an IP address. It is an administratively defined rule applied to an IP address in order to divide it into subnet and host IDs.*

For example, the IP address 10.15.3.154 with the subnet mask 255.255.255.0 produces the network ID equal to 10, the subnet ID equal to 15.3, and the host ID equal to 154.

The way a subnet mask is defined does not require the set bits in a subnet mask to be contiguous. In other words, subnet masks with alternating 0s and 1s such as 255.240.255.0 are theoretically possible. But are they practically usable?

To answer this question, let's see what the host ID and subnet ID become if we use an IP address of 10.35.63.45 with two subnet masks, 255.255.240.0 and 255.252.15.192. The bit patterns of the IP address and both subnet masks are shown in Figures 1.14 and 1.15. Figure 1.14 shows how the contiguous subnet mask divides the IP address into the network, subnet, and host IDs. Figure 1.15 shows how the noncontiguous subnet mask divides the IP address into the network, subnet, and host IDs. Notice that there are now two subnet IDs and two host IDs. In fact, the two subnet IDs are essentially a single noncontiguous subnet ID; likewise, the two host IDs are a single noncontiguous host ID.

Aside from looking rather scary, noncontiguous subnet masks would bring an administrative nightmare if they became widely used. Imagine assigning IP addresses on the interfaces of hosts that use a noncontiguous subnet mask. For

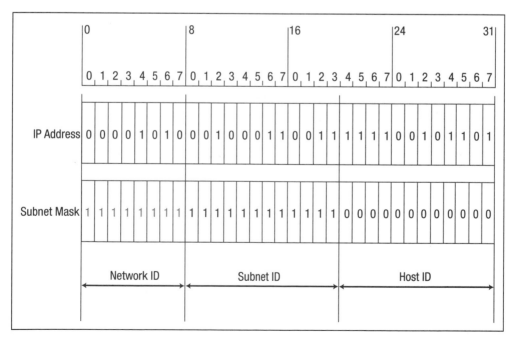

Figure 1.14   Contiguous subnet mask example.

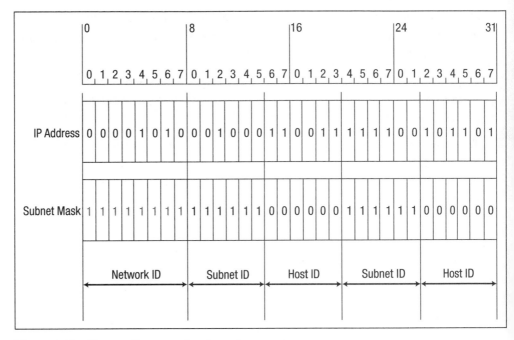

Figure 1.15   Noncontiguous subnet mask example.

example, if the last IP address allocated is 10.192.3.63 and the subnet mask is 255.240.255.192, then the next available IP address is 10.193.3.0—which is very inconvenient. The administrative overhead and complications in routing are primary reasons why noncontiguous subnet masks are not used.

Subnetting introduced so-called *default subnet masks*. These masks have to be used if no other subnet masks are explicitly specified. The default subnet masks are dependent on network classes. For all class A IP addresses, the default subnet mask is 255.0.0.0; for class B, it is 255.255.0.0; and, for class C, it is 255.255.255.0. Notice that the default subnet masks do not allocate any bits of an IP address for a subnet ID. In a way, they preserve the pure classful division of an IP address into network and host IDs.

Throughout this book, I will use the term *classful network address* when referring to the network addresses with the default subnet masks. Examples are 10.0.0.0/8, 172.16.0.0/16, and 192.168.1.0/24.

Later developments of subnetting permitted *supernets*, which are defined as network addresses whose subnet masks (which, of course, are contiguous) have a smaller number of set bits than the default subnet masks of the corresponding classful network addresses. Examples of supernets are 8.0.0.0 248.0.0.0, 172.16.0.0 255.240.0.0, 192.168.0.0 255.255.0.0, and so on. Supernets can be used to aggregate several classful network addresses for routing purposes. The most typical example of a supernet is the *default address* or *default network*, which corresponds to 0.0.0.0 0.0.0.0.

NOTE: The term supernet can be used only in the context of tclassful IP addressing.

Subnetting keeps all special-purpose IP addresses as previously defined ; the only difference is that the term *network ID* is now *network and subnet IDs*. For example, if the IP address is 10.10.4.1 and the subnet mask is 255.255.0.0, then the directed broadcast address is 10.10.255.255 and the network address is 10.10.0.0. If subnetting is used, a network address is also called a *subnet address*.

NOTE: If subnetting is used, then assigning of an IP address to an interface must be accompanied by specifying the respective subnet mask.

Modern or "Classless" IP Addressing

The culmination of IP addressing redesign comes in the form of so-called *classless* IP addressing. Classless IP addressing puts an end to unicast network classes A, B, and C. The bit pattern of the first bits of an IP address no longer predefines any default division of the IP address into network and host IDs. Any IP address can be arbitrarily divided into a *network prefix* and a host ID.

Both network prefix and host ID must be contiguous, and a network prefix must precede a host ID. The division of an IP address into a network prefix and a host ID is achieved by specifying a *network prefix length*.

A network prefix, like a network ID or subnet ID, identifies a segment. A host ID identifies the interface of a host that connects the host to the segment. The interfaces of hosts connected to the same segment must have unique host IDs and the same network prefix.

A notation that becomes more and more widely used to denote network prefixes is to specify an IP address whose host ID bits are 0s in dotted decimal notation followed by a slash followed by a network prefix length in decimal notation. For example: 10.10.0.0/16.

NOTE: Network prefixes historically stem from network addresses specified using contiguous subnet masks. Indeed, a contiguous subnet mask can be unequivocally expressed by specifying the number of set bits, —that is, the prefix length. Thus, there is an unambiguous relation between contiguous subnet masks and prefix lengths. Quite often, network prefixes are expressed using old notation (specifying an IP address with host ID bits all cleared) followed by the corresponding contiguous subnet mask. The example of a network prefix shown above in the old notation looks like 10.10.0.0 255.255.0.0. In this book, however, I will refrain from using the old notation and will stick to the modern one, unless it is specifically necessary to use the old notation.

The classless notation preserves all special-purpose IP addresses, with the only difference being that the network ID is replaced with the network prefix. The following is a recap of the meanings of the special-purpose IP address in the classless version of IP addressing:

- The network prefix whose bits are all 0s denotes *this network*. An IP address whose network prefix bits are 0s can be used only as the source IP address.

- The IP address whose bits are all 0s denotes *this host* on *this network*. This address can be used only as a source IP address.

- The IP address whose bits are all 1s, or 255.255.255.255 in dotted decimal notation, is called a *local broadcast address*. The local broadcast address can be used only as a destination IP address. It addresses all hosts on a segment.

- The IP address whose host ID bits are all 1s is called a *directed broadcast address*. A directed broadcast address can appear as a destination IP address only. It addresses all hosts on a segment whose network prefix is equal to the network prefix of the directed broadcast address.

- A host ID whose bits are all 0s is reserved to denote the network prefix. It can be used neither as a source nor as a destination IP address.

- Any IP address whose first octet is equal to 127 is called a *loopback address*. This address always addresses the host itself.

The usage of the special-purpose IP addresses remains unchanged. Notice that the term *network address* was removed; it was replaced with the term *network prefix*.

NOTE: *If classless IP addressing is used, then an interface must be configured with an IP address and the length of the network prefix, to which all hosts on the segment adhere. Typically, the length is specified using an "old-fashioned" subnet mask whose number of set bits is equal to the network prefix length.*

The length of a network prefix defines the maximum number of hosts that the network prefix allows. The formula that establishes the relation between the network prefix length and the number of hosts it allows is:

$$N = 2^{(32 - L)} - 2$$

where N is the number of hosts and L is the network prefix length.

As an example, let's calculate how many hosts prefixes whose length is 29 allow:

$$N = 2^{(32 - 29)} - 2 = 2^3 - 2 = 8 - 2 = 6$$

If the network prefix is 10.1.1.0/29, then the available IP addresses are 10.1.1.1 through 10.1.1.6. Addresses 10.1.1.0 and 10.1.1.7 are the network prefix and the directed broadcast address, respectively.

A network prefix length equal to 31 is useless:

$$N = 2^{(32-31)} - 2 = 2^1 - 2 = 2 - 2 = 0$$

Indeed, this prefix length allocates only 1 bit for the host ID, which, if set, produces the directed broadcast address and, if cleared, produces the network prefix itself.

A special case presents the network prefix length equal to 32. It appears to be invalid:

$$N = 2^{(32-32)} - 2 = 2^0 - 2 = 1 - 2 = -1$$

Nevertheless, this prefix length is valid and serves a special purpose. A network prefix with a length of 32 denotes an *individual host address*. Such a network prefix is not a regular IP address; it is still a network prefix. As we'll see in upcoming chapters devoted to routing, this type of network prefix often plays an important role.

The formula shown above is not very useful. In practice, the task is usually reversed: Given the number of hosts, deduce the required prefix length. The reversed formula is rather complex:

$$L = 32 - \log_2 (N + 2)$$

The good news is that the number of practically useful network prefixes is very limited. The excessive number of hosts connected to the same segment is very undesirable. In real life, segments with more than 200 hosts should be rare. In any case, for all practical purposes, 2,000 seems to be the maximum number of hosts on a single segment. Given this limit, the calculated maximum number of hosts and the corresponding network prefix lengths shown in Table 1.4 produce a good tool for planning network address allocation.

Notice that Table 1.4 also shows old-style subnet masks corresponding to the prefix lengths.

I must say, however, that, even with the advent of classless IP addressing, the issues associated with IP address allocation and subsequent routing problems did not become much simpler compared to what they were in the case of the classful version. The classless version is still a sort of a "patch" of the original IP addressing design and, as such, does not cure all of the problems. We will see in upcoming chapters devoted to routing protocols and redistribution that even classless IP addressing can still become a major headache.

Table 1.4   The relation between a network prefix length and the number of hosts it allows.

Number Of Hosts	Prefix Length	Corresponding Subnet Mask
1	/32	255.255.255.255
up to 2	/30	255.255.255.252
up to 6	/29	255.255.255.248
up to 14	/28	255.255.255.240
up to 30	/27	255.255.255.224
up to 62	/26	255.255.255.192
up to 126	/25	255.255.255.128
up to 254	/24	255.255.255.0
up to 510	/23	255.255.254.0
up to 1,022	/22	255.255.252.0
up to 2,046	/21	255.255.248.0

Secondary IP Addresses

The original idea behind a network prefix was to uniquely identify an individual network segment. Likewise, a host ID is supposed to uniquely identify a network interface of a host. It was also assumed that neither a single segment nor a single host would require more than one identification, whether a network prefix or host ID. Somehow, this clear and neat concept became distorted by the introduction of so-called *secondary IP addresses*.

A secondary IP address is an additional IP address that is assigned to an interface of a router or host that has already been assigned an IP address. If a secondary IP address is present, then the original IP address is called the *primary IP address*. There can be multiple secondary IP addresses on the same interface. A secondary IP address may or may not have the same network prefix as the primary IP address. Moreover, the network prefix length of a secondary IP address does not have to be the same as that of the primary IP address. If, however, the network prefix of a secondary IP address coincides with the network prefix of the primary IP address, then its host ID must be different from that of the primary IP address.

Secondary IP addresses were introduced to overcome IP address-allocation problems associated with the limitations of classful IP addressing and routing. In addition, secondary IP addresses are often used when migrating from classful IP addressing to classless IP addressing. Usually, secondary IP addresses are considered (or, at least, must be considered) a temporary measure.

The biggest shortcoming of secondary IP addresses is that they create more problems than they solve. In upcoming chapters, we'll examine how different routing protocols handle secondary IP addresses. In most cases, it is definitely not graceful.

Although a temporary solution, secondary IP addresses have, in many cases, somehow become a *de facto* standard way of performing IP address allocation. Looking at the transition that secondary IP addresses made from temporary to "normal," it is really amazing how right the person who said "there is nothing more permanent than temporary" was.

Private IP Addresses

Every IP address that appears in the Internet must be officially acquired, because doing so guarantees that the same IP address will not be duplicated. Duplicate IP addresses, if they existed, would make some hosts inaccessible, which renders the whole idea of the Internet as a worldwide public network useless.

Some IP addresses, however, are guaranteed to never appear in the Internet. No authority responsible for allocation of IP addresses can ever assign any of these IP addresses to networks connected to the Internet. These IP addresses are called *private IP addresses*.

The document that specifies which IP addresses are private, what they are for, and how they should be used is RFC 1918 "Address Allocation for Private Internets." According to RFC 1918, the network prefixes 10.0.0.0/8, 172.16.0.0/12, and 192.168.0.0/16 describe all of the private IP addresses.

In the examples in this book, I will stick to using private IP addresses whenever possible.

Terminology

In this book, I will stick to using the term *network prefix* as opposed to *network address* or *subnet address* unless the specifics of the subject require otherwise. I will also use the terms *supernet* and *classful network address* when discussing technologies that require classful IP addressing.

Finally, regardless of the context, whether classful or classless, I will use the modern network prefix notation (an IP address in dotted decimal notation followed by a slash followed by the length of the network prefix). In the classful context, however, the network prefix length is to be interpreted as the number of set bits of the subnet mask. Such an interpretation is adequate because noncontiguous subnet masks are not used and are not discussed in this book.

> **NOTE:**   *Many sources use the term* network prefix *in spite of the version of IP addressing discussed, whether classful or classless. Although I totally support this approach, in this book, I make a distinction because both types of IP addressing are discussed, and it would often be too confusing to use the same terminology regardless of the context.*

Unicast IP Routing Model

We've discussed most IP components, so it is time to discuss how IP datagrams are delivered via a network that can consist of multiple segments. This section, however, deals only with *unicast* IP routing. *Multicast* IP routing, although it shares some of the concepts with unicast IP routing, is a completely separate issue. It is discussed in Chapter 9.

Routing is the IP function responsible for delivering the datagrams throughout a network. If the network consists of a single segment, routing is simple. The IP modules of the communicating hosts can use the link layer modules to exchange the datagrams directly through the segment that interconnects them.

If multiple segments are interconnected with a single router, the function of routing becomes more complex. Somehow, the hosts must be aware of the router to be able to use it for their intersegment communications. The task of the router, though, is still simple: From the router's perspective, all hosts reside on the directly connected segments, and the router can use its link layer modules to facilitate the hosts' communications.

If multiple segments are interconnected with multiple routers, the function of routing becomes quite challenging. Not only must hosts know of the presence of the routers, but routers must also know of each other and what segments are available behind them.

The following sections explain in detail the techniques and router component that enable IP routing in arbitrarily interconnected networks.

Prefix-Based Routing—IP routing is *prefix based*. This means that, when IP chooses through which interface the datagram must be sent and which next hop router must receive it for further delivery, it looks only at the network prefix of the destination IP address. No attention is paid to the host ID.

Destination-Based Routing—IP routing is *destination based*, which means that routing decisions are made based only on destination addresses. Source IP addresses are not taken into account.

IP Routers

IP routers are intrinsic components of IP-based networks. Their main function is forwarding IP datagrams from segment to segment until they arrive to the final destination.

So far, we know that the protocol stack on the IP routers must include modules of the link and Internet layers to sustain the forwarding function. We also know why only modules of the link and Internet layers are required, and why modules of the transport and application layers are optional. This knowledge, however, is not enough to understand how IP routers make forwarding decisions.

Therefore, now it is time to thoroughly examine the mechanics of how IP routers make such decisions. We'll start with a formal definition of an IP router, from which we'll gradually cover the rest of the related material.

First, we need a few words about network interfaces. Network interfaces are link layer entities that connect hosts and routers to segments. A network interface, from the IP perspective, is essentially a combination of a NIC and its driver.

Exclusively for the purpose of formally defining an IP router, a distinction is made between *input interfaces* and *output interfaces*. Datagrams are received on input interfaces and are sent out of output interfaces. The same interface can be input and output at the same time.

IP Router Definition

An IP router is an intermediate network device that receives datagrams on its input interfaces and forwards them towards their destination out of output interfaces.

In this section, I use the term *IP router*, intending to emphasize that all of the considerations made apply to IP routers and do not necessarily apply to other routers, such as those that route IPX, AppleTalk, and so on. Throughout this book, however, I will use the term *router* (without "IP") to refer to IP routers. This should not create a conflict as, except for in Chapter 2, the book deals only with IP-related technology. Chapter 2 discusses bridging and hence does not deal with routers at all (except for the fact that bridging is configured on Cisco *routers*).

Essential Router Components

From the IP routing perspective, a router has three components: a set of input and output interfaces, a data structure called a *routing table*, and a *routing engine*.

We already know what input and output interfaces are. A routing table is a special data structure that contains information about what network prefixes are available via which output interfaces. The routing table is maintained by the IP module.

NOTE: *A routing table does not have a predefined structure. Vendors have a lot of freedom to tailor the routing tables in their IP implementation for the best results. Nevertheless, some components of a routing table are intrinsic and are always present in some form in every routing table. These components are explained below.*

A routing table consists of *routing table entries*. A routing table entry always contains at least three fields: a network prefix, a reference to the output interface through which the network prefix can be reached, and the IP address of the next-hop router to which the traffic destined for the network prefix must be forwarded. If the network prefix is reachable directly through one of the router's interfaces, then the IP address of the next-hop router field in the corresponding routing table entry is left blank. A routing table can contain two or more entries whose network prefix fields are identical. Each of these entries, however, must have a unique combination of the other two fields—the output interface and the IP address of the next-hop router.

The combination of a network prefix, the reference to the output interface, and the IP address of the next-hop router, if present, is called a *route*. Hence, a routing table entry describes a route. A route is said to be *pointing* to the referenced output interface. If the IP address of the next-hop router field is present, the route is also said to be pointing to the IP address of the next-hop router, or simply to the next-hop router.

If a router implements ToS routing, then each routing entry has to have a ToS field that specifies the characteristic of the route. Refer back to Table 1.2 for the possible values of the ToS field. All other fields in a routing entry (if they are present) are optional. We'll consider some of the optional fields in the course of this book.

A routing engine is the aggregate of a router's hardware and software that receives datagrams from input interfaces, makes routing decisions based on the datagrams' destination addresses and the routing table, and sends the datagrams out of the corresponding output interfaces towards their destinations.

A routing engine uses the routing algorithm to make routing decisions. Upon execution, the routing algorithm advises the routing engine as to how the datagram must be handled—whether it must be forwarded and how, or whether it must be dropped as no route is known for the destination.

Routing Algorithms

As we know, there are two major versions of IP addressing—classful and classless. The difference between the two is significant; hence, we have two versions of routing algorithm—classful and classless.

Both algorithms perform a common procedure: the comparison between an IP address and network prefix. From my personal experience, I've noticed a confusion with regard to how the comparison is made. Therefore, before getting down to the details of both routing algorithms, I would like to explain how the comparison is made.

The Rules of Comparison

The bits 0 through the prefix length minus 1 of a network prefix are called *significant*. The comparison between a network prefix and an IP address is made bit by bit between the significant bits and the corresponding bits of the IP address. A match exists between the network prefix and IP address only if the value of *every* significant bit of the network prefix is equal to the value of the corresponding bit of the IP address.

Figure 1.16 demonstrates the comparison between IP address 10.35.63.45 and network prefix 10.32.0.0/14. Because the significant bits of the network prefix have exactly the same values as the corresponding bits of the IP address, the network prefix matches the IP address.

Sometimes, it is necessary to compare two network prefixes, as opposed to a network prefix and an IP address. Two network prefixes are considered the same if their lengths are the same and the value of each significant bit of one network prefix is equal to that of the corresponding significant bits of the other network prefix.

Classless Routing Algorithm

The classless routing algorithm makes no assumptions with regard to how IP address allocation is performed. In other words, no attention is paid to network classes A, B, and C.

The classless routing algorithm consists of three steps, with the third step being optional. The algorithm takes a destination IP address and the routing table as arguments and returns zero, one, or several routing table entries that can be used to forward the datagram. If no routing table entries are returned, then the datagram must be dropped, because the routing table does not contain sufficient information to forward the datagram.

The three steps of the classless routing algorithm:

* *Basic Match*—This step, the destination IP address is compared against the network prefixes of the routing in this table's entries. Those entries whose network prefixes do not match the destination IP address are discarded. As a result of this step; table entries whose network prefixes match the destination IP address are routed.

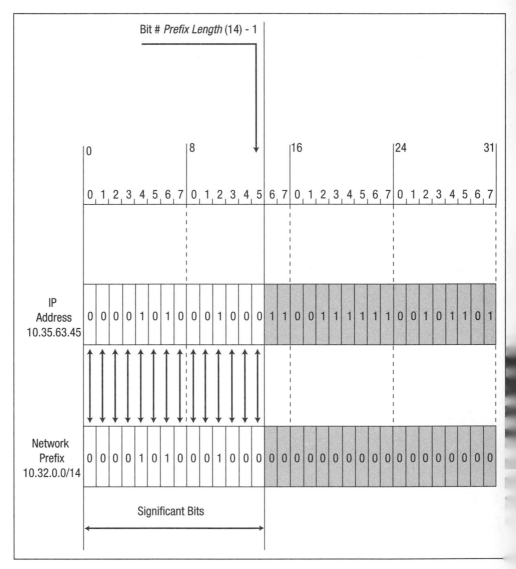

Figure 1.16   Network prefix 10.32.0.0/14 matches IP address 10.35.63.45 because the value of every significant bit of the network prefix is equal to that of the corresponding bits of the IP address.

- *Longest Match*—This step takes the routing table entries that are left after the Basic Match step and keeps only those that have the highest prefix length. This step can keep several entries only if they have the same length.

- *Weak ToS* (optional)—This step compares the ToS value carried in the ToS octet of the datagram header against the ToS values specified in the routing table entries that are left from the Longest Match step. The routing table entries whose ToS value coincides with the ToS value in the datagram header are kept, and all other entries are discarded. If there is no entry with such a ToS, then only the routing table entries whose ToS is normal (0000 in binary) are kept. All others are discarded.

If any of the steps returns no routing table entries, the algorithm quits and advises the routing engine to drop the datagram.

To understand better what actually happens in the steps of the algorithm, let's consider several examples. In the examples, we won't use the ToS field because it is rare and because it is not practically useful.

Suppose we have a router whose routing table has the entries shown in Table 1.5. Notice that entries 4 and 6 have identical network prefix fields and output interface fields. However, the next-hop router fields are different, which makes simultaneous existence of these routing table entries possible.

Suppose the router receives a datagram destined for IP address 10.35.63.45. Following are the results of each step of the algorithm:

- The Basic Match step keeps routing table entries 1, 2, 4, and 6 and discards entries 3, 5, 7, 8, and 9.
- The Longest Match step keeps table entries 4 and 6 because they boast the longest network prefixes.

Thus, the algorithm returns routing table entries 4 and 6 as the result of its operation.

Suppose now that a datagram destined for IP address 10.255.5.1 arrives. Following are the results of each step of the algorithm:

Table 1.5   The routing table of a hypothetical router.

Entry #	Network Prefix	Output Interface	Next-Hop Router
1	8.0.0.0/5	Ethernet 0	192.168.1.1
2	10.1.0.0/16	TokenRing 0	192.168.2.1
3	172.0.0.0/8	Serial 0	172.16.1.1
4	10.32.0.0/14	Ethernet 1	10.32.1.10
5	10.32.1.0/24	Ethernet 1	-
6	10.32.0.0/14	Ethernet 1	10.32.1.11
7	192.168.1.0/24	Ethernet 0	-
8	192.168.2.0/24	TokenRing 0	-
9	172.16.1.0/30	Serial0	-

- The Basic Match step keeps routing only table entry 1 and discards all other entries.

- The Longest Match step keeps table entry 1.

Therefore, the datagram is sent out of the interface Ethernet 0 to the next-hop router 192.168.1.1.

In the last example, a datagram that is destined for IP address 9.1.1.1 arrives. Following are the results of each step of the algorithm:

- The Basic Match step keeps only routing table entry 1 and discards all other entries.

- The Longest Match step keeps table entry 1.

Like in the previous example, the datagram is forwarded to the next-hop router 192.168.1.1 through the Ethernet 0 interface>

Classful Routing Algorithm

Unlike the classless routing algorithm, the classful one makes the following assumptions:

- Unicast network classes exist; hence, every IP address belongs to one of them.

- IP address allocation must be contiguous within a classful network address. This means that for any two hosts whose interfaces are assigned IP addresses that belong to the same classful network address, there must be a path through segments addressed within the same classful network address. In other words, two hosts whose interfaces are addressed within the same classful network address cannot be separated completely by a segment or group of segments that is not addressed in the same classful network address.

- Supernets exist and can appear in the routing table.

For example, host H1 and H2 in Figure 1.17 cannot communicate if routers R1 and R2 use the classful routing algorithm, because segment 3 (which is addressed in classful network address 172.16.0.0/16) completely separates segments 1 and 2 (both are addressed in classful network address 10.0.0.0/8).

Like the classless routing algorithm, the classful one consists of three steps: the Basic Match, Longest Match, and Weak ToS (which, again, is optional). As before, the algorithm takes a destination IP address and the routing table as arguments and returns zero, one, or several routing table entries that can be used to forward the datagram. In fact, the difference between the two algorithms lies only at the Basic Match step. For that reason, I will explain only the Basic Match step of the classful routing algorithm; the other steps can be taken from the description of the classless routing algorithm.

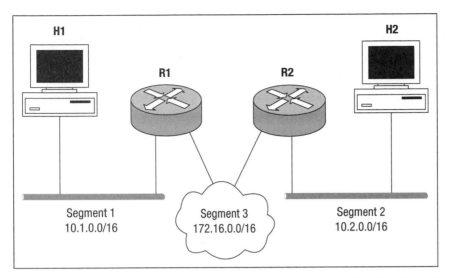

Figure 1.17 This network is "Illegal" from the perspective of the classful routing algorithm.

- The Basic Match step of the classful routing algorithm first determines the classful network address of the destination IP address. If the IP address of any router's interfaces belongs to the same classful network, then all routing entries whose network prefix fields contain supernets are discarded. After that, the algorithm compares the destination IP address against network prefixes of the routing entries that were not discarded, keeping only those that match the IP address.

If any of the steps of the classful routing algorithm returns no routing entries, the algorithm quits and returns no routing entries.

TIP: *It is convenient to think of a router that uses classful routing protocol as if it "knows" too much about the networks to which it is directly connected. It assumes that the destination is unreachable if it is connected to a certain classful network and if it does not have a nonsupernet route for an IP address that belongs to this classful network. Notice that, the router may have a route for the network prefix equal to the classful network address (such as 10.0.0.0/8), in which case this route is used if no other "more specific" route appears in the routing table.*

To understand how the classful routing algorithm differs from the classless one, let's use the same examples as we used in the previous section. A datagram destined for IP address 10.35.63.45 arrives on one of the router's input interfaces. Following are the results of each step of the algorithm:

- The Basic Match step first figures out that the classful network address to which the destination IP address belongs is 10.0.0.0/8. The presence of routing table entry 5 indicates that the router is directly connected to a segment addressed within the classful network address 10.0.0.0/8; therefore, table entries 1 and 3 are discarded because they are supernets. After that, the algorithm compares the destination IP address against the routing table entries that are left in the routing table, keeping table entries 2, 4, and 6, and discarding table entries 5, 7, 8, and 9.

- The Longest Match step keeps table entries 4 and 6 because they boast the longest network prefixes.

Like before, routing table entries 4 and 6 are returned as the result of the algorithm operation.

A datagram destined for IP address 10.255.5.1 arrives. Following are the results of each step of the algorithm:

- The Basic Match step first figures out that the classful network address to which the destination IP address belongs is 10.0.0.0/8. The presence of routing table entry 5 indicates that the router is directly connected to a segment addressed within the classful network address 10.0.0.0/8; therefore, table entries 1 and 3 are discarded because, they are supernets. After that, the algorithm compares the destination IP address against the routing table entries that are left in the routing table and discards all of them. The Basic Match step returns no table entries, therefore, the algorithm quits and returns no routes which advises the router to drop the datagram.

Notice in the case of the classful routing algorithm that the datagram is dropped because the router is connected to a segment addressed within network 10.0.0.0/8 yet does not have a nonsupernet route for the destination IP address.

A datagram that is destined for IP address 9.1.1.1 arrives. Following are the results of each step of the algorithm:

- The Basic Match step first figures out that the classful network address to which the destination IP address belongs is 9.0.0.0/8. The router is not connected to any segment addressed within classful network address 9.0.0.0/8; therefore, no routing table entries are discarded. The algorithm compares the destination IP address against the routing table entries and keeps table entry 1, which is returned as a result of the Basic Match step.

- The Longest Match step keeps table entry 1.

This time, however, the classful routing algorithm behaves in exactly the same way as the classless routing algorithm. This happens because the router does not have any interface addressed within classful network address 9.0.0.0/8; therefore, all supernet routing table entries are preserved.

After the Algorithm Is Done

After the algorithm—whether classless or classful—is finished, the datagram must either be forwarded or dropped. As we know, the datagram must be dropped if the algorithm returns no routing table entries.

If the routing algorithm returns no routing table entries, then there are two choices: A single routing table entry is returned or multiple routing table entries are returned.

The way the routing engine handles a single routing table entry is obvious. It uses the output interface and the IP address of the next-hop router (if not blank) to forward the datagram towards its destination. But how does the routing engine handle multiple routing entries? It is actually up to the designers of the router to answer this question. They can decide to use only one routing table entry, let's say the first one, and ignore all of the others, or they can decide to use all of the routing table entries.

This latter case requires explanation. Obviously, multiple routing table entries cannot be used simultaneously to forward a single datagram. However, they can be used to forward subsequent datagrams so that each datagram is sent using the routing information contained in the routing table entry that was least recently used (a technique called *load balancing*).

Load Balancing

Load balancing has two major approaches. The first approach specifies that datagrams destined for a network prefix for which the routing algorithm returns multiple routing table entries be sent using these entries in a round-robin fashion. This approach is called *per-packet load balancing*.

The other approach requires the routing engine to randomly choose the routing table entry when the *first* datagram destined for its destination IP address arrives at the router. All subsequent datagrams destined for this IP address will be forwarded using the information in the chosen routing table entry. This approach is called *per-destination load balancing*, and it is the preferred approach if the router is required to perform load balancing.

Methods of Populating Routes into the Routing Table

The existence of the routing table on a router at least requires methods of adding routing table entries. Methods of modifying and removing routing table entries are also required, because the routing information can change in the course of the router operation.

The routing table can be maintained in three ways:

- If an operational interface on a router is assigned an IP address and a network prefix length, then a routing table entry that contains the resulting network prefix and references the interface in the output interface field is created. The next-hop router field is left blank. The created route is called *directly connected*. If the network prefix part of the interface's IP address is changed, the routing table entry is automatically modified to reflect this change. If the interface goes down or becomes administratively disabled, the routing table entry is removed.

- Routing table entries can be created, modified, and removed manually (via an administrative action). The routing table entries created manually are called *static*; likewise, the routes described by these entries are called *static routes*.

- Routing table entries can be created, modified, and removed by means of special auxiliary protocols called *routing protocols*. A single router can implement multiple routing protocols. The routing table entries created by routing protocols are called *dynamic*; likewise, the routes described by these entries are called *dynamic*.

A routing table entry that is being added must meet certain requirements before it is actually inserted into the routing table. If it does not meet the requirements, it is not inserted.

The requirements are as follows:

- The output interface to which the routing table entry points must be operational. For example, if an interface is physically disconnected or administratively disabled, no entry that points to this interface can be added to the routing table.

- If the IP address of the next-hop router is used, the IP address must belong to one of the network prefixes configured on the router's interfaces. Otherwise, the entry is not added.

An ambiguity can arise if two or more sources of routing information try to insert routing table entries for the same network prefix. A similar situation occurs if one or more sources of routing information tries to insert a routing table entry for the same network prefix for which an entry in the routing table already exists and was created by a different source. In both cases, the ambiguity is resolved by prioritizing the sources of routing information. The source with the highest priority is allowed to insert its routing table entry, and all other sources are ignored. If an entry for the network prefix already exists, it is replaced with the new entry only if the source of the new entry has higher priority than the source that created the existing entry.

Notice that an ambiguity is detected *only* by comparing the network prefixes of the routes in conflict. The other two fields—that is, the output interface and the next-hop router—are not compared. This may appear to contradict to the previously made statement that two or more routes for the *same* network prefix can simultaneously exist in the routing table providing the other two fields produce a unique combination for each of these routes. To make this possible, a co-existence condition of multiple routes for the same network prefix is introduced; the condition specifies that only the same source can install multiple routes for the same network prefix. But again, these routes are subject to the described ambiguity check. For example, if a single route whose source has a higher priority than the source of the multiple routes for the same network prefix is submitted for installation in the routing table, it supersedes *all* of the multiple routes for that network prefix.

The priorities are called *administrative distances* of the sources of routing information. The administrative distances range from 0 through 255. The smaller the administrative distance, the higher the priority of the corresponding source of routing information. The connected routes always have the highest priority, that is 0. Except for a few cases, administrative distances of sources of routing information can be changed from their default values.

A router usually keeps track of the administrative distances by means of an extra field in each routing table that stores the value of the administrative distance of the source that inserted the routing table entry. This way, whenever an entry for a certain network prefix is being installed and another entry already exists for that network prefix, the router always knows the administrative distance of the source that created the existing entry and thus can resolve the ambiguity.

The administrative distance of the source of routing information is often associated with the routing table entries it creates. Therefore, it is common practice to say "the administrative distance of a routing table entry" or "the administrative distance of a route."

For example, suppose the routing table of a router consists of the routing table entries shown in Table 1.6.

limited, especially compared with the amount of interaction between the end node itself and source-route bridges.

We examine bridging in this book for two reasons. First, bridging is available on Cisco routers—that is, a Cisco router can be configured as a bridge, whether transparent or source-route. Second, bridging being configured on Cisco routers affects the operation of IP and (what's more important) the operation of the main function of IP routers: routing IP traffic. (Also, aren't you excited to know more about bridging and how it's done on Cisco routers?)

MAC Addresses

Very much like Internet datagrams, LAN frames—often called *MAC frames* in honor of the MAC sublayer of the data link layer—bear two addresses: source and destination. These addresses are called *MAC addresses*.

The structures of the MAC addresses used in most LAN technologies are very similar. Most of them are 48 bits long, with certain bit patterns reserved to denote some predefined destinations, such as all nodes on a segment (broadcast) and the like. The primary purpose of the MAC addresses is to identify the nodes residing on the network segments, so the MAC addresses are usually burned into the read-only memory (ROM) chips located on the nodes' network interface cards (NICs). Some NICs allow the burned MAC address to be redefined and/or additional MAC addresses to be assigned.

Because we'll deal only with Ethernet and token ring in this book, it makes sense to limit ourselves to examining the specifics of only Ethernet and token ring MAC addresses.

Like typical MAC addresses, Ethernet and token ring MAC addresses are 48 bits long. The major difference between the two addresses is the bit order within the individual bytes (from a transmission point of view). Compared to Ethernet, token ring MAC addresses have the reversed bit order. The example below explains the difference:

```
Ethernet:   00000000.11001100.10101111
TokenRing:  00000000.00110011.11110101
```

If an Ethernet or token ring MAC address consists of all 1s, this address is called *broadcast*; a MAC frame destined for the broadcast address is received by all nodes on the segment onto which it is sent.

Table 1.6   The contents of the routing table of a hypothetical router.

Entry #	Network Prefix	Output Interface	Next-Hop Router	Administrative Distance
1	8.0.0.0/5	Ethernet0	192.168.1.1	100
2	10.1.0.0/16	TokenRing0	192.168.2.1	150
3	172.0.0.0/8	Serial0	172.16.1.1	150
4	10.32.0.0/14	Ethernet1	10.32.1.10	200
5	10.32.1.0/24	Ethernet1	-	0
6	10.32.0.0/14	Ethernet1	10.32.1.11	100
7	192.168.1.0/24	Ethernet0	-	0
8	192.168.2.0/24	TokenRing0	-	0
9	172.16.1.0/30	Serial0	-	0

Suppose a source of routing information whose administrative distance is 1 tries to install a route for network prefix 10.32.1.0/28. The entry is inserted because the routing table does not contain an entry for that network prefix. Although network prefix 10.32.1.0/24 contained in entry 5 looks much like the new network prefix, its length (24) is smaller than the length of the new network prefix (28), which makes the network prefixes different.

If a source of routing information whose administrative distance is 150 tries to insert a routing table entry for network prefix 8.0.0.0/5, it fails, because entry 1 already contains this network prefix and its administrative distance is 100 (which is lower than 150).

Interior vs. Exterior Routing Protocols

Routing protocols represent the most widely used method of populating routing information into the routing tables on the routers. Routing protocols are preferred over static routing for two primary reasons:

- Routing protocols significantly reduce the amount of administrative effort that is associated with maintaining up-to-date routing information on the router.

- Routing protocols are specifically made to react to changes in the network topology and therefore are much less susceptible to creating problems associated with the incorrect modification of routing information and outdated routing information. They usually make necessary changes in routing information much faster than humans can.

Routing protocols operate by exchanging routing information. Usually, two routers employing the same routing protocol must reside on the same segment to be able to exchange routing information using this protocol. The aggregate of all of the networks—in which routers exchange routing information using the same protocol—is called the *routing domain* of this protocol. IP routing protocols can be categorized multiple ways. One of the ways has to do with the routing domains of different protocols.

An *autonomous system* is defined as a group of networks under the same administrative authority. If an autonomous system is connected to the Internet, it must present to the other autonomous systems consistent reachability information for the destinations located inside of it. Examples of autonomous systems are large corporate networks, large university networks, and networks of Internet Service Providers (ISPs).

Autonomous systems can employ multiple routing protocols to exchange routing information. The routing protocols that are used to exchange routing information inside autonomous systems are called *interior gateway protocols (IGPs)*. The routing domains of IGPs do not cross the boundaries of autonomous systems.

The routing protocols that are used to exchange the routing information among interconnected autonomous systems are called *exterior gateway protocols (EGPs)*. The routing domains of EGPs span multiple autonomous systems. If the autonomous systems are connected to the Internet, the routing domains of EGPs they use can span the whole Internet.

Classless Inter-Domain Routing (CIDR)
The explosive growth of the Internet and subsequent IP addressing requirements were the primary reasons for the advent of classless IP addressing. As it became more and more difficult to allocate IP addresses for new networks that were connected to the Internet, it became clear that the unicast network classes no longer sufficed.

After classless IP addressing was introduced, a new methodology for allocating IP addresses and routing in the Internet was designed. This new methodology is called *CIDR*.

The primary focus of CIDR is EGPs. EGPs belong to their own area of routing technology. This area is quite different from IGP routing, and it is worth a separate book. For that reason, we won't discuss any EGPs and associated issues here.

For more information on CIDR, refer to RFC 1519 "Classless Inter-Domain Routing (CIDR): An Address Assignment and Aggregation Strategy" and RFC 1518 "An Architecture for IP Address Allocation with CIDR." In addition, RFC 1812 provides a good introduction to CIDR.

Filtering

A typical function of modern routers is traffic filtering, whereby a router decides whether to forward or drop a datagram based on certain administratively defined criteria. Usually, traffic filtering is performed by using access lists as traffic filters. Access lists are logical expressions that specify the desired filtering criteria.

A Note about Hosts

The IP modules of hosts have all three elements of a router: the network interfaces, the routing table, and the routing engine. However, the complexity of these elements in the case of hosts is diminished.

Hosts usually have only a single interface as opposed to routers, which rarely have a single interface. The routing table of a host is used in exactly the same way as the routing table of a router; however, its structure may not contain as many vendor-specific fields, which can be essential for routers. The routing engine of hosts does not have to be as "performance-centric" as the routing engine of the routers. On hosts, IP is only a supplementary part of the operating system, whereas on routers, it is a main component that carries out the primary function of routers.

The most typical IP configuration of hosts is based on the concept of the *default gateway*. The default gateway is an IP address of a router to which the host sends all traffic destined for the segments other than the one on which the host resides. The most typical host routing table comprises only two entries—one directly connected for the network prefix of the segment on which the host resides, and the other one for the default address—that is 0.0.0.0/0. The first entry points to the NIC of the host and blank next-hop router; the second one points to the same NIC and the default gateway. As the second entry is for the network prefix with the length of zero, it will match all IP addresses. Thus, if the host wants to send traffic to an IP address that does not belong to the network prefix of the local segment, it will forward it to the router whose IP address is reference in the routing table entry pointing to 0.0.0.0/0.

The route for the default address is itself often called a *default route* or even *default gateway*. The latter is rarely confusing because the context usually unambiguously implies whether the route or the IP address is being discussed.

NOTE: *The routing table comprising only the default route, and connected routes should typically appear on hosts with a single NIC. Host with multiple NICs should typically have other routes too.*

Hosts and routers also have different requirements. The document that specifies the requirements for hosts is RFC 1122. "Requirements for Internet Hosts—Communication Layers." The requirements for routers are set forth in RFC 1812.

Internet Control Message Protocol

Internet Control Message Protocol (ICMP) is an auxiliary protocol that is used to report error conditions that occur on the Internet layer and to send control messages that are relevant to the Internet layer. ICMP PDUs are often called *error* or *control messages*. The distinction is made based on whether the message reports an error or carries control information.

ICMP messages are transmitted encapsulated into IP datagrams. In other words, ICMP uses the IP datagram transmission service. Nevertheless, ICMP resides on the Internet layer and is, an integral part of IP, although it is considered a separate protocol.

NOTE: *One can think of ICMP not as a separate protocol but as a part of IP. In this case, the ICMP messages should be considered a continuation of the IP datagram headers. This makes ICMP compliant with the multilayer communication model, but, aside from this, it does not seem to serve any other purpose.*

ICMP Control Messages

ICMP resides on the Internet layer, meaning that the transmission of ICMP control messages is not guaranteed. ICMP messages can get lost or become corrupted en route to the destination. If ICMP is used to report an error, the ICMP message is sent to the IP address that appears as the source address in the header of the datagram that caused the error. No message is sent to the destination of the datagram. The IP module on the source machine, upon receipt of the ICMP error message, should take appropriate steps to notify the upper-layer protocols of the error condition. The network node, whose ICMP module generated the error message, does not try to correct the problem.

Each individual ICMP message has its own format. Nevertheless, all ICMP messages share a common part consisting of three fields located at the beginning of the ICMP message. These fields are as follows:

- An 8-bit Type field which identifies the type of the message

- An 8-bit Code field, which provides further information regarding the message

- A 16-bit Checksum field, which is used to verify the integrity of the whole ICMP message

In addition, ICMP messages that report errors always include the header and the first 64 bits of the payload of the datagram that caused the error. Table 1.7 provides information on possible values for the Type field.

Table 1.7   ICMP message types.

TYPE Field	Type Description
0	Echo Reply
1	Unassigned
2	Unassigned
3	Destination Unreachable
4	Source Quench
5	Redirect
6	Alternate Host Address
7	Unassigned
8	Echo
9	Router Advertisement
10	Router Selection
11	Time Exceeded
12	Parameter Problem
13	Timestamp
14	Timestamp Reply
15	Information Request
16	Information Reply
17	Address Mask Request
18	Address Mask Reply
19	Reserved (for Security)
20-29	Reserved (for Robustness Experiment)
30	Traceroute
31	Datagram Conversion Error
32	Mobile Host Redirect
33	IPv6 Where-Are-You
34	IPv6 I-Am-Here
35	Mobile Registration Request
36	Mobile Registration Reply
37-255	Reserved

This chapter provides information only on the most common ICMP messages. Detailed information on all of the ICMP messages currently defined can be found in RFC 792, "Internet Control Message Protocol," and RFC 1700, the latest "Assigned Numbers" document (latest as of this writing).

Echo and Echo Reply

Echo and Echo Reply messages are control messages that are used for testing host reachability through the network. A host, upon receiving an ICMP Echo message, should reply using an ICMP Echo Reply message. An ICMP Echo message can contain optional data, in which case the corresponding ICMP Echo Reply message should contain the same data for verification purposes. The Code field always contains 0.

A popular network testing and troubleshooting tool, *ping*, uses ICMP Echo messages. Unlike most network applications that require both communicating hosts to have software modules responsible for receiving and sending data, ping uses the "built-in" replying capability of IP. In other words, ping can always be used to check the reachability of IP hosts, regardless of what software is installed on them for some reason.

Destination Unreachable

Destination Unreachable is an error message that is sent back to the source host if the datagram cannot be delivered to the destination for some reason.

The Code field is used to indicate why the datagram cannot be delivered. Table 1.8 shows the values the Code field can have.

Table 1.8   The Code values of the ICMP Destination Unreachable error message.

CODE	Description
0	Net Unreachable
1	Host Unreachable
2	Protocol Unreachable
3	Port Unreachable
4	Fragmentation Needed and DF (Don't Fragment) Bit Was Set
5	Source Route Failed
6	Destination Network Unknown
7	Destination Host Unknown
8	Source Host Isolated
9	Communication with Destination Network Is Administratively Prohibited

(continued)

Table 1.8   *The Code values of the ICMP Destination Unreachable error message (continued).*

CODE	Description
10	Communication with Destination Host Is Administratively Prohibited
11	Destination Network Unreachable for Type of Service
12	Destination Host Unreachable for Type of Service

Depending on the value of the Code field, the ICMP Destination Unreachable message can be sent by either an intermediate router or the final destination. For instance, the message with a Code equal to 0, "Net Unreachable," is sent by an intermediate router only if it doesn't know a route to the destination. However, the message with a Code equal to 3, "Port Unreachable," is sent by the destination host itself if the upper-layer protocol port, for which the data is destined, is not available.

Source Quench

The Source Quench message is used when IP needs to perform congestion control. An intermediate router or the destination host usually sends an ICMP Source Quench message for every datagram that it has to drop. The source, upon receiving a Source Quench message, lowers the rate at which it sends the datagrams and keeps lowering the rate as long as it receives the Source Quench messages. Because there is no ICMP message to indicate that the originator of the Source Quench messages is relieved, the host begins increasing the rate when it stops receiving the Source Quench messages. It continues to do so until it either reaches the maximum rate or starts receiving the Source Quench messages again. According to RFC 1812, the use of the Source Quench messages is strongly discouraged.

Redirect

If a router receives a datagram destined for an IP address for which there is a better route through another router, the router may send an ICMP Redirect message back to the source of the datagram. The ICMP Redirect message contains the IP address of the best router en route to the destination and the first 64 bits of the datagram. Even though the router sends an ICMP Redirect message, it routes the datagram.

Although ICMP Redirect messages appear to be a good idea, they have a major shortcoming. Suppose a router receives a datagram from another router and suppose it knows that there is a better route to the destination through a third router. The router forwards the datagram and sends an ICMP Redirect message to the source and not to the "confused" router. But there is really nothing that the source can do about it, because it does not have control over the "confused" router.

Time Exceeded

The ICMP Time Exceeded message is sent by an intermediate router if it either receives a datagram whose TTL field holds 0 or if it itself reduces the TTL field value of a datagram in its memory to 0. The router drops the datagram and sends an ICMP Time Exceeded message back to the source of the datagram.

Link Layer Addressing Considerations

When IP needs to deliver a datagram, it first finds out the IP address of the nexthop to which the datagram needs to be delivered. The nexthop can be a router or the final destination (as in the case of hosts interconnected with a single segment).

The next step for IP is to request the appropriate link layer module to deliver the datagram to the next hop via the intermediate segment. Therefore, among other things, IP must somehow let the link layer module know the link layer identification of the next hop. The only thing that IP knows of the next hop is its IP address, which is meaningless from the perspective of the link layer. Therefore, IP must perform mapping of the next-hop IP address to its link layer identification.

The diversity of modern link layer technologies is substantial, which significantly complicates the task of mapping an IP address to the corresponding link layer identification. Several approaches currently exist, each of which was specifically developed to perform mapping of IP addresses to link layer identifications for a number of link layer technologies of similar nature.

Before we consider the popular ways of mapping IP addresses to link layer identifications, let's first see how various link layer technologies can be categorized from the IP perspective.

All link layer technologies can be categorized into three groups:

- *Broadcast networks*—Allow transmitting a single link layer frame to all of the devices connected to a single segment. Examples of broadcast networks are most local area networks (LANs), such as Ethernet, TokenRing, and FDDI.

- *Point-to-point networks*—Have only two devices interconnected with a single segment. Examples of point-to-point networks are leased lines and circuit switched connections (such as Integrated Services Digital Network ISDN).

- *Non-Broadcast Multiple Access (NBMA) networks*—Allow interconnecting multiple devices; however, they do not provide for sending a single link layer frame destined for all devices on the segment. Examples of NBMA networks are Frame Relay and X.25.

For each of these categories of link layer technologies, IP takes a separate approach to map IP addresses to the corresponding link layer identifications.

For broadcast networks, the approach is called *address resolution*. Address resolution is usually implemented in the form of an auxiliary address-resolution protocol that performs the mapping of IP addresses to link layer identifiers for IP. When IP needs to map an IP address to the corresponding link layer identifier, it invokes the address-resolution protocol, which transmits a link layer broadcast frame that carries a request inquiring as to which device the specified IP address belongs. The frame is destined for the link layer broadcast address and therefore is received by all devices on the segment. The device that possesses the IP address sends a reply back to the device that issued the request. Upon receipt of the reply, the address-resolution protocol module returns the resolved link layer identifier to the IP module.

The majority of broadcast networks are LANs. The link layer identifiers of the devices connected to LANs are implemented as link layer addresses, most often referred to as *Media Access Control (MAC) addresses*, named after the MAC sublayer of the data link layer of OSI/RM.

For LANs, there is a single address-resolution protocol based on the described approach. This protocol is called *Address Resolution Protocol (ARP)*. ARP performs mapping of IP addresses to the corresponding MAC addresses. In addition to transmitting address-resolution requests and replies over a LAN segment, ARP maintains a cache of recently acquired mappings. Most devices on a LAN do not get disconnected for rather long periods; that's why it makes sense to memorize once-resolved mappings in a cache. Nevertheless, a once-established mapping between an IP address and a MAC address can change. It can be a result of a NIC replacement or an IP address being removed from one host's interfaces and transferred to another host. In any case, the once-resolved mappings cannot be stored in the ARP cache forever. This issue is addressed by a timer that ARP maintains for each ARP cache entry; upon expiration of the timer, ARP removes the cache entry. Usually, if a network device receives a packet from another device, the timer associated with the corresponding ARP cache entry is reset. This way, ARP won't time out the entry, which is guaranteed to be up to date, as the IP address and MAC address of the corresponding device are contained in the frames received from it, which confirms the validity of the ARP entry. The formal specification of ARP is presented in RFC 826, "An Ethernet Address Resolution Protocol."

For point-to-point networks, there is really no need for address resolution, because it is *a priori* knowledge that the segment has only two devices. Therefore, unless a datagram is destined for the device's own IP address assigned to the point-to-point interface, it must be transmitted to the other end device.

For NBMA networks, a single approach of mapping IP addresses to the corresponding link layer identifiers does not exist. Sometimes, these technologies allow connected devices to "advertise" whatever Internet layer information they desire; in this case, a technique similar to ARP can be used to resolve the IP addresses to the link layer identifiers. However, this time, there is no request; a device has to "advertise" its IP address and its link layer identity. An example of a protocol that uses this approach is *Inverse Address Resolution Protocol (Inverse ARP)*. If, however, the advertisement service is not provided by an NBMA network, the mapping is performed manually. Typically, the number of devices connected to NBMA networks is limited. Thus, it is usually not too difficult to perform all mappings manually.

Final Notes

This section explains the notation used in the book and what's contained in this book's listings.

Notation of the Router Commands

When explaining the format of router commands, I will stick to using a notation that is very similar to that used in the Cisco documentation. The notation is as follows:

- **Boldface** is used to denote mandatory command elements that must be entered as shown.

- *<Italics in angle brackets>* is used to denote the mandatory command elements that supply values. Values have no predefined format and can consist of alphanumeric (and possibly some other) characters.

- [Text in square brackets] is used to denote optional command elements.

- **Bolded** words in curly brackets separated by vertical bars—such as **{Choice1|Choice2|Choice3}**—specify a mandatory element of the command, which consists of choices (the words). In this example, there are three choices: Choice1, Choice2, and Choice3. One of these must be entered as a part of the command.

- If the previous element is shown in square brackets and is not bolded—such as [{Choice1|Choice2|Choice3}]—this indicates an optional command element consisting of choices.

As you can see, the only difference between Cisco notation and that used in this book is that this book uses angle brackets in addition to italicized text to denote the command elements that supply values. I believe it's important to emphasize the functional role of these elements in a clearer way.

Throughout the book, I use full router commands instead of abbreviated commands. However, I encourage you to use the abbreviated versions whenever possible, as it saves a lot of time.

Listings

Listings are always shown stripped of irrelevant commands. For example, if the section in which the listing appears deals with configuring the Ethernet 0 interface for IP and the complete configuration of the router looks as shown in Listing 1.1, then the configuration that you'll see will look like the code snippet shown below Listing 1.1.

Listing 1.1   Router R1's configuration.

```
!
version 11.0
service password-encryption
service udp-small-servers
service tcp-small-servers
!
hostname R1
!
enable secret 5 $1$wnKY$/E6fuwaPIlU8S/GDGMai91
!
no ip domain-lookup
!
interface Ethernet0
 ip address 10.2.0.1 255.255.255.0
!
interface Serial0
 no ip address
 shutdown
 no fair-queue
!
interface Serial1
 no ip address
 shutdown
!
interface TokenRing0
 no ip address
 shutdown
!
!
line con 0
 exec-timeout 0 0
line aux 0
```

```
 transport input all
line vty 0 4
 exec-timeout 0 0
 password 7 0822455D0A16
 login
!
end
```

Router R1's configuration is as follows:

```
interface Ethernet0
 ip address 10.2.0.1 255.255.255.0
```

The router outputs are also stripped of their irrelevant parts unless it makes the output too difficult to recognize.

In the listings, I will often shade and italicize the elements that are directly relevant to the discussed subject. I will also use comments in the listings. The comments begin with an exclamation point (!); any line that begins with an exclamation point is ignored by the Cisco IOS command line interface. Therefore, the comments are safe to enter.

Immediate Solutions

In this section, we examine how IP addressing is configured on router interfaces, details of some specific interfaces, and how access lists are defined and used.

Configuring IP Addressing on an Interface

Configuring an IP address on an interface is simple. It consists of issuing the command **ip address** <*IP address*> <*subnet mask*> in the interface configuration mode. The parameter <*IP address*> is the representation of the desired IP address in dotted decimal notation. The parameter <*subnet mask*> is a subnet mask in dotted decimal notation that is used to assign the desired network prefix length.

NOTE: Throughout this book, the parameters <IP address>, <subnet mask>, and <wildcard mask> are assumed to be always specified using dotted decimal notation.

It is possible to assign an arbitrary number of secondary IP addresses on a single interface. To do that, the command described above must be followed by the keyword **secondary**.

On a LAN interface, assigning an IP address is usually all that needs to be done to configure it for IP (aside from bringing it up using the command **no shutdown**).

Configuring a Frame Relay Interface

To understand the issues associated with a typical NBMA network, let's consider configuring a serial interface of a Cisco router for a Frame Relay connection.

Frame Relay is a packet-switching technology. Frame Relay defines two types of nodes: *data terminal equipment (DTE)* and *data communication equipment (DCE)*. DTE devices are the user devices, such as routers, bridges, and hosts; DCE devices are the devices that constitute Frame Relay networks, such as Frame Relay switches.

Because the transmission service provided by Frame Relay is optimized for speed, the Frame Relay switches only detect errors in frames; they do not attempt to retransmit corrupted frames. The retransmission is left for the upper-layer protocols.

Frame Relay allows multiplexing multiple logical connections (called *virtual circuits*) over a single physical connection. Currently, Frame Relay defines *permanent virtual circuits (PVCs)*, which are statically configured in a Frame Relay network. *Switched virtual circuits (SVCs)* are in a proposed state. Frame Relay uses numeric *data link circuit identifiers (DLCIs)* to identify the PVCs. From the IP perspective, a DLCI is a link layer identifier of the device on the other end of the PVC.

Frame Relay supports a special service called l*ocal management interface (LMI)*. LMI is used to exchange the management information between the Frame Relay DTE and DCE. An example of management information is the status of an existing PVC. LMI uses a predefined PVC so that both the DTE and DCE can exchange the management information even when no PVC has been defined. There are different versions of LMI, and Cisco IOS supports three: Cisco, ANSI Annex D, and ITU-T Q.933 Annex A. For example, the default LMI, called Cisco LMI, uses PVC 1023.

Two techniques are available to perform a mapping between a DLCI and the IP address of the device on the other end of the PVC: inverse ARP and manual mapping.

A serial interface can be configured for Frame Relay in two ways. One way is to perform all configuration under the serial interface itself. The other way is to define only the encapsulation and optional LMI type under the interface and then use *subinterfaces*. A subinterface is essentially a logical interface that inherits most parameters (such as encapsulation) from its parent interface. From the IP perspective, a subinterface is not different from a regular interface.

Subinterfaces are of two types: point-to-point and multipoint. A point-to-point subinterface can be configured with only a single PVC, and a multipoint subinterface can be configured with multiple PVCs. The point of having subinterfaces will become clear in later chapters, when we discuss dynamic routing protocols. For now, we'll just examine how to configure the subinterfaces.

Performing Frame Relay Configuration on an Interface

A basic configuration of a serial interface for Frame Relay without subinterfaces consists of the following steps (all steps are performed in the interface configuration mode):

1. Configure the Frame Relay encapsulation using the command **encapsulation frame-relay**.

2. Optionally, specify the LMI type, using the command **frame-relay lmi-type** *<lmi-type>*. The LMI type of the interface *must* coincide with the LMI type defined on the Frame Relay switch to which the router's serial interface is connected.

3. Assign an IP address using the command **ip address** *<IP address>* *<subnet-mask>*.

4. To perform manual mapping of the IP address of the router on the other end of the PVC to the local DLCI, use the command **frame-relay map ip** *<IP address> <DLCI>* [broadcast]. The optional parameter [broadcast] requires the router to forward packets destined for the IP broadcast address to that PVC. Notice that this parameter does not change the NBMA nature of the Frame Relay network.

Inverse-ARP in enabled on the interface by default. Therefore, if manual mapping is not performed, the router tries to use Inverse ARP to resolve the remote router's IP address. To enable Inverse ARP explicitly use the command **frame-relay inverse-arp ip** *<DLCI>*.

NOTE: *The commands **frame-relay map ip** and **frame-relay inverse-arp ip** are not mutually exclusive. They can be used simultaneously in the cases when multiple PVCs are configured on a single interface.*

In Figure 1.18, the LMI types and DLCIs are different on both sides of the connection through the Frame Relay network. This is possible because they both have a local significance between the DTE (the routers in our case) and DCE, the Frame Relay switches (not shown).

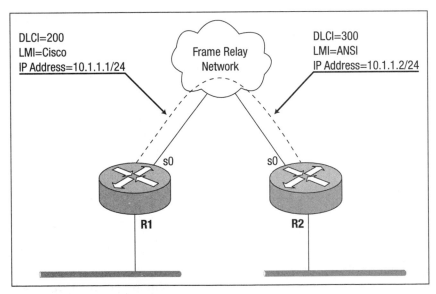

Figure 1.18   Two routers connected over a Frame Relay network.

The partial configurations of both routers are shown below. The configurations rely on manual mapping of the IP addresses onto the corresponding DLCIs.

Router R1's configuration is as follows:

```
interface Serial0
 ip address 10.1.1.1 255.255.255.0
 encapsulation frame-relay
 frame-relay map ip 10.1.1.2 200 broadcast
```

Router R2's configuration is as follows:

```
interface Serial0
 ip address 10.1.1.2 255.255.255.0
 encapsulation frame-relay
 frame-relay lmi-type ansi
 frame-relay map ip 10.1.1.1 300 broadcast
```

NOTE: *The configurations are partial because they do not reflect configurations of the routers' interfaces connected to the Ethernet segments, which are also present in Figure 1.18.*

Inverse ARP is enabled by default, so no specific commands appear in the router's configuration. Thus, the configurations of routers R1 and R2 using Inverse ARP look like the configurations shown in the above code snippets except for the lines showing the command **frame-relay map ip**—these lines do not exist in the case of Inverse ARP.

Performing Frame Relay Configuration on a Subinterface

Frame Relay configuration using a subinterface consists of the following steps:

1. Configure Frame Relay encapsulation on the appropriate serial interface using the command **encapsulation frame-relay** in interface configuration mode.

2. Optionally, specify the LMI type for the whole interface using the command **frame-relay lmi-type** *<lmi-type>* in interface configuration mode.

3. Define one or several point-to-point or multipoint subinterfaces (you can use both types of subinterfaces in a single router's configuration) using the command **interface Serial** *<Interface #>.<Subinterface #>* **point-to-point**, or **interface Serial** *<Interface #>.<Subinterface #>* **multipoint**, respectively. The parameter *<Interface #>* is the number of a physical serial

interface; the parameter *<Subinterface #>* is the number of the local subinterface you wish to configure. After this command is issued, the command line interface transfers to subinterface configuration mode, in which the rest of the configuration is done.

4. Assign an IP address to each subinterface using the command **ip address** *<IP address> <subnet mask>*.

5. For point-to-point subinterfaces, assign a DLCI using the command **frame-relay interface-dlci** *<DLCI>*. Once you've done this, the router will automatically establish a mapping between the whole subnet (to which the assigned IP address belongs) and the DLCI. For multipoint subinterfaces, choose whether the interface uses Inverse ARP or static mapping for address resolution. For Inverse ARP, use the command **frame-relay interface-dlci** *<DLCI>*. To define static mapping, use the command **frame-relay map ip** *<remote IP address> <DLCI>*. This command can be optionally followed by the keyword **broadcast**, which allows sending datagrams destined for the IP broadcast addresses.

Figure 1.19 shows an example of a Frame Relay network to which the routers are connected using subinterfaces. Listings 1.2 through 1.4 show the interface configurations of all three routers.

Listing 1.2   Router R1's configuration.

```
interface Serial0
 no ip address
 encapsulation frame-relay

! The subinterface is configured with static mapping
interface Serial0.1 multipoint
 ip address 10.1.0.1 255.255.255.0
 frame-relay map ip 10.1.0.2 200 broadcast

! The subinterface uses Inverse ARP
interface Serial0.2 multipoint
 ip address 10.2.0.1 255.255.255.0
 frame-relay interface-dlci 100
```

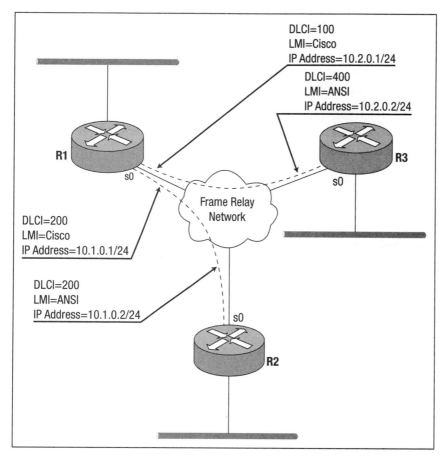

Figure 1.19   Multiple routers are configured for Frame Relay using subinterfaces.

Listing 1.3   Router R2's configuration.

```
interface Serial0
 no ip address
 encapsulation frame-relay
 frame-relay lmi-type ansi

! For point-to-point subintefaces the
! mapping is performed automatically
interface Serial0.1 point-to-point
 ip address 10.1.0.2 255.255.255.0
 frame-relay interface-dlci 300
```

Listing 1.4   Router R3's configuration.

```
interface Serial0
 no ip address
 encapsulation frame-relay
 frame-relay lmi-type ansi

! The subinterface uses Inverse ARP
interface Serial0.1 multipoint
 ip address 10.2.0.2 255.255.255.0
 frame-relay interface-dlci 400
```

Understanding and Configuring a Loopback Interface

The Loopback interface is a logical interface defined only in a router's memory. The Loopback interface has two important features.

- The Loopback interface never goes physically and logically down.

NOTE: *The state of the interface can be determined by looking at the first line of the output of the command* ***show interfaces*** *<Interface ID> <Interface #>. For example, in the case of a Loopback interface, this line looks like "Loopback0 is up, line protocol is up". The first "up" refers to the physical state of the interface; the "line protocol is up" refers to the logical one.*

- Unlike a regular interface, the Loopback interface is not used to connect a router to any network segment.

The Loopback interface has numerous uses, many of which will be considered in the course of this book. For now, we'll just examine the guidelines for the configuration of the Loopback interface.

A Loopback interface is created in a router's memory by using the command **interface Loopback** *<Interface #>*. The parameter *<Interface #>* is the desired number of the created Loopback interface. Multiple Loopback interfaces can be created on a single router. A Loopback interface can be assigned an IP address just like a regular interface. A router can originate datagrams from a Loopback interface using the interface's IP address. Likewise, datagrams can be destined for a Loopback interface's IP address.

A sample configuration of a Loopback interface is shown in the code snippet below

```
interface Loopback0
 ip address 192.168.1.1 255.255.255.0
```

> **NOTE:** *A Loopback interface must not be confused with a IP Loopback address.*

A Loopback interface can be removed using the command **no interface Loopback** *<Interface #>*.

Understanding and Configuring a Tunnel Interface

A Tunnel interface is another example of a logical interface that exists in a router's memory. Unlike a Loopback interface, however, a Tunnel interface is used to transmit network traffic:

The idea behind a Tunnel interface is that it is possible to encapsulate any type of traffic into IP datagrams. The last two lines in Table 1.3 show that two protocols whose PDUs can also be carried inside the payload of IP datagrams are IP itself and general routing encapsulation (GRE). The first protocol is specifically designed to allow encapsulation of an arbitrary protocol's PDUs into another protocol's PDUs, such as IP datagrams. The other protocol is IP, which means that IP datagrams can be encapsulated inside IP datagrams.

Cisco makes use of these two encapsulations in the form of the Tunnel interface. When traffic must be sent out of a Tunnel interface, the router encapsulates this traffic into IP using the encapsulation type administratively defined for the Tunnel interface. By default, the encapsulation is GRE. The available encapsulations are shown in Table 1.9.

Table 1.9   Encapsulation types available for the Tunnel interface.

Keyword	Description
aurp	AURP TunnelTalk AppleTalk encapsulation
cayman	Cayman TunnelTalk AppleTalk encapsulation
dvmrp	DVMRP multicast tunnel
eon	EON-compatible CLNS tunnel
gre	GRE protocol
ipip	IP over IP encapsulation
iptalk	Apple IPTalk encapsulation
nos	IP over IP encapsulation (KA9Q/NOS compatible)

Of these encapsulations, only GRE (denoted by the keyword **gre**) can be used to pass arbitrary traffic through the participating Tunnel interfaces. There are two different IP over IP encapsulations—**ipip** and **nos**; they can be used to pass only IP through Tunnel interfaces. Other types of encapsulations are for special purposes and are irrelevant for this book.

NOTE: *The operation of a Tunnel interface assumes that IP routing works properly in the network, so that the encapsulated traffic can be passed between the participating routers.*

The following steps must be used to configure a Tunnel interface on a router:

1. Create a Tunnel interface using the command **interface tunnel** *<Interface #>*. The parameter *<Interface #>* indicates the number of the created interface.

2. Assign the source IP address for the Tunnel interface using the command **tunnel source** *<IP address>*. The *<IP address>* parameter is the source IP address of the datagrams that carry the encapsulated traffic. Alternatively, the parameter *<IP address>* can be replaced by the parameter *<Interface #>*, which specifies the existing router interface. If the latter version of the command is used, the Tunnel interface will use the IP address of the specified interface.

3. Assign the destination IP address for the Tunnel interface using the command **tunnel destination** *<IP address>*. The encapsulated traffic is passed between the local router and the remote router to which the IP address specified in the command **tunnel destination** belongs.

A Tunnel interface, like a regular interface, has two states—physical and logical A Tunnel interface is always physically up, because it's a logical interface; hence it does not have physical components that can be down. Unlike a Loopback inter face, however, a Tunnel interface can be logically down. A Tunnel interface i logically down if 1) the command **tunnel source** *<Interface>* references the in terface that is logically or physically down, and 2) the command **tunnel destina tion** *<IP address>* references an unreachable IP address.

The code snippet below shows a sample configuration of a Tunnel interface tha uses regular IP over IP encapsulation:

```
interface Tunnel0
 ip address 192.168.1.1 255.255.255.0
 tunnel source 10.0.0.2
 tunnel destination 10.0.0.3
 tunnel mode ipip
```

1. Internet Protocol (IP)

Configuring IP Unnumbered

IP addressing has an interesting feature that actually allows a segment not to be assigned any network prefix. This feature is called *IP unnumbered*. The primary purpose of IP unnumbered is to conserve IP address space. Usually, IP unnumbered is used on point-to-point links, such as a serial connection over a dedicated line.

To configure an interface for IP unnumbered, the command **ip unnumbered** *<Interface>* must be used instead of the command **ip address** *<IP address> <subnet mask>*. Once this command is issued, the interface is assumed to have the same IP address as the interface specified in the parameter *<Interface>*. The interface of the router on the other end of the point-to-point connection must be configured regularly; however, the IP address assigned to it must belong to the same network prefix as the IP address of the interface specified in the parameter *<Interface>* of the command **ip unnumbered**.

Figure 1.20 shows an example of the network in which the routers are configured with IP unnumbered over the serial link between them.

The code snippets below show the routers' configurations.

Router R1's configuration is as follows:

```
interface Ethernet0
 ip address 10.1.0.1 255.255.255.0

interface Serial0
 ip unnumbered Ethernet0
```

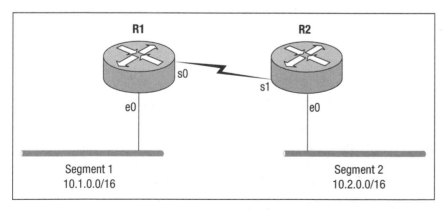

Figure 1.20   Routers are configured with IP unnumbered on their interfaces interconnected with the serial link.

Router R2's configuration is as follows:

```
interface Ethernet0
 ip address 10.2.0.1 255.255.255.0

interface Serial1
 ip address 10.1.0.2 255.255.255.0
```

Configuring and Understanding ProxyARP

ProxyARP is an extension of a regular ARP that allows a router to accept ARP requests for IP addresses belonging to network prefixes for which it has routes. When a router detects an ARP request for a reachable IP address that does not belong to the network prefix of the segment on which the ARP request was issued, the router replies with the MAC address of its interface attached to this segment. Once the traffic destined for that IP address starts arriving on the router's interface, the router performs regular routing.

In other words, the idea behind ProxyARP is that the router pretends that it is the remote destination by supplying its own MAC address for the remote IP address.

On Cisco routers, ProxyARP is enabled by default. To disable it, use the command **no ip proxy-arp** in LAN interface configuration mode. To re-enable it back, use the command **ip proxy-arp**.

Hosts resort to ProxyARP in two cases:

- The IP address of the host's interface is assigned a network prefix whose length is smaller than that of the router's interface. For example, the host's IP address is 10.1.0.100/8, whereas the IP address of the router's interface is 10.1.0.1/24. Obviously, the host will use ARP for every host whose IP address belongs to network prefix 10.0.0.0/8.

- The host is configured with the IP address of the default gateway equal to its own IP address. In this case, the host will use ARP for *every* IP address.

ProxyARP is really a bad idea and as such must be avoided whenever possible. If ProxyARP is used, the hosts generate superfluous broadcast traffic, as they use ARP for IP addresses for which they otherwise wouldn't. Higher-level broadcast traffic causes higher CPU utilization of all devices on the segment.

Using Access Lists to Filter Traffic

An access list is a logical expression that specifies one or more match conditions against which certain characteristics of network traffic are compared. Each condition is accompanied by one of two actions: **permit** or **deny**. When an access list is used, a router cycles through match conditions, comparing them against the values—such as the values of the fields of datagram headers or parameters in routing updates—carried in the network traffic. As soon as the router finds a match, it stops the cycle and returns the action that accompanies the condition that was matched.

Access lists have numerous applications, many of which we'll consider in the course of this book. One of these applications—to filter the traffic the router forwards—is the subject of this section.

When a router filters traffic using access lists, it compares the match conditions against the values of the fields of datagram headers. If this process returns **deny**, the datagram is dropped; otherwise, it is forwarded in accordance with the results of the routing algorithm.

Using Standard Access Lists

Standard access lists allow only comparison of the *source* IP address against a specified match condition.

Standard access lists for filtering network traffic are configured using two steps:

1. Create an access list using the command **access-list** *<AL number>* **{permit|deny}** *<source IP address> <wildcard mask>*. The *<AL number>* parameter is the access list number ranging from 1 through 99. The *<wildcard mask>* parameter specifies how the *<source IP address>* parameter is compared against the source IP address carried in the datagram header. The *<wildcard mask>* parameter represents a 32-bit value whose cleared bits denote the bits of the *<source IP address>* parameter, which must be compared against the corresponding bits of the source IP address of the datagram. All other bits are ignored. The *<source IP address>* and *<wildcard mask>* parameters are specified using the dotted decimal notation.

   An alternative notation can be used to specify the *<source IP address>* and *<wildcard mask>* parameters if the latter is equal to either 0.0.0.0 or 255.255.255.255. If the *<wildcard mask>* parameter is equal to 0.0.0.0, the alternative notation is **host** *<source IP address>*. The keyword **host** indicates that all of the bits are significant; hence, **host** matches only the source IP address that is identical to the *<source IP address>* parameter. If the *<wildcard mask>* parameter is equal to 255.255.255.255, then the alternative notation for both parameters is the single keyword **any**. It signifies that none of the bits must be compared; hence, **any** matches any source IP address.

An access list can consist of multiple lines, which is achieved by entering multiple **access-list** commands with the same *<AL number>* parameter. Any access list contains an implicit **access-list** *<AL number>* **deny any** at the end. This line is always invisible.

NOTE: *Nonexistent access lists, if used, always return the **permit** action. In other words, nonexistent access lists are equivalent to **access-list** <AL number> **permit any**.*

---

2. Apply the access list in the interface configuration mode using the command **ip access-group** *<AL number>* [{in|out}]. If the last optional parameter is **in**, the access list is called *inbound*, which means that only the datagrams that the router *receives* through the interface are checked against the access list. If the last parameter is either blank or **out**, the access list is called *outbound*, which means that only the datagrams that the router is about to *send* out of the interface are checked against the access list.

NOTE: *You can have separate **ip access-group** <AL Number> **in** and **ip access-group** <AL Number> **out** commands on a single interface.*

TIP: *It makes sense to specify more-specific match criteria at the beginning of an access list. For example, if you want to allow only a single host on a certain subnet to access some server located behind a router, compose an access list that first specifies the host's IP address with the **permit** condition, then the subnet address with the **deny** condition, and then use the keyword **any** with the **permit** condition.*

WARNING!   **The lines that constitute an access list cannot be removed individually. If you try to remove an individual line (even if it was the last command that you entered) using the no form of it, you will remove the entire access list.**

Let's examine how router R in Figure 1.21 should be configured to allow only host H3 to communicate with host H1.

Listing 1.5 shows the configuration of router R1 from Figure 1.21. Pay attention to the order of the conditions in access list 1. It demonstrates the technique described in the tip above.

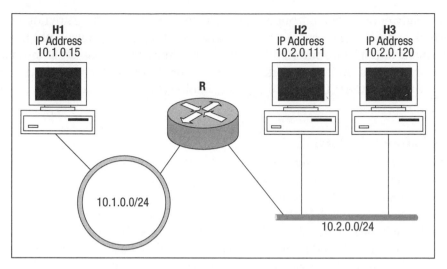

Figure 1.21   Router R allows only host H3 to communicate with host H1.

Listing 1.5   Router R1's configuration.

```
interface Ethernet0
 ip address 10.2.0.1 255.255.255.0

interface TokenRing0
 ip address 10.1.0.1 255.255.255.0
 ip access-group 1 out
 ring-speed 16

access-list 1 permit host 10.2.0.120
access-list 1 deny   10.2.0.0 0.0.0.255
access-list 1 permit any
```

In this particular configuration, we do not need the last **access list 1 permit any** line. It was added in case other segments are connected to router R1 and may need access to host H1.

The command **ping 10.1.0.15** issued on host H2 fails, as shown in the code snippet below:

```
C:\>ping 10.1.0.15

Pinging 10.1.0.15 with 32 bytes of data:

Reply from 10.2.0.1: Destination net unreachable.
Reply from 10.2.0.1: Destination net unreachable.
```

Interestingly enough, the output of ping indicates that the packets are not simply silently dropped by the router. (If that were the case, the output would be "Request timed out.") The router returns ICMP Destination Unreachable messages whose type is 0x0D in hexadecimal or 13 in decimal, which does not correspond to any "official" ICMP Destination Unreachable types. (See Table 1.8 earlier in this chapter.)

Using Extended Access Lists

Extended access lists provide more flexibility than standard access lists in terms of which characteristics of a datagram can be matched. Standard access lists allow only matching of the source address of a datagram. Extended access lists provide a means to match both source and destination addresses, the destination protocol (such as TCP, UDP, and ICMP), protocol-specific characteristics (such as TCP or UDP ports), and much more. The same procedure defined for standard access lists applies when using extended access lists for filtering user data traffic. The format of an extended access list follows:

access-list *<AL number>* **{permit|deny}** *<protocol> <source IP address> <source wildcard mask> <destination IP address> <destination wildcard mask>* [protocol-specific parameters]

In the case of extended access lists, the parameter *<AL number>* ranges from 100 through 199.

The parameter *<protocol>* can be either the IP protocol number—that is, the value passed in the Protocol field of an IP datagram header—or the name of a protocol. Some currently available protocol names are shown in Table 1.10.

Table 1.10   Protocol names available with extended access lists.

Name	Description
ip	Any of the Internet Protocol Suite Protocol (which means that the router will not analyze the Protocol field)
tcp	TCP
udp	UDP
icmp	ICMP
igrp	Cisco's IGRP routing protocol
eigrp	Cisco's EIGRP routing protocol
ospf	OSPF routing protocol
gre	Cisco's GRE tunneling
ipinip	IP in IP tunneling

(continued)

Table 1.10   Protocol names available with extended access lists (continued).

Name	Description
igmp	IGMP
nos	KA9Q NOS-compatible IP over IP tunneling
ahp	Authentication Header Protocol
esp	Encapsulation Security Payload
pcp	Payload Compression Protocol

NOTE: The information presented in Table 1.10 was taken from a router running IOS Version 12.0(2a). Depending on the version of IOS that your routers run, some of these keywords may not be available. Future releases of the Cisco IOS may support more keywords.

Only the protocols that use IP datagram delivery services are supported. For example, the routing protocol RIP is not available because it relies on UDP for delivery of its PDUs.

The combinations *<source IP address>* **255.255.255.255** and *<destination IP address>* **255.255.255.255** can be replaced by the keyword **any**; likewise, the combinations *<source IP address>* **0.0.0.0** and *<destination IP address>* **0.0.0.0** can be replaced by **host** *<IP address>*. For protocol-specific options, see the Cisco documentation.

Let's modify the network traffic-filtering task for the network in Figure 1.21. This time, we will allow host H1 to access only the Telnet and Daytime services on host H3. All other communication between any two hosts on the network must be fully available.

Listing 1.6 demonstrates one of the ways in which this task can be performed. The last four bolded lines show the extended access list defined for the task. It is applied as an inbound network traffic filter on the interface TokenRing 0.

Listing 1.6   Router R's configuration.

```
interface Ethernet0
 ip address 10.2.0.1 255.255.255.0

interface TokenRing0
 ip address 10.1.0.1 255.255.255.0
 ip access-group 100 in
 ring-speed 16
```

```
access-list 100 permit tcp any host 10.2.0.120 eq telnet
access-list 100 permit tcp any host 10.2.0.120 eq daytime
access-list 100 deny    ip any host 10.2.0.120
access-list 100 permit ip any any
```

If we try to ping host H3 from host H1, ping fails (see the following code snippet). The extended access list applied as an inbound network traffic filter on router R1 disallows host H1 to ping host H3, as follows:

```
C:\>ping 10.2.0.120

Pinging 10.2.0.120 with 32 bytes of data:

Reply from 10.1.0.1: Destination net unreachable.
Reply from 10.1.0.1: Destination net unreachable.
```

However, Telnetting from host H1 to host H3 is successful (see the following code snippet). The access list does not block Telnet traffic from host H1 to host H3, as follows:

```
C:\>telnet 10.2.0.120
Trying 10.2.0.120...
Connected to 10.2.0.120.  Escape key is Ctrl-].

Welcome to the Telnet Service on THUNDER

Username:
```

Listing 1.7 shows that both ping and Telnet succeed if they are used to access host H2 from host H1. Neither Telnet nor ping packets are blocked by the access list if they are destined for host H2.

Listing 1.7   The output of the commands telnet 10.2.0.111 and ping 10.2.0.111 issued on host H1.

```
C:\>ping 10.2.0.111

Pinging 10.2.0.111 with 32 bytes of data:

Reply from 10.2.0.111: bytes=32 time<10ms TTL=127
Reply from 10.2.0.111: bytes=32 time<10ms TTL=127
Reply from 10.2.0.111: bytes=32 time<10ms TTL=127
Reply from 10.2.0.111: bytes=32 time<10ms TTL=127
```

```
C:\>telnet 10.2.0.111
Trying 10.2.0.111...
Connected to 10.2.0.111.  Escape key is Ctrl-].

Welcome to the Telnet Service on HUGEWAVE

Username:
```

Using Named Access Lists

In Cisco IOS Version 11.2, a new format of access lists was introduced. This new format is called *named access-lists* because, instead of a number, a name can be used to identify an access list. The functionality behind named access lists remains the same as the functionality of regular standard and extended access lists.

To create a named access list, follow these steps:

1. Create an access list header using the command **ip access-list {standard|extended}** *<AL name>*. After you enter this command, the command line interface is transferred to access list configuration mode. The parameter *<AL name>* signifies the name of the access list; unlike the number, it can contain any alphanumeric characters.

2. In access list configuration mode, enter one or several match clauses. The format of the match clauses depends on whether the access list is standard or extended. In both cases, the match clauses have the same format as the part of the regular standard or extended access list from the word **permit** or **deny** up to the end of the access list.

NOTE: *A named access list is terminated with an implicit **deny any** condition at the end.*

TIP: *Instead of the parameter <AL name>, you can use a number, just as with regular access lists. For standard access lists, the number can be in the range from 1 through 99; for extended access lists, the number can be in the range from 100 through 199.*

For example, Listing 1.8 shows a standard named access list, which is an equivalent of the standard access list from Listing 1.5; likewise, Listing 1.9 shows an extended named access list, an equivalent of the extended access list from Listing 1.6.

Listing 1.8   Router R configured with a standard named access list.

```
interface Ethernet0
 ip address 10.2.0.1 255.255.255.0

interface TokenRing0
 ip address 10.1.0.1 255.255.255.0
 ip access-group StdNAL out
 ring-speed 16

ip access-list standard StdNAL
 permit 10.2.0.120
 deny    10.2.0.0 0.0.0.255
 permit any
```

Listing 1.9   Router R configured with an extended named access list.

```
interface Ethernet0
 ip address 10.2.0.1 255.255.255.0

interface TokenRing0
 ip address 10.1.0.1 255.255.255.0
 ip access-group ExtNAL in
 ring-speed 16

ip access-list extended ExtNAL
 permit tcp any host 10.2.0.120 eq telnet
 permit tcp any host 10.2.0.120 eq daytime
 deny    ip any host 10.2.0.120
 permit ip any any
```

Chapter 2

Transparent and Source-Route Bridging

If you need an immediate solution to:	See page:
Configuring Transparent Bridging	126
Configuring Source-Route Bridging	147
Configuring Source-Route Translational Bridging	176

In Depth

Bridges are devices whose functionality lies at the link layer of the Internet model. Although the Internet model does define the link layer, the Internet technologies and their development focus primarily on the internet and transport layers. The link layer is really a formality; its presence simply acknowledges the networking technologies that are essential to the internet layer's internet protocol (IP) operation. However, no further specification is made; instead, the Internet technology and development rely on the link layer technologies that are either already available or are currently under development.

Therefore, it makes sense to explain bridging in terms of the open systems interconnection reference model (OSI/RM), as opposed to the Internet model. OSI/RM provides quite a developed framework for its two lower layers—the data link layer and the physical layer—which are a rough equivalent of the link layer of the Internet model. For example, the specification provided for the data link layer breaks the data link layer into two sublayers—the logical link control (LLC) sublayer and the media access control (MAC) sublayer.

The network layer of OSI/RM is a very close equivalent of the internet layer of the Internet model. Therefore, it's legitimate to say that IP, from the OSI/RM point of view, belongs to the network layer. Because IP is the book's main subject, whatever we discuss must be viewed from its perspective. And, as we agreed that bridging should be explained in terms of OSI/RM, we must understand which place IP itself occupies in OSI/RM.

The details behind the physical and data link layers and the data link layer's two sublayers are beyond the scope of this book. Nevertheless, one aspect of the MAC sublayer—MAC addressing—is crucial understanding how bridging works. Thus, it will be discussed in subsequent sections.

The Concept of Bridging

The concept of bridging is simple—bridges interconnect physical segments on the data link layer. This makes several segments appear to the network layer protocols (such as IP) as a single segment.

Bridging is primarily used to interconnect physical segments with large numbers of end nodes. The typical example of this type of segments is a local area network,

(LAN). Although bridging can be used to interconnect other types of physical networks, such as wide area networks (WANs) or metropolitan-area networks (MANs), it is used mostly in LAN environments.

The pure bridging concept does not specify any further details with regard to how the segments must be interconnected, whether end nodes are required to be aware of the bridging, and so on. These details are left to the discretion of the designers of individual bridging technologies.

From the generality of the bridging concept, two principal bridging approaches have emerged. The first approach declares that the bridging operation must not be visible to the end nodes on the segments interconnected by means of bridging. This approach created the foundation for the *transparent bridging* technology, which is discussed in subsequent sections. On the contrary, the second approach requires awareness and involvement on the side of the end nodes. If some end nodes are not aware of the bridging, they won't be able to communicate if they reside on segments interconnected by bridging. From the second approach emerged a technology called *source-route bridging*, which is also discussed in subsequent sections.

We should pause to explain a bit of the bridging-related terminology. A device that interconnects physical segments by means of bridging is called a *bridge*. Bridge interfaces are called *ports*. I will call a single physical segment without bridges a *LAN segment*. (It's a *LAN* segment, not simply a *segment* because both transparent bridging and source-route bridging are used to interconnect LANs. Thus, it makes sense to make *LAN* the distinguisher between segments in the IP-related subjects and the bridging-related ones.) Likewise, a number of segments interconnected only with bridges are *bridged LANs*.

NOTE: *The recent term* switching *or* layer two switching *simply means* bridging. *Likewise,* switches *or* layer two switches *are* bridges.

Why Do We Discuss Bridging?

You must be wondering why we are discussing bridging (a data link layer technology) in a book about IP (a network layer technology) and Cisco routers (clearly not bridges, which nowadays are marketed as switches).

Furthermore, bridging, although clearly a link layer technology, does not provide many services to the internet layer (or the network layer of OSI/RM for that matter) and thus to IP. Transparent bridging is totally "transparent" to IP, and, although source-route bridging does require certain interaction with IP, it's still very

Both Ethernet and token ring MAC addresses have two special-purpose bits. The purpose of the first bit is to denote whether the frame addresses a single node, (in which case the bit is cleared), or a group of nodes, (in which case the bit is set). This bit is often referred to as the *group/individual* bit. The MAC addresses whose group/individual bit is cleared are called *unicast* MAC addresses; likewise, the MAC addresses whose group/individual bit is set are called *multicast* MAC addresses.

The second special-purpose bit is used to denote the origin of the MAC address. If the bit is cleared, then the address was officially acquired from Institute of Electrical and Electronics Engineers (IEEE); if it's set, then the address is administratively assigned locally. The latter also means that no officially assigned MAC address, with the exception of the broadcast MAC address, can have this bit cleared.

These two special bits are located in the first byte (in the transmission order) of both Ethernet and token ring MAC addresses. Figure 2.1 shows the exact location of the two bits in both cases.

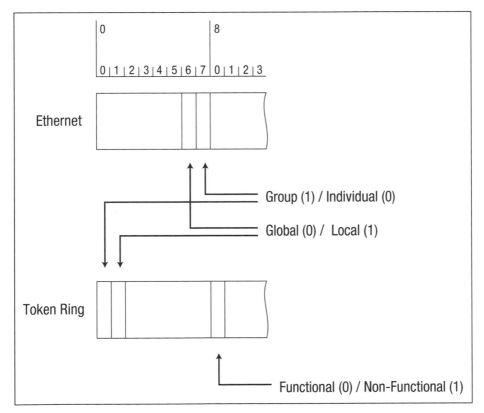

Figure 2.1   Special bits in Ethernet and token ring MAC addresses.

In the case of token ring, the multicast MAC addresses are subdivided as *functional* and *nonfunctional*. This subdivision is accomplished by means of one extra bit (shown in Figure 2.1) that when cleared indicates that the multicast address is functional. If the bit is set, the address is nonfunctional.

NOTE: *The functional/nonfunctional bit has no meaning in the context of unicast token ring MAC addresses.*

Functional MAC addresses are primarily used for purposes specific to token ring technology. There are cases, however, when certain functional MAC addresses are allocated for other technologies, although the allocation is done by the authority that manages the token ring functional address space.

Of all possible functional MAC addresses, only 31 are defined—a rather small number. This limited number explains why applications that are not a part of the token ring technology must be specifically allocated functional MAC addresses through the central authority. Many of the functional MAC addresses are shared among different network applications.

The trouble with token ring multicast MAC addresses is that most token ring controllers do not support them. Instead, they support only the 31 functional MAC addresses, one of which can be used for all multicasting purposes.

NOTE: *Chapter 9 has more information on how multicast is implemented on token ring networks.*

Transparent Bridging

Transparent bridging is a standard way of interconnecting LANs. It's fully defined in the IEEE standard 802.1D, *Information Technology—Telecommunications and Information Exchange Between Systems—Local Area Networks—Media Access Control (Mac) Bridges*. The standard has also been adopted by ISO as International Standard ISO/IEC 10038.

As mentioned before, transparent bridging does not require any involvement on the side of the hosts. In other words, a host sending a frame to another host, which is located behind a transparent bridge, won't even know that the frame will cross the bridge.

To make such transparent operation possible, transparent bridges follow certain rules when forwarding packets and implement a special bridging protocol, which will be discussed shortly.

Before we get down to the rules that transparent bridges follow, it's important to mention that—unlike some other types of bridges—transparent bridges can have an unlimited number of ports.

No Reverse Forwarding

The first rule that transparent bridges follow is that they never forward a frame back onto the segment on which it was received. In future, I will further refer to this rule as *no reverse forwarding*. The idea behind no reverse forwarding is simple: If the destination is located on the segment from which the frame arrived, it will obviously receive the frame, and thus there is no need to duplicate the frame. In the network example shown in Figure 2.2, if host H1 sends host H3 a frame bridge, B1 must not forward it back onto segment 1.

As the end nodes do not know anything about the bridges interconnecting the segments, they won't notify the bridges about their (end nodes') locations. Thus, in order to assure that the frames are delivered to their destinations, a bridge should flood the frames through all its ports except for the one on which the frames were received.

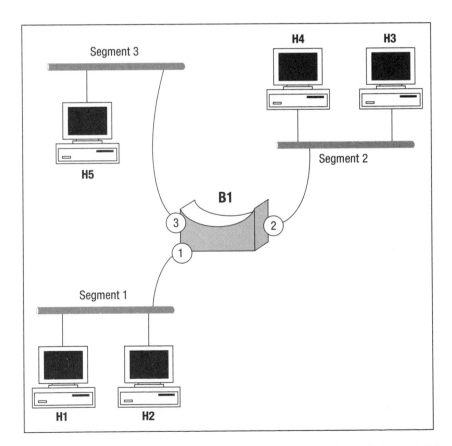

Figure 2.2 If host H1 sends a frame to host H3, the bridge won't forward it back onto segment 1. The bridge's ports are labeled as circles with numbers inside.

The Filtering Database

Obviously, the described operation of a bridge is not optimal. The frames are forwarded onto all segments regardless of the location of the actual destinations, which creates an excess of traffic on the segments that do not contain the destinations. One way to eliminate this traffic is to have the bridge memorize the MAC addresses and the ports on which they appeared in the arriving frames as the source addresses. This way, the bridge will subsequently forward onto the corresponding ports only those frames that are destined for the remembered MAC addresses. The bridge will still flood the frames destined for unknown MAC addresses as well as the frames destined for the broadcast and possibly multicast MAC addresses through all its ports.

The data structure that bridges use to store the MAC addresses and the ports is called a *filtering database*. The entries in the filtering database have two fields: the MAC address and the port through which the traffic destined for that MAC address must be sent. In the future, I will refer to these fields as *the address field* and *the port field*, respectively. The format of both fields is numeric, with the address field storing the value of the MAC address and the port field storing the number of the port. The designers are free to implement any numbering scheme for the ports on their bridges.

The two types of filtering database entries are *dynamic* and *static*. Dynamic entries are created and maintained in the filtering database by the bridge itself as it observes the source MAC addresses of the frames traversing it. For each dynamic entry, the bridge keeps a timer that, upon expiration, causes the bridge to remove the entry. The timer expires after it reaches an administratively defined value called the *aging time*. The default aging time is 300 seconds. The bridge resets the timer each time a frame whose source MAC address is equal to the address field of the entry crosses the bridge. If such a frame appears on a port different from the one referenced by the port field of the filtering database entry, the port field is updated with the new value. The purpose of the timer is to allow end nodes to be moved from one segment of a bridged LAN to another without forever preventing them from receiving traffic.

The process that runs on a bridge and is responsible for populating the filtering database with dynamic entries is called a *learning process*.

Static entries are entered to the filtering database manually by network administrators. Bridges do not keep timers for static entries as they do for dynamic entries. Also, static entries take precedence over dynamic entries (that is, a dynamic entry cannot be created if a static entry has the same MAC address).

Suppose the MAC address of hosts H1, H2, H3, H4, and H5 from Figure 2.2 are 0002.0000.0001 through 0002.0000.0005 (locally assigned addresses; the local/global bit is set; the value of the last octet of the MAC address is equal to the number of the host). The filtering database of bridge B1 should then look like the one shown in Table 2.1.

The bridges—which feature only a filtering database and implement the no reverse forwarding rule—still suffer from a major shortcoming: They do not support redundant bridged LAN topologies. In redundant topologies, such bridges continuously produce duplicated frames and may proliferate them to such an extent that the bridged LAN becomes nonfunctional.

To understand the problem better, let's have a look at Figure 2.3. Two bridges, B1 and B2, interconnect segments 1 through 3. The reason why two bridges are used when one would suffice is redundancy: If one bridge fails, the other one takes over. (At least, that's what we wish.)

Let's consider what happens if the bridges obey only the no reverse forwarding rule and implement filtering databases.

Suppose host H1 sends out a frame destined for host H2's MAC address. Both bridges receive the frame and, because their filtering databases contain no entry for host H2's MAC address, they flood the frame over their other two ports (2 and 3). At the same time, the bridges create a filtering database entry for host H1's MAC address pointing to port 1 on both bridges. The first outcome of this flooding procedure is that host H2 receives two copies of the original frame instead of one. Things get worse after the bridges start receiving each other's copies of the frame on ports 2 and 3, which causes both bridges to correct the filtering database entry that they created for host H1's MAC address. Depending on the segment from which the frame is last received, the updated entries may point either to port 2 or 3; whichever port it is, it's incorrect. Unless host H2 replies, the bridges will keep forwarding the copies of the frame through the two ports that are not

Table 2.1   The filtering database of bridge B1 from Figure 2.2.

Address	Port
0002.0000.0001	1
0002.0000.0002	1
0002.0000.0003	2
0002.0000.0004	2
0002.0000.0005	3

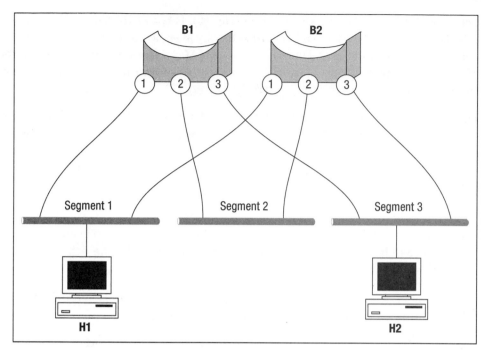

Figure 2.3   The redundant LAN topology can cause duplication and proliferation of traffic unless some ports on the bridges are "disabled" for receiving and sending.

referenced in the filtering database entry for host H1's MAC address. The port field of this entry will keep being updated, and the number of frames will double with each iteration of this process. If host H2 replies, the process stops as a filtering database entry is created for host H2's MAC address, and the bridges will forward all accumulated frames to host H2. At the same time, host H2's reply may not be forwarded onto the correct segment, depending on what port is referenced in the filtering database entries that bridges B1 and B2 have for host H1's MAC address after the last iteration of the flooding procedure.

The problem is much more straightforward if host H1, instead of sending a frame destined for host H2's MAC address, issues a broadcast frame such as an address resolution protocol (ARP) request. The bridges will keep flooding the copies of the broadcast frame through the other two ports, and soon the number of frames will increase to the extent that no communication is possible.

The problem just described is called a *bridging loop*. Bridging loops emerge when there are active redundant paths in bridged LANs. Therefore, bridging operations require a loop-free topology—that is, a topology without active redundant paths. Transparent bridges implement a special bridging protocol that is sometimes called the *spanning tree protocol (STP)* and ensures a loop-free topology in a bridged LAN. However, I will use the term *bridging protocol* because it is the term used in IEEE standard 802.1D.

The Bridging Protocol and Spanning Tree Algorithm

The spanning tree algorithm and bridging protocol were invented by Radia Perlman while she was working for Digital Equipment Corporation (DEC). Originally, the protocol was implemented on DEC bridges. Later, the protocol was adopted with minor changes by IEEE, and its technical specification was stipulated in the IEEE 802.1D standard. Thus, we have two versions of the protocol: DEC and IEEE 802.1D.

The goal of the bridging protocol is to allow the bridges to exchange the information that is necessary to establish a loop-free topology in a bridged LAN. The spanning tree protocol defines *bridge protocol data units (BPDUs)*. BPDUs come in two types: *configuration BPDUs* and *topology change notification BPDUs*. Bridges use configuration BPDUs to communicate the topology information so that a loop-free topology can be established in the bridged LAN. Topology change notification BPDUs are used to notify certain bridges of a change in the bridged LAN topology.

The topology that results from the operation of the spanning tree protocol is called a *spanning tree*. The bridges use the spanning tree algorithm to establish the spanning tree topology in the bridged LAN by means of prohibiting certain ports from accepting and forwarding bridged traffic. Those ports are said to be in the *blocking state*. Likewise, the ports that are allowed to accept and forward bridged traffic are said to be in the *forwarding state*. Ports in the blocking state still accept BPDUs.

The Spanning Tree Algorithm

The operation of the spanning tree algorithm requires the following parameters to be defined on bridges:

- Each bridge on a bridged LAN has a unique ID. A bridge ID is a numeric parameter.

- Each port on a bridge has an ID. A port ID is a numeric parameter unique for each port within the bridge.

- A cost is associated with each bridge port. A port cost is a numeric parameter.

The spanning tree algorithm produces the following results:

- Among all bridges in a bridged LAN, the bridge with the smallest ID (the highest priority) is "elected" as the *root bridge*.

- Each bridge—except for the root bridge—chooses a single port that produces the "shortest path" to the root bridge. This port is called the *root port*.

- For each segment of a bridged LAN, a single bridge is "elected" as the *designated bridge*. The designated bridge chooses a single port called the *designated port* that connects it to the segment on which it is the designated bridge.

- All the ports on every bridge that are neither the root port, or designated ports are placed into the blocking state. The root port and the designated ports are placed into the forwarding state.

NOTE: *The meaning of the terms* elected *and* shortest path *will be explained later in this section.*

These results of the spanning tree algorithm produce a spanning tree topology in a bridged LAN.

Let's now discuss the operation of the spanning tree algorithm and the bridging protocol.

The configuration BPDUs convey the information that is necessary for the operation of the spanning tree algorithm. The information that configuration BPDUs carry includes:

- The root bridge ID as known by the transmitting bridge

- The cost of the shortest known path from the transmitting bridge to the root bridge

- The ID of the bridge that transmitted the BPDU

- The ID of the port through which the BPDU was transmitted

BPDUs are destined for a special multicast MAC address that is permanently allocated by IEEE for the bridging protocol. (For the purposes of this section, this information is enough. Detailed information about BPDUs is provided in the "BPDUs" section later in this chapter.)

When a bridge transmits a BPDU onto a segment, it is received by all bridges residing on that segment. However, bridges never forward received BPDUs; instead, they use the information in the received BPDUs to adjust the parameters that are used when creating their own BPDUs.

Every bridge on a bridged LAN keeps track of the root bridge ID and the cost of the shortest known path to the root bridge. These parameters on the root bridge are equal to its own ID and 0, respectively. For every port, a bridge also keeps a copy of the last BPDU either transmitted or accepted on the port.

2. Transparent and Source-Route Bridging

NOTE: *The copy of a BPDU stored by a bridge for a port includes only the four parameters of the BPDU discussed before. Aside from these, the BPDU contains some other parameters, but these are not stored for the port.*

When a bridge receives a BPDU, it compares it with the BPDU it stores for the port on which the new BPDU was received to find out whether the new BPDU supersedes the existing one or vice versa. The bridge uses the following comparison procedure:

1. The BPDU with the smaller root ID supersedes the other.

2. If the root IDs of BPDUs are equal, the costs of the path to the root are compared. The BPDU with the smaller cost of the path to the root supersedes the other.

3. If the costs of the path to the root are equal, the transmitting bridge IDs are compared. The BPDU with the smaller transmitting bridge ID supersedes the other.

4. If the transmitting bridge IDs are equal, the port IDs are compared. The BPDU with the smaller port ID supersedes the other.

If the new BPDU supersedes the existing one, the existing one is discarded and the new BPDU is accepted and stored for the port. The bridge then checks if the root ID of the port's new BPDU is smaller than the bridge-wide root ID parameter; if it is, the latter is replaced with the new, smaller value. After that, the bridge chooses the root port among the ports whose BPDUs root IDs are equal to the bridge's root ID parameter. The port that produces the smallest sum of the port cost and the cost of the path to the root in its BPDU becomes the root port. If two or more ports produce the same smallest sum, the one with the smallest port ID becomes the root port. The calculated sum replaces the bridge-wide cost of the path to the root parameter.

The bridge creates its own BPDU from the bridge-wide root ID and the cost of the path to the root. It makes the transmitting bridge ID equal to its own ID, and the port ID equal to the port over which the BPDU is transmitted. After the BPDU is created, the bridge compares it against the BPDUs stored for each port using the comparison procedure described earlier in this section. If the created BPDU supersedes any port's BPDU, the port's BPDU is replaced with the created BPDU. In addition, the bridge makes those ports designated ports and transmits the created BPDU over those ports.

Finally, when a bridge is first connected to a bridged LAN, it assumes itself to be the root bridge. It starts transmitting BPDUs carrying the root ID equal to the bridge's ID, the cost of the path to the root equal to 0, the transmitting bridge ID equal to the bridge's ID, and the port ID equal to the ID of the port through which the BPDU is sent. As it receives replies from the other bridges, it keeps adjusting its parameters until they are coherent with the established topology.

Notice that bridges in a bridged LAN originally don't know which one of them will become the root bridge. As they exchange configuration BPDUs, they start finding out their IDs. During this process, the bridges give up the earlier-discovered candidate root IDs in favor of the new, smaller values. Eventually, every bridge finds the smallest bridge ID. The bridge with this smallest ID becomes what was earlier termed the "elected" root bridge.

As the bridges exchange BPDUs, they also elect a single designated bridge for each segment. This is the bridge whose BPDU supersedes the BPDUs of all other bridges connected to this segment.

Figure 2.4 shows a bridge that receives a new BPDU on port 1. The new BPDU supersedes port 1's BPDU, which causes the bridge to adjust its parameters.

Having adjusted its parameters, the bridge creates its own BPDU and transmits it over the ports whose BPDUs are superseded by the bridge-wide BPDU. The bridge replaces the BPDUs of those ports with the new BPDU. The results of this process are shown in Figure 2.5.

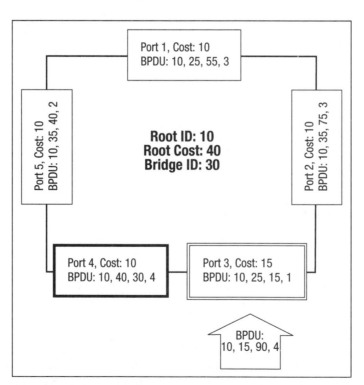

Figure 2.4   A new BPDU arrives on port 1. The current root port has a double border; the designated ports are shown with a thick border.

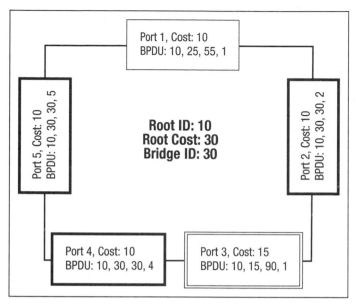

Figure 2.5 The bridge adjusts its parameters in accordance with the parameters of the arrived BPDU. The new root port is shown with a double border; the new designated ports are shown with a thick border.

The question that may naturally arise concerns why BPDUs also carry the port ID. It's obvious that eventually, all BPDUs will carry the same root ID. It is possible that two or more bridges can have the same cost of the path to the root. But, the bridge ID is guaranteed to be unique on every bridge. Then why is the transmitting bridge ID not enough to unambiguously tell if one BPDU supersedes another?

A bridge must rely on the port ID as the tiebreaker in three cases. The first case is when two bridges are connected to two segments. Obviously, one of the bridges produces BPDUs that supersede the BPDUs of the other, based either on the cost of the path to the root or on the transmitting bridge ID. If the other bridge has to choose one of the two ports connected to these two segments as the root port, it would have to use the port ID of the BPDUs stored for these ports as the tiebreaker. This case is demonstrated in Figure 2.6.

Notice that, in Figure 2.6, bridge B3 chooses port 2 (but not port 1) as the root port. This happens because the BPDU that bridge B3 stores on port 2 (after bridge B2 sent its BPDUs over segments 2 and 3) supersedes the BPDU stored on port 3 by the value of the port ID (2 against 3).

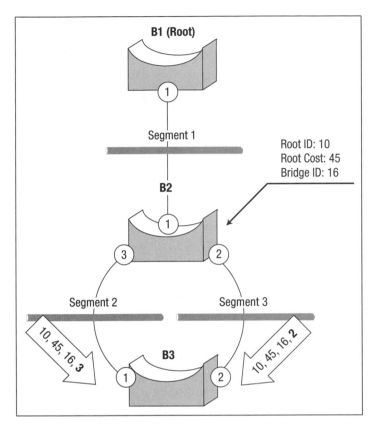

Figure 2.6   Bridges B2 and B3 are both connected to segments 2 and 3. Bridge B3 must rely on the port ID parameter carried in bridge B2's BPDUs to make one of its two ports the root port.

The second case is when two ports on the same bridge are connected to a single segment. If there are no other bridges on this segment, or the other bridge's BPDUs are superseded by the first bridge's BPDUs, it must decide which port to make designated. As the bridge transmits a BPDU through one of the ports, it ultimately receives it on the other port. Obviously, the BPDU of the port with the smaller port ID supersedes that of the other port. Thus, the port with the smaller ID becomes the designated port. An example of this case is shown in Figure 2.7.

The final case arises when two ports on a bridge are connected to a single segment to which the designated bridge is connected with only one port. If the bridge has to choose one of these ports as the root port, it must use the port IDs as the tiebreaker. Notice that this presents a deviation from the regular procedure, whereby the tie was resolved by examining the contents of the ports' BPDUs

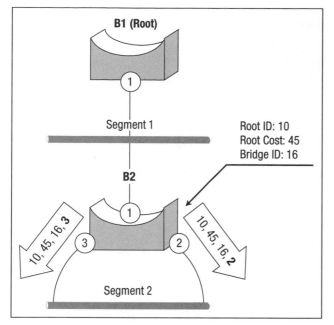

Figure 2.7   Bridge B2 is connected to segment 2 with two ports 2 and 3; it makes port 2
the designated port as its BPDU supersedes that of port 3.

This time, both ports have identical BPDUs. An example of this case is shown in
Figure 2.8.

NOTE: *The root bridge is the designated bridge on every segment to which it is attached. Usually, all ports on
the root bridge are designated. Exceptions are only the ports connected to the same segment. In this case, the
ports with smaller port IDs are the designated ports.*

Handling the Failures

The described operation of the spanning tree algorithm handles only additions of
new segments and bridges. It does not handle failures and removals of segments
and bridges.

To handle such failures and removals, the spanning tree algorithm defines additional parameters and procedures.

First, the root bridge is required to transmit BPDUs through its designated ports
on a regular basis. The interval between successive transmissions of BPDUs on
the same port is called a *hello time*. The default value of the hello time is 2 seconds. The bridges downstream from the root bridge are required to transmit their

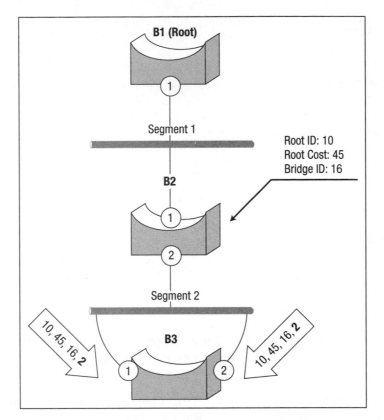

Figure 2.8   Bridge B3 is connected to segment 2 with two ports; the designated bridge
(bridge B2) is connected to segment 2 with only one port. Bridge B3 must use
its own ports' IDs to choose the root port.

BPDUs through their designated ports following the receipt of a BPDU on the
root port.

In addition, bridges are required to maintain a special timer on the root port and
the ports that are not designated (that is, the ports in the blocking state) to allow
monitoring the BPDUs received on these ports. This timer is called a *message age
timer*, and it expires when it reaches the administratively configured *maximum
age* parameter. (The default value of this parameter is 20 seconds.) The message
age timer is reset each time a BPDU—which either is equal to or supersedes the
one stored on the port—is received on the port. The message age timer is not
reset to 0, however, but is instead reset to the value of an additional parameter
called a *message age*, which is carried in the BPDU.

The message age parameter of the BPDUs transmitted by the root bridge is always equal to 0. The bridges downstream from the root bridge make the message

age parameter in their BPDUs equal to the message age timer of the root port plus the administratively defined value called *message age increment*. The default message age increment is equal to 1.

Once a message age timer expires on any of a bridge's ports, the bridge removes the BPDU associated with the port and tries to become the designated bridge on this port by transmitting its own BPDU through it. It may or may not succeed depending on the parameters of the other bridges' BPDUs connected to the same segment.

If the message age timer expires on the root port, the bridge recalculates the root ID and the cost of the path to the new root.

Transition from Blocking to Forwarding

As mentioned earlier, only the root port and the designated ports on a bridge are in the forwarding state. All other ports are in the blocking state. In addition, ports on a bridge can be in the *administratively disabled state*, which simply means that the port is turned off. It cannot receive and transmit any traffic, including BPDUs.

Because of the changes in a bridged LAN, a port on a bridge can change the state from blocking to forwarding. For example, if a message age timer expires on a port in the blocking state, which causes the bridge to become the designated bridge on this segment, the port must change the state from blocking to forwarding. Another example is a port that is enabled by the bridge administrator. The disabled port is first put into the blocking state, and—if the bridge's BPDU on that port supersedes the BPDUs of all other bridges on this segment—the port will be put into the forwarding state.

The nature of the spanning tree algorithm and bridging protocol is such that the topology changes may be temporary. Thus, they may not adequately reflect the spanning tree topology that will eventually be settled in the bridged LAN. Therefore, making an abrupt transition in port states from blocking to forwarding can lead to temporary bridging loops. As we know, bridging loops are dangerous and must be avoided whenever possible.

So, the spanning tree algorithm introduces two additional port states—*listening* and *learning*. A port that tries to make a transition from the blocking to the forwarding state is first put into the listening state. During the listening state, the port is not allowed to accept or transmit bridged traffic. It may, however, transmit BPDUs, provided it is the designated port for the segment to which it is attached. The port is held in the listening state for a period called a *forward delay*. The forward delay is administratively configured, and its default value is 15 seconds. If, during the listening state, the port wasn't put back in the blocking state, the port enters the learning state. During the learning state, the port is still not allowed to forward or receive bridged traffic. The difference between the learning and listening periods is that the bridge starts the learning process on the port and begins populating the filtering database with the MAC addresses of end nodes located on the segment attached to the port. The port is held in the learning state for the duration of the forward delay. Finally, if the port is not put back in the blocking state during the learning state, it enters the forwarding state.

Topology Change Notification

During the stable operation of a bridged LAN, the bridges use the aging time value to age out entries in the filtering database. The aging time by default is 300 seconds (a rather long period of time, but one that is justified because, under stable bridged LAN operation, this long aging time can cause temporary nonreachability of an end node only after it was moved from one segment to another). Right after the topology of a bridge LAN has changed, this justification no longer holds true. On the contrary, there is a high probability that some stations moved from the perspective of some bridges. Therefore, it makes sense to use a shorter aging time during a certain period right after the detection of the bridged LAN topology change. The shorter aging time is equal to the forward delay.

NOTE: *Topology change occurs in three cases: when a port makes a transition from the learning state to forwarding, from forwarding to blocking, and from learning to blocking.*

It is possible that, if a topology change occurs in some part of a bridged LAN, not all of the bridges will be able to detect it. To notify the rest of the bridges of the topology change, the bridges implement the following procedure. The bridge that detects the topology change starts regularly transmitting a topology change notification BPDU onto the segment attached to its root port. The interval between successive transmissions of the topology change notification BPDUs is equal to the hello time. The bridge keeps transmitting the topology change notification BPDUs until it receives the configuration BPDU on the root port that carries the *topology change acknowledgment flag* set. The designated bridge of the segment onto which the topology change notification BPDUs are transmitted first sets the topology change acknowledgement flag in its BPDU it will transmit through the port attached to this segment. Then it itself starts regularly transmitting topology change notification BPDUs through its root port until it receives a configuration BPDU carrying the topology change acknowledgement flag. Does it schedule the topology change flag, or it necessarily replies,even if it has not seen a BPDU on the root port lately? It's the first one. This process continues until it reaches the root bridge.

The root bridge—upon receipt of a topology change notification BPDU or if it itself generated a topology change—starts the *topology change timer*. Until this timer expires, the root bridge sets the *topology change flag* in the configuration BPDUs it transmits. The bridges downstream from the root bridge copy the value of the topology change flag into their own configuration BPDUs. As long as the root bridge transmits the configuration BPDUs with the topology change flag set, all bridges on the bridged LAN must use the shorter aging time, which is equal to the forward delay (by default 15 seconds).

The topology change timer expires when it reaches the value equal to the sum of the maximum age (by default 20 seconds) and forward delay (by default 15 seconds). In other words, the default value at which the topology change timer expires is equal to 35 seconds.

BPDUs

Before examining the format of the BPDU, we need to understand what bridge and port IDs are.

Bridge IDs are eight octets (64 bits) long. Bridge IDs consist of two fields: the bridge priority and the bridge's MAC address, which are two octets (16 bits) and six octets (48 bits) long, respectively. Every bridge must have at least one MAC address.

When two bridge IDs are compared, the priorities are compared first, and the bridge ID with the smaller bridge priority is considered smaller. If the bridge priorities are equal, then the MAC addresses are compared. As the MAC addresses are distributed by IEEE, they are guaranteed to be unique. Bridge priorities are administratively configurable. The default value of the bridge priority is 32768.

NOTE: *It is common practice to force the root election in favor of a certain bridge by assigning it the bridge priority of 1000. Typically, such a bridge is the most powerful bridge, which is placed in the relative center of the network. To make the bridged LAN less vulnerable to the failure of the root bridge, another similarly robust and placed bridge is assigned the bridge priority of 2000. This backup bridge is often referred to as a secondary root bridge. (Notice that this is not official terminology of the IEEE 802.1D standard.) All other bridges are left with their default priorities.*

The port ID is two octets (16 bits) long and also consists of two parts: the port priority and internal port ID, each of which is one octet (8 bits) long. When two port IDs are compared, the port priorities are compared first, and the port ID with the smaller port priority is considered smaller. If the port priorities are equal, the internal port IDs are compared, and the port ID with the smaller internal port ID is considered smaller. Port priorities are administratively configurable; their default value is 128.

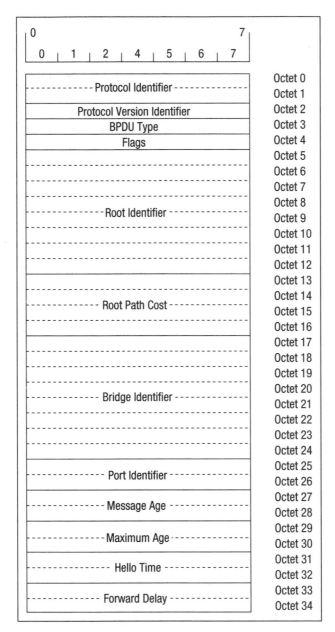

Figure 2.9   The format of the configuration BPDU.

Figure 2.9 shows the format of the configuration BPDU.

Following are the descriptions of the BPDU fields in the order of their appearance in the diagram:

The protocol identifier field is 16 bits long and always carries the value of 0.

The protocol version identifier field is 8 bits long and always carries the value of 0.

The BPDU type field is 8 bits long. For the configuration BPDUs, the field always carries the value of 0.

The flags field is 8 bits long. Bit 0 denotes the topology change flag, and bit 7 of the flags field denotes the topology change acknowledgement flag.

NOTE: *The IEEE 802.1D standard references the aforementioned bits as "Bit 1" and "Bit 8." This is because in the standard the bits in an octet are counted 1 through 8. In this book, I adhere to the practice accepted in Internet-related documents to count the bits in an octet 0 through 7.*

The root identifier field is eight octets (64 bits) long. It carries the value of the bridge ID (consisting of the bridge priority [2 bytes] and the bridge's MAC addresses [6 bytes]) that the bridge transmitting the configuration BPDU believes to be the root bridge of the spanning tree.

The root path cost field is four octets (32 bits) long. It carries the cost of the best-known path from the bridge that transmits the configuration BPDU to the bridge believed to be the root of the spanning tree.

The bridge identifier field is eight octets (64 bits) long and carries the ID of the bridge that transmits the configuration BPDU. As before, the bridge ID consists of the bridge priority (2 bytes) and the bridge's MAC addresses (6 bytes).

The port identifier field is two octets (16 bits) long and carries the port ID through which the BPDU was transmitted.

The message age field is two octets (16 bits) long and carries the value of the message age timer of the transmitting bridge's root port incremented by the message age increment value. You can think of this value as the time elapsed since the root bridge transmitted its BPDU, which triggered the bridges downstream to create and send their BPDUs.

The maximum age field is two octets (16 bits) long and carries the value of the maximum age parameter configured on the bridge.

The hello time field is two octets (16 bits) long and carries the value of the hello time configured on the bridge.

The forward delay field is two octets (16 bits) long and carries the value of the forward delay configured on the bridge.

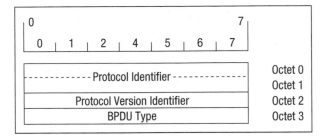

Figure 2.10   The format of the topology change notification BPDU.

The format of the topology change notification BPDU is shown in Figure 2.10.

The first two fields of the topology change notification BPDU are identical to those of the configuration BPDU. The BPDU type field is also 8 bits long, although, in the case of topology change notification BPDUs, it carries the value of 0x80.

BPDUs are encapsulated into IEEE 802.3 frames, with the Destination Service Access Point (DSAP) and Source Service Access (SSAP) values equal to 0x42 (equal to 01000010 in binary, which is symmetric regardless of the bit transmission order). BPDUs are sent to the multicast MAC address equal to 0180.C200.0000 (hexadecimal).

For Further Study

To find out more about the spanning tree algorithm and the bridging protocol, I highly recommend Radia Perlman's book, *Interconnections*, which not only comprehensively covers bridging but also extensively explains routing and the issues associated with it, plus some other important network-related subjects. The book is definitely worth reading if you want to understand how modern networks work.

In addition, if you are involved in practical work with bridges (including switches), I recommend that you acquire a copy of the IEEE 802.1D standard. Understanding some situations may require reading about the individual details that are covered only in the standard. I do, however have to warn you: The document is incredibly difficult to read and requires some knowledge of the C programming language. The text of the standard is not free, it must be purchased from IEEE. For more information about purchasing the standard, visit IEEE's Web site at **www.ieee.org**.

Source-Route Bridging

Source-route bridging was designed by IBM for interconnecting token ring segments into a bigger LAN. Originally, source-route bridging was deemed as a universal method of creating large-scale networks, including corporate networks. Eventually, though, it became clear that, in most cases, source-route bridging cannot meet the requirements that many clients have for their large-scale corporate networks. Nevertheless, source-route bridging, although having failed to become a method for creating large-scale networks, leaves a significant legacy of numerous source-route bridged network deployments.

Like a transparently bridged LAN, a source-route bridged LAN consists of multiple token ring segments interconnected with (source-route) bridges. As in the case of transparent bridging, source-route bridging allows redundant paths to exist within a single source-route bridged LAN, which can be utilized to recover from network component failures. Besides this, no similarity exists between source-route and transparent bridging.

The concept of source-route bridging is based upon the following premises:

- The headers of token ring frames that must traverse source-route bridges contain routing information that is used by the bridges to forward the frame through the source-route bridged LAN from the source to the destination. Routing information describes precisely which bridges and segments the frame must traverse to arrive at the destination.

NOTE: *If two nodes reside on a single token ring segment, the routing information field is not inserted into the token ring frames exchanged by the nodes.*

- The source node is responsible for inserting the routing information into the headers of the token ring frames that must be delivered through source-route bridges.
- Source-route bridging requires each node to be able to discover and memorize routing information to the destinations accessible through source-route bridges.

These premises make source-route bridging quite "nontransparent" compared to transparent bridging. A node on a source-route bridged LAN is pretty much involved from the bridging perspective, whereas a node on a transparently bridged LAN knows nothing about the presence of bridging.

A source-route bridged LAN is required to be administratively configured as follows:

- Each ring should be assigned a unique number.
- Each bridge should be assigned a number unique within each ring to which the bridge is connected.

The original IBM specification defined a source-route bridge as a data link layer device that interconnects precisely two token ring segments. In other words, a "pure" source-route bridge cannot interconnect three or more token ring segments.

In many cases, this is a significant limitation in terms of the design of source-route bridged LANs. To overcome this limitation, several methods were developed to be compliant with source-route bridging. We'll consider these methods after we examine the basics of the source-route bridging operation.

Routing Information Field (RIF)

Routing information is stored in the header of the token ring frames in the form of the *Routing Information Field*, well known by its acronym *RIF*. The format of the RIF is shown in Figure 2.11.

As mentioned earlier, not every token ring frame requires routing information—only those that have to cross source-route bridges do. Subsequently, not every token ring frame carries the RIF in its header. Thus, there must be a way to distinguish between frames that carry the RIF and those that don't.

The distinction is made by utilizing the group/individual bit in the source MAC address of a token ring frame. Obviously, multiple nodes can't possibly send a single frame; thus, the group/individual meaning of the bit makes no sense in the context of a source address. So, it was decided to use the bit in source-route bridging environments to indicate the presence or absence of a RIF. If the bit is set, the RIF is present, and otherwise if it is not. In the source-route bridging context, the bit is called the *routing information indicator (RII)*.

NOTE: *A frame containing a RIF is not a special token ring frame. It can be a regular frame, containing a fully functional, upper-layer protocol protocol data unit (PDU), such as an IP datagram.*

Following is a brief description of the fields stored in the route control subfield of a RIF.

The first 3 bits of the RIF are called *broadcast bits*, sometimes also called *broadcast indicators*. The broadcast bits indicate whether the frame is used to discover a route to the destination or if it already contains all necessary routing information. If all 3 bits are cleared, the frame contains a route; otherwise, the pattern of bits indicates which method must be used to discover the route. The available values are shown in Table 2.2. The meanings of these values (as well as that of the route discovery methods they signify) will be discussed in the "Routing Information Discovery And Use" section later in this chapter.

Length is a 5-bit-long field, that specifies the total length of the RIF in bytes. Only even numbers between 2 and 30 are allowed. The total length covers the first five fields, plus optional route designators. The number of route designators is equal to the number of source-route bridges the frames must cross plus one. The IBM

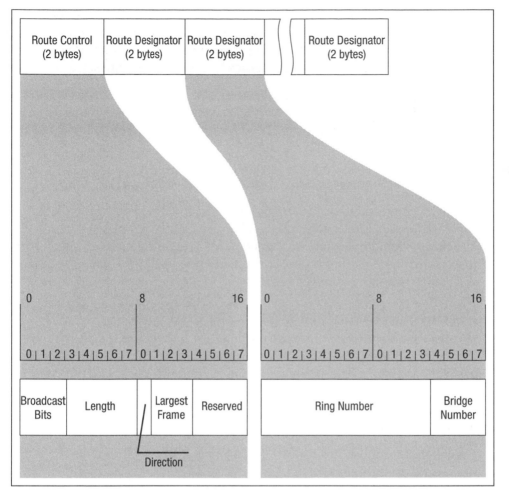

Figure 2.11   The structure of the RIF field.

specification limits the maximum number of the bridges a frame can cross to seven. As the size of the first five fields and each of route designators is equal to 2 bytes, the effective maximum value that the length fields can take is equal to 18— 2 bytes for the first five fields+ 2 bytes multiplied by (7+1).

Table 2.2   The meaning of the broadcast bits.

Broadcast Bits	Description
000	Specific route (nonbroadcast)
100	All routes broadcast
110	Single route broadcast

The direction field is only 1 bit long and indicates in which direction the route designators should be interpreted. When cleared, the interpretation of route designators must be performed in the transmission order. When set, it requires the bridges to start interpretation from the last transmitted route designator and move towards the first one.

The largest frame field is 3 bits long and specifies the minimal maximum transmission unit (MTU) size among all bridges along the route contained in a RIF. In other words, this value indicates the largest possible frame that can be sent along the route carried in the route designators. Table 2.3 shows the values this field can have and the respective MTU sizes and maximum IP datagram sizes.

Finally, route designator is a 16-bit-long field that describes an element of the route to the destination. Route designator consists of two subfields: ring number and bridge number (which are 12 and 4 bits long, respectively). The lengths of these subfields yield the ranges for ring and bridge numbers, which are 0 through 4095 and 0 through 15, respectively.

Routing Information Discovery and Use

As mentioned earlier, broadcast bits denote whether a RIF already contains a route, or that the frame is used to discover one. As Table 2.2 showed, if the broadcast bits are cleared, the frame contains a route. In this case, the route is expressed as a sequence of route designators. Table 2.2 also contained two nonzero combinations of broadcast bits patterns, which designate two different approaches for route discovery.

We will first examine how route discovery processes work and then how source-route bridges use routes.

Table 2.3   *The relation between largest frame values, the frame MTUs, and maximum IP datagram sizes.*

Largest Frame Size	MTU	Maximum IP Datagram Size
000	552	508
001	1064	1020
010	2088	2044
011	4136	4092
100	8232	8188

All Routes Broadcast (All Routes Explorer)

The first way to discover a route to a destination is denoted by the broadcast bit pattern equal to 100 in binary. The type of packet whose broadcast bits carry this value is called the *all routes broadcast* or *all routes explorer*. Such frames are called all routes *broadcast* (and the bits are called *broadcast*) because the frames whose RIFs carry this broadcast bit pattern are supposed to be sent to the broadcast MAC address (that is, 0xFFFFFFFFFFFF in hexadecimal notation).

> **NOTE:**   Both terms are equivalent and can be used interchangeably. In this book, I will use the term all routes explorer *because it identifies the functionality of such frames more distinctively. It emphasizes that these frames are not simply broadcasts, but that they are also intended to discover a route to the destination. All routes broadcast sounds more broadcast-like, which sometimes can be confusing.*

All routes explorers are used by nodes as follows. Once a node needs to find out a route to a certain destination residing behind one or more source-route bridges, it sends out an all routes explorer, which contains information identifying the destination. The all routes explorer contains a RIF with no route designators. All of the source-route bridges connected to the token ring segment on which the node resides receive the all routes explorer and forward it onto the other token ring segments to which they are attached. Source-route bridges on these other segments receive one or more copies of the original all routes explorer and forward them further onto the token ring segments to which they are attached. As the bridges forward the copies of the all routes explorer, they also attach route designators indicating the ring from which the copy was received, the receiving bridge number, and the number of the segment onto which the copy is forwarded. Eventually, one copy (or more) of the all routes explorers arrive at the destination. The destination picks one of them and, using the route recoded by the source-route bridges, sends the source a reply.

Obviously, there are redundant LAN configurations such that, if the source-route bridges blindly forwarded received copies of all routes explorers onto the segments to which they are attached, a broadcast storm would be created. To avoid broadcast storms, source-route bridges use the following rules when processing and forwarding all routes explorers:

- If an all routes explorer does not contain any route designators, the source-route bridge forwards a copy of the all routes explorer onto the other segment to which it is attached. Two route designators are added to this copy. The first route designator contains the number of the token ring segment from which the original all routes explorer arrived and the number of the source route bridge itself. The second route designator contains the number of the ring onto which the copy is forwarded. The bridge number subfield in the second route designator is left blank.

- If an all routes explorer contains route designators, the source-route bridge creates a copy of the all routes explorer only if the ring number of the second segment to which the bridge is attached does not appear in the route designators. If the ring number does appear in the route designators, no copy is created and the all routes explorer is silently dropped. If the source route bridge creates a copy of the all routes explorer, it fills out the bridge number subfield of the last route designator with its own number and adds one more route designator that contains the blank bridge number and the ring number of the segment onto which the copy is forwarded.

Figure 2.12 demonstrates how source-route bridges in redundant LAN configurations create multiple copies of a single all routes explorer. The source-route bridges are labeled BX, with X corresponding to the bridge number that is placed into the bridge number subfield of route designators. The token ring segments are labeled RYYY, with YYY corresponding to the ring numbers placed into the ring number subfield of route designators.

End node H1, in an attempt to find out a route to destination end node H2, creates an all routes explorer (shown as an arrow labeled EXP0) and transmits it over segment R100. This all routes explorer does not contain any route designators yet. Each of the source-route bridges B1 and B2 receives the all routes explorer and forwards a copy of it onto segment R200. This makes two copies (shown as arrows labeled EXP1 and EXP2). Each bridge inserts two route designators into

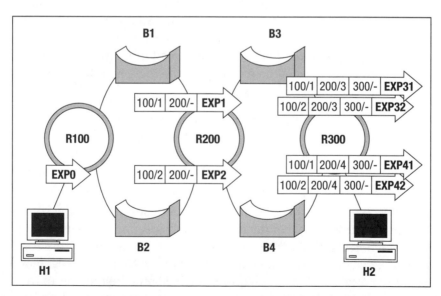

**Figure 2.12   In the redundant source-route bridged LAN, node H2 receives multiple
copies of the all routes explorer created by node H1.**

the copy it creates. The route designators are shown as rectangles with ring and bridge numbers inside attached to the ends of arrows EXP1 and EXP2. Each of the source-route bridges B3 and B4 picks the two copies of the all routes explorer from segment R200 and creates two new copies that it sends over segment R300, to which end node H2 is attached. Source-route bridges B3 and B4 fill out the blank bridge number subfield in the last route designator of each copy they create and add one more route designator. This makes four copies of the all routes explorer on segment R300; the copies are labeled EXP31, EXP32, EXP41, and EXP42. Thus, end node H2 receives four copies of the original explorer.

Because the destination can receive multiple copies of the all routes explorer, each containing a different route, it must decide which one to reply to. Would that be the first copy, or maybe the one that boasts the shortest route?

This question has no definitive answer. In fact, the implementers of source-route bridging modules of end nodes are free to choose whatever method they desire. In most cases though, the first copy is picked regardless of the route it contains.

The final question is: What is the all routes explorer? So far, we know that it must be destined for a broadcast address. In this case, how does the destination know that the all routes explorer is intended for it?

Actually, an all routes explorer contains a PDU of an upper-layer protocol. This PDU must specify the details of the destination so that once the destination receives the all routes explorer, it can recognize the explorer was sent to it and not to any other node.

In the case of IP, all routes explorers typically carry ARP requests.

Single Route Broadcast (Spanning Explorer)

The second way to discover a route to a destination is designated by the broadcast bits, value equal to 110 in binary. If this value appears in a RIF of a token ring frame, the frame is called a *single route broadcast* or *spanning explorer*. Such frames are also supposed to carry the broadcast MAC address as the destination address.

NOTE: *For the same reason as in the case of the all routes explorers, I will use the term spanning explorer in this book.*

The route discovery process using spanning explorers is somewhat similar to the one with all routes explorers. A node wishing to discover a route to a certain destination behind one or more source-route bridges sends out a spanning explorer. The source-route bridges on the token ring segment receive the spanning explorer, but instead of forwarding it onto the segments to which they are attached, the source-route bridges forward it only onto the segments that are specifically configured for spanning explorers. This configuration is done on the source-route bridges' interfaces, not on the segments. The configuration of source-route bridges' interfaces must be done in such a way that allows a spanning explorer issued by any end node to reach any other node. Similarly to handling all routes explorers, source-route bridges insert route designators as the forward spanning explorer throughout the LAN.

Source-route bridges may or may not verify the ring numbers stored in route designators when deciding whether to forward a spanning explorer. Although it is assumed that the interfaces of source-route bridges are configured so that redundant copies of spanning explorers aren't created, a mistake in configuration can easily create a broadcast storm if source-route bridges completely ignore the ring numbers stored in the RIF. For example, if two source-route bridges that interconnect two token ring segments are configured to process spanning explorers on both token ring interfaces, then a broadcast storm will arise as soon as the bridges receive a spanning explorer on any of the token ring segments. The reason is that one of the bridges will pick up the copy of the spanning explorer forwarded by the other bridge; it will then forward it back to the segment from which it was received by the second bridge. The same is going to happen to the other bridge. Luckily, the limitation in the RIF size makes such a broadcast storm short lived. If, however, the source-route bridges verified the ring numbers, no broadcast storm would emerge. On the other hand, disregarding the ring numbers reduces the spanning explorer processing time.

NOTE: Even if source-route bridges do check ring numbers before forwarding spanning explorers, it only helps prevent spanning explorers from ending up in bridging loops. Duplicate copies of spanning explorers can still arrive if source-route bridges are not properly configured to handle spanning explorers.

If source-route bridges are properly configured for handing spanning explorers, the destination receives only one copy of the original spanning explorer.

NOTE: Spanning explorers created by any end node must be able to reach any other node on the LAN. In addition, no redundant copies of a spanning explorer can be created as it is forwarded throughout the LAN. The topology that sustains this type of operation is called spanning tree, which explains the name—spanning explorers.

In small networks, it is usually fairly easy to figure out which ports on which source-route bridges must be configured to accept and send spanning explorers and which must not be. As the size of the network gets bigger, however, this task becomes increasingly difficult to accomplish.

To avoid human mistakes and to accommodate for potential changes of the topology of a source-route bridged LAN, a variation of the STP is used. This variation is called *automatic spanning tree (AST)*, and it is used in only source-route bridged environments to enable or disable processing spanning explorers on bridges' ports.

AST uses the standard IEEE 802.1D BPDUs to communicate the topology information. Once a port is put into a blocking state as the result of AST operation, the bridge can no longer receive or send spanning explorers through this port. Likewise, if a port is put into a forwarding mode, the bridge does send and receive spanning explorers on that port. None of the states affects any other traffic received and sent by the port in any way.

Multiport Source-Route Bridges

According to the IBM specification, source-route bridges have only two ports. This can become a considerable obstacle, which, in order to be bypassed, can require a significant amount of additional equipment (that is, source-route bridges and token ring segments).

A neat solution was devised, and it allows multiport source-route bridges to be created without violating the IBM specification. The idea of the solution is to create an abstraction called a *virtual ring* in a multiport source-route bridge's memory that allows presenting the bridge as multiple two-port bridges interconnected with the virtual ring. The operation of such a bridge counts the virtual ring as a regular ring and thus inserts an extra route designator into all routes and spanning explorers crossing the bridge.

Figure 2.13 demonstrates the implementation of a multiport source-route bridge using the concept of a virtual ring.

IP and ARP in the Presence of Source-Route Bridging

Source-route bridging operation requires quite an involvement on the side of end nodes. End nodes must know of the presence of source-route bridging, and they must assume that they can be separated by source-route bridges. They also have to agree on which type of route discovery mechanism to use: all routes explorers or spanning explorers. In addition, end nodes may need a method to verify if the destinations they want to reach are behind source-route bridges or if they reside on the same segment. Because both all routes and spanning explorers traverse the whole LAN and thus create additional broadcast traffic, it would be unwise to always blindly use them even if the destination is on the same segment. All routes explorers make the situation even more undesirable because their operation can produce multiple copies of a single all routes explorer.

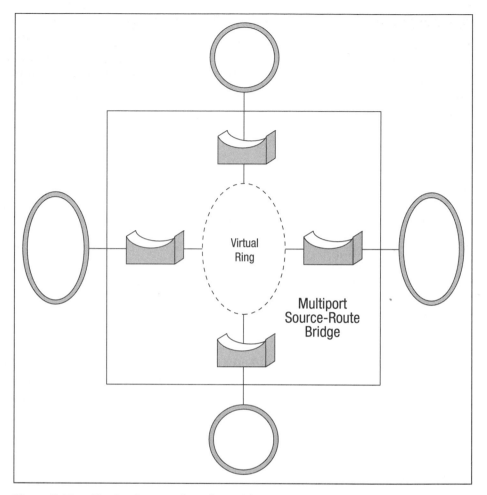

Figure 2.13   The implementation of a multiport source-route bridge based on the use of a virtual ring.

The way IP and ARP work in source-route bridging environments is documented in RFC 1042, "A Standard for the Transmission of IP Datagrams over IEEE 802 Networks." In brief, the document states the following:

- IP and ARP are both required to be able to utilize the source-route bridging functionality.

- When ARP is used to resolve an IP address to an appropriate MAC address, it first should use a local broadcast—that is, a frame destined for the broadcast address but containing no RIF (RII = 0). If within a reasonable amount of time no reply is received, then ARP should try either an all routes explorer or a single route explorer.

- Contrary to those of ARP, IP broadcasts should be sent using only spanning explorers.

Alternatives to Pure Source-Route Bridging

As mentioned before, IBM originally intended source-route bridging to be—and then positioned it as—the universal method of interconnecting large networks. Although it failed to become such a method, source-route bridging was deployed by some organizations on a rather large scale. Obviously, being universal means that it had to work over large distances, which often separate parts of large networks, especially corporate networks—one of whose primary goals is to interconnect branches. The technologies that are used to interconnect networks over large distances are WANs. Thus, source-route bridging must work not only over token ring segments, but also over WAN connections.

The variation of source-route bridging that works over types of media other than token ring, such as WANs, is called *remote source-route bridging (RSRB)*. IBM's version of RSRB is based on so-called *half bridges* that, when interconnected with a WAN link, behave as a single two-port source-route bridge.

RSRB

Half bridges are not available on Cisco routers. Instead, Cisco came up with its own version of RSRB. Cisco's RSRB is based on virtual rings—the abstraction that, as we know, is also used to implement multiport source-route bridges. This time, though, the virtual ring is "extended" between two or more routers interconnected with non-token ring networks and acting as source-route bridges. The individual token ring segments to which routers may be connected still appear as interconnected with the virtual ring with multiple two-port source-route bridges.

The virtual ring is extended using other networking technologies. The source-route bridged traffic, which is to be forwarded onto the virtual ring, is encapsulated into the PDUs of the network over which the virtual ring is extended.

Let's consider the example of a source-route bridged network, shown in Figure 2.14.

Routers R1, R2, and R3, which act as source-route bridges interconnecting the token ring segments on which they reside, are themselves interconnected via the WAN. Figure 2.15 shows how the same topology looks from the RSRB perspective.

All of the token ring segments appear to be interconnected with the virtual ring via two-port source-route bridges. The rectangles labeled R1, R2, and R3 show the "boundaries" of the original routers.

Data Link Switching

There is an alternative to RSRB called data link switching (DLSw). DLSw provides for only source-route bridging of Systems Network Architecture (SNA) and Network Basic Input/Output System (NetBEUI) traffic. Thus, IP cannot be source-route bridged over DLSw networks; for that reason, we won't consider the details of the technology.

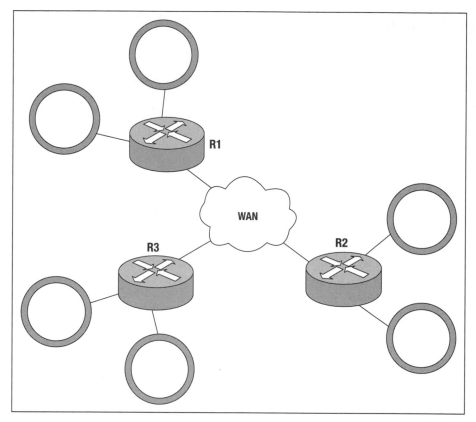

Figure 2.14   Routers R1, R2, and R3 which act as source-route bridges, are interconnected with the WAN.

I mentioned DLSw for two reasons. First, it is a more flexible and reliable alternative to RSRB (and thus is always worth considering when you are implementing RSRB networks). Second, DLSw can use IP to deliver source-route bridged traffic. Thus, there is a connection between DLSw and IP, although sort of reversed.

Cisco routers implement an extended version of DLSw called *DLSw+*.

The details of the DLSw technology can be found in RFC 1795, "Data Link Switching: Switch-to-Switch Protocol AIW DLSw RIG: DLSw Closed Pages, DLSw Standard Version 1.0."

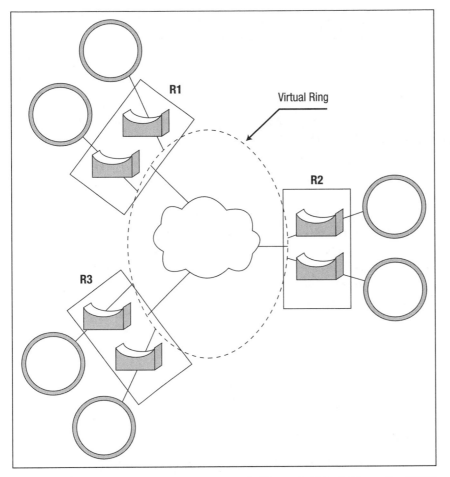

Figure 2.15   The way the topology shown in Figure 2.14 looks from the RSRB
perspective.

2. Create a bridge group using the command **bridge** *<bridge group #>* **protocol** *<bridging protocol>* in global configuration mode. The parameter *<bridge group #>* allows you to define several bridge groups within the same router, where each bridge group behaves as a separate bridge. The *<protocol>* parameter provides a choice of three bridging protocols: **ieee**, **dec**, and **ibm** of which only **ieee** and **dec** can be used for transport bridging. The first, **ieee**, is the IEEE 802.1D-compliant bridging protocol. The second, **dec**, is the original bridging protocol developed at Digital Equipment Corporation on which IEEE 802.1D is based. The last, **ibm**, is the IBM version of STP used in source-route bridging environments.

3. Assign the appropriate interfaces to the created bridge group using the command **bridge-group** *<group number>* in interface configuration mode.

As explained before, a single router cannot be configured for transparent bridging and routing of the same routed protocol (IP in our case) simultaneously unless it is configured with CRB or IRB. Therefore, all configurations, except those for CRB and IRB, share the same command: **no ip routing**. A Cisco router by default routes IP and does not route all other routed protocols (but it does not bridge them either). Hence, the command **ip routing** is a part of the default router configuration. If present, it is not displayed when you are viewing the router configuration. Therefore, if you are interested in configuring a router for bridging IP traffic, the command **no ip routing** is easy to omit, but it's difficult to detect that it's missing. While IP routing is on, the router will try to route—as opposed to bridge—the IP traffic. Since the router won't give you a hint about what's going on by displaying the command **ip routing**, troubleshooting can become frustrating. The bottom line is that if you have to configure transparent bridging of IP traffic and CRB or IRB are not an option, make sure **no ip routing** appears in the router configuration.

WARNING!   Keep in mind that most configurations presented in this chapter expose the command no ip routing because the book itself is about IP and thus we consider bridging as a way to provide connectivity for IP.

In real life, though, bridging is rarely configured to provide connectivity for IP; therefore, the command no ip routing is unlikely to be needed. The good news is that, aside from this command, no changes are usually needed to the router configurations of this chapter if they are to be used to bridge non-IP traffic.

Typical applications for bridging are so called nonroutable protocols, such as NetBEUI, LAT, and so on. Once you have configured bridging, these protocols are typically bridged by default.

If you needed to bridge a routed protocol other than IP, you most typically would have to repeat the IP-specific steps but only for this protocol. For example, if you need to bridge IPX and would like to use one of the configurations found in this chapter that contains the command no ip routing, make sure that the command ipx routing is not present in the router configuration (by default it is not, but if you see it, you can turn it off using the command no ipx routing).

These considerations hold true in the case of a source-route bridging configuration. For specific details, however, see the sections devoted to source-route bridging.

Let's consider an example that will help you understand the above guidelines and how they should be applied. Figure 2.16 shows a router that is used to bridge IP traffic between two segments. The configuration of router R1 is shown in Listing 2.1.

Listing 2.1   Router R1's configuration.

```
! Don't use this command unless
! IP must be bridged:
no ip routing

bridge 1 protocol ieee

interface Ethernet0
 bridge-group 1

interface Ethernet1
 bridge-group 1
```

As discussed in the "In Depth" section of this chapter, transparent bridges maintain the filtering database that stores the MAC addresses and bridge ports against which the MAC addresses appeared. The command **show bridge** *<group number>* displays the contents of the filtering database. If the parameter *<group number>* is omitted, the router displays the filtering databases for each defined bridge group.

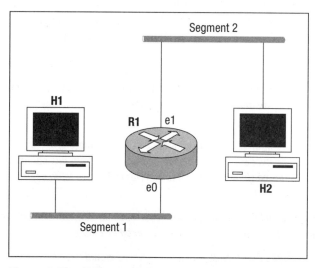

Figure 2.16   Using a single router as a bridge between two Ethernet segments.

Listing 2.2 demonstrates the output of the command **show bridge** entered on router R1 from Figure 2.16.

Listing 2.2   The output of the command show bridge entered on router R1.

```
R1#show bridge

Total of 300 station blocks, 295 free
Codes: P - permanent, S - self

Bridge Group 1:

    Address       Action    Interface     Age   RX count   TX count
0260.8c4c.1132    forward   Ethernet1      3          41         32
0060.5cc4.f4c5    forward   Ethernet0      0         475          0
0060.b01a.9e1c    forward   Ethernet0      3         500        202
```

The Age field indicates the number of minutes since a frame was last sent from or received at the corresponding MAC address. The fields RX count and TX count specify the number of frames received from and transmitted to the MAC address.

TIP: *Although routing is turned off, individual interfaces can still be assigned IP addresses using the command **ip** **address** <ip address> <subnet mask>. This makes the router accessible via the network for management purposes.*

If multiple interfaces belong to a single bridge group, assign only a single IP address on one of the interfaces. Avoid assigning IP addresses on every interface within the same bridge group.

Using Multiple Bridge Groups

It is possible to configure multiple bridge groups on a single Cisco router. As mentioned in the previous section, multiple Ethernet groups behave as separate bridges.

The following guidelines should be used to configure a Cisco router for bridging IP traffic using multiple bridge groups:

1. Disable IP routing using the command **no ip routing** in global configuration mode.

2. Create multiple bridge groups using the command **bridge** <*group number*> **protocol** <*protocol*>. The parameter <*group number*> must have a unique value for each group.

3. Assign the interfaces to the appropriate bridge groups using the command **bridge-group** <*group number*> in interface configuration mode.

Let's consider the situation shown in Figure 2.17 as an example. The configuration of router R1 is shown in Listing 2.3.

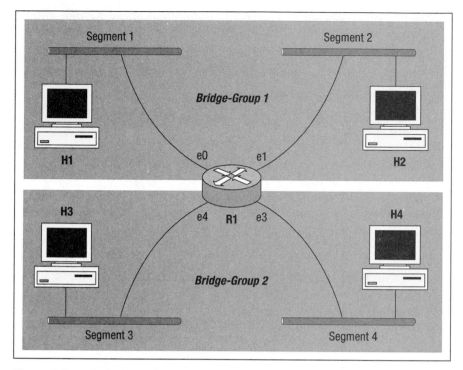

Figure 2.17   A single router configured with multiple bridge groups.

Listing 2.3   Router R1's configuration.

```
! Don't use this command unless
! IP must be bridged:
no ip routing

bridge 1 protocol ieee
bridge 2 protocol ieee

interface Ethernet0
 bridge-group 1

interface Ethernet1
 bridge-group 1

interface Ethernet2
 bridge-group 2

interface Ethernet3
 bridge-group 2
```

Although all four segments are connected via a single router, there can be no communication between the pair of segments 1 and 2 and the pair of segments 3 and 4. Even if all hosts use IP addresses from the same subnet address, hosts H1 or H2 cannot communicate with either host H3 or H4 because the two pairs reside on different bridged LANs.

If the command **show bridge** is used on router R1 without parameters, it displays two filtering databases, as shown in Listing 2.4.

Listing 2.4   The output of the command show bridge entered on router R1.

```
R1#show bridge

Total of 300 station blocks, 295 free
Codes: P - permanent, S - self


Bridge Group 1:

     Address         Action    Interface      Age    RX count    TX count
  0260.8c4c.1132    forward    Ethernet1       3          41          32
  0060.5cc4.f4c5    forward    Ethernet0       0         475           0
  0060.b01a.9e1c    forward    Ethernet0       3         500         202


Bridge Group 2:

  0060.97fb.566a    forward    Ethernet3       0           5           4
  0260.8ca3.28cd    forward    Ethernet2       0          41          10
```

Configuring Mixed-Media Transparent Bridging

It's possible to configure bridging over non-LAN types of media or between two different LAN types, such as Ethernet and token ring.

Configuring bridging over non-LAN types of media is done for two primary purposes. The first is to provide a data link layer network connection for protocols that cannot be routed, such as NetBEUI or LAT. The other is to provide redundant paths for higher-speed primary bridged media, such as Fast Ethernet.

Unlike bridging over non-LAN types of media, bridging between dissimilar LAN types, especially token ring and Ethernet, does not have a strong justification. Transparent bridging between token ring and Ethernet has much in common with so-called *translational bridging* between token ring and Ethernet, and these are discussed at the end of this chapter.

NOTE: *Transparently bridged traffic cannot be forwarded through a tunnel interface.*

Bridging over HDLC

The easiest way to configure bridging over non-LAN media is to do it over an HDLC connection. It is not different from configuring LAN interfaces for bridging; thus, the guidelines presented so far can be used to perform this task.

Figure 2.18 shows an example of how two Cisco routers can be used to bridge traffic between two Ethernet segments over a serial link. The configurations of routers R1 and R2 are shown in Listings 2.5 and 2.6, respectively.

Listing 2.5   Router R1's configuration.

```
! Don't use this command unless
! IP must be bridged:
no ip routing
bridge 1 protocol ieee

interface Ethernet0
 bridge-group 1

interface Serial0
 bridge-group 1
```

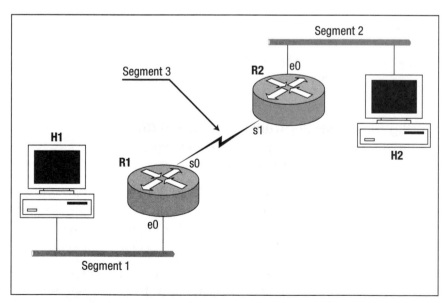

Figure 2.18   Bridging two Ethernet segments using two routers connected via a serial link configured with HDLC encapsulation.

Listing 2.6   Router R2's configuration.

```
! Don't use this command unless
! IP must be bridged:
no ip routing
bridge 1 protocol ieee

interface Ethernet0
 bridge-group 1

interface Serial1
 bridge-group 1
```

The command **show bridge** entered on either router produces typical output (shown in Listings 2.7 and 2.8); however, instead of pointing to a LAN interface, they point to a serial interface.

Listing 2.7   Router R1's configuration.

```
R1#show bridge

Total of 300 station blocks, 296 free
Codes: P - permanent, S - self

Bridge Group 1:
```

Address	Action	Interface	Age	RX count	TX count
0260.8c4c.1132	forward	Serial0	0	15	4
0060.b01a.9e1c	forward	Ethernet0	0	10	10
00e0.b064.30a9	forward	Ethernet0	1	30	0
0260.8ca3.28cd	forward	Serial0	0	42	4

Listing 2.8   Router R2's configuration.

```
R2#show bridge

Total of 300 station blocks, 296 free
Codes: P - permanent, S - self

Bridge Group 1:
```

Address	Action	Interface	Age	RX count	TX count
0260.8c4c.1132	forward	Ethernet0	0	19	6
0060.b01a.9e1c	forward	Serial1	0	12	11
00e0.b064.30a9	forward	Serial1	1	30	0
0260.8ca3.28cd	forward	Ethernet0	0	42	4

2. Transparent and Source-Route Bridging

Bridging over Frame Relay

Configuring bridging over other types of serial interface encapsulations, such as Frame Relay, requires a little more involvement from the network administrator in terms of configuration effort.

The following guidelines allow you to configure an interface with Frame Relay encapsulation for transparent bridging of IP traffic:

1. Disable IP routing using the command **no ip routing** in global configuration mode.

2. Create a bridge group using the command **bridge** *<group number>* **protocol** *<protocol>* in global configuration mode.

3. Configure a serial interface for Frame Relay using the command **encapsulation frame-relay** and, if necessary, **frame-relay lmi-type** *<LMI type>*. It's entirely up to you whether to use subinterfaces. If you use subinterfaces, they can be either point-to-point or multipoint, whichever is more suitable for your needs.

4. Using the command **bridge-group** *<group number>* in interface configuration mode, assign the bridge group on all involved interfaces, including any Frame Relay subinterfaces.

5. If you use multipoint subinterfaces or no subinterfaces, use the command **frame-relay map bridge** *<DLCI>* **broadcast** to map the bridging function to the appropriate Frame Relay DLCI. (It's done automatically for point-to-point subinterfaces right after the command **bridge-group** *<group number>* is entered in the corresponding subinterface configuration mode.)

NOTE: *The keyword **broadcast** must be used to allow bridges to exchange BPDUs.*

The example in Figure 2.19 shows how two routers can be used to bridge IP traffic between two Ethernet segments over a Frame Relay PVC. Listings 2.9 and 2.10 show the configurations of routers R1 and R2 with multipoint subinterfaces.

Listing 2.9   Router R1's configuration with a multipoint subinterface.

```
! Don't use this command unless
! IP must be bridged:
no ip routing
bridge 1 protocol ieee

interface Ethernet0
 bridge-group 1

interface Serial0
```

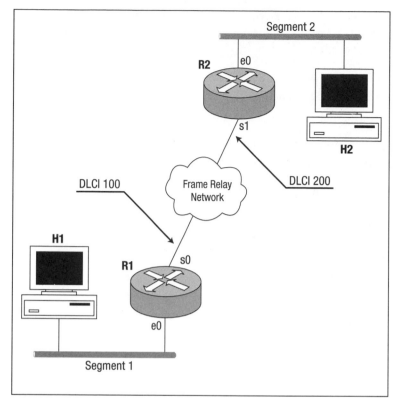

Figure 2.19 Bridging two Ethernet segments using two routers connected via a Frame
Relay network.

```
encapsulation frame-relay
frame-relay lmi-type ansi

interface Serial0.1 multipoint
frame-relay map bridge 100 broadcast
bridge-group 1
```

Listing 2.10   Router R2's configuration with a multipoint subinterface.

```
! Don't use this command unless
! IP must be bridged:
no ip routing
bridge 1 protocol ieee

interface Ethernet0
bridge-group 1
```

```
interface Serial1
 encapsulation frame-relay
 frame-relay lmi-type ansi

interface Serial1.1 multipoint
 frame-relay map bridge 200 broadcast
 bridge-group 1
```

Alternatively, point-to-point subinterfaces can be used, in which case the configurations of the routers become as shown in Listings 2.11 and 2.12.

Listing 2.11   Router R1's configuration with a point-to-point subinterface.

```
! Don't use this command unless
! IP must be bridged:
no ip routing
bridge 1 protocol ieee

interface Serial0
 encapsulation frame-relay
 frame-relay lmi-type ansi

interface Serial0.1 point-to-point
 frame-relay interface-dlci 100
 bridge-group 1
```

Listing 2.12   Router R2's configuration with a point-to-point subinterface.

```
! Don't use this command unless
! IP must be bridged:
no ip routing
bridge 1 protocol ieee

interface Serial1
 encapsulation frame-relay
 frame-relay lmi-type ansi

interface Serial1.1 point-to-point
 frame-relay interface-dlci 200
 bridge-group 1
```

The outputs of the command **show bridge** issued on both routers are shown in Listings 2.13 and 2.14. As you might expect, some of the lines point to subinterfaces instead of LAN interfaces.

Listing 2.13   The output of the command show bridge entered on router R1.

```
R1#show bridge

Total of 300 station blocks, 296 free
Codes: P - permanent, S - self

Bridge Group 1:

    Address        Action    Interface     Age    RX count    TX count
  0260.8c4c.1132   forward   Serial0.1     2           11           4
  0060.97fb.566a   forward   Ethernet0     0           73           4
  0060.b01a.9e1c   forward   Ethernet0     0           39           9
  0260.8ca3.28cd   forward   Serial0.1     0           36          10
```

Listing 2.14   The output of the command show bridge entered on router R2.

```
R2#show bridge

Total of 300 station blocks, 296 free
Codes: P - permanent, S - self

Bridge Group 1:

    Address        Action    Interface     Age    RX count    TX count
  0260.8c4c.1132   forward   Ethernet0     0           12           4
  0060.97fb.566a   forward   Serial1.1     0           73           4
  0060.b01a.9e1c   forward   Serial1.1     0           34           9
  0260.8ca3.28cd   forward   Ethernet0     0           36          10
```

Configuring CRB

The purpose of CRB is to allow the same router to be used for simultaneous bridging and routing of the same type of traffic, such as IP. CRB is enabled using the command **bridge crb** in global configuration mode. After that, the command **no ip routing** is no longer necessary. With IP routing on and CRB enabled, some interfaces on a router can be configured for routing IP, and some can be configured for bridging. The guidelines for configuring bridging are the same as described in the "Configuring Transparent Bridging" section but without the command **no ip routing**.

Figure 2.20 shows a router configured to bridge IP traffic between segments 1 and 2 and to route IP traffic between segments 3 and 4. Router R1's configuration is shown in Listing 2.15.

2. Transparent and Source-Route Bridging

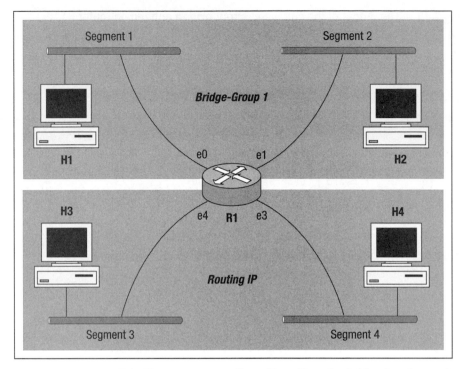

Figure 2.20   Enabling CRB on a router allows IP traffic to be bridged and routed independently.

Listing 2.15   Router R1's configuration with CRB.

```
! The command no ip routing is no longer needed

bridge crb
bridge 1 protocol ieee

interface Ethernet0
 bridge-group 1

interface Ethernet1
 bridge-group 1

interface Ethernet2
 ip address 10.0.1.1 255.255.255.0

interface Ethernet3
 ip address 10.0.2.1 255.255.255.0
```

TIP: *When you use the command **bridge crb**, all protocols including IP are bridged on the interfaces configured for bridging. To re-enable routing of IP on the interfaces configured for bridging, use the command **bridge** <group number> **route ip**. After that, all interfaces that are configured with this bridge group will route IP.*

Configuring IRB

IRB allows the same type of traffic to be passed between the bridging and routing processes on a router. Once a router is configured for IRB using the command **bridge irb** in global configuration mode, a special interface called a *bridge virtual interface (BVI interface)*, becomes available for every bridge group defined on the router. Like before, the bridge groups are defined using the command **bridge** *<bridge group>* **protocol {ieee|dec}**.

To change to BVI interface configuration mode, the command **interface BVI** *<bridge group>* must be entered in bridge configuration mode. This command transfers the command line interface into interface configuration mode with typical configuration options, such as assigning the interface an IP address.

If the BVI interface is configured for IP, its IP address must belong to the network prefix used on the bridged segments. The hosts connected to the bridged segments can use the BVI interface's IP address as their next-hop router, such as the default gateway.

Figure 2.21 shows a configuration in which router R1 is used to route IP traffic between segment 3 and two bridged segments (1 and 2). Router R1's configuration is shown in Listing 2.16.

Listing 2.16   Router R1's configuration with a BVI interface.

```
! The command no ip routing is no longer needed

bridge irb
bridge 1 protocol ieee
 bridge 1 route ip

interface Ethernet0
 bridge-group 1

interface Ethernet1
 bridge-group 1

interface Ethernet2
 ip address 10.0.1.1 255.255.255.0

interface BVI1
 ip address 10.0.2.1 255.255.255.0
```

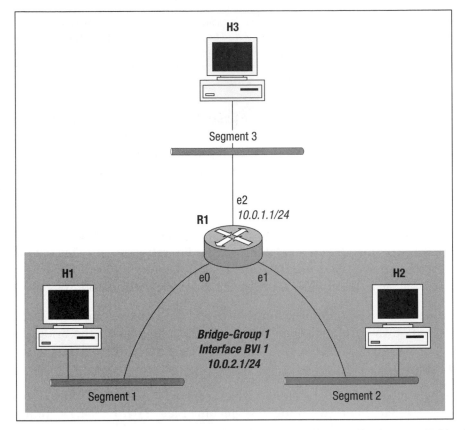

Figure 2.21   Router R1 is configured for IRB, which allows routing between bridged groups and single interfaces within the same router.

NOTE: *IRB requires the command* **bridge** *<group number>* **route ip** *in order to pass the bridged traffic to the corresponding BVI interface. Without this command, the router will not attempt to route IP traffic to or from the bridge group.*

Tuning the Spanning Tree Parameters

This section provides an example of how certain parameters on Cisco routers configured as bridges can be changed to modify the active topology created by the operation of the spanning tree algorithm and STP.

Let's take the configuration shown in Figure 2.22 as an example and examine what active topology is achieved by default and how we can possibly improve it by tuning some bridge parameters. Listings 2.17 through 2.19 show the configurations of routers R1, R2, and R3, respectively.

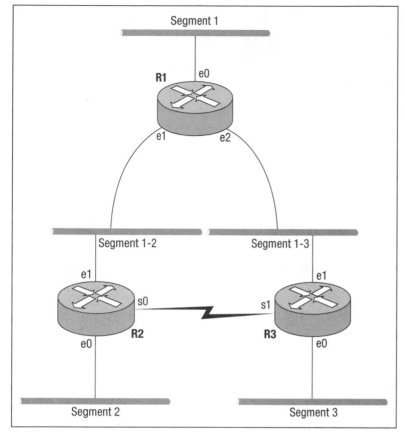

Figure 2.22 A bridged LAN implemented with three Cisco routers configured for bridging.

Listing 2.17 Router R1's configuration.

```
! Don't use this command unless
! IP must be bridged:
no ip routing
bridge 1 protocol ieee

interface Ethernet0
 bridge-group 1

interface Ethernet1
 bridge-group 1

interface Ethernet2
 bridge-group 1
```

Listing 2.18   Router R2's configuration.

```
! Don't use this command unless
! IP must be bridged:
no ip routing
bridge 1 protocol ieee

interface Ethernet0
 bridge-group 1

interface Serial0
 bridge-group 1

interface Ethernet1
 bridge-group 1
```

Listing 2.19   Router R3's configuration.

```
no ip routing
bridge 1 protocol ieee

interface Ethernet0
 bridge-group 1

interface Serial1
 bridge-group 1

interface Ethernet1
 bridge-group 1
```

So far, we have not examined the spanning tree topology defined as the result of spanning tree algorithm operation. One reason for not doing this was that the configurations we examined consisted of a maximum of two bridges connected via a single link. All ports on such bridges should be put into a forwarding state. However, now we have three bridges, each connected to two other ones. This means that at least one port on one of the bridges must be put into a blocking state.

The command that is used to examine the spanning tree information on a router (configured as a bridge) is **show spanning-tree** [*<bridge group number>*]. The *<bridge group>* parameter is optional. If omitted, it causes the command to display the spanning tree information for all bridge groups defined on the router.

Listings 2.20 through 2.22 show the outputs of the command **show spanning-tree** entered on all three routers.

Immediate Solutions

Configuring Transparent Bridging

Originally, bridging for IP could be configured on Cisco routers only if IP routing was turned off. It wasn't very convenient, and soon Cisco came up with a version of IOS that supported so-called *concurrent routing and bridging (CRB)*. In CRB, a router can be configured to simultaneously bridge and route the same protocol, such as IP, although those are two completely independent processes. In other words, with CRB enabled, bridged traffic can be forwarded among only those interfaces configured for bridging, and routed traffic can be forwarded among only those interfaces configured for routing. (An interface in the case of CRB can be configured for only routing or bridging—not both.)

A router with CRB enabled acted as two devices in a single box: a router and a bridge. Although CRB did make the lives of those who needed bridging configuration on a router a little bit easier, CRB was still far from perfect. Soon, another solution followed. It was called *integrated routing and bridging (IRB)*. With IRB enabled, a router could not only be configured for routing and bridging of the same protocol, but it could also forward traffic between the interfaces configured for bridging and the interfaces configured for routing.

Luckily, CRB and IRB added only a few commands in addition to those that were used to configure a router for bridging only. The existing commands were sort of extended by the new commands, which added the missing functionality.

Thus, we'll first consider how to configure Cisco routers for pure bridging of IP, and then we'll see how the CRB- and IRB-related commands expand the capabilities of a router.

Using a Single Bridge Group on a Single Router

Cisco IOS allows several independent virtual bridges to be created inside a single Cisco router. Each virtual bridge behaves as a separate transparent bridge in terms of bridging traffic among the ports it controls. The virtual bridges are configured as *bridge groups*. In other words, a bridge group represents a single virtual bridge.

The following guidelines should be used to configure a Cisco router with a single bridge group (for IP bridging only):

1. Disable IP routing using the command **no ip routing** in global configuration mode.

```
Port 2 (Ethernet0) of bridge group 1 is forwarding
   Port path cost 100, Port priority 128
   Designated root has priority 32768, address 0000.0000.1000
   Designated bridge has priority 32768, address 0000.0000.1000
   Designated port is 2, path cost 0
   Timers: message age 0, forward delay 0, hold 0

Port 4 (Serial0) of bridge group 1 is forwarding
   Port path cost 100, Port priority 128
   Designated root has priority 32768, address 0000.0000.1000
   Designated bridge has priority 32768, address 0000.0000.1000
   Designated port is 4, path cost 0
   Timers: message age 0, forward delay 0, hold 0

Port 3 (Ethernet1) of bridge group 1 is forwarding
   Port path cost 100, Port priority 128
   Designated root has priority 32768, address 0000.0000.1000
   Designated bridge has priority 32768, address 0000.0000.1000
   Designated port is 3, path cost 0
   Timers: message age 0, forward delay 0, hold 0
```

Listing 2.22   The output of the command show spanning-tree entered on router R3.

```
R3#show spanning-tree 1

Bridge Group 1 is executing the IEEE compatible Spanning Tree protocol
   Bridge Identifier has priority 32768, address 0000.0000.2000
   Configured hello time 2, max age 20, forward delay 15
   Current root has priority 32768, address 0000.0000.1000
   Root port is 5 (Serial1), cost of root path is 100
   Topology change flag not set, detected flag not set
   Times:  hold 1, topology change 30, notification 30
           hello 2, max age 20, forward delay 15, aging 300
   Timers: hello 0, topology change 0, notification 0

Port 2 (Ethernet0) of bridge group 1 is forwarding
   Port path cost 100, Port priority 128
   Designated root has priority 32768, address 0000.0000.1000
   Designated bridge has priority 32768, address 0000.0000.2000
   Designated port is 2, path cost 100
   Timers: message age 0, forward delay 0, hold 0

Port 5 (Serial1) of bridge group 1 is forwarding
   Port path cost 100, Port priority 128
   Designated root has priority 32768, address 0000.0000.1000
   Designated bridge has priority 32768, address 0000.0000.1000
```

```
    Designated port is 4, path cost 0
    Timers: message age 1, forward delay 0, hold 0

Port 3 (Ethernet1) of bridge group 1 is forwarding
    Port path cost 100, Port priority 128
    Designated root has priority 32768, address 0000.0000.1000
    Designated bridge has priority 32768, address 0000.0000.2000
    Designated port is 3, path cost 100
    Timers: message age 0, forward delay 0, hold 0
```

Let's assume that router R1 is the most powerful of all three routers and that we want the majority of traffic to go through this router. In other words, we want R1 to become the root bridge. The root bridge is the designated bridge for all segments to which it is attached; thus, it will be more likely to forward the majority of bridged traffic.

However, line 4 of the output received on router R2 tells us that R2 is the root bridge. Why? Because we did not change the default bridge priorities. So, the bridges used their MAC addresses to decide which should become the root bridge. Router 2 has a MAC address equal to 0000.0000.1000. Routers R1 and R2 have MAC addresses equal to 0010.1111.1111 and 0000.0000.2000, respectively. R2's MAC address has the smallest value, and that's why R2 became the root bridge.

Another nuisance of the active spanning tree topology is that both serial interfaces on R2 and R3 are in forwarding mode, whereas the Ethernet2 interface on router R1 is in blocking mode. The explanation is simple: The path cost configured on both serial interfaces and all Ethernet interfaces is equal to 100. Therefore, because the serial interface on router R3 provides the shortest path to the root bridge, it is put into forwarding mode, which ultimately puts the redundant interface (Ethernet) into the blocking state.

The easiest way to change the produced spanning tree topology is to set an appropriate bridge priority value on R1. The default value of the bridge priority is equal to 32768. Therefore, setting router R1's bridge priority to any value lower than this guarantees it will become the root of the spanning tree.

The command that changes the bridge priority is **bridge** *<group number>* **priority** *<new priority>*. (This command changes the bridge priority only for the corresponding bridge group.)

Let's examine what happens when we change the bridge priority on router R1 to the value of 1000. The outputs of the command **show spanning-tree** issued on all three routers are shown in Listings 2.23 through 2.25. To make the output more readable, I skipped over the lines that are not relevant to our discussion.

Listing 2.23   The output of the command show spanning-tree entered on router R1.

```
R1#show spanning-tree 1

Bridge Group 1 is executing the IEEE compatible Spanning Tree protocol
   Bridge Identifier has priority 1000, address 0010.1111.1111
   ...
   We are the root of the spanning tree
   ...


Port 6 (Ethernet0) of bridge group 1 is forwarding
   ...


Port 7 (Ethernet1) of bridge group 1 is forwarding
   ...


Port 8 (Ethernet2) of bridge group 1 is forwarding
   ...
```

Listing 2.24   The output of the command show spanning-tree entered on router R2.

```
R2#show spanning-tree 1

Bridge Group 1 is executing the IEEE compatible Spanning Tree protocol
   Bridge Identifier has priority 32768, address 0000.0000.1000
   ...
   Current root has priority 1000, address 0010.1111.1111
   Root port is 2 (Ethernet0), cost of root path is 100
   ...


Port 2 (Ethernet0) of bridge group 1 is forwarding
   ...


Port 4 (Serial0) of bridge group 1 is forwarding
   ...


Port 3 (Ethernet1) of bridge group 1 is forwarding
   ...
```

Listing 2.25   The output of the command show spanning-tree entered on router R3.

```
R3#show spanning-tree 1

Bridge Group 1 is executing the IEEE compatible Spanning Tree protocol
   Bridge Identifier has priority 32768, address 0000.0000.2000
```

```
...
Current root has priority 1000, address 0010.1111.1111
Root port is 2 (Ethernet0), cost of root path is 100
...


Port 2 (Ethernet0) of bridge group 1 is forwarding
...


Port 5 (Serial1) of bridge group 1 is blocking
...


Port 3 (Ethernet1) of bridge group 1 is forwarding
...
```

Now the spanning topology reflects what we want. R1 is the root bridge, and only the Ethernet ports are in forwarding mode.

TIP: *It is possible (although undesirable) to change the burned MAC address of an Ethernet interface on a Cisco router. To do this, you have to use the command **mac-address** <new MAC address> in interface configuration mode.*

NOTE: *The MAC address values that appeared in the output of the command **show spanning-tree** were assigned using the command **mac-address** <new MAC address>. This was done to simplify the explanation of the spanning tree recalculation process. In addition, the path cost value on the serial interfaces was changed from its default value using the command **bridge** <group number> **path-cost 100** to force the interface into a forwarding state (for the purposes of our discussion). Although the default path-cost value on a serial interface is higher than that on an Ethernet interface, it may not adequately reflect the actual bandwidth of the serial interface and, therefore, may require adjusting.*

Configuring Source-Route Bridging

Configuring source-route bridging is covered in the sections below.

Configuring Source-Route Bridging for Two Interfaces

The very basic configuration of source-route bridging on a Cisco router is accomplished using the command **source-bridge** *<this ring #> <bridge #> <other ring #>* in the token ring interface configuration mode. The parameter *<this ring #>* specifies the ring number of the segment to which this interface is attached. The parameter *<bridge #>* specifies the bridge number of the router. The parameter *<other ring #>* specifies the ring number of the other interface configured for source-route bridging.

This command requires a counter command entered on another token ring interface of the same router. The parameters *<this ring #>* and *<other ring #>* must be in reverse order in the counter command.

> **WARNING!**   **If source-route bridging is configured for IP, then the command no ip routing must be present in the router's configuration. Otherwise, the router will still route IP, as opposed to source-route bridge it.**
>
> **Source-route bridging itself is rarely used for IP; thus, the command no ip routing is unlikely to be needed. Typical source-route bridging applications are SNA and NetBIOS (over NetBEUI). Both are nonroutable protocols.**

Let's consider the example shown in Figure 2.23. Router R1 is used as a source-route bridge to interconnect the two token ring segments to which it is attached. The router has bridge number 5, and the token ring segments have ring numbers 100 and 200. Listing 2.26 shows R1's configuration.

Listing 2.26   Router R1's configuration.

```
! Don't use this command unless
! IP must be bridged:
no ip routing

interface TokenRing0
 ring-speed 16
 source-bridge 100 5 200
```

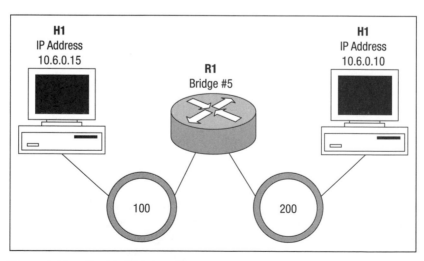

Figure 2.23   Router R1 is configured as a source-route bridge to interconnect the two token ring segments.

```
interface TokenRing1
 ring-speed 16
 source-bridge 200 5 100
```

Notice the order of the rings in the commands **source-bridge**.

Configuring Source-Route Bridging Using a Virtual Ring

A virtual ring is necessary if a router has more than two token ring interfaces that must be interconnected using source-route bridging. In this case, the individual token ring interfaces are "connected" to a virtual ring.

Follow these steps to configure source-route bridging using a virtual ring to bridge IP traffic:

1. Turn off IP routing using the command **no ip routing** in global configuration mode.

2. Define a virtual ring using the command **source-bridge ring-group** *<virtual ring #>* in global configuration mode. The parameter *<virtual ring #>*is numeric and ranges from 1 through 4095. It defines the ring number parameter carried in the RIFs of source-route bridged frames crossing the virtual ring.

3. Connect individual token ring interfaces on the router to the virtual ring using the command **source-bridge** *<local ring #> <bridge #> <virtual ring #>* in interface configuration mode. The parameter *<local ring #>* defines the ring number for the token ring segment to which the interface is attached. This parameter is numeric and also ranges from 1 through 4095. The *<bridge #>* parameter is numeric and ranges from 1 through 15. It defines the bridge number for the virtual bridge that interconnects the physical token ring segment with the virtual ring. The parameter *<virtual ring #>* is the one defined in Step 1.

To see how the guidelines apply, let's consider the same network we examined in the previous section (refer back to Figure 2.23), only this time we'll require router R1 to interconnect the token ring segments using the virtual ring with the number equal to 10. Listing 2.27 shows the revised configuration of the router.

Listing 2.27   Router R1's configuration.

```
! Don't use this command unless
! IP must be bridged:
no ip routing

source-bridge ring-group 10
```

```
interface TokenRing0
 ring-speed 16
 source-bridge 100 5 10

interface TokenRing1
 ring-speed 16
 source-bridge 200 15 10
```

NOTE: *A virtual ring counts as a regular token ring segment from the source-route bridging perspective. As such, it has a ring number. Therefore, a router configured with a virtual ring will insert one extra route designator into the RIF of spanning and all routes explorers it forwards. If an environment in which such a router is used spans multiple source-route bridge hops, the seven-hop limitation for source-route bridging can be exceeded, which consequently will make some nodes unable to communicate.*

If you encounter this problem, consider using alternatives, such as two interface source-route bridging configurations, RSRB or DLSw+.

Understanding the **multiring ip** Command

If a router is connected to a source-route bridged LAN, by default it won't encapsulate ARP requests into either all routes or spanning explorers. Thus, the ARP requests won't be able to reach hosts behind source-route bridges. This situation is shown in Figure 2.24. Router R1 interconnects the source-route bridged LAN consisting of two rings and source-route bridge B1 with the rest of the network (shown as a cloud). By default, router R1's ARP requests won't reach the hosts (such as host H1) behind bridge B1.

In this case, the router must be specifically configured to use either all routes or spanning explorers when issuing ARP requests. This is achieved using the command **multiring ip** [{all-routes|spanning}] in token ring interface configuration mode. The parameter [{all-routes|spanning}] specifies the type of explorers the router should use. This parameter is optional; if omitted, it defaults to spanning.

NOTE: *The command **multiring ip** also affects the behavior of dynamic routing protocols. Typically, routing protocols exchange routing information by sending it to either the broadcast address or a certain multicast address. If a dynamic routing protocol's PDUs are to be sent through a token ring interface attached to a source-route bridged LAN, the command **multiring ip** must be used to make the router encapsulate the PDUs into either all routes or spanning explorers. Otherwise, the router uses plain token ring broadcasts, which cannot cross source-route bridges. The other routers separated from this router by source-route bridges won't be able to receive those PDUs.*

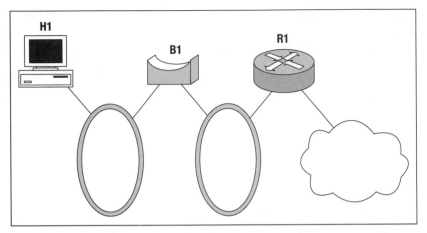

Figure 2.24   Router R1 must be specifically configured to encapsulate ARP requests into explorers that would allow it to reach hosts on the ring behind bridge B1.

Configuring RSRB

Cisco's version of RSRB is based on the use of virtual rings. The virtual ring is extended using other network technologies, thereby allowing source-route bridged traffic to be exchanged between participating routers acting as source-route bridges.

Examples of the networking technologies that can be used to extend virtual rings on the Cisco routers are shown in Table 2.4.

The configuration of RSRB on Cisco routers is done on a peer-to-peer basis. Two Cisco routers are said to be *peers* if there is a non-source-route bridged connection between them that can transparently carry source-route bridged traffic. The connection between peers is established on a point-to-point basis (that is, only two routers can be peers). The connection between peers is often called a *peer relation*.

Although only two routers can form a peer relation, more than two routers can maintain a single virtual ring by means of multiple peer relations between each other. Figure 2.25 demonstrates the concept.

Although peer connections don't have to produce fully meshed topology for RSRB to work correctly, it is desirable, especially if the routers utilize AST.

If multiple routers maintain a single virtual ring, the peer relations do not have to be established using the same encapsulation. For example, a single router can be configured with one virtual ring and three peer relations, so that the first peer relation uses direct encapsulation, the second one TCP, and the third one FST.

Table 2.4   Examples of networking technologies that can be used to encapsulate source-route bridged traffic.

Technology	Explanation
Direct encapsulation	Source-route bridged traffic is encapsulated directly into PDUs of the interface over which the virtual ring is extended.
Frame Relay	Source-route bridged traffic is encapsulated into Frame Relay PDUs.
TCP	Source-route bridged traffic is sent over a TCP/IP connection between participating routers.
Fast-switched TCP	Similar to TCP, only faster. The router uses fast switching to forward the token ring frames between the token ring interfaces and the TCP connection.
Fast-Sequenced Transport (FST)	Source-bridged traffic is encapsulated directly into IP datagrams, whose headers have the "don't fragment" (DF) bit set and the protocol field with a value of 90.

The peer relations are configured on a pair of routers using the command **source-bridge remote-peer** *<virtual ring #>* followed by parameters specifying the details of the encapsulation and often the remote peer identification.

The next five sections explain the details of the RSRB encapsulations shown in Table 2.4.

Configuring RSRB Using Direct Encapsulation

One of the simplest ways to configure RSRB is with direct encapsulation. With this type of RSRB, the source-route bridged traffic that should cross the virtual ring is encapsulated directly into the PDUs of the physical interfaces over which the virtual ring is extended. For example, if the virtual ring is extended over an Ethernet segment interconnecting two routers, then the source-route bridged token ring traffic is encapsulated into Ethernet frames (SNAP encapsulation, Ethernet Type = 1996).

To perform that task, follow these steps:

1. Turn off IP routing using the command **no ip routing** in global configuration mode.

2. Create a virtual ring using the command **source-bridge ring-group** *<virtual ring #>* in global configuration mode. The parameter *<virtual ring #>* is numeric and ranges from 1 through 4095. It denotes the ring number parameter of the virtual ring passed or recorded in the RIFs of the token ring frames sent to and received from the virtual ring.

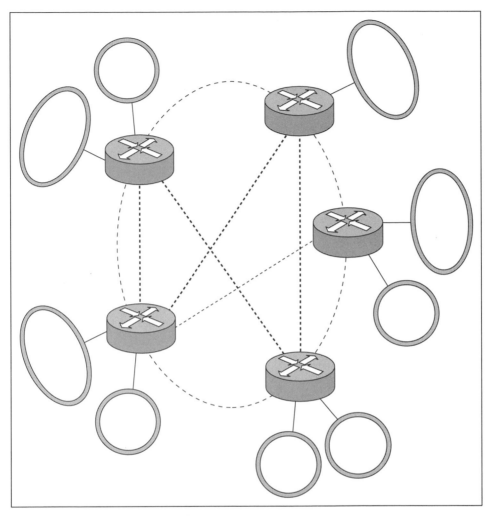

Figure 2.25   More than two routers maintain a single virtual ring by means of multiple peer connections between each other.

3. Specify the interface over which the traffic crossing the virtual ring must be sent using the command **source-bridge remote-peer** *<virtual ring #>* **interface** *<interface ID>* *<interface #>* in global configuration mode. The parameter *<virtual ring #>* must be equal to the parameter *<virtual ring #>* from Step 1. The parameters *<interface ID>* and *<interface #>* denote the interface over which the remote peer is available. The available values of the parameter *<interface ID>* depend on the router model and installed physical interfaces. Some possible values are shown in Table 2.5.

Table 2.5   Examples of direct encapsulation available on Cisco routers.

Interface Type	Comments
Serial	Uses Cisco HDLC encapsulation.
FDDI	Must specify the remote peer's MAC address.
Token ring	Must specify the remote peer's MAC address.
Vlan	Must specify the remote peer's MAC address.
Ethernet	Must specify the remote peer's MAC address.
FastEthernet	Must specify the remote peer's MAC address.
Null	Drops all traffic that must be forwarded through the virtual ring.

NOTE: If a LAN interface (such as FDDI, token ring, and Vlan) is used, then the parameter <interface #> must be followed by the MAC address of the remote peer.

Multiple **source-bridge remote-peer** commands can be used with the same *<virtual ring #>* parameter to establish multiple peer connections. All of the peers are considered to be interconnected with the same virtual ring whose number is equal to the value of the parameter *<virtual ring #>*.

NOTE: Only a single peer connection can be established through a single serial interface. Multiple peer connections can be established through a single LAN interface by using the command **source-bridge remote-peer** several times with the same <interface ID> and <interface #> parameters followed by different MAC addresses.

4. Establish a connection between individual token ring interfaces and the virtual ring using the command **source-bridge** *<this ring #> <bridge #> <virtual ring #>* in interface configuration mode. The parameter *<this ring #>* defines the ring number for the token ring segment to which the token ring interface is attached. The parameter *<bridge #>* defines the bridge number.

NOTE: When connecting a token ring interface with a virtual ring, the bridge is a virtual entity. Although Cisco routers allow you to assign the same bridge number when connecting physical token ring interfaces to a virtual ring, try to avoid doing this.

The parameter *<virtual ring #>* is equal to the parameter of the same name defined on Step 1.

Let's consider the example of the network shown in Figure 2.26. The configurations of routers R1 and R2 are shown in Listings 2.28 and 2.29, respectively.

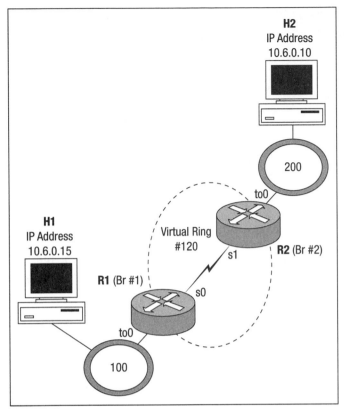

Figure 2.26 Routers R1 and R2, acting as source-route bridges, are interconnected with a serial link over which virtual ring 120 is extended.

Routers R1 and R2 are supposed to maintain the virtual ring with number 120 over a serial link interconnecting them. The serial interfaces on the routers are configured with HDLC encapsulation.

Listing 2.28   Router R1's configuration.

```
! Don't use this command unless
! IP must be bridged:
no ip routing

source-bridge ring-group 120
source-bridge remote-peer 120 interface Serial0

interface Serial0
 mtu 4464

interface TokenRing 0
 ring-speed 16
 source-bridge 100 1 120
```

Listing 2.29   Router R2's configuration.

```
! Don't use this command unless
! IP must be bridged:
no ip routing

source-bridge ring-group 120
source-bridge remote-peer 120 interface Serial1

interface Serial1
 mtu 4464

interface TokenRing0
 ring-speed 16
 source-bridge 200 2 120
```

Notice that the MTU size of the serial interfaces on both routers was made equal to the MTU size of the token ring interface. The latter was acquired from the output of the command **show interfaces TokenRing 0**.

A good way to verify the status of the peer connection is by examining the output of the command **show source-bridge**. The sample output of this command entered on router R1 from Figure 2.26 is shown in Listing 2.30.

Listing 2.30   The output of the command **show source-bridge** entered on router R1.

```
R1#show source-bridge

Local Interfaces:                              receive     transmit
          srn bn  trn r p s n  max hops        cnt         cnt      drops
To0       100  1  120 *   f    7  7  7          2375        2286       0

Global RSRB Parameters:
 TCP Queue Length maximum: 100

Ring Group 120:
  No TCP peername set, TCP transport disabled
  Maximum output TCP queue length, per peer: 100
  Peers:            state   bg lv  pkts_rx  pkts_tx  expl_gn   drops TCP
   IF  Serial0     open       3       0        8        1         0 n/a
  Rings:
   bn: 1  rn: 100  local   ma: 4007.0d26.0a46 TokenRing0    fwd: 2187
   bn: 2  rn: 200  remote  ma: 4007.0d26.0c15 IF  Serial0    fwd: 0

Explorers: ------ input ------        ------ output ------
          spanning  all-rings   total    spanning  all-rings  total
To0            109        79     188           8         91     99
```

```
Explorer fastswitching enabled
Local switched: 109        flushed 0         max Bps 38400

    rings       inputs        bursts       throttles     output drops
     To0         109            0              0              0
```

The part of the output that interests us is shaded, and it's here we'll find the word *open* (it's italicized), which indicates that the peer connection through interface Serial0 is operational. If the status of a connection is "closed," this does not necessarily indicate a problem with establishing a connection. If no traffic has been forwarded through the virtual ring, the status of the peer connection remains closed. In this case, make sure some traffic is definitely sent through the virtual ring and check the status again. If it's still closed, then it's time to troubleshoot the connection.

Another possible value for the peer connections is "dead." This clearly indicates a problem with the connection.

TIP: *If the connection for some reason cannot be established (the status remains closed), you can try troubleshooting the problem using the command **debug source bridge**. Although avoid using this command on production routers.*

Let's consider another example in which a virtual ring is extended using direct encapsulation. Figure 2.27 shows the source-route bridged network in which routers R1 and R2, acting as source-route bridges, extend the virtual ring whose number is 120 over an Ethernet segment. Listings 2.31 and 2.32 show the configurations of both routers.

Listing 2.31   Router R1's configuration.

```
! Don't use this command unless
! IP must be bridged:
no ip routing

source-bridge ring-group 120
! The MAC address is that of interface Ethernet 0 on router R2
source-bridge remote-peer 120 interface Ethernet0 00e0.b064.30a9

interface Ethernet0
! no shutdown -- the interface must be up

interface TokenRing0
 ring-speed 16
 source-bridge 100 1 120
```

2. Transparent and Source-Route Bridging

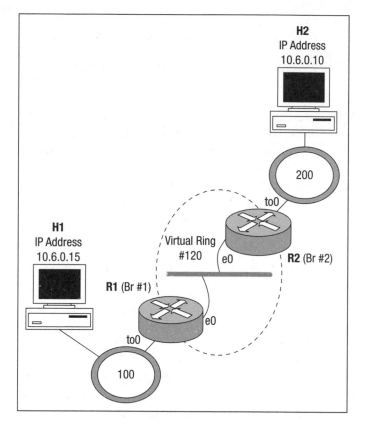

Figure 2.27   Routers R1 and R2, acting as source-route bridges, are interconnected via an Ethernet segment over which virtual ring 120 is extended.

Listing 2.32   Router R2's configuration.

```
! Don't use this command unless
! IP must be bridged:
no ip routing

source-bridge ring-group 120
! The MAC address is that of interface Ethernet 0 on router R1
source-bridge remote-peer 120 interface Ethernet0 00e0.b064.5063

interface Ethernet0
! no shutdown -- the interface must be up

interface TokenRing0
 ring-speed 16
 source-bridge 200 2 120
```

Notice that this time, we used a slightly different version of the command **source-bridge remote-peer**. It was followed by the remote peer's Ethernet MAC address.

TIP: *The values of MAC addresses for the command **source-bridge remote-peer** can be obtained from the output of the command **show interfaces**.*

Let's try an experiment. Let's make host H1 send host H2 a frame that is bigger than the MTU of the Ethernet segment (1,500 bytes). We know that, in the case of transparent bridging, such a frame would be silently dropped. But will this happen in the case of source-route bridging?

We can make host H1 send a large frame to host H2 using the command **ping**. In the lab in which the configuration from Figure 2.27 was tried, host H1 was a Windows NT machine. In Windows NT, the command **ping** has the parameter –l followed by the size of the buffer that **ping** sends. If the size of the buffer is set to 3,000 bytes, then the frame carrying the ICMP echo request still fits the token ring's MTU size but does not fit the Ethernet's MTU size.

The results of the command **ping –l 3000** issued on host H1 are shown in Listing 2.33. To our surprise, host H1 receives replies from host H2.

Listing 2.33 **The output of the command ping –l 3000 10.6.0.10 indicates that host H2 is accessible, regardless of the smaller MTU size of the intermediate segment.**

```
C:\>ping -l 3000 10.6.0.10

Pinging 10.6.0.10 with 3000 bytes of data:

Request timed out.
Reply from 10.6.0.10: bytes=3000 time=10ms TTL=128
Reply from 10.6.0.10: bytes=3000 time=10ms TTL=128
Reply from 10.6.0.10: bytes=3000 time=10ms TTL=128
```

Why did the smaller MTU size of the Ethernet segment not prevent the larger token ring frames from being exchanged by the hosts? The answer lies in the length subfield of the RIF of frames crossing the virtual ring extended over the Ethernet segment. When host H1 issued the first ARP request to resolve host H2's IP address into its MAC address, the ARP request was encapsulated into an all routers explorer. (By default, Windows NT uses all routes explorers to send ARP requests.) When the all routes explorer arrived at router R1, router R1 adjusted the length subfield stored in the RIF of the explorer before sending it over the virtual ring. It made the value of the length subfield smaller than the MTU size of

Ethernet. (In fact, it made it equal to 512 bytes.) This value was eventually passed back to host H1 in the ARP reply from host H2. Host H1 took notice of the value and, when creating the first ping packet, instead of producing a single large datagram, it created several fragments whose encapsulated size was smaller or equal to the returned length subfield value. Thus, host H1 never sent a large frame to host H2. Of course, if host H1 sent host H2 a token ring frame that was bigger than the MTU of Ethernet, this frame would be dropped by router R1. (IP fragmentation does not apply because router R1 does not act as an IP router but rather acts as a source-route bridge).

Nevertheless, the described process is quite a departure from the way such situations are handled by transparent bridging, in which case hosts would never adjust the smallest MTU size value for their IP communication. The experiment demonstrates that the overhead of source-route bridging at the end nodes does have some positive sides. For example, it simplifies the smallest MTU size discovery process.

Configuring RSRB with Frame Relay Encapsulation

A virtual ring can be extended over serial links configured with Frame Relay encapsulation. In this case, the source-route bridged traffic is directly encapsulated into Frame Relay PDUs.

The following guidelines allow configuring RSRB (for IP) with Frame Relay encapsulation:

1. Turn off IP routing using the command **no ip routing** in global configuration mode.

2. Create a virtual ring using the command **source-bridge ring-group** *<virtual ring #>* in global configuration mode. The parameter *<virtual ring #>* is numeric and ranges from 1 through 4095.

3. Specify the interface over which the traffic crossing the virtual ring must be sent using the command **source-bridge remote-peer** *<virtual ring #>* **frame relay interface** *<interface ID> <interface #> <DLCI>* in global configuration mode. The parameter *<virtual ring #>* must be equal to the parameter *<virtual ring #>* from Step 1. The parameters *<interface ID>* and *<interface #>* denote the interface over which the remote peer is accessible through the Frame Relay network; the interface must be configured with Frame Relay encapsulation. Most likely, the parameter *<interface ID>* will be equal to **Serial**. The parameter *<DLCI>* denotes the DLCI of the PVC interconnecting the local router with the remote peer.

NOTE: *The parameters* <interface ID> *and* <interface #> *can reference a Frame Relay subinterface* **Serial0.1***.*

Multiple **source-bridge remote-peer** command can be used with the same *<virtual ring #>* parameter to establish multiple peer connections. All of the peers are considered to be interconnected with the same virtual ring whose number is equal to the value of the *<virtual ring #>* parameter.

4. Using the command **frame-relay map rsrb** *<DLCI>* **broadcast** in interface configuration mode, establish the mapping between RSRB and Frame Relay DLCI. Use this command for every serial interface, which provides access to the remote peers through the Frame Relay network.

5. Establish a connection between individual token ring interfaces and the virtual ring using the command **source-bridge** *<this ring #>* *<bridge #>* *<virtual ring #>* in interface configuration mode. The parameter *<this ring #>* defines the ring number for the token ring segment to which the token ring interface is attached. The parameter *<bridge #>* defines the bridge number. The parameter *<virtual ring #>* is equal to the parameter *<virtual ring #>* defined in Step 1.

The example of the network shown in Figure 2.28 demonstrates how two routers extend the virtual ring between each other via a Frame Relay network. Listings 2.34 and 2.35 show the configurations of both routers. Notice that router R1 is configured with a Frame Relay subinterface.

Listing 2.34   Router R1's configuration.

```
! Don't use this command unless
! IP must be bridged:
no ip routing

source-bridge ring-group 12
source-bridge remote-peer 12 frame-relay interface Serial0.1 102

interface Serial0
 mtu 4464
 encapsulation frame-relay
 frame-relay lmi-type ansi

interface Serial0.1 multipoint
 mtu 4464
 frame-relay map rsrb 102 broadcast

interface TokenRing0
 ring-speed 16
 source-bridge 100 1 12
```

Listing 2.35   Router R2's configuration.

```
! Don't use this command unless
! IP must be bridged:
no ip routing

source-bridge ring-group 12
source-bridge remote-peer 12 frame-relay interface Serial0 201

interface Serial0
 mtu 4464
 encapsulation frame-relay
 frame-relay lmi-type ansi
 frame-relay map rsrb 201 broadcast

interface TokenRing0
 ring-speed 16
 source-bridge 200 2 12
```

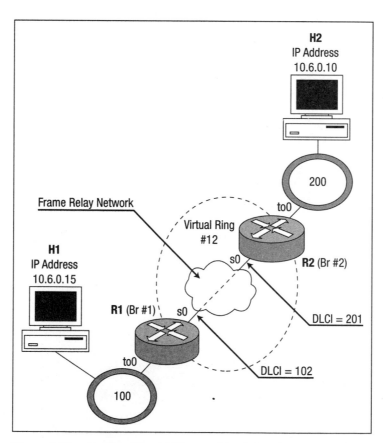

Figure 2.28   **Routers R1 and R2 use virtual ring #12 extended through a Frame Relay network.**

> **NOTE:** Notice the use of the command **mtu 4464** in the configuration of both routers. As it is possible to change the MTU size of a serial interface, it makes sense to make it equal to the MTU size of the token ring interfaces connected to the virtual ring. In our case, the token ring interface on both routers is **TokenRing0**, the serial interfaces are **Serial0.1** on router R1 and **Serial0** on router R2, and the virtual ring number is 12.
>
> If the current MTU size of the serial interface is less than 2,104 bytes, the routers produce the following message right after the command **source-bridge remote-peer** is entered: **WARNING! RSRB: MTU size of Frame Relay interface should be > 2104**.

Configuring RSRB over a TCP Connection

It is possible to extend a virtual ring over a TCP connection between two routers. The guidelines for configuring RSRB (for IP) over TCP are as follows:

1. Turn off IP routing using the command **no ip routing** in global configuration mode.

2. Create a virtual ring using the command **source-bridge ring-group** *<virtual ring #>* in global configuration mode. The parameter *<virtual ring #>* is numeric and ranges from 1 through 4095.

3. Using the command **source-bridge remote-peer** *<virtual ring #>* **tcp** *<local IP address>* in global configuration mode, specify which IP address the router has to use when establishing peer connections. The parameter *<virtual ring #>* is equal to the one defined in Step 2. The parameter *<local IP address>* is equal to the IP address of one of the router's interfaces, which must be accessible from the routers with which the connections are established.

4. Create one or several peer connections using the command **source-bridge remote-peer** *<virtual ring #>* **tcp** *<remote IP address>*. The parameter *<virtual ring #>* is equal to the one defined in Step 2. The parameter *<remote IP address>* is equal to the IP address of an interface of the router with which the connection is established.

> **NOTE:** The parameters <local IP address> and <remote IP address> must be accessible from the remote and local routers, respectively. Depending on which interfaces these IP addresses reside, this may require IP routing to be enabled on the local and remote routers.

To see how the guidelines are to be applied, let's consider the network example shown in Figure 2.29. Three TCP connections forming a full mesh among the routers are established to extend the virtual ring. Listings 2.36 through 2.38 show the configurations of all three routers.

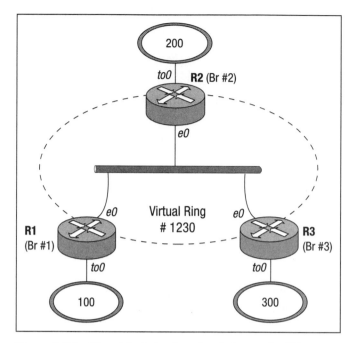

Figure 2.29   The virtual ring is extended over the Ethernet segment among all three routers.

Listing 2.36   Router R1's configuration.

```
! Don't use this command unless
! IP must be bridged:
no ip routing

source-bridge ring-group 1230
source-bridge remote-peer 1230 tcp 192.168.1.1
source-bridge remote-peer 1230 tcp 192.168.1.2
source-bridge remote-peer 1230 tcp 192.168.1.3

interface Ethernet0
 ip address 192.168.1.1 255.255.255.0

interface TokenRing0
 ring-speed 16
 source-bridge 100 1 1230
```

Listing 2.37   Router R2's configuration.

```
! Don't use this command unless
! IP must be bridged:
no ip routing
```

```
source-bridge ring-group 1230
source-bridge remote-peer 1230 tcp 192.168.1.1
source-bridge remote-peer 1230 tcp 192.168.1.2
source-bridge remote-peer 1230 tcp 192.168.1.3

interface Ethernet0
 ip address 192.168.1.2 255.255.255.0

interface TokenRing0
 ring-speed 16
 source-bridge 200 2 1230
```

Listing 2.38   Router R3's configuration.

```
! Don't use this command unless
! IP must be bridged:
no ip routing

source-bridge ring-group 1230
source-bridge remote-peer 1230 tcp 192.168.1.1
source-bridge remote-peer 1230 tcp 192.168.1.2
source-bridge remote-peer 1230 tcp 192.168.1.3

interface Ethernet0
 ip address 192.168.1.3 255.255.255.0

interface TokenRing0
 ring-speed 16
 source-bridge 300 3 1230
```

Notice that in this example, the peer connections produce full mesh.

Configuring RSRB over a Fast-Switched TCP Connection
RSRB over a fast-switched TCP connection is very similar to RSRB over a regular TCP connection. The router uses fast switching to forward token ring frames between the token ring interfaces and the fast-switched TCP connection.

Configuring RSRB with FST Encapsulation
FST is really a direct encapsulation of token ring frames into IP datagrams. The protocol number field carried in such IP datagrams is equal to 90.

Fast really means that the router uses fast switching when forwarding IP datagrams. Fast switching requires IP routing function; therefore, RSRB over FST cannot be used for source-route bridging of IP traffic.

FST does not provide any reliability assurance, such as reordering out-of-sequence datagrams, eliminating duplicated datagrams, and retransmitting lost datagrams. Moreover, FST does not even allow fragmentation; this is ensured by setting the DF bit in the datagrams carrying the source-route bridged traffic.

The following guidelines should be used to configure RSRB with FST encapsulation:

1. Make sure IP routing is on; if it's off, re-enable it using the command **ip routing** in global configuration mode.

2. Create a virtual ring using the command **source-bridge ring-group** *<virtual ring #>* in global configuration mode. The parameter *<virtual ring #>* is numeric and ranges from 1 through 4095.

3. Using the command **source-bridge fst-peername** *<local IP address>* in global configuration mode, specify which IP address the router has to use when establishing peer connections. The parameter *<local IP address>* is equal to the IP address of one of the router's interfaces, which must be accessible from the routers with which the connections are established.

4. Create one or several peer connections using the command **source-bridge remote-peer** *<virtual ring #>* **fst** *<remote IP address>*. The parameter *<virtual ring #>* is equal to the one defined in Step 2. The parameter *<remote IP address>* is equal to the IP address of an interface of the router with which the connection is established.

NOTE: *The parameters* <local IP address> *and* <remote IP address> *must be accessible from the remote and local routers, respectively.*

Let's see how the routers from the example shown in Figure 2.29 can be configured with RSRB with FST encapsulation instead of TCP encapsulation. Listings 2.39 through 2.41 show the configurations of all three routers.

Listing 2.39   Router R1's configuration.

```
! ip routing is required for FST

source-bridge ring-group 1230
source-bridge fst-peername 192.168.1.1
source-bridge remote-peer 1230 fst 192.168.1.2
source-bridge remote-peer 1230 fst 192.168.1.3

interface Ethernet0
 ip address 192.168.1.1 255.255.255.0

interface TokenRing0
 ring-speed 16
 source-bridge 100 1 1230
```

Listing 2.40   Router R2's configuration.

```
! ip routing is required for FST

source-bridge ring-group 1230
source-bridge fst-peername 192.168.1.2
source-bridge remote-peer 1230 fst 192.168.1.1
source-bridge remote-peer 1230 fst 192.168.1.3

interface Ethernet0
 ip address 192.168.1.2 255.255.255.0

interface TokenRing0
 ring-speed 16
 source-bridge 200 2 1230
```

Listing 2.41   Router R3's configuration.

```
! ip routing is required for FST

source-bridge ring-group 1230
source-bridge fst-peername 192.168.1.3
source-bridge remote-peer 1230 fst 192.168.1.1
source-bridge remote-peer 1230 fst 192.168.1.2

interface Ethernet0
 ip address 192.168.1.3 255.255.255.0

interface TokenRing0
 ring-speed 16
 source-bridge 300 3 1230
```

Use the guidelines for configuring RSRB over TCP for configuring RSRB over fast-switched TCP.

Configuring Spanning Explorers

Configuring spanning explorers manually and using AST are covered in the next two sections.

Configuring Spanning Explorers Manually

Individual token ring interfaces on a Cisco router can be configured for process-ing spanning explorers using the command **source-bridge spanning**. This com-mand, however, must be used with care as its placement on the wrong interfaces can lead to duplicate spanning explorers and potentially to source-route bridging loops (short lived).

An example of a redundant source-route bridged network is shown in Figure 2.30. Listings 2.42 and 2.43 show the configuration of both routers.

Routers R1 and R2, acting as source-route bridges, are required to process spanning explorers. Because the network is redundant, spanning explorers cannot be enabled on both token ring interfaces of both routers. One possible configuration, however, is to enable spanning explorers on both token ring interfaces of a single router and to leave the other router with spanning explorers disabled on its token ring interfaces. This ensures that there is a single route between the two token ring segments that spanning explorers can traverse.

Listing 2.42   Router R1's configuration.

```
! Don't use this command unless
! IP must be bridged:
no ip routing

interface TokenRing0
 ring-speed 16
 source-bridge 100 1 200
 source-bridge spanning

interface TokenRing1
 ring-speed 16
 source-bridge 200 1 100
 source-bridge spanning
```

Listing 2.43   Router R2's configuration.

```
! Don't use this command unless
! IP must be bridged:
no ip routing

interface TokenRing0
 ring-speed 16
 source-bridge 100 2 200

interface TokenRing1
 ring-speed 16
 source-bridge 200 2 100
```

Configuring Spanning Explorers Using Automatic Spanning Tree AST

Configuring AST is very similar to configuring transparent bridging. The following procedure shows the steps that should be followed to configure a router acting as a source-route bridge to run AST:

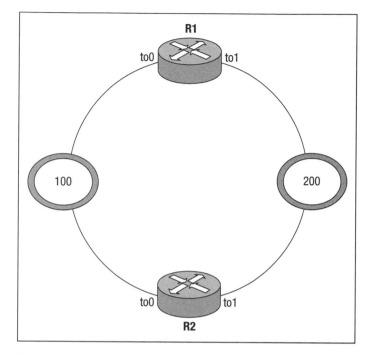

Figure 2.30   A redundant source-route bridged network.

1. Create an AST process on the router using the command **bridge**
   <bridge group #> **protocol ibm**. In general, the parameter *<bridge
   group#>* allows multiple bridge processes to be created inside a single
   router; different interfaces then can be assigned to different bridge
   processes using this number. It has local significance and is not communicated between the routers or/and bridges.

NOTE: *Although the parameter <bridge Group #> can be different on different bridges, it makes sense to
keep it identical for consistency purposes. In addition, only a single command **bridge** <bridge Group #>
protocol ibm is allowed. If you try to enter a subsequent command using a different <bridge Group #>
parameter, the router will respond with the message **Bridge Group** <bridge Group #> **is running the IBM
protocol already** and the command won't be accepted.*

---

2. Optionally assign the bridge process a priority using the command
   bridge *<bridgegroup #>* **priority** *<priority>*. The parameter *<bridge
   group #>* must be equal to the parameter *<bridge Group #>* from Step
   1. The parameter *<priority>* is numeric and can range from 0 through
   65535. It denotes the bridge priority parameter communicated between
   the bridges and is used to force the election of the root of the spanning
   tree in favor of the bridge with the lowest priority. By default, the
   bridge priority is 32768.

3. Start the bridge process on individual token ring interfaces using the command **source-bridge spanning** <*bridge group #*> [**path-cost** <*path-cost*>]. The parameter <*bridge group #*> must be equal to the parameter <*bridge group #*> from Step 1. The optional parameter <*path-cost*> can be used to assign an AST path cost on the interface. The bridge process uses this value when calculating the distance from the root.

NOTE: *A virtual ring is automatically included in the bridge process, provided at least one physical token ring interface on which AST is enabled is interconnected with the virtual ring. No command exists to start AST on the virtual ring. This also means that the port cost values associated with the virtual interfaces cannot be changed.*

Let's consider the example of the network shown in Figure 2.31. Listings 2.44 through 2.47 show the configurations of all four routers configured for AST operation. The commands directly relevant to AST configuration are bolded.

Routers R1, R2, R3, and R4 are configured as source-route bridges. As they are interconnected with redundant paths, the individual interfaces participating in source-route bridging must be appropriately configured for forwarding and blocking spanning explorers. The easiest way to do that is to create an AST process on the routers, which will take care of the individual interfaces.

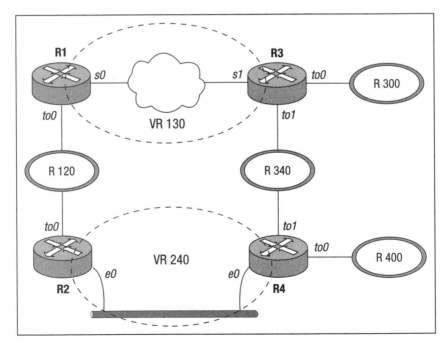

Figure 2.31 A sample source-route bridged network configuration that can benefit from using AST.

Listing 2.44   Router R1's configuration.

```
! Don't use this command unless
! IP must be bridged:
no ip routing

source-bridge ring-group 130
source-bridge remote-peer 130 frame-relay interface Serial0 103

interface Serial0
 encapsulation frame-relay
 frame-relay map rsrb 103 broadcast
 frame-relay lmi-type ansi

interface TokenRing0
 ring-speed 16
 source-bridge 120 1 130
 source-bridge spanning 60

bridge 60 protocol ibm
```

Listing 2.45   Router R2's configuration.

```
! Don't use this command unless
! IP must be bridged:
no ip routing

source-bridge ring-group 240
source-bridge remote-peer 240 tcp 10.1.0.2
source-bridge remote-peer 240 tcp 10.1.0.1

interface Ethernet0
 ip address 10.1.0.1 255.255.255.0

interface TokenRing0
 ring-speed 16
 source-bridge 120 2 240
 source-bridge spanning 60

bridge 60 protocol ibm
```

Listing 2.46   Router R3's configuration.

```
! Don't use this command unless
! IP must be bridged:
no ip routing
```

```
source-bridge ring-group 130
source-bridge remote-peer 130 frame-relay interface Serial1 301

interface Serial1
 encapsulation frame-relay
 frame-relay map rsrb 301 broadcast
 frame-relay lmi-type ansi

interface TokenRing0
 ring-speed 16
 source-bridge 300 3 130
 source-bridge spanning 60

interface TokenRing1
 ring-speed 16
 source-bridge 340 3 130
 source-bridge spanning 60

bridge 60 protocol ibm
```

Listing 2.47   Router R4's configuration.

```
! Don't use this command unless
! IP must be bridged:
no ip routing

source-bridge ring-group 240
source-bridge remote-peer 240 tcp 10.1.0.1
source-bridge remote-peer 240 tcp 10.1.0.2

interface Ethernet0
 ip address 10.1.0.2 255.255.255.0

interface TokenRing0
 ring-speed 16
 source-bridge 400 4 240
 source-bridge spanning 60

interface TokenRing1
 ring-speed 16
 source-bridge 340 4 240
 source-bridge spanning 60

bridge 60 protocol ibm
```

AST supports the command **show spanning** optionally followed by the parameter *<bridge group #>*. As with transparent bridging, this command displays the state of spanning tree that the bridge group has at the moment.

For example, when the **show spanning** command was entered on router R4, the output shown in Listing 2.48 was generated. This output indicates that the bridging process running on router R4 perceives itself as the root of the spanning tree.

Listing 2.48 The output of the command **show spanning 60** entered on router R4 indicates that the router is the root bridge of the spanning tree.

```
R4#show spanning 60

Bridge Group 60 is executing the IBM compatible Spanning Tree protocol
  Bridge Identifier has priority 32768, address 0000.0c32.3a08
  Configured hello time 2, max age 10, forward delay 4
  We are the root of the spanning tree
  Topology change flag not set, detected flag not set
  Times:  hold 1, topology change 30, notification 30
          hello 2, max age 10, forward delay 4, aging 300
  Timers: hello 1, topology change 0, notification 0

Port 1904 (TokenRing0) of bridge group 60 is forwarding
   Port path cost 16, Port priority 128
   Designated root has priority 32768, address 0000.0c32.3a08
   Designated bridge has priority 32768, address 0000.0c32.3a08
   Designated port is 1904, path cost 0, peer 0
   Timers: message age 0, forward delay 0, hold 0

Port 1544 (TokenRing1) of bridge group 60 is forwarding
   Port path cost 16, Port priority 128
   Designated root has priority 32768, address 0000.0c32.3a08
   Designated bridge has priority 32768, address 0000.0c32.3a08
   Designated port is 1544, path cost 0, peer 0
   Timers: message age 0, forward delay 0, hold 0

Port 0F04 (spanRSRB) of bridge group 60 is forwarding
   Port path cost 250, Port priority 128
   Designated root has priority 32768, address 0000.0c32.3a08
   Designated bridge has priority 32768, address 0000.0c32.3a08
   Designated port is 0F04, path cost 0, peer 0
   Timers: message age 0, forward delay 0, hold 0
```

Listing 2.49 shows the outout of the command **show spanning** entered on router R1. The bridging process on router R1 assumes that the shortest path to the root is through port 0821, which corresponds to the virtual port residing on the virtual ring (denoted as **spanRSRB** in the output). The TokenRing0 interface of the router is in the blocking state.

Listing 2.49   The output of the command show spanning 60 entered on router R1.

```
R1#show spanning 60

Bridge Group 60 is executing the IBM compatible Spanning Tree protocol
   Bridge Identifier has priority 32768, address 0207.0d26.0ac6
   Configured hello time 2, max age 10, forward delay 4
   Current root has priority 32768, address 0000.0c32.3a08
   Root port is 0821 (spanRSRB), cost of root path is 266
   Topology change flag not set, detected flag not set
   Times:  hold 1, topology change 30, notification 30
           hello 2, max age 10, forward delay 4, aging 300
   Timers: hello 0, topology change 0, notification 0

Port 0781 (TokenRing0) of bridge group 60 is blocking
   Port path cost 16, Port priority 128
   Designated root has priority 32768, address 0000.0c32.3a08
   Designated bridge has priority 32768, address 0207.0d26.0c95
   Designated port is 0782, path cost 250, peer 0
   Timers: message age 2, forward delay 0, hold 0

Port 0821 (spanRSRB) of bridge group 60 is forwarding
   Port path cost 250, Port priority 128
   Designated root has priority 32768, address 0000.0c32.3a08
   Designated bridge has priority 32768, address 0200.0c19.302a
   Designated port is 0823, path cost 16, peer 0
   Timers: message age 3, forward delay 0, hold 0
```

So far, we have not forced any router to become the root of the spanning tree. Let's now add the command **bridge 60 priority 1000** into the configuration of router R2, which should make it the root of the spanning tree. Listing 2.50 shows the updated configuration.

Listing 2.50   Router R2's configuration modified to make the router the root bridge of the spanning tree.

```
! Don't use this command unless
! IP must be bridged:
no ip routing

source-bridge ring-group 240
source-bridge remote-peer 240 tcp 10.1.0.2
source-bridge remote-peer 240 tcp 10.1.0.1
```

```
interface Ethernet0
 ip address 10.1.0.1 255.255.255.0

interface TokenRing0
 ring-speed 16
 source-bridge 120 2 240
 source-bridge spanning 60

bridge 60 protocol ibm
bridge 60 priority 1000
```

Listing 2.51 shows the output of the command **show spanning 60** entered on router R1 after router R2 was updated with the new configuration. Notice the change in the states of the ports and how the priority of the new root is reflected in the output.

Listing 2.51 **The output of the command show spanning 60 entered on router R1 reflects the new root and shows the change in the state of some ports.**

```
R1#show spanning 60

Bridge Group 60 is executing the IBM compatible Spanning Tree protocol
   Bridge Identifier has priority 32768, address 0207.0d26.0ac6
   Configured hello time 2, max age 10, forward delay 4
   Current root has priority 1000, address 0207.0d26.0c95
   Root port is 0781 (TokenRing0), cost of root path is 16
   Topology change flag not set, detected flag not set
   Times:  hold 1, topology change 30, notification 30
           hello 2, max age 10, forward delay 4, aging 300
   Timers: hello 0, topology change 0, notification 0

Port 0781 (TokenRing0) of bridge group 60 is forwarding
   Port path cost 16, Port priority 128
   Designated root has priority 1000, address 0207.0d26.0c95
   Designated bridge has priority 1000, address 0207.0d26.0c95
   Designated port is 0782, path cost 0, peer 0
   Timers: message age 2, forward delay 0, hold 0

Port 0821 (spanRSRB) of bridge group 60 is forwarding
   Port path cost 250, Port priority 128
   Designated root has priority 1000, address 0207.0d26.0c95
   Designated bridge has priority 32768, address 0207.0d26.0ac6
   Designated port is 0821, path cost 16, peer 0
   Timers: message age 0, forward delay 0, hold 0
```

Configuring Source-Route Translational Bridging

Source-route bridging is defined only for token ring networks. Nevertheless, a technology exists that allows source-route bridging to be translated into transparent bridging and vice versa, making it possible to merge a transparently bridged LAN with a source-route bridged LAN. This technology is called source-route translational bridging.

The "translation" is not particularly seamless, however. First, as discussed in the "In Depth" section earlier in this chapter, the Ethernet and token ring MAC addresses have a different order of bits in bytes. Therefore, a bridge must translate the token ring bit order to Ethernet, and vice versa. An example of such a translation is shown in Figure 2.32.

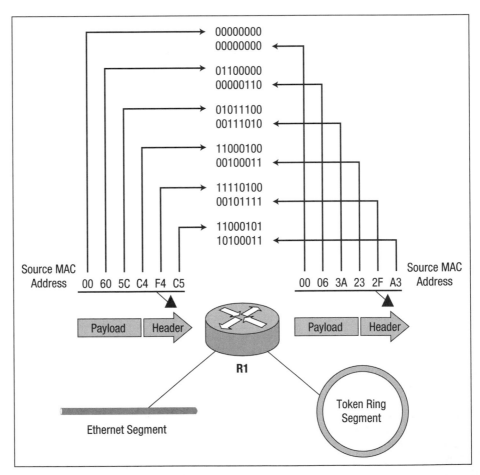

Figure 2.32   A router that is used to bridge traffic between a token ring segment and an Ethernet segment translates the bit order in the bytes of the MAC addresses.

The translation itself wouldn't be a big problem unless ARP saved a copy of the source MAC address in its own PDU. From the perspective of the data link layer, ARP's PDU is a payload of a MAC frame. Therefore, a bridge (a data link layer device) won't look into the payload and translate the copy of MAC address in it as well. The ARP module at the destination uses the copy of the source MAC address stored in the received ARP PDU and not the one from the header of the MAC frame, which was translated by the bridge. Thus, the destination replies using the nontranslated version of the MAC address, which becomes translated upon reaching the bridge. Thus, the MAC frame containing the ARP reply never reaches the host that issued the ARP request.

The described problem cannot be resolved even by setting all of the necessary ARP entries manually (which would be too much hassle anyway). The manual ARP entries do not create necessary RIF cache entries in the source-route bridging entity running on the hosts. Thus, the hosts wouldn't even try to resort to source-route bridging, which is necessary for communication.

Listing 2.52 shows router R1's configuration for the network example depicted in Figure 2.33, which shows .

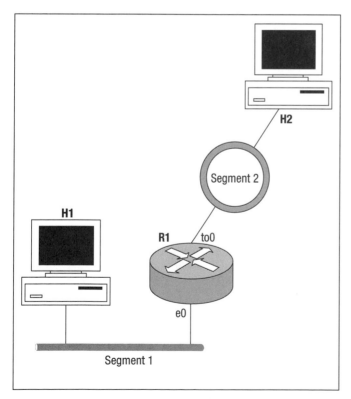

Figure 2.33 Router R1 performs (userless) translational bridging of IP traffic between the Ethernet segment and the token ring segment.

Listing 2.20 The output of the command show spanning-tree entered on router R1.

```
R1#show spanning-tree 1

Bridge Group 1 is executing the IEEE compatible Spanning Tree protocol
  Bridge Identifier has priority 32768, address 0010.1111.1111
  Configured hello time 2, max age 20, forward delay 15
  Current root has priority 32768, address 0000.0000.1000
  Root port is 7 (Ethernet1), cost of root path is 100
  Topology change flag not set, detected flag not set
  Times:  hold 1, topology change 30, notification 30
          hello 2, max age 20, forward delay 15, aging 300
  Timers: hello 0, topology change 0, notification 0

Port 6 (Ethernet0) of bridge group 1 is forwarding
  Port path cost 100, Port priority 128
  Designated root has priority 32768, address 0000.0000.1000
  Designated bridge has priority 32768, address 0010.1111.1111
  Designated port is 6, path cost 100
  Timers: message age 0, forward delay 0, hold 0

Port 7 (Ethernet1) of bridge group 1 is forwarding
  Port path cost 100, Port priority 128
  Designated root has priority 32768, address 0000.0000.1000
  Designated bridge has priority 32768, address 0000.0000.1000
  Designated port is 2, path cost 0
  Timers: message age 0, forward delay 0, hold 0

Port 8 (Ethernet2) of bridge group 1 is blocking
  Port path cost 100, Port priority 128
  Designated root has priority 32768, address 0000.0000.1000
  Designated bridge has priority 32768, address 0000.0000.2000
  Designated port is 2, path cost 100
  Timers: message age 2, forward delay 0, hold 0
```

Listing 2.21 The output of the command show spanning-tree entered on router R2.

```
R2#show spanning-tree 1

Bridge Group 1 is executing the IEEE compatible Spanning Tree protocol
  Bridge Identifier has priority 32768, address 0000.0000.1000
  Configured hello time 2, max age 20, forward delay 15
  We are the root of the spanning tree
  Topology change flag not set, detected flag not set
  Times:  hold 1, topology change 30, notification 30
          hello 2, max age 20, forward delay 15, aging 300
  Timers: hello 1, topology change 0, notification 0
```

Listing 2.52   Router R1's configuration.

```
no ip routing
source-bridge ring-group 1000
source-bridge transparent 1000 200 15 1
bridge 1 protocol ieee

interface Ethernet0
 bridge-group 1

interface TokenRing0
 ring-speed 16
 source-bridge 100 1 1000
```

WARNING!   *AST cannot be enabled on the virtual interfaces connecting a transparent bridge with a virtual ring.*

Chapter 3

Static Routing

If you need an immediate solution to:	See page:
Understanding the **ip routing** Command	181
Using Connected Interfaces to Perform Basic Routing	181
Understanding the Administrative Distance of Connected Routes	182
Configuring Basic Static Routing	183
Changing the Administrative Distances of Static Routes	186
Using an Output Interface Instead of a Next-Hop Router in Static Routes	191
Configuring Classless Routing	195
Understanding the Longest Match Concept	198
Configuring a Default Route	200
Configuring Individual Host Routes	202
Configuring Equal-Cost Load Balancing Using Static Routing	203
Configuring Unequal-Cost Load Balancing Using Static Routing	208

In Depth

Static routing is a method of populating routes into the routing table by an administrative action. In other words, routes are entered manually.

NOTE: *The word* manually *has a rather broad meaning in the context of networked devices. It typically means that something is done through the router command-line interface, but it can also pertain to actions performed through Simple Network Management Protocol (SNMP). For example, static routes can be configured on a router through an SNMP agent, such as HP OpenView.*

By default, static routes receive the administrative distance of 1, which can be changed to any value in the range from 1 through 255. Static routes with an administrative distance of 255 are never placed into the routing table.

As we know from Chapter 1, a route won't be inserted into the routing table if the route's output interface is physically or logically down. In the case of static routes, the output interface may not be entered explicitly. Typically, specifying the network prefix and the internet protocol (IP) address of the next-hop router en route to the network prefix creates a static route. The router itself then figures out what output interface it should use.

Immediate Solutions

Understanding the **ip routing** Command

Routing of IP traffic is enabled on Cisco routers by default. If necessary, however, IP routing can be turned off using the command **no ip routing** in global configuration mode. The command **ip routing**—again issued in global configuration mode—re-enables IP routing.

NOTE: *Because the **ip routing** command is a part of the default command set on Cisco routers, it does not appear in the router's configuration. On the contrary, the command **no ip routing** does appear in the router's configuration.*

Using Connected Interfaces to Perform Basic Routing

If a single router is used to perform routing among segments that are directly attached to it, no extra routing configuration is required. The router automatically places into the routing table the network prefixes of the IP addresses from all the active interfaces. *Active* in this context means that the corresponding interface is physically and logically up, which can be verified by using the command **show ip interfaces** *<interface ID> <interface #>*. A sample output of this command is shown below:

```
R1#show interfaces ethernet 0
Ethernet0 is up, line protocol is up
...
```

"Ethernet is up" means that the interface is physically up, and "line protocol is up" means that the interface is logically up. Suppose that the interface is assigned an IP address of 10.1.1.1. By using the **show ip route** command (the output of which is shown in Listing 3.1), we can verify that the IP address appears in the routing table.

Listing 3.1   The routing table of router R1.

```
R1#show ip route
...

10.0.0.0/24 is subnetted, 3 subnets
C       10.2.2.0 is directly connected, TokenRing0
C       10.1.1.0 is directly connected, Ethernet0
C       10.0.255.0 is directly connected, Serial1
```

In some cases, an interface can be physically up but logically down. If this happens, the network prefix associated with the interface is removed from the routing table. For example, if a router uses an Ethernet transceiver to connect to a hub, the corresponding Ethernet interface—for example, Ethernet0—is always physically up, as long as the transceiver is working properly. If the transceiver is disconnected from the hub, the interface on the router goes "logically down." An example of such a situation is shown below:

```
R1#show interfaces ethernet 0
Ethernet0 is up, line protocol is down
```

The output of the **show ip route** command shown below confirms that the network prefix is removed from the routing table:

```
R1#show ip route
...
10.0.0.0/24 is subnetted, 2 subnets
C       10.2.2.0 is directly connected, TokenRing0
C       10.0.255.0 is directly connected, Serial1
```

The hosts that are connected to segments interconnected with a single router must have routes pointing to the IP addresses assigned on the corresponding router interfaces. For example, all of the hosts on a segment can have a single default route pointing to the IP address of the router's interface attached to the segment.

Understanding the Administrative Distance of Connected Routes

Connected routes are created by a nameless source of routing information whose administrative distance is equal to 0. This is the "best" possible administrative distance, meaning that no other source of routing information is trusted more than connected routes. The administrative distance of connected routes cannot be changed.

Configuring Basic Static Routing

The source of routing information other than connected routes becomes necessary if a network has more than one router. One such source is static routing.

To configure static routing on a router, follow these steps:

1. Identify the network prefixes of the networks that are accessible through other routers.

2. Create a static route for each of the identified network prefixes using the command **ip route** *<remote network address> <subnet mask> <next-hop router>* in global configuration mode.

Although this seems a simple, two-step procedure, you may encounter a few pitfalls when configuring static routing. First, be sure to consider the traffic going to the destination as well as the traffic coming back. This factor is especially important when you are configuring a router that routes traffic among networks, none of which is directly attached to it. Let's consider the example depicted in Figure 3.1.

First, let's assume that routers R1 and R3 are configured correctly. Then, assume that host H1 on segment 1 must be able to communicate with host H2 on segment 2 and that, to make this happen, the network administrator of router R2 creates a static route as shown below:

```
R2(config)#ip route 10.0.2.0 255.255.255.0 10.0.255.3
```

This route works fine when a datagram from host H1 destined for host H2 arrives to router R2. Router R2 then performs a routing-table lookup that yields the IP address of router R3's interface Serial0, to which router R2 then forwards the datagram. Router R3 identifies the destination IP address as belonging to a directly connected network that is available through interface Ethernet0. Thus, Router R3 completes the delivery of the datagram to host H2. After the datagram is delivered to host H2, host H2 replies to host H1 with its own datagram, which it sends back to router R3.

If router R3 is configured correctly, it forwards the datagram to router R2. However, this time, router R2 does not know a route to the destination network (that is, segment 1). Therefore, router R2 drops the datagram. To correct the problem, another static route must be created on router R2, as shown below:

```
R2(config)#ip route 10.0.1.0 255.255.255.0 10.0.254.1
```

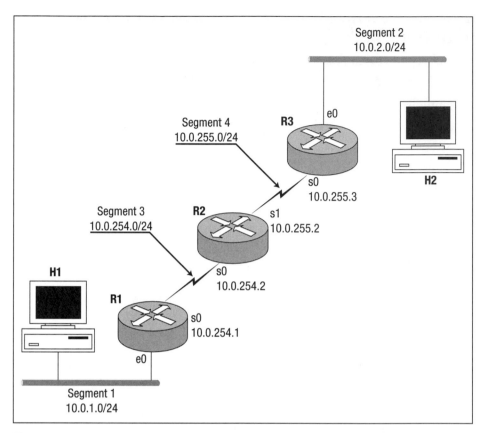

Figure 3.1   A router is used to route traffic between two remote networks.

Configurations that require static routing rarely involve only one router. Configuring static routing on a single router therefore creates only one-way connectivity. The datagram is delivered to the destination, but, when the destination replies, the router at the other end won't know the route to the original source. Therefore, the reply is dropped. For example, suppose that router R1 in Figure 3.2 has the following static routing entry:

```
ip route 10.0.2.0 255.255.255.0 10.0.254.2
```

However, router R2 does not have any static-routing entries configured. The communication initiated from host H1 to host H2 fails, because the reply sent by host H2 is dropped by router R2. Again, this can be easily corrected by entering a static route on router R2, as shown below:

```
R2(config)#ip route 10.0.1.0 255.255.255.0 10.0.254.1
```

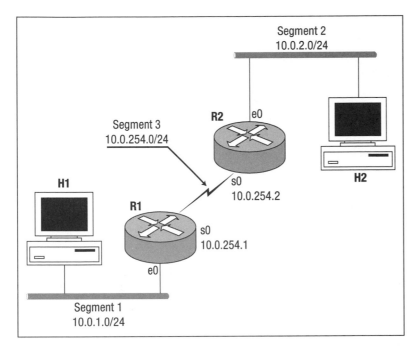

Figure 3.2   Only router R1 is configured with a static route for segment 2.

Interestingly enough, this simple problem can sometimes be difficult to diagnose. If, for example, the **ping** command is used on router R1 to verify the accessibility of host H2, host H2 may appear to be perfectly accessible. However, if the same **ping** command is used on host H2 to verify the accessibility of the Ethernet inter- face on router R1, it times out. At first, such symptoms may look like a one-way connectivity problem: Traffic goes from router R1 to host H2 normally, but not from host H2 back to router R1. Because this happens at router R1 and because host H2 cannot access anything behind router R1, it appears that router R1 is having some sort of a configuration problem. If we think carefully, however, these suspicions will turn out to be groundless. First, **ping** on router R1 shows that host H2 is accessible, which means that **ping** is receiving replies. Thus, we know that it's not a one-way connectivity problem. To send the ICMP echo messages generated by **ping**, the router uses the interface that is the closest to the destina- tion. In our case, this interface is Serial0, which is directly connected to segment 3. Router R2 is also directly connected to segment 3; thus, it has a (connected) route to segment 3. When host H2 replies, the replies are sent to the IP address that is configured on interface Serial0 of router R1, for which router R2 has the route. If host H2 sends **ping** packets destined for the IP address configured on interface Ethernet0 of router R1, the packets are dropped because router R2 does not have a route for this network.

Usually, this confusion occurs because an IP address is often associated with the whole router instead of a particular interface of that router. In the case of hosts, this usually isn't a problem, because hosts normally don't have multiple interfaces. On the contrary, routers rarely have a single interface.

Finally, another important consideration is the host configuration. Static routing won't work without an appropriate routing configuration on the hosts. All hosts that rely on routers must have routing entries pointing to the appropriate interfaces of the routers. Two administration errors that frequently go hand in hand are an incomplete host configuration and an incorrect static routing on the closest router. In other words, network administrators configuring static routing often do only half of the job: They configure only a single site, forgetting that this site needs to communicate with others.

Changing the Administrative Distances of Static Routes

Although the default administrative distance of static routes is equal to 1, it can be changed by specifying a new distance using the parameter *<distance>* in the command **ip route** *<remote network address>* *<subnet mask>* *<next-hop router>* *<distance>*. The parameter *<distance>* is numeric and can range from 1 through 255. If it is made equal to 255, the route is not inserted into the routing table; however, it will remain in the router's configuration.

As explained in Chapter 1, administrative distances of routes are used to resolve the conflict that results when a source of routing information tries to install a route for a network prefix for which another route already exists in the routing table. In these instances, the route with the smaller administrative-distance value will succeed, and the other route will be discarded.

NOTE: A router considers it a conflict only if the network prefixes of routes are the same, which includes the bits of network prefixes and their lengths. If the network prefixes have different lengths, they are considered to be different, even if their bits look the same. For example, network prefixes 10.1.0.0/16 and 10.1.0.0/24 have different lengths; thus, a separate route for each of these network prefixes can exist in the routing table of a router regardless of its administrative distance.

Let's consider a simple example to understand how administrative distances work. Suppose there is a router whose Ethernet0 interface is configured with IP address 10.1.0.1/24. If we try to enter static routes for network prefixes 10.1.0.0/16, 10.1.0.0/24, and 10.1.0.0/28, they will all be included in the router's configuration (as shown in Listing 3.2).

Listing 3.2   Router R1's configuration.

```
interface Ethernet0
 ip address 10.1.0.1 255.255.255.0

ip route 10.1.0.0 255.255.0.0 10.0.150.2
ip route 10.1.0.0 255.255.255.0 10.0.150.2
ip route 10.1.0.0 255.255.255.240 10.0.150.2
```

However, only the routes for network prefixes 10.1.0.0/16 and 10.1.0.0/28 are going to appear in the routing table. In Listing 3.3, which shows the routing table of router R1, the corresponding lines are shaded.

Listing 3.3   The routing table of router R1.

```
R1#show ip route
...

     10.0.0.0/8 is variably subnetted, 4 subnets, 4 masks
S        10.1.0.0/16 [1/0] via 10.0.150.2
S        10.1.0.0/28 [1/0] via 10.0.150.2
C        10.1.0.0/24 is directly connected, Ethernet0
```

Why does the static route for network prefix 10.1.0.0/24 not appear in the routing table? Because the administrative distance of the connected route (italicized line) corresponding to the interface Ethernet0 is 0, which is smaller than the default administrative distance of the static route (1). As the routes are for the same network prefix (10.1.0.0/24), only the one with the smaller administrative distance is included in the routing table.

Using administrative distances, you can create two static routes for the same network prefix so that only one of them is installed in the routing table. The question now is why anyone would bother creating static routes that are not installed into the routing table.

Interestingly enough, creating such routes does have some practical benefits. Suppose two routes for the same network prefix—but pointing to next-hop routers available through different interfaces—are configured on a router. The routes have different administrative distances, and so only the one with the smaller distance makes it to the routing table. Although the other route is not in the routing table, it remains in the router's configuration. Suppose that, at some point, there is a failure of the output interface through which the next-hop gateway of the installed route was available. As discussed in the "In Depth" section earlier in this chapter, all routes pointing to this output interface—including those that pointed to the next-hop routers available through this interface—are removed from the routing table. Thus, the route that was originally installed disappears. As soon as this happens, the other route (with the higher administrative distance) is installed instead. Thus, the network prefix becomes immediately available through another output interface and another next-hop router.

Duplicate static routes with higher administrative distances are sometimes called *floating routes*.

Floating static routes are often used when it's necessary to provide a backup for a certain connection. Figure 3.3 shows two routers connected using two serial links running in parallel between routers R1 and R2. The routers are configured as shown in Listings 3.4 and 3.5.

Listing 3.4   Router R1's configuration.

```
interface Ethernet0
 ip address 10.0.1.1 255.255.255.0

! Segment 3
interface Serial0
 ip address 10.0.254.1 255.255.255.0

! Segment 4
interface Serial1
 ip address 10.0.255.1 255.255.255.0

ip route 10.0.2.0 255.255.255.0 10.0.254.2
ip route 10.0.2.0 255.255.255.0 10.0.255.2 10
```

Listing 3.5   Router R2's configuration.

```
interface Ethernet0
 ip address 10.0.2.1 255.255.255.0

! Segment 4
interface Serial0
 ip address 10.0.255.2 255.255.255.0

! Segment 3
interface Serial1
 ip address 10.0.254.2 255.255.255.0

ip route 10.0.1.0 255.255.255.0 10.0.254.1
ip route 10.0.1.0 255.255.255.0 10.0.255.1 10
```

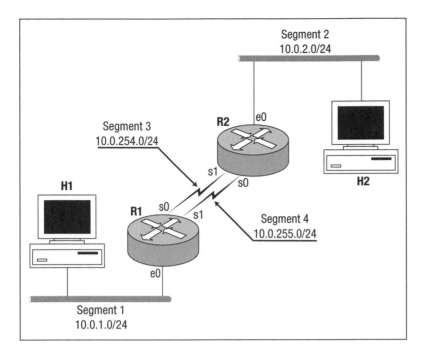

Figure 3.3 Segment 4 is used only when segment 3 fails.

If you examine the routing table on either router, you'll notice that the route with
the administrative distance of 10 was not added. (See Listings 3.6 and 3.7.)

Listing 3.6   The routing table of router R1.

```
R1#show ip route
...
     10.0.0.0/24 is subnetted, 4 subnets
S       10.0.2.0 [1/0] via 10.0.254.2
C       10.0.1.0 is directly connected, Ethernet0
C       10.0.254.0 is directly connected, Serial0
C       10.0.255.0 is directly connected, Serial1
```

Listing 3.7   The routing table of router R2.

```
R2#show ip route
...
     10.0.0.0/24 is subnetted, 4 subnets
C       10.0.2.0 is directly connected, Ethernet0
S       10.0.1.0 [1/0] via 10.0.254.1
C       10.0.254.0 is directly connected, Serial1
C       10.0.255.0 is directly connected, Serial0
```

As soon as segment 3 fails, the existing static route vanishes (along with the connected route that was associated with the corresponding serial interface), and the floating route kicks in instead. Listing 3.8 shows this process on both routers.

Listing 3.8   If segment 3 fails, the existing static route disappears from the routing table of both routers, and the floating route kicks in.

```
R1#
%LINEPROTO-5-UPDOWN: Line protocol on Interface Serial0, changed state to
down
%LINK-3-UPDOWN: Interface Serial0, changed state to down
R1#show ip route
...
     10.0.0.0/24 is subnetted, 3 subnets
S       10.0.2.0 [10/0] via 10.0.255.2
C       10.0.1.0 is directly connected, Ethernet0
C       10.0.255.0 is directly connected, Serial1

R2#
%LINEPROTO-5-UPDOWN: Line protocol on Interface Serial1, changed state to
down
%LINK-3-UPDOWN: Interface Serial1, changed state to down
R2#show ip route
...
     10.0.0.0/24 is subnetted, 3 subnets
C       10.0.2.0 is directly connected, Ethernet0
S       10.0.1.0 [10/0] via 10.0.255.1
C       10.0.255.0 is directly connected, Serial0
```

When segment 3 is restored, the original routes return and the floating routes disappear, as shown in Listing 3.9.

Listing 3.9   When segment 3 is restored, the floating route is superseded by the original route on both routers.

```
R1#
%LINK-3-UPDOWN: Interface Serial0, changed state to up
%LINEPROTO-5-UPDOWN: Line protocol on Interface Serial0, changed state to up
R1#show ip route
...
     10.0.0.0/24 is subnetted, 4 subnets
S       10.0.2.0 [1/0] via 10.0.254.2
C       10.0.1.0 is directly connected, Ethernet0
C       10.0.254.0 is directly connected, Serial0
C       10.0.255.0 is directly connected, Serial1
```

```
R2#
%LINK-3-UPDOWN: Interface Serial1, changed state to up
%LINEPROTO-5-UPDOWN: Line protocol on Interface Serial1, changed state to up
R2#show ip route
...
     10.0.0.0/24 is subnetted, 4 subnets
C       10.0.2.0 is directly connected, Ethernet0
S       10.0.1.0 [1/0] via 10.0.254.1
C       10.0.254.0 is directly connected, Serial1
C       10.0.255.0 is directly connected, Serial0
```

Using an Output Interface Instead of a Next-Hop Router in Static Routes

It is possible to configure a static route that doesn't point to the IP address of a next-hop router and points to an output interface instead. The command **ip route** *<remote network address> <subnet mask> <output interface>* creates a route of this type.

From a routing standpoint, the question of using an interface instead of a next-hop router may seem moot. How does the router using such a route know which next-hop router to choose?

The answer can be found rather easily, if we take a closer look at the connected routes in the routing table. These routes actually point to interfaces and *not* to the IP addresses of next-hop routers. In the case of connected routes, it's perfectly understandable because the router itself is the last step en route to these segments. No other router is needed. As discussed in Chapter 1, when the last-hop router needs to deliver a datagram to the final destination, it tries to resolve the destination's IP address to the corresponding link layer address, such as a Media Access Control (MAC) address in the case of Local Area Networks (LANs). If it succeeds, the router sends the datagram directly to the destination.

Static routes that point to interfaces actually behave as connected routes. The router assumes that these networks are directly connected and that all traffic destined for them terminates on the segment to which the router's corresponding interface is attached. Therefore, the router does not try to find a next-hop router and instead considers itself to be the last-hop router. Thus, the router tries to resolve the final destination's IP address to the appropriate link layer address using available methods, such as Addess Resolution Protocol (ARP) in the case of LANs.

3. Static Routing

For the purposes of our discussion, I will call static routes pointing to an interface *pseudo-connected*.

Although a pseudo-connected static route behaves very much like a regular connected route, there is a difference between the two: A connected route is derived from the IP address of the corresponding interface, whereas a pseudo-connected route is a static route and therefore no router's IP address is associated with it. Thus, the difference between the true connected routes and pseudo-connected routes is that the router always has an IP address from the network prefix of a true connected route and it does *not* have an IP address from the network prefix of a pseudo-connected route.

An example of a router configuration with a pseudo-connected route is shown below:

```
Interface Ethernet0
 ip address 10.1.0.1 255.255.255.0

ip route 172.16.0.0 255.255.0.0 Ethernet 0
```

This configuration produces two routes in the router's routing table: a connected route for network prefix 10.1.0.0/24 and a pseudo-connected route for network prefix 172.16.0.0/16. The router's Ethernet0 interface is assigned an IP address that belongs to the first network prefix. At the same time, the router doesn't have any IP address belonging to second network prefix configured on any of its interfaces.

NOTE: *The only case in which a router can have an IP address belonging to the network prefix of a pseudo-connected route is when this network prefix coincides with the network prefix of the output interface. However, this pseudo-connected route won't be installed in the routing table because of the connected route that is derived from the interface's IP address.*

Imagine now that this hypothetical router's Ethernet0 interface is attached to a segment on which some hosts' IP addresses belong to network prefix 172.16.0.0/16. The router can deliver datagrams destined for these hosts, but the hosts can't use the router to return their datagrams because the router does not have an IP address that the hosts can use as the next-hop router. The only way around this issue for the hosts is to resort to ProxyARP. Although the router doesn't have an IP address that can be used as the next-hop router, it can supply the MAC address of its Ethernet0 interface in its replies to ARP requests for the IP addresses it can reach.

Alternatively, instead of hosts relying on ProxyARP, there can be another router that can pick up the first router's ARP requests and reply with its own MAC address. This new router can serve as the ProxyARP server for the first router, and it can route the datagrams further towards the actual destination. From the perspective of the first router, however, the traffic still terminates on that segment.

For example, the two routers in Figure 3.4 are interconnected with a token ring segment. The routers are configured with pseudo-connected static routes for the networks located behind each other and pointing to their respective token ring interfaces.

Listings 3.10 and 3.11 show the configurations of both routers.

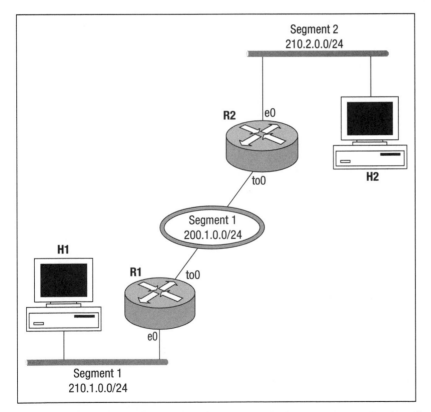

Figure 3.4   Two routers use static routes pointing to their token ring interfaces to forward the datagrams exchanged by hosts H1 and H2.

Listing 3.10   Router R1's configuration.

```
interface Ethernet0
  ip address 210.1.0.1 255.255.255.0

interface TokenRing0
  ip address 200.1.0.1 255.255.255.0
  ring-speed 16

ip route 210.2.0.0 255.255.255.0 TokenRing0
```

Listing 3.11   Router R2's configuration.

```
interface Ethernet0
  ip address 210.2.0.1 255.255.255.0

interface TokenRing0
  ip address 200.1.0.2 255.255.255.0
  ring-speed 16

ip route 210.1.0.0 255.255.255.0 TokenRing0
```

The routing tables of both routers are shown in Listings 3.12 and 3.13.

Listing 3.12   The routing table of router R1.

```
R1#show ip route
...
C    200.1.0.0 is directly connected, TokenRing0
S    210.2.0.0 is directly connected, TokenRing0
C    210.1.0.0 is directly connected, Ethernet0
```

Listing 3.13   The routing table of router R2.

```
R2#show ip route
...
C    200.1.0.0/24 is directly connected, TokenRing0
C    210.2.0.0/24 is directly connected, Ethernet0
S    210.1.0.0/24 is directly connected, TokenRing0
```

Notice how the real connected routes differ from the pseudo-connected static routes. The real connected routes are labeled with the letter C, which signifies *connected*, whereas the pseudo-connected routes are labeled with the letter S, which stands for *static*.

Suppose the **ping** command is used to verify if host H2 can be reached from host H1. If the **debug arp** command is issued on router R1, it produces the output shown in Listing 3.14, which demonstrates ProxyARP communication between the routers.

Listing 3.14   The output of the debug arp command entered on router R1.

```
R1#debug arp
ARP packet debugging is on
R1#
IP ARP: creating incomplete entry for IP address: 210.2.0.120
IP ARP: sent req src 200.1.0.1 0007.0d26.0a46,
                dst 210.2.0.120 0000.0000.0000 TokenRing0
IP ARP: rcvd rep src 210.2.0.120 0007.0d26.0c15,
 dst 200.1.0.1 TokenRing0
IP ARP: rcvd req src 200.1.0.2 0007.0d26.0c15,
 dst 210.1.0.50 TokenRing0
IP ARP: creating entry for IP address: 200.1.0.2,
 hw: 0007.0d26.0c15
IP ARP: sent rep src 210.1.0.50 0007.0d26.0a46,
                dst 200.1.0.2 0007.0d26.0c15 TokenRing0
```

First, router R1 uses ARP to resolve host H2's IP address to its MAC address. Router R2 replies with its token ring MAC address. The original **ping** packet that caused this exchange of ARP requests/replies is then delivered to host H2, and host H2 sends a reply. Router R2 now needs to know host H1's MAC address, so it issues an ARP request. It's now router R1's turn to reply with its own token ring MAC address.

Pseudo-connected static routes and secondary IP addresses are similar in that both tend to generate superfluous ARP broadcast traffic. In addition, pseudo-connected routes make the router's configuration more complex (and thus more susceptible to errors). Like secondary IP addresses, pseudo-connected routes should generally be considered as a temporary measure.

Configuring Classless Routing

The **ip classless** command (entered in global configuration mode) makes the router use the classless routing algorithm when making routing decisions. Depending on the version of IOS running on the router, this command may or may not be a part of the default router configuration.

> **NOTE:**   Typically, the **ip classless** command should be used in conjunction with the **ip subnet-zero** command. The latter command enables configuring the network prefixes, which from the perspective of classful routing appear as subnets whose subnet ID consists of all 0s. An example of such a network prefix is 10.0.0.0/ 16—without the **ip subnet-zero** command the command **ip address 10.0.0.1 255.255.0.0** produces an error if entered in interface configuration mode. In other words, if the **ip subnet-zero** command is not present in the router configuration, it is impossible to assign IP address whose "subnet ID" consists of all 0s on an interface.

If the **no ip classless** command appears in the router configuration, the router adheres to the classful routing algorithm.

> **NOTE:**   For more information on classful and classless routing algorithms, see Chapter 1.

Let's consider the example shown in Figure 3.5. Listings 3.15 and 3.16 show the configurations of routers R1 and R2.

Router R1 does not have a route for network prefix 150.1.2.0/24. Instead, it is configured with a static route for network prefix 150.0.0.0/8. However, the network prefixes of segments 1 and 2 belong to the same classful network address, 150.1.0.0/ 16. At the same time, router R1's interface, Ethernet0, is attached to segment 1;

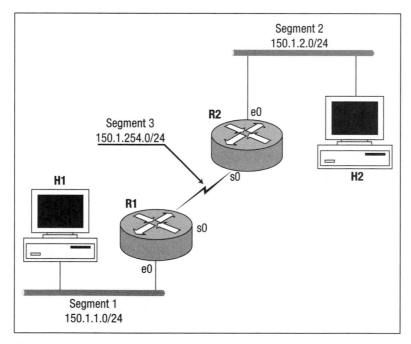

Figure 3.5   Router R1 is configured with a route for network prefix 150.0.0.0/8 pointing "towards" segment 2 behind router R2.

thus, router R1 considers itself connected to classful network address 150.1.0.0/16. Therefore, unless router R1 is configured with the classless routing algorithm, it cannot use the static route to forward datagrams towards segment 2.

Listing 3.15   Router R1's configuration.

```
interface Ethernet0
 ip address 150.1.1.1 255.255.255.0

interface Serial0
 ip address 150.1.254.1 255.255.255.0

ip route 150.0.0.0 255.0.0.0 150.1.254.2
```

Listing 3.16   Router R2's configuration.

```
interface Ethernet0
 ip address 150.1.2.1 255.255.255.0

interface Serial1
 ip address 150.1.254.2 255.255.255.0

ip route 150.1.1.0 255.255.255.0 150.1.254.1
```

At this point, router R1 does not have the **ip classless** command in its configuration. If the **ping** command is used to verify whether host H2 can be reached from host H1, it fails, as shown in Listing 3.17.

Listing 3.17   Ping issued on host H1 to verify if host H2 can be reached fails because the classful routing algorithm prevents router R1 from using the route for network prefix 150.0.0.0/8.

```
C:\>ping 150.1.2.120

Pinging 150.1.2.120 with 32 bytes of data:

Reply from 150.1.1.1: Destination host unreachable.
Reply from 150.1.1.1: Destination host unreachable.
Reply from 150.1.1.1: Destination host unreachable.
```

After the **ip classless** command is entered on router R1, the output of the **ping** command changes, as shown in Listing 3.18. The output indicates that host H2 is now reachable from host H1.

**Listing 3.18   After the routing algorithm on router R1 is changed from classful to class=
less, the ping from host H1 to host H2 goes through.**

```
C:\>ping 150.1.2.120

Pinging 150.1.2.120 with 32 bytes of data:

Reply from 150.1.2.120: bytes=32 time=40ms TTL=126
Reply from 150.1.2.120: bytes=32 time=30ms TTL=126
Reply from 150.1.2.120: bytes=32 time=30ms TTL=126
```

NOTE: *Despite the description of the **ip classless** command that you find in the Cisco documentation (which states that this command is always disabled by default), some later versions of the Cisco IOS have this command enabled by default.*

Understanding the Longest Match Concept

Both classless and classful routing algorithms are based on the concept of the longest match. In this section, I'll show you an example that demonstrates this concept.

Figure 3.6 shows the scheme of a rather weird network: Segment 4's network prefix is 10.1.0.0/24, whereas segment 2's is 10.1.0.0/16, a superset of the first. Furthermore, host H2's IP address coincides with the IP addresses assigned on router R1's interface Ethernet0.

The routers are configured as shown in Listing 3.19 and 3.20.

Listing 3.19   Router R1's configuration.

```
interface Ethernet0
 ip address 10.1.0.111 255.255.0.0

interface Serial0
 ip address 192.168.1.1 255.255.255.0

interface TokenRing0
 ip address 10.6.0.1 255.255.0.0
 ring-speed 16

ip classless
ip route 10.1.0.0 255.255.255.0 192.168.1.2
```

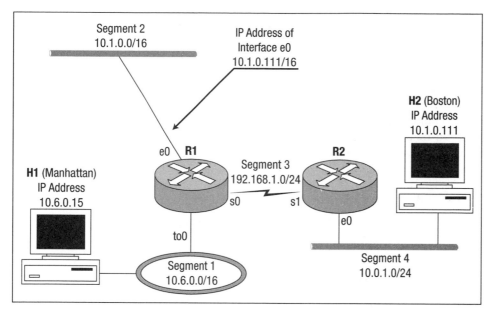

Figure 3.6 Router R1 is configured with a static route for network prefix 10.1.0.0/24. Although the IP address of its interface, Ethernet0, is 10.1.0.111/16, the traffic for this address is routed to host H2 because the static route provides a longer match.

Listing 3.20 Router R2's configuration.

```
interface Ethernet0
 ip address 10.1.0.1 255.255.255.0

interface Serial1
 ip address 192.168.1.2 255.255.255.0

ip classless
ip route 10.6.0.0 255.255.0.0 192.168.1.1
```

Disregarding the question about the actual viability of this network, let's see what happens if host H1 tries to communicate with IP address 10.1.0.111. (See Listing 3.21.)

Listing 3.21 The **telnet 10.1.0.111** command issued on host H1 clearly demonstrates that a connection is established with host H2 (Boston), not router R1.

```
C:\>telnet 10.1.0.111

Welcome to BOSTON!
```

```
IP address: 10.1.0.111/24

User Access Verification

Password:
```

Surprisingly, router R1 passes the connection further towards host H2 (Boston) instead of terminating it, ignoring the fact that its own interface, Ethernet0, is assigned the destination IP address of 10.1.0.111. The reason why can be easily determined by examining router R1's routing table, shown in Listing 3.22.

Listing 3.22   Router R1's routing table.

```
R1#show ip route
...
     10.0.0.0/8 is variably subnetted, 3 subnets, 2 masks
S        10.1.0.0/24 [1/0] via 192.168.1.2
C        10.1.0.0/16 is directly connected, Ethernet0
C        10.6.0.0/16 is directly connected, TokenRing0
C    192.168.1.0/24 is directly connected, Serial0
```

Notice that the lower administrative distance of the connected route created as the result of assigning interface Ethernet0 the IP address of 10.1.0.1/16 is no obstacle for the static route for network prefix 10.1.0.0/24. The latter is longer than the network prefix of the connected route; hence, both routes are included in the routing table. After that, the only criterion for resolving ambiguities is the length of the network prefixes of the routes in conflict. As the static route's network prefix has a more favorable (i.e., longer) length than that of the connected route, router R1 must use the static route for all destination IP addresses that its network prefix matches—as in the case with IP address 10.1.0.111.

Configuring a Default Route

A default route is a route for network prefix 0.0.0.0/0. In other words, this is a route that should be used if the network prefix of no other route matches the destination IP address.

A default route is configured using the command **ip route 0.0.0.0 0.0.0.0** *<next-hop router>* in global configuration mode.

It makes sense to accompany a default route with the **ip classless** command. According to the classful routing algorithm, a default route cannot be used to forward a datagram if:

- The datagram is destined for an IP address for which the router does not have a route
- One of the router's interfaces is assigned an IP address that belongs to the same classful network address to which the destination IP address belongs

An example of this situation is shown in Figure 3.7. The configuration of router R1 is shown in Listing 3.23. Router R1 connects a single stub network to the corporate network. All segments in the corporate network, including segment 1, are addressed within network prefix 10.0.0.0/8.

Router R1 is configured with a single default route that points to its counterpart router behind interface Serial0.

Listing 3.23   Router R1's configuration.

```
interface Ethernet0
 ip address 10.1.0.1 255.255.255.0

interface Serial0
 ip address 10.0.150.1 255.255.255.252

no ip classless

ip route 0.0.0.0 0.0.0.0 10.0.150.2
```

Right now, router R1 adheres to the classful routing algorithm, as indicated by the presence of the **no ip classless** command. Thus, router R1 is useless, as hosts on segment 1 cannot use it to reach any IP address within the corporate network. The **debug ip packet** command followed by the **ping 10.3.0.1** command produces the output shown in Listing 3.24, which confirms this fact.

Listing 3.24   The output of the **debug ip packet** command indicates that router R1 cannot route datagrams to destinations within the corporate network.

```
R1#debug ip packet
IP packet debugging is on
R1#ping 10.3.0.1

Type escape sequence to abort.
Sending 5, 100-byte ICMP Echos to 10.3.0.1, timeout is 2 seconds:

IP: s=10.1.0.1 (local), d=10.3.0.1, len 100, unroutable.
IP: s=10.1.0.1 (local), d=10.3.0.1, len 100, unroutable.
IP: s=10.1.0.1 (local), d=10.3.0.1, len 100, unroutable.
```

The problem is easily corrected by issuing the **ip classless** command on router R1 in global configuration mode.

3. Static Routing

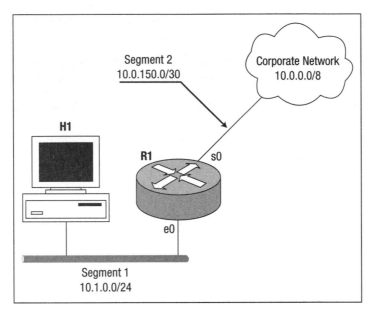

Figure 3.7   If router R1 is configured with only a default route pointing to its counterpart router on the other end of the serial connection, it can't use it for routing to destinations in the corporate network unless the **ip classless** command is present in its configuration.

Configuring Individual Host Routes

Using the command **ip route** *<IP address>* **255.255.255.255** *<next-hop router>*, you can configure an individual host route.

NOTE: Although "host route" suggests that the route is for a host, the IP address appearing in the command does not have to be an IP address of a host per se. For example, it can be the IP address of another router.

The router configured in Listing 3.25 has an individual host route for 200.2.0.120.

Listing 3.25   Router R1's configuration.

```
interface Serial0
 ip address 195.0.0.1 255.255.255.0

interface Serial1
 ip address 195.1.0.1 255.255.255.0

ip route 200.2.0.0 255.255.255.0 195.0.0.2
ip route 200.2.0.120 255.255.255.255 195.1.0.2
```

Notice in the routing table in Listing 3.26 that the router uses two different interfaces for routing traffic to a host whose address is 200.2.0.120 and to the other
hosts with IP addresses belonging to network prefix 200.2.0.0/24.

NOTE: *From the routing perspective, a host route is merely a regular route for a network prefix with the
maximum length (32). Thus, when in conflict, a host route always takes precedence over any other route
(regardless of what algorithm the router uses).*

Listing 3.26   The routing table of router R1.

```
R1#show ip route
...
C    195.1.0.0/24 is directly connected, Serial1
C    195.0.0.0/24 is directly connected, Serial0
C    200.1.0.0/24 is directly connected, TokenRing0
     200.2.0.0/24 is variably subnetted, 2 subnets, 2 masks
S       200.2.0.120/32 [1/0] via 195.1.0.2
S       200.2.0.0/24 [1/0] via 195.0.0.2
```

Individual host routes are often used either for debugging purposes or in case of
emergencies to provide access to critical network resources when the main route
to the network is no longer available.

Configuring Equal-Cost Load Balancing Using Static Routing

A router performs load balancing if it has up to six static routes going to the same
destination. (The number of routes over which a router can perform load balancing may change in future releases of the Cisco IOS.) The router assumes that all
routes have the same characteristics, such as bandwidth and delay, regardless of
what the actual characteristics are. Therefore, the router distributes the outgoing
traffic among multiple routes equally.

NOTE: *Notice that load balancing is performed over only the outgoing traffic. The router has no control over the
incoming traffic, which, regardless of the router's routing table, can always arrive on a single interface.*

Load balancing is enabled by default, and the default number of routes across
which a router can perform load balancing is four. This can be changed by using
the command **maximum-paths** *<# of routes>* in global configuration mode. The

parameter <# *of routes*> is numeric and can take values from 1 through 6. If it's made equal to 1, load balancing is turned off. In this case, the router will use the first route among the routes returned by the routing algorithm.

Let's consider the example of a network shown in Figure 3.8. Listings 3.27 and 3.28 show the configurations of the two routers. Routers R1 and R2 are interconnected with two parallel serial links.

Listing 3.27   Router R1's configuration.

```
interface Serial0
 ip address 195.0.0.1 255.255.255.0

interface Serial1
 ip address 195.1.0.1 255.255.255.0

interface TokenRing0
 ip address 200.1.0.1 255.255.255.0
 ring-speed 16

ip route 200.2.0.0 255.255.255.0 195.0.0.2
ip route 200.2.0.0 255.255.255.0 195.1.0.2
```

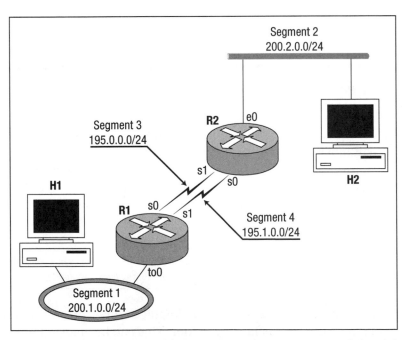

Figure 3.8   Two routers perform load balancing over two parallel serial connections.

Listing 3.28   Router R2's configuration.

```
interface Ethernet0
 ip address 200.2.0.1 255.255.255.0

interface Serial0
 ip address 195.1.0.2 255.255.255.0

interface Serial1
 ip address 195.0.0.2 255.255.255.0

ip route 200.1.0.0 255.255.255.0 195.0.0.1
ip route 200.1.0.0 255.255.255.0 195.1.0.1
```

Listings 3.29 and 3.30 show the routing tables of the routers.

Listing 3.29   The routing table of router R1.

```
R1#show ip route
...
C    195.1.0.0 is directly connected, Serial1
C    195.0.0.0 is directly connected, Serial0
C    200.1.0.0 is directly connected, TokenRing0
S    200.2.0.0 [1/0] via 195.0.0.2
               [1/0] via 195.1.0.2
```

Listing 3.30   The routing table of router R2.

```
R2#show ip route
...
C    195.1.0.0/24 is directly connected, Serial0
C    195.0.0.0/24 is directly connected, Serial1
S    200.1.0.0/24 [1/0] via 195.0.0.1
                  [1/0] via 195.1.0.1
C    200.2.0.0/24 is directly connected, Ethernet0
```

Notice how the routers display the presence of two or more routes for the same network prefix. They do not copy the network prefix for each route; instead, they leave blank all of the spaces normally occupied by the network prefix except for the first line.

Cisco routers can perform load balancing in two modes: per destination and per packet. The router performs per-destination load balancing if it is configured for fast switching of IP traffic. *Fast switching* means that the router maintains a cache of the destination addresses so that it does not perform a routing table lookup each time a datagram destined for the same address arrives on an interface. As long as an IP address remains in the cache, the router always uses the same output interface when forwarding datagrams to that address. You can specifically enable fast switching using the **ip route-cache** command. Normally, fast switching is enabled by default, and this command typically does not appear in the router configuration.

> **NOTE:** High-end Cisco routers, such as Route Switch Modules (RSM) in the Catalyst switches or Cisco series 7500 routers (especially those with VIP modules), have more fast-switching modes. For more information on these modes, refer to the Cisco documentation.

Per-packet load balancing is performed when fast switching is disabled. The router distributes the datagrams going to the same destination in a round-robin fashion among all the output interfaces that point to that destination. You can disable fast switching using the **no ip route-cache** command. Usually, this is not recommended because Cisco routers typically perform better with fast switching enabled, unless the traffic is too "bursty" or if it is sent across overflowed serial connections.

Temporarily disabling fast switching may be useful for one practical purpose, and that's examining IP traffic flow using the **debug ip packet** command. If fast switching is disabled, the **debug ip packet** command displays how the datagrams are actually forwarded. If fast switching is enabled, this command produces output only if the datagrams either originate from or are destined for the router itself.

By using **debug ip packet**, you can actually see how the load balancing is performed. For example, if host H1 in Figure 3.8 has an IP address of 200.1.0.15—and host H2 has an IP address of 200.2.0.120—the routers produce the output shown in Listings 3.31 and 3.32 when host H1 pings host H2. The alternating shaded and regular parts of the output demonstrate the equality of the performed load balancing.

Listing 3.31   The output of the debug ip packet command entered on router R1.

```
IP: s=200.1.0.15 (TokenRing0), d=200.2.0.120 (Serial0),
 g=195.0.0.2, len 82, forward
IP: s=200.2.0.120 (Serial0), d=200.1.0.15 (TokenRing0),
 g=200.1.0.15, len 64, forward
IP: s=200.1.0.15 (TokenRing0), d=200.2.0.120 (Serial1),
 g=195.1.0.2, len 82, forward
IP: s=200.2.0.120 (Serial1), d=200.1.0.15 (TokenRing0),
 g=200.1.0.15, len 64, forward
IP: s=200.1.0.15 (TokenRing0), d=200.2.0.120 (Serial0),
 g=195.0.0.2, len 82, forward
IP: s=200.2.0.120 (Serial0), d=200.1.0.15 (TokenRing0),
```

```
 g=200.1.0.15, len 64, forward
IP: s=200.1.0.15 (TokenRing0), d=200.2.0.120 (Serial1),
 g=195.1.0.2, len 82, forward
IP: s=200.2.0.120 (Serial1), d=200.1.0.15 (TokenRing0),
 g=200.1.0.15, len 64, forward
```

Listing 3.32   The output of the debug ip packet command entered on router R2.

```
IP: s=200.1.0.15 (Serial1), d=200.2.0.120 (Ethernet0),
 g=200.2.0.120, len 60, forward
IP: s=200.2.0.120 (Ethernet0), d=200.1.0.15 (Serial1),
 g=195.0.0.1, len 60, forward
IP: s=200.1.0.15 (Serial0), d=200.2.0.120 (Ethernet0),
 g=200.2.0.120, len 60, forward
IP: s=200.2.0.120 (Ethernet0), d=200.1.0.15 (Serial0),
 g=195.1.0.1, len 60, forward
IP: s=200.1.0.15 (Serial1), d=200.2.0.120 (Ethernet0),
 g=200.2.0.120, len 60, forward
IP: s=200.2.0.120 (Ethernet0), d=200.1.0.15 (Serial1),
 g=195.0.0.1, len 60, forward
IP: s=200.1.0.15 (Serial0), d=200.2.0.120 (Ethernet0),
 g=200.2.0.120, len 60, forward
IP: s=200.2.0.120 (Ethernet0), d=200.1.0.15 (Serial0),
 g=195.1.0.1, len 60, forward
```

Notice how the routers alternate the serial interfaces when forwarding the datagrams.

Load balancing does not necessarily require parallel links between two routers, and it is possible to configure static routes pointing to different next-hop routers (so that load balancing is performed). However, such configurations are quite complex and therefore susceptible to errors. As the number of static routes on involved routers grow, it becomes increasingly more difficult to achieve meaningful load balancing and to keep the router's configurations free of errors.

Usually, load balancing is automatically achieved using dynamic routing protocols, which can populate all necessary routes to the routing table to produce optimal performance. Load balancing using static routing is, therefore, usually limited to either parallel links or to very symmetrical configurations such as the one shown in Figure 3.9. It's easy to configure static routes on routers R1 and R4 so that the traffic going between segments 1 and 2 is split equally between two paths going through routers R2 and R3.

3. Static Routing

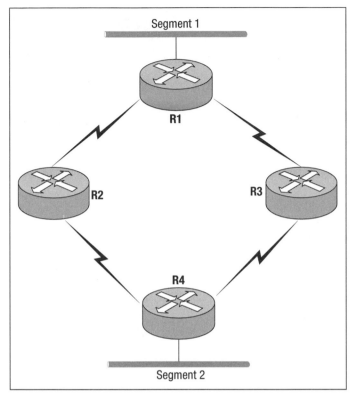

Figure 3.9   Four-router configuration, enables load balancing of the traffic between segments 1 and 2.

Configuring Unequal-Cost Load Balancing Using Static Routing

Although it may be difficult to believe, unequal-cost load balancing can be performed using static routing. Before we proceed to the solution itself, however, I would like to explain how I found out about it (see the Changing Paradigms sidebar).

Changing Paradigms

A while ago, I was a frequent visitor of a newsgroup titled **comp.dcom.sys.cisco**. Like many others, I sometimes asked questions and sometimes answered those of other participants.

Once, somebody asked if it was possible to perform unequal-cost load balancing using only static routes. Of course, according the Cisco router manuals, it was not. So that was my answer, as well as a few other participants'. On the next day, the person who posted the question said that he actually was able to do this impossible thing. When I saw the post, I was really intrigued. This seemed so unreal. But the person was right: He did achieve that.

The person's name was Steve Kann, and I have the pleasure to present his neat solution in my book. I also think that this incident teaches a valuable lesson: It's sometimes important to go beyond the existing paradigms and examine opportunities that may at first look impossible.

Thank you, Steve!

This solution is based on the very simple fact that the router actually splits the traffic among the routes for the same destination, not among the interfaces. For example, if a router has three routes for a certain destination pointing to one interface and two routes for the same destination pointing to another interface, the router sends three-fifths of the traffic over the first interface and two-fifths over the other. Obviously, this type of unequal-cost load balancing is limited in terms of a variety of ratios, because the router can split the traffic among not more than six routers. Table 3.1 shows several ratios that can be used when the bandwidth of the connections falls into the shown ratios.

Probably the easiest way to implement multiple static routes for the same destination through the same interface is to use secondary addresses on the counterpart router's interface and then point the static routes to these and the primary IP addresses.

As an example, let's consider the network shown in Figure 3.10.

Figure 3.10 shows that the serial connections between routers R1 and R2 have bandwidths equal to 768Kbps and 512Kbps. These two numbers relate to each other as 3/5 and 2/5. According to Table 3.1, the necessary traffic split ratio can be achieved using three routes pointing to the interfaces connected to the first link and two routes pointing to the interfaces connected to the second link.

Table 3.1   Traffic split ratios are achievable through varying the number of routes pointing to two different interfaces.

Load Split Ratios	Number Of Routes Pointing To Interface 1	Number Of Routes Pointing To Interface 2
1/3 and 2/3	1	2
1/4 and 3/4	1	3
1/5 and 4/5	1	4
1/6 and 5/6	1	5
2/5 and 3/5	2	3

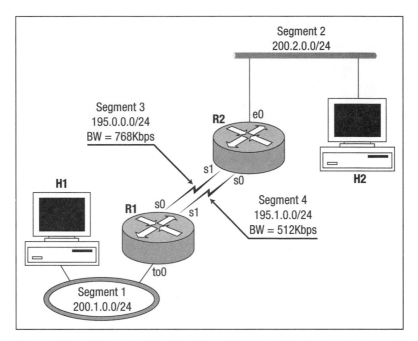

Figure 3.10 The actual bandwidths of the two links between router R1 and R2 are 768Kbps and 512Kbps.

Listings 3.33 and 3.34 show two sample configurations that, when entered on routers R1 and R2, will perform load splitting with the specified ratio.

Listing 3.33 Router R1's configuration.

```
interface Serial0
 ip address 195.0.0.1 255.255.255.0
 ip address 195.0.0.2 255.255.255.0 secondary
 ip address 195.0.0.3 255.255.255.0 secondary

interface Serial1
 ip address 195.1.0.1 255.255.255.0
 ip address 195.1.0.2 255.255.255.0 secondary

interface TokenRing0
 ip address 200.1.0.1 255.255.255.0
 ring-speed 16

ip route 200.2.0.0 255.255.255.0 195.0.0.4
ip route 200.2.0.0 255.255.255.0 195.0.0.5
ip route 200.2.0.0 255.255.255.0 195.0.0.6
ip route 200.2.0.0 255.255.255.0 195.1.0.3
ip route 200.2.0.0 255.255.255.0 195.1.0.4
```

Listing 3.34 Router R2's configuration.

```
interface Ethernet0
 ip address 200.2.0.1 255.255.255.0

interface Serial0
 ip address 195.1.0.3 255.255.255.0
 ip address 195.1.0.4 255.255.255.0 secondary

interface Serial1
 ip address 195.0.0.4 255.255.255.0
 ip address 195.0.0.5 255.255.255.0 secondary
 ip address 195.0.0.6 255.255.255.0 secondary

ip route 200.1.0.0 255.255.255.0 195.0.0.1
ip route 200.1.0.0 255.255.255.0 195.0.0.2
ip route 200.1.0.0 255.255.255.0 195.0.0.3
ip route 200.1.0.0 255.255.255.0 195.1.0.1
ip route 200.1.0.0 255.255.255.0 195.1.0.2
```

If fast switching is turned off, the **debug ip packet** command can be used to observe in what proportion the traffic is split between output interfaces Serial0 and Serial1. Listing 3.35 shows the output of the **debug ip packet** command entered on router R1. Notice how the router alternates the output interfaces. (The lines referencing interface Serial1 are shaded.)

Listing 3.35 The output of the **debug ip packet** command entered on router R1.

```
IP: s=200.2.0.120 (Serial0), d=200.1.0.15 (TokenRing0), ...
IP: s=200.2.0.120 (Serial0), d=200.1.0.15 (TokenRing0), ...
IP: s=200.2.0.120 (Serial0), d=200.1.0.15 (TokenRing0), ...
IP: s=200.2.0.120 (Serial1), d=200.1.0.15 (TokenRing0), ...
IP: s=200.2.0.120 (Serial1), d=200.1.0.15 (TokenRing0), ...
IP: s=200.2.0.120 (Serial0), d=200.1.0.15 (TokenRing0), ...
IP: s=200.2.0.120 (Serial0), d=200.1.0.15 (TokenRing0), ...
IP: s=200.2.0.120 (Serial0), d=200.1.0.15 (TokenRing0), ...
IP: s=200.2.0.120 (Serial1), d=200.1.0.15 (TokenRing0), ...
IP: s=200.2.0.120 (Serial1), d=200.1.0.15 (TokenRing0), ...
```

3. Static Routing

Chapter 4

Routing Information Protocol (RIP)

If you need an immediate solution to:	See page:
Understanding the Output of the **show ip route** Command	238
Modifying the Network Prefix Format	240
Understanding Candidate Default Routes and Gateways of Last Resort	242
Performing Basic RIP Configuration	249
Understanding How RIP Processes Routing Updates	252
Understanding the Relation between the Routing Table Contents and RIP Routing Updates	257
Understanding RIP Auto-Summarization	259
Using Individual Host Addresses	261
Configuring RIP to Originate a Default Route	264
Understanding How RIP Handles Secondary IP Addresses	265
Understanding How RIP Handles IP Unnumbered	272
Making RIP Passive on an Interface	280
Using Unicast Routing Updates with RIP	282
Changing the Administrative Distance of RIP Routing Updates	287
Performing Equal-Cost Load Balancing with RIP	294
Changing RIP Metrics	297
Adjusting RIP Timers	299
Using RIP in the Presence of NBMA Networks	300
Configuring RIP Version 2	303
Disabling RIP Version 2 Auto-Summarization	305
Understanding How RIP Versions 1 and 2 Can Be Used Together	312

In Depth

This chapter is devoted to the popular dynamic routing protocol, routing information protocol (RIP). RIP, an open protocol, is available in two versions—1 and 2. RIP version 1 is a classful routing protocol, and its classful nature pretty much ties it to classful Internet Protocol (IP) addressing. Therefore, this chapter will be full of classful terminology, such as *subnets*, *subnet masks*, *classful network addresses*, and so on. It's quite difficult to avoid this terminology, and replacing it with purely classless terminology—such as *network prefix* and *network prefix length*—would often complicate the explanations of certain subjects. Therefore, where it's more appropriate, I will use the classful terminology throughout this chapter.

RIP version 2 is a classless routing protocol, so when explaining it, I will try to adhere to the classless terminology as much as possible. Nevertheless, Cisco's implementation of RIP version 2 still inherits some classful features of RIP version 2, which again requires the classful terminology.

Distance-Vector Algorithm

RIP is based on a distance-vector algorithm that was first described by Ford and Fulkerson in their Flows in Networks (Princeton University Press, 1962). Their work was based on Bellman's equation from his book Dynamic Programming (Princeton University Press, 1957). Thus, the distance-vector algorithm is also called the Ford-Fulkerson algorithm or the Bellman-Ford algorithm.

An in-depth discussion of the pure distance vector algorithm lies beyond the scope of this book; instead we will look at a more network-specific version that is used in the dynamic routing protocols.

The task that the distance-vector algorithm solves is finding the shortest paths among the vertices of a graph. A graph is a mathematical abstraction in which vertices (or nodes) are interconnected by edges. Each edge has a cost of "using" it. A path between two vertices is a set of the intermediate edges and vertices interconnecting the two vertices. (This is an "intuitive" and somewhat ambiguous definition of the path. This definition, however, is sufficient for the purposes of our discussion. A precise definition would require introducing auxiliary terms and definitions, which would be irrelevant to this book.) The cost of a path is defined as the sum of the costs of the edges constituting it. The shortest path between two vertices is therefore the path with the smallest cost.

The distance-vector algorithm can be defined as the following set of rules:

- At the beginning of the algorithm operation each vertex only "knows" the paths to the *adjacent* vertices, that is, the vertices to which it is connected with the edges.

- During the algorithm operation the adjacent vertices "advertise" to each other the vertices that they can reach. Each advertisement consists of the destination vertex and the cost of the shortest path as known by the advertising vertex.

- Initially each vertex advertises only the adjacent vertices with the shortest path costs equal to the costs of the edges.

- Upon receipt of an advertisement, the vertex calculates the cost of the path to the advertised vertex through the advertising vertex as the sum of the cost of the edge leading to the advertising vertex and the path cost contained in the advertisement. After that the vertex checks if it already knows a path to the advertised destination vertex. If it doesn't or if the cost of the known path is greater than the calculated cost of the new path, the vertex memorizes the new path as the triplet of the destination vertex, its calculated path cost and the next-hop vertex, where the latter is equal to the advertising vertex. If the new path replaces an existing path, the existing path is discarded. If, however, the cost of the existing path is smaller or equal to the cost of the new path, the new path is discarded.

- After memorizing a new path, the vertex must advertise to the adjacent vertices the path's destination vertex and the path cost.

The described algorithm is mathematically proven to calculate the shortest paths between all pairs of the vertices in a finite time.

Notice that neither upon completion nor during the operation of the algorithm any vertex possesses the topological knowledge of any path. Each of the discovered paths is represented by only the destination vertex, the path cost and the next-hop vertex en route to the destination vertex; the path representation does not contain the intermediate vertices and edges. This is why the algorithm is called distance-vector—the path cost is the "distance" and the destination and next-hop vertices represent the direction, or the "vector".

After the algorithm finishes, its results can be used to "travel" between any two vertices of the graph. At the starting vertex, the "traveler" should look up the path to the destination vertex and move to the next-hop vertex specified in the path. At the next-hop vertex, the traveler should again look up the path to the destination vertex and move to the next-hop vertex specified in it. The traveler should continue this process until he or she reaches the destination vertex.

The described process is essentially routing. The paths contained at each vertex constitute the vertex's the routing table. Hence, the task that the distance-vector algorithm solves is populating the routing table with paths, or routes; as we know, that same task is solved by the dynamic routing protocols.

The dynamic routing protocols that are based on the described distance-vector algorithm are themselves most frequently referred to as the *distance-vector protocols*. Distance-vector protocols are probably the most widespread group of dynamic routing protocols—besides IP, most other network architectures, such as IPX, AppleTalk and DECNET, have associated distance-vector routing protocols.

The presented algorithm only lays a framework for the distance-vector protocols; the algorithm must be modified and possibly expanded to fit the requirements of the specific technology. The next several subsections describe the algorithm's modifications and most important aspects of its implementation, all tailored to the IP routing requirements. The last subsections of the In Depth section describe the implementation of the two versions of the popular distance-vector routing protocol called RIP.

IP Specific Distance-Vector Algorithm

In the IP specific version of the distance-vector algorithm the vertices represent the routers and the edges represent the interconnections between the routers. I specifically avoided the term "segments" because segments can interconnect more than two routers, whereas edges interconnect exactly two vertices. The interconnections, in this context, indicate the ability of two routers to perform mutual communication; hence the interconnections can be unequivocally represented by the edges.

As most real networks contain segments interconnecting more than two routers, we need to establish a relation between edges (or interconnections) and segments. From the IP routing point of view, there are three types of segments—point-to-point, broadcast and NBMA. As we might expect, each of these segment types requires a separate representation in the form of graph edges. These representations are described below:

- A point-to-point segment between two routers is an equivalent of a single edge between the two vertices representing the routers.

- A broadcast segment with multiple routers is an equivalent of a full mesh of edges among the vertices representing the routers.

- An NBMA segment interconnecting multiple routers is an equivalent of multiple edges interconnecting only those vertices that correspond to the routers, which can communicate with each other directly through the NBMA segment.

The goal of the IP specific version of the distance-vector algorithm is somewhat different from that of the generic version. The goal of the IP specific version is to discover the paths to the network prefixes (as opposed to the vertices in the generic version). Consequently the contents of the advertisements the routers exchange among each other is different too—instead of the vertices, the advertisements carry the network prefixes the advertising routers can reach. The path cost, which is now called the *metric*, is present unchanged in the advertisements and serves the same purpose—to compare paths for the same destination. (The smaller metric denotes the shorter path.) The exact calculation and representation of the metric, however, is left to the discretion of a particular routing protocol.

The routing protocol PDUs carrying network prefix advertisements of are called *routing updates*. The routing updates of most distance-vector routing protocols can carry advertisements of multiple network prefixes.

NOTE: *The terms advertisement and routing update are often used interchangeably. While there is a slight difference in the meanings of the two terms, such a use is usually unambiguous and acceptable.*

The network prefixes contained in routing updates are said to be *advertised* by the router. The advertised network prefixes are taken from the router's own interfaces (on which routing updates are processed) and received from the other routers in their routing updates. The process of receiving and accepting network prefixes carried in other routers' routing updates is called *learning*, and the accepted network prefixes are said to be *learned*. However, not all network prefixes in the routing updates that a router receives are accepted. The rules explaining which network prefixes are accepted and which are not will be set forth shortly.

The interfaces through which a router receives and sends routing updates must be specifically administratively configured to perform this task. The router neither receives nor sends routing updates through any other interfaces. Each interface configured for receiving and sending of routing updates is assigned a routing protocol specific *cost*, which has the following two uses:

- The router uses the interface cost in calculations of its own metrics for the network prefixes contained in the routing updates received through the interface

- The router uses the interface cost as the metric when advertising the network prefix assigned on the interface.

A router uses the following three-step procedure to decide whether to accept a network prefix contained in a received routing update:

1. The router first calculates its own metric for the advertised network prefix by combining the metric contained in the routing update with the cost of the interface through which the routing update was received. The exact

formula for calculating the router's own metric is routing protocol specific; the calculated value however *must* be greater than the metric contained in the routing update.

2. If the router does not have a route for the advertised network prefix, it accepts the network prefix and creates a new route for it. The router uses the IP address of the advertising router and the interface through which the routing update was received as the new route's next-hop router and output interface fields respectively. The router also stores the calculated metric in the routing protocol specific portion of the route (routing table entry).

NOTE: *Some routing protocols also pass the IP address of the next-hop router along with the advertised network prefixes in their routing updates. In this case, the router that accepts such a routing update creates a routing table entry pointing to this IP address as the next-hop router.*

---

3. If the router has a route for the advertised network prefix and the route was established by the same distance-vector protocol, the router compares the calculated metric with the metric contained in the existing route. If the calculated metric is lower than the existing one, the router discards the existing route and creates a new one as described in step 2. If, however, the new metric is greater than or equal to the existing one, the router simply discards the received routing update without modifying the routing table.

NOTE: *Although the router may have accepted the advertised network prefix, it still may not be able to create a routing table entry for it. This situation is explained in more detail in a later section, "Routing Table Maintenance Rules Revisited."*

After the advertised network prefix is accepted and the corresponding routing table entry is created, the router itself starts advertising the network prefix with the calculated metric. The router also advertises the network prefixes assigned on its interfaces, which were configured for sending and receiving of routing updates. As it was mentioned, the router advertises these network prefixes with the metrics equal to the costs of the respective interfaces.

Finally, upon start, before a router has received any routing updates, it advertises only those network prefixes assigned on its interfaces, which were configured for sending and receiving of routing updates. As it starts receiving routing updates from other routers, it populates the routing table with the advertised network prefixes, which it begins advertising itself. All routers on all segments will eventually learn all the network prefixes available throughout the network.

NOTE: *The distance-vector protocol based routing is sometimes called "routing by rumors" because the routers possess no knowledge of the intermediate segments and routers en route to the learned network prefixes.*

Handling Network Changes

In an ideally stable network, the routing table of every router should not change after it has been populated with routes created by a dynamic routing protocol. Of course, ideally stable networks do not exist. Every so often, any network becomes unstable at least temporarily as the result of additions, removals, or failures of network components. Therefore, distance-vector protocols must be able to adapt to changes in the network whenever they occur.

Adding new components is simple. If another router is connected to a network, it starts learning from its neighbors the routing information of the network. At the same time, it starts advertising the network prefixes from the segments to which it is directly connected, thus making other routers aware of these. If a new segment is connected to the network, the routers that it interconnects start sending and receiving routing updates over it. Eventually all routers throughout the network will recalculate existing routes and learn the new ones. In other words, no special means are necessary to handle network additions.

In contrast to adding network components, handling removals and failures is a bit more difficult. If a component, such as a segment or a router, disappears, the other routers won't learn that unless they are specifically notified. Such notifications are implemented in the form of the *regular routing updates*, which are an extension to the basic distance-vector protocol. All routers must exchange routing updates on a regular basis (for example, every 30 seconds). Whenever a route for a learned network prefix is installed in the router's routing table, the so-called timer (called *timeout*) is started for that route. If the router does not receive another update before the timeout timer expires, the route is removed from the routing table.

The Problem of Counting to Infinity

It takes the routers a certain amount of time to communicate among each other the information about network changes. Until the network changes are conveyed to every router, some segments of the network may not be accessible (because not all of the routers may have the correct "after the change" routes for these segments). The process of making the routing tables of all routers consistent is called *convergence*. Likewise, the routing protocol is said to be *converging* when it is adapting to a network change. The routing protocol is said *to have converged* once the routing on all routers becomes consistent.

Convergence time is defined as the time period between the moment a network change happens and the moment the routing protocol converges. Nevertheless, despite individual features, all distance-vector protocols suffer from the same problem, which increases their convergence times. This problem is called *counting to infinity*.

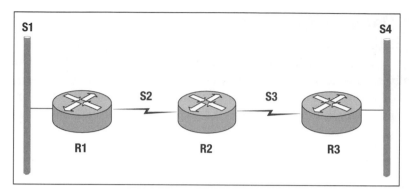

Figure 4.1   A network topology that demonstrates the counting-to-infinity problem.

To understand the counting-to-infinity problem, let's consider the network shown in Figure 4.1.

All three routers use the same distance-vector routing protocol. Let's assume that convergence is achieved (that is, that all three routers have learned the network prefixes of all four segments). As we know, the routers exchange regular routing updates in case something fails. For example, router R2 advertises segment S1 via both of its interfaces. Router R3, not having a better route for segment S1, picks up router R2's update. Because router R1 is directly connected to segment S1—and therefore is closer to segment S1—it ignores router R2's updates for segment S1. Likewise, router R3 also advertises segment S1 back to router R2, which of course is ignored by router R2 for the same reason. Suppose now that segment S2 fails. Router R2 starts a timeout timer for segment S1. Eventually, the timer expires, and router R2 stops considering segment S1 as available via router R1. Until this happens, router R2 continues to advertise segment S1 to router R3 via segment S3. The result is that router R3 does not even know that router R2 has stopped receiving updates from router R1. After router R2's timer for segment S1 expires, router R2 removes the corresponding route and is ready to consider an alternative route for that segment. As soon as router R3's update for segment S1 hits router R2, router R2 accepts it. A new route through router R3 is created for segment S1, only this time with a higher metric. Router R2 recalculates its own metric for this new route and sends it back to router R3 in the next regular update. Router R3 discovers that the routing update for segment S1 from router R2 now has a worse metric then before, so router R3 discards the routing update and starts the timeout timer for the existing route for segment S1. Until the timer expires, router R3 keeps sending routing updates carrying the old metric. After the timeout timer expires, router R3 removes the existing route and installs a new route based on the metric contained in router R2's routing updates. Now router R2 detects that the metric increased, so it starts the timeout timer again, and the whole process repeats. This process goes on indefinitely, and with each iteration, the metrics for segment S1 become worse—which nevertheless does not make the bogus route vanish.

The first step in resolving the problem is to consider any network prefix to be unreachable if the metric associated with it is greater than a certain value (infinity). (Thus, the problem is called *counting to infinity*.) As this value is reached, the corresponding network prefix is declared unreachable, which effectively causes the routers to remove the corresponding route from the routing table.

Although the routers eventually "count to infinity," this process takes time. During the counting-to-infinity process, the routers believe that a route for the affected network prefix is still available. Because two or more routers point to each other, this creates a loop such that, if any datagram is destined for the affected network prefix, it ends up being bounced among the routers until the Time-To-Live field in its header expires. During this period, the segment between the affected routers can become very congested, which in turn often makes the routers delay and even drop the useful traffic.

Distance-Vector Algorithm Refinements

A few techniques have been developed to eliminate or lessen the counting-to-infinity problem.

Split-Horizon Rule

This rule forbids a router from advertising a network prefix via the output interface of the route installed for the network prefix. In our example, the routers would have entirely avoided the counting-to-infinity problem if they had adhered to the split-horizon rule.

A more aggressive version of the split-horizon rule is known as the *split-horizon with poison reverse*. Unlike the regular version, the split-horizon with poison reverse rule instructs the router to advertise a network prefix via the output interface of the route for it but with the metric set to infinity.

Although the split-horizon rules are very important techniques in improving the convergence of distance-vector algorithms, they do not help in all situations. Let's consider the network shown in Figure 4.2 as an example.

Suppose all routers adhere to the split-horizon rule (either regular or with poisoned reverse). As in the previous example, segment S2 goes down. Eventually, router R2 times out the route for segment S1 via router R1. Until this happens, router R2 keeps advertising segment S1 to routers R3 and R4. In turn, routers R3 and R4 continue to advertise segment S1 to each other via segment S5. (Before segment S2 went down, routers R3 and R4 hadn't trusted each other's advertisements for segment S1 because they both had routes for the segment with better

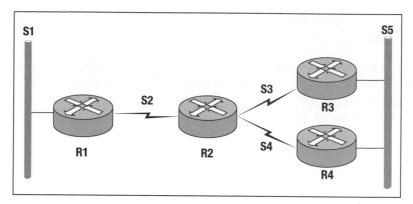

Figure 4.2   A network topology in which the split-horizon rule will not solve the counting-to-infinity problem.

metrics through router R2). As router R2 stops sending updates, routers R3 and R4 start their own timers for the route for segment S1 through router R2. When these timers expire, routers R3 and R4 pick up each other's advertisements for segment S1, establish bogus routes (again through each other), and advertise segment S1 back to router R2. This creates a temporary routing loop.

Holddowns

The *holddown* technique is even simpler than the split-horizon rule. For each route the router, in addition to the timeout timer, also maintains a holddown timer, which starts following the expiration of the timeout timer. However, in this instance, the route is not removed from the routing table after the timeout timer has expired. Instead, the router declares the corresponding network prefix to be unreachable by setting the route's metric to infinity. Until the holddown timer expires, the route cannot be removed from the routing table or modified, even if another routing update for that network prefix arrives.

The purpose of holddowns is to avoid the routing loops that are caused by routing updates originated by the routers that are not yet aware of the network change.

NOTE: *Although a metric associated with a route for which a holddown timer has been started is equal to infinity, the router keeps using the route (until it's removed from the routing table) to forward traffic. This happens because the routing algorithm (whether classful or classless) does not take the metrics of routes into account.*

Poisoned-Reverse Updates

An important improvement over plain holddowns involves making the router that placed a route for some network prefix into holddown also advertise this network prefix with the metric set to infinity. The routing updates carrying the metric of infinity are called *poison-reverse updates*. Poisoned-reverse updates are intended to force other routers in the network to put their routes for that network prefix into holddown also, even before they time out.

A router that receives a poison-reverse update for some network prefix reacts as follows:

- If the router has a route for this network prefix with a metric that is not equal to infinity (the route is *not* in holddown) and the source IP address of the poisoned-reverse update is equal to the IP address of the next-hop router of the route, the router places the route into holddown and sets the route's metric to infinity.

- If the router does not have a route for this network prefix, it ignores the poison-reverse update. This essentially means that the router does not create a route in a holddown for the network prefix.

NOTE: *Notice that, if a poison-reverse update is received from a router whose IP address is not equal to the IP address of the next-hop router in the routing table entry, the receiving router simply ignores the poisoned-reverse update. Otherwise, the receiving router might mistakenly put some route into holddown if it receives a poison-reverse update that resulted from some other router employing split-horizon with poison reverse.*

This second rule is important because it prevents the routers from reestablishing holddowns for routes for which holddowns have already expired. This could happen if some other routers in the network still maintain holddown timers for their routes for this network prefix, and thus still advertise it with the metric set to infinity.

The same rules apply to the routing updates that are generated by routers adhering to the split-horizon with poison reverse rule.

A more aggressive version of holddowns prescribes to put a route into holddown and set its metric to infinity whenever the next-hop router of the route *increases* the metric with which it advertises the network prefix. I called this version "more aggressive" because it only takes a mere increase in the metric, as opposed to a poisoned-reverse update, to trigger a holddown. A poisoned-reverse update, as we remember, is a routing update, which carries the advertised network prefix with the metric of infinity—the highest possible metric.

Triggered Updates

Another technique is triggered updates, which is a method that requires a router to send an update whenever the metrics of any route change. The purpose of triggered updates is to propagate the information about network failures as quickly as possible, so that no router mistakenly tries to advertise the network prefix from a failed network segment.

However, triggered updates must be employed with caution, because, if a segment goes down in a network with a large number of routers, an avalanche of triggered updates can occur. This massive amount of triggered updates can make the network virtually unavailable until all routers make their routing tables consistent throughout the network. Typically, a router must start a timer after it issues a triggered update, and this router may not send another triggered update until the timer expires. If, upon the expiration of this timer, the router still has to send another triggered update, it must first check if a regular routing update is due. If so, the router discards the triggered update and sends only the regular update.

Routing Table Maintenance Rules Revisited

In my personal experience, I notice that metrics are sometimes confused with administrative distances. In addition, metrics and administrative distances are sometimes mistakenly understood as being a part of the routing algorithm (classful or classless) that routers use to make routing decisions.

So far, there should be no confusion regarding the role of administrative distances. We introduced metrics in this chapter, so let's again revisit the routing table maintenance rules.

First, let's remember that routes for two different network prefixes can exist in the routing table regardless of the metrics associated with them and the administrative distances of the sources that created the routes. The conflict arises only if the network prefixes are the same, which means the significant bits are equal and the network prefix lengths are identical. If the latter is the case, then the following rules are used to resolve the ambiguity.

- The route whose metric is smaller is installed in the routing table, and the other route is discarded. If the metrics are identical, then both routes can be simultaneously installed in the routing table. The presence of two or more routes for the same network prefix results in load balancing of traffic destined for that network prefix (provided load balancing is enabled).

  All static routes have the fixed metric of zero.

  In the case of dynamic routing protocols, routing updates advertising the same network prefix will be considered different only if they arrived from different routers.

  Finally, some routing protocols may allow unequal-cost load balancing, which allows routes for the same network prefix but with different metrics to be installed in the routing table. We'll get back to this type of load balancing in Chapter 5, which is devoted to Internet Gateway Routing Protocol (IGRP).

- If the sources of the routing information are different, then the route whose source has a smaller administrative distance is installed in the routing table. The other route is discarded.

Because most sources of routing information can be assigned administrative distances manually, it is important to make sure that the administrative distances of two different sources do not coincide.

• Finally, after the routes are installed in the routing table, the router uses the routing algorithm (whether classful or classless) to forward arriving datagrams. The routing table is not allowed to contain any type of ambiguity.

The operation of a generic distance-vector routing protocol presented in the previous sections was explained without taking into account the possibility of the presence of other sources of routing information. If, however, some routing information source has an administrative distance that is smaller than that of a certain distance-vector routing protocol, it can prevent the latter from installing routes into the routing table. This fact prompts the question: Should the distance-vector protocol advertise network prefixes for which it failed to install routes? The answer is no, it must not. In other words, the necessary condition for advertising a learned network prefix is that the corresponding distance-vector protocol must first install a route for that network prefix.

Classful and Classless Routing Protocols

Another way to categorize routing protocols is by separating the classful and the classless ones.

Classful routing protocols do not send network prefix lengths in their routing updates. In terms of classful IP addressing, classful routing protocols do not send subnet masks in their routing updates. Instead, they rely on the information available at the router to "guess" the necessary subnetting information.

Unlike classful routing protocols, classless ones send full network prefix information (the network prefixes and their lengths) in their routing updates.

Classless routing protocols allow much flexibility in terms of dividing IP address space and assigning individual network prefixes in the network. For example, in regards to classful IP addressing, classless routing protocols permit using multiple subnet masks within a single classful network and allow discontinuous subnets.

NOTE: *The aforementioned features of classless routing protocols are normal from the classless IP addressing point of view.*

On the contrary, classful routing protocols impose rather strict requirements on how IP address space must be used and how IP addresses can be assigned.

First, let's discuss the types of addresses that can be passed in the routing updates of classful routing protocols:

- *Individual host addresses (such as 172.16.1.100/32)*—Support for individual host addresses is optional. For example, IGRP does not support individual host addresses.

- *Subnet addresses (such as 172.16.1.0/24)*—Because classful routing protocols do not pass subnet masks (network prefix lengths) in their routing updates, they can only "guess" the subnet mask by taking it from the interface, which belongs to the same classful network address to which the advertised subnet address belongs. For example, suppose a routing update carries address 172.20.5.0 and one of the interfaces on the router that receives the update is assigned the IP address of 172.20.35.1/28. The router takes the subnet mask (/28) and applies it to the address in the update. The result is the subnet address of 172.20.5.0/28.

- *Classful network addresses (such as 10.0.0.0/8)*—Typically, a classful routing protocol knows that an advertised address is a classful network address if no bits in the subnet part of the address are set. For example, if a router receives 172.22.0.0 in a routing update, it would guess that it is a classful network address.

- *Default addresses (such as 0.0.0.0/0)*—This is the simplest case. Whenever a router receives a routing update that contains 0.0.0.0, it knows that the update contains a default address.

Given all the guesswork that classful routing protocols must perform to adequately recognize the received network prefixes as belonging to one of these four categories, it is obvious that the flexibility of usage and allocation of IP address space managed by a classful routing protocol must be quite limited. The following rules must be enforced to ensure the correct operation of classful routing protocols:

- For every classful network address deployed, only a single subnet mask can be used throughout the network. For example, if network 10.0.0.0/8 is subnetted using subnet mask 255.255.255.0 (/24), this mask must be used on all segments comprised by the network. Different classful network addresses, however, can use different subnet masks. For example, it is allowable to deploy network address 172.19.0.0 with subnet mask 255.255.252.0 (/22) and network address 10.0.0.0 with subnet mask 255.255.255.0 (/24).

- The allocation of IP addresses must remain contiguous within the classful network boundaries. This means that, for every two segments with subnet addresses belonging to the same classful network address, there must be a path between them through segments, all of which are assigned subnet addresses of the same classful network address.

An example of a network that does not meet the second requirement is shown in Figure 4.3. The two gray areas denote the segments whose subnet addresses belong to classful network 10.0.0.0/8. The routing in this network cannot be handled by means of a classful routing protocol. Network 10.0.0.0/8 is noncontiguous because the two groups of segments addressed within network address 10.0.0.0/8 are completely separated by a segment addressed in another network address (192.168.5.0/24).

Finally, classful routers must summarize subnet and host addresses when they cross the classful network boundary. This means that, instead of sending a routing update that contains subnet and host addresses, the router must send an update containing only the classful network address. The metric in such an update is typically made equal to the smallest among the metrics of all subnet and host addresses that the router knows about.

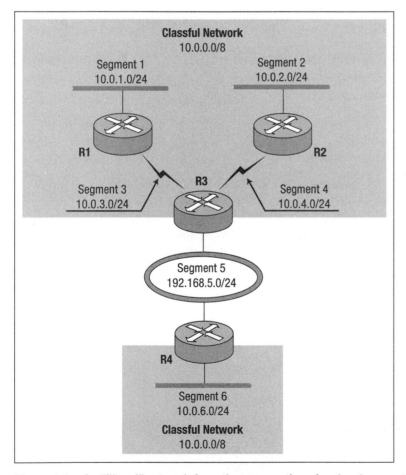

Figure 4.3   An "illegal" network from the perspective of a classless routing
             protocols network.

For example, if a router has four interfaces, three of which have IP addresses 10.0.1.1/24, 10.0.2.1/24, and 10.0.3.1/24, and the fourth interface has IP address 192.168.1.1/30, the router must not send a routing update containing individual subnets of network 10.0.0.0/8 through the fourth interface. Instead, all it can do is send an update that contains classful network address 10.0.0.0.

Details of RIP

As we've mentioned before, RIP is a distance-vector routing protocol. The very first implementation of RIP was in the form of the **routed** program developed at the University of California, Berkley, for BSD UNIX. Some other implementations are also available.

The early implementations of RIP differed in several details and hence lacked interoperability. In an effort to stipulate common requirements of RIP, the Internet Engineering Task Force (IETF) came up with a RIP specification, which was issued as Request for Comments (RFC)1058, "Routing Information Protocol."

RIP is a classful routing protocol primarily designed for small networks. If the network diameter of a routing protocol is defined as the longest path the routing protocol can handle, the network diameter of RIP is 16 router hops.

The operation of RIP is simple (if not primitive), and the protocol itself is easy to implement. Its simplicity notwithstanding, RIP became quite popular—a fact that can be primarily explained by its open nature and ease of implementation.

As the Internet advanced as the global public network, which eventually led to the advent of the classless IP addressing, RIP no longer sufficed as the routing protocol even for small networks. This initiated a further development of RIP, which resulted in RIP version 2—a classless RIP with slightly improved capabilities. RIP version 2 is documented in RFC 2453, "RIP Version 2" (the status of this RFC is the "Internet standard").

NOTE: RFC 2453 contains information on both versions of RIP. Furthermore, most information on RIP version 1 is simply copied from RFC 1058. Hence, it makes sense to read RFC 2453 only.

The following subsections provide an overview of both versions of RIP.

RIP Routing Update Format

RIP routing updates are encapsulated into User Datagram Protocol (UDP) packets destined for the local broadcast address (255.255.255.255). The source and destination UDP port in these packets is equal to 520 (decimal). Figure 4.4 shows the format of the RIP routing update.

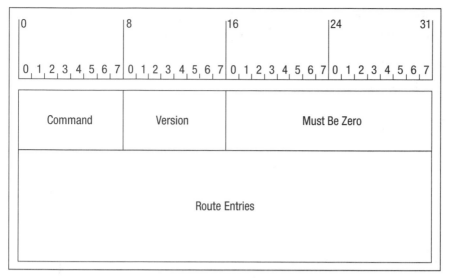

Figure 4.4   The format of the RIP routing update (RIP PDU).

The Command field is 1 octet long and can carry the values shown in Table 4.1.

Most typical RIP commands are **request** (1) and **response** (2). Routing updates that carry RIP requests must be handled in accordance with the following procedure:

- If the request contains route entries, create a RIP response with the same number of route entries. (The format of route entries will be explained shortly; for now we only need to know that route entries contain IP addresses representing the advertised or requested network prefixes and the corresponding metrics.) Copy the IP addresses from the request's route entries to the response's route entries. Look up the IP addresses contained in the request's route entries among the RIP managed routes using bit-by-bit comparison of all 32 bits (that is, ignoring the actual network prefix lengths). For each IP address for which a matching route is found, enter in the metric field of the response's corresponding route entry the value of the RIP metric contained in the route. For all IP addresses for which no matching routes are found, enter the value of 16 (infinity) in the metric fields of the response's corresponding route entries. Send the resulting RIP response back to the IP address, which appeared as the source IP address of the request.

NOTE: *The "managed by RIP entries" include the entries created by RIP and the entries whose network prefixes RIP can advertise (for example, connected).*

- If the request contains no entries, ignore it.

Table 4.1   The values the Command field of the RIP routing update can carry.

Value	Command	Description
1	**request**	The system that issued the RIP PDU requests the receiving system to send all or part of its routing table (handled by RIP only).
2	**response**	The RIP PDU contains network prefixes and associated metrics in accordance with the sending system's routing table. This PDU could be a response to a previously received request or a regular routing update.
3	**traceon**	Obsolete. Must be ignored.
4	**traceoff**	Obsolete. Must be ignored.
5	**reserved**	This value is used by Sun Microsystems for its own purposes. RIP entities by other vendors do not have to implement it and can safely ignore RIP PDUs carrying this value.

- If the request contains a single route entry whose IP address is equal to 0.0.0.0 and the metric field is set to 16, reply back with one or more RIP responses whose route entries carry all RIP managed network prefixes and their corresponding RIP metrics. If split-horizon is enabled on the interface through which the response is sent, the route entries must be created only for those network prefixes that pass the split-horizon rule.

An RIP request that carries route entries can arrive from a port other than 520. In this case, the response is given back to this port using a unicast routing update sent to the source IP address of the datagram that carried the request.

RIP updates that carry the **response** (2) command are either replies to RIP requests or regular RIP updates.

The Version field is 1 octet long and carries the version of RIP: It must be 1 for the original RIP and 2 for RIP version 2. (RIP version 2 is discussed in the "RIP Version 2" section later in this chapter.)

A route entry is 20 octets long and carries the advertised IP address and its metric. (The interpretation of what the IP address actually is presented in the next section.) A single RIP routing update can contain up to 25 route entries. Figure 4.5 shows the format of RIP route entries.

Theoretically, RIP is not an IP-only routing protocol. Therefore, a provisioning was made for RIP to carry routing information for more than one "routed" protocol. Each RIP entry, in theory, can contain routing information for a separate protocol, which is identified by the value contained in the Address Family Identifier field (2 octets long). For IP, this value is set to 2.

The next 2-octet field is reserved. In the case of RIP version 1, this field must be set to 0.

The last four 4-octet fields of the RIP entry shown in Figure 4.5 are IP specific. The IP Address field carries the advertised network prefix. This field is followed by two fields whose values must be equal to 0. Finally, the Metric field carries an RIP-specific metric of the advertised network prefix.

Network Prefixes That RIP Can Advertise

Being a typical classful routing protocol, RIP does not pass subnet masks along with IP addresses in its routing updates.

RIP can advertise all four types of IP addresses (discussed earlier in the "Classful and Classless Routing Protocols" section). RIP uses the following rules to recognize an advertised IP address as belonging to one of the four types:

1. If the advertised IP address belongs to a classful network address to which the IP address of one of the router's interface belongs, take the subnet mask from the interface and apply it to the advertised IP address. If any bits in the host ID part of the address are set, then the advertised IP address is a host address. Otherwise, it's a subnet address.

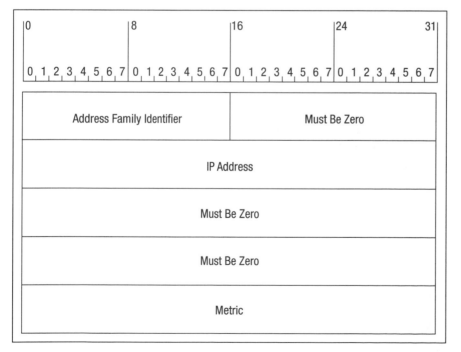

Figure 4.5   The format of the route entry in RIP routing updates.

2. If the advertised IP address belongs to a classful network address to which none of the router's IP addresses belongs, this is the classful network address. If any bits in the host part of the address are set, discard the address because it's illegal.

3. If the advertised IP address is equal to 0.0.0.0, this is the default address (that is, 0.0.0.0/0).

Of course, routers employing RIP must summarize of subnet and host addresses in routing updates that cross the corresponding classful network boundary.

RIP Metrics

RIP uses a hop count as the metric. The metric of 16 is considered infinity, and the network prefixes advertised with the metric of 16 are considered unreachable.

There is a little discrepancy in the way RFC 2453 requires the metrics to be processed and how it is implemented in Cisco IOS. According to RFC 2453, the metrics must be adjusted upon receipt of the routing updates. The formula that is used to calculate the new value of the metric is

$$M_N = \min(\, M_O + C, 16\,),$$

where M_N and M_O are the new and old metrics, and C is the cost of the interface over which the routing update was received. Typically, C is equal to 1.

Cisco routers do not modify the metrics that are received in the routing updates. Instead, they adjust the metrics in the routing updates that they themselves send. The routers use the same formula, but, if the resulting metric is equal to 16 (infinity), the network prefix is not advertised.

The discrepancy in handling metrics according to the standard and how it is implemented in Cisco IOS should not cause any significant issues.

RIP Stability Features

RIP employs split-horizon (either regular or poisoned-reverse—the decision is left to the discretion of the implementers) and triggered updates.

Cisco's version of RIP also uses holddowns, and the way they are implemented is explained in the "Cisco's Implementation of RIP timers" section later in this chapter.

RIP Timers

Upon expiration of the regular update timer, RIP routers send regular routing updates, and the timer is reset and restarted. (By default, the regular update timer expires every 30 seconds.)

The routers that are exchanging large amounts of routing updates tend to synchronize their regular update timers (unless the timers are completely independent of the router's CPU utilization). To avoid this synchronization, the routers are required to randomly change the expiration time of the regular update timer by adding or subtracting a small value within a range of 0 through 5 seconds. (This value is sometimes referred to as a *jitter time.*)

For each route RIP installs in the routing table, it maintains two timers: a timeout and a *garbage-collection* timer. These timers facilitate handling network changes associated with failures and removals of segments and routers. The direct result of both types of changes is that the associated network prefixes become either reachable or unreachable from different directions. Therefore, the routers have to adjust their routing tables accordingly.

When RIP installs a route into the routing table, it starts a timeout timer for this route. Every time a routing update for the network prefix of the route arrives from the next-hop router RIP resets the timeout timer. If the timeout timer for some entry expires, the metric associated with it is changed to 16 (infinity) and the garbage-collection timer is started for that entry. Until the garbage-collection timer expires, the route is advertised with the metric set to 16. By default, the expiration times for the timeout and garbage-collection timers are 180 and 120 seconds, respectively.

Alternatively, RIP can change the metric of a route to 16 and start the garbage-collection timer if it receives a poison-reverse update for the network prefix of the route from the router whose IP address appears as the IP address of the next-hop router.

Regardless of how the garbage-collection timer was started, if the router receives another routing update that reestablishes the route (the new routing update must carry a metric smaller than 16), the garbage-collection timer is stopped. The entry is then made operational with the new metric and possibly a new IP address of the next-hop router and new output interface (whichever applies).

Finally, RIP routers are required to maintain a separate timer for subsequent triggered updates. The value of the timer is chosen randomly within a range of 1 through 5 seconds. Until the timer expires, no triggered update can be sent. If a regular update is due when a triggered update can be sent (upon expiration of the timer), only the regular update is to be sent.

Cisco's Implementation of RIP Timers

Cisco's implementation of RIP supports holddowns, whose usage is governed by the following rules:

- If the timeout timer for some route expires, a Cisco router uses the procedure prescribed by the RIP standard (that is, it does not put the route into holddown). Instead, it starts a garbage-collection timer for the route. If the route is updated before the timer expires, the route is brought back to operation, and the garbage-collection timer is stopped. (The routing update that restores the route may not necessarily arrive from the original next-hop router and through the original interface.)

- If a router receives a poisoned-reverse update for a network prefix for which it has an RIP-installed route and the IP address of the next-hop router in the route is equal to the source IP address of the poisoned-reverse update, the route is placed into holddown. The router won't accept any routing updates for this network prefix until the holddown expires.

To sustain the operation of holddowns, Cisco's implementation of RIP uses a slightly different set of timers and corresponding expiration times.

For timing out routing entries, a regular timeout timer is used, and its expiration time is referred to in the Cisco documentation as the *invalid time*. By default, the invalid time is 180 seconds.

Cisco IOS represents the garbage-collection timer a bit differently. The timeout timer, upon reaching the invalid time, prompts the router to start advertising the network prefix with the metric of infinity. However, the timer itself is not stopped. When the timer reaches the *flush time*, the route is removed; only then is the timer stopped. If, during the timer operation, a routing update that updates the route arrives, the timer is stopped.

By default, the flush time is 240 seconds. You can think of the flush time as the sum of the expiration times of the timeout timer and the garbage-collection timer. If Cisco's implementation of RIP used a separate garbage-collection timer, then, by default, the garbage-collection timer expiration time would be 60 (240 - 180).

If a route is put into holddown, a separate holddown timer is started, which expires after 180 seconds (the default). This means that, after the holddown expires, the route is removed from the routing table.

NOTE: *Until the route is removed from the routing table, the router still uses it to forward datagrams destined for the network prefix of the route. This forwarding happens regardless of the metric value associated with the route, even if it's equal to infinity (16, in the case of RIP).*

RIP Version 2

RIP version 2 is not another protocol; it is actually a number of extensions to the original RIP specification that allow RIP to exchange more-detailed routing information and to perform some additional functions. These extensions are outlined in this section.

First, routers that employ RIP version 2 do not send routing updates to the broadcast address; rather, they send them to the multicast address 224.0.0.9 instead.

In the case of RIP version 2, the value carried in the Version field in the RIP update header is equal to 2.

RIP version 2 uses the extended route entry format shown in Figure 4.6.

The following paragraphs describe the fields of the RIP version 2 route entry.

The Address Family Identifier field is the same in RIP Version 2 as it was in Version 1.

The 2-octet Route Tag field replaces the reserved field whose value must be equal to 0 in RIP version 1. The field contains a value that allows RIP to identify the network prefix contained in the route entry as originated by a routing information source other than RIP and imported to RIP. No values are predefined for the Route Tag field. The network administrators are free to choose whether to use this field or not; if they do use it, the numbering is left to their discretion. Other uses of the Route Tag field are also allowed.

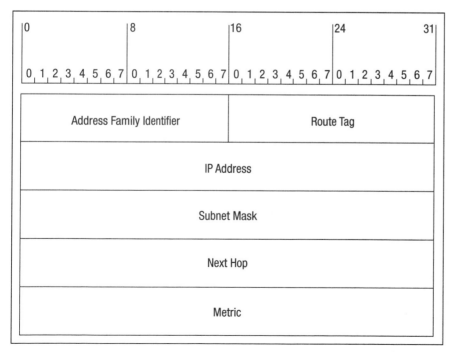

Figure 4.6   The format of an RIP version 2 route entry.

Routers that implement RIP version 2 must preserve the value of route tags as they re-advertise learned network prefixes.

Two 4-octet fields—IP Address and Subnet Mask—represent a network prefix and its length. The length of the network prefix is now passed in the routing updates, so the routers no longer "guess" network prefixes. In other words, routers that employ RIP version 2 do not use the rules presented earlier in the section "Network Prefixes That RIP Can Advertise."

The 4-octet Next Hop field carries the IP address of the router through which the advertised network prefix is best available. This field essentially allows routers to advertise network prefixes that are available through other routers. If the value carried in this field is equal to 0.0.0.0, the source IP address of the datagram that is carrying the routing update must be used as the next-hop IP address. If the value of this field is not 0.0.0.0, it must be directly accessible from the router that is receiving the routing update.

The 4-octet Metric field is the same in RIP version 2 as it was in version1.

RIP Version 2 Authentication

RIP version 2 provides for the optional authentication of routing updates. If it is used, the authentication information is passed in the first route entry of a routing update. The router that receives a routing update determines the presence of authentication by examining the Address Family Identifier field of the first route entry. If it's equal to 0xFFFF (hexadecimal), authentication information is contained in the route entry.

The format of the first route entry that contains authentication information is shown in Figure 4.7.

Currently, only clear text password authentication is documented and standardized. Clear text password authentication is indicated by setting the Authentication Type field equal to 2. The Authentication Data field carries the password, which must be padded with zeroes if it is shorter than 16 octets.

Interoperation of RIP Versions 1 and 2

The RIP standard (RFC 2453) requires that routers that implement RIP version 2 be configurable on a per-interface basis with the following four modes:

- RIP-1 mode, in which only RIP version 1 routing updates are sent
- RIP-1 compatibility mode, in which RIP version 2 routing updates are sent to the local broadcast address (255.255.255.255)
- RIP-2 mode, in which the RIP version 2 routing updates are sent to multicast address 224.0.0.9
- None (no RIP routing updates are sent)

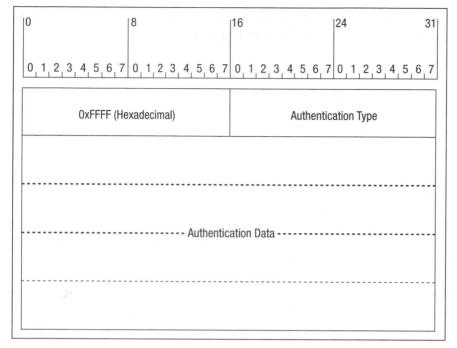

Figure 4.7   The optional Authentication field.

Immediate Solutions

The rest of this chapter is mostly devoted to RIP configuration and operation tasks specific to Cisco routers. The very beginning of the chapter, however, explains two important Cisco-specific subjects: the interpretation of the output of the **show ip route** command and the meaning and use of candidate default routes and the "gateway of last resort."

WARNING!   Throughout the "Immediate Solutions" section in this chapter, we will often resort to various debug commands to better understand what's happening on the routers. I must warn you, however, that it is very dangerous to use certain debug commands on the production routers. Examples of such debug commands are debug ip rip, debug ip igrp transactions, and so on. These commands are very processor intensive; using them on a moderately loaded router can easily lead to extremely high CPU usage on the router. During this high CPU-usage period, the router becomes very slow at processing production traffic and won't accept any input, even from the console. Typically, the only measure that helps in such situations is a restart of the router. This obviously causes disruption of network operation for the duration of the router restart.

Understanding the Output of the **show ip route** Command

The **show ip route** command is used to display the routing table of a Cisco router. We already used this command in Chapter 3 when discussing static routing. In Chapter 3, however, the routing tables of the routers contained only static and connected routes, so the output of the **show ip route** command was pretty simple.

From this chapter on, we'll be dealing with all three sources of routing information: connected routes, static routes, and dynamic routing protocols. The latter make the routing table—and, hence, the output of the **show ip route** command—more diverse. So it's now time to discuss the **show ip route** command in more detail.

Figure 4.8 shows the sample output of the **show ip route** command.

The first six lines of the output are always the same: They present the legend for the letters that precede the routing table entries and signify the source of routing information that created the routing table entry. Among the routing information sources are connected routes (signified by the letter *C*), static routes (signified by *S*), routes created by routing protocols RIP (*R*) and IGRP (*I*), and so on.

```
                        Source of Routing Information
                        That Installed Route

R1#show ip route
Codes: C - connected, S - static, I - IGRP, R - RIP, M - mobile, B - BGP
       D - EIGRP, EX - EIGRP external, O - OSPF, IA - OSPF inter area
       N1 - OSPF NSSA eternal type 1, N2 - OSPF NSSA external type 2
       E1 - OSPF external type 1, E2 - OSPF external type 2, E - EGP
       i - IS-IS, L1 - IS-IS level-1, L2 - IS-IS level-2, * - candidate default
       U - per-user static route, o - QDR

Gateway of last resort is not set

R      192.168.4.0/24 [120/1] via 192.168.3.1. 00:00:27, Serial0
R      192.168.5.0/24 [120/1] via 192.168.3.1. 00:00:00, Serial0
       10.0.0.0/24 is subnetted, 1 subnets   ──────── Indicates That This Classful
S         10.0.1.0 [1/0] via 192.168.1.5                Network Is Subnetted
C      192.168.3.0/24 is directly connected, Serial0
S      172.0.0.0/8 [1/0] via 192.168.3.5   ──────────── Supernet Route
R      192.168.6.0/24 [120/2] via 192.168.3.1. 00:00:00, Serial0
C      192.168.1.0/24 is directly connected, Ethernet0
R      192.168.2.0/24 [120/2] via 192.168.3.1, 00:00:00, Serial0


   Network Prefix      Metric    Next-Hop Router      Output Interface
                                 IP Address

            Administrative       Time Elapsed Since
            Distance of Route    Route Was Last Updated
```

Figure 4.8   A sample output of the show ip route command.

NOTE: *The number of lines in the legend (six, in our example) may vary depending on the version of IOS.*

The next line (which in Figure 4.8 reads "Gateway of last resort is not set") denotes the default router that the router should use if it receives a datagram destined for an IP address for which it does not have any route. The "gateway of last resort" is essentially an implicit route for a network prefix 0.0.0.0/0, although, unlike for the latter, no routing entry is displayed for the gateway of last resort. If the gateway of last resort is set, it is indicated in this line of the output of the **show ip route** command.

NOTE: *The section "Understanding Candidate Default Routes and Gateways of Last Resort," comprehensively explains the meaning of gateways of last resort and candidate default routes.*

Each routing table entry is displayed using a separate line, each of which (unless it is a part of a group of lines indicating load balancing or a connected route) contains the following elements (in order of appearance):

- The indicator that specifies the source of routing information that created the routing table entry. Typically, the indicator is a single letter that can optionally be followed by one or more letters or digits that provide details specific to the source of the routing information. Both the indicators and their options are explained in the legend lines.

- The network prefix for which the routing table entry is created. (The available network prefix formats are explained in the next section.)

- The administrative distance of the routing table entry.

- The routing information source-specific metric. In the case of static routes, this entry carries the value of 0.

- The IP address of the next-hop router en route to the network prefix.

- The time elapsed since the routing table entry was last updated.

- The output interface to be used to send datagrams destined for IP addresses matched by the network prefix.

TIP: *While examining how different dynamic routing protocols work, we'll often use the **show ip route** command. If you decide to repeat those experiments, or even to conduct your own experiments, the routing table may not always exhibit the contents you expect. This can happen for three reasons: You did something wrong, your expectations are wrong, or it takes time for the dynamic routing protocol to converge. Although the first two reasons may not be easy to correct, the third one has a simple solution: Just type in* "clear ip route". *This command clears the contents of the routing table, which in most cases causes the router to request the routing information from its neighbors. This may speed up the process of acquiring the correct routing information by the router tremendously, especially in the case of "slow" routing protocols, such as RIP and IGRP.*

Modifying the Network Prefix Format

The network prefix can be displayed using three formats: bit-count, decimal, and hexadecimal. The default format in the later versions of IOS is bit-count, which is the format that is used throughout this book (a network prefix is shown as an IP address followed by a slash followed by the network prefix length expressed as a decimal number). Decimal format is the old-style format, in which both the IP address and the subnet mask are shown using dotted decimal notation. In hexadecimal format, the IP address is shown using dotted decimal notation, but the subnet mask is shown using hexadecimal notation (eight hexadecimal digits prefixed by "0x"). You can change the network prefix format for the duration of the terminal session using the **terminal ip netmask-format {bit-count|decimal| hexadecimal}** command in exec mode (either user or privileged). Listing 4.1 shows the output of the **show ip route** command after the **terminal ip netmask-format decimal** command was entered on the router.

Listing 4.1   The output of the **show ip route** command after the network prefix format was changed to decimal.

```
R2#show ip route
...
R   192.168.1.0 255.255.255.0 [120/2] via 192.168.4.1, 00:00:12, Serial1
C   192.168.2.0 255.255.255.0 is directly connected, Ethernet0
R   192.168.3.0 255.255.255.0 [120/1] via 192.168.4.1, 00:00:13, Serial1
C   192.168.4.0 255.255.255.0 is directly connected, Serial1
R   192.168.5.0 255.255.255.0 [120/1] via 192.168.4.1, 00:00:13, Serial1
R   192.168.6.0 255.255.255.0 [120/2] via 192.168.4.1, 00:00:13, Serial1
```

Listing 4.2 shows the output of the same command, but after the **terminal ip netmask-format hexadecimal** command was entered.

Listing 4.2   The output of the **show ip route** command after the network prefix format was changed to hexadecimal.

```
R2#show ip route
...
R   192.168.1.0 0xFFFFFF00 [120/2] via 192.168.4.1, 00:00:12, Serial1
C   192.168.2.0 0xFFFFFF00 is directly connected, Ethernet0
R   192.168.3.0 0xFFFFFF00 [120/1] via 192.168.4.1, 00:00:12, Serial1
C   192.168.4.0 0xFFFFFF00 is directly connected, Serial1
R   192.168.5.0 0xFFFFFF00 [120/1] via 192.168.4.1, 00:00:12, Serial1
R   192.168.6.0 0xFFFFFF00 [120/2] via 192.168.4.1, 00:00:12, Serial1
```

The desired network prefix format can be permanently assigned on a per-terminal basis using the **ip netmask-format {bit-count|decimal|hexadecimal}** command in line configuration mode. The following snippet of code shows how to change the network prefix format to hexadecimal for the console of a router:

```
line con 0
 ip netmask-format hexadecimal
```

NOTE: *The expression "permanently assigned" means that the assigned network prefix format is not reset to the default after the terminal session is terminated or the router is reloaded. It does not assume an irretrievable change.*

---

4. Routing Information Protocol (RIP)

Understanding Candidate Default Routes and Gateways of Last Resort

Cisco's version of the routing algorithm (whether classful or classless) is extended by the concept of the gateway of last resort.

The gateway of last resort is essentially a router that receives the traffic whose destination has no match in the router's routing table. This concept is very similar to the concept of the default gateway or default router of hosts. There is a functional difference, however, between the hosts' default gateway and the routers' gateway of last resort. Hosts typically have small routing tables and thus use the default gateway intensively. On the contrary, routers typically have comprehensive routing tables, and thus should rarely use the gateway of last resort—keeping it as just that, a last resort.

Stemming from this functional difference, there is also an "administrative" difference between the hosts' default gateway and the routers' gateway of last resort. Hosts usually don't have a large choice of next-hop routers. Most hosts can access only one or two routers—a fact that naturally leads to making the IP addresses of these routes the default gateways on the hosts. Unlike hosts, most routers have several next-hop routers, and which they choose one is the closest to the traffic destination. Therefore, it would be natural to provide routers with a number of potential gateways of last resort and allow them to choose the best depending on circumstances.

A typical application of the gateway of last resort concept on routers is the connections to the Internet. The number of routes in the Internet is huge, and making the routers of every network connected to the Internet learn of all of them would create excessive loads on these routers. This can all be avoided by utilizing the gateway of last resort on these routers. After all, if the destination of some traffic isn't found inside the network, it can be accessible only through the Internet.

NOTE: *That's not to say that gateway of the last resort is always one and only solution for routing IP traffic to the Internet.*

If a network has only a single connection to the Internet, obviously all routers should forward Internet-destined traffic to this connection. If, however, the network has multiple connections to the Internet, the routers can try to split the traffic among these connections.

An example of a network with multiple Internet connections is shown in Figure 4.9.

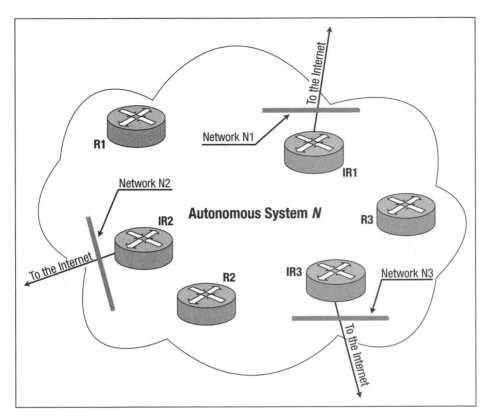

Figure 4.9   Autonomous system *N* has multiple connections to the Internet.

Segments N1, N2, and N3 lead to the Internet. The routers in the network can choose through which of these three segments they'll forward traffic to the Internet. For example, router R1 can choose segment N1, if, among the routes for segments N1, N2, and N3, the route for segment N1 on router R1 boasts the smallest metric. Likewise, routers R2 and R3 may choose segments N2 and N3, respectively, for the same reason. If router R1 is separated from segment N1 only by router IR1, router IR1 becomes the gateway of last resort. In any case, the gateway of last resort for router R1 is the router whose IP address is contained in the route for segment N1.

The routers in autonomous system *N* have routes for segments N1, N2, and N3, so they can use these routes to choose their preferred gateways of last resort. This brings us to the concept of *candidate default routes*, which are routes that allow the routers to choose the gateway of last resort. Obviously, candidate default routes must point to the network prefixes of segments that do provide "default" access.

For a Cisco router to choose the gateway of last resort, it must first choose the best among the candidate default routes (if any). Let's first discuss how candidate default routes get to a router's routing table.

Candidate default routes on Cisco routers are created in three ways:

- All routes for network prefix 0.0.0.0/0 become the candidate default route. These can be either static routes (including pseudo-connected routes, that is, static routes pointing to an interface) or routes created by dynamic routing protocols, such as RIP.

- By entering one or several **ip default-network <IP address>** commands in global configuration mode. All routes (whether dynamic, static, or connected) whose network prefixes are equal to the **<IP address>** parameter of the commands become candidate default routes.

- Some routing protocols (IGRP, for example) advertise some network prefixes as exterior. If routes are created for exterior network prefixes, those routes become candidate default routes.

The routers use the following algorithm to choose the "best" candidate default route:

1. If any candidate default connected or pseudo-connected routes are present, exclude them from the list of examined candidate default routes. (The administrative distance of pseudo-connected routes is not important.) The exception is pseudo-connected routes for network prefix 0.0.0.0/0, which must be kept.

2. If several candidate default routes exist, only the ones with the smallest administrative distance are kept. If there is only one candidate default route with the smallest administrative distance, it is chosen and the algorithm finishes.

3. Among the candidate default routes kept as a result of Step 1, the ones with the smallest metric are chosen. If there is only one candidate default route with the smallest metric, it is chosen and the algorithm finishes.

4. If several candidate default routes are kept as a result of Step 2, choose the one that was created first.

After the candidate default route is chosen, the router uses the following rules to decide whether to create the gateway of last resort:

- If no candidate default routes were excluded in Step 1 (connected and/or pseudo-connected), the router creates the gateway of last resort.

- If any routes were excluded in Step 1 (connected and/or pseudo-connected) and the chosen candidate default route is a static route, the algorithm creates the gateway of last resort.

- If routes were excluded in Step 1 (connected and/or pseudo-connected) and the chosen candidate default route is a dynamic route, the algorithm does not create the gateway of last resort.

Finally, if the router decides to create the gateway of last resort, it makes it equal to the IP address of the next-hop router of the chosen candidate default route. The router declares this IP address the gateway of last resort to the network prefix of this route. (This essentially means that the router presumes that the traffic for unknown destinations must be forwarded towards this network prefix by the gateway of last resort.) If, however, the chosen candidate default route is a static route for network prefix 0.0.0.0/0 pointing to an interface, the IP address of the gateway of last resort is made 0.0.0.0, and all the traffic forwarded to the gateway of last resort is sent to this interface. (This is identical to how the router uses a pseudo-connected route.)

The described rules are rather complex, so let's consider a few examples.

The first example is shown in Listing 4.3.

Listing 4.3   The routing table of router R1.

```
R1#show ip route
...
Gateway of last resort is 10.0.1.1 to network 192.168.31.0

I*   192.168.31.0/24 [100/10576] via 10.0.1.1, 00:00:05, Serial0
I*   192.168.41.0/24 [100/10676] via 10.0.1.1, 00:00:06, Serial0
I    192.168.200.0/24 [100/10676] via 10.0.1.1, 00:00:06, Serial0
     10.0.0.0/24 is subnetted, 7 subnets
I       10.0.10.0 [100/8576] via 10.0.1.1, 00:00:06, Serial0
I       10.0.2.0 [100/10576] via 10.0.1.1, 00:00:06, Serial0
I       10.0.3.0 [100/10476] via 10.0.1.1, 00:00:06, Serial0
C       10.1.2.0 is directly connected, TokenRing0
I       10.2.2.0 [100/10639] via 10.0.1.1, 00:00:06, Serial0
C       10.0.1.0 is directly connected, Serial0
I       10.0.4.0 [100/10576] via 10.0.1.1, 00:00:06, Serial0
C    192.168.100.0/24 is directly connected, Ethernet0
```

This routing table contains two candidate default routes (the italicized lines). Notice the asterisk right after the letter designating the source of routing information that created the routes (in this case IGRP). The asterisk denotes candidate default routes.

NOTE: *The details of IGRP and how to configure it to produce candidate default routes are covered in Chapter 6.*

The router chooses the first route because its metric is the best. Both routers are created by IGRP, so their administrative distances are the same (100, the first number in the brackets). This is reflected in the shaded line, which references the IP address of the next-hop router from the first route (actually, the IP address of the next-hop router is the same in both routes) as the gateway of last resort to the network prefix of this route.

Suppose the following command was added to the router's configuration:

```
ip default-network 192.168.100.0
```

This command makes the connected route through interface Ethernet0 a candidate default route. The routing table of the router changes, as shown in Listing 4.4.

Listing 4.4   The routing table of router R1.

```
R1#show ip route
...
Gateway of last resort is not set

I*   192.168.31.0/24 [100/10576] via 10.0.1.1, 00:00:35, Serial0
I*   192.168.41.0/24 [100/10676] via 10.0.1.1, 00:00:36, Serial0
I    192.168.200.0/24 [100/10676] via 10.0.1.1, 00:00:36, Serial0
     10.0.0.0/24 is subnetted, 7 subnets
I       10.0.10.0 [100/8576] via 10.0.1.1, 00:00:36, Serial0
I       10.0.2.0 [100/10576] via 10.0.1.1, 00:00:36, Serial0
I       10.0.3.0 [100/10476] via 10.0.1.1, 00:00:36, Serial0
C       10.1.2.0 is directly connected, TokenRing0
I       10.2.2.0 [100/10639] via 10.0.1.1, 00:00:36, Serial0
C       10.0.1.0 is directly connected, Serial0
I       10.0.4.0 [100/10576] via 10.0.1.1, 00:00:36, Serial0
C*   192.168.100.0/24 is directly connected, Ethernet0
```

The new candidate default route is connected (the last line in the listing), so it becomes excluded in the first step of the algorithm. Because the chosen candidate default route is a dynamic route, the router won't create a gateway of last resort, which is reflected in the shaded line of the listing.

Let's now add two more commands:

```
ip route 172.30.0.0 255.255.0.0 192.168.100.40
ip default-network 172.30.0.0
```

The first command creates a static route for network prefix 172.30.0.0/16; the second makes it a candidate default route. Listing 4.5 shows the new routing table of the router.

Listing 4.5 The routing table of router R1.

```
R1#show ip route
...
```
Gateway of last resort is 192.168.100.40 to network 172.30.0.0
```
I*   192.168.31.0/24 [100/10576] via 10.0.1.1, 00:00:28, Serial0
S*   172.30.0.0/16 [1/0] via 192.168.100.40
I*   192.168.41.0/24 [100/10676] via 10.0.1.1, 00:00:28, Serial0
I    192.168.200.0/24 [100/10676] via 10.0.1.1, 00:00:28, Serial0
     10.0.0.0/24 is subnetted, 7 subnets
I       10.0.10.0 [100/8576] via 10.0.1.1, 00:00:28, Serial0
I       10.0.2.0 [100/10576] via 10.0.1.1, 00:00:28, Serial0
I       10.0.3.0 [100/10476] via 10.0.1.1, 00:00:28, Serial0
C       10.1.2.0 is directly connected, TokenRing0
I       10.2.2.0 [100/10639] via 10.0.1.1, 00:00:28, Serial0
C       10.0.1.0 is directly connected, Serial0
I       10.0.4.0 [100/10576] via 10.0.1.1, 00:00:29, Serial0
C*   192.168.100.0/24 is directly connected, Ethernet0
```

The new chosen candidate default route is static (its administrative distance is smaller than that of the two IGRP routes). In addition, although the candidate default connected route still exists, the router creates the gateway of last resort. (See the shaded line.)

Now let's get back to the state of the router when it had the routing table shown in Listing 4.3 (that is, before we made a connected route a candidate default route and then added a candidate default static route). This time, we are going to add the following two commands to the router's configuration:

```
ip route 172.16.0.0 255.255.0.0 Ethernet0 240
ip default-network 172.16.0.0
```

The first command creates a pseudo-connected route; the second one makes it a candidate default route. The new routing table of router R1 is shown in Listing 4.6.

Listing 4.6 The routing table of router R1.

```
R1#show ip route
...
```
Gateway of last resort is not set
```
I*   192.168.31.0/24 [100/10576] via 10.0.1.1, 00:01:12, Serial0
S*   172.16.0.0/16 is directly connected, Ethernet0
I*   192.168.41.0/24 [100/10676] via 10.0.1.1, 00:01:13, Serial0
I    192.168.200.0/24 [100/10676] via 10.0.1.1, 00:01:13, Serial0
     10.0.0.0/24 is subnetted, 7 subnets
```

4. Routing Information Protocol (RIP)

```
I     10.0.10.0 [100/8576] via 10.0.1.1, 00:01:13, Serial0
I     10.0.2.0 [100/10576] via 10.0.1.1, 00:01:13, Serial0
I     10.0.3.0 [100/10476] via 10.0.1.1, 00:01:13, Serial0
C     10.1.2.0 is directly connected, TokenRing0
I     10.2.2.0 [100/10639] via 10.0.1.1, 00:01:13, Serial0
C     10.0.1.0 is directly connected, Serial0
I     10.0.4.0 [100/10576] via 10.0.1.1, 00:01:13, Serial0
C  192.168.100.0/24 is directly connected, Ethernet0
```

The new look of the routing table confirms that even a pseudo-connected candidate default route (the second shaded line) won't let a chosen dynamic candidate default route be used to create the gateway of last resort.

Our final experiment consists of adding one more command to the last state or router's configuration. This one command is:

```
ip route 0.0.0.0 0.0.0.0 TokenRing0
```

The routing table's new state is shown in Listing 4.7.

Listing 4.7   The routing table of router R1.

```
R1#show ip route
...
```
Gateway of last resort is 0.0.0.0 to network 0.0.0.0

```
I*  192.168.31.0/24 [100/10576] via 10.0.1.1, 00:00:29, Serial0
S*  172.16.0.0/16 is directly connected, Ethernet0
I*  192.168.41.0/24 [100/10676] via 10.0.1.1, 00:00:30, Serial0
I   192.168.200.0/24 [100/10676] via 10.0.1.1, 00:00:30, Serial0
    10.0.0.0/24 is subnetted, 7 subnets
I     10.0.10.0 [100/8576] via 10.0.1.1, 00:00:30, Serial0
I     10.0.2.0 [100/10576] via 10.0.1.1, 00:00:30, Serial0
I     10.0.3.0 [100/10476] via 10.0.1.1, 00:00:30, Serial0
C     10.1.2.0 is directly connected, TokenRing0
I     10.2.2.0 [100/10639] via 10.0.1.1, 00:00:30, Serial0
C     10.0.1.0 is directly connected, Serial0
I     10.0.4.0 [100/10576] via 10.0.1.1, 00:00:31, Serial0
C  192.168.100.0/24 is directly connected, Ethernet0
S*  0.0.0.0/0 is directly connected, TokenRing0
```

Although the new candidate default route is pseudo-connected, it was not excluded in Step 1 of the algorithm. Because it's static, the router used it to create the gateway of last resort. (Notice the IP address of the gateway of last resort.)

Performing Basic RIP Configuration

Performing the basic configuration of RIP on a Cisco router is simple. The procedure is as follows:

1. Create an RIP routing process on the router using the **router rip** command in global configuration mode. This command transfers the command-line interface in RIP configuration mode.

NOTE: *Typically a Cisco router can run several processes of the same routing protocol. This is different in the case of RIP—there can be only one RIP process on a single router.*

---

2. Specify the interfaces that the RIP routing process will use to receive and send its routing updates using one or several of the **network** *<IP address>* commands. The <IP address> parameter must be a classful network address (such as 10.0.0.0, 172.16.0.0, and so on.). All operational interfaces whose IP addresses belong to the specified classful network addresses will be used by RIP to process routing updates. (The interfaces that are either down or administratively disabled won't be used by RIP.) RIP will advertise the network prefixes configured on the interfaces specified using the **network** *<IP address>* command.

NOTE: *The <IP address> parameter accepts any IP address, not just the classful ones. The router, however, will strip off any digits that reside behind the classful part of the address. For example, even if you enter "**network 172.20.10.0**", the router will keep only **network 172.20.0.0**, which will appear in its configuration.*

Step 2 requires some clarification. It is a common misbelief that the **network** command defines the network prefixes (or, using classful terminology, network and subnet addresses) that RIP should advertise. It's easy to prove that such a statement is wrong by entering a "network" command followed by a classful network address to which none of the router interface's IP addresses belong. The result is that the router won't advertise this classful network address.

The network statement indeed defines only the interfaces through which RIP receives and sends its routing updates. The network prefixes that RIP advertises are derived from the IP addresses of those interfaces.

NOTE: *One can argue that since the **network** command makes the router derive the network prefixes from only those interfaces whose IP addresses belong to the specified classful network address, it essentially does define the network prefixes that RIP advertises. I believe this is a dangerous concept to follow because it distorts the sequence and interdependency of the events: The command first defines the interfaces and only then are the network prefixes derived.*

---

4. Routing Information Protocol (RIP)

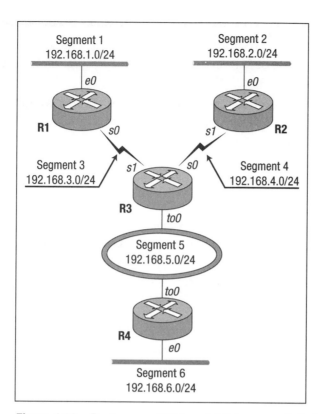

Figure 4.10   Routers use RIP to establish connectivity in the network.

Let's examine the network example shown in Figure 4.10. All routers use RIP to establish overall connectivity in the network.

The configurations of all four routers are shown in Listings 4.8 through 4.11.

Listing 4.8   Router R1's configuration.

```
interface Ethernet0
 ip address 192.168.1.1 255.255.255.0

interface Serial0
 ip address 192.168.3.2 255.255.255.0

router rip
 network 192.168.1.0
 network 192.168.3.0
```

Listing 4.9   Router R2's configuration.

```
interface Ethernet0
 ip address 192.168.2.1 255.255.255.0
```

```
interface Serial1
 ip address 192.168.4.2 255.255.255.0

router rip
 network 192.168.2.0
 network 192.168.4.0
```

Listing 4.10   Router R3's configuration.

```
interface Serial0
 ip address 192.168.4.1 255.255.255.0

interface Serial1
 ip address 192.168.3.1 255.255.255.0

interface TokenRing0
 ip address 192.168.5.1 255.255.255.0
 ring-speed 16

router rip
 network 192.168.3.0
 network 192.168.4.0
 network 192.168.5.0
```

Listing 4.11   Router R4's configuration.

```
interface Ethernet0
 ip address 192.168.6.1 255.255.255.0

interface TokenRing0
 ip address 192.168.5.2 255.255.255.0
 ring-speed 16

router rip
 network 192.168.5.0
 network 192.168.6.0
 network 172.20.0.0
```

Let's examine the routing table of router R1, for example. To do that, we have to use the **show ip route** command, the output of which is shown in Listing 4.12.

Listing 4.12   The routing table of router R1.

```
R1#show ip route
...
R   192.168.4.0/24 [120/1] via 192.168.3.1, 00:00:05, Serial0
R   192.168.5.0/24 [120/1] via 192.168.3.1, 00:00:06, Serial0
R   192.168.6.0/24 [120/2] via 192.168.3.1, 00:00:06, Serial0
```

```
C   192.168.1.0/24 is directly connected, Ethernet0
R   192.168.2.0/24 [120/2] via 192.168.3.1, 00:00:06, Serial0
C   192.168.3.0/24 is directly connected, Serial0
```

Pay attention to the routes labeled with the letter R: These are created by RIP. Notice that, although the RIP part of router R4's configuration contains the statement **network 172.20.0.0** (the shaded line in Listing 4.11), the network prefix 172.20.0.0/16 does not appear in router R1's routing table. The reason is that none of router R4's interfaces has an IP address that belongs to 172.20.0.0/16.

Understanding How RIP Processes Routing Updates

Let's now conduct an experiment. Let's disconnect router R4 from the network and see what will happen to the RIP process at router R3. To do that, we'll use the **debug ip rip** command. Listing 4.13 shows a sample output of this command entered on router R3 before router R4 was disconnected.

Listing 4.13   A sample output of the debug ip rip command on router R3.

```
R3#debug ip rip
RIP protocol debugging is on
R3#
19:16:41: RIP: sending v1 update to 255.255.255.255 via
    Serial0 (192.168.4.1)
19:16:41:    network 192.168.5.0, metric 1
19:16:41:    network 192.168.6.0, metric 2
19:16:41:    network 192.168.1.0, metric 2
19:16:41:    network 192.168.3.0, metric 1
19:16:41: RIP: sending v1 update to 255.255.255.255 via
    Serial1 (192.168.3.1)
19:16:41:    network 192.168.4.0, metric 1
19:16:41:    network 192.168.5.0, metric 1
19:16:41:    network 192.168.6.0, metric 2
19:16:41:    network 192.168.2.0, metric 2
19:16:42: RIP: sending v1 update to 255.255.255.255 via
    TokenRing0 (192.168.5.1)
19:16:42:    network 192.168.4.0, metric 1
19:16:42:    network 192.168.1.0, metric 2
19:16:42:    network 192.168.2.0, metric 2
19:16:42:    network 192.168.3.0, metric 1
19:16:54: RIP: received v1 update from 192.168.4.2 on Serial0
19:16:54:    192.168.2.0 in 1 hops
19:17:03: RIP: received v1 update from 192.168.5.2 on TokenRing0
19:17:03:    192.168.6.0 in 1 hops
```

```
19:17:04: RIP: received v1 update from 192.168.3.2 on Serial1
19:17:04:    192.168.1.0 in 1 hops
```

Each line of the output in this example starts with a timestamp, which records the actual time when the event denoted by the line happened. The presence and format of the timestamps is dependent upon the statement **service timestamps debug {datetime|uptime}** in the router's configuration (in global configuration mode). If no such statement appears, then the router does not produce timestamps; otherwise, depending whether the last parameter is **datetime** or **uptime**, the router will put either the time of day or the time elapsed since it was powered up or reloaded.

NOTE: *The **service timestamps** command has more options. Please see the Cisco documentation.*

Depending on the version of IOS, the **service timestamps debug** command may or may not be present in the router configuration by default. In the case of the output presented in the listings in this section, the **service timestamps debug datetime** command was explicitly entered on router R3.

The rest of the output of the **debug ip rip** command is pretty much self-explanatory. The command displays the contents of the received and sent routing updates.

Notice in Listing 4.13 that the shaded lines show that a routing update was received from a router with the IP address of 192.168.5.2. This IP address is assigned on TokenRing0 of router R4. This is the last update router R3 receives from router R4; right after the routing update was received by router R3, router R4 was disconnected from segment 5.

Listing 4.14 shows the output of the **debug ip rip** command after router R4 was disconnected.

Listing 4.14   The output of the debug ip rip command shows what happens after router R4 becomes unavailable.

```
19:17:09: RIP: sending v1 update to 255.255.255.255 via Serial0
(192.168.4.1)
19:17:09:    network 192.168.5.0, metric 1
19:17:09:    network 192.168.6.0, metric 2
19:17:09:    network 192.168.1.0, metric 2
19:17:09:    network 192.168.3.0, metric 1
19:17:09: RIP: sending v1 update to 255.255.255.255 via Serial1
(192.168.3.1)
19:17:09:    network 192.168.4.0, metric 1
19:17:09:    network 192.168.5.0, metric 1
19:17:09:    network 192.168.6.0, metric 2
```

```
19:17:09:    network 192.168.2.0, metric 2
19:17:09: RIP: sending v1 update to 255.255.255.255 via TokenRing0
(192.168.5.1)
19:17:09:    network 192.168.4.0, metric 1
19:17:09:    network 192.168.1.0, metric 2
19:17:09:    network 192.168.2.0, metric 2
19:17:09:    network 192.168.3.0, metric 1
19:17:22: RIP: received v1 update from 192.168.4.2 on Serial0
19:17:22:    192.168.2.0 in 1 hops
19:17:33: RIP: received v1 update from 192.168.3.2 on Serial1
19:17:33:    192.168.1.0 in 1 hops
19:17:36: RIP: sending v1 update to 255.255.255.255 via Serial0
(192.168.4.1)
...
19:19:55: RIP: sending v1 update to 255.255.255.255 via Serial0
(192.168.4.1)
19:19:56:    network 192.168.5.0, metric 1
19:19:56:    network 192.168.6.0, metric 2
19:19:56:    network 192.168.1.0, metric 2
19:19:56:    network 192.168.3.0, metric 1
19:19:56: RIP: sending v1 update to 255.255.255.255 via Serial1
(192.168.3.1)
19:19:56:    network 192.168.4.0, metric 1
19:19:56:    network 192.168.5.0, metric 1
19:19:56:    network 192.168.6.0, metric 2
19:19:56:    network 192.168.2.0, metric 2
19:19:56: RIP: sending v1 update to 255.255.255.255 via TokenRing0
(192.168.5.1)
19:19:56:    network 192.168.4.0, metric 1
19:19:56:    network 192.168.1.0, metric 2
19:19:56:    network 192.168.2.0, metric 2
19:19:56:    network 192.168.3.0, metric 1
19:20:09: RIP: received v1 update from 192.168.4.2 on Serial0
19:20:09:    192.168.2.0 in 1 hops
19:20:19: RIP: received v1 update from 192.168.3.2 on Serial1
19:20:19:    192.168.1.0 in 1 hops
!  The timeout timer for 192.168.6.0 has expired and router R3 started
!  advertising the network prefix with the metric of 16 (poisoned-reverse
!  updates).
19:20:23: RIP: sending v1 update to 255.255.255.255 via Serial0
(192.168.4.1)
19:20:23:    network 192.168.5.0, metric 1
19:20:23:    network 192.168.6.0, metric 16
19:20:23:    network 192.168.1.0, metric 2
19:20:23:    network 192.168.3.0, metric 1
19:20:23: RIP: sending v1 update to 255.255.255.255 via Serial1
```

```
(192.168.3.1)
19:20:23:    network 192.168.4.0, metric 1
19:20:23:    network 192.168.5.0, metric 1
19:20:23:    network 192.168.6.0, metric 16
19:20:23:    network 192.168.2.0, metric 2
19:20:24: RIP: sending v1 update to 255.255.255.255 via TokenRing0
(192.168.5.1)
19:20:24:    network 192.168.4.0, metric 1
19:20:24:    network 192.168.6.0, metric 16
19:20:24:    network 192.168.1.0, metric 2
19:20:24:    network 192.168.2.0, metric 2
19:20:24:    network 192.168.3.0, metric 1
!  Routers R1 and R2 picked up router R3's poisoned-reverse updates and
!  placed corresponding routes into holddown. The also started advertising
!  192.168.6.0 with the metric of 16.
19:20:24: RIP: received v1 update from 192.168.4.2 on Serial0
19:20:24:    192.168.2.0 in 1 hops
19:20:24:    192.168.6.0 in 16 hops (inaccessible)
19:20:24: RIP: received v1 update from 192.168.3.2 on Serial1
19:20:24:    192.168.6.0 in 16 hops (inaccessible)
19:20:24:    192.168.1.0 in 1 hops
19:20:39: RIP: received v1 update from 192.168.4.2 on Serial0
19:20:39:    192.168.2.0 in 1 hops
19:20:39:    192.168.6.0 in 16 hops (inaccessible)
19:20:46: RIP: received v1 update from 192.168.3.2 on Serial1
19:20:46:    192.168.6.0 in 16 hops (inaccessible)
19:20:46:    192.168.1.0 in 1 hops
19:20:49: RIP: sending v1 update to 255.255.255.255 via Serial0
(192.168.4.1)
19:20:49:    network 192.168.5.0, metric 1
19:20:49:    network 192.168.6.0, metric 16
19:20:49:    network 192.168.1.0, metric 2
19:20:49:    network 192.168.3.0, metric 1
19:20:49: RIP: sending v1 update to 255.255.255.255 via Serial1
(192.168.3.1)
19:20:49:    network 192.168.4.0, metric 1
19:20:49:    network 192.168.5.0, metric 1
19:20:49:    network 192.168.6.0, metric 16
19:20:49:    network 192.168.2.0, metric 2
19:20:49: RIP: sending v1 update to 255.255.255.255 via TokenRing0
(192.168.5.1)
19:20:49:    network 192.168.4.0, metric 1
19:20:49:    network 192.168.6.0, metric 16
19:20:49:    network 192.168.1.0, metric 2
19:20:49:    network 192.168.2.0, metric 2
19:20:49:    network 192.168.3.0, metric 1
```

```
19:21:06: RIP: received v1 update from 192.168.4.2 on Serial0
19:21:06:    192.168.2.0 in 1 hops
19:21:06:    192.168.6.0 in 16 hops (inaccessible)
19:21:14: RIP: received v1 update from 192.168.3.2 on Serial1
19:21:14:    192.168.6.0 in 16 hops (inaccessible)
19:21:14:    192.168.1.0 in 1 hops
!  Router R4 is connected back to the network; it begins advertising
!  192.168.6.0 again
19:21:15: RIP: received v1 update from 192.168.5.2 on TokenRing0
19:21:15:    192.168.6.0 in 1 hops
!  Router R3 did not place route for 192.168.6.0 in holddown. So it
!  changes the metric to the value carried in router R4's updates.
19:21:18: RIP: sending v1 update to 255.255.255.255 via Serial0
(192.168.4.1)
19:21:18:    network 192.168.5.0, metric 1
19:21:18:    network 192.168.1.0, metric 2
19:21:18:    network 192.168.3.0, metric 1
19:21:18: RIP: sending v1 update to 255.255.255.255 via Serial1
(192.168.3.1)
19:21:18:    network 192.168.4.0, metric 1
19:21:18:    network 192.168.5.0, metric 1
19:21:18:    network 192.168.2.0, metric 2
19:21:18: RIP: sending v1 update to 255.255.255.255 via TokenRing0
(192.168.5.1)
9:21:18:    network 192.168.4.0, metric 1
9:21:18:    network 192.168.1.0, metric 2
9:21:18:    network 192.168.2.0, metric 2
9:21:18:    network 192.168.3.0, metric 1
!  Contrary to the behavior of router R3, routers R1 and R2 did place
!  their routes for 192.168.6.0 in holddown; thus they keep advertising
!  192.168.6.0 with the metric of 16 until the holddown timer expires.
9:21:35: RIP: received v1 update from 192.168.4.2 on Serial0
9:21:35:    192.168.2.0 in 1 hops
9:21:35:    192.168.6.0 in 16 hops (inaccessible)
9:21:40: RIP: received v1 update from 192.168.3.2 on Serial1
9:21:40:    192.168.6.0 in 16 hops (inaccessible)
9:21:40:    192.168.1.0 in 1 hops
9:21:43: RIP: received v1 update from 192.168.5.2 on TokenRing0
9:21:43:    192.168.6.0 in 1 hops
```

Because Listing 4.14 is quite long, I put comments inside of it. The comments, in shaded lines and beginning with an exclamation point, explain what is happening from the perspective of router R3.

If we examined the routing table of router R3 right after the timeout timer had expired for the route for network prefix 192.168.6.0/24, it would look as shown in

Listing 4.15. The line that denotes the route is shaded. Notice the words "is possibly down;" they indicate that a garbage-collection timer has been started for the route.

Listing 4.15   The routing table of router R3 shows that the garbage-collection timer has been started for the route for network prefix 192.168.6.0/24.

```
R3#show ip route
...
C   192.168.4.0/24 is directly connected, Serial0
C   192.168.5.0/24 is directly connected, TokenRing0
R   192.168.6.0/24 is possibly down, routing via 192.168.5.2, TokenRing0
R   192.168.1.0/24 [120/1] via 192.168.3.2, 00:00:25, Serial1
R   192.168.2.0/24 [120/1] via 192.168.4.2, 00:00:12, Serial0
C   192.168.3.0/24 is directly connected, Serial1
```

Although router R3 believes the route for 192.168.6.0/24 is possibly down, it is preserved in the routing table. The routing algorithm doesn't check metrics and other attributes (mostly specific to the source of routing information) when making routing decisions. Therefore, the route is still used to forward the datagrams destined for 192.168.6.0/24.

Understanding the Relation between the Routing Table Contents and RIP Routing Updates

As we learned in the "In Depth" section, RIP won't advertise network prefixes for which it failed to install routes into the routing table. How can the RIP process on a router fail to install a route for a network prefix that was learned from another router? The only instance in which RIP would fail to install a route for such a network prefix is when another route created by a source of routing information whose administrative distance is lower than that of RIP (RIP's administrative distance is 120) has already installed a route for the network prefix. For example, it could be a static route with the default administrative distance (1).

To understand the situation better, we'll use the network scheme from the previous section (Figure 4.10). Listing 4.16 shows the contents of the regular updates router R3 sends over segment 5, which right now contains network prefix 192.168.1.0/24.

Listing 4.16   The content of the routing update that router R3 sends over segment 5.

```
R3#debug ip rip
RIP protocol debugging is on
R3#
...
RIP: sending v1 update to 255.255.255.255 via TokenRing0 (192.168.5.1)
```

4. Routing Information Protocol (RIP)

```
network 192.168.4.0, metric 1
network 192.168.1.0, metric 2
network 192.168.2.0, metric 2
network 192.168.3.0, metric 1
```

If we enter a static route for network prefix 192.168.1.0/24 on router R3 using the following command, the content of the routing updates sent by router R3 over segment 5 changes, as shown in Listing 4.17:

```
ip route 192.168.1.0 255.255.255.0 192.168.3.2
ip route 192.168.2.0 255.255.255.0 192.168.4.2
```

Listing 4.17   The content of the routing updates that router R3 sends over segment 5 no longer contains network prefix 192.168.1.0/24.

```
R3#debug ip rip
RIP protocol debugging is on
R3#
...
RIP: sending v1 update to 255.255.255.255 via TokenRing0 (192.168.5.1)
    network 192.168.4.0, metric 1
    network 192.168.3.0, metric 1
```

The reason for this change becomes apparent if we look at the routing table of router R3, shown in Listing 4.18. The shaded lines show the static routes, which replaced the RIP routes for network prefixes 192.168.1.0/24 and 192.168.2.0/24. This means that RIP can no longer advertise these network prefixes because it can't install routes for them. The ability to install a route for a network prefix is, as we know, a necessary condition for a distance-vector protocol to be able to advertise this network prefix.

Listing 4.18   The routing table of router R3.

```
R3#show ip route
...
C  192.168.4.0/24 is directly connected, Serial0
C  192.168.5.0/24 is directly connected, TokenRing0
R  192.168.6.0/24 [120/1] via 192.168.5.2, 00:00:07, TokenRing0
S  192.168.1.0/24 [1/0] via 192.168.3.2
S  192.168.2.0/24 [1/0] via 192.168.4.2
C  192.168.3.0/24 is directly connected, Serial1
```

Understanding RIP Auto-Summarization

RIP, being a classful routing protocol, summarizes subnets and individual host addresses in the routing updates that cross the corresponding classful network boundary. In other words, all individual network prefixes, such as subnets and individual host addresses, are replaced by a single network prefix equal to the classful network address. An example of this situation is shown in Figure 4.11.

Router R can exchange routing updates that carry Serial 1 and Serial 2 subnets and individual host addresses with its neighbors as long as the updates are communicated via its interfaces. If an update must be sent through interface Serial 0, all individual subnets and host routes that belong to classful network 10.0.0.0/8 are replaced with a single network prefix: 10.0.0.0/8 itself.

To see what happens in real life, let's modify the network we used in the previous section (as shown in Figure 4.12).

Only the configurations of routers R1, R2, and R3 have changed. The new configurations are shown in Listings 4.19 through 4.21.

Listing 4.19   Router R1's configuration.

```
interface Ethernet0
  ip address 10.0.1.1 255.255.255.0

interface Serial0
  ip address 10.0.3.2 255.255.255.0

router rip
  network 10.0.0.0
```

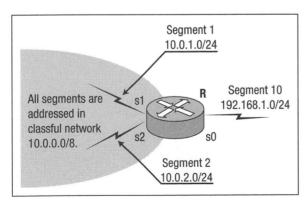

Figure 4.11   Router R performs auto summarization of subnets and individual host routes in the routing updates sent through interface Serial0.

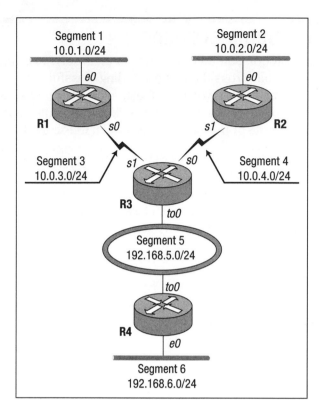

Figure 4.12   Routers R1, R2, and R3 now have interfaces whose IP addresses belong to classful network address 10.0.0.0/8.

Listing 4.20   Router R2's configuration.

```
interface Ethernet0
 ip address 10.0.2.1 255.255.255.0

interface Serial1
 ip address 10.0.4.2 255.255.255.0

router rip
 network 10.0.0.0
```

Listing 4.21   Router R3's configuration.

```
interface Serial0
 ip address 10.0.4.1 255.255.255.0

interface Serial1
 ip address 10.0.3.1 255.255.255.0
```

```
interface TokenRing0
 ip address 192.168.5.1 255.255.255.0
 ring-speed 16

router rip
 network 10.0.0.0
 network 192.168.5.0
```

If we examine the routing table of router R4 now, we'll notice that it became much smaller, as Listing 4.22 reveals.

Listing 4.22   The routing table of router R1 still contains routes for all individual network prefixes.

```
R1#show ip route
...
R   192.168.5.0/24 [120/1] via 10.0.3.1, 00:00:18, Serial0
    10.0.0.0/24 is subnetted, 4 subnets
R      10.0.2.0 [120/2] via 10.0.3.1, 00:00:19, Serial0
C      10.0.3.0 is directly connected, Serial0
C      10.0.1.0 is directly connected, Ethernet0
R      10.0.4.0 [120/1] via 10.0.3.1, 00:00:19, Serial0
R   192.168.6.0/24 [120/2] via 10.0.3.1, 00:00:19, Serial0
```

If we examine the routing table of router R4, however, we'll notice that it became much smaller:

```
R4#show ip route
...
C   192.168.5.0/24 is directly connected, TokenRing0
R   10.0.0.0/8 [120/1] via 192.168.5.1, 00:00:29, TokenRing0
C   192.168.6.0/24 is directly connected, Ethernet0
```

All individual network prefixes that still have separate routes in router R1's routing table are replaced with a single summary route for classful network address 10.0.0.0/8.

Using Individual Host Addresses

As mentioned in the "In Depth" section, RIP can advertise individual host addresses (or network prefixes whose length is /32) in the routing updates. Like regular network prefixes, individual host addresses cannot be advertised outside of the corresponding classful network address. For example, individual host address 10.1.0.1/32 can be advertised by RIP over only those segments whose network prefixes belong to 10.0.0.0/8; beyond 10.0.0.0/8, only 10.0.0.0/8 itself can be advertised by RIP.

If the condition of contiguous address space is met, the individual host addresses are configured using the following procedure:

1. Define a loopback interface using the command **interface loopback** *<number>* in global configuration mode.

2. Assign an IP address to the loopback interface using the command **ip address** *<IP address>* 255.255.255.255. The *<IP address>* parameter must belong to the classful network addresses defined under the **router rip** configuration using the command **network** *<classful IP address>*.

For example, let's add loopback addresses on routers R1, R2, and R3 from Figure 4.12 and assign them IP addresses of 10.0.0.1/32, 10.0.0.2/32, and 10.0.0.3/32, respectively. The new configurations of routers R1 through R3 are shown in Listings 4.23 through 4.25. (The lines that contain the loopback interface configuration are italicized.)

Listing 4.23   Router R1's configuration.

```
interface Loopback0
 ip address 10.0.0.1 255.255.255.255

interface Ethernet0
 ip address 10.0.1.1 255.255.255.0

interface Serial0
 ip address 10.0.3.2 255.255.255.0

router rip
 network 10.0.0.0
```

Listing 4.24   Router R2's configuration.

```
interface Loopback0
 ip address 10.0.0.2 255.255.255.255

interface Ethernet0
 ip address 10.0.2.1 255.255.255.0

interface Serial1
 ip address 10.0.4.2 255.255.255.0

router rip
 network 10.0.0.0
```

Listing 4.25 Router R'3 configuration.

```
interface Loopback0
 ip address 10.0.0.3 255.255.255.255

interface Serial0
 ip address 10.0.4.1 255.255.255.0

interface Serial1
 ip address 10.0.3.1 255.255.255.0

interface TokenRing0
 ip address 192.168.5.1 255.255.255.0
 ring-speed 16

router rip
 network 10.0.0.0
 network 192.168.5.0
```

Now we should be able to see these addresses as individual host addresses in the router's routing table. For example, let's examine the routing table of router R3, shown in Listing 4.26.

Listing 4.26 The routing table of router R3 indicates the presence of routes for individual host addresses configured on the loopback interfaces of routers R1, R2, and R3.

```
R3#show ip route
...
C  192.168.5.0/24 is directly connected, TokenRing0
   10.0.0.0/8 is variably subnetted, 7 subnets, 2 masks
R     10.0.0.2/32 [120/1] via 10.0.4.2, 00:00:04, Serial0
R     10.0.2.0/24 [120/1] via 10.0.4.2, 00:00:04, Serial0
C     10.0.0.3/32 is directly connected, Loopback0
C     10.0.3.0/24 is directly connected, Serial1
R     10.0.0.1/32 [120/1] via 10.0.3.2, 00:00:20, Serial1
R     10.0.1.0/24 [120/1] via 10.0.3.2, 00:00:20, Serial1
C     10.0.4.0/24 is directly connected, Serial0
R  192.168.6.0/24 [120/1] via 192.168.5.2, 00:00:23, TokenRing0
```

The shaded lines in Listing 4.26 show the routes for the created individual host addresses. The first and third shaded lines show routing table entries installed by RIP. The second shaded line shows the entry for the local Loopback0 interface and individual host address 10.0.0.3/32, which was assigned on the interface.

If we display the routing table of router R4, we won't see the routes for the individual host addresses, as we should expect. Here is what the routing table of router R4 looks like:

```
R4#show ip route
...
C  192.168.5.0/24 is directly connected, TokenRing0
R  10.0.0.0/8 [120/1] via 192.168.5.1, 00:00:01, TokenRing0
C  192.168.6.0/24 is directly connected, Ethernet0
```

Configuring RIP to Originate a Default Route

To make a router advertise the default address (0.0.0.0/0), the **default-information originate** command must be entered under the **router rip** configuration.

NOTE: *When a router advertises network prefix 0.0.0.0/0, it is sometimes said to "originate a default route."*

For example, let's assume that router R4 in Figure 4.12 is also connected to the Internet. Let's also assume that we want to allow every host at every location in the network to access the Internet, which can be accomplished by making router R4 advertise the default route.

Listing 4.27 shows the changed configuration of router R4.

Listing 4.27   Router R4's configuration.
```
interface Ethernet0
 ip address 192.168.6.1 255.255.255.0

interface TokenRing0
 ip address 192.168.5.2 255.255.255.0
 ring-speed 16

router rip
 network 192.168.5.0
 network 192.168.6.0
 default-information originate
```

Let's have a look at the routing table of router R3, shown in Listing 4.28.

Listing 4.28   The routing table of router R3.
```
R3#show ip route
...
```

```
Gateway of last resort is 192.168.5.2 to network 0.0.0.0

C   192.168.5.0/24 is directly connected, TokenRing0
    10.0.0.0/8 is variably subnetted, 7 subnets, 2 masks
R      10.0.0.2/32 [120/1] via 10.0.4.2, 00:00:23, Serial0
R      10.0.2.0/24 [120/1] via 10.0.4.2, 00:00:23, Serial0
C      10.0.0.3/32 is directly connected, Loopback0
C      10.0.3.0/24 is directly connected, Serial1
R      10.0.0.1/32 [120/1] via 10.0.3.2, 00:00:11, Serial1
R      10.0.1.0/24 [120/1] via 10.0.3.2, 00:00:11, Serial1
C      10.0.4.0/24 is directly connected, Serial0
R   192.168.6.0/24 [120/1] via 192.168.5.2, 00:00:24, TokenRing0
R*  0.0.0.0/0 [120/1] via 192.168.5.2, 00:00:24, TokenRing0
```

Notice that the routing table of router R3 now contains a route for network prefix 0.0.0.0/0. In addition to the letter *R* (indicating that the route was learned via RIP) is an asterisk, which suggests that the route is a candidate default route. Notice also that the "gateway of last resort" preceding the routing table entries now points to the IP address of router R4's interface TokenRing0.

NOTE: *Right now, the configuration of router R4 does not provide any routing to the Internet. Although router R3 and the other routers in the network will now forward all traffic for which they don't have more-explicit routes to router R4, router R4 won't know what to do with it. In reality, router R4 would be connected to the Internet with one of its interfaces. If that's router R4's only connection to the Internet, then a single static route for the default address would suffice. For example, **ip route 0.0.0.0 0.0.0.0 Serial1**.*

Understanding How RIP Handles Secondary IP Addresses

The Cisco version of RIP supports secondary IP addresses in the following manner. If an interface on a router is configured with secondary IP addresses and the classful network addresses to which the secondary IP addresses belong appear in the **network** statements under the **router rip** configuration, the router will advertise those addresses. But, in addition to that, the router may send multiple routing updates at a time through the interface with secondary IP addresses such that:

• The number of routing updates sent at a time is equal to the number of classful network addresses to which the secondary IP addresses belong (counting only those classful network addresses that also appear in the **network** statements under the **router rip** configuration).

- Each routing update is sent in a datagram with the source IP address equal to the first (in the order of the appearance in the router's configuration) IP address of each classful network address. The first routing update is always sent with the interface's primary IP address as the source IP address. If one or more secondary IP addresses belong to the same classful network address to which the primary IP address belongs, none of them is used as the source IP address of a routing update.

- Each routing update contains the known (learned and originated) subnet and host addresses of the classful network to which the source IP address of the routing update belongs. In addition to that, the routing update contains the classful network addresses, which are 1) learned from other routers and 2) appear in the **network** statements under the **router rip** configuration. The latter, however, are placed into the routing update only if the IP addresses of one or more of the router's interfaces belong to these classful network addresses.

- The routing update does not contain any of the subnets to which the secondary IP addresses of the interface belong. The routing update also does not contain any known classful network addresses if the IP addresses that belong to them appear as the secondary or primary IP addresses of only the interface through which the routing update is sent.

This surely sounds a bit too convoluted, but there is a justification for why it happens this way.

To preserve the contiguousness of each of the classful networks, the RIP process generates a separate routing update for every classful network to which the secondary IP addresses of the interface belong. It generates only a single routing update per each classful network address (as opposed to every subnet of each classful network address) to reduce the amount of broadcast traffic. A single routing update per a classful network address is sufficient to pass the subnetting information in the routing updates whose source IP address belongs to this classful network address.

To understand better what routing updates RIP generates on interfaces with secondary IP addresses and how it helps preserve the integrity of classful network addresses, let's consider the network shown in Figure 4.13.

Classful networks 172.16.0.0/16 and 172.20.0.0/16 span both sides of segment 1, which is itself addressed with network prefix 192.168.1.0/24. In other words, the two classful networks become separated, which begets discontiguous subnets that are unsupported by classful routing protocols. The cure is foul secondary IP addresses.

To see the full picture of how RIP handles secondary IP addresses, we'll configure more secondary IP addresses on the Ethernet0 interfaces of routers R2 and R3 than

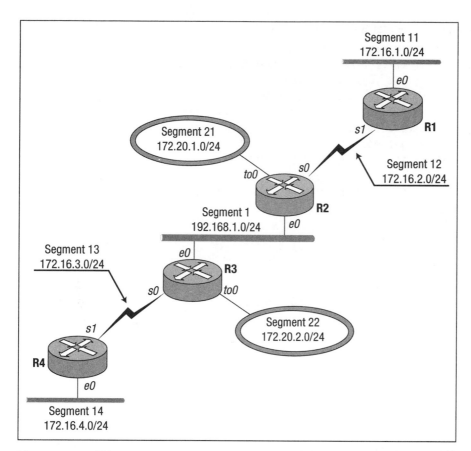

Figure 4.13 This network is impossible to implement using RIP unless secondary IP addresses are configured on the routers' interfaces that are connected to segment 1.

necessary. We'll create several subnets of 172.16.0.0/16, several IP addresses of 172.20.100.0/24, and several subnets of classful network 172.30.0.0/16 (which is present nowhere else). Listings 4.29 through 4.32 show the configurations of routers R1 through R4, respectively.

Listing 4.29 Router R1's configuration.

```
interface Ethernet0
 ip address 172.16.1.1 255.255.255.0

interface Serial1
 ip address 172.16.2.2 255.255.255.0

router rip
 network 172.16.0.0
```

Listing 4.30   Router R2's configuration.

```
interface Ethernet0
 ip address 172.16.120.2 255.255.255.0 secondary
 ip address 172.16.110.2 255.255.255.0 secondary
 ip address 172.16.100.2 255.255.255.0 secondary
 ip address 172.20.100.6 255.255.255.0 secondary
 ip address 172.20.100.4 255.255.255.0 secondary
 ip address 172.20.100.2 255.255.255.0 secondary
 ip address 172.30.150.6 255.255.255.0 secondary
 ip address 172.30.200.4 255.255.255.0 secondary
 ip address 172.30.100.2 255.255.255.0 secondary
 ip address 192.168.1.2 255.255.255.0

interface Serial0
 ip address 172.16.2.1 255.255.255.0

interface TokenRing0
 ip address 172.20.1.1 255.255.255.0
 ring-speed 16

router rip
 network 172.16.0.0
 network 172.20.0.0
 network 172.30.0.0
 network 192.168.1.0
```

Listing 4.31   Router R3's configuration.

```
interface Ethernet0
 ip address 172.16.120.1 255.255.255.0 secondary
 ip address 172.16.110.1 255.255.255.0 secondary
 ip address 172.16.100.1 255.255.255.0 secondary
 ip address 172.20.100.3 255.255.255.0 secondary
 ip address 172.20.100.5 255.255.255.0 secondary
 ip address 172.20.100.1 255.255.255.0 secondary
 ip address 172.30.150.5 255.255.255.0 secondary
 ip address 172.30.200.3 255.255.255.0 secondary
 ip address 172.30.100.1 255.255.255.0 secondary
 ip address 192.168.1.1 255.255.255.0

interface Serial0
 ip address 172.16.3.1 255.255.255.0

interface TokenRing0
 ip address 172.20.2.1 255.255.255.0
 ring-speed 16
```

```
router rip
 network 172.16.0.0
 network 172.20.0.0
 network 172.30.0.0
 network 192.168.1.0
```

Listing 4.32   Router R4's configuration.

```
interface Loopback0
 ip address 10.0.1.1 255.255.255.0

interface Ethernet0
 ip address 172.16.4.1 255.255.255.0

interface Serial1
 ip address 172.16.3.2 255.255.255.0

router rip
 network 172.16.0.0
 network 10.0.0.0
```

The alternating shaded and italicized groups of lines in the configurations of routers R2 and R3 (Listings 4.30 and 4.31) show the secondary IP addresses. Each group (either shaded or italicized) shows the IP addresses belonging to the same classful network address.

Notice that router R4's configuration (Listing 4.32) also contains the Loopback0 interface, which is assigned the IP address of 10.0.1.1/24. Obviously, router R4 instead will advertise classful network address 10.0.0.0/8 to the other routers, as no router R4's interface but interface Loopback0 has an IP addresses that belongs to 10.0.0.0/8.

We have configured the routers, so it's time to check if the configurations do the job. Let's examine the routing table of router R1, shown in Listing 4.33.

Listing 4.33   The routing table of router R1.

```
R1#show ip route
...
   172.16.0.0/24 is subnetted, 7 subnets
R    172.16.4.0 [120/3] via 172.16.2.1, 00:00:18, Serial1
C    172.16.1.0 is directly connected, Ethernet0
C    172.16.2.0 is directly connected, Serial1
R    172.16.3.0 [120/2] via 172.16.2.1, 00:00:18, Serial1
R    172.16.120.0 [120/1] via 172.16.2.1, 00:00:18, Serial1
R    172.16.110.0 [120/1] via 172.16.2.1, 00:00:18, Serial1
R    172.16.100.0 [120/1] via 172.16.2.1, 00:00:18, Serial1
```

```
R   172.20.0.0/16 [120/1] via 172.16.2.1, 00:00:18, Serial1
R   172.30.0.0/16 [120/1] via 172.16.2.1, 00:00:18, Serial1
R   10.0.0.0/8 [120/3] via 172.16.2.1, 00:00:18, Serial1
R   192.168.1.0/24 [120/1] via 172.16.2.1, 00:00:18, Serial1
```

The routes that we are interested in seeing are shown as shaded lines; without the secondary IP addresses, we won't be able to see the presence of these routes in the routing table of router R1. The italicized lines show the routes for the subnets of classful network address 172.16.0.0/16 that we configured on the Ethernet0 interfaces of routers R2 and R3. Also notice the presence of a route for network 10.0.0.0/8. We would see this route even if routers R2 and R3 weren't configured with the secondary IP addresses.

Let's also examine the routing table of router R2, shown in Listing 4.34.

Listing 4.34   The routing table of router R2.

```
R2#show ip route
...
    172.16.0.0/24 is subnetted, 7 subnets
R      172.16.4.0 [120/2] via 172.16.120.1, 00:00:15, Ethernet0
R      172.16.1.0 [120/1] via 172.16.2.2, 00:00:27, Serial0
C      172.16.2.0 is directly connected, Serial0
R      172.16.3.0 [120/1] via 172.16.120.1, 00:00:15, Ethernet0
C      172.16.120.0 is directly connected, Ethernet0
C      172.16.110.0 is directly connected, Ethernet0
C      172.16.100.0 is directly connected, Ethernet0
    172.20.0.0/24 is subnetted, 3 subnets
C      172.20.1.0 is directly connected, TokenRing0
R      172.20.2.0 [120/1] via 172.20.100.3, 00:00:15, Ethernet0
C      172.20.100.0 is directly connected, Ethernet0
    172.30.0.0/24 is subnetted, 3 subnets
C      172.30.150.0 is directly connected, Ethernet0
C      172.30.200.0 is directly connected, Ethernet0
C      172.30.100.0 is directly connected, Ethernet0
R   10.0.0.0/8 [120/2] via 192.168.1.1, 00:00:17, Ethernet0
                [120/2] via 172.16.120.1, 00:00:17, Ethernet0
                [120/2] via 172.20.100.3, 00:00:16, Ethernet0
                [120/2] via 172.30.150.5, 00:00:16, Ethernet0
C   192.168.1.0/24 is directly connected, Ethernet0
```

Like router R1, router R2 has the exact routing information for the subnets of classful network addresses 172.16.0.0/16 and 172.20.0.0/16. Again, this wouldn't be possible without the secondary IP addresses. But, in addition to this, the routing table of router R2 exhibits false load balancing (the shaded lines). Why?

To understand why, let's see what routing updates router R2 receives on its Ethernet0 interface. The output of the **debug ip rip** command is shown in Listing 4.35.

Listing 4.35   The output of the debug ip rip command on router R2.

```
R2#debug ip rip
RIP protocol debugging is on
R2#
...
RIP: received v1 update from 192.168.1.1 on Ethernet0
    172.16.0.0 in 1 hops
    172.20.0.0 in 1 hops
    10.0.0.0 in 2 hops
RIP: received v1 update from 172.16.120.1 on Ethernet0
    172.16.4.0 in 2 hops
    172.16.3.0 in 1 hops
    172.20.0.0 in 1 hops
    10.0.0.0 in 2 hops
RIP: received v1 update from 172.20.100.3 on Ethernet0
    172.20.2.0 in 1 hops
    172.16.0.0 in 1 hops
    10.0.0.0 in 2 hops
RIP: received v1 update from 172.30.150.5 on Ethernet0
    172.16.0.0 in 1 hops
    172.20.0.0 in 1 hops
    10.0.0.0 in 2 hops
...
```

Router R3 advertises network prefix 10.0.0.0/8 in each routing update it sends over segment 1. Router R3 sends four routing updates at a time. (The number of routing updates is equal to the number of classful network addresses configured on its Ethernet0 interface.) To router R2, the advertised network prefix 10.0.0.0/8 contained in the routing updates appears to be available through four separate routers with the same metric. As we'll find out in the "Performing Equal-Cost Load Balancing with RIP" section later in this chapter, the load balancing condition is met. Thus, router R2 installs four routes for 10.0.0.0/8. Moreover, router R2 will try to perform load balancing using these parallel routes, assuming it sends datagrams to three different next-hop routers. In fact however, all of the datagrams will arrive at router R3.

Listing 4.35 also confirms the rules explained in the beginning of the section. The number of the routing updates sent at a time is equal to the number of classful network addresses. Each update is sent in a datagram whose source IP address is equal to the first (in order of appearance) IP address of the corresponding classful network. Each routing update contains the subnets of the classful network address to which the source IP address of the routing update belongs. Each routing update contains the known classful network addresses, except for 172.30.0.0/30, because it appears only on interface Ethernet0, the interface through which the routing update is sent.

Although secondary IP addresses do help resolve some issues inherent to the classful routing protocols, they are still not a very good idea. Mixing them with RIP doesn't make them any better. At least three relatively serious shortcomings of this mixture become apparent from our experimenting:

- In the presence of secondary IP addresses, RIP tends to generate superfluous routing updates. Routing updates are sent as broadcasts, which affects the CPU performance of every node on the segment.

- The logic behind how RIP chooses from which of the secondary IP addresses to originate routing updates is complex. Even worse, it's dependent upon the order in which the secondary IP addresses appear in the router's configuration. If any hosts listen to RIP routing updates and the IP addresses of those hosts belong to the secondary subnet or network addresses, they may not receive routing updates.

- The extraneous information (load balancing) in the routing tables can sometimes be generated by RIP when handling secondary IP addresses. This adds to the administrative overhead associated with maintaining the network.

The bottom line is try to avoid secondary IP addresses, with or without RIP.

Understanding How RIP Handles IP Unnumbered

RIP handles unnumbered interfaces pretty nicely, actually. RIP does not advertise the link that uses IP unnumbered for an obvious reason: The link is not assigned any network prefix. But RIP still forwards routing updates through the link. In other words, using IP unnumbered with RIP is in fact a good idea if conservation of IP address space is a consideration.

Figure 4.14 shows a modified network diagram in which a new branch is added to the existing network and the link between routers R4 and R5 is configured using IP unnumbered.

Listings 4.36 through 4.38 show the configurations of routers R4 through R6.

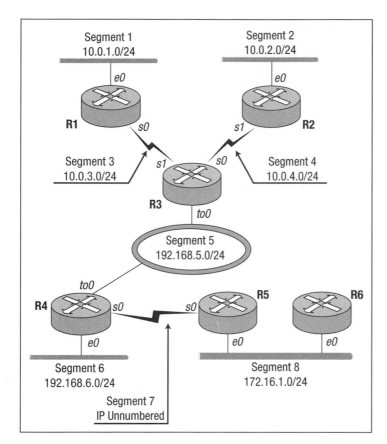

Figure 4.14 Interface Serial0 on router R5 is configured using IP unnumbered.

Listing 4.36 Router R4's configuration.

```
interface Ethernet0
 ip address 192.168.6.1 255.255.255.0

interface Serial0
 ip address 172.16.1.3 255.255.255.0

interface TokenRing0
 ip address 192.168.5.2 255.255.255.0
 ring-speed 16

router rip
 network 172.16.0.0
 network 192.168.5.0
 network 192.168.6.0
```

Listing 4.37   Router R5's configuration.

```
interface Ethernet0
 ip address 172.16.1.1 255.255.255.0

interface Serial0
 ip unnumbered Ethernet0

router rip
 network 172.16.0.0
```

Listing 4.38   Router R6's configuration.

```
interface Loopback0
 ip address 172.16.2.1 255.255.255.0

interface Ethernet0
 ip address 172.16.1.2 255.255.255.0

router rip
 network 172.16.0.0
```

Notice that only router R5 actually implements IP unnumbered. Interface Serial0 on this router is assigned the same IP address as interface Ethernet0. Router R4's interface Serial0 is assigned an available IP address from the network prefix 172.16.1.0/24. This IP address is 172.16.1.3. Router R6's interface Ethernet0 is assigned the IP address of 172.16.1.2, another available IP address from the same network prefix. Thus, segments 7 and 8 share the same network prefix.

Let's now examine the routing tables of routers R1, R4, R5, and R6. These are shown in Listings 4.39 through 4.42.

Listing 4.39   The routing table of router R1.

```
R1#show ip route
...
R   172.16.0.0/16 [120/2] via 10.0.3.1, 00:00:06, Serial0
R   192.168.5.0/24 [120/1] via 10.0.3.1, 00:00:07, Serial0
    10.0.0.0/24 is subnetted, 4 subnets
R     10.0.2.0 [120/2] via 10.0.3.1, 00:00:07, Serial0
C     10.0.3.0 is directly connected, Serial0
C     10.0.1.0 is directly connected, Ethernet0
R     10.0.4.0 [120/1] via 10.0.3.1, 00:00:07, Serial0
R   192.168.6.0/24 [120/2] via 10.0.3.1, 00:00:07, Serial0
```

Listing 4.40   The routing table of router R4.

```
R4#show ip route
...
```

```
    172.16.0.0/24 is subnetted, 2 subnets
C      172.16.1.0 is directly connected, Serial0
R      172.16.2.0 [120/2] via 172.16.1.1, 00:00:03, Serial0
C   192.168.5.0/24 is directly connected, TokenRing0
R   10.0.0.0/8 [120/1] via 192.168.5.1, 00:00:12, TokenRing0
C   192.168.6.0/24 is directly connected, Ethernet0
```

Listing 4.41   The routing table of router R5.

```
R5#show ip route
...
    172.16.0.0/24 is subnetted, 2 subnets
C      172.16.1.0 is directly connected, Ethernet0
R      172.16.2.0 [120/1] via 172.16.1.2, 00:00:09, Ethernet0
R   192.168.5.0/24 [120/1] via 172.16.1.3, 00:00:28, Serial0
R   10.0.0.0/8 [120/2] via 172.16.1.3, 00:00:28, Serial0
R   192.168.6.0/24 [120/1] via 172.16.1.3, 00:00:28, Serial0
```

Listing 4.42   The routing table of router R6.

```
R6#show ip route
...
    172.16.0.0/24 is subnetted, 2 subnets
C      172.16.1.0 is directly connected, Ethernet0
C      172.16.2.0 is directly connected, Loopback0
R   192.168.5.0/24 [120/2] via 172.16.1.1, 00:00:07, Ethernet0
R   10.0.0.0/8 [120/3] via 172.16.1.1, 00:00:07, Ethernet0
R   192.168.6.0/24 [120/2] via 172.16.1.1, 00:00:07, Ethernet0
```

The routing tables of all routers seem to be consistent. Router R1 has a summary route for classful network address 172.16.0.0/16; routers R4 through R6 have routes for all configured subnets of 172.16.0.0/16.

Let's now do some connectivity checking. Let's first ping addresses 172.16.1.1 through 172.16.1.3 and 172.16.2.1 from router R1 and then from router R4. Listings 4.43 and 4.44 show the results of the experiment.

Listing 4.43   The results of pinging addresses 172.16.1.1 through 172.16.1.3 and 172.16.2.1 from router R1.

```
R1#ping 172.16.1.1
Type escape sequence to abort.
Sending 5, 100-byte ICMP Echos to 172.16.1.1, timeout is 2 seconds:
!!!!!
Success rate is 100 percent (5/5), round-trip min/avg/max = 4/5/8 ms

R1#ping 172.16.1.2
```

```
Type escape sequence to abort.
Sending 5, 100-byte ICMP Echos to 172.16.1.2, timeout is 2 seconds:
!!!!!
Success rate is 100 percent (5/5), round-trip min/avg/max = 4/12/36 ms

R1#ping 172.16.1.3
Type escape sequence to abort.
Sending 5, 100-byte ICMP Echos to 172.16.1.3, timeout is 2 seconds:
!!!!!
Success rate is 100 percent (5/5), round-trip min/avg/max = 4/4/8 ms

R1#ping 172.16.2.1
Type escape sequence to abort.
Sending 5, 100-byte ICMP Echos to 172.16.2.1, timeout is 2 seconds:
!!!!!
Success rate is 100 percent (5/5), round-trip min/avg/max = 8/8/8 ms
```

Listing 4.44   The results of pinging addresses 172.16.1.1 through 172.16.1.3 and 172.16.2.1 from router R4.

```
R4#ping 172.16.1.1
Type escape sequence to abort.
Sending 5, 100-byte ICMP Echos to 172.16.1.1, timeout is 2 seconds:
.....
Success rate is 0 percent (0/5)

R4#ping 172.16.1.2
Type escape sequence to abort.
Sending 5, 100-byte ICMP Echos to 172.16.1.2, timeout is 2 seconds:
.....
Success rate is 0 percent (0/5)

R4#ping 172.16.1.3
Type escape sequence to abort.
Sending 5, 100-byte ICMP Echos to 172.16.1.3, timeout is 2 seconds:
.....
Success rate is 0 percent (0/5)

R4#ping 172.16.2.1
Type escape sequence to abort.
Sending 5, 100-byte ICMP Echos to 172.16.2.1, timeout is 2 seconds:
.....
Success rate is 0 percent (0/5)
```

Why is the pinging of the addresses so successful if carried out on router R1 but such a mess on router R4? How is it possible at all? After all, although pinging is done from router R1, the ping packets (Internet Control Message Protocol— ICMP— echoes and echo replies) still go through router R4.

The answer is pretty simple (as usual). As was explained earlier, because of the nature of IP unnumbered, routers R4, R5, and R6 appear to be connected to the same link layer medium, whereas in reality they are not. Therefore, when router R6 receives a datagram from router R4 with the source IP address equal to the IP address of router R4's interface Serial0, router R6 tries to reply by first issuing an Address Resolution Protocol (ARP) request for this IP address. Router R5 does not pass the ARP request to router R4: ARP PDUs cannot traverse routers. At the same time, router R5 does not perform proxy ARP in the case of IP unnumbered. Therefore, router R6's ARP request times out. Router R6 does not have an IP address to media access control (MAC) address mapping, so it won't issue a reply. This explains why router R4 does not receive replies for its pings for the two addresses of router R6.

Router R5 appears to be somewhat confused. On one hand, it is directly connected to router R4 via its Serial0 interface, and thus it could reply upon receipt of the ping packets from router R4. On the other hand, the pinged (destination) IP address does not belong to interface Serial0 but rather to interface Ethernet0. The source IP address belongs to the network prefix to which the destination IP address belongs. Therefore, just like router R6, router R5 tries first to resolve the mapping between the source address in the ping packets (172.16.1.3) to the corresponding (nonexistent) MAC address using ARP. Obviously, those ARP requests time out just like before.

Listing 4.45 shows the output of the commands **debug arp** and **debug ip packet detail** on router R5 while the command **ping 172.16.1.1** was in progress on router R4.

Listing 4.45   The output of the **debug arp** and **debug ip packet detail** commands on router R5 while pinging address 172.16.1.1 from router R4.

```
R5(config)#access-list 100 permit icmp any any
R5(config)#^Z
R5#debug arp
ARP packet debugging is on
R5#debug ip packet detail 100
IP packet debugging is on (detailed) for access list 100
R5#
IP: s=172.16.1.3 (Serial0), d=172.16.1.1, len 100, rcvd 4
  ICMP type=8, code=0
IP: s=172.16.1.1 (local), d=172.16.1.3 (Ethernet0), len 100, sending
  ICMP type=0, code=0
IP ARP: creating incomplete entry for IP address: 172.16.1.3
```

```
IP ARP: sent req src 172.16.1.1 0060.5cc4.f4fe,
   dst 172.16.1.3 0000.0000.0000 Ethernet0
IP: s=172.16.1.1 (local), d=172.16.1.3 (Ethernet0), len 100,
   encapsulation failed
  ICMP type=0, code=0
IP: s=172.16.1.3 (Serial0), d=172.16.1.1, len 100, rcvd 4
  ICMP type=8, code=0
IP: s=172.16.1.1 (local), d=172.16.1.3 (Ethernet0), len 100, sending
  ICMP type=0, code=0
IP ARP throttled out the ARP Request for 172.16.1.3
IP: s=172.16.1.1 (local), d=172.16.1.3 (Ethernet0), len 100,
   encapsulation failed
  ICMP type=0, code=0
...
```

TIP: *The command that was used to examine the IP processing on router R5 is **debug ip packet detail** <access-list>. The <access-list> parameter allows using an access list to limit the amount of information processed and produced by this **debug** command. Using the **debug** command followed by an access-list number has two benefits. First, it reduces the load on the router's CPU that is associated with processing the **debug** command. Second, it filters out irrelevant information, which otherwise often makes the output much more difficult to understand. In our example, this irrelevant information would be RIP routing updates, which would appear in the output unless we filtered them with **access-list 100**. The first line of Listing 4.45 actually shows how **access-list 100** was created.*

The first shaded line in Listing 4.45 shows that router R4's ping packet arrived on interface Serial0 of router R5. The second shaded line shows that router R5 forms a reply, but instead of sending it back to interface Serial0, it tries to send it over interface Ethernet0. The three shaded lines that follow show that router R5 issues an ARP request for IP address 172.16.1.3 through interface Ethernet0. The last shaded line reads "encapsulation failed," which, in the case of local area network (LAN) interfaces, typically means that the previously issued ARP request has timed out. The output of the **show arp** command entered on router R5, shown here, confirms that:

```
R5#show arp
Protocol Address      Age (min) Hardware Addr  Type  Interface
Internet 172.16.1.1       -   0060.5cc4.f4fe ARPA  Ethernet0
Internet 172.16.1.3       0   Incomplete     ARPA
Internet 172.16.1.2      112  0060.5cc4.f4c5 ARPA  Ethernet0
```

Finally, it's still unclear why router R4 cannot receive ping replies for its own IP address (172.16.1.3). Interestingly enough, Cisco's implementation of IP over a Cisco High-Level Data Link Control (HDLC) connection requires the router to actually forward the datagram to the other-end router even if it's destined for the

IP address of the serial interface itself. As the datagrams carrying ping packets arrive to router R5, router R5 can't forward them back to router R4 because it perceives the source IP address as locally accessible through interface Ethernet0. Thus, just like before, router R5 resorts to ARP, whose requests simply time out. And, just like before, router R4 receives no replies.

Listing 4.46 shows the sequence of the events on router R5 while router R4 was pinging its own IP address of 172.16.1.3.

Listing 4.46 The output of the commands **debug arp** and **debug ip packet detail** issued on router R5 while router R4 was pinging its own IP address (172.16.1.3).

```
IP: s=172.16.1.3 (Serial0), d=172.16.1.3 (Ethernet0), g=172.16.1.3,
  len 100, forward
  ICMP type=8, code=0
IP ARP: creating incomplete entry for IP address: 172.16.1.3
IP ARP: sent req src 172.16.1.1 0060.5cc4.f4fe,
  dst 172.16.1.3 0000.0000.0000 Ethernet0
IP: s=172.16.1.3 (Serial0), d=172.16.1.3 (Ethernet0), len 100,
  encapsulation failed
  ICMP type=8, code=0
```

The **ping** command on Cisco routers provides an option that allows you to change the source IP address. Let's see if pinging, say, 172.16.1.1 will succeed if we change the source IP address from the default address of 172.16.1.3 to that of router R4's TokenRing0 interface. Listing 4.47 shows the results of this experiment. The shaded lines show the essential parts of the output. (The rest of the output is kept for reference. It's not relevant to the discussed subject, although without it the output would be rendered unrecognizable.)

Listing 4.47 The results of pinging 172.16.1.1 after changing the source IP address from 172.16.1.3 to that of router R4's TokenRing0 interface.

```
R4#ping ip
Target IP address: 172.16.1.1
Repeat count [5]:
Datagram size [100]:
Timeout in seconds [2]:
Extended commands [n]: yes
Source address or interface: 192.168.5.2
Type of service [0]:
Set DF bit in IP header? [no]:
Validate reply data? [no]:
Data pattern [0xABCD]:
Loose, Strict, Record, Timestamp, Verbose[none]:
```

```
Sweep range of sizes [n]:
Type escape sequence to abort.
Sending 5, 100-byte ICMP Echos to 172.16.1.1, timeout is 2 seconds:
!!!!!
Success rate is 100 percent (5/5), round-trip min/avg/max = 4/4/4 ms
```

NOTE: *Alternatively, you can create a "totally unnumbered" connection, in which case the interfaces on both ends of the connection are unnumbered. For example, in Figure 4.14 router R4 could be configured with the* **ip unnumbered TokenRing0** *command. This configuration is supported by RIP and all other dynamic routing protocols available on Cisco routers. Furthermore, this configuration is preferred if the use of unnumbered interfaces in necessary.*

This time, pinging is successful.

Making RIP Passive on an Interface

RIP can be made passive on an interface by using the command **passive-interface** <*interface*> in the **router rip** configuration.

If RIP is made passive on an interface, the router won't send routing updates through it. Nevertheless, the router will still receive routing updates on that interface, and it will advertise the network prefix configured on this interface through other interfaces (unless they are also made passive).

To better understand how passive interfaces work, let's consider an example. In the example, we'll use the network scheme from Figure 4.12. We are going to make RIP on router R3 passive on interface TokenRing0. Thus, we expect router R4 to stop seeing network 10.0.0.0; aside from this, nothing else should change. Routers R1 and R2 should still have routes for the network prefix of segment 6, located behind router R4.

The configurations of routers R1, R2, and R4 are as they were in Listings 4.23, 4.24, and 4.11, respectively. The configuration of router R3 is shown in Listing 4.48.

Listing 4.48   Router R3's configuration.

```
interface Loopback0
 ip address 10.0.0.3 255.255.255.255

interface Serial0
 ip address 10.0.4.1 255.255.255.0

interface Serial1
 ip address 10.0.3.1 255.255.255.0
```

```
interface TokenRing0
 ip address 192.168.5.1 255.255.255.0
 ring-speed 16

router rip
 passive-interface TokenRing0
 network 10.0.0.0
 network 192.168.5.0
```

If we examine the routing table of router R4 (shown below), we'll see that the route for network 10.0.0.0/8 is gone:

```
R4#show ip route
...
C  192.168.5.0/24 is directly connected, TokenRing0
C  192.168.6.0/24 is directly connected, Ethernet0
```

But the routing tables of routers R1, R2, and R3 remain intact. As an example, the routing table of router R1 is shown in Listing 4.49.

Listing 4.49   The routing table of router R1.

```
R1#show ip route
...
R  192.168.5.0/24 [120/1] via 10.0.3.1, 00:00:08, Serial0
    10.0.0.0/8 is variably subnetted, 7 subnets, 2 masks
R     10.0.0.2/32 [120/2] via 10.0.3.1, 00:00:09, Serial0
R     10.0.2.0/24 [120/2] via 10.0.3.1, 00:00:09, Serial0
R     10.0.0.3/32 [120/1] via 10.0.3.1, 00:00:09, Serial0
C     10.0.3.0/24 is directly connected, Serial0
C     10.0.0.1/32 is directly connected, Loopback0
C     10.0.1.0/24 is directly connected, Ethernet0
R     10.0.4.0/24 [120/1] via 10.0.3.1, 00:00:09, Serial0
R  192.168.6.0/24 [120/2] via 10.0.3.1, 00:00:09, Serial0
```

The shaded line in Listing 4.49 shows that the route for segment 6 still exists.

The reasonable question is: Why would anyone bother making RIP passive on an interface? This question has several possible answers:

- If only a single router is connected to a LAN segment and no hosts rely on RIP, it makes sense to make RIP passive on the router's interface connected to the segment. Doing so lets you avoid sending unnecessary broadcast traffic in the form of the RIP routing updates onto this segment.

- Hosts, especially those with multiple network interface cards (NICs) that rely on RIP must be configured with RIP made passive on all interfaces. It's possible that such hosts may produce routing updates carrying a smaller

4. Routing Information Protocol (RIP)

metric for the segment that they can reach. In this case, some traffic that should normally go through the routers can become directed through the hosts. This jeopardizes the hosts' primary function. You must thus avoid this by making RIP passive on those hosts on all their interfaces.

Using Unicast Routing Updates with RIP

RIP can be configured to send routing updates to a specified unicast address by using the command **neighbor <IP address>** in the **router rip** configuration. The *<IP address>* parameter is the IP address to which the routing updates must be sent. This address must reside on one of the directly connected segments. If it doesn't, and is instead located behind other routers, the router will still forward routing updates to this IP address, which makes no sense from the perspective of routing.

However, the **neighbor <IP address>** command does not prevent RIP from sending broadcast routing updates via the interface through which the specified IP address is available.

The **neighbor** command is especially useful when used in conjunction with the **passive-interface** command. Let's consider an example, which helps demonstrate how these two commands can be used together.

In the previous section, we made RIP passive on router R3's interface TokenRing0. This caused router R4 to be unable to receive routing updates for network 10.0.0.0 from router R3. Let's now add the command **neighbor 192.168.5.2** under the **router rip** configuration of router R3. Doing so should restore router R4's ability to receive routing updates for network 10.0.0.0. Listing 4.50 shows router R3's new configuration. (As before, the configurations of routers R1, R2, and R4 are as they were in Listings 4.23, 4.24, and 4.11, respectively.)

Listing 4.50   Router R3's configuration.

```
interface Loopback0
 ip address 10.0.0.3 255.255.255.255

interface Serial0
 ip address 10.0.4.1 255.255.255.0

interface Serial1
 ip address 10.0.3.1 255.255.255.0

interface TokenRing0
 ip address 192.168.5.1 255.255.255.0
 ring-speed 16
```

```
router rip
 passive-interface TokenRing0
 network 10.0.0.0
 network 192.168.5.0
 neighbor 192.168.5.2
```

The command **neighbor 192.168.5.2** is shaded; the italicized line shows the **passive-interface TokenRing0** command.

After we've changed router R3's configuration, the routing table of router R4 (shown below) again shows the route for network 10.0.0.0:

```
R4#show ip route
...
C  192.168.5.0/24 is directly connected, TokenRing0
R  10.0.0.0/8 [120/1] via 192.168.5.1, 00:00:04, TokenRing0
C  192.168.6.0/24 is directly connected, Ethernet0
```

Let's now try to investigate in more detail what's happening on the routers configured with the **neighbor** command under the **router rip** configuration. To do that, we'll modify our network as shown in Figure 4.15.

4. Routing Information Protocol (RIP)

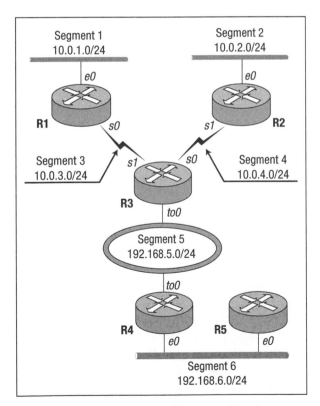

Figure 4.15   Router R5 is added on segment 6.

Router R5 is added on segment 6. It has only interface Ethernet0 enabled, and this interface is assigned the IP address of 192.168.6.2/24.

Furthermore, we also are going to add the **neighbor 192.168.5.1** command under the **router rip** configuration of router R4 as well as the **neighbor 192.168.6.2** command under the **router rip** configuration of router R3. The first command should make router R4 send router R3 unicast routing updates, and the second should make router R3 send routing updates to the IP address of router R5, which is not directly accessible from router R3.

The new configurations of routers R3 and R4 and the configuration of router R5 are shown in Listings 4.51 through 4.53.

Listing 4.51   Router R3's new configuration.

```
interface Loopback0
 ip address 10.0.0.3 255.255.255.255

interface Serial0
 ip address 10.0.4.1 255.255.255.0

interface Serial1
 ip address 10.0.3.1 255.255.255.0

interface TokenRing0
 ip address 192.168.5.1 255.255.255.0
 ring-speed 16

router rip
 passive-interface TokenRing0
 network 10.0.0.0
 network 192.168.5.0
 neighbor 192.168.6.2
 neighbor 192.168.5.2
```

Listing 4.52   Router R4's new configuration.

```
interface Ethernet0
 ip address 192.168.6.1 255.255.255.0

interface TokenRing0
 ip address 192.168.5.2 255.255.255.0
 ring-speed 16

router rip
 network 192.168.5.0
 network 192.168.6.0
 neighbor 192.168.5.1
```

Listing 4.53   Router R5's configuration.

```
interface Loopback0
 ip address 172.16.1.1 255.255.255.0

interface Ethernet0
 ip address 192.168.6.2 255.255.255.0

router rip
 network 192.168.6.0
```

Let's now see what's happening on router R3. To do that, we'll use two commands: **debug ip rip** and **debug ip packet detail 100**. Listing 4.54 shows the output of these two commands issued on router R3.

Listing 4.54   The output of the **debug ip rip** and **debug ip packet detail 100** commands on router R3.

```
R3(config)#access-list 100 permit udp any any eq rip
R3(config)#^Z
R3#debug ip rip
RIP protocol debugging is on
R3#debug ip packet detail 100
IP packet debugging is on (detailed) for access list 100
R3#
RIP: sending v1 update to 192.168.6.2 via TokenRing0 (192.168.5.1)
   network 10.0.0.0, metric 1
   network 192.168.6.0, metric 2
IP: s=192.168.5.1 (local), d=192.168.6.2 (TokenRing0), len 72, sending
 UDP src=520, dst=520
RIP: sending v1 update to 192.168.5.2 via TokenRing0 (192.168.5.1)
   network 10.0.0.0, metric 1
IP: s=192.168.5.1 (local), d=192.168.5.2 (TokenRing0), len 52, sending
 UDP src=520, dst=520
IP: s=192.168.5.2 (TokenRing0), d=255.255.255.255, len 52, rcvd 2
 UDP src=520, dst=520
RIP: received v1 update from 192.168.5.2 on TokenRing0
   192.168.6.0 in 1 hops
IP: s=192.168.5.2 (TokenRing0), d=192.168.5.1 (TokenRing0), len 52, rcvd 3
 UDP src=520, dst=520
RIP: received v1 update from 192.168.5.2 on TokenRing0
   192.168.6.0 in 1 hops
```

Listing 4.54 is divided into five parts—one italicized, two shaded, and two nonshaded. The italicized part shows the commands that were used to produce the output. For more information on these commands, please see the tip in the "Understanding How RIP Handles IP Unnumbered" section earlier in this chapter.

4. Routing Information Protocol (RIP)

The first shaded parts (and the following nonshaded one) show two routing updates that router R3 sends. The routing update shown in the shaded part is weird:
It's destined for the IP address of router R5 (192.168.6.2), which is not directly
accessible from router R3. The routing update shown in the nonshaded part is a
regular unicast routing update that router R3 sends to router R4.

The second shaded part (and the following nonshaded one) shows two routing
updates received from router R4. Notice that the content of the updates is identical. The only difference between the updates is the destination IP addresses: The
first update was sent to the broadcast address, the second one to the IP address
of router R3's TokenRing0 interface.

TIP: *We needed the **debug ip packet detail 100** command to see which IP addresses the received routing
updates were actually sent to.*

Let's see what results the **debug ip rip** command produces on router R5. Listing
4.55 shows the output of the command.

Listing 4.55   The output of the debug ip rip command issued on router R5.

```
R5(config)#access-list 100 permit udp any any eq rip
R5(config)#^Z
R5#debug ip rip
RIP protocol debugging is on
R5#debug ip packet detail 100
IP packet debugging is on (detailed) for access list 100
R5#
IP: s=192.168.6.1 (Ethernet0), d=255.255.255.255, len 72, rcvd 2
  UDP src=520, dst=520
RIP: received v1 update from 192.168.6.1 on Ethernet0
    192.168.5.0 in 1 hops
    10.0.0.0 in 2 hops
IP: s=192.168.5.1 (Ethernet0), d=192.168.6.2, len 72, rcvd 0
  UDP src=520, dst=520
RIP: ignored v1 update from bad source 192.168.5.1 on Ethernet0
```

The shaded part of Listing 4.55 shows a regular routing update that router R5
receives from router R4. The last three lines of the listing show the bogus routing
update from router R3. The last line clearly indicates that router R3 ignores the
update because the IP address of "next-hop-router-to-be" is not directly accessible from router R5. As we remember from Chapter 1, this is a necessary condition for a routing table entry to be created.

Although sending routing updates to IP addresses that are not directly accessible may seem weird, doing so does have one practical use. If the goal of the

destination of such routing updates is not routing but instead gathering information for, say, management purposes, the existence of this type of routing update is well justified.

Unicast routing updates (sent to directly accessible neighbors) can be quite handy in two cases:

- Unicast routing updates can be used in LANs to reduce the amount of broadcast traffic. If the number of RIP neighbors remains the same over long periods of time, it makes sense to fully mesh them using the **neighbor** commands, thereby eliminating the part of broadcast traffic caused by RIP updates.

- If it is undesirable to expose the exact routing information to every node on the segment, unicast routing update can provide a basic level of security. This is a rather weak security measure in the case of shared networks (such as an Ethernet segment made of hubs). A simple LAN analyzer connected to a shared segment can be effectively used to intercept even unicast routing updates. In switched LANs, however, the measure becomes much stronger because the switches do not flood unicast traffic over all their ports; instead, they only forward the traffic to the ports on which the actual destinations reside.

In addition, some network technologies may not support broadcast traffic. In that case, unicast routing updates can be used to provide for RIP operation over such networks.

Changing the Administrative Distance of RIP Routing Updates

So far, we know how to use administrative distances with static routes. Now it's time to discuss how administrative distances are used with the dynamic routing protocol, RIP.

It is possible to change the administrative distances of the routes RIP that creates, both on a per RIP neighbor and per destination basis. To do that, the command **distance** <*new AD*> [<IP address> <wildcard mask> [<standard access-list #>]] should be used under the **router rip** configuration. The command can be entered multiple times to specify different administrative distances for different neighbors. The order in which the **distance** commands appear in the router's configuration is significant.

The <*new AD*> parameter is used to specify the numeric value of the new administrative distance (from 1 through 255). If the value of 255 is specified, this prevents the eligible routers from being installed in the routing table. All other parameters are optional; if none of them is specified, the **distance** command changes the administrative distance of all RIP routes to the specified value.

The *<IP address>* and *<wildcard mask>* parameters are used to specify the RIP neighbors whose routing updates must be treated with the specified administrative distance. These parameters have dotted decimal format. The *<wildcard mask>* parameter presents a 32-bit binary value, the set bits of which denote that the corresponding bits in the *<IP address>* parameter must be ignored during comparison. It's equivalent to the *<wildcard mask>* parameter that is used in the access-list syntax. For example, the combination 192.168.100.0 0.0.0.255 chooses all hosts on the segment, provided the segment's network prefix (subnet address) is 192.168.100.0/24. These two parameters must be used together in only the shown order. They can be optionally followed by the last parameter, *<standard access-list>*.

The *<standard access-list>* parameter specifies the access list that is used to select specific network prefixes from the specified neighbors' routing updates. Only network prefixes that pass the access list with the **permit** result are considered selected. The routes for these selected network prefixes will be created with the specified administrative distance. The network prefixes that pass the access list with the **deny** result are not affected by the command. Thus, routes for them will be created with the default administrative distance, unless they are affected by another **distance** command. The *<standard access-list>* parameter can take as the number of a standard access list the name of a named standard access list if the latter is available in the version of IOS running on the router. The *<standard access-list>* parameter can be used only in conjunction with the two other optional parameters (*<IP address>* and *<wildcard mask>*) in the shown order.

Finally, there can be only one **distance** command per pair *<IP address> <wildcard mask>* with or without the *<standard access-list>* parameter. Subsequent **distance** commands with the same pair of the *<IP address> <wildcard mask>* parameters (with different *<standard access-list>* parameters or even without them) overwrite each other.

> **WARNING!**   *The order in which the **distance** commands appear in the router's configuration is crucial. Only the value supplied in the first command that matches the candidate route will be used; all subsequent commands are ignored.*

Let's consider an example that helps us understand how the **distance** command works.

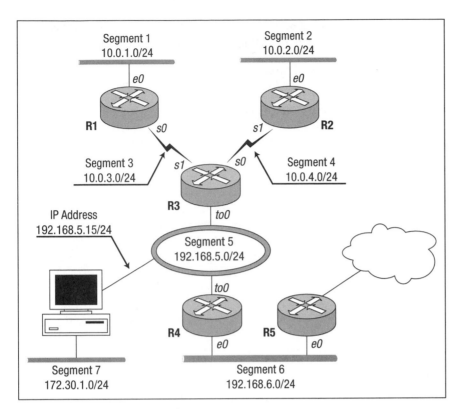

Figure 4.16   Host H1 and router R5 advertise extraneous addresses using RIP; routers R3 and R4 employ the **distance** command to defeat those addresses.

Figure 4.16 shows our favorite network scheme modified once again. This time, host H1 (with multiple NICs) is connected to segment 5, and router R5 is connected to segment 6. Host H1 advertises the network prefix of extraneous segment 7. Router R5 advertises a number of network prefixes; we are interested in only those that begin with 192.168. Thus, our tasks are is to get rid of the network prefix of extraneous segment 7 and to pick the correct network prefixes from router R5's update, while effectively ignoring all other network prefixes that router R5 might advertise.

Let's also require that the routes for the network prefixes, which router R4 learns from router R3, be created with the administrative distance of 200.

Before any configuration related to administrative distances is done, routers R1, R2, R3, and R4 are configured as shown in Listings 4.15, 4.16, 4.25, and 4.6, respectively. To know what we are fighting with, let's first take a look at the routing table of router R4, shown in Listing 4.56.

Listing 4.56   The routing table of router R4 before we change the administrative distances of the neighbors that advertise extraneous addresses.

```
R4#show ip route
...
R   192.168.150.0/24 [200/1] via 192.168.6.2, 00:00:15, Ethernet0
R   172.17.0.0/16 [1/1] via 192.168.6.2, 00:00:16, Ethernet0
R   172.19.0.0/16 [1/1] via 192.168.6.2, 00:00:16, Ethernet0
R   172.18.0.0/16 [1/1] via 192.168.6.2, 00:00:16, Ethernet0
R   172.20.0.0/16 [1/1] via 192.168.6.2, 00:00:16, Ethernet0
R   172.30.0.0/16 [1/2] via 192.168.5.15, 00:00:10, TokenRing0
R   192.168.200.0/24 [200/1] via 192.168.6.2, 00:00:16, Ethernet0
R   192.168.250.0/24 [200/1] via 192.168.6.2, 00:00:16, Ethernet0
C   192.168.5.0/24 is directly connected, TokenRing0
R   10.0.0.0/8 [1/1] via 192.168.5.1, 00:00:19, TokenRing0
C   192.168.6.0/24 is directly connected, Ethernet0
R   192.168.50.0/24 [200/1] via 192.168.6.2, 00:00:16, Ethernet0
R   192.168.100.0/24 [200/1] via 192.168.6.2, 00:00:16, Ethernet0
```

The shaded lines show the extraneous routes; the shaded italicized line shows the route for the network prefix advertised by host H1. The nonshaded italicized lines show the route for network prefixes advertised by router R5 that we seek to preserve.

Let's start with router R4. It's the only router that exchanges routing updates with router R5. Thus, we are first going to create a standard access list that produces a match with the **permit** result for all prefixes that begin with 192.168 (the preserved network prefixes). Then, we are going to create two separate **distance** commands—one for the preserved network prefixes and one for all others. The first **distance** command should assign the administrative distance of 200 to all the routes for the preserved network prefixes. The second **distance** command should assign the administrative distance of 255 to the routes for the other network prefixes, which will effectively prevent these routes from being installed in the routing table.

Host H1's advertisements of the extraneous network prefix affect two routers—R3 and R4. Thus, measures must be taken on both of these routers. The easiest way to defeat host H1's advertisements is to treat them with the administrative distance of 255. The resulting routes won't make it into the routing table. This requires two **distance** commands: One will preserve the favorable administrative distance of routes that result from routing updates exchanged by routers R3 and R4; the other one will discriminate the extraneous routes from segment 8.

Listings 4.57 and 4.58 show the new configurations of routers R3 and R4.

Listing 4.57 Router R3's new configuration.

```
interface Loopback0
 ip address 10.0.0.3 255.255.255.255

interface Serial0
 ip address 10.0.4.1 255.255.255.0

interface Serial1
 ip address 10.0.3.1 255.255.255.0

interface TokenRing0
 ip address 192.168.5.1 255.255.255.0
 ring-speed 16

router rip
 network 10.0.0.0
 network 192.168.5.0
 distance 200 192.168.5.2 0.0.0.0
 distance 255 192.168.5.0 0.0.0.255
```

Listing 4.58 Router new R4's configuration.

```
interface Ethernet0
 ip address 192.168.6.1 255.255.255.0

interface TokenRing0
 ip address 192.168.5.2 255.255.255.0
 ring-speed 16

router rip
 network 192.168.5.0
 network 192.168.6.0
 distance 255 192.168.6.2 0.0.0.0 2
 distance 200 192.168.5.1 0.0.0.0
 distance 255 192.168.5.0 0.0.0.255

access-list 1 permit 192.168.0.0 0.0.255.255

access-list 2 deny  192.168.0.0 0.0.255.255
access-list 2 permit any
```

The shaded line in router R4's configuration (Listing 4.58) shows the **distance** command that discriminates the routes for network prefixes advertised by router R5 that do not begin with 192.168. The last parameter of the command is the number of the access list that selects those network prefixes with the **permit** result. The last two lines of Listing 4.58 are about access list 2.

Notice that router R4's configuration also contains access list 1 (presently unused). We'll discuss access list 1 later in this section.

Let's examine the routing tables of routers R3 and R4 after we change to their configurations. Listings 4.59 and 4.60 show the new contents of the routing tables for routers R3 and R4, respectively.

Listing 4.59   The routing table of router R3.

```
R3#show ip route
...
R  192.168.150.0/24 [200/2] via 192.168.5.2, 00:00:04, TokenRing0
R  192.168.200.0/24 [200/2] via 192.168.5.2, 00:00:05, TokenRing0
R  192.168.250.0/24 [200/2] via 192.168.5.2, 00:00:05, TokenRing0
C  192.168.5.0/24 is directly connected, TokenRing0
   10.0.0.0/8 is variably subnetted, 7 subnets, 2 masks
R     10.0.2.0/24 [120/1] via 10.0.4.2, 00:00:05, Serial0
R     10.0.0.2/32 [120/1] via 10.0.4.2, 00:00:05, Serial0
C     10.0.3.0/24 is directly connected, Serial1
C     10.0.0.3/32 is directly connected, Loopback0
R     10.0.1.0/24 [120/1] via 10.0.3.2, 00:00:04, Serial1
R     10.0.0.1/32 [120/1] via 10.0.3.2, 00:00:04, Serial1
C     10.0.4.0/24 is directly connected, Serial0
R  192.168.6.0/24 [200/1] via 192.168.5.2, 00:00:05, TokenRing0
R  192.168.50.0/24 [200/2] via 192.168.5.2, 00:00:05, TokenRing0
R  192.168.100.0/24 [200/2] via 192.168.5.2, 00:00:07, TokenRing0
```

Listing 4.60   The routing table of router R4.

```
R4#show ip route
...
R  192.168.150.0/24 [120/1] via 192.168.6.2, 00:00:16, Ethernet0
R  192.168.200.0/24 [120/1] via 192.168.6.2, 00:00:16, Ethernet0
R  192.168.250.0/24 [120/1] via 192.168.6.2, 00:00:16, Ethernet0
C  192.168.5.0/24 is directly connected, TokenRing0
R  10.0.0.0/8 [200/1] via 192.168.5.1, 00:00:07, TokenRing0
C  192.168.6.0/24 is directly connected, Ethernet0
R  192.168.50.0/24 [120/1] via 192.168.6.2, 00:00:16, Ethernet0
R  192.168.100.0/24 [120/1] via 192.168.6.2, 00:00:16, Ethernet0
```

The shaded lines in both routing tables show the routes for the network prefixes that routers R3 and R4 advertise to each other. As we wanted, the administrative distance of these routers did become 200 (the first number in the brackets). Neither routing table shows a route for the extraneous network prefixes: They are all gone. So, we can conclude that the configurations of routers R3 and R4 did the job.

Let's do a simple experiment. Let's enter the command **distance 150 192.168.6.2 0.0.0.0 1** under the **router rip** configuration of router R4. We'd expect that the new command should remove the old command, **distance 255 192.168.6.2 0.0.0.0 2**. But why would we want to do that?

The most probable answer is that we might mistakenly think that the new command can coexist with the old one. After all, the two commands do have different access-list numbers. However, if these two commands could coexist, the routes for the preserved network prefixes advertised by router R5 would be created with the administrative distance of 150, whereas the routes for the other network prefixes still wouldn't be able to make it to the routing table. (Notice access list 1 is reversed access list 2.)

Let's see what happens in real life. Listing 4.61 shows the configuration of router R4 after the command **distance 150 192.168.6.2 0.0.0.0 1** was entered.

Listing 4.61 The configuration of router R4 after the command **distance 150 192.168.6.2 0.0.0.0 1** was entered.

```
interface Ethernet0
 ip address 192.168.6.1 255.255.255.0

interface TokenRing0
 ip address 192.168.5.2 255.255.255.0
 ring-speed 16

router rip
 network 192.168.5.0
 network 192.168.6.0
 distance 150 192.168.6.2 0.0.0.0 1
 distance 200 192.168.5.1 0.0.0.0
 distance 255 192.168.5.0 0.0.0.255

access-list 1 permit 192.168.0.0 0.0.255.255
access-list 2 deny  192.168.0.0 0.0.255.255
access-list 2 permit any
```

The first result is that, unfortunately, the rules that govern the behavior of the **distance** command (which were explained above) remain in effect. (It's unfortunate because adding the command was actually a pretty good idea.) The second result becomes obvious after we display the routing table of router R4 after we made the change (shown in Listing 4.62).

Listing 4.62 The routing table of router R4.

```
R4#show ip route
...
R  192.168.150.0/24 [150/1] via 192.168.6.2, 00:00:03, Ethernet0
R  172.17.0.0/16 [120/1] via 192.168.6.2, 00:00:03, Ethernet0
R  172.19.0.0/16 [120/1] via 192.168.6.2, 00:00:03, Ethernet0
```

```
R  172.18.0.0/16 [120/1] via 192.168.6.2, 00:00:03, Ethernet0
R  172.20.0.0/16 [120/1] via 192.168.6.2, 00:00:03, Ethernet0
R  192.168.200.0/24 [150/1] via 192.168.6.2, 00:00:03, Ethernet0
R  192.168.250.0/24 [150/1] via 192.168.6.2, 00:00:03, Ethernet0
C  192.168.5.0/24 is directly connected, TokenRing0
R  10.0.0.0/8 [200/1] via 192.168.5.1, 00:00:03, TokenRing0
C  192.168.6.0/24 is directly connected, Ethernet0
R  192.168.50.0/24 [150/1] via 192.168.6.2, 00:00:04, Ethernet0
R  192.168.100.0/24 [150/1] via 192.168.6.2, 00:00:04, Ethernet0
```

A quick look at the italicized lines of the new routing table reveals that the routes for the preserved network prefixes (192.168.X.X) did receive the administrative distance of 150, as we desired. However, the routes for the other network prefixes that were previously suppressed are now back with the default administrative distance of 120 (the shaded lines).

Performing Equal-Cost Load Balancing with RIP

RIP on Cisco routers can install multiple routes for the same network prefix, providing all routes have the same RIP metric. The number of such routes is controlled by the command **ip maximum paths** under the **router rip** configuration, which can take whole-number values in the range of 1 through 6. By default, the number of maximum routes for the same destination is four.

By installing routes for the same network, RIP essentially initiates load balancing of the outgoing IP traffic that is destined for this network prefix across these routes. Notice, though, that, because the router has no control over the incoming traffic, it may still take a single route depending on the routing tables of the routers returning the traffic.

To see RIP-initiated load balancing in action, let's consider the network example shown in Figure 4.17.

The routers' configurations are shown in Listings 4.63 through 4.65.

Listing 4.63   Router R1's configuration.

```
interface Serial0
 ip address 10.0.2.2 255.255.255.0

interface TokenRing0
 ip address 10.0.1.1 255.255.255.0
 ring-speed 16

router rip
 network 10.0.0.0
```

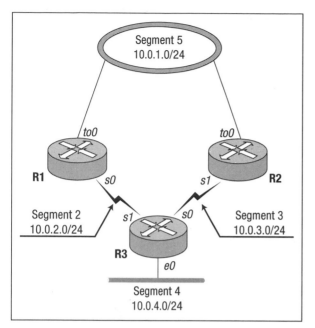

Figure 4.17   Router R3 has two parallel links leading to segment 1, so it can use them to perform load balancing.

Listing 4.64   Router R2's configuration.

```
interface Serial1
 ip address 10.0.3.2 255.255.255.0

interface TokenRing0
 ip address 10.0.1.2 255.255.255.0
 ring-speed 16

router rip
 network 10.0.0.0
```

Listing 4.65   Router R3's configuration.

```
interface Ethernet0
 ip address 10.0.4.1 255.255.255.0

interface Serial0
 ip address 10.0.3.1 255.255.255.0

interface Serial1
 ip address 10.0.2.1 255.255.255.0

router rip
 network 10.0.0.0
```

4. Routing Information Protocol (RIP)

Listing 4.66   The routing table of router R3.

```
R3#show ip route
...
     10.0.0.0/24 is subnetted, 4 subnets
C    10.0.2.0 is directly connected, Serial1
C    10.0.3.0 is directly connected, Serial0
R    10.0.1.0 [120/1] via 10.0.3.2, 00:00:10, Serial0
              [120/1] via 10.0.2.2, 00:00:06, Serial1
C    10.0.4.0 is directly connected, Ethernet0
```

In Listing 4.66, the two shaded lines indicate load balancing: two routes for the same destination.

Surprisingly (or not, if we remember RIP's simplistic metrics), we'll discover load balancing on all three routers. Let's, for example, have a look at router R1's routing table, shown in Listing 6.67.

Listing 4.67   Router R1's routing table also exhibits two routes for the same destination—this time for segment 3.

```
R1#show ip route
...
     10.0.0.0/24 is subnetted, 4 subnets
C    10.0.2.0 is directly connected, Serial0
R    10.0.3.0 [120/1] via 10.0.1.2, 00:00:19, TokenRing0
              [120/1] via 10.0.2.1, 00:00:17, Serial0
C    10.0.1.0 is directly connected, TokenRing0
R    10.0.4.0 [120/1] via 10.0.2.1, 00:00:17, Serial0
```

Route R1's routing table also shows two routes for the same destination (segment 3). If we examined the routing table of router R2, we'd also discover two routes (but for segment 2).

The reason is simple. Topologically, the example network is a triangle, with the routers being the vertices and segments 1, 2, and 3 the edges. From every router, there is always a segment to which the traffic can take two paths (the other two segments). RIP assigns the cost of 1 to every segment, so the routers can't tell the difference between these two paths. In our case, however, the simplicity of RIP's metrics makes the bandwidth-abundant Token Ring segment equal to a narrow serial link.

Nevertheless, the load balancing in the case of routers R1 and R2 is nothing more than an administrative nuisance and is not harmful. The load balancing occurs only for traffic destined for the serial links (which is an unlikely event).

Changing RIP Metrics

Sometimes, it is desirable to force RIP to choose one route over another. For example, if two routers have two parallel links between them, one of which has a smaller bandwidth, we may want to make RIP prefer the one with the higher bandwidth. As we already know, RIP is not particularly discerning about the network segments on which it works. To RIP, they all have the metric of 1, regardless of their actual characteristics. Therefore, instead of making the link with the higher bandwidth the only route to the destination, RIP will perform equal-cost load balancing over both links, which we may not want. For example, if the bandwidth of the second link is three times smaller than that of the first link, the combined bandwidth is smaller than the bandwidth of the first link alone.

Cisco IOS provides a powerful command to change the default metric of 1 that RIP uses for every interface that it services. The command, **offset-list**, is available under the **router rip** configuration.

This command does not change the RIP cost of an interface, per se. Instead, it selectively applies a specified offset to change the metrics of advertised network prefixes in incoming or outgoing RIP updates. (*Selectively* means that the command allows you to specify which network prefixes get the changed metrics.) Optionally, the command can be used on individual interfaces.

The format of the command is **offset-list** *<access-list>* **{in|out}** *<offset>* [*<interface>*]

The *<access-list>* parameter can be 0, a number of a standard IP access list, or the name of a standard IP access list (if it's supported). If an existing access list is specified, the offset is applied to only those routes matched by the access list. If the access list does not exist or if 0 is used, the offset is applied to all routes.

The second parameter must be either **in** or **out**. If **in** is used, the offset is applied to the network prefixes in the incoming RIP updates. If **out** is used, the offset is applied to the network prefixes in the routing updates sent by the router.

The *<interface>* parameter is optional and specifies the interface to which the operation of the offset list should be limited. If specified, it makes RIP apply the offset only to those network prefixes in the routing updates that are received from or sent through the specified interface. The logic behind the access-list functionality remains the same.

The Cisco documentation calls the **offset-list** commands that specify an interface *extended offset-lists*. The extended offset lists take precedence over nonextended offset lists; therefore, if the same routing update is matched by both commands, only the offset specified in the extended one is applied.

For each interface, you can enter separate **offset-list ... in** and **offset-list ... out** commands. In addition, you can configure a single separate set of the nonextended **offset-list ... in** and **offset-list ... out** commands. If a subsequent **offset-list** command is entered, it overwrites the existing one with the matching {in|out} and *<interface> <interface#>* parameters.

For example, let's assume that the bandwidth of segment 3 in Figure 4.17 is three times smaller than that of segment 2. Currently, router R3 performs load balancing over both segments. Our task is to increase the metric that router R3 uses for this segment from the default value of 1 to 3, using the **offset-list** command. The new configuration of router R3 is shown in Listing 4.68.

Listing 4.68   The configuration of router R3.

```
interface Ethernet0
 ip address 10.0.4.1 255.255.255.0

interface Serial1
 ip address 10.0.2.1 255.255.255.0

router rip
 offset-list 0 in 3 Serial0
 network 10.0.0.0
```

The new state of router R3's routing table is shown below:

```
R3#show ip route
...
    10.0.0.0/24 is subnetted, 4 subnets
C    10.0.2.0 is directly connected, Serial1
C    10.0.3.0 is directly connected, Serial0
R    10.0.1.0 [120/1] via 10.0.2.2, 00:00:25, Serial1
C    10.0.4.0 is directly connected, Ethernet0
```

The evidence of load balancing that we saw in the example in the previous section has disappeared. If we look at the routing updates that router R3 receives on interface Serial0 (shown below), we will see that the metric of network prefix 10.0.1.0/24 became 4—that is, it is increased by 3—just as we configured:

```
R3#debug ip rip
RIP protocol debugging is on
R3#
RIP: received v1 update from 10.0.3.2 on Serial0
    10.0.1.0 in 4 hops
RIP: received v1 update from 10.0.2.2 on Serial1
    10.0.1.0 in 1 hops
```

Adjusting RIP Timers

RIP timers can be changed from the default values by using the command **timers basic <update> <invalid> <holddown> <flush>** *[<sleep time>]* in the **router rip** configuration.

The *<update>*, *<invalid>*, *<holddown>*, and *<flush>* parameters are measured in seconds and can accept values in the range from 0 through 4294967295.

The *<update>* parameter is the time between regular routing updates. The *<invalid>*, *<holddown>*, and *<flush>* parameters represent invalid, holddown, and flush times, respectively. Use the following guidelines to modify the **<invalid>**, *<holddown>*, and *<flush>* parameters:

- The invalid time value should be at least three times the value of the update time.
- The holddown value should be at least three times the value of the update time.
- The flush value should be greater than the value of the invalid time.

The optional *<sleep time>* parameter is measured in milliseconds and can accept values in the range from 1 through 4294967295. This parameter represents the expiration time of the triggered update timer.

The default values for these parameters are shown in Table 4.2.

WARNING! Typically, the timers of a dynamic routing protocol should not be changed. The designers of the protocol have extensively experimented and tested these very sensitive parameters to devise the optimal values for them. You should change timers only in instances when no other measures can help.

Table 4.2 The default expiration times for Cisco's implementation of RIP timers.

Timer Name	Expiration Time
Update	30 seconds
Invalid	180 seconds
Holddown	180 seconds
Flush	240 seconds
Sleep Time	0 milliseconds

4. Routing Information Protocol (RIP)

Using RIP in the Presence of NBMA Networks

Configuring routing protocols on Cisco routers over NBMA networks, such as Frame Relay, presents a special case that differs to a certain extent from configuring the same protocols over most other media. This is because NBMA networks do not support broadcast-type traffic. Most routing protocols, however, send their routing updates to either broadcast or multicast addresses, which—not being supported by NBMA networks—require workarounds.

These workaround techniques become especially obvious in the case of Open Shortest Path First (OSPF), which we'll examine in Chapter 6. Although the distance vector-based routing protocols are not as particular with regard to NBMA networks, they may still present some surprises, especially in NBMA networks that aren't fully meshed.

Let's consider the network shown in Figure 4.18.

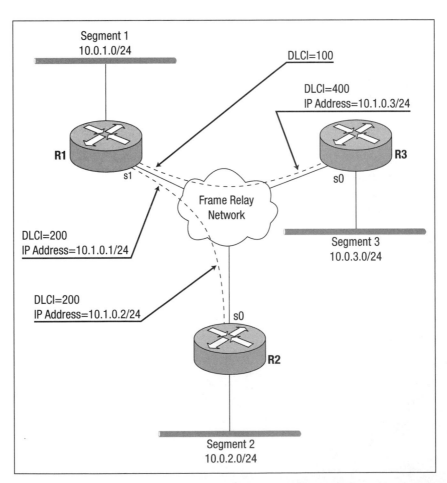

Figure 4.18   The routers are connected via a Frame Relay network that isn't fully meshed.

The routers are interconnected via a Frame Relay network that isn't fully meshed. For some unknown reason, router R1 is not allowed to use subinterfaces for the two permanent virtual circuits (PVCs) connecting it with routers R2 and R3. (That's why router R1's callout for the PVC between routers R1 and R3 doesn't show an IP address, only the Data Link Control Identifier—DLCI.)

All three routers are configured with RIP. According to what we already know, RIP will be unable to establish overall connectivity in the network because the split-horizon rule will prevent router R1 from re-advertising the network prefixes that it learns from router R2 to router R3, and vice versa. These network prefixes must be advertised over the same interface through which they were learned.

Still, let's have a look at what happens in real life. Listings 4.69 through 4.71 show the configurations of all three routers.

Listing 4.69   Router R1's configuration.

```
interface Ethernet0
 ip address 10.0.1.1 255.255.255.0

interface Serial1
 ip address 10.1.0.1 255.255.255.0
 encapsulation frame-relay
 frame-relay map ip 10.1.0.2 200 broadcast
 frame-relay map ip 10.1.0.3 100 broadcast

router rip
 network 10.0.0.0
```

Listing 4.70   Router R2's configuration.

```
interface Ethernet0
 ip address 10.0.2.1 255.255.255.0

interface Serial0
 ip address 10.1.0.2 255.255.255.0
 encapsulation frame-relay
 frame-relay map ip 10.1.0.1 200 broadcast

router rip
 network 10.0.0.0
```

Listing 4.71   Router R3's configuration.

```
interface Ethernet0
 ip address 10.0.3.1 255.255.255.0
```

```
interface Serial0
 ip address 10.1.0.3 255.255.255.0
 encapsulation frame-relay
 frame-relay map ip 10.1.0.1 400 broadcast

router rip
 network 10.0.0.0
```

Let's examine the routing table of router R2, shown below:

```
R2#show ip route
...
    10.0.0.0/24 is subnetted, 4 subnets
C    10.0.2.0 is directly connected, Ethernet0
R    10.0.3.0 [120/2] via 10.1.0.1, 00:00:09, Serial0
R    10.0.1.0 [120/1] via 10.1.0.1, 00:00:09, Serial0
C    10.1.0.0 is directly connected, Serial0
```

We assume that, because of the split horizon performed by router R1, we shouldn't see a router for segment 3. Nevertheless, the routing table contains a route for the network prefix of segment 3. Why?

The answer is simple: For interfaces with frame relay encapsulation, by default Cisco IOS disables split-horizon for RIP version 1 and 2 and IGRP. (For frame-relay subinterfaces however, by default Cisco IOS enables split-horizon for these protocols.) Let's have a look at the output of the show ip interface Serial1 command entered on router R1:

```
R1#show ip interface Serial1
Serial1 is up, line protocol is up
 Internet address is 10.1.0.1/24
 Broadcast address is 255.255.255.255
...
 Split horizon is disabled
...
```

Don't, however, expect to ping segment 3 from router R2 (nor segment 2 from router R3). Although the routing works fine and hosts on segments 2 and 3 would be able to communicate with each other without any problems, routers R2 and R3 won't be able to ping segments 3 and 2, respectively. The reason is that routers use the IP address of the interface that is closest to the destination, which is Serial0 on both routers. The ICMP echoes produced by ping arrive at the pinged segment fine, but the replies won't go back: Routers R2 and R3 don't have the appropriate **frame-relay map ip** commands for each other. If you add these commands, this issue will not exist (but the commands won't help anything else).

Configuring RIP Version 2

Cisco IOS, beginning with version 11.2, supports RIP version 2. To enable pure RIP version 2, the **version 2** command must be entered under the **router rip** configuration.

As we know from the "In Depth" section, RIP version 2 is a classless routing protocol. Thus, the restriction of one subnet mask per classful network address is no longer present in the case of RIP version 2—a normal condition in classless IP addressing. Let's see how it works.

We'll use the new network topology shown in Figure 4.19.

Segments 1 through 5 are assigned network prefixes of different lengths (/22, /25, and /30), and all of the network prefixes belong to the same classful network address (10.0.0.0/8).

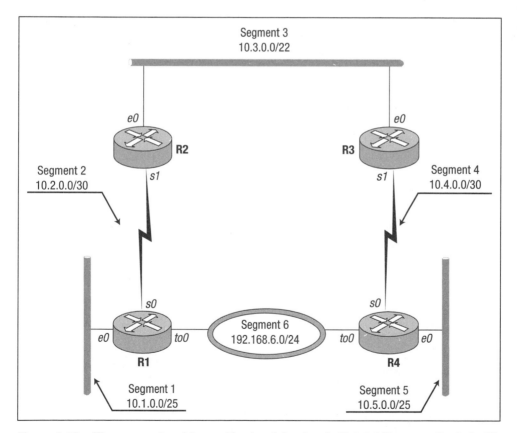

Figure 4.19   The segments addressed in classful network 10.0.0.0/8 are configured with network prefixes of different lengths: /22, /25, and /30.

Listings 4.72 through 4.75 show the configurations of all four routers.

Listing 4.72   Router R1's configuration.

```
interface Ethernet0
 ip address 10.1.0.1 255.255.255.128

interface Serial0
 ip address 10.2.0.1 255.255.255.252

interface TokenRing0
 ip address 192.168.6.1 255.255.255.0
 ring-speed 16

router rip
 version 2
 network 10.0.0.0
 network 192.168.6.0
```

Listing 4.73   Router R2's configuration.

```
interface Ethernet0
 ip address 10.3.0.1 255.255.252.0

interface Serial1
 ip address 10.2.0.2 255.255.255.252

router rip
 version 2
 network 10.0.0.0
```

Listing 4.74   Router R3's configuration.

```
interface Ethernet0
 ip address 10.3.0.2 255.255.252.0

interface Serial1
 ip address 10.4.0.2 255.255.255.252

router rip
 version 2
 network 10.0.0.0
```

Listing 4.75   Router R4's configuration.

```
interface Ethernet0
 ip address 10.5.0.1 255.255.255.128
```

```
interface Serial0
 ip address 10.4.0.1 255.255.255.252

interface TokenRing0
 ip address 192.168.6.2 255.255.255.0
 ring-speed 16

router rip
 version 2
 network 10.0.0.0
 network 192.168.6.0
```

Notice the **version 2** statement under the **router rip** configuration of all four routers. Let's now examine the routing table of router R4, shown in Listing 4.76.

Listing 4.76   The routing table of router R4.

```
R4#show ip route
...
     10.0.0.0/8 is variably subnetted, 6 subnets, 4 masks
R    10.2.0.0/30 [120/2] via 10.4.0.2, 00:00:00, Serial0
R    10.3.0.0/22 [120/1] via 10.4.0.2, 00:00:00, Serial0
R    10.0.0.0/8 [120/1] via 192.168.6.1, 00:00:23, TokenRing0
R    10.1.0.0/25 [120/3] via 10.4.0.2, 00:00:00, Serial0
C    10.4.0.0/30 is directly connected, Serial0
C    10.5.0.0/25 is directly connected, Ethernet0
C  192.168.6.0/24 is directly connected, TokenRing0
```

The shaded lines show network prefixes that belong to network 10.0.0.0/8 and are learned via RIP version 2. They all have different lengths, which demonstrates the classless nature of RIP version 2.

NOTE: *The reason why 10.0.0.0/8 appears in the routing table will be explained in the next section.*

Disabling RIP Version 2 Auto-Summarization

The most important feature of RIP version 2 is its classless nature. Speaking in terms of classful IP addressing, it translates to two important classfully impossible features:

• Routers that employ RIP version 2 can advertise subnets with more than one mask per classful network address (we examined an example of this in the previous section).

- RIP version 2 can advertise subnets in the routing updates that cross the corresponding classful network boundary.

The first feature is important because it allows you to allocate of the network prefixes whose lengths adequately reflect the maximum number of hosts that can reside on each segment. This, in turn, facilitates the conservation of IP address space.

The second feature is important because it provides for optimal routing and supports discontiguous IP address space. Let's see how these two concepts can be implemented with RIP version 2.

By default, RIP version 2 on Cisco routers performs auto-summarization of subnets in the routing updates that cross the corresponding classful network boundary, thereby disabling the second classless feature of RIP version 2. To turn off this "classful" behavior of RIP version 2, the **no auto-summary** command must be used in the **router rip** configuration.

In the example in the previous section, the routing table of router R4 exhibited a route for network prefix 10.0.0.0/8 through router R1. This was because router R1 summarized network prefixes that belong to classful network 10.0.0.0/8 in its routing updates sent through interface TokerRing0. The summary address is the classful network 10.0.0.0/8 itself. In the case of RIP version 2, it is specifically advertised as network prefix 10.0.0.0/8, which also includes the prefix length. Upon receipt of router R1's advertisements, router R4 installed a route for 10.0.0.0/8, because, from a classless perspective, it's just another network prefix with nothing specific about it.

Likewise, router R4 advertises the 10.0.0.0/8 summary address through its TokenRing0 interface. Therefore, if we examined router R1's routing table, we would also discover a route for network prefix 10.0.0.0/8, only this time through router R4. At the same time, network prefix 10.0.0.0/8 is the only network prefix for which routers R1 and R4 have routes through Token Ring segment 6. For example, the route for network prefix 10.5.0.0/25 at router R1 points towards router R2 through interface Serial0, whereas it's clearly best accessible through Token Ring segment 0. Likewise, the route for network prefix 10.1.0.0/25 at router R4 points towards router R3 through interface Serial0 of router R4.

The output of the **traceroute 10.1.0.1** command issued on router R4 (shown below) confirms that traffic destined for segment 1 takes two extra router hops:

```
R4#traceroute 10.1.0.1
 ...
 1 10.4.0.2 4 msec 4 msec 4 msec
 2 10.3.0.1 12 msec 4 msec 4 msec
 3 10.2.0.1 176 msec * 4 msec
```

The reason for this nonoptimal routing is that the RIP version 2 processes on routers R1 and R4 won't currently advertise any network prefixes of network 10.0.0.0/8 (except for 10.0.0.0/8 itself) through their TokenRing0 interfaces.

This is easy to correct by using the **no auto-summary** command in the **router rip** configuration to disable RIP version 2 auto-summarization on routers R1 and R4. After that change, the routing table of router R4 will appear as shown in Listing 4.77.

Listing 4.77   The routing table of router R4 after the **no auto-summary** command has been entered on routers R1 and R4 in the **router rip** configuration.

```
R4#show ip route
...
   10.0.0.0/8 is variably subnetted, 5 subnets, 3 masks
R    10.2.0.0/30 [120/1] via 192.168.6.1, 00:00:29, TokenRing0
R    10.3.0.0/22 [120/1] via 10.4.0.2, 00:00:02, Serial0
R    10.1.0.0/25 [120/1] via 192.168.6.1, 00:00:29, TokenRing0
C    10.4.0.0/30 is directly connected, Serial0
C    10.5.0.0/25 is directly connected, Ethernet0
C    192.168.6.0/24 is directly connected, TokenRing0
```

This time, the routing table of router R4 shows no signs of a route for network prefix 10.0.0.0/8. In addition, the routing table shows optimal routes for network prefixes 10.1.0.0/25 and 10.2.0.0/30 (the two shaded lines).

The output of the **traceroute 10.1.0.1** command entered on router R4 now shows only one router hop, router R1:

```
R4#traceroute 10.1.0.1
...
 1 192.168.6.1 4 msec * 4 msec
```

Let's consider another example that demonstrates how RIP version 2 can be used to implement a network with IP address allocation, which, speaking in terms of classful IP addressing, is called *discontiguous subnetting*. An example of such a network is shown in Figure 4.20. Segments 1, 2, 3, 4, and 6, addressed within classful network address 10.0.0.0/8, are separated by Token Ring segment 5, whose network prefix is 192.168.5.0/24. This network is impossible to implement using classful routing protocols, such as RIP version 1 and IGRP. Nevertheless, to classless RIP version 2, this IP address allocation presents no problem, provided auto-summarization is disabled.

To make the example a bit more interesting, we'll also require every router to have a loopback interface with the IP address of 10.0.0.X/32, where X corresponds to the router's number.

4. Routing Information Protocol (RIP)

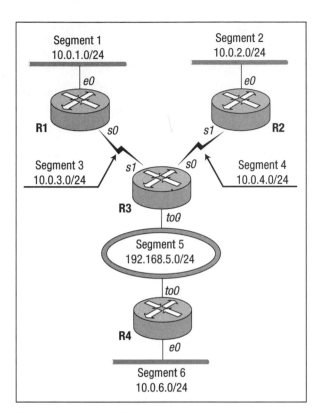

Figure 4.20 The "illegal" network (from the perspective of classful RIP version 1) can nevertheless be handled by classless RIP version 2.

To support this addressing scheme, routers R3 and R4 should be configured with **no auto-summary** in the **router rip** parts of their configurations. Listings 4.78 through 4.81 show the configurations of all four routers.

Listing 4.78   Router R1's configuration.

```
interface Loopback0
 ip address 10.0.0.1 255.255.255.255

interface Ethernet0
 ip address 10.0.1.1 255.255.255.0

interface Serial0
 ip address 10.0.3.2 255.255.255.0

router rip
 version 2
 network 10.0.0.0

ip classless
```

Listing 4.79   Router R2's configuration.

```
interface Loopback0
 ip address 10.0.0.2 255.255.255.255

interface Ethernet0
 ip address 10.0.2.1 255.255.255.0

interface Serial1
 ip address 10.0.4.2 255.255.255.0

router rip
 version 2
 network 10.0.0.0

ip classless
```

Listing 4.80   Router R3's configuration.

```
interface Loopback0
 ip address 10.0.0.3 255.255.255.255

interface Serial0
 ip address 10.0.4.1 255.255.255.0

interface Serial1
 ip address 10.0.3.1 255.255.255.0

interface TokenRing0
 ip address 192.168.5.1 255.255.255.0
 ring-speed 16

router rip
 version 2
 network 10.0.0.0
 network 192.168.5.0
 no auto-summary

ip classless
```

Listing 4.81   Router R4's configuration.

```
interface Loopback0
 ip address 10.0.0.4 255.255.255.255

interface Ethernet0
 ip address 10.0.6.1 255.255.255.0
```

4. Routing Information Protocol (RIP)

```
interface TokenRing0
 ip address 192.168.5.2 255.255.255.0
 ring-speed 16

router rip
 version 2
 network 10.0.0.0
 network 192.168.5.0
 no auto-summary

ip classless
```

The shaded lines in the configurations of routers R3 and R4 (Listings 4.80 and 4.81) show the **no auto-summary** command. Notice that this command is not present in the other routers' configurations.

To see if the configurations of the routers do the job, let's examine the routing tables of routers R1 and R4, shown in Listings 4.82 and 4.83, respectively.

Listing 4.82   The routing table of router R1.

```
R1#show ip route
...
R  192.168.5.0/24 [120/1] via 10.0.3.1, 00:00:08, Serial0
     10.0.0.0/8 is variably subnetted, 9 subnets, 2 masks
R     10.0.0.2/32 [120/2] via 10.0.3.1, 00:00:08, Serial0
R     10.0.2.0/24 [120/2] via 10.0.3.1, 00:00:08, Serial0
R     10.0.0.3/32 [120/1] via 10.0.3.1, 00:00:08, Serial0
C     10.0.3.0/24 is directly connected, Serial0
C     10.0.0.1/32 is directly connected, Loopback0
C     10.0.1.0/24 is directly connected, Ethernet0
R     10.0.6.0/24 [120/2] via 10.0.3.1, 00:00:09, Serial0
R     10.0.0.4/32 [120/2] via 10.0.3.1, 00:00:09, Serial0
R     10.0.4.0/24 [120/1] via 10.0.3.1, 00:00:09, Serial0
```

Listing 4.83   The routing table of router R4.

```
R4#show ip route
...
C  192.168.5.0/24 is directly connected, TokenRing0
     10.0.0.0/8 is variably subnetted, 9 subnets, 2 masks
R     10.0.0.2/32 [120/2] via 192.168.5.1, 00:00:06, TokenRing0
R     10.0.2.0/24 [120/2] via 192.168.5.1, 00:00:06, TokenRing0
R     10.0.0.3/32 [120/1] via 192.168.5.1, 00:00:06, TokenRing0
R     10.0.3.0/24 [120/1] via 192.168.5.1, 00:00:06, TokenRing0
R     10.0.0.1/32 [120/2] via 192.168.5.1, 00:00:06, TokenRing0
R     10.0.1.0/24 [120/2] via 192.168.5.1, 00:00:06, TokenRing0
C     10.0.6.0/24 is directly connected, Ethernet0
```

```
R    10.0.4.0/24 [120/1] via 192.168.5.1, 00:00:06, TokenRing0
C    10.0.0.4/32 is directly connected, Loopback0
```

The shaded lines in both listings show the routing table entries that wouldn't be possible if RIP version 1 were used instead of RIP version 2.

The discussed classless features of RIP version 2 notwithstanding, Cisco's implementation of it still lacks some key classless elements. For example, from the standpoint of classless IP addressing, network prefix 172.16.0.0/12 presents nothing special. (On the contrary, from the classful IP addressing standpoint, it is a supernet.) An IP address that belongs to this network prefix can be assigned on a router interface. In addition, if the router runs RIP version 2, the router's operating system must provide the means to turn on the RIP version 2 operation on that interface.

Let's see if this holds true in the case of Cisco IOS by adding another loopback interface on router R4 and assigning it the IP address 172.16.0.1/12. Then, using the **network 172.16.0.0** command, we'll try to enable RIP version 2 on this loopback interface. If Cisco's RIP version 2 is really classless, it should begin advertising this network prefix to the other routers.

Listing 4.84 shows the modified configuration of router R4.

Listing 4.84 The configuration of router R4 in which an attempt is made to make RIP version 2 advertise the "supernet" network prefix of interface Loopback1.

```
interface Loopback0
 ip address 10.0.0.4 255.255.255.255

interface Loopback1
 ip address 172.16.0.1 255.240.0.0

interface Ethernet0
 ip address 10.0.6.1 255.255.255.0

interface TokenRing0
 ip address 192.168.5.2 255.255.255.0
 ring-speed 16

router rip
 version 2
 network 10.0.0.0
 network 172.16.0.0
 network 192.168.5.0
 no auto-summary

ip classless
```

The shaded lines show the discussed commands.

If we examine the routing table of another router in the network, we won't see a route for network prefix 172.16.0.0/12. As an example, the routing table of router R3 is shown in Listing 4.85.

Listing 4.85   The routing table of router R3 shows no signs of a route for network prefix 172.16.0.0/12.

```
R3#show ip route
...
C  192.168.5.0/24 is directly connected, TokenRing0
   10.0.0.0/8 is variably subnetted, 9 subnets, 2 masks
R    10.0.2.0/24 [120/1] via 10.0.4.2, 00:00:09, Serial0
R    10.0.0.2/32 [120/1] via 10.0.4.2, 00:00:09, Serial0
C    10.0.3.0/24 is directly connected, Serial1
C    10.0.0.3/32 is directly connected, Loopback0
R    10.0.1.0/24 [120/1] via 10.0.3.2, 00:00:09, Serial1
R    10.0.0.1/32 [120/1] via 10.0.3.2, 00:00:09, Serial1
R    10.0.6.0/24 [120/1] via 192.168.5.2, 00:00:09, TokenRing0
R    10.0.0.4/32 [120/1] via 192.168.5.2, 00:00:09, TokenRing0
C    10.0.4.0/24 is directly connected, Serial0
```

In Chapter 7, we'll consider a method of making RIP version 2 a little more "classless."

Understanding How RIP Versions 1 and 2 Can Be Used Together

Cisco's implementation of RIP allows using both versions simultaneously on a per-interface basis. Two commands are used to enable the processing of the desired RIP version on an interface. The first command is **ip rip send version {1|2}**, which enables sending the desired version of RIP routing updates via the corresponding interface. The second command is **ip rip receive version {1|2}**, which allows the router to receive and process the desired version of RIP routing updates. Both commands should be entered in interface configuration mode.

TIP: *The full format of the command is **ip rip {receive|send} version {1|2}** [{1|2}], which allows you to specify exactly which version of RIP you want the router to use when sending and receiving RIP routing updates on a particular interface. The last parameter is optional and allows you to use both versions simultaneously. However, exercise care if both versions are specified, because the router will double the number of routing updates (it will have to create a separate routing update for each version).*

Regardless of which version of RIP is specified in the **version** command under the **router rip** configuration, the command **ip rip {receive|send} version {1|2} [{1|2}]** is still available and takes precedence. In other words, the **version** command under the **router rip** configuration specifies the default version, whereas the **ip rip {receive|send} version {1|2} [{1|2}]** specifies the version that should be used on individual interfaces when sending or receiving the RIP routing updates.

4. Routing Information Protocol (RIP)

Chapter 5

Interior Gateway Routing Protocol (IGRP)

If you need an immediate solution to:	See page:
Performing Basic IGRP Configuration	328
Understanding How IGRP Processes Routing Updates	331
Understanding How IGRP Handles Secondary IP Addresses	335
Understanding and Changing IGRP Metrics	341
Performing Equal- and Unequal-Cost Load Balancing with IGRP	344
Configuring IGRP to Originate a Default Route	349
Adjusting IGRP Timers	356
Modify the IGRP Metric Weights	356

In Depth

This chapter is devoted to Interior Gateway Routing Protocol (IGRP), the interior gateway routing protocol. This is a Cisco-proprietary, distance-vector routing protocol (so the algorithm theory set forth in Chapter 4 fully applies to IGRP).

Like RIP, IGRP is a classful routing protocol. Hence, much of this chapter will contain classful terminology—subnets, classful network addresses, and so on.

IGRP

IGRP is similar to RIP in that it's a rigid classful protocol, but it differs in that IGRP was designed to handle networks of virtually any size. The network diameter of IGRP is 255.

NOTE: The network diameter *of a routing protocol was previously defined as the length of the longest route (measured in router hops) that the routing protocol could handle.*

Although IGRP's stability features (such as split-horizon, holddowns, and so on) make it slower to converge than RIP, its slowness is well compensated for by its much higher stability.

IGRP uses quite sophisticated metrics that take into account various characteristics of routes, such as minimum bandwidth, total delay, and so forth.

Because IGRP is Cisco proprietary, it cannot be found on non-Cisco devices such as other vendors' routers or Unix machines.

IGRP Routing Update Format

IGRP routing updates are encapsulated directly into Internet Protocol (IP) datagrams and consist of a header and route entries. The Protocol field in the headers of datagrams that carry IGRP routing updates holds the value of 9. The datagrams are destined for the local broadcast address (255.255.255.255).

The format of the IGRP routing update is shown in Figure 5.1.

The 4-bit Version field always carries the value of 1.

The 4-bit Opcode field can take two values: 1 (update) and 2 (request). The Opcode field performs a function similar to that of the Command field in RIP routing

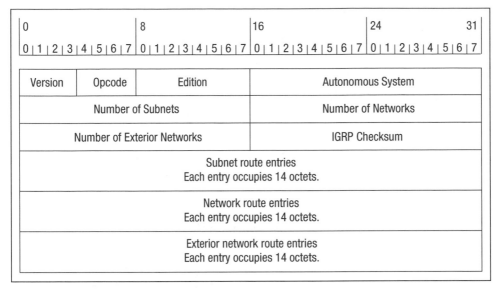

Figure 5.1   The format of the IGRP routing update.

updates. A router uses the request Opcode (2) to request routing information from its neighbors, which typically occurs when a router initializes or if it loses the routing information (for example, because someone entered the **clear ip route** * command). The neighbors that choose to answer the routing update carrying the request Opcode (2) reply with routing updates carrying the update Opcode (1).

The update Opcode (1) is also used in the regular routing updates.

The routing updates carrying the request Opcode (2) are not supposed to have any route entries. In addition, the only non-zero fields in those updates are Version, Opcode, and Autonomous System; all other fields must be set to 0.

NOTE: *Unlike IGRP requests, RIP requests can carry route entries, which means that the source of the request wants routing information for only those network prefixes that it put in the route entries. The primary reason for this difference between the two protocols is that RIP is an open protocol and, as such, it is often implemented on hosts, which seek a basic level of dynamic routing. These hosts may not want to know all available routing information, because processing it might cause excessive CPU overhead. Instead, such hosts may want routing information for only the destinations that they intend to communicate with. That's why RIP requests allow the hosts to specify these specific destinations. On the contrary, because IGRP is Cisco proprietary, it's unlikely ever to be implemented on hosts. Hence, the designers of the protocol sought the most economic implementation (as opposed to the most flexible), trying to limit the adverse impact on the network while completely meeting the routing requirements.*

The Edition field is 8 bits long and carries the current edition of the routing update. Each time IGRP changes the contents of the routing updates that it sends over the same interface, it increments the value carried in the Edition field. This helps other routers detect and ignore obsolete routing updates.

NOTE: *The Edition field is a rather questionable means to detect obsolete routing information. There are scenarios in which it won't help at all, if not make the things worse. Most probably, the real IGRP implementation ignores the field. Nevertheless, the routers do modify it as described.*

The 16-bit Autonomous System field denotes the IGRP process ID on the router that issued the routing update. The neighbors can exchange routing updates only if they run IGRP processes with the same ID. This field is called Autonomous System because typically if routing in a large network is handled by IGRP, all routers are configured with the same IGRP process ID. Hence, this number essentially denotes the autonomous system of the network.

NOTE: *The Autonomous System number is not related to the globally administered Autonomous System numbers that denote autonomous systems in the Internet. The latter Autonomous System numbers are used in BGP configuration.*

The 16-bit Number Of Subnets field denotes the number of route entries carrying the subnets of the classful network to which the IP address of the interface through which the routing update is sent. These entries must appear right after the header of the routing update.

The 16-bit Number Of Networks field denotes the number of route entries carrying the advertised classful network addresses. These entries must appear right after the subnet route entries of the routing update.

The 16-bit Number Of Exterior Networks field denotes the number of route entries carrying the exterior network addresses. (The meaning of "exterior network addresses" will be explained later in this chapter.) These entries must appear right after the network route entries of the routing update.

Any of these last three fields can hold a value of 0 (which means that the corresponding route entries are not present in the routing update).

Finally the 16-bit IGRP Checksum field carries a checksum that covers the IGRP header and all route entries. (IGRP uses the same checksum algorithm as UDP.) Upon receipt of an IGRP routing update, the router must first verify the integrity of the update by recalculating the IGRP checksum and comparing it with the value carried in this field. If the values coincide, the router can further process the update; otherwise, it must drop the update.

IGRP Route Entries

The format of the IGRP route entry is shown in Figure 5.2.

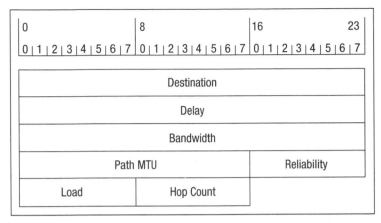

Figure 5.2   The format of the IGRP route entry.

The first field of the route entry (Destination) is the advertised network prefix. Interestingly enough, it's only 3 octets long (as opposed to a regular IP address, which is 4 octets long). Nevertheless, the information contained in this field is enough for classful IGRP to correctly set a route for the advertised network prefix.

IGRP uses the following rules to interpret the value of the Network Prefix field.

- If the route entry is a subnet route entry, IGRP interprets the contents of the Destination field as the last 3 octets of the advertised network prefix. It takes the first octet from the IP address of the interface over which the update was received. IGRP recognizes the route entry as a subnet route entry if its number is less than or equal to the value of the Number Of Subnets field (providing the entries in these fields are enumerated starting with 1). (In other words, if the route entry appears among the subnet route entries, it is a subnet route entry.)

- If the route entry is a network route entry, IGRP interprets the contents of the Destination field as the first 3 octets of the advertised classful network address. (The fourth octet of any classful network address is equal to 0.) IGRP recognizes a route entry as a network route entry if its number is greater than the value of the Number Of Subnets field and less than or equal to the sum of the values of the Number Of Subnets and Number Of Networks fields. (In other words, if the route entry appears among the network route entries, it is a network route entry.)

- If the route entry is an exterior network route entry, IGRP interprets the contents of the Destination field as the first 3 octets of the advertised classful network address. (The interpretation is identical to that of the network route entry.) IGRP recognizes a route entry as an exterior network route entry if its number is greater than the sum of the values of the Number Of Subnets and

Number Of Networks fields and less than or equal to the sum of the values of the Number Of Subnets, Number Of Networks, and Number Of Exterior Networks fields. (In other words, if the route entry appears among the network route entries, it is a network route entry.)

> **NOTE:**   Although the interpretation of the values of the Destination fields in the network and exterior network route entries is the same, the use of the resulting network prefixes is slightly different. This will be thoroughly discussed in the "Types of Addresses IGRP Can Advertise" section later in this chapter.

The 3-octet Delay field carries the value of logical delay of the route to the advertised network prefix, measured in tens of microseconds.

The 3-octet Bandwidth field carries the value of the largest inverse logical bandwidth en route to the network prefix encoded in the Destination field.

The 2-octet Path MTU field carries the value of the smallest MTU size of the route to the advertised network prefix.

> **NOTE:**   The Path MTU field provides routers with the ability to keep track of MTU sizes en route to various destinations within the IGRP routing domain. This capability immensely facilitates the greatly encouraged MTU discovery process mentioned in Chapter 1. Nevertheless, this valuable feature of IGRP remains useless unless the routers can communicate the discovered MTU sizes to the hosts.

The 1-octet Reliability field carries the value of the reliability of the route to the advertised network prefix.

Load is also a 1-octet field, and it carries the value of the average load of the route to the advertised network prefix.

Hop Count is a 1-octet subnet of a classful network address (providing it has one or more interfaces) whose IP field carries the number of the router hops in the route to the advertised network prefix.

The details of how routers calculate the values for the Delay, Bandwidth, Reliability, and Load fields are explained in the "IGRP Metrics" section later in this chapter.

Types of Addresses IGRP Can Advertise

A router can advertise two types of network prefixes via IGRP: classful network addresses, and subnets of classful network addresses (providing the router has one or more interfaces whose IP addresses belong to these classful network addresses).

As IGRP is a classful routing protocol, it won't pass network prefix lengths (subnet masks) in the routing updates. Thus, it can advertise subnets of a classful network address through only those interfaces whose IP addresses belong to this classful network address.

The IGRP routers cannot advertise the default address (0.0.0.0/0) and individual host addresses (192.168.1.1/32, for example).

Instead of the default address, IGRP can advertise so-called *exterior network prefixes*, or simply *exterior networks*. Exterior networks typically provide access to the Internet, or to another network, which is assumed to have additional routes. Thus, the traffic sent to unknown destinations can be forwarded through the exterior networks. Exterior networks are advertised in the exterior network route entries. The router that advertises exterior networks can be used as the default router by the routers that accept its routing updates.

An example of exterior networks is shown in Figure 5.3. Networks N1, N2, and N3 can be advertised by IGRP as exterior.

If a router that receives a routing update with exterior network route entries accepts the network prefixes contained in them, it labels the resulting routes as

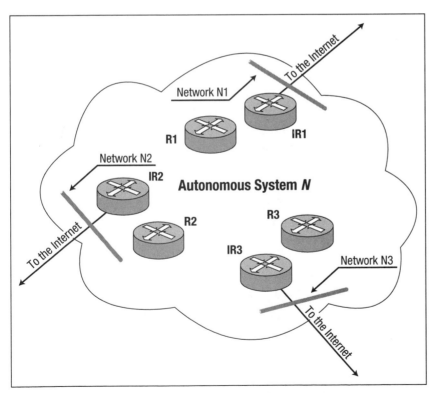

Figure 5.3   Routes for networks N1, N2, and N3 are exterior.

candidate default. Notice, however, that if IGRP accepts routing updates that advertise exterior networks and then installs the corresponding candidate default routes, those routes may not necessarily be utilized as the default routes.

NOTE: *To understand how routers use candidate default routes, refer to the "Understanding Candidate Default Routes and Gateway of Last Resort" section in Chapter 4.*

Aside from this, the network prefixes advertised in the network route entries do not differ from those advertised in the exterior network route entries. Both can be used to advertise only classful network addresses, and both, if accepted, cause the router to create routing table entries that point to the advertising router as the next-hop router.

IGRP Metrics

As mentioned before, IGRP uses rather sophisticated metrics to discriminate amongst different routes.

IGRP routers obey the following rules when creating and modifying route metrics:

- When advertising a network prefix assigned on one of the interfaces on which IGRP operates, the router calculates the metric for it using the parameters of the interface. The router is said to *originate* the route for such network prefixes.

- When creating a route for a network prefix learned from another IGRP router, the router calculates the new metric using the parameters passed in the route entry of the routing update and the parameters of the interface through which the update was received. The router also uses this new metric to advertise this network prefix.

- The router advertises a classful network address with the metric equal to the smallest among the metrics of all routes for subnets of the classful address. If the router does not know of any subnets of this classful network address, then one of the first two rules applies.

NOTE: *The last rule basically means that summary addresses are created with the smallest known metric.*

IGRP metrics are 32-bit values. The value of 4294967295 decimal (0xFFFFFFFF) denotes infinity. When calculating the values of the metrics, IGRP uses the following formula:

$$M_{IGRP} = \left[k1 * B_{IGRP} + \frac{k2 * B_{IGRP}}{256 - L} + k\,3 * D_{IGRP} \right] * \frac{k5}{R + k4}$$

If, however, $k2$ is equal to 0, the formula is reduced to

$$M_{IGRP} = k1*B_{IGRP} + \frac{k2*B_{IGRP}}{256-L} + k3*D_{IGRP}$$

where M_{IGRP} is the calculated metric. Following is the explanation of the parameters of the formula.

B_{IGRP} is the inverse logical bandwidth of the route. If the router originates the route, the inverse logical bandwidth is calculated using the following formula:

$$B_{IGRP} = \frac{10^7}{BW}$$

where BW is the value of the logical bandwidth (measured in kilobits per second) of the interface on which the advertised network prefix is configured. The value of B_{IGRP} is placed in the Bandwidth field of the corresponding route entry in the routing updates.

If the router recalculates the metric for a network prefix that it learned from another router, it compares the inverse logical bandwidth of the interface through which the update was received with the value carried in the Bandwidth field of the corresponding route entry of the routing update. Whichever is greater becomes the new value for B_{IGRP}. When advertising this network prefix, the router will place this value into the Bandwidth field of its routing updates.

NOTE: *The purpose of the described operation is to keep track of the smallest logical bandwidth en route to the advertised network prefix. Because the bandwidth's values passed in the IGRP routing updates are "inverted," the comparison selects the greater value as opposed to the psychologically expected smaller one.*

D_{IGRP} is the cumulative logical route delay measured in tens of microseconds. If the router originates the route, the logical delay is calculated using the following formula:

$$D_{IGRP} = \frac{DLY}{10}$$

where DLY is the logical delay (in microseconds) of the interface on which the advertised network prefix is configured. The value of D_{IGRP} is placed in the Delay field of the corresponding route entry in the routing updates.

If the router recalculates the metric for a network prefix that it learned from another router, it calculates the new value for D_{IGRP} as a sum of the D_{IGRP} of the interface through which the routing update was received and the value of the Delay field of the route entry in the original routing update.

The new calculated value is placed into the Delay field of the router's own routing updates advertising the network prefix.

NOTE: The purpose of D_{IGRP} is to keep track of the total logical delay of the route to the network prefix.

If the router originates the network prefix, L is the IGRP load of the interface on which the network prefix is assigned. This parameter is dynamically measured by IGRP and is expressed as an integer value in the range of 1 through 255, with 1 as the minimally loaded interface and 255 being the 100 percent loaded interface. The value of L is placed in the Load field of the corresponding route entry in the routing updates.

If the router recalculates the metric for a network prefix that it learned from another router, it makes L equal to the larger of the values of the IGRP load of the interface through which the original routing update was received and the Load field in the corresponding route entry of this routing update. The new calculated value is placed into the Load field of the router's own routing updates advertising the network prefix.

NOTE: The purpose of L is to keep track of the most loaded segment en route to the network prefix.

R is the IGRP reliability of the segment to which the corresponding interface is attached. This is another parameter measured dynamically by IGRP itself. Similar to L, R is expressed as an integer value from 0 through 255, with 0 being the minimally reliable segment and 255 the 100 percent reliable segment.

If the router originates a network prefix, R is taken from the interface on which the network prefix is assigned. This value is placed in the Reliability field of the corresponding route entry in the routing updates. If the router recalculates the metric for a network prefix that it learned from another router, it makes R equal to the smaller of the values of the IGRP load of the interface through which the original routing update was received and the Reliability field in the corresponding route entry of this routing update. The new calculated value is placed into the Reliability field of the router's own routing updates advertising the network prefix.

NOTE: The purpose of R is to keep track of the least reliable segment en route to the network prefix.

All of the aforementioned variables of the IGRP formula for calculating metrics can be expressed using the following equations:

- $B_{new} = \min(B_{int}, B_{update})$
- $D_{new} = D_{int} + D_{update}$
- $L_{new} = \max(L_{int}, L_{update})$
- $R_{new} = \min(R_{int}, R_{update})$

where the values indexed with *new* are the calculated values, those indexed with *int* are the values associated with the interface through which the routing update was received, and those indexed with *update* are the values from the corresponding route entry of the routing update.

Parameters *k1*, *k2*, *k3*, *k4*, and *k5* are administratively configurable weights. Their default values are shown in Table 5.1.

When applied, the default values of the weights reduce the formula for calculating the IGRP metrics to $M_{IGRP} = B_{IGRP} + D_{IGRP}$.

NOTE: Although not used in the metric calculations, MTU size is also recalculated whenever the router originates a network prefix or re-advertises a network prefix learned from another router. The recalculated value is stored in the Path MTU field of the corresponding route entry of the sent routing updates. If the router originates a network prefix, the Path MTU field is assigned the value of the MTU size of the interface on which the network prefix is assigned. For learned and re-advertised network prefixes, the Path MTU field carries the smallest of the values of the MTU size of the interface through which the original routing update was received and the Path MTU value in the route entry of this route update.

Unequal-Cost Load Balancing

IGRP's unique feature is the ability to perform unequal-cost load balancing. This feature is based on the premise that a router employing IGRP is allowed to have multiple routes with different metrics for the same network prefix. If that's the case, the router will share the traffic destined for the network prefix among the routes proportionally to their metrics.

Table 5.1   The default values of the IGRP metric weights.

Weight	Default Value
k1	1
k2	0
k3	1
k4	0
k5	0

Typically, if a routing process has two or more routes for the same destination, it installs to the routing table only the one with the smallest metric and discards all others. If two or more routes have equally small metrics, they can all be installed in the routing table, which, as we know, results in equal-cost load balancing.

IGRP handles routes with the same smallest metric just like any other source of routing information, thereby producing equal-cost load balancing. If, however, IGRP has several routes for the same destination but with different metrics, it may not necessarily get rid of the routes with the metric greater than the smallest metric.

Among several (IGRP) routes for the same destination, one or more produce the smallest metric. We'll call these routes the *best local routes*. (Why the term *local* is needed will become clear shortly.) Obviously, the best local routes are always installed into the routing table.

NOTE: *The number of the best local routes installed in the routing table must be smaller than or equal to the administratively configurable number of maximum parallel paths.*

The remaining routes whose metric is greater than the metric of the best local routes will be called *candidate routes*. The candidate routes, which pass the following two feasibility conditions, are also installed into the routing table:

- The next-hop router in the candidate route should have a route for the destination with a metric smaller than that of the best local route (the best metric).

NOTE: *The router applying this feasibility condition calculates the metric of the best route at the next-hop router using the values of the corresponding route entry of the routing update received from the next-hop router.*

- The metric of the candidate route must be less than or equal to the metric of the local best route multiplied by the administratively configurable value called a *multiplier*. The multiplier value can be whole numbers between 1 and 128.

NOTE: *By default, the multiplier is equal to 1, which disables unequal-cost load balancing.*

An example of unequal-cost load balancing is presented in the "Performing Equal and Unequal-Cost Load Balancing with IGRP" section later in this chapter.

IGRP Timers

IGRP routers send regular routing updates upon expiration of the update timer. After the update timer expires, it's reset and restarted. By default, the update timer expires every 90 seconds.

To avoid synchronization of the update timers, the routers randomly change the expiration time of the regular update timer by subtracting a small value (a *jitter time*) of up to 20 percent of the configured update timer expiration time. If the expiration time is left at the default, the interval between the succeeding regular routing updates randomly ranges from 72 through 90 seconds (20 percent of 90 seconds = 18 seconds; 90 − 18 = 72 seconds).

The router starts a timeout timer for every IGRP route installed in the routing table, and the timeout timer is reset each time the route is updated by an incoming routing update. If the timeout timer for some route reaches the *invalid time* (270 seconds by default), the route's metric is changed to infinity (4294967295 decimal), and the route itself is placed into holddown. The route cannot be modified until the timer reaches the value equal to the sum of the invalid time and the holddown time (280 seconds by default). When the timer reaches the *flush* time (630 seconds by default), the route is removed from the routing table.

NOTE: *The flush time can be configured to be greater than the sum of the invalid and holddown times. In that case, if the timeout timer exceeds the sum of the invalid and holddown times, the route can be updated. But, until it is updated, it's still advertised with the metric of infinity (4294967295 decimal).*

If a router has an IGRP route for a certain network prefix and receives a poisoned-reverse update from the router whose IP address is the next-hop router, the route's metric is changed to infinity (4294967295 decimal), the route itself is put into holddown, and the holddown timer is started for the route. Until the holddown timer expires, the router won't update the route. After the holddown timer expires (after the holddown time), the route is either removed from the routing table or updated.

5. Interior Gateway Routing Protocol (IGRP)

Immediate Solutions

As we've mentioned, IGRP is very similar to RIP in that both are classful, distance-vector routing protocols. And the differences they do have don't much affect the configuration and operation of the protocols on Cisco routers. Thus, it makes sense to examine only those configuration and operation tasks that are different for IGRP and RIP, and to simply list the tasks that are identical.

The following list shows the configuration and operation tasks that are identical for IGRP and RIP:

- Handling IP unnumbered

- Using unicast routing updates

- Changing the administrative distance of routing updates

- Using IGRP and RIP in the presence of NBMA networks

(One task, however, cannot be performed with IGRP: It's impossible to make IGRP advertise host addresses.)

The following sections show the configuration and operation tasks that are specific to IGRP.

Performing Basic IGRP Configuration

Basic IGRP configurations are very similar to basic RIP configurations. To configure IGRP, follow these steps:

1. Create an IGRP routing process on the router using the **router igrp** <*AS* #> command in global configuration mode. The numeric <*AS* #> parameter ranges from 1 through 65535 and represents the desired autonomous system number. The primary purpose of this parameter is to allow the creation of multiple IGRP processes on a single router. The specified value must be the same on the routers that are expected to exchange IGRP routing updates. As we learned in the "In Depth" section, this value is communicated between IGRP neighbors in the routing updates.

    This command transfers the command line interface into IGRP configuration mode for the specified autonomous system.

2. Specify the interfaces that the IGRP routing process will use to receive and send its routing updates using one or several **network** *<IP address>* commands. The *<IP address>* parameter must be a classful network address (such as 10.0.0.0 and 172.16.0.0). To process routing updates, IGRP will use all operational interfaces whose IP addresses belong to the specified classful network addresses. (The interfaces that are either down or administratively disabled won't be used.) IGRP will advertise the network prefixes configured on the interfaces specified using the **network** *<IP address>* command.

The meaning of the **network** command in the case of IGRP is exactly the same as it was in the case of RIP.

To see how these guidelines apply, let's use the network scheme shown in Figure 5.4.

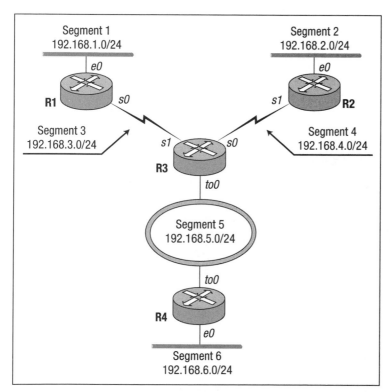

Figure 5.4   This network demonstrates a basic IGRP configuration.

The configurations of all four routers are shown in Listings 5.1 through 5.4.

Listing 5.1   The configuration of router R1.

```
interface Ethernet0
 ip address 192.168.1.1 255.255.255.0

interface Serial0
 ip address 192.168.3.2 255.255.255.0

router igrp 1
 network 192.168.1.0
 network 192.168.3.0
```

Listing 5.2   The configuration of router R2.

```
interface Ethernet0
 ip address 192.168.2.1 255.255.255.0

interface Serial1
 ip address 192.168.4.2 255.255.255.0

router igrp 1
 network 192.168.2.0
 network 192.168.4.0
```

Listing 5.3   The configuration of router R3.

```
interface Serial0
 ip address 192.168.4.1 255.255.255.0

interface Serial1
 ip address 192.168.3.1 255.255.255.0
 ring-speed 16

interface TokenRing0
 ip address 192.168.5.1 255.255.255.0

router igrp 1
 network 192.168.3.0
 network 192.168.4.0
 network 192.168.5.0
```

Listing 5.4   The configuration of router R4.

```
interface Ethernet0
 ip address 192.168.6.1 255.255.255.0
```

```
interface TokenRing0
 ip address 192.168.5.2 255.255.255.0
 ring-speed 16

router igrp 1
 network 192.168.5.0
 network 192.168.6.0
```

Let's examine the routing table of router R1 (shown in Listing 5.5).

Listing 5.5   The routing table of router R1.

```
R1#show ip route
...
I    192.168.4.0/24 [100/10476] via 192.168.3.1, 00:00:30, Serial0
I    192.168.5.0/24 [100/8539] via 192.168.3.1, 00:00:31, Serial0
I    192.168.6.0/24 [100/8639] via 192.168.3.1, 00:00:31, Serial0
C    192.168.1.0/24 is directly connected, Ethernet0
I    192.168.2.0/24 [100/10576] via 192.168.3.1, 00:00:31, Serial0
C    192.168.3.0/24 is directly connected, Serial0
```

The routing table represents the complete routing information for our network. Notice that this time, the lines that show the routes for the learned network prefixes begin with the letter *I*, which stands for IGRP.

Understanding How IGRP Processes Routing Updates

IGRP processes routing updates differently than RIP does. To see the difference, let's use the **debug ip igrp transactions** command, which is similar to **debug ip rip**.

We'll use the network scheme that we used in the previous section (refer back to Figure 5.4). The routes' configurations remain the same as shown in Listings 5.1 through 5.4.

We are going to issue the **debug ip igrp transactions** command on router R3, wait until a routing update arrives from router R4, disconnect router R4, wait until router R3 times out the route for 192.168.6.0/24, and then, right after that, reconnect router R4 to the network and see what happens.

Listing 5.6 shows the output of the **debug ip igrp transactions** command entered on router R3.

Listing 5.6   The output of the **debug ip igrp transactions** command issued on router R3.

```
R3#debug ip igrp transactions
IGRP protocol debugging is on
R3#
```

```
!          The last routing update from router R4.
1:29:43: IGRP: received update from 192.168.5.2 on TokenRing0
1:29:43:        network 192.168.6.0, metric 1163 (neighbor 1100)
!          Router R3 is still unaware of router R4's unavailability;
!          So, router R3 keeps sending regular routing updates advertising
!          192.168.6.0.
1:29:52: IGRP: sending update to 255.255.255.255 via Serial0 (192.168.4.1)
1:29:52:        network 192.168.5.0, metric=688
1:29:52:        network 192.168.6.0, metric=1163
1:29:52:        network 192.168.1.0, metric=8576
1:29:52:        network 192.168.3.0, metric=8476
1:29:52: IGRP: sending update to 255.255.255.255 via Serial1 (192.168.3.1)
1:29:52:        network 192.168.4.0, metric=8476
1:29:52:        network 192.168.5.0, metric=688
1:29:52:        network 192.168.6.0, metric=1163
1:29:52:        network 192.168.2.0, metric=8576
1:29:52: IGRP: sending update to 255.255.255.255 via TokenRing0
(192.168.5.1)
1:29:52:        network 192.168.4.0, metric=8476
1:29:52:        network 192.168.1.0, metric=8576
1:29:52:        network 192.168.2.0, metric=8576
1:29:52:        network 192.168.3.0, metric=8476
1:29:59: IGRP: received update from 192.168.3.2 on Serial1
1:29:59:        network 192.168.1.0, metric 8576 (neighbor 1100)
1:30:24: IGRP: received update from 192.168.4.2 on Serial0
1:30:24:        network 192.168.2.0, metric 8576 (neighbor 1100)
...
!          The last regular routing update carrying 192.168.6.0/24 before
!          router R3 times out the route for it.
1:33:59: IGRP: sending update to 255.255.255.255 via Serial0 (192.168.4.1)
1:34:00:        network 192.168.5.0, metric=688
1:34:00:        network 192.168.6.0, metric=1163
1:34:00:        network 192.168.1.0, metric=8576
1:34:00:        network 192.168.3.0, metric=8476
1:34:00: IGRP: sending update to 255.255.255.255 via Serial1 (192.168.3.1)
1:34:00:        network 192.168.4.0, metric=8476
1:34:00:        network 192.168.5.0, metric=688
1:34:00:        network 192.168.6.0, metric=1163
1:34:00:        network 192.168.2.0, metric=8576
1:34:00: IGRP: sending update to 255.255.255.255 via TokenRing0
(192.168.5.1)
1:34:00:        network 192.168.4.0, metric=8476
1:34:00:        network 192.168.1.0, metric=8576
1:34:00:        network 192.168.2.0, metric=8576
1:34:00:        network 192.168.3.0, metric=8476
```

```
1:34:31: IGRP: received update from 192.168.4.2 on Serial0
1:34:31:         network 192.168.2.0, metric 8576 (neighbor 1100)
1:35:01: IGRP: received update from 192.168.3.2 on Serial1
1:35:01:         network 192.168.1.0, metric 8576 (neighbor 1100)
1:35:25: IGRP: edition is now 8
!         Router R3 has already timed out the route for 192.168.6.0/24
!         The routing update for 192.168.6.0/24 is poisoned-reverse
!         (i.e. metric=4294967295(IGRP infinity)).
1:35:25: IGRP: sending update to 255.255.255.255 via Serial0 (192.168.4.1)
1:35:25:         network 192.168.5.0, metric=688
1:35:25:         network 192.168.6.0, metric=4294967295
1:35:25:         network 192.168.1.0, metric=8576
1:35:25:         network 192.168.3.0, metric=8476
1:35:25: IGRP: sending update to 255.255.255.255 via Serial1 (192.168.3.1)
1:35:25:         network 192.168.4.0, metric=8476
1:35:25:         network 192.168.5.0, metric=688
1:35:25:         network 192.168.6.0, metric=4294967295
1:35:25:         network 192.168.2.0, metric=8576
1:35:25: IGRP: sending update to 255.255.255.255 via TokenRing0
(192.168.5.1)
1:35:25:         network 192.168.4.0, metric=8476
1:35:25:         network 192.168.6.0, metric=4294967295
1:35:25:         network 192.168.1.0, metric=8576
1:35:25:         network 192.168.2.0, metric=8576
1:35:25:         network 192.168.3.0, metric=8476
!         Routers R1 and R2 pick up the poisoned-reverse update and because
!         the metric of the routes for 192.168.6.0/24 went down (infinity)
!         they immediately issue triggered updates for 192.168.6.0/24
!         (if you examine the timestamps, you'll notice that this time
!         there is no gap between router R3's regular (poisoned-reverse)
!         update and the (poisoned-reverse) updates sent by router R1 and R2.
1:35:25: IGRP: received update from 192.168.4.2 on Serial0
1:35:25:         network 192.168.2.0, metric 8576 (neighbor 1100)
1:35:25:         network 192.168.6.0, metric 4294967295 (inaccessible)
1:35:26: IGRP: received update from 192.168.3.2 on Serial1
1:35:26:         network 192.168.6.0, metric 4294967295 (inaccessible)
1:35:26:         network 192.168.1.0, metric 8576 (neighbor 1100)
1:35:58: IGRP: received update from 192.168.4.2 on Serial0
1:35:58:         network 192.168.2.0, metric 8576 (neighbor 1100)
1:35:58:         network 192.168.6.0, metric 4294967295 (inaccessible)
1:36:13: IGRP: received update from 192.168.3.2 on Serial1
1:36:13:         network 192.168.6.0, metric 4294967295 (inaccessible)
1:36:13:         network 192.168.1.0, metric 8576 (neighbor 1100)
!         Router R4 is back; it's again advertising 192.168.6.0/24 with
!         the original metric.
```

```
1:36:28: IGRP: received update from 192.168.5.2 on TokenRing0
1:36:28:          network 192.168.6.0, metric 1163 (neighbor 1100)
!          Unlike RIP, IGRP ignores R4's routing update. Unlike RIP, IGRP
!          places timed out routes into holddown (not only those for which
!          a poisoned-reverse update was received). Router R3 keeps sending
!          poisoned-reverse updates for 192.168.6.0/24.
1:36:40: IGRP: sending update to 255.255.255.255 via Serial0 (192.168.4.1)
1:36:40:          network 192.168.5.0, metric=688
1:36:40:          network 192.168.6.0, metric=4294967295
1:36:40:          network 192.168.1.0, metric=8576
1:36:40:          network 192.168.3.0, metric=8476
1:36:41: IGRP: sending update to 255.255.255.255 via Serial1 (192.168.3.1)
1:36:41:          network 192.168.4.0, metric=8476
1:36:41:          network 192.168.5.0, metric=688
1:36:41:          network 192.168.6.0, metric=4294967295
1:36:41:          network 192.168.2.0, metric=8576
1:36:41: IGRP: sending update to 255.255.255.255 via TokenRing0
(192.168.5.1)
1:36:41:          network 192.168.4.0, metric=8476
1:36:41:          network 192.168.6.0, metric=4294967295
1:36:41:          network 192.168.1.0, metric=8576
1:36:41:          network 192.168.2.0, metric=8576
1:36:41:          network 192.168.3.0, metric=8476
```

As before, because of the length of the listing, I placed comments right into it. They are the shaded lines, and they explain what's happening from the perspective of router R3.

The most important observation that we can make from this experiment is that, unlike RIP, IGRP places timed-out routes into holddown. Remember that, after RIP timed out the route for 192.168.6.0/24 (Listing 4.14 in Chapter 4.) and then received a routing update again carrying this network prefix, RIP killed the garbage-collection timer it held for the route and began advertising 192.168.6.0/24 as normal. Routers R1 and R2 did put their routes for 192.168.6.0/24 into holddown because they previously received poisoned-reversed updates from R3. (Let's recall that this isn't a feature of standard RIP and that this feature is specific to Cisco's version.) IGRP puts even the timed-out routes into holddown, thereby refusing to accept positive routing updates for the affected network prefixes until the holddown timer expires.

If we examine the routing table of router R3 right after it received the new positive update for 192.168.6.0/24 from router R4, we'll see that it still declares the route for the network prefix to be "possibly down" (the shaded line in Listing 5.7).

Listing 5.7   The routing table of router R3 confirms that the route for 192.168.6.0/24 is still in holddown.

```
R3#show ip route
...
C    192.168.4.0/24 is directly connected, Serial0
C    192.168.5.0/24 is directly connected, TokenRing0
I    192.168.6.0/24 is possibly down, routing via 192.168.5.2, TokenRing0
I    192.168.1.0/24 [100/8576] via 192.168.3.2, 00:00:50, Serial1
I    192.168.2.0/24 [100/8576] via 192.168.4.2, 00:01:06, Serial0
C    192.168.3.0/24 is directly connected, Serial1
```

Understanding How IGRP Handles Secondary IP Addresses

Similarly to RIP, IGRP advertises the subnets and classful network addresses to which the secondary IP addresses assigned on an interface belong, provided they have corresponding **network** statements under the **router igrp** configuration.

Similarly to RIP, IGRP may generate multiple routing updates per a regular update interval for the interface with secondary IP addresses, although the rules that IGRP follows are slightly different than those that RIP follows:

- The number of routing updates generated per a regular update interval is equal to the number of classful network addresses to which the primary and secondary IP addresses belong. (The only classful network addresses that count are those that also appear in the **network** statements under the **router igrp** configuration.)

NOTE: Notice that the updates are generated but not yet sent. IGRP decides which routing updates to send in accordance with the last rule of this bulleted list.

- Each routing update is encapsulated into a datagram with the source IP address equal to the first IP address (in the order of the appearance in the router's configuration) of each classful network address.
- The first routing update is always encapsulated into a datagram with the interface's primary IP address as the source IP address. If one or more secondary IP addresses belong to the same classful network address to which the primary IP address belongs, none of them is used as the source IP address of a routing update.

- Only the routing update that is encapsulated into a datagram whose source IP address is equal to the interface's primary IP address can contain IGRP network and external network route entries. It can also contain any subnet entries, providing the subnets in them do not coincide with the subnet to which the primary and secondary IP addresses of the interface belong.

- The routing updates that are encapsulated into datagrams whose source IP addresses are among the interface's secondary IP addresses can contain only subnet entries. These routing updates cannot contain subnet route entries for the subnets to which the interface's secondary and primary IP addresses belong.

NOTE: It's possible that some of these routing updates contain no route entries.

- Only the routing updates that contain route entries are sent. Routing updates without any entries are discarded.

Sending IGRP routing updates in datagrams whose source IP addresses are among the interface's secondary IP addresses preserves the contiguous nature of each of the classful network addresses to which the secondary IP addresses belong. You can notice, however, that IGRP does a better job than RIP: IGRP does not pack as much routing information into the routing updates whose source IP addresses are among the secondary IP addresses. This results in a smaller number of sent routing updates and less confusion at the end of the routers that receive the routing updates.

Let's use the same network scheme that we used in Chapter 4 when we examined how RIP handles secondary IP addresses. The network scheme is shown in Figure 5.5.

Classful networks 172.16.0.0/16 and 172.20.0.0/16 span both sides of segment 1, and, because they are separated by segment 1 addressed with network prefix 192.168.1.0/24, they cannot be handled by IGRP. As in the case of RIP, the cure— secondary IP addresses—is simple and repulsive at the same time.

Just as in the case of RIP, we'll configure more secondary IP addresses than necessary on the Ethernet0 interfaces of routers R2 and R3. We'll create several subnets of 172.16.0.0/16, several IP addresses of 172.20.100.0/24, and several subnets of a classful network 172.30.0.0/16 that isn't present anywhere else. Listings 5.8 through 5.11 show the configurations of routers R1 through R4, respectively.

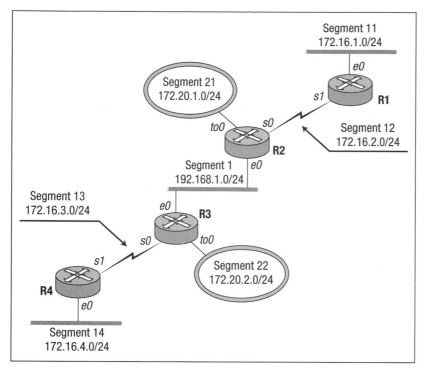

Figure 5.5 This network is impossible to implement using IGRP unless secondary IP addresses are configured on the routers' interfaces connected to segment 1.

Listing 5.8 The configuration of router R1.

```
interface Ethernet0
 ip address 172.16.1.1 255.255.255.0

interface Serial1
 ip address 172.16.2.2 255.255.255.0

router igrp 1
 network 172.16.0.0
```

Listing 5.9 The configuration of router R2.

```
interface Ethernet0
 ip address 172.16.120.2 255.255.255.0 secondary
 ip address 172.16.110.2 255.255.255.0 secondary
 ip address 172.16.100.2 255.255.255.0 secondary
 ip address 172.20.100.6 255.255.255.0 secondary
 ip address 172.20.100.4 255.255.255.0 secondary
 ip address 172.20.100.2 255.255.255.0 secondary
```

```
ip address 172.30.150.6 255.255.255.0 secondary
ip address 172.30.200.4 255.255.255.0 secondary
ip address 172.30.100.2 255.255.255.0 secondary
ip address 192.168.1.2 255.255.255.0

interface Serial0
ip address 172.16.2.1 255.255.255.0

interface TokenRing0
ip address 172.20.1.1 255.255.255.0
ring-speed 16

router igrp 1
network 172.16.0.0
network 172.20.0.0
network 172.30.0.0
network 192.168.1.0
```

Listing 5.10   The configuration of router R3.

```
interface Ethernet0
ip address 172.16.120.1 255.255.255.0 secondary
ip address 172.16.110.1 255.255.255.0 secondary
ip address 172.16.100.1 255.255.255.0 secondary
ip address 172.20.100.3 255.255.255.0 secondary
ip address 172.20.100.5 255.255.255.0 secondary
ip address 172.20.100.1 255.255.255.0 secondary
ip address 172.30.150.5 255.255.255.0 secondary
ip address 172.30.200.3 255.255.255.0 secondary
ip address 172.30.100.1 255.255.255.0 secondary
ip address 192.168.1.1 255.255.255.0

interface Serial0
ip address 172.16.3.1 255.255.255.0

interface TokenRing0
ip address 172.20.2.1 255.255.255.0
ring-speed 16

router igrp 1
network 172.16.0.0
network 172.20.0.0
network 172.30.0.0
network 192.168.1.0
```

Listing 5.11   The configuration of router R4.

```
interface Loopback0
 ip address 10.0.1.1 255.255.255.0

interface Ethernet0
 ip address 172.16.4.1 255.255.255.0

interface Serial1
 ip address 172.16.3.2 255.255.255.0

router igrp 1
 network 172.16.0.0
 network 10.0.0.0
```

The alternating shaded and italicized groups of lines in routers' R2 and R3 configurations (shown in Listings 5.9 and 5.10) show the secondary IP addresses. Each group (either shaded or italicized) shows the IP addresses belonging to the same classful network address.

As with RIP, router R4's configuration (shown in Listing 5.11) also contains the Loopback0 interface, which is assigned the IP address of 10.0.1.1/24. We expect router R4 to advertise classful network address 10.0.0.0/8 instead to the other routers, as no other router R4 interface has an IP address belonging to 10.0.0.0/8.

If we examine router R1's routing table (shown in Listing 5.12), we'll see it contains all of the required routing information.

Listing 5.12   The routing table of router R1.

```
R1#show ip route
...
     172.16.0.0/24 is subnetted, 7 subnets
I       172.16.4.0 [100/10676] via 172.16.2.1, 00:01:13, Serial1
C       172.16.1.0 is directly connected, Ethernet0
C       172.16.2.0 is directly connected, Serial1
I       172.16.3.0 [100/10576] via 172.16.2.1, 00:01:13, Serial1
I       172.16.120.0 [100/8576] via 172.16.2.1, 00:01:13, Serial1
I       172.16.110.0 [100/8576] via 172.16.2.1, 00:01:13, Serial1
I       172.16.100.0 [100/8576] via 172.16.2.1, 00:01:13, Serial1
I     172.20.0.0/16 [100/8539] via 172.16.2.1, 00:01:13, Serial1
I     172.30.0.0/16 [100/8576] via 172.16.2.1, 00:01:13, Serial1
I     10.0.0.0/8 [100/11076] via 172.16.2.1, 00:01:13, Serial1
I     192.168.1.0/24 [100/8576] via 172.16.2.1, 00:01:13, Serial1
```

However, if we examine the routing table of router R2 (shown in Listing 5.13), we won't find the presence of any load balancing, which we saw in the case of RIP.

Router R2's routing table looks as clean as that of router R1, thanks to the more sophisticated rules that IGRP follows to generate routing updates for the secondary IP addresses of the interface.

Listing 5.13   The routing table of router R2.

```
R2#show ip route
...
     172.16.0.0/24 is subnetted, 7 subnets
I       172.16.4.0 [100/8676] via 172.16.120.1, 00:01:12, Ethernet0
I       172.16.1.0 [100/8576] via 172.16.2.2, 00:00:35, Serial0
C       172.16.2.0 is directly connected, Serial0
I       172.16.3.0 [100/8576] via 172.16.120.1, 00:01:12, Ethernet0
C       172.16.120.0 is directly connected, Ethernet0
C       172.16.110.0 is directly connected, Ethernet0
C       172.16.100.0 is directly connected, Ethernet0
     172.20.0.0/24 is subnetted, 3 subnets
C       172.20.1.0 is directly connected, TokenRing0
I       172.20.2.0 [100/1163] via 172.20.100.3, 00:01:12, Ethernet0
C       172.20.100.0 is directly connected, Ethernet0
     172.30.0.0/24 is subnetted, 3 subnets
C       172.30.150.0 is directly connected, Ethernet0
C       172.30.200.0 is directly connected, Ethernet0
C       172.30.100.0 is directly connected, Ethernet0
I    10.0.0.0/8 [100/9076] via 192.168.1.1, 00:01:12, Ethernet0
C    192.168.1.0/24 is directly connected, Ethernet0
```

Finally, let's examine the output of the **debug ip igrp transactions** command issued on router R2 (shown in Listing 5.14). As we expect, only the routing update encapsulated into the datagram whose source IP address is equal to the primary IP address of the interface contains IGRP network route entries (the first four shaded lines). (Pay attention to the keyword *network* in front of the lines denoting route entries.) The other routing updates contain only subnet entries (denoted by *subnet*). Notice that the last update (the two shaded lines at the end of the listing) is suppressed: It contains no route entries. This routing update contains no route entries because it's sent in the datagram whose source IP address is 172.30.150.6/16 belonging to classful network address 172.30.0.0/16. The only interface that is configured with subnets of this classful network address is the interface through which the routing update is sent.

Listing 5.14   The output of the debug ip igrp transactions command issued on router R2.

```
R2#debug ip igrp transactions
IGRP protocol debugging is on
R2#
...
IGRP: received update from 192.168.1.1 on Ethernet0
```

```
      network 172.16.0.0, metric 1200 (neighbor 1100)
      network 172.20.0.0, metric 1163 (neighbor 688)
      network 10.0.0.0, metric 9076 (neighbor 8976)
IGRP: received update from 172.16.120.1 on Ethernet0
      subnet 172.16.4.0, metric 8676 (neighbor 8576)
      subnet 172.16.3.0, metric 8576 (neighbor 8476)
IGRP: received update from 172.20.100.3 on Ethernet0
      subnet 172.20.2.0, metric 1163 (neighbor 688)
...
IGRP: sending update to 255.255.255.255 via Ethernet0 (192.168.1.2)
      network 172.16.0.0, metric=1100
      network 172.20.0.0, metric=688
IGRP: sending update to 255.255.255.255 via Ethernet0 (172.16.120.2)
      subnet 172.16.1.0, metric=8576
      subnet 172.16.2.0, metric=8476
IGRP: sending update to 255.255.255.255 via Ethernet0 (172.20.100.6)
      subnet 172.20.1.0, metric=688
IGRP: sending update to 255.255.255.255 via Ethernet0 (172.30.150.6) -
suppressing null update
...
```

Understanding and Changing IGRP Metrics

As we learned in the "In Depth" section, IGRP operates with logical bandwidth, delay, reliability, and load of the interface.

These values are easy to examine using the **show interfaces** *<interface>* *<interface #>* command. An example of this command's output is shown in Listing 5.15.

Listing 5.15   The output of the **show interfaces Ethernet0** command shows the current values of logical bandwidth, delay, reliability, and load.

```
R2#show interfaces Ethernet0
Ethernet0 is up, line protocol is up
  Hardware is Lance, address is 00e0.b064.30a9 (bia 00e0.b064.30a9)
  Internet address is 192.168.200.1/24
  MTU 1500 bytes, BW 10000 Kbit, DLY 1000 usec,
     reliability 255/255, txload 1/255, rxload 1/255
...
```

The shaded lines show the current values of all five parameters.

The default values of the delay and bandwidth can be changed using the **delay** *<new delay>* and **bandwidth** *<new bandwidth>* commands. The numeric *<new delay>*

parameter can range from 1 through 16777215, and the assigned delay is measured in tens of microseconds. The numeric *<new bandwidth>* parameter can range from 1 through 10000000, and the assigned bandwidth is measured in kilobits per second.

Let's now try to calculate the metric with which router R4 in Figure 5.6 will see the network prefix of segment 1 (10.0.1.0/24).

To do calculations, we need to know the values of the logical bandwidth and delay of all the interfaces involved. Listing 5.16 shows the interesting (at least to us) parts of the output of the **show ip interfaces** command entered on each of the four routers.

Listing 5.16   The output of the show ip interfaces command on routers R1 through R4.

```
R1#show interfaces Ethernet0
...
  Internet address is 10.0.1.1/24
  MTU 1500 bytes, BW 10000 Kbit, DLY 1000 usec,
...
R2#show interfaces TokenRing0
...
  Internet address is 10.0.2.2/24
  MTU 4464 bytes, BW 16000 Kbit, DLY 630 usec,
...
R3#show interfaces Serial1
...
  Internet address is 10.0.3.2/24
  MTU 1500 bytes, BW 64 Kbit, DLY 20000 usec,
...
R4#show interfaces Ethernet0
...
  Internet address is 10.0.4.2/24
  MTU 1500 bytes, BW 10000 Kbit, DLY 1000 usec,
...
```

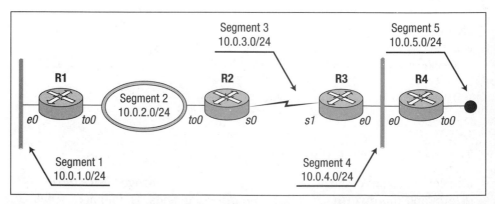

Figure 5.6   The network scheme that helps us understand how IGRP calculates metrics.

The minimum bandwidth along the route is 64Kbps, the bandwidth of the serial link between routers R2 and R3. To calculate the IGRP metric, however, we are interested in the inverse logical bandwidth, which is:

$$B_{IGRP} = \frac{10^7}{64} = 156,250$$

The total delay is equal to the sum of the delays of all the involved segments. To get the true IGRP delay value, we have to divide the logical delay of the interface by 10: $D_{IGRP} = 100 + 63 + 2,000 + 100 = 2,263$.

The resulting IGRP metric is as follows:

$$M_{IGRP} = 156,250 + 2,263 = 158,513.$$

Let's see if this is correct. Listing 5.17 shows the output of the **show ip route** command entered on router R4.

Listing 5.17 The output of the show ip route command confirms that the calculated metric of network prefix 10.0.1.0/24 coincides with the actual one.

```
R4#show ip route
...
     10.0.0.0/24 is subnetted, 5 subnets
I       10.0.2.0 [100/158413] via 10.0.4.1, 00:00:09, Ethernet0
I       10.0.3.0 [100/158350] via 10.0.4.1, 00:00:09, Ethernet0
I       10.0.1.0 [100/158513] via 10.0.4.1, 00:00:10, Ethernet0
C       10.0.4.0 is directly connected, Ethernet0
C       10.0.5.0 is directly connected, Loopback0
```

Number 158513 in the shaded line shows the actual metric of the route for network prefix 10.0.1.0/24.

Sometimes it is necessary to adjust the metric of some route. This can be done in two ways: change the logical bandwidth of one or more involved interfaces, or change the logical delay of one or more interfaces. Which one should we use?

Because the logical bandwidth of the route is not cumulative, changing it is not a good way to tune the metrics of IGRP routes. The routers really keep track of the smallest logical bandwidth (the largest inverse logical bandwidth), so increasing or decreasing the logical bandwidth of a single interface will work only if the current logical bandwidth of the interface is the smallest. Should there appear another interface en route to the network prefix whose logical bandwidth is smaller than the configured one, the effort becomes useless.

On the contrary, logical delay is a cumulative parameter, and changing it—even on a single interface—changes the logical delay of the whole route.

In addition, any changes to the logical bandwidth and delays must be consistent. You can use the following guidelines when adjusting these values:

- The logical bandwidth of an interface must adequately represent its physical bandwidth. For example, for Ethernet, whose physical bandwidth is 10Mbps, the logical bandwidth must be equal to 10000 (Kbps). Typically, the default logical bandwidth of an interface adequately reflects its physical bandwidth. The exception is the serial interface, for which the logical bandwidth must be adjusted in accordance with the bandwidth of the line to which the interface is connected.

- If a change is necessary in either logical delay or bandwidth, it must be done on a per-segment basis. In other words, all router interfaces connected to the same physical segment should be configured with the same logical bandwidth and delay.

Performing Equal- and Unequal-Cost Load Balancing with IGRP

Equal-cost load balancing with IGRP occurs in the same way as it does with RIP. When IGRP installs several routes for the same network prefix in the routing table, the router will perform equal-cost load balancing across them. As with RIP, IGRP equal-cost load balancing is controlled by the command **maximum-paths** <# *of routes*> available under the **router igrp** configuration, where the numeric <# *of routes*> parameter can take values from 1 through 6.

The network scheme that we are going to use to see how IGRP performs load balancing is similar to the one we used for RIP. It's shown in Figure 5.7.

Once we've reconfigured the routers from Figure 5.7, as shown in Listings 5.18 through 5.20, we'll still see load balancing at router R3, just as with RIP. The routing table of router R3 should look like the one shown in Listing 5.21.

Listing 5.18   Router R1's configuration.

```
interface Serial0
 ip address 10.0.2.2 255.255.255.0

interface TokenRing0
 ip address 10.0.1.1 255.255.255.0
 ring-speed 16

router igrp 1
 network 10.0.0.0
```

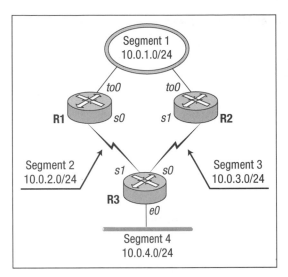

Figure 5.7   Router R3 can forward traffic destined to segment 1 using two routes—
through segments 2 and 3.

Listing 5.19   Router R2's configuration.

```
interface Serial1
 ip address 10.0.3.2 255.255.255.0

interface TokenRing0
 ip address 10.0.1.2 255.255.255.0
 ring-speed 16

router igrp 1
 network 10.0.0.0
```

Listing 5.20   Router R3's configuration.

```
interface Ethernet0
 ip address 10.0.4.1 255.255.255.0

interface Serial0
 ip address 10.0.3.1 255.255.255.0

interface Serial1
 ip address 10.0.2.1 255.255.255.0

router igrp 1
 network 10.0.0.0
```

Listing 5.21   The routing table of router R3 from Figure 5.7.

```
R3#show ip route
...
     10.0.0.0/24 is subnetted, 4 subnets
C       10.0.2.0 is directly connected, Serial1
C       10.0.3.0 is directly connected, Serial0
I       10.0.1.0 [100/8539] via 10.0.3.2, 00:00:57, Serial0
                 [100/8539] via 10.0.2.2, 00:01:12, Serial1
C       10.0.4.0 is directly connected, Ethernet0
```

The routing tables of routers R1 and R2, however, won't show any signs of load balancing this time. (Remember, that we saw load balancing on all three routers when they were configured with RIP.) For example, the routing table of router R1 is shown here:

```
R1#show ip route
...
     10.0.0.0/24 is subnetted, 4 subnets
C       10.0.2.0 is directly connected, Serial0
I       10.0.3.0 [100/8539] via 10.0.1.2, 00:01:03, TokenRing0
C       10.0.1.0 is directly connected, TokenRing0
I       10.0.4.0 [100/8576] via 10.0.2.1, 00:00:05, Serial0
```

This example demonstrates the superiority of IGRP metrics over those of RIP. IGRP knows the difference between two segments (2 and 3) with unequal bandwidth (which, as we know, is controlled by the **bandwidth** statement).

As we discussed in the "In Depth" section, IGRP possesses the unique feature of being able to install multiple routes with unequal metrics for the same destination. The router uses these routes to perform unequal-cost load balancing by splitting the traffic across the multiple routes in proportion with the routes' metrics. Let's see how it works.

For two or more routes for the same network prefix but with unequal metrics to be installed into the routing table, it is necessary to meet the feasibility conditions (described in the "In Depth" section). Remember that the second feasibility condition is controlled by the value of a multiplier that is administratively assigned. This multiplier is assigned a value using the command **variance** *<multiplier>*, accepting whole numbers from 1 through 128.

Suppose that, in our network shown in Figure 5.7, the bandwidths of segments 2 and 3 are 768Kbps and 512Kbps, respectively. Thus, our task is to first adjust the logical bandwidth on all three routers for segments 2 and 3. Then we must determine the metrics with which router R3 will perceive segment 1 through segments 2 and 3. Finally, based on that, we need to determine the value for the **variance** command to enable unequal-cost load balancing on router R3.

Obviously, for each of the routes, the minimum bandwidth is equal to the bandwidth of the respective serial link (768Kbps and 512Kbps in our example). The logical delays of the TokenRing0, Serial0, and Serial1 interfaces on routers R1, R2, and R3 are 630ms, 20000ms, and 20000ms, respectively.

The metric of the first route is:

$$M_1 = \frac{10^7}{768} + \frac{20000}{10} + \frac{630}{10} = 13020 + 2000 + 63 = 15083$$

The metric of the second route is:

$$M_2 = \frac{10^7}{512} + \frac{20000}{10} + \frac{630}{10} = 19531 + 2000 + 63 = 21594$$

To meet the first feasibility condition, the next-hop router of the second route must have a route for segment 1 with a metric smaller than that of the first route (15020). Although it's obvious that router R2—being directly connected to segment 1—produces a smaller metric, let's calculate it anyway:

$$M = \frac{10^7}{16000} + \frac{630}{10} = 625 + 63 = 688$$

NOTE: *This metric cannot be displayed by using the **show ip route** command. This is the metric with which router R2 advertises the network prefix of segment 1.*

Router R2's IGRP metric for directly connected Token Ring segment 1 is smaller than the metric of the best route for the same segment on router R3. Thus, the first feasibility condition is met. To meet the second feasibility condition, we should first calculate the value for the **variance** command. Let's call the value x; then,

$M_2 < M_1 * x$; $21594 < 15083 * x$; $x < 21594/15083 = 1.43....$

The closest whole number greater than 1.43 is 2. Thus, the command **variance 2** must enable unequal-cost load balancing at router R3 for traffic destined for segment 1. Let's see if this works. The new configurations of all three routers are shown in Listings 5.22 through 5.24.

Listing 5.22   Router R1's configuration.

```
interface Serial0
 ip address 10.0.2.2 255.255.255.0
 bandwidth 768

interface TokenRing0
 ip address 10.0.1.1 255.255.255.0
 ring-speed 16

router igrp 10
 network 10.0.0.0
```

Listing 5.23   Router R2's configuration.

```
interface Serial1
 ip address 10.0.3.2 255.255.255.0
 bandwidth 512

interface TokenRing0
 ip address 10.0.1.2 255.255.255.0
 ring-speed 16

router igrp 10
 network 10.0.0.0
```

Listing 5.24   Router R3's configuration.

```
interface Ethernet0
 ip address 10.0.4.1 255.255.255.0

interface Serial0
 ip address 10.0.3.1 255.255.255.0
 bandwidth 512

interface Serial1
 ip address 10.0.2.1 255.255.255.0
 bandwidth 768

router igrp 10
 variance 2
 network 10.0.0.0
```

Listing 5.25 shows the routing table of router R3, which confirms that our calculations and subsequent router R3 configuration are correct.

Listing 5.25   The routing table of router R3.

```
R3#show ip route
...
     10.0.0.0/24 is subnetted, 4 subnets
C       10.0.2.0 is directly connected, Serial1
C       10.0.3.0 is directly connected, Serial0
I       10.0.1.0 [100/15083] via 10.0.2.2, 00:00:17, Serial1
                 [100/21594] via 10.0.3.2, 00:00:34, Serial0
C       10.0.4.0 is directly connected, Ethernet0
```

Configuring IGRP to Originate a Default Route

As we saw in the "In Depth" section, IGRP communicates default routing information using exterior network route entries. To make IGRP advertise one or more network prefixes as exterior networks, one or more **ip default-network** *<IP address>* commands must be used in global configuration mode. In general, the *<IP address>* parameter defines the network prefix the routes for which are tendered to become candidate default routes. In the case of IGRP, the *<IP address>* parameter can be only a classful network address (not a subnet address) that IGRP knows of.

IGRP can know of such a network prefix because it learned of it from some other router or because it itself originates it. (In the latter case, the value of the *<IP address>* parameter must also appear in the **network** statement under the **router igrp** configuration.)

To see the guidelines at work, let's consider the hypothetical corporate network shown in Figure 5.8.

The network consists of the "headquarters" with two routers (RH1 and RH2), and four branches, (Br1 through Br4), each with a single router. Branches Br3 and Br4 provide connectivity with the Internet via segments 31 and 41 through two Internet routers (IG1 and IG2).

Routers IG1 and IG2 are not a part of the corporate network. We know only the IP addresses assigned on their Ethernet0 interfaces—192.168.31.50 and 192.168.41.50, respectively.

Our task is to configure the six corporate routers so that each of them would send Internet traffic to the closest Internet router.

With IGRP, the task is easy. All we need to do is to make routers R3 and R4 advertise segments 31 and 41 as exterior routes. In addition to that, we'll also

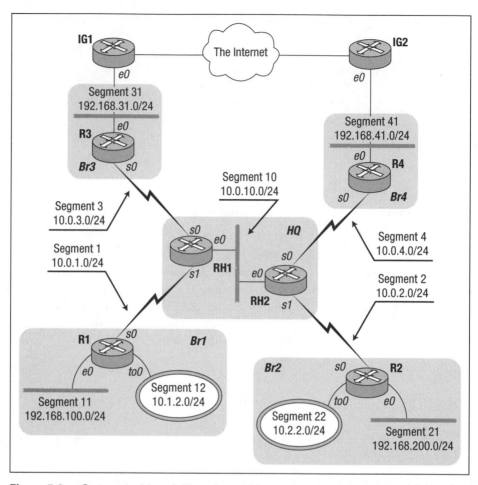

Figure 5.8   Segments 31 and 41 each provide a point of access to the Internet; the routers in the autonomous system advertise them as IGRP exterior routes.

need to set the gateways of last resort on these two routers to be Internet routers IG1 and IG2.

Listings 5.26 through 5.31 show the configurations of all four routers.

Listing 5.26   The configuration of router RH1.

```
interface Ethernet0
 ip address 10.0.10.1 255.255.255.0

interface Serial0
 ip address 10.0.3.1 255.255.255.0

interface Serial1
 ip address 10.0.1.1 255.255.255.0
```

```
router igrp 10
 network 10.0.0.0
```

Listing 5.27   The configuration of router RH2.

```
interface Ethernet0
 ip address 10.0.10.2 255.255.255.0

interface Serial0
 ip address 10.0.4.1 255.255.255.0

interface Serial1
 ip address 10.0.2.1 255.255.255.0

router igrp 10
 network 10.0.0.0
```

Listing 5.28   The configuration of router R1.

```
interface Ethernet0
 ip address 192.168.100.1 255.255.255.0

interface Serial0
 ip address 10.0.1.2 255.255.255.0

interface TokenRing0
 ip address 10.1.2.1 255.255.255.0
 ring-speed 16

router igrp 10
 network 10.0.0.0
 network 192.168.100.0
```

Listing 5.29   The configuration of router R2.

```
interface Ethernet0
 ip address 192.168.200.1 255.255.255.0

interface Serial0
 ip address 10.0.2.2 255.255.255.0

interface TokenRing0
 ip address 10.2.2.1 255.255.255.0
 ring-speed 16
```

```
router igrp 10
 network 10.0.0.0
 network 192.168.200.0
```

Listing 5.30   The configuration of router R3.

```
interface Ethernet0
 ip address 192.168.31.1 255.255.255.0

interface Serial0
 ip address 10.0.3.2 255.255.255.0

router igrp 10
 network 10.0.0.0
 network 192.168.31.0

ip default-network 192.168.31.0
ip route 0.0.0.0 0.0.0.0 192.168.31.50
```

Listing 5.31   The configuration of router R4.

```
interface Ethernet0
 ip address 192.168.41.1 255.255.255.0

interface Serial0
 ip address 10.0.4.2 255.255.255.0

router igrp 10
 network 10.0.0.0
 network 192.168.41.0

ip default-network 192.168.41.0
ip route 0.0.0.0 0.0.0.0 192.168.41.50
```

The shaded lines in the configurations of routers R3 and R4 show the commands that are essential for this task. The first shaded line in each configuration makes the connected route associated with the Ethernet0 interface becomes a candidate default route. It also makes IGRP advertise the network prefix of the interface as an exterior network.

The resulting candidate default connected route does not lead to the assignment of the gateway of last resort. The assignment is taken care of by the second command, which forcefully makes the IP address of the corresponding Internet router become the gateway of last resort.

If we examine the routing table of router R3, shown in Listing 5.32, we'll see the results of the configuration.

Listing 5.32   The routing table of router R3.

```
R3#show ip route
...
Gateway of last resort is 192.168.31.50 to network 0.0.0.0

C*   192.168.31.0/24 is directly connected, Ethernet0
I*   192.168.41.0/24 [100/10676] via 10.0.3.1, 00:00:27, Serial0
I    192.168.200.0/24 [100/10676] via 10.0.3.1, 00:00:27, Serial0
     10.0.0.0/24 is subnetted, 7 subnets
I       10.0.10.0 [100/8576] via 10.0.3.1, 00:00:27, Serial0
I       10.0.2.0 [100/10576] via 10.0.3.1, 00:00:27, Serial0
I       10.1.2.0 [100/10539] via 10.0.3.1, 00:00:27, Serial0
C       10.0.3.0 is directly connected, Serial0
I       10.2.2.0 [100/10639] via 10.0.3.1, 00:00:27, Serial0
I       10.0.1.0 [100/10476] via 10.0.3.1, 00:00:27, Serial0
I       10.0.4.0 [100/10576] via 10.0.3.1, 00:00:27, Serial0
I    192.168.100.0/24 [100/10576] via 10.0.3.1, 00:00:27, Serial0
S*   0.0.0.0/0 [1/0] via 192.168.31.50
```

The shaded line confirms that the gateway of last resort is router IG1. The three italicized lines show the candidate default routes.

Let's also examine the routing tables of routers RH1, RH2, and R1, shown in Listings 5.33 through 5.35, respectively.

Listing 5.33   The routing table of router RH1.

```
RH1#show ip route
...
Gateway of last resort is 10.0.3.2 to network 192.168.31.0

I*   192.168.31.0/24 [100/8576] via 10.0.3.2, 00:00:23, Serial0
I*   192.168.41.0/24 [100/8676] via 10.0.10.2, 00:00:10, Ethernet0
I    192.168.200.0/24 [100/8676] via 10.0.10.2, 00:00:10, Ethernet0
     10.0.0.0/24 is subnetted, 7 subnets
C       10.0.10.0 is directly connected, Ethernet0
I       10.0.2.0 [100/8576] via 10.0.10.2, 00:00:11, Ethernet0
I       10.1.2.0 [100/8539] via 10.0.1.2, 00:00:34, Serial1
C       10.0.3.0 is directly connected, Serial0
I       10.2.2.0 [100/8639] via 10.0.10.2, 00:00:11, Ethernet0
C       10.0.1.0 is directly connected, Serial1
I       10.0.4.0 [100/8576] via 10.0.10.2, 00:00:11, Ethernet0
I    192.168.100.0/24 [100/8576] via 10.0.1.2, 00:00:35, Serial1
```

Listing 5.34 The routing table of router RH2.

```
RH2#show ip route
...
Gateway of last resort is 10.0.4.2 to network 192.168.41.0

     10.0.0.0/24 is subnetted, 7 subnets
C       10.0.10.0 is directly connected, Ethernet0
C       10.0.2.0 is directly connected, Serial1
I       10.0.3.0 [100/8576] via 10.0.10.1, 00:00:50, Ethernet0
I       10.1.2.0 [100/8639] via 10.0.10.1, 00:00:50, Ethernet0
I       10.2.2.0 [100/8539] via 10.0.2.2, 00:00:37, Serial1
I       10.0.1.0 [100/8576] via 10.0.10.1, 00:00:50, Ethernet0
C       10.0.4.0 is directly connected, Serial0
I     192.168.100.0/24 [100/8676] via 10.0.10.1, 00:00:50, Ethernet0
I*    192.168.41.0/24 [100/8576] via 10.0.4.2, 00:00:24, Serial0
I*    192.168.31.0/24 [100/8676] via 10.0.10.1, 00:00:50, Ethernet0
I     192.168.200.0/24 [100/8576] via 10.0.2.2, 00:00:37, Serial1
```

Listing 5.35 The routing table of router R1.

```
R1#show ip route
...
Gateway of last resort is 10.0.1.1 to network 192.168.31.0

I*    192.168.31.0/24 [100/10576] via 10.0.1.1, 00:00:24, Serial0
I*    192.168.41.0/24 [100/10676] via 10.0.1.1, 00:00:24, Serial0
I     192.168.200.0/24 [100/10676] via 10.0.1.1, 00:00:24, Serial0
     10.0.0.0/24 is subnetted, 7 subnets
I       10.0.10.0 [100/8576] via 10.0.1.1, 00:00:24, Serial0
I       10.0.2.0 [100/10576] via 10.0.1.1, 00:00:24, Serial0
I       10.0.3.0 [100/10476] via 10.0.1.1, 00:00:24, Serial0
C       10.1.2.0 is directly connected, TokenRing0
I       10.2.2.0 [100/10639] via 10.0.1.1, 00:00:24, Serial0
C       10.0.1.0 is directly connected, Serial0
I       10.0.4.0 [100/10576] via 10.0.1.1, 00:00:25, Serial0
C     192.168.100.0/24 is directly connected, Ethernet0
```

Notice that the routing tables of routers RH1 and RH2 show the two candidate default routes created by IGRP (the second and third shaded lines in each listing). Each router chose the route with the smaller metric, and from this route it created the gateway of last resort. The two routes pointing to different next-hop routers (routers R3 and R4) provide a measure of redundancy should any of the next-hop routers fail. As the IGRP process removes the failed route, the router automatically reconfigures the gateway of last resort in accordance with the remaining candidate default route.

On router R1, however, the two IGRP candidate default routes point to the same next-hop router, leaving router R1 with no redundancy in case of the serial link failure.

This network example also provides an excellent opportunity to see how routers label different types of IGRP routes in the output of the **debug ip igrp transactions** command. The output of this command issued on router R1 is shown in Listing 5.36.

Listing 5.36 The output of the **debug ip igrp transactions** command issued on router R1.

```
R1#debug ip igrp transactions
IGRP protocol debugging is on
R1#
IGRP: sending update to 255.255.255.255 via Ethernet0 (192.168.100.1)
      network 192.168.200.0, metric=10676
      network 10.0.0.0, metric=688
      exterior 192.168.31.0, metric=10576
      exterior 192.168.41.0, metric=10676
IGRP: sending update to 255.255.255.255 via Serial0 (10.0.1.2)
      subnet 10.1.2.0, metric=688
      network 192.168.100.0, metric=1100
IGRP: sending update to 255.255.255.255 via TokenRing0 (10.1.2.1)
      subnet 10.0.10.0, metric=8576
      subnet 10.0.2.0, metric=10576
      subnet 10.0.3.0, metric=10476
      subnet 10.2.2.0, metric=10639
      subnet 10.0.1.0, metric=8476
      subnet 10.0.4.0, metric=10576
      network 192.168.200.0, metric=10676
      network 192.168.100.0, metric=1100
      exterior 192.168.31.0, metric=10576
      exterior 192.168.41.0, metric=10676
IGRP: received update from 10.0.1.1 on Serial0
      subnet 10.0.10.0, metric 8576 (neighbor 1100)
      subnet 10.0.2.0, metric 10576 (neighbor 8576)
      subnet 10.0.3.0, metric 10476 (neighbor 8476)
      subnet 10.2.2.0, metric 10639 (neighbor 8639)
      subnet 10.0.4.0, metric 10576 (neighbor 8576)
      network 192.168.200.0, metric 10676 (neighbor 8676)
      exterior network 192.168.31.0, metric 10576 (neighbor 8576)
      exterior network 192.168.41.0, metric 10676 (neighbor 8676)
...
```

Notice the keywords *subnet, network,* and *exterior* at the beginning of the lines showing advertised network prefixes.

Adjusting IGRP Timers

IGRP timers can be changed from the default values by using the command **timers basic** *<update> <invalid> <holddown> <flush>* [<sleep time>] in the **router igrp** *<AS #>* configuration mode.

The parameters *<update>*, *<invalid>*, *<holddown>*, and *<flush>* are measured in seconds and can accept values from 0 through 4294967295.

The *<update>* parameter is the time between regular routing updates. The *<invalid>*, *<holddown>*, and *<flush>* parameters represent invalid, holddown, and flush times, respectively. Use the following guidelines when modifying these parameters:

- The invalid time should be at least three times the value of the update time.
- The holddown time should be at least three times the value of the update time.
- The flush time should be greater than or equal to the sum of the invalid and holddown times.

NOTE: The IGRP flush time is not an equivalent of the RIP flush time. For more information, refer to the subsections devoted to the RIP and IGRP timers in the "In Depth" section.

The optional *<sleep time>* parameter represents the triggered update timer expiration time. It is measured in milliseconds and can accept values from 1 through 4294967295.

The default values for these parameters are shown in Table 5.2.

WARNING!   Typically, the timers of a dynamic routing protocol should not be changed. The designers of the protocol have extensively tested these sensitive parameters to devise their optimal values. You should consider changing timers only in cases when no other measures can help.

Modifying the IGRP Metric Weights

The **metric weights 0** <k1> <k2> <k3> <k4> <k5> command provides means to modify theweights of the formula for calculating the IGRP metrics. Each of the <k> parameters is integer and ranges from 0 to 4294967295. The default values of the IGRP metric weights are shown in Table 5.1.

Table 5.2   The default expiration times for Cisco's IGRP timers.

Timer Name	Expiration Time
Update	90 seconds
Invalid	270 seconds
Holddown	280 seconds
Flush	630 seconds
Sleep Time	0 milliseconds

Chapter 6

Enhanced Interior Gateway Routing Protocol (EIGRP)

If you need an immediate solution to:	See page:
Performing Basic EIGRP Configuration	385
Understanding the **show ip eigrp topology** Command	391
Understanding the **show ip eigrp neighbors** Command	392
Understanding the Output of the **show ip eigrp interfaces** Command	393
Using the Extended **network** Command of IOS 12.0(X)T	394
Understanding Basic DUAL Operation	399
Understanding How EIGRP Handles Secondary IP Addresses	408
Disabling EIGRP on an Interface	412
Understanding How EIGRP Works across NBMA Networks	412
Configuring Route Summarization with EIGRP	416
Modifying the Active Time	422

In Depth

Enhanced Interior Gateway Routing Protocol (EIGRP) is a Cisco-proprietary distance-vector routing protocol. Unlike RIP version 2, EIGRP is not an extension of IGRP; rather, it is a completely different protocol.

Despite being proprietary, EIGRP is very popular, thanks to its fast convergence.

In fact, it is often called an "advanced" distance-vector protocol because of its fast convergence and stability features. But what kind of protocol is EIGRP exactly?

By the representation of routing information, EIGRP is still a distance-vector protocol: Network prefixes are accompanied by metrics and next-hop routers (i.e. distances and vectors). Similarly to other distance-vector protocols, EIGRP does not possess complete knowledge of the actual network topology.

However, the algorithm on which EIGRP is based is not Bellman-Ford, but DUAL, the *diffusing update algorithm*. DUAL itself originates from Edsger Dijkstra's and C. S. Scholten's 1980 work *Termination Detection for Diffusing Computations*. DUAL is backed by many mathematical works, the most important of which is *Loop-Free Routing Using Diffusing Computations* by J. J. Garcia-Luna-Aceves.

NOTE: *The latter work can be of great help if you want a comprehensive understanding of DUAL concepts. The work can be purchased from ACM/IEEE's Web site at **www.acm.org/pubs/contents/journals/ton/**. (The exact location of the document is **www.acm.org/pubs/citations/journals/ton/1993-1-1/p130-garcia-luna-aceves/**.) Although the work contains a lot of mathematics, don't be afraid. The formulas contain only very basic arithmetic operations.*

Finally, EIGRP is built on a rather broad conceptual framework, which allowed a separate version of EIGRP to be created for three different protocols: IP, IPX, and AppleTalk. In this book, we'll examine only the IP version (often referred to as *IP EIGRP*). Regardless of the version, though, some EIGRP components remain unchanged. (For example, all versions use DUAL.)

Diffusing Update Algorithm (DUAL)

DUAL lies in the core of EIGRP, so let's consider it first. We'll start with pure DUAL and later examine the EIGRP-related changes in it.

The routing protocols based on the Bellman-Ford distance-vector algorithm tend to have two fundamental problems:

* Routing loops
* Counting to infinity

Both of these problems stem from the fact that routers know nothing about the actual network topology. All they know is what network prefixes are available through which of their neighbors. Whenever a change in the network occurs, routers try to switch routes based on the new metrics as they become available. Until convergence is reached, metrics may not correctly reflect the actual costs of routes, which can lead to routing loops. The first measure to avoid routing loops is to introduce infinity, essentially a metric, that if reached denotes that the network prefix is inaccessible. Infinity is rarely reached immediately. Typically-routers need to go through a number of iterations before setting a metric to infinity. The time during which the routers perform these iterations makes convergence longer. To facilitate faster convergence, distance-vector protocols employ a number of auxiliary techniques, such as the split-horizon rule, poison-reverse updates, triggered updates, and holddowns.

Let's recall what information routers learn from each other and how they use it. Routers, in the case of the Bellman-Ford distance-vector algorithm, exchange routing updates carrying network prefixes that they can reach. Each network prefix in a routing update is accompanied by a metric reflecting how far away the router that sends the routing update perceives itself to be from the network prefix. The router that receives a routing update uses the metric in the update to calculate its own metric. In most cases, the new metric incorporates the cost of the interface over which the routing update is received (or more precisely, the interface through which the potential next-hop router is available; typically, these interfaces coincide). If the produced metric is the smallest for the network prefix, the router creates a route for the network prefix. The route points to the router that sent the routing update and contains the newly calculated metric. This metric is further used by the router in its own routing updates for the network prefix.

6. Enhanced Interior Gateway Routing Protocol (EIGRP)

NOTE: *Certain routing protocols allow a router to specify a different next-hop router in the routing updates. If this is the case, then the route is established not through the router that sent the routing update, but through the router specified in the routing update.*

Notice, that in this scenario, the router that receives the routing update discards a piece of very valuable information—the advertising router's metric. The router uses it to calculate its own metric only, but after that, the advertising router's metric is forgotten.

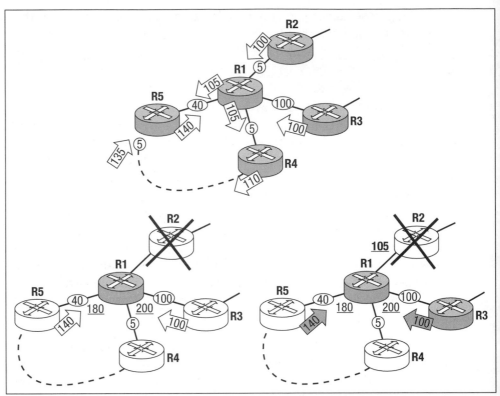

Figure 6.1   The two router R1's perceptions (on the bottom) of the part of the network
(on the top) after router R2's failure; in the one on the left, router R1 does not
have its neighbors' metrics, in the one on the right it does.

So the question is: What's so valuable in the reported distance ? Let's have a look at Figure 6.1, which depicts three views on the same part of some network with router R1 in the middle. We'll focus on router R1 and its routing options for some network prefix NP. The view on the top shows the network before a failure of router R1's neighbor, R2, through which router R1 had a route for network prefix NP. The arrows with numbers show with what metric the router (which the arrow touches) advertises network prefix NP over the respective segment. The numbers in the ovals show the costs of the segments. For simplicity, we'll assume that the routers calculate their own metrics by summarizing the metric in the routing update with the cost of the segment through which the update was received. Router R1 originally chose router R2 as the next-hop router for network prefix NP because router R2's advertised metric (100), being summarized with the cost of the segment (5), produced the smallest value (100 + 5 = 105).

The location of routers R4 and R5 is such that whichever path they choose to forward traffic destined for network prefix NP, this path must lie through router R1. For example, router R5 might forward such traffic directly to router R1 through the segment interconnecting the two routers. Or, it can choose an alternative path, which is shown in Figure 6.1 as a dashed curve. This path first brings the traffic to router R4, which then forwards it to router R1. As Figure 6.1 shows, the metric of the route through the alternative path is smaller than the metric of the direct route through router R1, hence router R5 chooses the alternative route over the direct one. Indeed, router R5 receives routing updates from router R1 and from its other neighbor on the alternative path; despite router R1's lower advertised metric (105), router R4 chooses the route through the other neighbor, because the neighbor's advertised metric (135), being summarized with the cost of the segment leading to the neighbor (5), produces a smaller value (135 + 5 = 140) than the metric of the route through router R1 (105 + 40 = 145).

The two views—one on the left and the other one on the right—show router R1's perception of the network after it detected router R2's failure. The difference between the views is that in the view on the left, router R1 is assumed to have discarded its neighbors' advertised metrics for network prefix NP, whereas in the view on the right, it is assumed to have remembered them.

In the left view, router R1 faces a dilemma—two routers that recently advertised network prefix NP are routers R3 and R5. Nevertheless, despite the smaller resulting metric of the route for network prefix NP through router R5, router R1 can't rely on this metric, as it can be outdated. So, router R1 should go through regular stability procedures, such as holddowns, triggered updates, and so on, to make sure it won't fall a victim of outdated metric information. (The light backgrounds of router R1's neighbors reflect router R1's lack of knowledge of the neighbors' metrics.)

In the right, router R1 has remembered the metrics with which all its neighbors advertised network prefix NP. So, upon detection of router R2's failure, router R1 can immediately tell that it can't rely on the better metric of router R5 because its advertised metric (135) is greater than router R1's own metric (105) through failed router R2. This essentially means that router R5 was originally located further away from network prefix NP than router R1. Contrary to that, router R3's advertised metric is 100, which is smaller than 105; hence, router R3 was originally closer to network prefix NP. Nevertheless, despite router R3's original vicinity to network prefix NP, the poor metric of the route through it (200 compared with 180, the metric of the route through router R5) prevents router R1 from switching to this route. (In this view the light background of routers R4 and R4 denotes that router R1 considers them to be further away from network prefix NP than router R1 itself. The darker background of router R3 denotes that router R1 is aware that router R3 is closer to network prefix NP than router R1 itself.)

In this particular scenario, router R1 still does not know for sure if it can or cannot use router R5 as the new next-hop router for network prefix NP, because it still does not know why router R5's advertised metric is greater than router R1's own metric. Maybe the reason is that router R5's route goes through that of router R1 (which is the case) hence, re-establishing the route through router R5 will create a routing loop. Or maybe router R5's route is simply longer; but nevertheless, it does not lie through router R1, in which case re-establishing a route through it should be fine.

So far, it may appear that router R1's knowledge of its neighbors' own metrics for network prefix NP presents no advantage. We will now prove otherwise.

Let's imagine that the cost of the segment interconnecting routers R1 and R3 were 10. Originally, router R1 would still have a route through router R2. But after router R2's failure, router R1 could immediately choose router R3 as the new next-hop router because router R3 would produce a new best metric (110 versus router R5's 180) and it is originally closer to network prefix NP than router R1 itself (router R3's metric of 100 versus router R1's metric of 105). The latter essentially means that there is no way a routing loop can be created if router R1 establishes a route through router R3.

Notice that the immediate switch to a new next-hop router is possible because router R1 kept track of its neighbors' advertised metrics for network prefix NP. These metrics allow router R1 in certain cases to immediately conclude that there is a loop-free route through another neighbor.

NOTE: *Detailed explanations of why and under which circumstances a router can conclude that there is a readily available alternative route for a destination, as well as the proof of that, are set forth in* Loop-Free Routing Using Diffusing Computations *by J. J. Garcia-Luna-Aceves.*

Keeping track of a router's neighbors' metrics is what constitutes the core of DUAL's approach. Compared to DUAL's approach, the Bellman-Ford distance-vector algorithm appears to be somewhat nearsighted. DUAL's approach of taking a deeper look at their nearest ecosphere allows acquiring topological knowledge that's often sufficient enough to make fast routing decisions, the ability crucial for achieving faster convergence.

Topology Table

DUAL requires the routers to remember their neighbors' metrics for the network prefixes they advertise. In DUAL terminology, the advertised metrics are called *reported distances*. Obviously, each router for every network prefix it advertises has a reported distance, which is equal to the metric of the route for the network prefix.

A router stores the reported distances of its neighbors in a separate database, which is called a *topology table*. The topology table consists of network prefix records, which hold information about network prefixes that the router learned from its neighbors. Each network prefix record also contains one or more subrecords for the routers that advertised it. Each subrecord contains the advertising router's IP address and the router's reported distance for the network prefix.

Whenever a router receives a routing update from its neighbor, in addition to performing regular routing table maintenance procedures, the router checks if it has a record for the advertised network prefix in its topology database. If it doesn't, it creates one. Then the router checks if there is a subrecord for the neighbor's IP address. If so, it updates it with the reported distance of the neighbor, providing it changed. If there is no subrecord, the router creates one.

As we remember, the routing table contains only "the best" routes; that is, the routes created based on the routing updates whose metrics combined with the costs of the output interfaces produced the smallest values. Unlike the routing table, the topology table contains records for all neighbors advertising each network prefix regardless of whether the neighbor becomes the next-hop router or not. For example, suppose Table 6.1 shows part of the routing table of a router, which was created by a hypothetic distance-vector protocol; then the router's topology table may look similar to the one shown in Table 6.2.

Table 6.1   Router R's routing table.

Network Prefix	Next-Hop Router	Metric
10.1.1.0/24	10.0.1.2	100
10.1.2.0/24	10.0.1.2	120
10.1.8.0/24	10.0.2.1	130

Table 6.2   Router R's topology table.

Network Prefix	Neighbor	Reported Distance (Neighbor's Metric)	Local Metric
10.1.1.0/24, FD = 100			
	10.0.5.1	80	130
	10.0.4.1	103	200
	10.0.1.2 *	95	100
	10.0.8.1	70	120
10.1.2.0/24, FD = 110			
	10.0.1.2 *	115	120
	10.0.5.1	120	170
	10.0.4.1	123	220
10.1.8.0/24, FD = 130			
	10.0.2.1 *	125	130
	10.0.8.1	90	140

NOTE: *The routing table and the topology table shown in Tables 6.1 and 6.2, respectively .are not related to the example we just considered.*

The routing table should also contain a column for the output interface. The output interface is not important for our discussion, and thus for simplicity, it is not shown in the routing table. The topology table does not have to contain references to the output interfaces because they are uniquely identified by the neighbors' IP addresses.

The router's local metric (the last column in Table 6.1) is shown for reference. It may or may not be stored in the topology table.

Notice that each network prefix is potentially accessible through multiple neighbors. The IP addresses of the neighbors that are the next-hop routers are followed by an asterisk (*).

In addition, each network prefix record contains the so-called *feasible distance* (denoted *FD*) of the network prefix. The feasible distance is the smallest metric the router has had for the network prefix. In Table 6.2, the feasible distances for the three network prefix records are shown right after the network prefixes. Notice that the ID for network prefix 10.1.1.0/24 is 100, the same as the metric of the current route, whereas the feasible distance for network prefix 10.1.2.0/24 is 110, which is smaller than the current route's metric (120). This means that the router previously had a better route for network prefix 10.1.2.0/24, but something happened that made the router change the metric to the greater value. Nevertheless, the feasible distance for the network prefix stayed the same.

NOTE: *In the example, the metric of router R1's route for network prefix NP through failed router R2 was the original feasible distance.*

The topology table is crucial for DUAL operation data structure, it's time to consider DUAL itself.

DUAL

Whenever a router detects a change in the cost or status of an interface, and/or in the status of one of its neighbors, it runs the *Feasibility Condition (FC)* procedure outlined below for the network prefix that the change can affect.

Feasibility Condition

1. Find the smallest among the metrics of all possible routes for the network prefix through every neighbor for which there is a subrecord in the topology table entry for the network prefix. This is done by calculating the smallest combination of every neighbor's reported distance with the cost of the respective output interface. Formally, $D_{min} = \min(C_N + RD_N)$, for every

neighbor N. D_{min} is the calculated value, RD_N is the neighbor N's reported distance for the network prefix, and C_N is the cost of the interface through which neighbor N is accessible.

NOTE: $C_N + RD_N$ may not necessarily be the sum of the two values. Furthermore, as we'll find out soon, the real-life DUAL-based protocol EIGRP uses a more complex formula to combine a neighbor's reported distance with the cost of the interface. But this is not really important. What's important is that the combination must have a greater value than the RD. In other words, a greater value denotes a longer path.

---

2. The router can immediately choose as the new successor any neighbor whose RD when combined with the cost of the output interface is equal to D_{min} and whose reported distance is smaller than or equal to the FD of the network prefix. Formally, neighbor N can become a new next-hop router if $RD_N + C_N = D_{min}$ and $RD_N \leq FD$. The neighbors who meet these two conditions are called *feasible successors.*

In the router finds a feasible successor, it establishes a new route for the network prefix through the feasible successor, which at that point becomes a new next-hop router. A next-hop router in the DUAL terminology is referred to as a *successor.* D_{min} becomes the metric of the new route and the router's RD for the network prefix. If the reported distance is different from the previous one, the router sends a routing update with the new reported distance to all its neighbors.

NOTE: If the original next-hop router is available, it can also become a feasible successor.

The router calculates the new feasible distance as the minimum of the previous feasible distance and the new route metric (that is, $FD_{new} = \min(FD_{old}, D_{min})$).

If the router cannot find a feasible successor for the network prefix, it sets the new metric and feasible distance equal to the combined values of the current next-hop router's reported distance and the cost of the interface through which it is available. If the current next-hop router is not available or if the interface or network through which it was available failed, the new metric and feasible distance are made equal to infinity. After that, the router sends a query to each of its neighbors inquiring if they know routes for the network prefix. The query contains the affected network prefix and its newly calculated reported distance. Until the router receives replies from *all* of its neighbors, it can change neither the existing route nor the feasible distance. Once the router receives all replies, it first sets its feasible distance for the network prefix to infinity,. Then it updates the topology table with the reported distances the neighbors returned in their replies and runs the feasibility condition procedure again. As the feasible distance is equal to infinity, the router essentially chooses the neighbor whose reported distance when combined with the cost of the output interface produces the smallest value as the new successor for the network prefix. Obviously the router's new feasible distance and reported distance are made equal to the new route metric. If however, all neighbors returned reported distances equal to infinity, the router declares the network prefix inaccessible.

If a router receives an update or a query, it first updates its topology table with the neighbor's RD contained in the update or query. Then it runs the feasibility condition procedure for the network prefix contained in the update or query. If the feasibility condition is met, the router updates its neighbors with its new reported distance if it changed; if the router received a query (as opposed to an update) it also sends a reply to the neighbor that issued the query. The reply contains the router's updated reported distance for the network prefix. If the feasibility condition is not met, the router itself starts the procedure outlined in the previous paragraph.

Eventually, all routers affected by the network change will update their topology tables and will be able to either figure out new routes for the network prefix or declare it inaccessible.

The process in which the routers issue queries and replies in order to find out an optimum route is called a *diffusing computation*. As the routers issue queries, the area in which the routers perform a diffusing computation is growing. As they receive replies, the area shrinks.

A router is said to maintain the *passive state* for a network prefix if the feasibility condition for that network prefix is met. Likewise, a router is said to be in the *active state* for a network prefix if the feasibility condition is not met. This, in turn, means that the router participates in a diffusing computation for that network prefix. Once the router in the active state has received replies from all of the neighbors to which it sent the queries were sent, it again becomes passive for the network prefix.

A router that already performs a diffusing computation can receive additional queries and/or updates or can detect an interface cost or status change that can affect the network prefix for which the router is in the active state. In theory, it is possible for the router to start a separate diffusing computation for such an event. This, however, potentially leads to high memory consumption and high CPU utilization. Thus, to avoid having a router perform multiple diffusing computations, a special algorithm was devised that ensures the router participates in only one diffusing computation at a time. The algorithm, although an important component of DUAL, does not change the routing concepts of DUAL, and therefore we won't discuss it in this book.

NOTE: *For those interested in the details of the aforementioned algorithm, see* Loop-Free Routing Using Diffusing Computations *by J. J. Garcia-Luna-Aceves.*

Finally, routers, upon discovering each other, exchange routing updates carrying network prefixes that they can reach and the respective metrics. If a new router is connected to the network, it should send an update to its neighbors carrying network prefixes to which it is directly connected.

Final Notes

Before we get down to EIGRP, a few interesting observations can be made with regard to DUAL:

- First, despite the common belief that DUAL handles only negative network changes, DUAL actually reacts on all network changes. For example, if a metric of a route becomes smaller (a positive change), DUAL still runs the feasibility condition procedure. In the case of the positive network changes, the feasibility condition may result in decreasing the values of the feasible distances of the affected network prefixes.

- If the network change is negative (such as a loss of a neighbor, an interface going down, and an interface cost increasing) but the FC remains satisfied, the feasible distances of the affected network prefixes stay the same, even if the metrics of the routes have increased.

- The term "feasible successor" really makes sense only while the FC procedure is being executed. In a stable network, when the router doesn't run the feasibility condition procedure, the term "feasible successor" is meaningless. Also, a router must not have a successor for a feasible successor to come into play.

NOTE: *I've heard many times how people call routers whose reported distance for some network prefix is smaller than the feasible distance of some router feasible successors for that network prefix.*

- There are two types of events that make a router run the feasibility condition procedure: changes in the cost or status of an interface or neighbor and receipt of an update or query. The latter type of event however always stems from the first one. In other words there is always a router that first detects an event of the first type, which triggers an event of the second type—an update or query.

- If a router sends a routing update for a network prefix carrying the reported distance equal to infinity, the routers that receive the routing can either remove the subrecord for the router, or change update the stored reported distance to infinity. Whatever action they choose this will have the same effect.

6. Enhanced Interior Gateway Routing Protocol (EIGRP)

Protocol Overview

Unlike RIP and IGRP, EIGRP does not rely on regular updates. Instead, EIGRP uses incremental updates, which are sent only when a network change occurs and only for the affected network prefixes.

As we know, RIP and IGRP handle network failures and component removals by timing out the routes for the affected network prefixes. Timing out is possible because the routers exchange regular routing updates, and—if they miss a certain number of regular routing updates for some network prefix—they conclude that the network prefix is no longer available through the known next-hop router. (The route times out.)

Because EIGRP does not use regular routing updates, it can't resort to timing out routes. Instead, EIGRP requires the routers to keep track of their neighbors that are directly reachable. The routers regularly send hello messages out of all interfaces configured for EIGRP operation. Upon receipt of a hello message, a router knows that the neighbor that sent the message is functional. If hello messages haven't been received from a neighbor for a period of time called the *hold time*, the neighbor is declared down and all the routes associated with the neighbor must be recalculated. As we know, routers recalculate these routes using DUAL.

EIGRP Metrics

Being a distance-vector protocol, EIGRP uses metrics to advertise network prefixes. EIGRP calculates metrics in a manner similar to IGRP: Upon acceptance of an advertised network prefix, a router calculates the new route metric by combining the advertised metric and the cost of the interface over which the routing update was received.

The exact formula for calculating EIGRP metrics is the same as that of IGRP. Like IGRP, EIGRP does not advertise the calculated metric but instead advertises the individual components used in the metric calculation—the bandwidth, delay, reliability, and load of the path. The bandwidth, reliability, and load are calculated in exactly the same way as in the case of IGRP. However, the EIGRP delay component differs from that of IGRP, as demonstrated by the equation

$$D_{EIGRP} = D_{IGRP} * 256$$

Thus, the resulting EIGRP metric is 256 times greater than the same IGRP metric.

TIP: *For simplicity, you can think of the EIGRP metric as simply the IGRP metric multiplied by 256.*

DUAL in IP EIGRP

So far, we learned how a generic implementation of DUAL works. This essentially means that the DUAL we studied doesn't take into consideration the IP addressing rules and restrictions. As it turns out, the IP addressing rules can lead to some optimizations with regard to the propagation of DUAL queries and replies.

As we remember, if a router goes active for a network prefix, it starts querying its neighbors in an attempt to find out if they know a better route for the network prefix. Depending on what routing information the neighbors have for the network prefix, some of them can also go active for the network prefix. This results in more queries, which in turn can cause even more queries. Until all these queries are replied to, the routers in the network can't change their existing routes for the network prefix, which are most likely incorrect.

If the segment on which the network prefix is assigned failed completely, generic DUAL would cause all routers to receive queries. If the network were large, this could take a rather long time to reply to the queries and would cause some congestion in the network.

In the case of IP networks, some routers can't possibly know of certain network prefixes, and thus propagating queries beyond such routers is meaningless. For example, if a router performs summarization of IP network prefixes on the classful boundary, the router that learns the summary network prefix won't possibly know the individual network prefixes. All routers behind this router will be oblivious to the individual network prefixes either. Therefore, it won't make sense to propagate queries for an individual network prefix through these routers.

Table 6.3 outlines the rules that apply when a router receives a query.

EIGRP Transport Protocols and Their PDUs

EIGRP as a routing protocol relies on two transport protocols to perform its own operation: the hello protocol and the reliable transport protocol (RTP). Routers

Table 6.3   Query processing rules.

Query Sender	Queried Network Prefix	Action
Any neighbor (except for the successor) of the network prefix	A route exists for the network prefix; the network prefix is in the passive state.	Reply with the current best metric for the network prefix.

(continued)

Table 6.3 Query processing rules **(continued).**

Query Sender	Queried Network Prefix	Action
The successor of the network prefix	A route exists for the network prefix; the network prefix is in either state—passive or active.	Choose a new successor among the existing feasible successors and reply with the new best metric; create a route for the network prefix through the new successor. If there are no feasible successors, start querying all neighbors (except for the old successor).
Any neighbor	No route exists for the network prefix.	Reply with the metric equal to infinity.
Any neighbor (except for the successor) of the network prefix	A route exists for the network prefix; the network prefix is in the active state.	If there is no successor (RD and most typical case), reply with the metric equal to infinity; otherwise, reply with the current best metric.

use the hello protocol to discover and monitor neighbors, and they use RTP to exchange routing information and to perform diffusing calculations.

Both the hello protocol and RTP are encapsulated directly into IP datagrams with the protocol field carrying the value of 88 (decimal) assigned to Cisco EIGRP. The PDUs of both protocols have the same structure, shown in Figure 6.2.

The Version field is 8 bits long and carries the current version of EIGRP. It should always be 2.

The Opcode field is also 8 bits long and is used to denote the type of the PDU. Table 6.4 lists the possible values of the Opcode field.

NOTE: *The last Opcode (6) is used only in IPX EIGRP operation. It appears in Table 6.4 for the sole purpose of representing all possible Opcodes.*

The Checksum field is 16 bits long and contains the checksum covering the whole EIGRP PDU. (It does not cover the IP and link layer headers.) The checksum algorithm is the same as that of UDP.

The 32-bit Flags field has the structure shown in Figure 6.3.

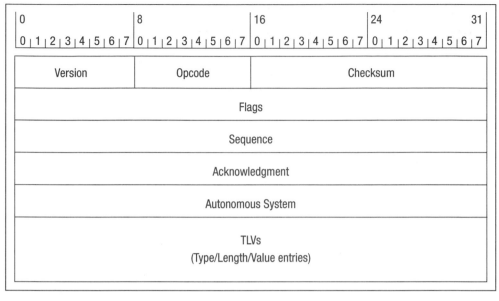

Figure 6.2   The format of the EIGRP PDUs.

Table 6.4   The EIGRP Opcode values.

Value	Type
1	Update
3	Query
4	Reply
5	Hello/Acknowledgment
6	IPX SAP

NOTE: *Some sources (including Sniffer) indicate that this 32-bit field actually comprises two fields—Reserved and Flags (in the transmission order), each occupying 16 bits.*

When set, the Initial Update Indicator is used to specify that the EIGRP PDU is the first update sent to a new neighbor. The Conditionally Receive Mode Indicator is used in RTP operation.

The 32-bit Sequence and Acknowledgment fields are used in RTP operation. (Their usage will be discussed shortly.)

The 32-bit Autonomous System field carries the value of the EIGRP autonomous system that is configured on the router that issues the EIGRP PDU. Only the routers with identical EIGRP autonomous system numbers perceive each other as neighbors.

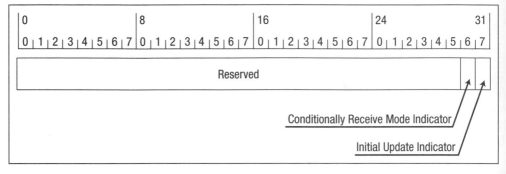

Figure 6.3   The structure of the EIGRP Flags field.

TIP: *The EIGRP autonomous system numbers mean the same as IGRP autonomous system numbers.*

The EIGRP PDU can optionally contain one or several type/length/value entries. Depending on the EIGRP PDU type (the Opcode field), the contained TLV entries can carry various pieces of data, which can range from the IOS version of the router to the advertised network prefixes. The TLV entries make EIGRP and its transport protocols very versatile: New TLV entries can be easily incorporated to accommodate new features.

All TLV entries have the generic structure shown in Figure 6.4.

The 8-bit Protocol ID field represents the protocol-specific version of EIGRP (IP, IPX, or AppleTalk) for which the data contained in the TLV entry is addressed. Alternatively, the data can be protocol independent, in which case the field carries the value of 0.

The 8-bit Type Code field denotes the individual, protocol-specific type of data contained in the TLV entry. The possible combinations of the Protocol ID and Type Code fields are shown in Table 6.5.

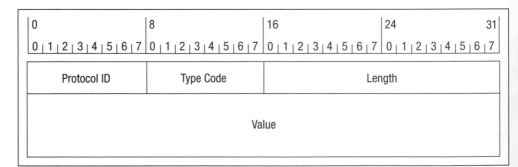

Figure 6.4   The format of the EIGRP TLVs.

Table 6.5   *The combinations of the values that the Protocol ID and Type Code fields can carry.*

Protocol ID	Type Code	TLV Type
General TLV Types (Protocol ID = 0x00)		
0x00	0x01	EIGRP parameters
0x00	0x02	Sequence
0x00	0x04	IOS and EIGRP versions of the sending router
0x00	0x05	Next multicast sequence
IP-specific TLV types (Protocol ID = 0x01)		
0x01	0x02	Internal network prefixes
0x01	0x03	External network prefixes

NOTE: *The protocol IDs for AppleTalk and IPX are equal to 0x02 and 0x03, respectively. The values of the Type Code field for these protocols are similar to those of IP.*

The 16-bit Length field carries the length of the TLV entry in octets (8-bit bytes).

Finally, the Value field is of variable length and carries the TLV type-specific information.

The EIGRP Hello Protocol

The EIGRP hello protocol is used to discover new neighbors and to remove lost ones.

A router transmits EIGRP hello messages through all of its ports on which EIGRP operation is enabled. The hello messages are destined for multicast IP address 224.0.0.10 (which is the address globally assigned for Cisco EIGRP).

Upon receipt of the first hello message, the router registers its sender as a new neighbor. No additional communication is required to establish a neighbor relation between the two routers.

NOTE: *Until the sender receives the countering hello message from the receiving router, the neighbor relation remains unidirectional. In other words, the sender may not yet consider the receiving router to be a neighbor. This inconvenience is typically resolved quickly and usually does not cause any problems.*

The routers keep track of their neighbors by maintaining a hold timer for each of them. Each time a hello message arrives from a neighbor, the hold timer associated with that neighbor is reset. If the router misses enough hello messages for the hold timer to expire, the neighbor is declared to be lost, and EIGRP executes DUAL for the affected network prefixes.

The routers keep track of their neighbors by means of the EIGRP neighbor table, which contains various neighbor information, such as the neighbor's IP address, the interface against which the neighbor appears, the neighbor's hold time, and so on.

NOTE: *The hold time entry in the neighbor table allows the router to maintain different hold times for each neighbor.*

Hello messages have the format shown in Figure 6.5. The hello message consists of the EIGRP header and two TLV entries.

The header carries an Opcode of 5. All other fields—except for the Version, Checksum, and Autonomous System fields—are equal to 0.

Both TLV entries are of the general type.

The first TLV entry carries the essential parameters of EIGRP: the k-weights of the EIGRP metric calculation formula and the hold time. The latter allows the routers to maintain different hold times for each of the neighbors.

The second TLV entry contains information regarding the versions of IOS and EIGRP of the sending router.

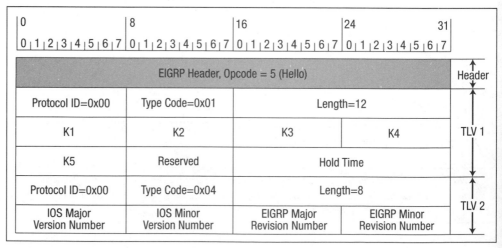

Figure 6.5   The format of EIGRP hello packets.

RTP

RTP is used for sending routing updates and for performing diffusing calculations. RTP operates with updates, queries and replies, and acknowledgments, which are distinguished by the appropriate value of the Opcode field. The updates and queries can be sent to the EIGRP multicast address as well as to the (unicast) IP addresses of individual neighbors. The acknowledgments and replies are always sent to the unicast IP addresses. Regardless of whether the destination is unicast or multicast, the updates, queries, and replies must be acknowledged by each neighbor. The use of acknowledgments ensures the reliable operation of RTP.

Routers maintain the reliable operation of RTP by observing and properly assigning the sequence and acknowledgment numbers in the exchanged EIGRP PDUs. The router keeps single-sequence numbering for each EIGRP process. After the router has sent an update, query, or reply, it increases the sequence number by one. All of the router's neighbors must acknowledge receiving the PDU (update, query, or reply) in one of two ways:

- The neighbor can transmit an acknowledgment back to the sender. The Acknowledgment field in the acknowledgment must carry the value of the Sequence field in the acknowledged PDU. If a response is required for the acknowledged PDU (such as a reply for a query), it must also carry the Acknowledgment field with the value equal to the value of the Sequence field in the acknowledged PDU.

- The neighbor can transmit its own update, query, or reply back to the sender. As in the case of the acknowledgment, the Acknowledgment field in the transmitted PDU must carry the value of the Sequence field in the acknowledged PDU.

Figure 6.6 shows an example that demonstrates both methods of acknowledging PDUs. First, router R1 sends router R2 a query whose Sequence field is equal to 10. Router R2 then replies with an acknowledgment whose Acknowledgment field is equal to 10. After that, it sends router R1 a reply whose Acknowledgment field is also equal to 10. The reply's Sequence field is equal to 7, and router R1 acknowledges router R2's reply with its acknowledgment with 7 in the Acknowledgment field. Later on, router R1 sends a multicast update whose Sequence field is equal to 11 (the previous sequence number increased by one). Router R2 replies back with a poison-reversed update (which will be discussed shortly) with the Acknowledgment field equal to 11 and the Sequence field equal to 8. Router R1 acknowledges router R2's update with an acknowledgment carrying 8 in the Acknowledgment field.

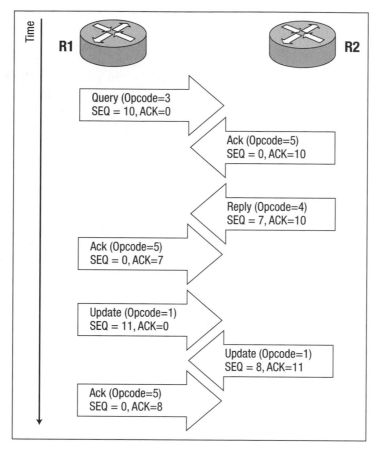

Figure 6.6   An example of the RTP operation.

The exact use of sequence and acknowledgment numbers in various EIGRP PDUs is shown in Table 6.6.

NOTE: Although not a part of RTP, hello messages are included in the table to show how they differ from acknowledgments whose Opcode is also equal to 5.

Table 6.6   The usage of sequence and acknowledgment numbers in various EIGRP PDUs.

PDU	Sequence Number	Acknowledgment Number
Multicast update or query	Current sequence number	0
Unicast update, query, or reply	Current sequence number	Last neighbor's sequence number, or 0 if no PDU has been received from neighbor
Acknowledgment	0	Last neighbor's sequence number
Hello message	0	0

Handling Retransmissions

If the router expecting an acknowledgment from a certain neighbor does not receive one within a period of time called a *retransmission timeout (RTO)*, it retransmits the unacknowledged PDU directly to the IP address of the nonresponding neighbor. The router will continue retransmitting the PDU until the neighbor sends back an acknowledgment. The router can retransmit the PDU 16 times even if the hold timer for the nonresponding neighbor has expired during the retransmissions. The router will continue retransmitting the PDU if the hold timer does not expire by the 16th retransmission. If the neighbor still does not reply, the router declares the neighbor to be lost.

The router maintains a separate RTO for each neighbor. To calculate an RTO, the router first measures a roundtrip time (RTT) for each RTP transaction. The RTT is defined as the difference between the time when an EIGRP PDU was sent and the time when the acknowledgment was received. The router keeps measuring an RTT for every acknowledged EIGRP PDU. Each time an RTT has been measured, the router uses it to calculate what is called the *smoothed roundtrip time (SRTT)* using the following formula:

$$SRTT_{new} = SRTT_{prev} * 0.8 + RTT * 0.2$$

where $SRTT_{prev}$ is the previously calculated SRTT.

Finally, the RTO is calculated as follows:

$$RTO = 6 * \max(SRTT, PI)$$

where PI is what is known as a *pacing interval*, a special value that is individually calculated for each EIGRP PDU sent out of the interface. (The pacing interval is used to prevent EIGRP from taking over all available bandwidth of the interface during convergence. We'll discuss how the pacing interface is used and calculated shortly.)

The calculated RTO is used for only the first retransmission. The router will recalculate the RTO each time a subsequent retransmission is required in accordance with the following formula:

$$RTO_{new} = RTO_{prev} * 1.5$$

where RTO_{prev} is the RTO calculated for the previous retransmission.

However, RTO can be neither smaller than 200 milliseconds nor greater than 5 seconds. Given this condition, the real formula for recalculating RTO is:

$$RTO_{new} = \min(5 \text{ sec.}, \max(200 \text{ ms}, RTO_{prev} * 1.5))$$

Pacing Packets

During convergence periods, EIGRP tends to generate an overwhelming number of PDUs, which can consume most of the available bandwidth of some slow links unless the rate at which PDUs are transmitted is reduced.

NOTE: *The term PDU used in this section refers to EIGRP PDUs only.*

When an EIGRP process on a router creates PDUs, the router does not send them immediately; instead, it puts them into the output queue of the output interface. Likewise, the PDUs from the output queue are not sent at the first possible opportunity either. For each PDU, the router calculates the PI for which the PDU must sit in the queue before it can be sent.

The PI for each PDU is calculated based on the PDU size, the interface's bandwidth, and the percentage of that bandwidth that EIGRP is allowed to consume. The percentage is an administratively configured value (let's denote it *EBP*, for *EIGRP bandwidth percentage*), which, by default, is equal to 50%. Using these three components, the router calculates the PI for the PDU using the following formula:

$$PI = \frac{S_{PDU}}{BW} * EBP$$

where S_{PDU} is the EIGRP PDU size in bits, and BW is the bandwidth of the interface in bits per second (bps). EBP is measured in fractions of 1. (For example, the default, 50%, is equal to 0.5.)

Stuck In Active Condition

It is possible that a router won't receive a reply from some neighbor after becoming active for a network prefix and having issued queries. Obviously, the router will retransmit the query, and if it still does not receive a reply, it will have to keep retransmitting the query until it receives one. As we remember, a router can't become passive for a network prefix until it receives replies from all of the neighbors to which the queries have been sent. Hence, the just-described router is in condition called *stuck in active (SIA)*. SIA essentially means that the router can't change the state of some network prefix to passive because at least one neighbor has not replied to a previously sent query.

Obviously, a router cannot be in the active state forever. To resolve this issue, the router declares itself to be stuck in active after a certain time threshold called the *active time*. If a neighbor does not reply to a previously issued query within the active time, the router declares the neighbor dead and stops waiting for its reply.

NOTE: *If a router detects a neighbor loss before the active time is reached, the stuck in active condition is not declared. Instead, the router handles a neighbor loss (which essentially has the same consequences).*

EIGRP Stability Features

EIGRP implements two of the most common distance-vector stability features: poison-reverse updates and the split-horizon rule.

As usual, poison-reverse updates are updates that advertise network prefixes with the metric of infinity. In EIGRP, infinity is indicated by advertising the delay of the route equal to 4,294,967,295 (0xFFFFFFFF hexadecimal).

EIGRP uses both the regular split horizon and split horizon with poisoned-reverse.

The exact usage of the split-horizon rule in EIGRP varies slightly depending on whether the EIGRP PDU is an update or a query. The next two sections explain the differences in split-horizon rule usage as well as poisoned-reverse updates.

Updates

A router uses updates in the following cases:

- If it finds out a new network prefix is included in EIGRP operation (as the result of a new interface being brought up, or because the router received an update for a network prefix from one of its neighbors)
- If the metric of an existing network prefix changes
- To update a new neighbor of known network prefixes
- As the result of the split horizon with poisoned-reverse rule

When a router discovers a new neighbor (the first hello message arrives from an unknown neighbor), it sends an update directly to the IP address of this neighbor. The EIGRP header of the update carries the initial update flag set, and this update must be acknowledged by the new neighbor as part of the RTP operation. The new neighbor replies with a poisoned-reverse update for the network prefixes for which it installed routes through the interface via which it received the initial update. The new neighbor should send the poisoned-reverse update to the multicast EIGRP address, unless split horizon is disabled on the output interface. If the latter is the case, the router must send the poisoned-reverse update directly to the IP address of the router that sent the initial update.

The process really comprises two stages, because—to the new neighbor—the existing routers are also new neighbors. Thus, each pair of routers must exchange initial updates followed by the poison-reverse updates, all acknowledged.

Unless the update is an initial update or retransmission, it is sent to the multicast EIGRP update. All routers that receive the update and established routes for the advertised network prefixes through the interface via which they received the update must reply with the poisoned-reverse update for those network prefixes.

The use of the poisoned-reverse updates described in the three previous paragraphs results from the split-horizon rule with the poisoned reverse mentioned in the last bullet point in the beginning of this section. The way the rule manifests itself in EIGRP differs from the way it typically does in regular distance vector routing protocols, such as RIP. In RIP, for example, the rule (if observed) would cause the router to regularly transmit poisoned-reverse routing updates, whereas in EIGRP it happens only once. The reason for this is that EIGRP does not use regular routing updates.

When sending EIGRP updates, the routers must also observe the regular split-horizon rule. This essentially means that routers may not send updates through the interfaces referenced as output interfaces in the routes for the network prefixes advertised in the updates. Of course, this applies only if the split-horizon rule is not turned off on the corresponding output interface.

The updates carry routing information encoded as internal and external IP route TLV entries. An update can contain none, one, or several IP route TLVs (both external and internal are allowed in the same update).

The internal IP route TLV entries describe the routing information originated by EIGRP. Figure 6.7 shows the format of internal IP route TLV entries.

The 32-bit Next Hop Router IP Address field is used to specify the IP address of the next-hop router. If this field is equal to 0 (most typical case), the sender's IP address is to be used as the IP address of the next-hop router.

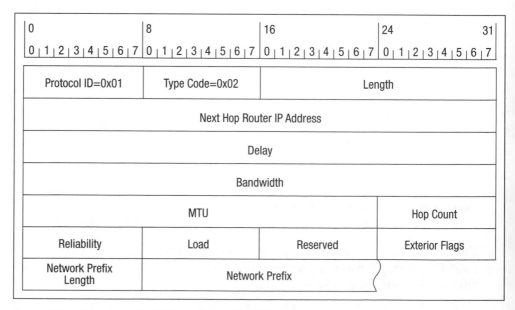

Figure 6.7   The format of internal IP route TLV entries.

The Delay, Bandwidth, Reliability, Load, MTU, and Hop Count fields have identical meanings to the same fields in IGRP updates, with one exception. In EIGRP, the size of the Delay and Bandwidth fields is 32 bits, whereas it is 24 in IGRP. The same considerations that were set forth for IGRP apply to these fields because they get updated while being propagated from router to router.

The 8-bit Reserved field must always carry the value of 0.

The 8-bit Exterior Flags field denotes whether the route for the network prefix must become the candidate default or not. The field has only two significant bits; all other bits must remain clear. The field's structure is shown in Figure 6.8.

The Candidate Default Indicator bit if set specifies that the route for the network prefix in the TLV entry if created through the advertising router must be labeled as candidate default. (A similar function in IGRP is performed by the exterior network route entries.) The function of the External Route Indicator flag is unclear.

NOTE: *Most sources specify that the Exterior Flags field is available only in the external IP route TLV entries. Furthermore, the popular LAN analyzer Sniffer shows only the field in the external IP route TLV entries. If Sniffer decodes internal IP route TLV entries, it labels the field as Reserved. This is not correct. The field does function in internal IP route TLV entries. This can be easily verified by configuring a router with the **ip default-network** command followed by some network prefix and then having the router advertise the network prefix out. The Sniffer trace will show that the value of the field does contain the Candidate Default Indicator bit set (the value of the Reserved field in the Sniffer trace will be equal to 0x02).*

The last two fields—Network Prefix Length and Network Prefix—describe the network prefix carried in the TLV entry. The Network Prefix Length field carries the length of the network prefix; the field's size is eight bits. The Network Prefix field carries the bits of the network prefix; the size of this field is variable—it is equal to the smallest number of octets sufficient to accommodate all of the bits of the network prefix (the size of this field ranges from 1 to 4 octets).

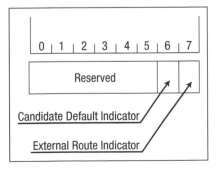

Figure 6.8   **The structure of the Exterior Flags field.**

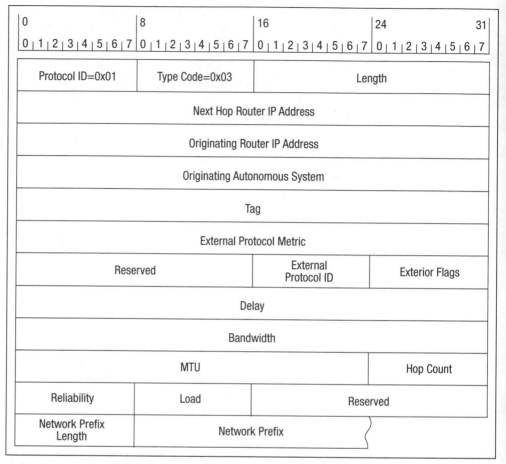

Figure 6.9   The format of external IP route TLV entries.

External IP route TLV entries describe the routing information that was imported into EIGRP as the result of a process called *redistribution*. Figure 6.9 shows the format of external IP route TLV entries.

Redistribution is comprehensively covered in Chapter 8. Thus, we will postpone discussing the details of external IP route TLV entries until then.

Queries and Replies

The usage of queries and replies is explained in the DUAL section of this chapter.

The structure of EIGRP queries and replies is essentially the same as the structure of EIGRP updates: They consist of the EIGRP header followed by one or several internal and/or external IP route TLV entries.

The queries carry IP route TLV entries for the network prefixes in the active state. If a router becomes active for a network prefix for which it makes the feasible distance equal to infinity, it issues queries that carry the delay equal to 4,294,967,295 (0xFFFFFFFF hexadecimal) to denote infinity.

The replies carry the best metric that the replying router knows for the network prefix. Of course, this metric can equal infinity if the replying router doesn't know a route for the network prefix or failed to discover one.

The split-horizon rule, if enabled, applies to queries. Thus, if a query for a network prefix is received from the successor and the query changed the state of the network prefix to active, the receiving router won't send its query back to the interface on which the successor's query was received.

Immediate Solutions

Although EIGRP is a completely different protocol from RIP version 1 and 2 and IGRP, certain EIGRP configuration and operation tasks are identical to those of these protocols. To avoid wasting space in the book, I've compiled a list of these tasks:

- EIGRP handles IP unnumbered in the same way as RIP and IGRP do. For more information, see the section "Understanding How RIP Handles IP Unnumbered" in Chapter 4.

- Auto-summarization is disabled by the **no auto-summary** command, which has the identical meaning and usage as the **no auto-summary** command in RIP version 2. As with RIP version 2, this command can be used in EIGRP to create noncontiguous classful networks and to perform optimized routing. For more information, see the section "Disabling RIP Version 2 Auto-Summarization" in Chapter 4.

- The administrative distance of EIGRP routes can be changed by the **distance** command, which has two formats. The first format is the same as that of the **distance** command available under RIP and IGRP. The second format requires information that isn't presented until Chapter 7, so it will be covered there.

- EIGRP metrics are changed in the same way as in IGRP (that is, by using the **bandwidth** and **delay** commands). The same usage rules apply.

- The *k*-parameters present in the EIGRP formula for calculating metrics can be changed using the same **metric weights** command available for IGRP.

- Performing equal- and unequal-cost load balancing with EIGRP is the same as with IGRP.

- EIGRP can be configured to originate default routes in exactly the same way as with IGRP. See the section "Configuring IGRP to Originate a Default Route" in Chapter 5.

In addition, the **neighbor** command does not appear to be functional with EIGRP.

Throughout this chapter, I will concentrate only on the unique features of EIGRP configuration and operation.

Performing Basic EIGRP Configuration

The basic configuration of EIGRP is identical to that of IGRP, except for the command **router eigrp** *<AS #>*. (The keyword **eigrp** replaces the keyword **igrp**.) The meaning of the *<AS #>* parameter as well as the values it can take are identical to those of the *<AS #>* parameter of the **router igrp** *<AS#>* command.

The following guidelines for basic EIGRP configuration mostly repeat those of IGRP:

1. Create an EIGRP routing process on the router using the **router igrp** *<AS #>* command in global configuration mode. The *<AS #>* parameter is numeric and ranges from 1 through 65535. As with IGRP, it represents the desired AS number, and its primary purpose is to allow the creation of multiple EIGRP processes on a single router. The specified value must be the same on the routers that are expected to participate in EIGRP routing. This value is communicated among EIGRP neighbors in all of the exchanged EIGRP PDUs.

   This command transfers the command-line interface into EIGRP configuration mode for the specified AS.

2. Specify the interfaces on which the EIGRP process must run using one or several **network** *<IP address>* commands. The *<IP address>* parameter must be a classful network address (such as 10.0.0.0, 172.16.0.0, and so forth). All operational interfaces whose IP addresses belong to the specified classful network addresses will be included into EIGRP operation. (The interfaces that are either down or administratively disabled won't be used by EIGRP.) EIGRP will advertise the network prefixes configured on the specified interfaces using the **network** *<IP address>* command.

The meaning of the **network** command in EIGRP is exactly the same as in RIP and IGRP. For more information on the specifics of this command, see the section "Performing Basic RIP Configuration" in Chapter 4.

The description of basic EIGRP configuration reveals a rather significant shortcoming: Although EIGRP as a protocol is capable of propagating any network prefixes, its configuration inherits the old classful **network** command, which limits the network prefixes that EIGRP can advertise to only those that are shorter than the network prefixes of the corresponding classful network addresses. Let's consider router R in Figure 6.10 as an example. The **network** command can make the EIGRP process advertise only network prefixes 192.168.4.0/24 and 192.168.0.192/28. Network prefix 192.168.128.0/20 won't be advertised because the corresponding classful address (192.168.128.0/24).

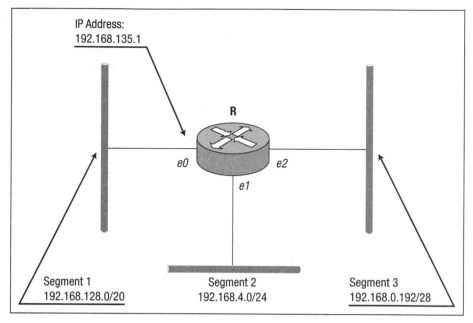

IP Address:
192.168.135.1

R

e0   e2

e1

Segment 1   Segment 2   Segment 3
192.168.128.0/20   192.168.4.0/24   192.168.0.192/28

Figure 6.10   Interface Ethernet0 of router R is configured with network prefix
192.168.128.0/20, which is shorter than the corresponding classful
network address (192.168.128.0/24).

Interestingly enough, this restriction affects only the network prefixes, not the
interfaces. In other words, it is possible to make EIGRP send and receive EIGRP
PDUs on an interface whose network prefix is shorter than the corresponding
classful network address. It appears that Cisco routers use two different approaches to the inclusion of interfaces into an EIGRP process and to the decision
of which network prefixes should be advertised. These two approaches can be
described as follows:

- When a router decides whether to include an interface into EIGRP operation,
  it compares only those bits that belong to the classful part of the interface's
  IP address against the corresponding bits in the <*IP address*> parameters
  specified in the **network** commands. The router completely disregards the
  length of the network prefix to which the IP address belongs, even if it is
  shorter than the network prefix of the classful network address.

- The router includes only those network prefixes that belong to the classful
  network addresses specified in the network commands and whose lengths
  are shorter than or equal to the network prefix lengths of the corresponding
  classful addresses.

For example, interface Ethernet0 of router R from Figure 6.10 is assigned the IP
address 192.168.135.1 (which, combined with subnet mask 255.255.240.0 (/20),

produces network prefix 192.168.128.0/20). The "classful bits" of this IP address are 192.168.135. Thus, the **network 192.168.135.0** command will include the interface into EIGRP operation. In other words, the EIGRP process on router R will send and receive EIGRP PDUs on this interface. The interface's network prefix, however, still won't be advertised through the other interfaces because of the difference in the inclusion of interfaces in EIGRP operation and the decision of which network prefixes to advertise.

Returning to basic EIGRP configuration, let's consider an example that should help clarify most of the important EIGRP features. We'll use the network scheme shown in Figure 6.11.

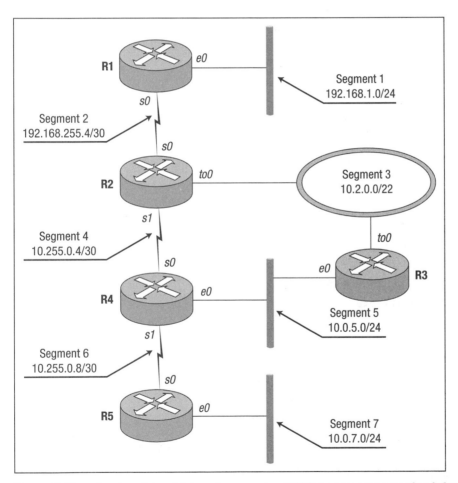

Figure 6.11   A network in which routers employ EIGRP to propagate routing information.

The configurations of all five routers are shown in Listings 6.1 through 6.5.

Listing 6.1   Router R1's configuration.

```
interface Ethernet0
 ip address 192.168.1.1 255.255.255.0

interface Serial0
 ip address 192.168.255.5 255.255.255.252

router eigrp 1
 network 192.168.1.0
 network 192.168.255.0
```

Listing 6.2   Router R2's configuration.

```
interface Serial0
 ip address 192.168.255.6 255.255.255.252

interface Serial1
 ip address 10.255.0.5 255.255.255.252

interface TokenRing0
 ip address 10.2.0.1 255.255.252.0
 ring-speed 16

router eigrp 1
 network 10.0.0.0
 network 192.168.255.0
```

Listing 6.3   Router R3's configuration.

```
interface Ethernet0
 ip address 10.0.5.1 255.255.255.0

interface TokenRing0
 ip address 10.2.0.2 255.255.252.0
 ring-speed 16

router eigrp 1
 network 10.0.0.0
```

Listing 6.4   Router R4's configuration.

```
interface Ethernet0
 ip address 10.0.5.2 255.255.255.0
```

```
interface Serial0
 ip address 10.255.0.6 255.255.255.252

interface Serial1
 ip address 10.255.0.9 255.255.255.252

router eigrp 1
 network 10.0.0.0
```

Listing 6.5   Router R5's configuration.

```
interface Ethernet0
 ip address 10.0.7.1 255.255.255.0

interface Serial0
 ip address 10.255.0.10 255.255.255.0

router eigrp 1
 network 10.0.0.0
```

As you can see, the configurations contain nothing fancy. All routers are configured very similarly to what they would be configured if we used IGRP or RIP instead.

Let's first have a look at the routing table of one of the routers, router R2, whose routing table is shown in Listing 6.6.

Listing 6.6   The routing table of router R2.

```
R2#show ip route
...
     10.0.0.0/8 is variably subnetted, 6 subnets, 4 masks
C       10.2.0.0/22 is directly connected, TokenRing0
D       10.0.0.0/8 is a summary, 00:11:40, Null0
D       10.0.7.0/24 [90/2237184] via 10.2.0.2, 00:06:15, TokenRing0
D       10.0.5.0/24 [90/297728] via 10.2.0.2, 00:06:18, TokenRing0
C       10.255.0.4/30 is directly connected, Serial1
D       10.255.0.8/30 [90/2211584] via 10.2.0.2, 00:06:15, TokenRing0
D     192.168.1.0/24 [90/2195456] via 192.168.255.5, 00:06:12, Serial0
     192.168.255.0/24 is variably subnetted, 2 subnets, 2 masks
C       192.168.255.4/30 is directly connected, Serial0
D       192.168.255.0/24 is a summary, 00:06:13, Null0
```

As we might expect, the EIGRP-learned routes are labeled with the letter D.

NOTE: *The choice might seem a bit strange at first because there is no letter D in EIGRP. Unfortunately, E had already been assigned to EGP by the time EIGRP was introduced. This is rather ironic because nobody seems to use EGP anymore, whereas EIGRP is quite popular.*

Notice one interesting route, which in Listing 6.6 is shown as the shaded line. Because the line begins with the letter D, the route was created by EIGRP. The route, however, points to the Null0 interface; in addition, it is described as a "summary." Why is this happening?

The reason is that, although EIGRP is a classless routing protocol, it inherits some pretty classful features, which (unless specifically turned off) often manifest themselves in some unusual ways. The route was created by EIGRP because EIGRP also operates on interfaces whose IP addresses do not belong to classful network address 10.0.0.0/8. By default, EIGRP summarizes subnets of all classful networks when advertising them over interfaces whose IP addresses belong to different classful networks. Thus, this route is indeed for summary address 10.0.0.0/8.

But why does the route point to the Null0 interface? As we remember, all traffic that must be sent over a null interface is dropped, which actually happens to be very convenient when it is necessary to create a route for a summary address. A summary address is used to represent a group of network prefixes in a terse form. A summary address essentially means a network prefix that is short enough to provide a match for any IP address belonging to the group of network prefixes the summary address summarizes. Consequently, the network prefix of a summary address is shorter any network prefix it summarizes. Thus, a route for the summary address may coexist with routes for any other network prefixes that it summarizes. Obviously, a router that advertises a summary address may not have routes for all possible summarized network prefixes. Some of them may simply not be used yet. This remains unknown to the routers that learn only the summary address from the router. Thus, if these routers must forward traffic that is destined for any IP address matched by the summary address, they will forward the traffic to the router advertising the summary address. Should this router have a route for this traffic other than the summary address route, the router will use it and forward the traffic further towards the destination. If the router does not have a route, it has no choice but to use the summary address route whose output interface is Null. Thus, the router drops the traffic. This behavior is exactly what we expect from a summary address. Moreover, by having a summary address route point to the Null interface, this behavior is achieved absolutely naturally through the use of the routing algorithm alone (whether the employed routing algorithm is classful or classless).

Let's now take a look at the routing table of router R1, which is shown in Listing 6.7.

Listing 6.7   The routing table of router R1.

```
R1#show ip route
...
D    10.0.0.0/8 [90/2185984] via 192.168.255.6, 00:12:23, Serial0
C    192.168.1.0/24 is directly connected, Ethernet0
```

```
     192.168.255.0/24 is variably subnetted, 2 subnets, 2 masks
C        192.168.255.4/30 is directly connected, Serial0
D        192.168.255.0/24 is a summary, 00:13:56, Null0
```

Notice that the only EIGRP-learned route (the shaded line) is for network prefix 10.0.0.0/8, which is the summary address advertised by router R2.

Interestingly, this route is not the only EIGRP-installed route. Router R2 itself has a route for a summary address—192.168.255.0/24. This happens because the serial connection between routers R1 and R2 uses a network prefix whose length is /30. EIGRP on router R1 is also configured for network 192.168.1.0/24 (which appears on other functioning interfaces of router R1), so router R1 automatically creates a route for summary address 192.168.255.0/24, in case it discovers neighbors on these other interfaces.

Understanding the **show ip eigrp topology** Command

The **show ip eigrp topology** command can be used to display the EIGRP topology table. Listing 6.8 shows the output of this command entered on router R2.

Listing 6.8   The EIGRP topology table of router R2.

```
R2#show ip eigrp topology
IP-EIGRP Topology Table for process 1

Codes: P - Passive, A - Active, U - Update, Q - Query, R - Reply,
       r - Reply status

P 10.2.0.0/22, 1 successors, FD is 176128
        via Connected, TokenRing0
P 10.0.0.0/8, 1 successors, FD is 176128
        via Summary (176128/0), Null0
P 10.0.7.0/24, 1 successors, FD is 2237184
        via 10.2.0.2 (2237184/2221056), TokenRing0
        via 10.255.0.6 (2707456/2195456), Serial1
P 10.0.5.0/24, 1 successors, FD is 297728
        via 10.2.0.2 (297728/281600), TokenRing0
        via 10.255.0.6 (2195456/281600), Serial1
P 192.168.1.0/24, 1 successors, FD is 2195456
        via 192.168.255.5 (2195456/281600), Serial0
P 192.168.255.4/30, 1 successors, FD is 2169856
        via Connected, Serial0
P 192.168.255.0/24, 1 successors, FD is 2169856
        via Summary (2169856/0), Null0
P 10.255.0.4/30, 1 successors, FD is 2169856
        via Connected, Serial1
```

```
P 10.255.0.8/30, 1 successors, FD is 2211584
        via 10.2.0.2 (2211584/2195456), TokenRing0
        via 10.255.0.6 (2681856/2169856), Serial1
```

Similar to the output of the **show ip route** command, the output of the **show ip eigrp topology** command always begins with several lines that explain various letters that are used in the output to denote certain important elements of the actual topology table.

Right after these explanatory lines, the actual topology table records are shown, and each topology table record is described using two or more lines. The first line begins with a single letter denoting the state of the network prefix (for example, P stands for "passive" and A for "active"). The state is followed by the network prefix itself in the bit count notation. The network prefix is in turn followed by the number of successors, which then is followed by the current FD. This concludes the first line. All subsequent lines describe the subrecords for the neighbors that advertised the network prefix.

Each of these lines begins with the IP address of the neighbor. The IP address is followed by two numbers in parentheses: The first number is the locally calculated metric through the neighbor, and the second is the RD of the neighbor. The line concludes with the reference to the output interface through which the neighbor is accessible.

TIP: *As we know from the "In Depth" section, the router keeps track of all neighbors that have advertised each network prefix with a reported distance other than infinity. The presented command however, displays only the subrecords for the neighbors whose reported distance is smaller than the router's feasible distance for the network prefix. You can still display all of the neighbors by using the **show ip eigrp topology all-links** command.*

Understanding the **show ip eigrp neighbors** Command

The **show ip eigrp neighbors** command displays the neighbor table of the router. Listing 6.9 shows the output of this command entered on router R2.

Listing 6.9   The output of the show ip eigrp neighbors command issued on router R2.

```
R2#show ip eigrp neighbors
IP-EIGRP neighbors for process 1
H    Address                Interface    Hold Uptime    SRTT    RTO   Q   Seq
                                         (sec)          (ms)         Cnt  Num
2    10.2.0.2               To0          11 00:10:20    511    3066   0   5
1    10.255.0.6             Se1          12 00:13:37    48      288   0   16
0    192.168.255.5          Se0          14 00:14:37    32      200   0   2
```

The output consists of nine columns. The first column, "H," shows the number of each EIGRP neighbor. Because the output of the **show ip eigrp neighbors** command is sorted by the IP addresses of the neighbors (the second column), the numbers most probably won't be sequential. The second column, "Address," contains the IP addresses of the neighbors. The third column, "Interface," shows the interfaces through which the neighbors are accessible. The next column, "Hold," shows the remaining hold time for each neighbor. The "Uptime" column shows for how long the neighbors have been known. The "SRTT" column actually shows the SRTT for the neighbor. The "RTO" column shows the RTO for the neighbor. The next column, "Q," shows the number of outstanding queries to be sent to the neighbor. The last column, "Seq," represents the sequence number of the last update, query, or reply received from the neighbor.

Understanding the Output of the **show ip eigrp interfaces** Command

The **show ip eigrp interfaces** command can be used to display the interfaces on which EIGRP operates. The output of this command issued on router R2 is shown in Listing 6.10.

Listing 6.10   The output of the **show ip eigrp interfaces** command issued on router R2.

```
R2#show ip eigrp interfaces
IP-EIGRP interfaces for process 1
```

Interface	Peers	Xmit Queue Un/Reliable	Mean SRTT	Pacing Time Un/Reliable	Multicast Flow Timer	Pending Routes
Se1	1	0/0	48	0/15	119	0
To0	1	0/0	511	0/10	2544	0
Se0	1	0/0	32	0/15	143	0

The output of the command consists of seven columns. The first column, "Interface", lists the interfaces on which EIGRP is operational. The next column, "Peers," shows how many EIGRP neighbors are available through the interface. The "Xmit Queue Un/Reliable" column shows the number of EIGRP PDUs outstanding in the interface queue for unreliable transmissions (the first number) and reliable transmissions (the second number). The "Mean SRTT" column shows the mean SRTT in seconds. The "Pacing Time Un/Reliable" column shows the interface's pacing intervals for unreliable EIGRP PDUs (hello messages and acknowledgements) and reliable ones (updates, queries, and replies). The pacing time is shown for the EIGRP PDUs whose size is equal to the MTU size of the interface. The "Multicast Flow Timer" column shows the maximum number of seconds in which EIGRP will send EIGRP PDUs destined for the EIGRP multicast address (224.0.0.10) through the interface. The last column, "Pending Routes," shows the number of network prefixes for which the updates have already been created and placed in the output queue of the interface but haven't been sent yet.

6. Enhanced Interior Gateway Routing Protocol (EIGRP)

Using the Extended **network** Command of IOS 12.0(X)T

The early-deployment release of Cisco IOS version 12.0(X)—where X is the minor IOS version number, labeled with letter T (e.g., 12.0(7)T)—features an extended version of the **network** command available under the **router eigrp** configuration. This extended version allows more classless configuration of EIGRP, the details of which will be explained shortly.

The extended version has the syntax **network** *<IP address> <wildcard mask>*. The two parameters are used to specify the interfaces on which the EIGRP process should operate. The *<wildcard mask>* parameter is used to specify the significant bits of the parameter *<IP address>* in the following way: The cleared bits (bits equal to 0) in the *<wildcard mask>* parameter denote significant bits in the *<IP address>* parameter. (Likewise, the set bits [bits equal to 1]) in the *<wildcard mask>* parameter denote so-called "don't care" bits in the *<IP address>* parameter.) The router chooses the interfaces on which EIGRP should operate by comparing the significant bits of the *<IP address>* parameter of the network commands against the corresponding bits of the IP addresses of the interfaces. If all of the significant bits of one of the **network** commands coincide with the IP address of an interface, this interface is included into EIGRP operation.

The *<wildcard mask>* parameter is very similar to a subnet mask with all bits inverted. Like a subnet mask, the *<wildcard mask>* parameter must be contiguous.

TIP: *If you type in a contiguous subnet mask instead of a wildcard mask, the router will convert it to the corresponding wildcard mask. For example, if you type in "255.240.0.0", the router's configuration will show 0.15.255.255. The router will also reset all bits in the <IP address> parameter whose corresponding bits in the <wildcard mask> parameter are equal to 1. For example, if you type in "network 10.1.1.1 255.255.0.0", the router's configuration will show* **network 10.1.0.0 0.0.255.255**.

The addition of the *<wildcard mask>* parameter eliminates the classful behavior of EIGRP, in which EIGRP advertises network prefixes only if they are as long as or longer than the network prefixes of the corresponding classful addresses.

To better understand how this new feature of EIGRP works, let's consider the network example shown in Figure 6.12.

This network features network prefixes 172.24.0.0/13, 172.20.0.0/14, 172.18.0.0/15, and 192.168.128.0/20. All of these network prefixes are shorter than the corresponding classful network addresses (172.24.0.0/16, 172.20.0.0/16, 172.18.0.0/16, and 192.168.128.0/24). Network prefixes 172.24.0.0/13 and 172.20.0.0/14, however, appear only on routers R1 and R2 running IOS version 11.3(11a) and 12.0(9), respectively. Network prefixes 172.18.0.0/15 and 192.168.128.0/20 appear on router R3, which runs IOS version 12.0(7)T, which features the extended **network** command.

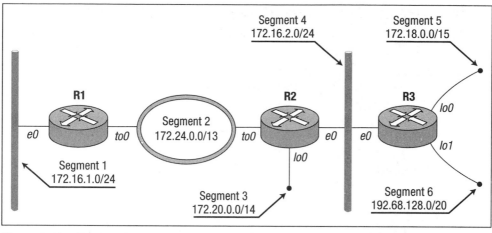

Figure 6.12   Routers R1 and R2 run IOS version 11.3(11a) and 12.0(9), respectively, whereas router R3 runs IOS version 12.0(7)T, which features the extended version of the **network** command.

Listings 6.11 through 6.13 show the configurations of routers R1 through R3.

Listing 6.11   Router R1's configuration.

```
interface Ethernet0
 ip address 172.16.1.1 255.255.255.0

interface TokenRing0
 ip address 172.28.1.1 255.248.0.0
 ring-speed 16

router eigrp 1
 network 172.16.0.0
 network 172.24.0.0
 network 172.28.0.0
 no auto-summary

ip classless
```

Listing 6.12   Router R2's configuration.

```
interface Loopback0
 ip address 172.22.1.1 255.252.0.0

interface Ethernet0
 ip address 172.16.2.1 255.255.255.0
```

6. Enhanced Interior Gateway Routing Protocol (EIGRP)

```
interface TokenRing0
 ip address 172.28.1.2 255.248.0.0
 ring-speed 16

router eigrp 1
 network 172.16.0.0
 network 172.20.0.0
 network 172.22.0.0
 network 172.24.0.0
 network 172.28.0.0
 no auto-summary

ip classless
```

Listing 6.13   Router R3's configuration.

```
interface Loopback0
 ip address 172.19.1.1 255.254.0.0

interface Loopback10
 ip address 192.168.129.1 255.255.240.0

interface Ethernet0
 ip address 172.16.2.2 255.255.255.0

router eigrp 1
 network 172.16.0.0 0.15.255.255
 network 192.168.129.1 0.0.0.0
 no auto-summary

ip classless
```

The shaded lines in router R3's configuration (Listing 6.13) show the **network** commands in the new format. The italicized lines in the configurations of routers R1 and R2 (Listings 6.11 and 6.12) show all the possible network prefixes that can potentially match network prefixes 172.24.0.0/13 and 172.20.0.0/14 (an attempt to make routers R1 and R2 advertise these network prefixes).

Listings 6.14 through 6.16 show the routing tables of all three routers.

Listing 6.14   The routing table of router R1.

```
R1#show ip route
...
     172.16.0.0/24 is subnetted, 2 subnets
C       172.16.1.0 is directly connected, Ethernet0
```

```
D       172.16.2.0 [90/297728] via 172.28.1.2, 00:11:15, TokenRing0
D       192.168.128.0/20 [90/425728] via 172.28.1.2, 00:00:45, TokenRing0
D       172.18.0.0/15 [90/425728] via 172.28.1.2, 00:00:45, TokenRing0
C       172.24.0.0/13 is directly connected, TokenRing0
```

Listing 6.15   The routing table of router R2.

```
R2#show ip route
...
        172.16.0.0/24 is subnetted, 2 subnets
D          172.16.1.0 [90/297728] via 172.28.1.1, 02:49:16, TokenRing0
C          172.16.2.0 is directly connected, Ethernet0
D       192.168.128.0/20 [90/409600] via 172.16.2.2, 02:38:46, Ethernet0
D       172.18.0.0/15 [90/409600] via 172.16.2.2, 02:38:47, Ethernet0
C       172.20.0.0/14 is directly connected, Loopback0
C       172.24.0.0/13 is directly connected, TokenRing0
```

Listing 6.16   The routing table of router R3.

```
R3#show ip route
...
        172.16.0.0/24 is subnetted, 2 subnets
D          172.16.1.0 [90/323328] via 172.16.2.1, 00:02:46, Ethernet0
C          172.16.2.0 is directly connected, Ethernet0
C       192.168.128.0/20 is directly connected, Loopback10
C       172.18.0.0/15 is directly connected, Loopback0
```

Notice that none of the routing tables shows EIGRP routes for network prefixes 172.24.0.0/13 and 172.20.0.0/14. These network prefixes are shorter than the network prefixes of the classful network addresses (that is, 172.24.0.0/16 and 172.20.0.0/16), and they appear only on routers R1 and R2, none of which runs IOS 12.0.7T.

The disability to advertise token ring segment 2's network prefix 172.24.0.0/13 notwithstanding, routers R1 and R2 can exchange routing updates through this segment. Listing 6.17 shows the output of the **show ip eigrp neighbors** command entered on both routers.

Listing 6.17   The output of the **show ip eigrp neighbors** command entered on routers R1 and R2.

```
R1#show ip eigrp neighbors
IP-EIGRP neighbors for process 1
H  .Address                Interface    Hold Uptime   SRTT   RTO  Q   Seq
                                        (sec)         (ms)        Cnt Num
0   172.28.1.2             To0          14 00:46:27   10     200  0   43
```

```
R2#show ip eigrp neighbors
IP-EIGRP neighbors for process 1
H   Address                    Interface   Hold Uptime     SRTT   RTO  Q  Seq
                                           (sec)           (ms)        Cnt Num
0   172.16.2.2                 Et0         14 00:36:19     16     200  0  5
1   172.28.1.1                 To0         13 00:46:48     14     200  0  18
```

The shaded lines show that routers R1 and R2 do perceive each other as EIGRP neighbors.

If we examine the outputs of the **show ip eigrp topology** command entered on both routers (Listings 6.18 and 6.19), we won't see the presence of network prefix 172.24.0.0/13 (configured on the TokenRing0 interface of both routers).

Listing 6.18   The output of the show ip eigrp topology command entered on router R1.

```
R1#show ip eigrp topology
...
P 172.16.1.0/24, 1 successors, FD is 281600
        via Connected, Ethernet0
P 172.18.0.0/15, 1 successors, FD is 425728
        via 172.28.1.2 (425728/409600), TokenRing0
P 172.16.2.0/24, 1 successors, FD is 297728
        via 172.28.1.2 (297728/281600), TokenRing0
P 192.168.128.0/20, 1 successors, FD is 425728
        via 172.28.1.2 (425728/409600), TokenRing0
```

Listing 6.19   The output of the show ip eigrp topology command entered on router R2.

```
R2#show ip eigrp topology
...
P 172.16.1.0/24, 1 successors, FD is 297728
        via 172.28.1.1 (297728/281600), TokenRing0
P 172.18.0.0/15, 1 successors, FD is 409600
        via 172.16.2.2 (409600/128256), Ethernet0
P 172.16.2.0/24, 1 successors, FD is 281600
        via Connected, Ethernet0
P 192.168.128.0/20, 1 successors, FD is 409600
        via 172.16.2.2 (409600/128256), Ethernet0
```

However, the EIGRP topology database of router R3 (shown in Listing 6.20) contains network prefixes 192.168.128.0/20 and 172.18.0.0/15 labeled as "Connected." Both these network prefixes are shorter than the corresponding classful network addresses (that is, 192.168.128.0/24 and 172.18.0.0/16). But, because of the new format of the **network** command, they are added to the topology table and are advertised by router R3.

Listing 6.20   The output of the show ip eigrp topology command entered on router R3.

```
R3#show ip eigrp topology
IP-EIGRP Topology Table for AS(1)/ID(192.168.129.1)

Codes: P - Passive, A - Active, U - Update, Q - Query, R - Reply,
       r - Reply status

P 172.16.1.0/24, 1 successors, FD is 323328
        via 172.16.2.1 (323328/297728), Ethernet0
P 172.18.0.0/15, 1 successors, FD is 128256
        via Connected, Loopback0
P 172.16.2.0/24, 1 successors, FD is 281600
        via Connected, Ethernet0
P 192.168.128.0/20, 1 successors, FD is 128256
        via Connected, Loopback10
```

Notice that the first line of the **show ip eigrp topology** output changed in IOS version 12.0(X)T.

> *WARNING!   Although the described feature of EIGRP appears to be nice, I wouldn't recommend using either this or any other early-deployment release of IOS in a production network. Early-deployment releases, while boasting new robust features, also tend to contain many new bugs. For example, I discovered one such bug while I was configuring router R2. At a certain point, I had to change the IP address on interface Loopback0. The new IP address, however, did not remove the network prefix corresponding to the previous IP address from the routing table. In other words, the routing table contained two connected routes for the new and old network prefixes, both pointing to interface Loopback0. After I removed interface Loopback0 and then re-created it with the desired IP address, the routing table was fixed.*
>
> *However, don't despair. The features typically introduced in early-deployment releases become available in the next major releases of IOS as standard (providing they proved to be valuable and viable). For example, the described feature of EIGRP will most probably become a standard feature in version 12.1.*

Understanding Basic DUAL Operation

In this section, we'll consider an example that shows some basic DUAL operation.

The network that we are going to use is shown in Figure 6.13.

Notice the numbers in ovals shown over the segments interconnecting the routers. They display the values of the **delay** command that was issued under the configurations of the respective interfaces on the routers. (The numbers are 10 times smaller

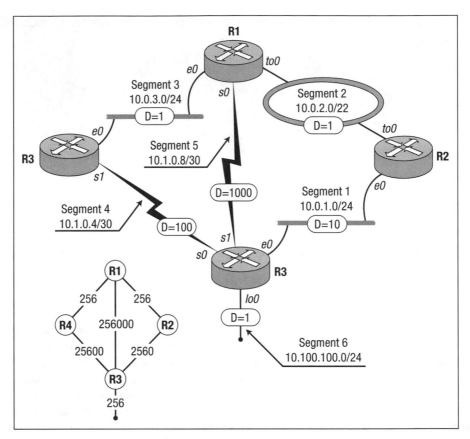

Figure 6.13 If router R1 loses its current next-hop router for network prefix 10.100.100.0/24 (segment 6), it must resort to DUAL to switch to router R4 as the new next-hop router.

than the actual logical delays of the interface, which can be displayed by the **show interfaces** command.) In addition, to make calculating EIGRP metrics easier, the routers are configured to ignore the logical bandwidths of the interfaces. This was achieved by means of the **metric weights 0 0 0 1 0 0** command, available under the **router eigrp** configuration.

The actual topology of the network is shown as the small graph in the left bottom corner of Figure 6.13. The numbers on the links show the actual EIGRP costs of the interfaces (which, in our case, are equal to D*256). The logical bandwidths are ignored, so the total metric of any path in the graph can be easily calculated by summarizing the costs of the edges constituting the path.

The configurations of all four routers are shown in Listings 6.21 through 6.24. Notice the shaded lines showing the **delay** and **metric weights** commands.

Listing 6.21   Router R1's configuration.

```
interface Ethernet0
 ip address 10.0.3.1 255.255.255.0
 delay 1

interface Serial0
 ip address 10.1.0.9 255.255.255.252
 delay 1000

interface TokenRing0
 ip address 10.0.2.1 255.255.255.0
 delay 1
 ring-speed 16

router eigrp 1
 network 10.0.0.0
 metric weights 0 0 0 1 0 0
```

Listing 6.22   Router R2's configuration.

```
interface Ethernet0
 ip address 10.0.1.2 255.255.255.0
 delay 10

interface TokenRing0
 ip address 10.0.2.2 255.255.255.0
 delay 1
 ring-speed 16

router eigrp 1
 network 10.0.0.0
 metric weights 0 0 0 1 0 0
```

Listing 6.23   Router R3's configuration.

```
interface Loopback0
 ip address 10.100.100.1 255.255.252.0
 delay 1

interface Ethernet0
 ip address 10.0.1.1 255.255.255.0
 delay 10

interface Serial0
 ip address 10.1.0.5 255.255.255.252
 delay 100
```

```
interface Serial1
 ip address 10.1.0.10 255.255.255.252
 delay 1000

router eigrp 1
 network 10.0.0.0
 metric weights 0 0 0 1 0 0
```

Listing 6.24   Router R4's configuration.

```
interface Ethernet0
 ip address 10.0.3.2 255.255.255.0
 delay 1

interface Serial1
 ip address 10.1.0.6 255.255.255.252
 delay 100

router eigrp 1
 network 10.0.0.0
 metric weights 0 0 0 1 0 0
```

To simplify the example, we'll examine only DUAL operation on router R1 for network prefix 10.100.100.0.

In the network, router R1 can forward traffic destined for network prefix 10.100.100.0/24 (segment 6) using three possible paths—through router R2, through router R3, and through router R4. Obviously, because the metric of the route through router R1 is the smallest of the three, router R1 originally chooses router R2 as the next-hop router. The evidence of this can be seen in the output of the **show ip route eigrp** command, shown below (the output was trimmed off all routes except the one for network prefix 10.100.100.0/24):

```
R1#show ip route eigrp
...
D      10.100.100.0/22 [90/3072] via 10.0.2.2, 00:05:42, TokenRing0
```

So, right now, router R1 is in the passive state for network prefix 10.100.100.0/24, and the feasible distance is equal to the metric of the route through router R2— that is 3072. (As we remember, the feasible distance is the smallest metric the router has had for the network prefix during the last passive state for the network prefix.)

Among the other two routers (R3 and R4) only R3 has the reported distance that is smaller than the feasible distance of router R1. This is no surprise because router R3 is a directly connected router to network prefix 10.100.100.0/24. Router R4's reported distance is greater than the feasible distance, so it won't be present in router R1's topology table. This is confirmed by the following output of the command **show ip eigrp topology** entered on router R1:

```
R1#show ip eigrp topology
...
P 10.100.100.0/22, 1 successors, FD is 3072
        via 10.0.2.2 (3072/2816), TokenRing0
        via 10.1.0.10 (256256/256), Serial0
```

Notice that router R4's IP address does not appear in the entry.

> **NOTE:** The IP address of router R4 is not present in the topology table because originally, when routers R4 and R1 just established the neighbor relationship, router R1 sent router R4 an initial update containing network prefix 10.100.100.0/22. In addition, router R4 could not counter it with a smaller metric, so it replied with a poison-reverse update. The latter essentially means that router R4 informs router R1 that it will not forward traffic destined for 10.100.100.0/22 and instead leaves this task to router R1. Even the output of the **show ip eigrp topology all-links** command won't show a subrecord for router R4.

Suppose the TokenRing0 interface of router R2 fails. Obviously, router R2 stops being router R1's EIGRP neighbor. This affects router R1's route for network prefix 10.100.100.0/24, so router R1 should run DUAL.

Listing 6.25 shows the output of **debug ip routing**, **debug eigrp fsm**, and **debug eigrp packet update reply query** commands. The **debug ip routing** command shows the changes the router makes to its routing table, the **debug eigrp fsm** command shows the transactions of DUAL, and the **debug eigrp packet update reply query** command shows the EIGRP PDUs generated as the result of DUAL operation. The **debug eigrp packet update reply query** command's output does not include hellos and acknowledgments.

To make it easier to understand the output, I included my comments in the output. The comments begin with an exclamation point. In addition, I shaded the lines generated by DUAL, and italicized the lines corresponding to the routing table changes. The lines corresponding to the generation of EIGRP PDUs are left unchanged. The output is also trimmed of irrelevant lines; those were replaced with ellipses.

Listing 6.25 The output of the three **debug** commands issued on router R1 showing the operation of DUAL when neighbor R2 disappears.

```
R1#debug ip routing
IP routing debugging is on
R1#debug eigrp fsm
```

```
EIGRP FSM Events/Actions debugging is on
R1#debug eigrp packet update reply query
EIGRP Packets debugging is on
    (UPDATE, QUERY, REPLY)
R1#
!
! Dual notices the loss of neighbor R2.
!
DUAL: linkdown(): start - 10.0.2.2 via TokenRing0
...
DUAL: Destination 10.100.100.0/22
!
! Originally network prefix 10.100.100.0/22 was available through
! neighbor R2. With the loss of neighbor R2, router performs feasibility
! condition procedure, which yields router R3 as the feasible successor.
!
DUAL: Find FS for dest 10.100.100.0/22. FD is 3072, RD is 3072
DUAL:   10.0.2.2 metric 4294967295/4294967295
DUAL:   10.1.0.10 metric 256256/256 found Dmin is 256256
!                                   ^^^^     ^^^^^^
! *** Feasibility Condition ***
! The router advertising network prefix 10.100.100.0/22 with the
! value of Dmin is R3. At the same time the reported distance of
! R2 is 256, which is less than the existing feasible distance
! 3072. Hence, right now R3 is a feasible successor.
! *** Feasibility Condition MET ***
!
RT: delete route to 10.100.100.0 via 10.0.2.2, eigrp metric [90/3072]
RT: no routes to 10.100.100.0
DUAL: Removing dest 10.100.100.0/22, nexthop 10.0.2.2
RT: add 10.100.100.0/22 via 10.1.0.10, eigrp metric [90/256256]
!
! The new route pointing to neighbor R3 is installed
!
DUAL: RT installed 10.100.100.0/22 via 10.1.0.10
DUAL: Send update about 10.100.100.0/22.   Reason: metric chg
DUAL: Send update about 10.100.100.0/22.   Reason: new if
DUAL: linkdown(): finish
...
EIGRP: Sending UPDATE on Ethernet0
...
EIGRP: Sending UPDATE on Serial0 nbr 10.1.0.10
...
!
! An update is sent to 10.0.3.2, an IP address of neighbor R4.
!
```

```
EIGRP: Received UPDATE on Ethernet0 nbr 10.0.3.2
...
DUAL: dest(10.100.100.0/22) not active
!
! Neighbor R4, which originally sent router R1 a poison-reverse
! update for network prefix 10.100.100.0/22 when neighbor R2 was
! available, now sees that its own metric is smaller than the new
! metric of router R1. So, instead of sending R1 a poison-reverse
! update, it sends it a regular update carrying a smaller metric
! that the current metric of router R1.
!
DUAL: dual_rcvupdate(): 10.100.100.0/22 via 10.0.3.2 metric 26112/25856
DUAL: Find FS for dest 10.100.100.0/22. FD is 3072, RD is 256256
DUAL:    10.1.0.10 metric 256256/256
DUAL:    10.0.3.2 metric 26112/25856not found Dmin is 26112
!                               ^^^^     ^^^^^
! *** Feasibility Condition ***
! Now, the new Dmin is advertised only by neighbor R4, whereas its
! reported distance is greater than the feasible distance of router
! R1. Therefore, the feasibility condition is not met, which makes
! router R1 to enter the active state for network prefix 10.100.100.0/22
! *** Feasibility Condition NOT MET ***
!
DUAL: Dest 10.100.100.0/22 entering active state.
DUAL: Set reply-status table. Count is 2.
DUAL: Not doing split horizon
...
EIGRP: Sending QUERY on Ethernet0
...
EIGRP: Sending QUERY on Serial0 nbr 10.1.0.10
...
EIGRP: Received REPLY on Ethernet0 nbr 10.0.3.2
...
DUAL: dual_rcvreply(): 10.100.100.0/22 via 10.0.3.2 metric 26112/25856
DUAL: Count is 2
DUAL: Clearing handle 0, count is now 1
EIGRP: Received REPLY on Serial0 nbr 10.1.0.10
...
DUAL: dual_rcvreply(): 10.100.100.0/22 via 10.1.0.10 metric 256256/256
DUAL: Count is 1
DUAL: Clearing handle 1, count is now 0
DUAL: Freeing reply status table
!
! Router R1 has received replies from all neighbors. Thus, it sets
```

```
! feasible distance (FD) equal to infinity, and once again runs the
! feasibility condition procedure, which, this time yields neighbor
! R4 as the new successor.
!
DUAL: Find FS for dest 10.100.100.0/22. FD is 4294967295, RD is 256256 found
DUAL: RT installed 10.100.100.0/22 via 10.1.0.10
!                                          ^^^^^^^^^
!                                          neighbor R4
!
RT: del 10.100.100.0/22 via 10.1.0.10, eigrp metric [90/256256]
RT: add 10.100.100.0/22 via 10.0.3.2, eigrp metric [90/26112]
DUAL: RT installed 10.100.100.0/22 via 10.0.3.2
DUAL: Send update about 10.100.100.0/22.   Reason: metric chg
DUAL: Send update about 10.100.100.0/22.   Reason: new if
...
EIGRP: Sending UPDATE on Ethernet0
...
EIGRP: Sending UPDATE on Serial0 nbr 10.1.0.10
...
```

The new topology table record for network prefix 10.100.100.0/22 is shown below:

```
R1#show ip eigrp topology
...
P 10.100.100.0/22, 1 successors, FD is 26112
        via 10.0.3.2 (26112/25856), Ethernet0
        via 10.1.0.10 (256256/256), Serial0
```

The corresponding routing table entry is shown below:

```
R1#show ip route eigrp
...
D       10.100.100.0/22 [90/26112] via 10.0.3.2, 00:00:41, Ethernet0
```

The handling of a reappearance of neighbor R2 is shown in Listing 6.26, which is formatted and commented the same way as Listing 6.25.

Listing 6.26   The output of the three debug commands issued on router R1 showing the operation of DUAL when neighbor R2 reappears.

```
R1#debug ip routing
IP routing debugging is on
R1#debug eigrp fsm
EIGRP FSM Events/Actions debugging is on
R1#debug eigrp packet update reply query
```

```
EIGRP Packets debugging is on
    (UPDATE, QUERY, REPLY)
R1#
...
EIGRP: Received UPDATE on TokenRing0 nbr 10.0.2.2
...
DUAL: dest(10.100.100.0/22) not active
!
! Neighbor R2 sends router R1 a routing update containing the
! previous reported distance. Router R1 runs feasibility condition
! procedures.
!
DUAL: dual_rcvupdate(): 10.100.100.0/22 via 10.0.2.2 metric 3072/2816
DUAL: Find FS for dest 10.100.100.0/22. FD is 26112, RD is 26112
DUAL:    10.0.3.2 metric 26112/25856
DUAL:    10.0.2.2 metric 3072/2816
DUAL:    10.1.0.10 metric 256256/256 found Dmin is 3072
!                                ^^^^      ^^^^
! *** Feasibility Condition ***
! The new Dmin is available through neighbor R2; at the same time
! neighbor R2's reported distance is smaller than the current feasible
! distance of router R1. Hence, neighbor R2 supersedes neighbor R4 as
! the successor; the new Dmin becomes the new feasible distance.
! *** Feasibility Condition MET ***
!
DUAL: RT installed 10.100.100.0/22 via 10.0.3.2
RT: del 10.100.100.0/22 via 10.0.3.2, eigrp metric [90/26112]
RT: add 10.100.100.0/22 via 10.0.2.2, eigrp metric [90/3072]
DUAL: RT installed 10.100.100.0/22 via 10.0.2.2
DUAL: Send update about 10.100.100.0/22.  Reason: metric chg
DUAL: Send update about 10.100.100.0/22.  Reason: new if
...
EIGRP: Sending UPDATE on TokenRing0
...
EIGRP: Sending UPDATE on Ethernet0
! This update  ^^^^^^ will be received by the previous successor
! neighbor R4.
...
EIGRP: Sending UPDATE on Serial0 nbr 10.1.0.10
...
EIGRP: Received UPDATE on Ethernet0 nbr 10.0.3.2
!              ^^^^^^             ^^^^^^^^
! Neighbor R4 replies back with a poison-reverse update
...
!
! Router R1 receives the poison-reverse update from neighbor R4.
```

6. Enhanced Interior
Gateway Routing
Protocol (EIGRP)

```
! Router R1 has to run feasibility condition procedure once again.
!
DUAL: dual_rcvupdate(): 10.100.100.0/22 via 10.0.3.2 metric 4294967295/
4294967295
DUAL: Find FS for dest 10.100.100.0/22. FD is 3072, RD is 3072
DUAL:    10.0.2.2 metric 3072/2816
DUAL:    10.0.3.2 metric 4294967295/4294967295
DUAL:    10.1.0.10 metric 256256/256 found Dmin is 3072
!                                      ^^^^     ^^^^
! *** Feasibility Condition ***
! This time the feasibility condition procedure yield no new results.
! Neighbor R2 remains the successor.
! *** Feasibility Condition MET ***
!
DUAL: Removing dest 10.100.100.0/22, nexthop 10.0.3.2
DUAL: RT installed 10.100.100.0/22 via 10.0.2.2
...
```

Understanding How EIGRP Handles Secondary IP Addresses

6. Enhanced Interior Gateway Routing Protocol (EIGRP)

As we know from Chapter 5, IGRP—when compared to RIP—significantly optimizes the propagation of routing information about secondary IP addresses. EIGRP goes even further by not only optimizing the propagation of routing information but also by simplifying the configuration and maintenance of secondary IP addresses.

With EIGRP, the secondary IP addresses are no longer required to be defined in a specific order. Moreover, the primary IP addresses of a router's interface connected to the same segment may not belong to the same network prefix. The only requirement is that the set of the network prefixes to which the primary and secondary IP addresses belong must be the same on the routers' interfaces connected to the same segment.

To see how secondary IP addresses can be used with EIGRP, let's consider the network example shown in Figure 6.14.

This network scheme is identical to the network schemes that we used to examine how RIP and IGRP behave in the presence of secondary IP addresses.

This time, however, we won't configure enormous numbers of secondary IP addresses on the Ethernet0 interfaces of routers R2 and R3. Instead, we'll configure the minimal number of secondary IP address, but we'll place them in a different order on each router.

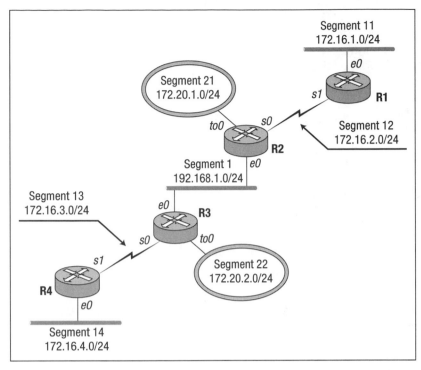

Figure 6.14 The secondary IP addresses must be used on segment 1 to preserve the contiguousness of classful network addresses 172.16.0.0/16 and 172.20.0.0/16.

Listings 6.27 through 6.30 show the configurations of all four routers.

Listing 6.27   Router R1's configuration.

```
interface Ethernet0
 ip address 172.16.1.1 255.255.255.0

interface Serial1
 ip address 172.16.2.2 255.255.255.0

router eigrp 1
 network 172.16.0.0
```

Listing 6.28   Router R2's configuration.

```
interface Ethernet0
 ip address 192.168.1.1 255.255.255.0 secondary
 ip address 172.16.100.1 255.255.255.0 secondary
 ip address 172.20.100.1 255.255.255.0

interface Serial0
```

```
    ip address 172.16.2.1 255.255.255.0

interface TokenRing0
 ip address 172.20.1.1 255.255.255.0
 ring-speed 16

router eigrp 1
 network 172.16.0.0
 network 172.20.0.0
 network 192.168.1.0
```

Listing 6.29   Router R3's configuration.

```
interface Ethernet0
 ip address 172.20.100.2 255.255.255.0 secondary
 ip address 192.168.1.2 255.255.255.0 secondary
 ip address 172.16.100.2 255.255.255.0

interface Serial0
 ip address 172.16.3.1 255.255.255.0

interface TokenRing0
 ip address 172.20.2.1 255.255.255.0
 ring-speed 16

router eigrp 1
 network 172.16.0.0
 network 172.20.0.0
 network 192.168.1.0
```

Listing 6.30   Router R4's configuration.

```
interface Ethernet0
 ip address 172.16.4.1 255.255.255.0

interface Serial1
 ip address 172.16.3.2 255.255.255.0

router eigrp 1
 network 172.16.0.0
```

The shaded lines in the configurations of routers R2 and R3 (Listings 6.28 and 6.29) show the primary IP addresses configured in the Ethernet0 interface of both routers. Notice that the primary IP addresses belong to different network prefixes.

Listing 6.31 shows the routing table of router R4. Notice that, despite the different primary IP addresses assigned on interfaces Ethernet0 of routers R2 and R3, router R4 can see the network prefixes behind router R2 (the shaded lines in Listing 6.15).

Listing 6.31   The routing table of router R4.

```
R4#show ip route
...
D     192.168.1.0/24 [90/2195456] via 172.16.3.1, 00:01:15, Serial1
D     172.20.0.0/16 [90/2185984] via 172.16.3.1, 00:55:41, Serial1
      172.16.0.0/24 is subnetted, 5 subnets
C        172.16.4.0 is directly connected, Ethernet0
D        172.16.1.0 [90/2733056] via 172.16.3.1, 00:01:11, Serial1
D        172.16.2.0 [90/2707456] via 172.16.3.1, 00:01:11, Serial1
C        172.16.3.0 is directly connected, Serial1
D        172.16.100.0 [90/2195456] via 172.16.3.1, 00:03:45, Serial1
```

Let's also examine the routing tables of routers R2 and R3, shown in Listings 6.32 and 6.33.

Listing 6.32   The routing table of router R2.

```
R2#show ip route
...
      172.16.0.0/16 is variably subnetted, 6 subnets, 2 masks
D        172.16.4.0/24 [90/2221056] via 172.16.100.2, 00:01:43, Ethernet0
D        172.16.0.0/16 is a summary, 00:04:35, Null0
D        172.16.1.0/24 [90/2195456] via 172.16.2.2, 00:55:41, Serial0
C        172.16.2.0/24 is directly connected, Serial0
D        172.16.3.0/24 [90/2195456] via 172.16.100.2, 00:01:43, Ethernet0
C        172.16.100.0/24 is directly connected, Ethernet0
      172.20.0.0/16 is variably subnetted, 4 subnets, 2 masks
D        172.20.0.0/16 is a summary, 00:56:06, Null0
C        172.20.1.0/24 is directly connected, TokenRing0
D        172.20.2.0/24 [90/297728] via 172.16.100.2, 00:01:44, Ethernet0
C        172.20.100.0/24 is directly connected, Ethernet0
C     192.168.1.0/24 is directly connected, Ethernet0
```

Listing 6.33   The routing table of router R3.

```
R3#show ip route
...
      172.16.0.0/16 is variably subnetted, 6 subnets, 2 masks
D        172.16.4.0/24 [90/2195456] via 172.16.3.2, 00:57:24, Serial0
D        172.16.0.0/16 is a summary, 00:04:43, Null0
D        172.16.1.0/24 [90/2221056] via 172.20.100.1, 00:02:09, Ethernet0
D        172.16.2.0/24 [90/2195456] via 172.20.100.1, 00:02:09, Ethernet0
```

```
C        172.16.3.0/24 is directly connected, Serial0
C        172.16.100.0/24 is directly connected, Ethernet0
         172.20.0.0/16 is variably subnetted, 4 subnets, 2 masks
D        172.20.0.0/16 is a summary, 00:56:39, Null0
D        172.20.1.0/24 [90/297728] via 172.20.100.1, 00:02:09, Ethernet0
C        172.20.2.0/24 is directly connected, TokenRing0
C        172.20.100.0/24 is directly connected, Ethernet0
C     192.168.1.0/24 is directly connected, Ethernet0
```

The shaded lines show the routes for network prefixes that are available through subnetted segment 1. Notice that these routes on router R3 point on the primary IP address of router R2. Likewise, these routes on router R2 point on the primary IP address of router R3.

NOTE: However easy it may appear to resort to secondary IP addresses in the presence of EIGRP, first try to examine other options, such as disabling auto-summarization. Although simplified by EIGRP from an operational standpoint, secondary IP addresses are still conceptually false.

Disabling EIGRP on an Interface

Unlike with RIP and IGRP, the command **passive-interface** <*interface*> disables EIGRP completely on the specified interface. EIGRP will neither send hello messages on the interface nor receive them. All other EIGRP PDUs received on the interface are ignored as well.

This command, however, does not remove the network prefix of the interface from EIGRP operation. In other words, the network prefix is advertised, and, if the interface goes down, the router will query its neighbors for another route for the network prefix.

Understanding How EIGRP Works across NBMA Networks

Surprisingly, the split-horizon rule is in effect for EIGRP on NBMA networks, such as Frame Relay. This is different from RIP and IGRP, which, by default, do not always adhere to the split-horizon rule on NBMA networks.

Let's consider the example of the network shown in Figure 6.15. The routers are interconnected via a Frame Relay network with two permanent virtual circuits (PVCs): one PVC between routers R1 and R2, and the other between routers R1 and R3.

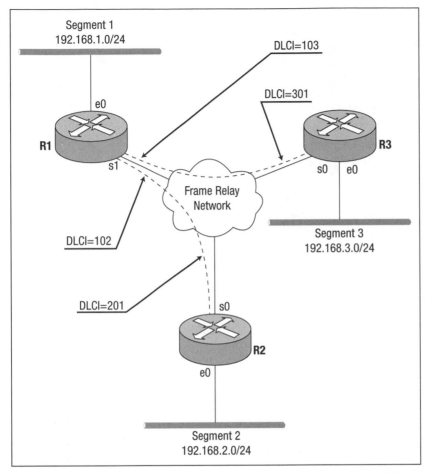

Figure 6.15 Routers R1, R2, and R3 are interconnected with a non-fully-meshed Frame Relay network.

Suppose it was decided to use a single network prefix for the whole Frame Relay network. This essentially means that no subinterfaces can be used on router R1 (subinterfaces assume different network prefixes). Thus, the configuration of all three routers would initially look as shown in Listings 6.34 through 6.36.

Listing 6.34 Router R1's configuration.

```
ip subnet-zero

interface Ethernet0
 ip address 192.168.1.1 255.255.255.0

interface Serial1
 ip address 192.168.255.1 255.255.255.240
```

```
encapsulation frame-relay
frame-relay map ip 192.168.255.2 102 broadcast
frame-relay map ip 192.168.255.3 103 broadcast
frame-relay lmi-type ansi

router eigrp 1
network 192.168.1.0
network 192.168.255.0
```

Listing 6.35   Router R2's configuration.

```
ip subnet-zero

interface Ethernet0
ip address 192.168.2.1 255.255.255.0

interface Serial0
ip address 192.168.255.2 255.255.255.240
encapsulation frame-relay
bandwidth 64
frame-relay map ip 192.168.255.1 201 broadcast
frame-relay lmi-type ansi

router eigrp 1
network 192.168.2.0
network 192.168.255.0
```

Listing 6.36   Router R3's configuration.

```
ip subnet-zero

interface Ethernet0
ip address 192.168.3.1 255.255.255.0

interface Serial0
ip address 192.168.255.3 255.255.255.240
encapsulation frame-relay
bandwidth 64
frame-relay map ip 192.168.255.1 301 broadcast
frame-relay lmi-type ansi

router eigrp 1
network 192.168.3.0
network 192.168.255.0
```

TIP: *Listings 6.34 through 6.36 begin with the **ip subnet-zero** command. This command is necessary because the Serial0 interface on all routers is assigned an IP address, that—from the classful IP addressing standpoint—belongs to a subnet whose ID is equal to 0 (192.168.255.0/28).*

Right now, no means are taken to disable the split-horizon rule on router R1's Serial0 interface; hence, router R2 won't see the network prefix assigned on router R3's Ethernet0 interface , and vice versa. Listing 6.37 shows the routing tables of both routers.

Listing 6.37   The routing tables of routers R2 and R3.

```
R2#show ip route
...
     192.168.255.0/24 is variably subnetted, 2 subnets, 2 masks
C       192.168.255.0/28 is directly connected, Serial0
D       192.168.255.0/24 is a summary, 00:15:50, Null0
D    192.168.1.0/24 [90/40537600] via 192.168.255.1, 00:11:45, Serial0
C    192.168.2.0/24 is directly connected, Ethernet0

R3#show ip route
...
     192.168.255.0/24 is variably subnetted, 2 subnets, 2 masks
C       192.168.255.0/28 is directly connected, Serial0
D       192.168.255.0/24 is a summary, 00:14:05, Null0
D    192.168.1.0/24 [90/40537600] via 192.168.255.1, 00:12:40, Serial0
C    192.168.3.0/24 is directly connected, Ethernet0
```

The command that is used to enable and disable the split-horizon rule for EIGRP is slightly different from the command for IGRP and RIP. For EIGRP, the command is **ip split-horizon eigrp** *<AS #>*. Thus, to disable the split-horizon rule in our case, we should enter the **no ip split-horizon eigrp 1** command under the **interface Serial1** configuration. The revised configuration of router R1 is shown in Listing 6.38.

Listing 6.38   Router R1's configuration.

```
ip subnet-zero

interface Ethernet0
 ip address 192.168.1.1 255.255.255.0

interface Serial1
 ip address 192.168.255.1 255.255.255.240
 encapsulation frame-relay
 no ip split-horizon eigrp 1
 frame-relay map ip 192.168.255.2 102 broadcast
```

```
frame-relay map ip 192.168.255.3 103 broadcast
frame-relay lmi-type ansi

router eigrp 1
 network 192.168.1.0
 network 192.168.255.0
```

After the **no ip split-horizon eigrp 1** command has been entered on router R1, routers R2 and R3 begin seeing the missing network prefixes (the shaded lines in Listing 6.39).

Listing 6.39   The routing tables of routers R2 and R3 after the split-horizon rule was disabled on router R1's Serial1 interface.

```
R2#show ip route
...
     192.168.255.0/24 is variably subnetted, 2 subnets, 2 masks
C       192.168.255.0/28 is directly connected, Serial0
D       192.168.255.0/24 is a summary, 00:23:19, Null0
D     192.168.1.0/24 [90/40537600] via 192.168.255.1, 00:05:07, Serial0
C     192.168.2.0/24 is directly connected, Ethernet0
D     192.168.3.0/24 [90/41049600] via 192.168.255.1, 00:05:07, Serial0

R3#show ip route
...
     192.168.255.0/24 is variably subnetted, 2 subnets, 2 masks
C       192.168.255.0/28 is directly connected, Serial0
D       192.168.255.0/24 is a summary, 00:21:03, Null0
D     192.168.1.0/24 [90/40537600] via 192.168.255.1, 00:04:56, Serial0
D     192.168.2.0/24 [90/41049600] via 192.168.255.1, 00:04:56, Serial0
C     192.168.3.0/24 is directly connected, Ethernet0
```

NOTE: *EIGRP does not adhere to the split-horizon used by RIP and IGRP. This also means that the split-horizon part of the output of the **show ip interface** command is irrelevant to EIGRP.*

Configuring Route Summarization with EIGRP

Being a classless routing protocol, EIGRP provides a powerful means to summarize advertised network prefixes in the form of the command **ip summary-address eigrp** *<AS #> <IP address> <subnet mask>*, which is available in interface configuration mode. The parameters *<IP address>* and *<subnet mask>* denote a summary network prefix that EIGRP will advertise out of the interface instead of any other network prefixes matched by the summary network prefix. The match occurs if all of the significant bits of the summary network prefix are equal to the corresponding bits of a network prefix and if the summary network prefix is shorter than or the same size as the network prefix. The network prefixes that are not matched by the summary network prefix are advertised as usual. The metric of the summary network prefix is equal to the smallest metric among all of the matched network prefixes.

Multiple **ip summary-address eigrp** *<AS #>* commands followed by different pairs of the *<IP address> <subnet mask>* parameters can be entered on a singe interface to create multiple summary network prefixes.

To see how the command works, let's modify the network scheme from the previous section, as shown in Figure 6.16.

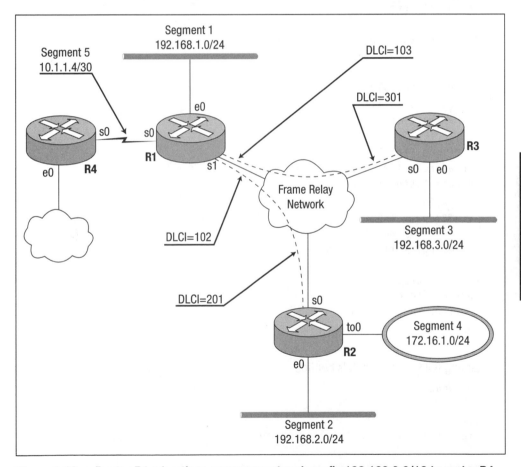

Figure 6.16   Router R1 advertises summary network prefix 192.168.0.0/16 to router R4 instead of all individual network prefixes matched by the summary network prefix.

On router R2, interface TokenRing0 was enabled and assigned IP address 172.16.1.1/24. Router R1 is now also connected to router R4, which is further connected to some other networks. In some circumstances, it may make sense to hide the individual network prefixes configured on routers R1, R2, and R3 from router R4 and the networks behind it. Thus, the **ip summary-address eigrp** command becomes quite handy.

The configuration of router R3 remains unchanged. Also, the configuration of router R4 is not really relevant, so I skipped it. Listings 6.40 and 6.41 show the new configurations of routers R1 and R2. Pay attention to the shaded line in router R1's configuration because it shows the **ip summary-address eigrp** command.

Listing 6.40   Router R1's configuration.

```
ip subnet-zero

interface Ethernet0
 ip address 192.168.1.1 255.255.255.0

interface Serial0
 ip address 10.1.1.5 255.255.255.252
 ip summary-address eigrp 1 192.168.0.0 255.255.0.0

interface Serial1
 ip address 192.168.255.1 255.255.255.240
 encapsulation frame-relay
 no ip split-horizon eigrp 1
 frame-relay map ip 192.168.255.2 102 broadcast
 frame-relay map ip 192.168.255.3 103 broadcast
 frame-relay lmi-type ansi

router eigrp 1
 network 10.0.0.0
 network 192.168.1.0
 network 192.168.255.0
```

Listing 6.41   Router R2's configuration.

```
ip subnet-zero

interface Ethernet0
 ip address 192.168.2.1 255.255.255.0

interface Serial0
 ip address 192.168.255.2 255.255.255.240
 encapsulation frame-relay
```

```
bandwidth 64
frame-relay map ip 192.168.255.1 201 broadcast
frame-relay lmi-type ansi

interface TokenRing0
 ip address 172.16.1.1 255.255.255.0
 ring-speed 16

router eigrp 1
 network 172.16.0.0
 network 192.168.2.0
 network 192.168.255.0
```

If we examine the routing table of router R4 (Listing 6.42), we won't find any routes for network prefixes 192.168.1.0/24, 192.168.2.0/24, 192.168.3.0/24, and 192.168.255.0/24. Instead, we'll see a route for only the summary network prefix 192.168.0.0/16 (the shaded line). In addition, we'll see a route for network 172.16.0.0/16 (the italicized line) because this network prefix is not matched by the summary network prefix and thus is advertised as usual.

Listing 6.42   The routing table of router R4.

```
R4#show ip route
...
D    172.16.0.0/16 [90/2697984] via 10.1.1.5, 00:15:41, Serial0
     10.0.0.0/8 is variably subnetted, 2 subnets, 2 masks
C       10.0.0.0/24 is directly connected, Ethernet0
C       10.1.1.4/30 is directly connected, Serial0
D    192.168.0.0/16 [90/2195456] via 10.1.1.5, 00:16:40, Serial0
```

The routing table, however, does not allow us to see the metric with which router R1 advertises the summary address to router R4. To see this metric, we can use the **show ip eigrp topology** command. The output of this command issued on router R4 is shown in Listing 6.43.

Listing 6.43   The EIGRP topology table of router R4.

```
R4#show ip eigrp topology
...
P 10.0.0.0/24, 1 successors, FD is 281600
        via Connected, Ethernet0
P 10.1.1.4/30, 1 successors, FD is 2169856
        via Connected, Serial0
P 192.168.0.0/16, 1 successors, FD is 2195456
        via 10.1.1.5 (2195456/281600), Serial0
P 172.16.0.0/16, 1 successors, FD is 2697984
        via 10.1.1.5 (2697984/2185984), Serial0
```

The shaded lines in Listing 6.43 show the topology table entry that corresponds to the summary network prefix. The second number in the parentheses shows the metric with which the network prefix is advertised by router R1.

Because router R1 has network prefixes matched by the summary network prefix, we can't use the **show ip route** command to see which one of them was used to create the metric for the summary network prefix. Most probably, it was one of the connected routes, for which the **show ip route** command won't show the EIGRP metric. As before, the **show ip eigrp topology** command can be used instead. The output of the command issued on router R1 is shown in Listing 6.44

Listing 6.44   The EIGRP topology table of router R1.

```
R1#show ip eigrp topology
...
P 10.0.0.0/24, 1 successors, FD is 2195456
        via 10.1.1.6 (2195456/281600), Serial0
P 10.0.0.0/8, 1 successors, FD is 2169856
        via Summary (2169856/0), Null0
P 10.1.1.4/30, 1 successors, FD is 2169856
        via Connected, Serial0
P 192.168.0.0/16, 1 successors, FD is 281600
        via Summary (281600/0), Null0
P 192.168.1.0/24, 1 successors, FD is 281600
        via Connected, Ethernet0
P 192.168.3.0/24, 1 successors, FD is 2195456
        via 192.168.255.3 (2195456/281600), Serial1
P 192.168.255.0/24, 1 successors, FD is 2169856
        via Summary (2169856/0), Null0
P 192.168.255.0/28, 1 successors, FD is 2169856
        via Connected, Serial1
P 172.16.0.0/16, 1 successors, FD is 2185984
        via 192.168.255.2 (2185984/176128), Serial1
```

The italicized lines show the topology table entries that correspond to the network prefixes that are summarized by the summary network prefix. The shaded entry is the one whose metric coincides with the metric that is used by router R1 to advertise the summary network prefix. This entry is for the network prefix configured on interface Ethernet0, which is well expected.

Why summarize with EIGRP? EIGRP does not use regular routing updates, so caring about minimizing routing overhead is irrelevant. In addition, setting up summary addresses involves a certain amount of administrative overhead, which in large environments better be minimized.

Routing overhead, however, is not entirely irrelevant in the case of EIGRP. It's true that the regular routing updates—which do cause significant overhead in the case of regular distance-vector protocols such as IGRP and RIP—are not a concern. What is a concern, though, is the EIGRP reaction on network changes. As we know, routers that use EIGRP, upon detection of a network change such as a neighbor or segment going down or a route metric change, check if the feasibility condition is still satisfied for the affected network prefixes (that is, if there are any feasible successors for the affected network prefixes). If the feasibility condition is not satisfied, the routers start querying each other if other routes exist to the affected network prefixes. The waves of queries and replies roll through the routers and segments interconnecting the routers. These waves have three negative effects. First, they may sometimes cause congestion on the segments, especially if the segments have low bandwidth. Second, the queries and replies may cause significant CPU utilization on the affected routers. Finally, until all replies are received, the routing tables cannot be updated on the routers, even if routes become available for the affected network prefixes.

Thus, in order to diminish the negative effect of queries and replies, the network area through which they can propagate should be limited.

This area becomes naturally limited when EIGRP routers perform summarization on the classful network boundaries, provided auto-summarization wasn't turned off. Obviously, individual subnets are unknown outside of the classful network. As the routers outside the classful network receive queries for the subnets of the classful network, they immediately reply with a metric equal to infinity, thereby preventing the queries from propagating further.

Alternatively, summarization can be accomplished manually, as we saw in this section. This helps reduce the query/reply propagation area in the same way as automatic summarization does.

Let's see how it works.

Suppose that, in our network example in Figure 6.16, the Ethernet0 interface of router R2 goes down, which causes router R2 to start querying its neighbors if they know of another route to the network prefix of segment 2 (192.168.2.0/24). No router knows another route for 192.168.2.0/24 spawning a query wave. The wave eventually reaches router R1, which forwards it further to router R4. Because router R1 summarizes all network prefixes beginning with 192.168 and advertises them as summary network prefix 192.168.0.0/16 to router R4, router R4 doesn't know a route for 192.168.2.0/24. So, it responds to R1's query for 192.168.2.0/24 with a reply carrying the metric of infinity. Listing 6.45 shows the process.

Listing 6.45   The output of the debug eigrp fsm command issued on router R4.

```
R4#debug eigrp fsm
EIGRP FSM Events/Actions debugging is on
R4#
DUAL: dest(192.168.2.0/24) not active
DUAL: dual_rcvquery():192.168.2.0/24 via 10.1.1.5 metric 4294967295/
4294967295, RD is 4294967295
DUAL: Send reply about 192.168.2.0/24 to 10.1.1.5
DUAL: Removing dest 192.168.2.0/24, nexthop 10.1.1.5
DUAL: No routes.  Flushing dest 192.168.2.0/24
```

Modifying the Active Time

The **timers active-time** {<*minutes*>|**disabled**} command, available under the **router eigrp** configuration, allows you to modify the EIGRP active time. The <*minutes*> parameter specifies the duration of active time in minutes; this parameter can range from 1 through 4294967295. Alternatively, the argument **disabled**, which disables the active time, can be used. This means that the router can wait indefinitely for a reply from a neighbor.

NOTE: The **timers active-time** command can be used without parameters. This form of the command is an equivalent of **timers active-time disabled**.

The modification is EIGRP routing process wide. The default value is three minutes.

WARNING!   It is not advisable to change the default EIGRP active time. Doing so must be considered the final measure; do it only when nothing else helps. If changed from the default, the configured active time must be consistent on all routers within the autonomous system.

Chapter 7

Open Shortest Path First (OSPF) Protocol

If you need an immediate solution to:	See page:
Performing Basic OSPF Configuration—Single Area	477
Using the Command **router-id** to Change the OSPF Router ID	483
Understanding the **show ip ospf interface** Command	484
Understanding the **show ip ospf neighbor** Command	485
Displaying the OSPF Link-State Database	486
Modifying OSPF Interface Costs	491
Using OSPF Router Priorities	492
Understanding How OSPF Handles IP Unnumbered	494
Understanding the **neighbor** Command	495
Performing Equal-Cost Load Balancing with OSPF	497
Configuring OSPF with Multiple Areas	497
Configuring OSPF to Originate the Default Gateway Route	506
Understanding the **show ip ospf border-routers** Command	507
Configuring OSPF Stub Areas	508
Understanding How OSPF Handles Secondary IP Addresses	510
Using Virtual Links to Connect Remote Areas	511
Using Virtual Links to Restore a Partitioned Backbone	517
Configuring OSPF over NBMA Networks	522
Configuring OSPF over Fully Meshed NBMA Networks	523
Configuring OSPF over Non-Fully Meshed NBMA Networks	526

In Depth

This chapter is devoted to an immensely popular dynamic routing protocol, Open Shortest Path First (OSPF).

Unlike the dynamic routing protocols we've already discussed, OSPF is not a distance-vector routing protocol. OSPF is a *link-state* dynamic routing protocol, which means that routing information is not represented in the form of vectors (network prefixes and how far away and in which direction they are located). Instead, link-state routing protocols possess the exact knowledge of the network topology from which they devise the routing table.

NOTE: *The routing protocols are called link state because the routers that use such protocols know the states of all the links in the routing protocol domain, and these states essentially describe the topology of the network.*

To better understand the difference between the two flavors of distance-vector algorithms that we've already studied—the Bellman-Ford algorithm and DUAL—and link-state algorithms, let's take a look at Figure 7.1.

Figure 7.1 consists of three shaded parts stacked on top of one another. The upper part shows the perception of the network by router R1, which employs a variation of the Bellman-Ford distance-vector algorithm. The only information that this router has are the network prefixes (shown as Ethernet-like segments labeled underneath), how far away they are, and in which direction.

The middle part again shows router R1's perception of the same network, but this time, the router employs a DUAL-based routing protocol. The router knows its directly reachable neighbors, how far away they are and in which direction, and the neighbors' distances (expressed as metrics) to all known network prefixes. As we can see, in addition to the shortest route for network prefix N4 lying through router R2 router R1 was also able to discover an alternative route, which lies through router R4. The metric of the shortest route is 22 (10+12), whereas the metric of the alternative route is 26 (10+16). Notwithstanding the higher metric, router R1 still considers the route through router R4 as alternative because the metric of router R4's own route for network prefix N4 is only 16, a lesser value than 22 (the metric of router R1's shortest route). Hence, router R4 is closer to network prefix N4 than router R1; thus, router R1 can momentarily switch to the route through router R4 should the route through router R2 become worse or

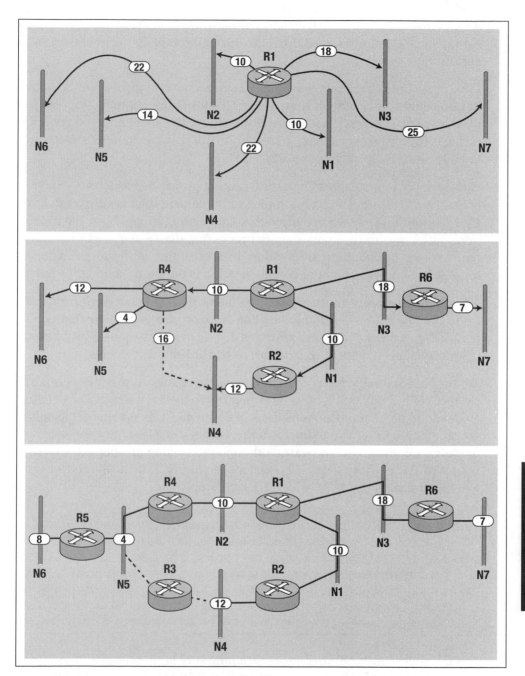

Figure 7.1   A network representation by the Bellman-Ford distance-vector algorithm,
DUAL, and link-state algorithms.

disappear. (Using the DUAL terminology introduced in Chapter 6, router R4 becomes a feasible successor if the route through router R2 becomes worse or disappears.)

Finally, the bottom part shows router R1's perception of the network employing a link-state routing protocol. Now router R1 knows the complete topology of the network. Thus, not only is it aware of the alternative route for network prefix N4 through router R4, but it also knows of the alternative routes for network prefixes N6 and N5 through router R2.

However, the superiority of link-state routing protocols has a price. Such protocols are typically much more complex to implement than are Bellman-Ford and DUAL-based distance-vector protocols. Calculating routes from the topological information generally involves more processing than is required to perform distance-vector calculations. In addition, to ensure that all routers have identical topological knowledge, more communication is necessary among the routers.

Although link-state protocols converge faster than Bellman-Ford protocols, the same can't be said when comparing link-state protocols to those that are DUAL-based. Experimental data demonstrates that, in most cases, the DUAL-based routing protocols converge at least as fast as the link-state protocols.

Yet the link-state routing paradigm is popular, thanks to the ubiquitous routing protocol OSPF, and OSPF owes its popularity to the openness of its specification. (Indeed, its very name contains the word "open.") This openness has allowed a multitude of different vendors, including Cisco, to successfully implement OSPF in their equipment and software. Although the routing protocols based on competing DUAL are fast, their only popular specimen is Enhanced Interior Gateway Routing Protocol (EIGRP), which is Cisco proprietary.

NOTE: Intermediate System to Intermediate System (IS-IS) is another popular link-state protocol. IS-IS and OSPF are equally popular among Internet Service Providers (ISPs); yet in corporate networks, OSPF seems to be more widely used. ISPs typically run two dynamic routing protocols in their networks—an IGP, such as OSPF or IS-IS, to maintain intranetwork routing and an EGP, usually BGP, to maintain routing with other ISPs. This book is devoted only to IGPs; therefore, given the ISP-centric application of IS-IS (that's not to say that IS-IS can't be used purely as an IGP) and that IS-IS does not use Internet Protocol (IP) as the transport, we won't consider IS-IS in detail. Nevertheless, Appendix F gives a brief overview of the protocol and provides IS-IS configuration guidelines.

OSPF has proven to be capable of sustaining very large networks that often comprise thousands of routers and segments. OSPF is fast, too; its convergence time rarely exceeds 1 minute.

In the core of OSPF, as well as any link-state protocol, lies Dijkstra's famous shortest-path algorithm, which is used to create routes from the topological information. Given the central place of Dijkstra's algorithm in the operation of link-state protocols, we'll first examine the algorithm, which should give us a feel for the core of link-state–protocol operation. After the algorithm we'll consider how real networks are modeled for processing by the algorithm. Only after that, do we consider the details of OSPF.

How Deep Is This "In Depth" Section?

OSPF is a large subject, much larger than any of the distance-vector routing protocols we've examined so far. It's much larger than even EIGRP. The OSPF specification consumes 244 pages, at least 200 of which are full of technical information. (For comparison, the total page count of the Routing Information Protocol (RIP) version 2 specification—which, in addition to the internals of RIP, sets forth the explanation of the Bellman-Ford distance-vector algorithm and its subsequent refinements—is only 39.)

Hence, there's absolutely no way I can comprehensively explain the OSPF operation in only one chapter of this book. I'm not at all attempting to excuse a poor job of explaining OSPF; I simply won't even try to give a comprehensive OSPF course. Instead, however, I'll strive to achieve the following goals in this chapter:

- I'll explain the central conceptual subjects of OSPF, such as Dijkstra's shortest-path algorithm and the OSPF network topology model.

- I'll present an overview of OSPF in which I'll also try to cover some questions that often arise from practical experience with the protocol.

- I'll supply the reference material, which can be useful in studying and working with the protocol. The reference material will include the formats of major link-state advertisement (LSA) types, the formats of OSPF protocol data units (PDUs), the interface, neighbor-state machines, and so on.

Whereas I'll try to make the material as useful as possible, it alone won't be enough for you to comprehensively understand the protocol and its operation. Therefore, I encourage you by all means to use other sources of OSPF information. Among those, I would like to recommend the following three:

- The most important source is the standard itself, Request for Comments (RFC) 2328, "OSPF Version 2". It's large, but don't let this sway you from reading it. It's written in perfectly understandable language and includes many examples that explain the key elements of OSPF operation. Although the word "complexity" is often used in conjunction with OSPF, the protocol is complex only in comparison with the relatively simple distance-vector protocols.

- The next source is the book *Interconnections* by Radia Perlman. Although the book does not delve deeply into the technical details of OSPF, it does provide a clear overview of the protocol and presents a very concise explanation of the link-state routing paradigm and related subjects. Let me again state that the book is a classic work on networking in general.

- Lastly, I highly recommend reading the book *OSPF: Anatomy of an Internet Routing Protocol* by John T. Moy (who is the editor of RFC 2178). The book provides a good description of OSPF in a friendlier manner than the RFC does. In addition, the book answers some questions that typically arise from reading the RFC and from working with the protocol. The book also gives some invaluable advice on operating the protocol.

Finally, a good network analyzer is indispensable when studying OSPF (as well as most other network-related subjects). An example of a good network analyzer is Sniffer by Network Associates, so if you have access to Sniffer, use it whenever possible. If you don't, you can get a trial version of SnifferPro, which should suffice for studying purposes. The trial version is available at Network Associates' Web site, **www.nai.com**.

Dijkstra's Shortest-Path Algorithm

Dijkstra's shortest-path algorithm operates over graphs—mathematical abstractions consisting of vertices interconnected with edges. Each edge connects precisely two vertices in one direction. Each edge has a cost associated with it, and each vertex can have any number of edges.

NOTE: *Strictly speaking, a graph in which edges have directions in called a digraph. Digraphs in which an edge is allowed to connect a vertex back to itself is called a loop-digraph. But because this book is not an introduction to the graph theory and to avoid infusing too many irrelevant terms to the main course of the book, I will use only the term graph (whose appearance in the book is very limited anyway). In addition, loop-digraphs are not used in the link-state algorithm; hence, we'll always presume that an edge leads to another vertex and never back to the same vertex.*

Vertices can be thought of as sites, and edges as transportation between the sites. The transportation is provided in only one direction and at a certain cost—in the direction and cost of the edge. For example, if an edge connects vertex A to vertex B, this essentially means that it's possible to move from vertex A to vertex B for the cost of the edge. This edge, however, does not permit a move back from vertex B to vertex A: Such a move requires another edge—from vertex B to vertex A.

A sample graph is shown in Figure 7.2. The vertices are depicted as thick-bordered circles labeled with capital letters inside. The graph contains five vertices, labeled A through E. The edges are depicted as arrow-headed lines that interconnect the vertices, and the costs of the edges are shown as the numbers in the ovals drawn on the tops of the edges.

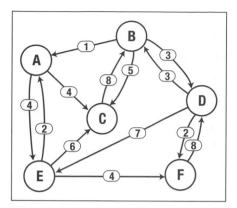

Figure 7.2 A sample graph.

Vertex X is said to be *adjacent* to vertex Y if there is an edge going from vertex X to vertex Y. For example, in Figure 7.2, vertex B is adjacent with vertex A. Notice, however, that the opposite may not be true; for example, vertex A is not adjacent with vertex B because there is no edge going from vertex A to vertex B.

A graph with many vertices can have multiple paths between two edges. Among them, the best path is defined as the path whose cumulative cost—calculated as the sum of the costs of the edges that constitute the path—is minimal. For example, in Figure 7.2, the shortest path from vertex D to vertex A lies through vertex D; its cost is 4. The reverse path (from vertex A to vertex D), however, is longer; it lies through vertices C and B and has a cost of 15.

At that point, however, we might ask ourselves: How did we arrive at the conclusion of what path was the shortest in the above example? Well, it was relatively easy to run through all possible paths, calculate their cumulative costs, and pick the one with the smallest cumulative cost. However, we must note that it was easy only because the graph is small. As the graph becomes larger, the amount of calculation grows exponentially. Soon, even the fastest computer would spend an unacceptably long time just running through all possible paths and calculating their costs.

Dijkstra's shortest-path algorithm solves the task of *quickly* finding the shortest path between any two vertices in an arbitrarily interconnected graph.

To operate, the algorithm uses two auxiliary data structures: a database of vertices for which the shortest path is found, and a database of candidate vertices for which the shortest path may have been found. We'll denote these databases as *Found* and *Candidate*. Both databases have identical structure: They contain two fields, which are the reference to a vertex and the cumulative cost of the path from the starting vertex to the referenced vertex.

NOTE: *To be exact, the databases should also have one more field containing the shortest path for each vertex. The link-state protocols, however, do not require this field, as their task is to populate the routing table with the routes, which have only metrics (essentially the cumulative costs of the paths), but not the exact paths themselves.*

The algorithm begins by putting the starting vertex to the Found database with the cumulative cost of 0, and all its adjacent vertices to the Candidate database with the cumulative costs equal to the costs of the respective edges. After that, the algorithm cycles through the following recursive steps:

1. Find a vertex in the Candidate database with the smallest cumulative cost. Move the vertex to the Found database.

2. Identify the vertices with which the moved vertex is adjacent.

3. Discard the moved vertex's adjacent vertices that have already been moved to the Found database.

4. For each of the moved vertex's adjacent vertices that have already been placed into the Candidate database, set the recorded cumulative cost equal to the smallest of its previously recorded cumulative cost and the sum of the cumulative cost of the moved vertex and the cost of the edge going from the moved vertex to the adjacent vertex. Formally,

$$C_{adj,new} = \min(\ C_{adj,old},\ C_{moved} + C_{edge}\ )$$

where

- $C_{adj,new}$ and $C_{adj,old}$ are, respectively, the new and old recorded cumulative costs of the adjacent vertex

- C_{moved} is the recorded cumulative cost of the moved vertex,

- C_{edge} is the cost of the edge going from the moved vertex to the adjacent one.

5. Place each adjacent vertex that appears in neither the Found database nor the Candidate database into the Candidate database. Set its cumulative cost equal to the sum of the cumulative cost of the moved vertex and the cost of the edge going from the moved vertex to the adjacent vertex. Formally,

$$C_{adj} = C_{moved} + C_{edge}$$

where C_{adj} is the cumulative cost of the adjacent vertex. The other two values are identical to those in the formula of Step 4.

6. If the Candidate database is empty, finish. Otherwise, return to Step 1 and proceed again.

To demonstrate how the algorithm works step by step, let's use it to calculate the shortest paths from vertex A to all other vertices in the graph in Figure 7.2.

The results of each iteration of the algorithm are shown in Figure 7.3. Each of the six iterations occupies a separate space and is labeled with its number (shown in parentheses in the top-left corner of the space). The vertices that have been placed in the Found database are shown with the thick border, and the vertices with the thin border have made it to only the Candidate database. The numbers in the ovals on top of the edges show the cumulative cost of the path from the starting vertex (in our case, vertex A) to the vertex to which the edge leads. (This convention is different than that in Figure 7.2, in which the numbers indicated the costs of the edges.) If the oval contains a question mark, this indicates that the vertex to which the edge leads already appears in the Found database and that, therefore, the cumulative cost is not calculated for it.

In addition, the top-right corner of each iteration shows the current contents of the Found and Candidate databases. The vertex that has just been placed into the Found database is marked with an asterisk (*), which appears to the right of the corresponding database record. Likewise, the vertices that have been either placed into the Candidate database or have updated existing records in it are marked with a sideways chevron (>) appearing on the right of the corresponding database records. If the cumulative cost is updated with a smaller value, the corresponding record in the Candidate database shows the old value, an arrow, and then the new value.

As we can see, the algorithm discovered the lengths of the shortest paths to every vertex in an orderly and rather simple fashion. Although it's not completely obvious from our example, the algorithm is also fast, especially when compared with the straightforward task of running through all possible paths and measuring their lengths.

The simplicity and speed of the algorithm qualify it for the central role in link-state algorithms—devising routes from the topology information.

OSPF

In this section, OSPF Network Topology Representations, OSPF Operations, and Link-State Advertisements are covered.

OSPF Network Topology Representation

Dijkstra's shortest-path algorithm works over graphs. Hence, to use the algorithm in link-state protocols, we must have a means to represent networks in the form of graphs.

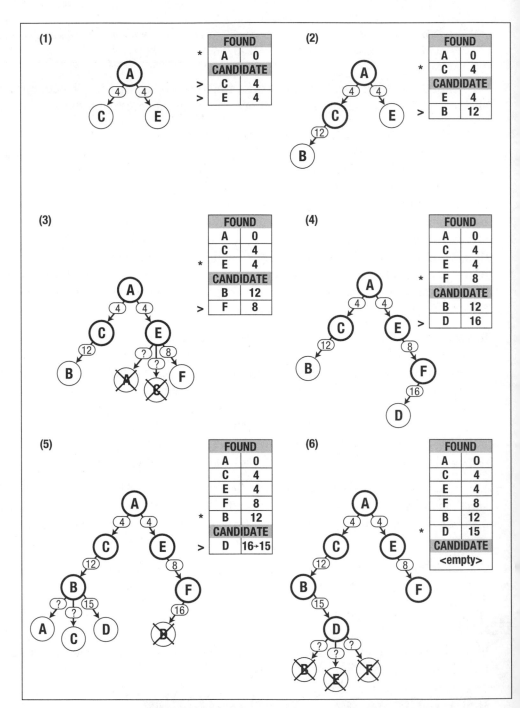

Figure 7.3   The results of each iteration of Dijkstra's shortest-path algorithm for the graph in Figure 7.2.

The important feature and limitation of graphs is that the edges in them connect only two vertices. This essentially makes it impossible to straightforwardly model a network in the form of a graph by representing routers as vertices and edges as segments between them, because many segments in real networks do interconnect more than two routers.

Therefore, modeling networks as graphs in link-state protocols must be somewhat more sophisticated. However, such modeling must preserve the paradigm of the graphs by which the vertices represent sites and the edges represent the means of transportation between the sites. In the case of computer networks, the sites are stop points for the network traffic—routers and segments. The edges reflect the direction and cost of network traffic delivery.

Interestingly enough, different link-state routing protocols feature different topological models to represent networks. For obvious reasons, we'll concentrate on only the model used in OSPF.

In the OSPF model, the routers are modeled as vertices. The segments, however, are modeled as vertices only if they are assigned network prefixes. Furthermore, if a segment is assigned more than one network prefix (which, for example, can be denoted by the presence of secondary IP addresses on router interfaces), OSPF models it using a separate vertex for each of the network prefixes. In other words, OSPF models the network prefixes rather than the segments as vertices. This is logical, because, in IP, a segment cannot receive any traffic if it does not have an assigned network prefix. Thus, there are no IP hosts on the segments, and the router interfaces are unnumbered. Such a segment cannot receive any traffic, so it is not a traffic stop point; hence, there is no need to model it as a vertex. Nevertheless, the "transportation" capability of such segments exists, so it is modeled using edges.

The edges among the vertices are placed based on the type of the segment. From the OSPF perspective, there are three types of segments:

- Point-to-point links

- Broadcast segments

- Fully or non-fully meshed nonbroadcast multiaccess networks (NBMAs)

NOTE: *In fact, these are not exactly OSPF types of segments but rather IP types of segments. OSPF, being a supplementary component of IP, simply "borrows" the IP classification of the segment types.*

In addition to these three segment types, OSPF distinguishes between transit and stub segments. Transit segments are segments to which more than one OSPF router is connected. Consequently, stub segments are segments on which only one OSPF router resides.

Finally, each router interface on which OSPF is enabled has an administratively configurable cost. (In OSPF, costs can range from 1 through 65535.) This cost is used in OSPF models to assign cost to the edges.

OSPF models stub segments are shown in Figure 7.4, regardless of which of the three types the segment belongs.

Both the router and the segment are modeled as vertices. A single edge connects the router vertex to the network vertex, and the cost of the edge is equal to the cost of the router's interface. There is no edge going back from the network vertex to the router vertex. This model is used for a simple reason. As per our discussion before, the vertices denote the stop points for the network traffic—the router and the network. The edge denotes the direction in which the router can forward the network traffic. Of course, the network traffic can and will come back from the segment, but the router is not concerned with how this traffic is going to reach it. Hence, if there is another edge going in the opposite direction, it would be of no use to the router. On the contrary, if the router must forward network traffic that is destined for the segment, it must know how to do this, which is reflected by the direction of the edge.

Figure 7.5 reveals three ways in which OSPF models point-to-point links. The choice of a particular method is dependent upon whether the routers' interfaces are assigned IP addresses, and, if so, whether the IP addresses belong to the same network prefix.

The graph labeled (a) shows how OSPF models unnumbered point-to-point links. The two routers are represented as vertices with two links mutually interconnecting the routers representing the link itself. The cost of each edge is equal to the cost of the interface from which the edge starts; the interfaces can be assigned different costs, which will result in the unequal costs of the edges. The two edges reflect the fact that the network traffic can travel between the routers in both directions. As the link is unnumbered, there is no network prefix vertex.

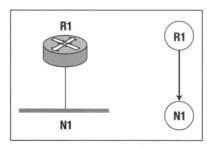

Figure 7.4   A graph representing stub segments in the OSPF model.

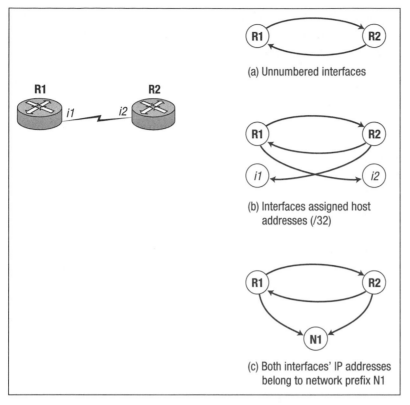

Figure 7.5   Depending on IP address assignment, OSPF models point-to-point links in three ways.

If the routers' interfaces are assigned host IP addresses (that is, network prefixes whose length is /32), OSPF models the link as the graph labeled (b). The routers are represented as vertices, and the link is represented as two edges that mutually interconnect the router vertices. In addition, two more vertices represent routers' interfaces as stub networks. Notice that the edges going to the interface vertices do not start at the vertices representing the routers to which the interfaces belong. Instead, each of the two edges starts at the vertex that represents the router on the other side of the link. The costs of each of the two edges starting at the router vertex are equal to the cost of the corresponding router interface. Again, the routers' interfaces may have unequal costs.

The two additional vertices are needed because the interfaces are assigned host IP addresses. Such interfaces are essentially stub segments, each featuring a network prefix with the length of /32. Hence, these network prefixes must be modeled as vertices. The edges going in only one direction signify that the network prefixes reside on stub segments.

Finally, the graph labeled (c) is used to model the point-to-point links in which the routers' interfaces are assigned IP addresses that belong to the same network prefix. As before, the routers are represented as two vertices. The representation of the link, like before, features the two edges, but with an extra vertex to which edges go from each of the router vertices. The costs of each of the two edges starting at the router vertex are equal to the cost of the corresponding router interface. This additional vertex is needed because the link is assigned a network prefix. Again, the two edges leading to the network prefix vertex reflect the fact that the network prefix is considered to reside on a stub segment. This is legitimate, because the transitional capability of the link is reflected by the two other edges going between the router vertices.

Transitional broadcast networks are modeled using the graph shown in Figure 7.6.

The routers and the network prefix of the segment are modeled as vertices. The pairs of edges that mutually interconnect each router vertex with the network prefix vertex reflect the transitional capability of the segment on which the network prefix resides. Each edge starting at the router vertex has a cost equal to the cost of the corresponding router interface. The costs of all edges starting at the network vertex are equal to 0.

NBMA networks represent a special case. Depending on whether the NBMA network is fully or non-fully meshed, OSPF can use two different models to represent it. Fully meshed NBMA networks can be represented as broadcast networks. (This is shown in the top part of Figure 7.6.) As in the case of broadcast networks, the costs of the edges that start at the router vertices are equal to the costs of the corresponding router interfaces. The costs of all edges starting at the network edge are equal to 0.

If, however, the NBMA network is not fully meshed, OSPF must represent it using the *point-to-multipoint* model. In the point-to-multipoint model, each connection between the routers is modeled as an unnumbered point-to-point link, shown in Figure 7.5(a). In addition, each router's interface is modeled as a stub segment;

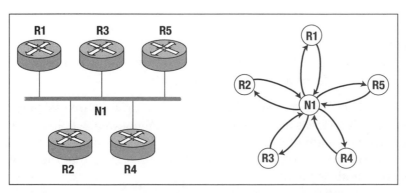

Figure 7.6   The graph that OSPF uses to model broadcast networks.

that is, it is represented as a vertex with an edge going to it from the router vertex. The costs of all edges starting at a router vertex are equal to the cost of the router's interface.

OSPF Operation Overview

So far, we know how OSPF routers model network topology and how they use the network topology information to devise OSPF routes, which are then placed into the routing table. Now it's time to discuss how the topological information is created, communicated, and stored by the routers in the network.

The OSPF routers create new topological information (or modify existing information) only when network changes occur. Network changes include changes in the states and costs of the segments and router interfaces, and changes in the states of the OSPF routers themselves.

In OSPF, the topology of the network is described, stored, and communicated in the form of LSAs. The content of the LSA describes an individual topological element of the network, such as a router, segment, or external destination. Just as there are different types of network topology elements (like routers and segments, to name a few), there are different types of LSAs, each corresponding to an individual type of network component. We'll examine the exact formats of LSAs in the upcoming sections of this and the next chapter.

Only OSPF routers can generate and modify LSAs; no other network components can. The router that generates an LSA is said to *originate* it, and only one router can originate a particular LSA (which is not to be confused with an LSA type; multiple OSPF routers can originate LSAs of the same type).

The OSPF routers store LSAs in the *link-state database*—a data structure whose purpose is to provide LSA storage and lookup functions—and they propagate the LSAs in the OSPF PDUs. (We'll consider the formats of all the OSPF PDUs in the course of this chapter.)

When a router generates a new LSA or modifies an existing one, it must communicate it to the routers that it can reach directly. Such routers are ordinarily called *neighbors*. Depending on the type of segment, however, the router may not communicate the LSA to all of its neighbors. (We'll later examine how the type of segment affects the communication between OSPF neighbors.) Upon receipt of the new or updated LSA, the neighbors first store it in their link-state databases and then communicate it to their neighbors. The neighbors, in turn, store the LSA and communicate it to their neighbors, and so on, until all of the routers in the network receive the LSA. Upon each iteration of this process, the routers observe two rules with regard to which of their neighbors must receive the LSA. The first rule has to do with the type of segment over which the neighbor is available. The second rule prevents the LSA from being forwarded back to the router from which it was received (similar to the split-horizon rule and the "no reverse forwarding" rule found in the bridging protocol that utilizes the spanning-tree algorithm).

This procedure of propagating new and changed LSAs is called *flooding*. The described flooding, however, suffers from two shortcomings. The first shortcoming is that, if the network has redundant paths, the routers would generate an enormous number of copies of the same LSA. Indeed, if a router resides on segments that each lead to the router that originated the LSA, this router would eventually receive at least two redundant copies of the LSA. On the next step, however, each of the redundant copies would be again multiplied when another router upstream from the originating router received the copies over different redundant paths. Soon, the whole network would be literally flooded by copies of the same LSA, and very likely to such an overwhelming extent that no communication would be possible, whether among the OSPF routers or of any other sort. As we know, most networks do have redundant connections, and—what's even more important—we want the dynamic routing protocol to take care of these redundant paths by utilizing them for load-balancing whenever possible and by switching to them when the main paths fail.

This shortcoming is best addressed by requiring that the OSPF routers not blindly forward the copies of the same LSA as they receive them, but store them for some period of time before propagating them further. If during this time an updated copy of the LSA arrives, it replaces the stored one. However, if the arriving copies are either identical to the stored one or outdated, they are simply discarded. This procedure effectively prevents the routers from overflowing the network with identical and outdated LSAs.

The second shortcoming is that the procedure does not provide for the reliable propagation of the LSAs. If a copy of the LSA gets lost (for example, as the result of a bad connection), the router that sent it wouldn't know about it. The most probable result of such a loss would be that all routers behind (and including) the router that failed to receive the copy wouldn't learn of the LSA. Exact knowledge of the network topology by all routers in the network is crucial for OSPF operation (as well as for the operation of any other link-state routing protocol), so this shortcoming must also be addressed before the procedure is implemented in the protocol.

This shortcoming is resolved by requiring that the OSPF routers acknowledge the receipt of LSAs. Before actually transmitting an LSA, an OSPF router sets a flag and starts a timer for each of its neighbors to which it should forward the LSA. The router can clear the flag only when an acknowledgment from the corresponding neighbor arrives. If one of the timers expires before the corresponding flag is cleared, the router restarts the timer and retransmits the LSA to the nonresponding neighbor. If the router receives no acknowledgment from that neighbor after a certain number of retries, it declares the neighbor dead.

The flooding procedure that includes these two procedural enhancements is called *reliable flooding*, and its implementation in OSPF will be detailed in upcoming sections.

OSPF Adjacencies

We have already emphasized several times the importance of reliable propagation of the topology information among the OSPF routers. One measure that helps achieve such reliable propagation is reliable flooding, which takes care of delivering LSAs to all of the OSPF routers in the network. However, reliable flooding doesn't take care of the discovery and monitoring of OSPF neighbors, nor does it prescribe to which neighbors the copies of the LSA must be forwarded. These two issues bring us to the next fundamental OSPF subject—*adjacencies*.

An OSPF adjacency is essentially a bidirectional relationship between two routers along which the routers propagate LSAs. Adjacencies are formed between two routers that are topologically modeled as two vertices mutually interconnected with two edges. For instance, two routers interconnected with a point-to-point link are modeled this way and therefore, form an adjacency.

NOTE: *A router that forms an adjacency with another router is said to be adjacent to this router. As the relationship is mutual, the other router is also adjacent to the first router.*

That said, the obvious question is: How do routers form adjacencies on broadcast and NBMA networks, especially on fully meshed ones that are modeled as broadcast networks? Routers connected to such networks are modeled as vertices that are mutually interconnected with a single vertex representing the network segment itself. Because the network, for obvious reasons, can't participate in OSPF routing, do routers that are connected to a broadcast or NBMA network segment not form adjacencies?

The answer to this question is no, they do form adjacencies, although in a slightly tricky way. To become adjacent on broadcast and NBMA network segments, the routers elect a single router as the *designated router* for the segment. The designated router represents the network segment vertex in the corresponding topological model—for example, in Figure 7.7(a) the designated router represents vertex N1. After that, every router forms an adjacency with the designated router.

NOTE: *Although the routers on a broadcast network do not become adjacent among each other (they do so only with the designated router) they do not forward all of the traffic to the designated router. The routers still forward the traffic to the router through which the traffic's destination is best reachable. In other words, the adjacency relationship affects only the propagation of LSA; it does not affect the traffic flow. We'll discuss how the routers find out which router provides the best route for which destination in the "Routing Table Calculation" section later in this chapter.*

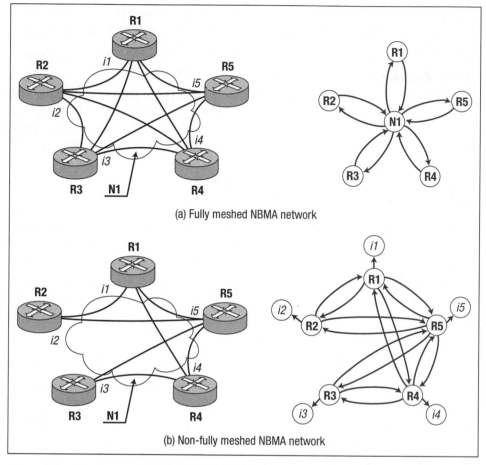

(a) Fully meshed NBMA network

(b) Non-fully meshed NBMA network

Figure 7.7   The two models that OSPF uses to represent NBMA networks.

To make OSPF routing over broadcast and NBMA networks more reliable, the routers also elect another router as the *backup designated router*, which takes over the responsibilities of the current designated router should it fail. The necessity for the backup designated router stems from the fact that, if the designated router fails, the routers on the segment must first detect the failure, elect a new designated router, and then go through the process of establishing adjacencies with it. In parallel with doing that, the routers must first remove the segment from the other routers' topological information by sending corresponding LSAs, and then reestablish it again by sending another set of LSAs.

If, however, the backup designated router is readily available, none of this needs to be done. Upon detecting the failure of the designated router, the routers would simply switch to the backup designated router, effectively making it a new designated router, and then elect a new backup designated router. None of this requires invalidating any piece of the topological information.

The routers use an auxiliary OSPF *hello* protocol to discover each other and form adjacencies. The details of the OSPF hello protocol and how it helps establish and maintain adjacencies will be explained in the upcoming sections.

OSPF Routing Hierarchy

A tight relationship exists between the contents of LSAs and IP addressing in the network. Apparently, the ultimate goal of OSPF is to maintain IP routing in the network, which boils down to the accuracy of the contents of the routers' routing tables at almost any moment. As we know, the routing table consists of routing entries, or routes, each of which contains a network prefix and the reference to the next-hop router and output interface through which the network prefix can be reached. Hence, in the case of OSPF routing, all these routing table components must be derived from the contents of the LSAs.

The larger the network, the larger the routers' routing tables will be, unless certain measures are taken. Consequently, we can conclude that, in the case of OSPF, the large size of the network also infers a large number of LSAs in the routers' link-state databases. This, in turn, causes a longer execution of Dijkstra's shortest-path algorithm and, as a result, higher CPU utilization on the routers as well as longer periods of network instability. Obviously, too large a network must be dealt with somehow.

The most typical approach to reducing a large network's impact on the convergence and overhead of routing protocols is summarization of network prefixes that belong to a common area. After such summarization, the routers beyond the common area perceive all destinations within the area via one or several summary network prefixes. This can dramatically reduce the number of router CPU cycles that are necessary to find the correct route for any destination within the area.

Apparently, the ability to do summarization imposes a certain constraint on the assignment of IP addresses. Summarization, in general, is governed by the principle that all destinations within an area must be assigned IP addresses that belong to one of the area summary network prefixes. (Speaking in terms of IP routing algorithms, every destination's IP address must be matched by one of the summary network prefixes.)

OSPF does support summarization. However, OSPF goes even further by not only requiring the enforcement of the described IP address-allocation principle but by also imposing a certain routing hierarchy.

If summarization needs to be done on a network whose routing is maintained by OSPF, the network must be divided into several areas, all of which must be connected to a single central area called the *OSPF backbone*. The actual connection of an area to the OSPF backbone is accomplished through the use of routers called *area border routers (ABRs)*. One or more interfaces of such a router must be connected to the segments that belong to the OSPF backbone; the remaining interfaces must be connected to the segments that belong to one or more (non-backbone) areas. In addition, no router can have interfaces connected to the segments that belong to different areas without at least one interface being connected to the segment that resides in the OSPF backbone.

All summarization of routing information within the OSPF routing domain—which is commonly referred to as an *autonomous system*—is handled by ABRs. ABRs originate LSAs of a special type to advertise summary network prefixes.

In addition, OSPF hierarchical routing allows external routing information to be injected into the OSPF autonomous system. Such external routing information can be routing information that has been created by routing protocols other than OSPF, or routing information imported from another OSPF autonomous system.

The routers that import external routing information are called *autonomous system boundary routers (ASBRs)*. ASBRs may reside in the OSPF backbone or in other areas, and they do not have to be connected to the backbone. Like ABRs, ASBRs originate LSAs of a special type to advertise external routing information.

Figure 7.8 demonstrates the interconnection between areas in an OSPF autonomous system and the placement of different types of routers.

In Figure 7.8, routers R2, R6, and R7 are ABRs, and routers R1 and R8 are ASBRs. Routers R3 and R5 are regular intra-area routers. The crossed-out router (R4) is not legitimate: Its interfaces are connected to segments that belong to different areas, whereas none of them is connected to a segment that resides in the OSPF backbone.

Areas in OSPF autonomous systems are enumerated using 32-bit integer values. Whereas regular areas can have any nonoverlapping numbers, the OSPF backbone's number must always be equal to 0. (This is why the OSPF backbone is quite often referred to as "Area 0.")

Dividing the OSPF autonomous system into areas also imposes the LSA storage, propagation, and processing rules that are outlined below. The purpose of these rules is to reduce as much as possible the number of LSAs that the routers in the autonomous system must process, and thereby reduce the amount of LSA processing and LSA-related memory allocation on the routers. Here are the rules:

- Each router has a separate link-state database for each area to which it is attached. Obviously, all the routers that are connected to the same area must have identical link-state databases for this area. When a router recalculates the routing table, it runs a separate Dijkstra shortest-path algorithm instance for each link-state database it has.

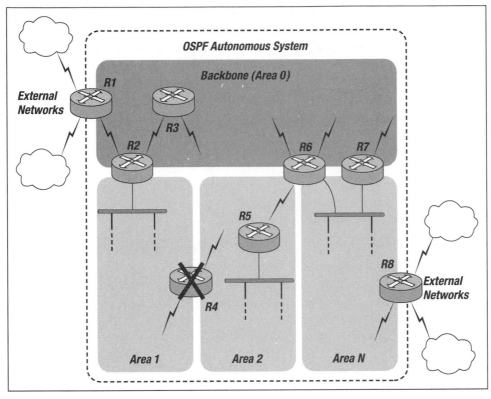

Figure 7.8   OSPF hierarchical routing.

- LSAs that describe the topology of an area are propagated only within their area. The routers attached to this area store these LSAs in the link-state database that corresponds to the area. When flooding of such LSAs occurs, the ABRs of the area are responsible for not propagating the LSAs beyond the area boundary.

- LSAs that describe the summary network prefixes of the destinations outside the area are originated by the ABRs of the area. For each area (including the OSPF backbone), an ABR originates a set of LSAs describing the summary network prefixes of all of the *other* areas in the OSPF autonomous system. These LSAs are flooded only within the area into which they are injected by the ABR and are stored only in the routers' link-state databases of that area.

NOTE: *Notice that the LSAs describing an area's own summary network prefixes are not injected back to the area.*

- LSAs that describe external routing information are originated by the ASBRs, are flooded throughout the autonomous system, and are stored in all of the link-state databases of each router.

Although the intention behind these rules is reducing the amount of LSA processing, the last rule may sometimes negate the effect of the other three rules because it states that the external routing information must be flooded throughout the whole OSPF autonomous system, area boundaries notwithstanding. Such flooding can in fact have a rather severe negative impact on the processing of routing information in certain areas if the autonomous system is connected to the Internet or to another large network that is not a part of the OSPF autonomous system. All network prefixes from the Internet or another large network are imported into the OSPF autonomous system in the form of LSAs carrying external routing information. In accordance with the last rule, these LSAs are flooded throughout the autonomous system. Hence, even the routers completely residing inside nonbackbone areas must be able to place them into their link-state databases and process them when necessary.

In the case of the OSPF backbone, the propagation of LSAs carrying external routing information is unavoidable because of the backbone's central role in the OSPF routing hierarchy. Hence, all of the routers that are connected to the OSPF backbone of an autonomous system into which large amounts of external routing information are imported must be robust enough to process all of this external routing information. Although this appears to be a legitimate requirement for the OSPF backbone, it may not be warranted for every area. Some areas may not functionally require all external routing information; hence, the routers in such areas do not need to be powerful enough to process all external routing information.

In OSPF, the areas that do not require the exact external routing information are called *stub*. Whereas regular areas receive all external routing information, stub areas do not receive any. Instead, they receive a single default route. Hence, the set of LSAs in stub areas is limited to only the LSAs that are originated within the area. Naturally, stub areas cannot contain any ASBRs.

However, the concept of OSPF stub areas does not cover the situation in which a small network whose routing is maintained by a non-OSPF routing protocol is connected to an OSPF autonomous system with a large amount of external routing information. Apparently, such a network cannot be made an OSPF stub area, because the routing information in it wasn't originated by OSPF and therefore is categorized as external routing information (which must be imported into the OSPF autonomous system via an ASBR, the presence of which is not allowed in an OSPF stub area). Under normal circumstances, such an area must be regular; therefore, all the external routing information that exists in the autonomous system is flooded into this area and is then imported into the area's routing protocol by the respective ASBR.

To address this situation, an extension of OSPF introduces the concept of *not-so-stubby areas (NSSA)*. The routing in an NSSA is performed in a manner similar to that of a stub area. No external routing information is injected into the area; instead, the area is supplied the default route by the area's ABRs. The ASBRs of the area (called *NSSA ASBRs*) use a special type of LSA to import the routing information originated by the network's routing protocol. These LSAs are flooded inside only the NSSA and are converted by the NSSA ABRs into standard LSAs for conveying external routing information.

Virtual Links

As mentioned, each area must be connected to the OSPF backbone. Nevertheless, in some situations, it may be physically impossible to connect an area to the backbone while being still possible to connect that area to another nonbackbone area. To address this type of situation, OSPF introduces the concept of a *virtual link*. A virtual link is established between two routers—one connected to the backbone and the other to the remote area—through a third common area, to which both routers must also be connected. The common area is called the virtual link's *transit area*. A virtual link acts similarly to a tunnel interface: Only the routers at the ends of the virtual link get the OSPF PDUs they send to each other through the virtual link, and the routers in the transit area deliver only the OSPF PDUs. Unlike the IP datagrams transferred through the tunnel interface, however, the IP datagrams carrying the OSPF PDUs sent over a virtual link are not encapsulated again into IP datagrams. Instead, they are routed like regular IP datagrams using the intra-area routing of the transit area.

NOTE: *Virtual links present the only case in which OSPF PDUs traverse multiple router hops.*

Virtual links are modeled as unnumbered point-to-point links whose two edges have the cost equal to the cost of the path between the two routers through the transit area. Once a virtual link is established between the router in the remote area and the backbone router, the router in the remote area essentially becomes connected to the backbone, which in turn makes it an ABR for the remote and transit areas.

OSPF virtual links are used only for conveying the routing information; they do not convey regular traffic between the remote area and the backbone. The regular traffic, like the IP datagrams carrying the OSPF PDUs sent over the virtual link, is routed using the intra-area routing of the transit area.

Besides remote areas, virtual links can be used to "repair" a partitioned backbone. The same rules apply as with connecting remote areas: The two partitions of the backbone can be interconnected by establishing a virtual link through a transit area between two routers, each residing in a different partition.

Traffic Flow in a Hierarchical OSPF Network

The routing hierarchy of a multiarea OSPF network casts certain patterns on the way the routed traffic traverses the network. These patterns are outlined below:

- Traffic whose source and destination resides within the same area traverses only this area, unless the area is the OSPF backbone and a better route for the destination exists, this route partially or completely goes through a transit area. If the latter is the case, the traffic traverses the transit area in addition to or instead of traversing the backbone.

- Traffic whose destination and source reside in different areas goes through the backbone, except in the following cases:

  - If two areas have one or several common ABRs, the traffic between the areas can bypass the backbone by going through one of these ABRs, providing the resulting route is more optimal. (The traffic still "touches" the backbone because the ABR is connected to the backbone. However, the traffic does not traverse any segment that resides in the backbone.)

  - If there is a better route for the destination and this route partially or completely goes through a transit area, the traffic traverses the transit area in addition to or instead of traversing the backbone.

- The traffic destined for an external destination goes to the ASBR that advertises the external destination. The ASBR is an internal to the OSPF routing domain destination, so the traffic gets to the ASBR in accordance with the above patterns.

LSAs

As mentioned, the purpose of LSAs is to describe network topology information. So let's discuss in more detail the structure of LSAs, their types, lifecycles, and so on.

The Structure of the LSA Header

Although different types of LSAs describe different types of topological information, all LSAs nonetheless have the same structure, which is shown in Figure 7.9.

All LSAs begin with the header, which is shown as the unshaded part in the LSA structure in Figure 7.9.

The 16-bit–long Link State Age field carries the value of the LSA age measured in seconds. When an instance of an LSA is created, its age is made equal to 0. Each second the LSA sits in the router's memory, its age is incremented by one. In addition, when the router floods the LSA out of an interface, it must increase the value of the Link State Age field in the transmitted copy by the value called *InfTransDelay*, which is local to the interface out of which the LSA is transmitted. (No standard default is imposed for this value; in Cisco IOS, the default value of InfTransDelay is 1, regardless of the interface type.) The maximum value that the Link State Age field can reach is called the *MaxAge*, which is equal to 1 hour (3,600 seconds).

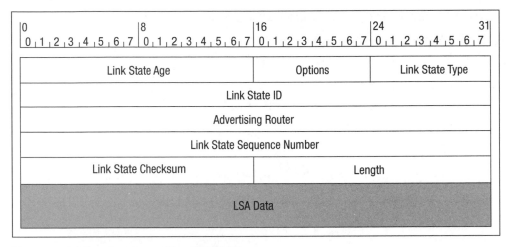

Figure 7.9   The structure of the OSPF LSA.

The 8-bit Options field describes the optional capabilities of the router that originates the LSA. This field has the structure shown in Figure 7.10.

The meanings of the individual bits of the Options field are shown in Table 7.1.

The 8-bit Link State Type field identifies the type of the LSA. Table 7.2 lists the common LSA types.

The different types of LSAs are often referenced by their values, as well. For example, as you can see in the table, there are two summary LSAs. To distinguish which one is actually meant, it's quite common to make a reference to "type 4 summary LSA," or even simply "type 4 LSA."

We'll discuss the structures of the particular LSA types in the upcoming sections.

The 32-bit Link State ID field is a component of the LSA's unique identification (the other components are the Link State Type and Advertising Router fields). Depending on the type of the LSA, this field is assigned the values shown in Table 7.3.

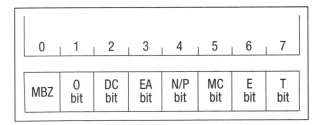

Figure 7.10   The structure of the Options field.

7. Open Shortest Path First (OSPF) Protocol

Table 7.1   The meanings of the individual bits of the Options field.

Bit	Meaning
0	The Opaque-LSA OSPF option, described in RFC 2370, "The OSPF Opaque LSA Option." If set, it denotes that the router supports Opaque-LSAs; otherwise, it doesn't.
DC	The Demand Circuit OSPF option, described in RFC 1793, "Extending OSPF to Support Demand Circuits." If set, it denotes that the router supports the demand circuits; otherwise, it doesn't.
EA	The External-Attributes-LSA OSPF option, described in D. Ferguson's *The OSPF External Attributes LSA*. It has the status of "work in progress." If set, the router will receive and forward External-Attributes-LSAs; otherwise, it won't.
N/P	NSSAs are documented.If set, this denotes that the LSA belongs to an NSSA; otherwise, it doesn't.
MC	The multicast extensions of OSPF, also known as MOSPF, described in RFC 1584, "Multicast Extensions to OSPF."
E	If set, denotes that the area to which the LSA belongs is a stub area.
T	If set, denotes that the router supports Type Of Service routing. Because Type Of Service routing is not in use, the bit is typically cleared.

Table 7.2   The types of LSAs.

Value	LSA Type	Description	Originated By
1	Router LSA	Describes the states of the router's interfaces	All OSPF routers
2	Network LSA	Lists the routers connected to the network	Designated routers
3	Summary LSA	Describes the summary network prefixes of an area	ABRs
4	Summary LSA	Describes ASBRs	ABRs
5	AS-External LSA	Describes the network prefixes that were imported into an OSPF autonomous system (that is, external network prefixes)	ASBRs
7	NSSA AS-External LSA	Describes network prefixes that were imported into an NSSA	NSSA ASBRs

Table 7.3   The values the Link State ID field is assigned depending on the LSA type.

LSA Type	Link State ID
1	The OSPF ID of the router that originates the LSA
2	The IP address of the designated router's interface connected to the segment
3	The destination network prefix
4	The OSPF ID of the ASBR
5 and 7	The destination network prefix

The 32-bit Advertising Router field carries the OSPF ID of the router that origi-nates the LSA.

The 32-bit Link State Sequence Number field carries the value that identifies the instance of the LSA. (Hereafter, I will refer to this field and its value as the sequence number.) The sequence number is treated as a signed integer, and an LSA's sequence number can be modified by only the router that originates the LSA. The very first instance of every LSA has the sequence number called *InitialSequenceNumber*, which is equal to 0x80000001 (that is, $-2^{31}+1$; 2^{31} is reserved and can never be used as a sequence number). Each time the router creates a new instance of the LSA, it increases its sequence number by one. The maximum value that the sequence number can attain is called the *MaxSequenceNumber*, which is equal to 0x7FFFFFFF ($2^{31}-1$). If the sequence number of any LSA reaches this value, the LSA must first be removed from the OSPF routing domain by the *premature aging process*, which I'll examine shortly. It can then be re-created with the InitialSequenceNumber.

NOTE: *Under normal conditions, MaxSequenceNumber won't be reached. If the router that originates the LSA created a new instance of it at the maximum allowed rate (every 5 seconds), it would take approximately 700 years to reach the MaxSequenceNumber. Therefore, if high sequence numbers appear on real routers, this may indicate some sort of hardware or software problem.*

The 16-bit Link State Checksum field holds the checksum that covers the whole contents of the LSA, excluding itself and the Link State Age field. The algorithm that is used to calculate the Link State Checksum is the same as the one used in ISO connectionless datagrams. This algorithm is commonly known as the Fletcher checksum.

NOTE: *The exact specification of the Fletcher checksum algorithm can be found in RFC 905, "ISO Transport Protocol Specification."*

The 16-bit Length field carries the size of the LSA in 8-bit octets.

Finally, the LSA Data field, which is not a part of the LSA header, carries the LSA type-specific information that actually describes the piece of the network topol-ogy. We'll consider the contents of different LSA types after we examine how routers create and maintain LSAs in the network.

The Purpose of the LSA Header

The LSA header has two purposes:

- It uniquely identifies the LSA. The three LSA header fields—Link State Type, Link State ID, and Advertising Router—provide sufficient information to differentiate any two LSAs.

- It helps identify the more recent of two instances of the same LSA. (The comparison rules are explained in the next section.)

- It helps sustain the "reliable" lifecycle of its LSA.

Comparison of Two Instances of the Same LSA

When comparing two instances of the same LSA (Link State Type, Link State ID, and Advertising Router are identical in both instances), the following rules help identify the more recent one:

- The instance with the highest sequence number is considered to be the most recent. If the instances' sequence numbers are identical, the next rule applies.

- The instance with the largest Link State Checksum value is considered to be more recent; if these values are the same, the next rule applies.

- The instance whose age is equal to MaxAge is considered to be the more recent; if neither's age is MaxAge, then the instance with the smaller age value is considered to be more recent.

- Otherwise, the instances are considered to be identical.

The LSA Lifecycle

When a router creates an LSA, it sets its sequence number equal to the InitialSequenceNumber and its Link State Age equal to 0. When it floods this LSA, it increments the Link State Age field in the copy sent out of an interface by the InfTransDelay value of that interface.

In addition, each second the LSA sits in each router's memory, its Link State Age is increased by one. If the LSA's Link State Age reaches the MaxAge value, which is equal to 3,600 seconds (1 hour), the router in the memory of which the LSA resides can no longer use the LSA in routing table calculations. Once the Link State Age of any LSA reaches MaxAge, the router refloods the LSA and keeps it in its memory only as long as necessary to complete the ongoing database synchronizations with the other routers. Once the link-state database synchronizations finish (or if there are no synchronizations), the LSA is removed from the router's memory after its flooding is complete (that is, acknowledgments are received from all of the routers to which the LSA was transmitted).

The router never increases the Link State Age of any LSA past MaxAge.

The router that originates an LSA must create a new instance of it when the LSA's Link State Age reaches the *LSRefreshTime* value, which is equal to 1,800 seconds (30 minutes). The router creates the new instance by increasing the LSA's sequence number by one and then reflooding the LSA. The LSRefreshTime is half the MaxAge time, so the LSA should remain in the router's link-state databases as long as it's maintained by the router that originated it.

Besides regular "refreshing" of the self-originated LSAs, the router must also create new instances of these LSAs when it detects the changes that affect the topology information conveyed in the LSAs. However, the router must wait at least *MinLSInterval* seconds (S seconds) after generating an instance of an LSA before generating another instance of this same LSA, even if it detected a change that affected the contents of the LSA. If the router detects multiple changes during MinLSInterval, the new instance will reflect the cumulative effect of the changes. The MinLSInterval is equal to 5 seconds.

In addition, if the router must remove a self-originated LSA from the routing domain, it uses the *premature aging procedure*, whereby the router first sets the LSA age equal to MaxAge and then floods it. The next section explains what happens when the other routers receive an LSA whose age is equal to MaxAge.

The Reliable Flooding Procedure

As discussed, routers use the reliable flooding procedure to propagate LSAs throughout areas and the OSPF routing domain. The type of LSA determines whether it is flooded only within the area in which it belongs or throughout the entire OSPF routing domain.

When flooding, routers send LSAs inside OSPF update PDUs. Multiple LSAs can be placed inside a single update. Each sent LSA must be acknowledged. Acknowledgments are sent inside OSPF acknowledgment PDUs, which can carry acknowledgments for multiple LSAs.

If an acknowledgment for a previously sent LSA is not received within the *RxmtInterval* time, configurable on a per-interface basis, the LSA is retransmitted.

Acknowledgments can be of two types—*delayed* and *direct*. When using delayed acknowledgments, a router sends acknowledgments at regular time intervals, as opposed to immediately transmitting them. Each time the router needs to acknowledge an LSA, it schedules an acknowledgment, which is then packed into an acknowledgment PDU that is sent at the next acknowledgment transmission time. Delayed acknowledgments are used in the majority of cases.

Direct acknowledgments are sent only to acknowledge duplicate LSAs. Direct acknowledgments are sent immediately.

On broadcast networks, the designated and backup designated routers send routing updates and delayed acknowledgments to the *AllSPFRouters address*, which is equal to 224.0.0.5. The other routers send updates and delayed acknowledgments to the *AllDRouters* address which is equal to 224.0.0.6. On other types of networks, the updates are sent directly to the IP address of each neighbor.

7. Open Shortest Path
First (OSPF) Protocol

Direct acknowledgments are always sent directly to the IP address of the router for which the acknowledgment is destined.

In some cases, a router can acknowledge receipt of a flooded LSA by sending an update PDU, as opposed to an acknowledgment PDU.

When a router receives an update, it uses the following procedure to decide the next step it must take with regard to the LSAs contained in the update:

1. The router retrieves the LSAs from the update one by one.

2. Having retrieved an LSA from the update, the router checks if it already has an instance of this LSA in its link-state database. To do this, it compares the Link State Type, Link State ID, and Advertising Router fields in the retrieved LSA with those of the LSAs that reside in its link-state database.

3. If the router finds an instance of the same LSA in its link-state database and if it was installed fewer than *MinLSArrival* seconds ago, the router discards the retrieved LSA without acknowledging it. The MinLSArrival is equal to 1 second.

4. If the LSA instance in the router's link-state database was installed more than MinLSArrival seconds ago and the retrieved instance is more recent than the one in the link-state database, the router installs the retrieved instance into the link-state database and discards the existing one. The router then floods the retrieved instance of the LSA and schedules a delayed acknowledgment for it. If the age of the retrieved instance (which has just been installed into the router's link-state database) is equal to MaxAge, the router keeps it in the link-state database as long as it is necessary to finish all ongoing link-state database synchronizations (if there are any). After that, the LSA is discarded after all the pending acknowledgments that resulted from the flooding of it are received.

   When flooding the new LSA instance, the router does not typically send it back to the router from which it was received. The only exception is designated routers, which must flood the LSA instance back through the interface on which it was received. Because the destination IP address of the update PDU that carries the flooded LSA instance is multicast, the router that originally sent the LSA instance to the designated router receives it, too.

5. If the router determines that the LSA instance it has in its database is more recent than the retrieved one, it must send an update with the database instance back to the router that flooded the retrieved instance.

Router LSAs (Type 1)

Router LSAs describe the states of the router's links in a particular area. They are originated by all OSPF routers without exception. An OSPF router generates a separate router LSA for every area to which it is attached. For example, if a router is an ABR whose two interfaces are attached to two segments that reside in the OSPF backbone and one interface to a segment that resides in another area, the router will originate two LSAs—one for the backbone and one for the area. The first LSA will describe the router's two interfaces connected to the segments in the backbone, and the second LSA will describe the router's single interface connected to the segment in the regular area. The routers, all of whose interfaces are connected to segments residing in the same area, originate a single router LSA.

Router LSAs are flooded throughout only the area for which they are created.

The structure of router LSAs is shown in Figure 7.11. It comprises the LSA header (whose Link State Type field carries the value of 1), the LSA Flags and Number Of Links fields, and one or several link entries.

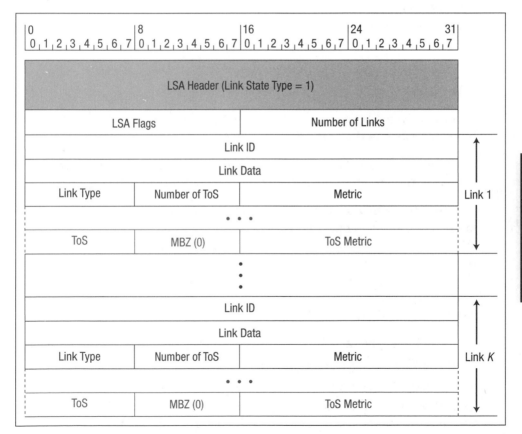

Figure 7.11   The structure of router LSAs (type 1).

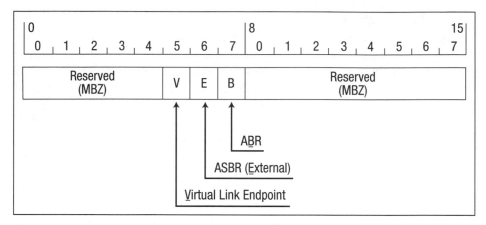

Figure 7.12   The structure of the LSA Flags field of the router LSA.

The 16-bit LSA Flags field has the structure shown in Figure 7.12. Only 3 bits out of 16 are defined; all other bits must be cleared at all times. The functions of these three defined bits are as follows:

- The V-bit, if set, denotes that the router has one or more virtual links established through the area for which the LSA was created.

- The E-bit, if set, denotes that the router is an ASBR.

- The B-bit, if set, denotes that the router is an ABR.

The 16-bit Number Of Links field carries the value equal to the number of router links described in the link entries.

Each link entry comprises five mandatory fields and up to four optional ToS fields. (These optional fields are shown with light contours in Figure 7.11.)

The first three fields—Link ID, Link Data, and Link Type—are closely interrelated. The interdependency between the values that these fields can accept is shown in Table 7.4. The first column shows the numeric value that the Link Type field can take, and the second provides the explanation of what link type the value actually signifies. Of these three fields, the Link Type, despite its placement in the link entry, actually defines the dependency. Hence, it makes sense to consider this field first.

The 8-bit Link Type field denotes the type of the router link. As Table 7.4 suggests, router links are of four different types.

The 32-bit Link ID field identifies the object to which the described link leads. This object may or may not be represented by another LSA. However, if it is represented by another LSA, the Link ID field carries the value of the Link State ID contained in the header of that LSA. (This facilitates the link-state lookup proce-

Table 7.4 Comparing the Link ID, Link Data, and Link Type fields.

Link Type	Link Type Description	Link ID	Link Data
1	Point-to-point link	OSPF ID of the router on the other end of the link	The MIB-II ifIndex value associated with the router's interface if the link is unnumbered; otherwise, the IP address of the interface
2	Connection to a transit network (broadcast or NBMA)	Designated router's IP address	The IP address of the interface
3	Connection to a stub network segment	Network prefix of the stub network segment	The subnet mask (not the network prefix length) of the network segment's network prefix
4	Virtual link	OSPF ID of the router on the other end of the link	The IP address of the interface through which the OSPF PDUs are sent to the router on the other end of the virtual link

dure that is invoked during the routing table building process by the procedure that implements Dijkstra's shortest-path algorithm.)

In most cases, the value of the 32-bit Link Data field helps resolve the IP address of the next-hop router in the routes created during the process of building the routing table.

The 8-bit Number Of ToS field denotes the number of optional ToS fields. The ToS fields are hardly used, which means that router LSAs do not usually have any optional ToS fields. Thus, the Number Of ToS field typically carries the value of 0. The ToS fields are supported to provide backward compatibility with the previous edition of the OSPF specification, RFC 1583.

The last mandatory field is the 16-bit Metric field, which carries the cost of the corresponding router link.

As mentioned in the beginning of this section, the router LSA represents the router vertex with outgoing edges in the OSPF topology model. Indeed, the router vertex is represented by the three LSA header fields that uniquely identify the LSA itself: Link State Type, Link State ID, and Advertising Router. The edges are encoded as link entries. The Metric field of the link entries represents the cost of the edge, and the Link ID field describes to which vertex the edge leads. The Link ID field contains either the Link State ID of another LSA (when the edge leads to another vertex) or the network prefix of a stub network (when the edge leads to a stub segment vertex).

Network LSAs (Type 2)

Network LSAs describe the routers connected to a transit broadcast or NBMA network segment. They are originated by the designated router for the network.

Network LSAs are flooded in the area in which the network resides and are stored in the routers' link-state databases for this area. The structure of network LSAs is shown in Figure 7.13.

The Link State Type field in the LSA header of the network LSA carries the value of 2.

The first field in the network LSA is the 32-bit Network Mask field, which actually carries the subnet mask (not the network prefix length) of the network prefix assigned on the segment. The network prefix is not explicitly contained in the network LSA; instead, as previously mentioned, the Link State ID in the LSA header of the network LSA carries the IP address of the designated router's interface attached to the network segment, thereby providing an unequivocal means to determine the actual network prefix assigned on the segment. (In other words, the network prefix is calculated by applying the value of the Network Mask field to the Link State ID; the length of the network prefix is equal to the number of set bits in the Network Mask field.)

Following the Network Mask field are the 32-bit Attached Router fields, the number of which is equal to the number of OSPF routers residing on the network

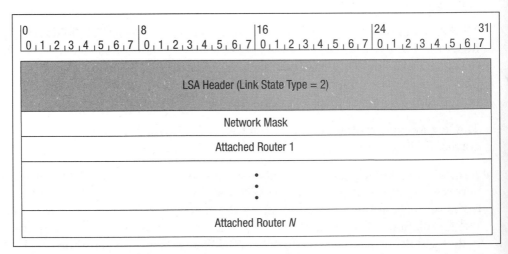

Figure 7.13   The structure of network LSAs (type 2).

segment, including the designated and backup designated routers. (To be exact, the number of Attached Router fields is equal to the number of OSPF routers with which the designated router is fully adjacent plus one, for the designated router itself. We'll consider the meaning of *fully adjacent* in the section "Establishing Adjacencies" later in this chapter.) Each Attached Router field carries the OSPF ID of the corresponding OSPF router.

Topologically, network LSAs correspond to the model that is used to represent the transit broadcast and NBMA network segments. The Link State ID and Network Mask fields represent identification for the network vertex; the Attached Router fields represent outgoing edges that point to the router vertices. Because the outgoing edges in the case of the network vertex have the cost of 0, network LSAs have no field that represents any sort of metric.

Summary LSAs (Types 3 and 4)

Summary LSAs describe the destinations that are located outside an area but inside the OSPF autonomous system. Type 3 summary LSAs describe interarea network prefixes, and type 4 summary LSAs describe ASBRs that are located outside the area. The LSAs of both types are originated by ABRs of the area. The ABRs flood the summary LSAs into the area only. Regardless of the type, each summary LSA describes precisely one destination.

NOTE: *Why type 4 summary LSAs are needed will become clear in the "Routing Table Calculation" section later in this chapter.*

To better understand how summary LSAs are generated, let's consider the example shown in Figure 7.14.

Let's begin with the summary LSAs that ABRs R1 and R2 inject into the OSPF backbone. From the perspective of ABR R1, the network prefixes in Areas 1 and 2 are located outside the OPSF backbone but in the areas to which it is attached. Likewise, ASBRs AR1 and AR3 are located outside the OSPF backbone but in the areas to which ABR R1 is attached. Hence, ABR R1 injects a number of type 3 LSAs for network prefixes inside Areas 1 and 2 and two type 4 LSAs for ASBRs AR1 and AR3.

In the "OSPF Operation Overview" section earlier in this chapter, it was mentioned that one of the primary purposes of dividing an OSPF autonomous system into areas was to decrease the routers' CPU utilization that results from running Dijkstra's shortest-path algorithm and the routing table lookup. The areas are supposed to have their IP addressing summarized with one or a few summary network prefixes. ABRs are the only routers that can legitimately perform such a summarization, which they do by originating type 3 summary LSAs.

7. Open Shortest Path First (OSPF) Protocol

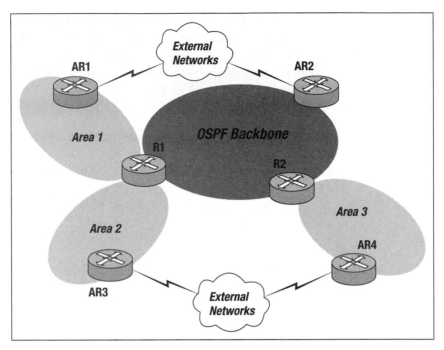

Figure 7.14   For each area to which the ABRs are attached, they generate summary LSAs
for the destinations that are located outside the area.

However, the summarization is not automatic. The area summary network prefixes, or *area ranges*, must be configured on each of the ABRs attached to the
area. Each of the ABRs hide all individual network prefixes that are matched by
any of the area summary network prefixes by originating type 3 LSAs for only the
area summary network prefixes. The ABR, however, doesn't originate a type 3
summary LSA for an area summary network prefix for which there are no routes
for the network prefixes that it matches. In addition, if the ABR has routes for
network prefixes of which none is matched by the configured area summary network prefixes, the ABR originates a type 3 summary LSA for each of these network prefixes.

Returning to Figure 7.14, suppose that ABR R1 has been configured for Area 1 with
two summary network prefixes—10.1.0.0/16 and 172.16.128.0/25. Also suppose that,
for Area 1, its routing table contains routes for network prefixes 10.255.1.1/32,
10.1.14.0/24, and 10.1.255.5/30. Therefore, ABR R1 will inject two type 3 summary
LSAs into the OSPF backbone—one for "unsummarized" network prefix 10.255.1.1/
32 and one for summary network prefix 10.1.0.0/16. Because it has no routes for
network prefixes that summary network prefix 172.16.128.0/25 can match, ABR R1
does not originate a type 3 summary LSA for it.

Suppose that, for Area 2, ABR R1 originates only one type 3 summary LSA—for network prefix 10.2.0.0/16. Therefore, in total, ABR R1 injects five summary LSAs—three of type 3 and two of type 4.

A similar process takes place on ABR R2, only it produces summary LSAs for Area 3 and ASBR AR4. Suppose ABR R2 injected exactly two summary LSAs into the backbone: one type 3 summary LSA for Area 3 summary network prefix 10.3.0.0/16, and one type 4 summary LSA for ASBR AR4. Hence, we have a total of seven summary LSAs: four type 3 summary LSAs for network prefixes in Areas 1, 2, and 3; and three type 4 summary LSAs for ASBRs AR1, AR2, and AR4.

Suppose that, for the OSPF backbone, ABRs R1 and R2 are configured with a single summary network prefix, 10.0.0.0/16 (the OSPF backbone is in Area 0, so the second octet is also 0), which matches all network prefixes that exist in the backbone. Thus, for Area 3, ABR R2 will originate one type 3 summary LSA for the backbone summary network prefix and one type 4 summary LSA for ASBR 3 located in the backbone. Because the destinations in Areas 1 and 2 are also located outside Area 3, ABR R2 must originate summary LSAs for them as well. The only network prefixes of Areas 1 and 2 that ABR R2 can possibly know of are the summary network prefixes produced from the type 3 summary LSAs originated by ABR R1. Hence, for each of these summary network prefixes (10.255.1.1/32, 10.1.0.0/16, and 10.2.0.0/16), ABR R2 will produce a type 3 summary LSA, which it will inject into Area 3. It will also originate new type 4 summary LSAs into Area 3 for ASBRs AR1 and AR2 that are known through ABR R1's type 4 summary LSAs.

A similar process takes place on ABR R1, but it happens twice in this case—once for Area 1 and once for Area 2. It's important to note that, in addition to originating type 3 summary LSAs for the backbone summary network prefix, ABR R1 originates type 3 summary LSAs into Area 2 for summary network prefixes of Area 1, and vice versa.

LSAs of both types have the same structure, which is shown in Figure 7.15.

The only difference between the types is found in the Link State Type field, which is equal to either 3 or 4, depending on the type.

The 32-bit Network Mask field is used only in type 3 LSAs, where it carries the subnet mask (not the network prefix length) of the summary network prefix (summary address). In the case of type 4 LSAs, this field must carry 0.

The 8-bit field must be zero (MBZ) field in Figure 7.15 is reserved and must carry 0.

The 24-bit Metric field carries the metric of the route for the destination that the summary LSA describes, which brings us to the question: How does the ABR originating the LSA produce the metric?

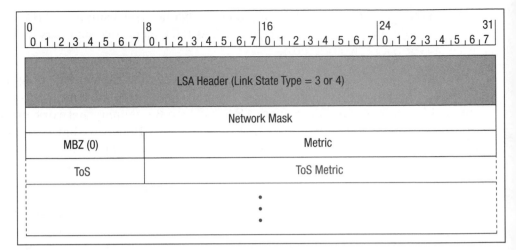

Figure 7.15   The structure of summary LSAs (types 3 and 4).

When an ABR originates a type 3 summary LSA for the configured summary net-work prefix, it first examines all its routes for the network prefixes matched by that summary network prefix. As we know, if no such routes exist, the summary LSA is not originated. However, if such routes do exist, the ABR sets the Metric field equal to the highest of the metrics of these routers.

NOTE: *This is opposite of what happens when the distance-vector protocols that we know—RIP, Internet Gateway Routing Protocol (IGRP), or EIGRP—advertise a summary network prefix. They use the smallest metric as opposed to the largest.*

If the ABR originates a type 3 summary LSA for a network prefix that is not matched by any of the configured summary network prefixes, it sets the Metric field equal to the metric of the route for which it has the network prefix.

But how does the ABR calculate the metrics for type 4 summary LSAs? As we know, the routing table contains routes for only network prefixes that are assigned on network segments, whereas type 4 summary LSAs advertise ASBRs (which are rout-ers and hence do not appear in the routing table). OSPF achieves this by perform-ing a little trick: making the router create auxiliary routing table entries for two types of routers—ABRs and ASBRs. The metrics of these routing table entries are used to produce the values for the Metric field in type 4 summary LSAs.

In the instance of Dijkstra's shortest-path algorithm running for an area, all sum-mary LSAs appear to be vertices similar to the ones that represent stub segments. To each of the stub vertices goes an edge from the ABR that injected the corre-sponding LSA into the area.

External and NSSA External LSAs (Types 5 and 7)

External LSAs describe destinations that are located outside the OSPF autonomous system. These LSAs are originated by the ASBRs and are flooded throughout the autonomous system, except for the stub areas and NSSAs.

The format of type 5 and 7 LSAs is shown in Figure 7.16.

Type 5 and 7 external LSAs are the subject of Chapter 8, so we'll consider them in more detail there.

Routing Table Calculation

As we know, LSAs describe the topological information of the OSPF routing domain. The routers then use this information to calculate the routing tables, which are used to forward network traffic towards its destination.

As we know from the "OSPF Operation Overview" section earlier in this chapter, each router has a separate link-state database for each area to which it is attached. Whenever the contents of the link-state database changes, the router runs Dijkstra's shortest-path algorithm to recalculate the OSPF routing table entries from the new contents of the link-state database. Dijkstra's shortest-path algorithm is executed for only the link-state database, which changed.

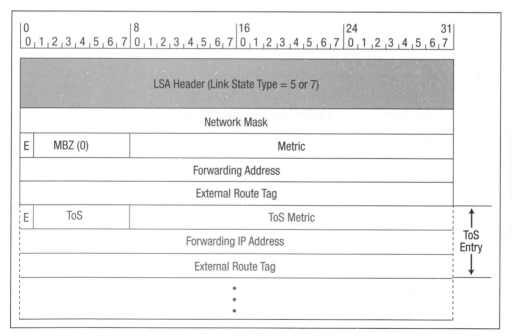

Figure 7.16 The structure of external network LSAs (types 5 and 7).

The following steps provide an overview of how a router calculates the routing table:

1. The router executes Dijkstra's shortest-path algorithm over the router and network LSAs contained in the link-state database whose contents have changed. The LSAs represent vertices; the link entries in the router LSAs and the Attached Router fields in the network LSAs represent edges. Unless the link entry is of type 3 (connection to a stub network), the router must check if the LSA to which the link entry points has a counter link entry pointing back to the link entry's LSA. If there is no counter link entry, the link entry is not used by Dijkstra's shortest path algorithm. For example, if a link entry in a router LSA is of type 2—a connection to a transit network—the Link Data field carries the IP address of the designated router. As we know, the IP address of the designated router is the Link State ID of the corresponding network LSA. Hence, the router should check if this network LSA contains the OSPF router ID of the router, which originated the router LSA. (The OSPF router ID is the Link State ID of the router LSA.)

NOTE: *This procedure prevents the routers from installing routes for the network prefixes of the links that are described in the outdated LSAs. For example, if some router disappears, it is possible that its router LSA stays in the link-state database of the other routers for some time. As we know, the routers will remove that LSA when its age reaches MaxAge; until then, however, the routers might try to use the LSA during the routing table recalculation process. To address this issue, the OSPF specification requires the routers to perform the described pruning procedure.*

The router produces intra-area routing table entries for all the network prefixes that are available within the area.

In addition, the router produces *router routing table entries* for all ABRs and ASBRs that reside in the area. These routing table entries are not used for forwarding traffic; they are used by only OSPF when creating inter-area routes as well as routes for the network prefixes that appear outside the OSPF routing domain (external routes).

If, during the process of building intra-area routes, the router encounters one or more virtual links set through the area, the router labels the area as transit.

NOTE: *The router itself does not have to be an end point of the virtual link to label the area as transit.*

2. The router then calculates inter-area routes from the summary LSAs of both types (3 and 4). ABRs calculate inter-area routes for only the OSPF backbone (Area 0).

When creating inter-area routes, the router must check if there is a router routing table entry (created in Step 1) for the ABR whose ID appears as the advertising router in the summary LSA. If no such entry exists, the inter-area route is not created.

For ASBRs, the routers create router routing table entries, which are not used for the forwarding traffic but are used internally by OSPF when creating external routes.

3. ABRs connected to transit areas must also check if there are any shorter routes through the transit areas for the destinations for which there are backbone inter-area and intra-area routes.

NOTE: *The ABRs, like all other routers, label areas as transit in Step 1. As mentioned, the router itself does not have to be an end point of the encountered virtual link to label the area as transit. Consequently, even if some ABR does not have any virtual links at all, it still must check for better routes through the area whose transit capability was conduced by a virtual link established by some of the other ABRs.*

---

4. Finally, the routers calculate routes for the external destinations from the type 5 external LSAs. When calculating external routes, the routers must check if they have router routing table entries for the ASBRs through which the external destinations are reachable. If they don't, the corresponding external route must not be created.

Notice that Dijkstra's shortest path algorithm is run only on Step 1 of the described procedure. Consequently, Step 1 is the most significant source of processing overhead associated with the recalculation of the OSPF part of the routing table. However, in Step 1, the router examines only router and network LSAs (type 1 and 2 LSAs) and ignores LSAs of other types. Hence, if a network change occurs that does not cause changes to the router and network LSAs, it is not necessary to run Step 1. To address this type of situation, the OSPF specification provides for so-called *incremental updates* of the routing table, whereby the router does not run Step 1 if a new summary, AS-external, or NSSA-external LSA arrives (type 3, 4, 5, and 7 LSAs). (There is a single case when a new summary LSA can cause an ABR attached to a transit area to run Step 1 as well.)

The described procedure is quite simplified compared to the actual routing table recalculation procedures as defined by the OSPF specification. Obviously, there are numerous nuances in the actual procedure that address all possible kinds of contingencies associated with invalid routing information that can still linger in the router's link-state database. To understand exactly all the checks and subroutines the routers must perform during the process of building the OSPF part of the routing table, please consult with the OSPF specification.

7. Open Shortest Path First (OSPF) Protocol

OSPF Adjacencies

OSPF adjacencies enforce OSPF topological models and serve as the paths for flooding LSAs.

Given the central role of adjacencies in the operation of OSPF, we need to get a rather thorough understanding of how adjacencies form. The next two sections are dedicated to this subject.

OSPF Interfaces

The interfaces on which OSPF operates are essential components in establishing adjacencies.

The OSPF specification defines a set of interface states and a number of events that make the interface transition from one state to another. The interface states define the PDUs that the router can receive and send over the interface. The interface's state together with the events causing the interface to transition from one state to another constitute the OSPF interface state machine, which is shown in Figure 7.17.

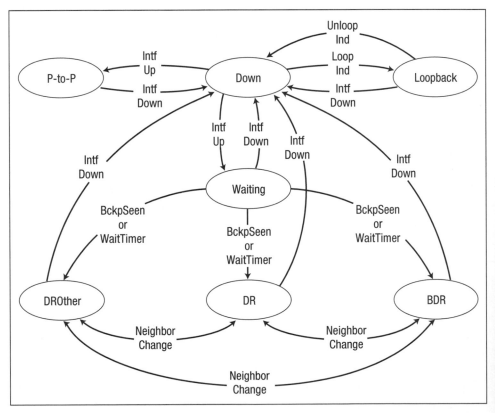

Figure 7.17   The OSPF interface state machine.

Every interface initializes in the *Down* state.

Depending on whether the network is broadcast or point-to-point, the interface can either transition to the *Point-to-Point* state (shown as P-to-P) or to the *Waiting* state. The event that causes the transition from the Down state to Waiting or Point-to-Point is *Interface#Up* (shown as Intf#Up); this event typically occurs when the interface is administratively enabled and/or when the link layer protocol indicates that the interface in functional.

From the Waiting state, the interface can transition into one of three states: *DR*, *BDR*, or *DROther*. The DR and BDR states denote that the router is the designated or backup designated router, respectively, for the segment to which the interface is attached. The DROther state indicates that the router is neither the designated nor backup designated router for the segment. The interface transitions from the Waiting state when one of two events occurs: *BackupSeen* (shown as BckpSeen) or *WaitTimer*. BackupSeen takes place when a router receives an OSPF hello carrying the ID of the designated or backup designated routers. The WaitTimer event occurs after the router fails to detect the existence of the designated and backup designated routers after waiting for a certain amount of time.

The transitions between DROther, DR, and BDR take place when the *NeighborChange* event occurs. The NeighborChange event is caused when the active designated or backup designated router disappears and when the priority of either designated or backup designated router changes to 0.

The *InterfaceDown* event (shown as IntfDown) always transitions the interface into the Down state, regardless of the interface's current state. The InterfaceDown event occurs as the result of an indication by the interface's link layer protocol of the interface's inoperability (the interface may have been physically disconnected from the medium) or following an administrative action whereby the interface is disabled.

NOTE: *The provided description of the events causing transitions among the states of the interface state machine is simplified. For a detailed description of the interface states and events, please refer to the OSPF specification (RFC 2328). The diagram in Figure 7.17 is exact; hence, you can refer to it when reading the OSPF specification.*

The shown interface state machine serves a very important role in the case of broadcast and fully meshed NBMA segments because it provides an unequivocal method of electing and maintaining the designated and backup designated routers for the segment. The description of the state machine and its visual representation shown in Figure 7.17 may not, however, be easily digestible from the human perspective. So, let's summarize what the interface state machine does once the designated and backup designated routers need to be elected. If multiple routers are connected to a segment on which no OSPF routers yet reside, the router with the highest OSPF priority becomes the designated router, and the router with the highest priority among the remaining routers becomes the backup designated router. If multiple routers have equal priorities and one of them must be elected the designated or backup designated router, the router whose interface connected to the segment has the IP address with the highest value becomes elected. If the designated router fails or if its priority is changed to 0, the backup designated router becomes the new designated router, and a new backup designated router is elected among the remaining routers. If a router whose priority is higher than that of the designated or backup designated router is connected to the segment, no re-election occurs.

Establishing Adjacencies

Upon detecting a neighbor available through an interface whose state is P-to-P, DROther, BDR, or DR, the router establishes an adjacency with the neighbor.

The OSPF specification defines a set of neighbor states and events that cause neighbors to transition from one state to another. Together, the states and events constitute the OSPF neighbor state machine, which is shown in Figure 7.18.

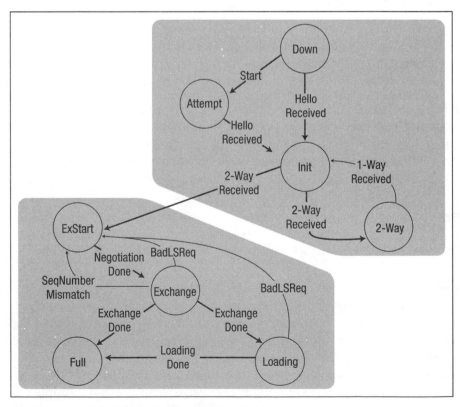

Figure 7.18   The OSPF neighbor state machine.

If during the database exchange process either router receives a database description PDU with 1) an unexpected sequence number, 2) the I-bit (init-bit) bit set, or 3) the value of the Options field different from that of the previously received database description PDUs, the state of the neighbor state machine is reset to the ExStart, and the routers start over the process of establishing adjacency. This event is called *SeqNumberMismatch*.

The last in the sequence of database description PDUs describing the router's entire link-state database must have the M-bit cleared. After both routers have transmitted database description PDUs with the M-bit cleared, the database exchange is completed and the neighbor state machine transitions to the Loading state.

In the Loading state, the routers request the most recent LSAs from each other using the link-state request PDUs in an effort to make their link-state databases identical. When a router receives a link-state request, it must reply back with one or several link-state updates carrying the requested LSAs. Each transmitted LSA must be acknowledged, just like during the reliable flooding procedure. Upon completion of this stage, the neighbor state machine transitions to the Full state, which denotes the full adjacency relationship between the routers.

The OSPF specification allows the routers to request missing and outdated LSAs and send updates carrying the most recent copies of LSAs during the database exchange process. Hence, by the time the database exchange process is completed, the Loading state may not be necessary because the routers may already have synchronized their link-state databases. In this case, the neighbor state machine transitions to the Full state, bypassing the Loading state, and the adjacency between the routers becomes Full.

If either router receives a request for an LSA that is not contained in the router's link-state database, the router's the neighbor state machine is reset to the ExStart state, and the router tries to reestablish adjacency with the neighbor that sent the request.

An example of how two routers synchronize their databases is shown in Figure 7.19.

Some events not shown in Figure 7.18 cause the neighbor state machine to transition to the Down state regardless of the current state. These events are *KillNeighbor, InactivityTimer,* and *LLDown*. The KillNeighbor event occurs when communication with the neighbor no longer becomes possible. The InactivityTimer event occurs when no hellos have been received from the neighbor for the last *RouterDeadInterval* seconds. (The RouterDeadInterval parameter is configurable on a per-interface basis.) The LLDown event occurs when the link layer module of the interface (the interface driver, essentially) reports that the interface is down. (Notice that these events bring the neighbor state machine down even after the state of full adjacency has been reached.)

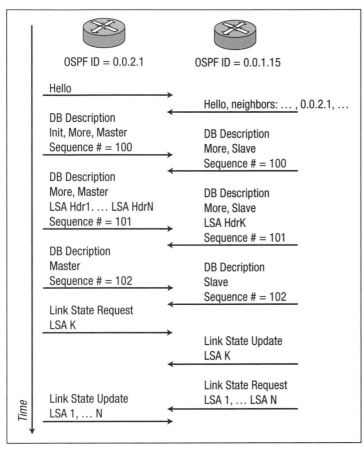

Figure 7.19   The process of link-state synchronization between two routers.

NOTE: *The provided description of the neighbor state machine is simplified. For a detailed description of the neighbor states and events causing transitions between these states, please refer to the OSPF specification. The diagram shown in Figure 7.18 is exact; hence, you can refer to it when reading the OSPF specification.*

OSPF PDU Formats

The following sections describe the formats of OSPF PDUs.

All OSPF PDUs consists of the uniform OSPF header and the PDU type-specific payload.

The structure of OSPF PDUs is shown in Figure 7.20.

The 8-bit Version field denotes the version of OSPF. It must carry a value of 2.

The 8-bit Type field denotes the type of the OSPF PDU. The possible types and the respective Type field values are shown in Table 7.5.

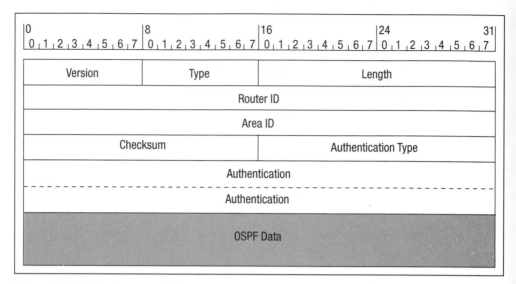

Figure 7.20   The format of OSPF PDUs.

Table 7.5   The types of OSPF PDUs and the corresponding values of the Type field.

Type	Description
1	OSPF Hello
2	Database Description
3	Link-State Request
4	Link-State Update
5	Link-State Acknowledgment

The 16-bit Length field carries the total length of the OSPF PDU measured in 8-bit octets.

The 32-bit Router ID field carries the OSPF ID of the router that sends the PDU.

The 32-bit Area ID field carries the ID of the area to which the PDU belongs. A PDU is considered to belong to an area if it traverses the segment residing within the area. The only exception is OSPF PDUs sent over virtual links. These PDUs always belong to the OSPF backbone regardless of which transit area they get delivered through.

The 16-bit Checksum field carries the standard IP checksum that covers all of the fields of the header, excluding the Checksum field itself, the 64-bit Authentication field, and the payload.

The 16-bit Authentication Type and 64-bit Authentication fields carry the values used in authenticating OSPF PDUs. (For details on OSPF authentication, please see OSPF specification RFC 2328.)

OSPF Hello PDUs

Figure 7.21 shows the format of OSPF hello PDUs.

The header of the OSPF hello carries the Type field equal to 1.

The 32-bit Network Mask field carries the 32-bit subnet mask (not the network prefix length) configured on the interface out of which the hello is sent.

The 16-bit Hello Interval field carries the number of seconds that the router waits between sending subsequent hellos.

The 8-bit Options field is identical to the Options field of the LSA header. The values that the Options field can accept are shown in Table 7.1 earlier in this chapter.

The 8-bit Router Priority field carries the value of the OSPF router priority configured on the interface out of which the hello is sent. The OSPF router priority is used during the designated and backup designated router election process on broadcast transit segments.

The 32-bit DeadInterval field specifies the maximum number of seconds that the neighbors must wait before declaring the router dead if it does not send regular OSPF hellos.

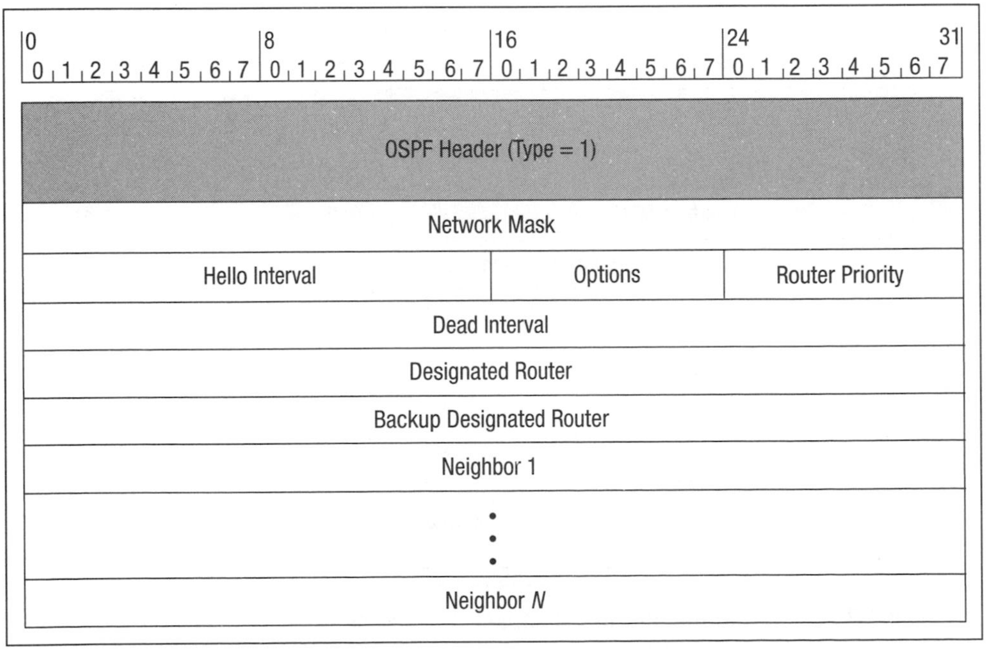

Figure 7.21   The format of OSPF hello PDUs.

The 32-bit Designated Router and Backup Designated Router fields carry the OSPF IDs of the designated and backup designated routers, respectively. If any of these routers does not exist, the corresponding field must be set to 0 (0.0.0.0).

The set of 32-bit Neighbor fields carries the OSPF IDs of the routers from which the OSPF hellos have been received within the last Dead#Interval seconds.

OSPF Database Description PDUs

The format of OSPF database description PDUs is shown in Figure 7.22.

The OSPF header of the database description PDU carries the Type field equal to 2.

The 16-bit Interface MTU field carries the maximum transmission unit (MTU) size of the interface out of which the database description PDU is sent.

The 8-bit Options field is identical to the Options fields of the LSA header. The values the Options field can take are shown in Table 7.1 earlier in the chapter.

The 8-bit Flags field is used during the database synchronization process. It has the structure shown in Figure 7.23.

The I-bit (or Init-bit), if set, indicates that this is the first in the sequence database description PDU.

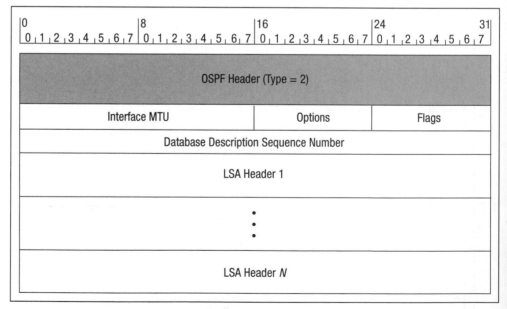

Figure 7.22   The format of OSPF database description PDUs.

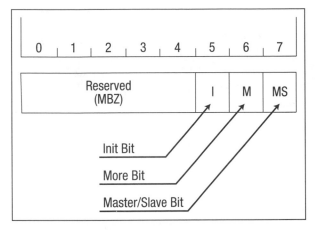

Figure 7.23   The format of the Flags field of the OSPF database description PDU.

The M-bit (or More-bit), if set, indicates that the router sending this database description PDU intends to send more. A cleared M-bit indicates that the router has transmitted all database description PDUs necessary to describe its entire link-state database.

The MS-bit (or Master/Slave-bit), if set, indicates that the router sending the database description PDU is the master; likewise, if this bit is cleared, it indicates that the router is the slave. The router with the higher OSPF router ID becomes the master; the other router becomes the slave.

The 32-bit Database Description Sequence Number field is used during the database exchange to preserve the order of the exchanged database description PDUs. The master generates the initial sequence number, which it places into its first database description PDU; after that, the master increases the sequence numbers by one in the subsequent database description PDUs that it sends. Upon receipt of the master's database description PDU, the slave must reply back with its own database description PDU whose sequence number is equal to that of the master's PDU. (In other words, only the master is concerned with generating the sequence numbers.)

Finally, the set of LSA Header fields carries the headers of the LSAs being stored in the router's link-state database. As we know, the LSA headers provide sufficient information to uniquely identify the LSA and to determine which of its instances is more recent.

OSPF Link-State Request PDUs

The structure of OSPF link-state request PDUs is shown in Figure 7.24.

The OSPF header of the link-state request carries the Type field equal to 3.

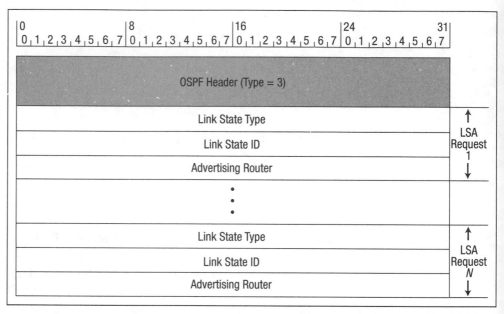

Figure 7.24   The format of OSPF link-state request PDUs.

The link-state request contains sets of three fields, which as we know, uniquely identify the LSA: Link State Type, Link State ID, and Advertising Router. As the router already knows which of its copies of LSAs are outdated, it does not have to specify the complete LSA headers in its requests.

OSPF Link-State Updates

The structure of link-state update PDUs is shown in Figure 7.25.

The OSPF header of the link-state update carries the Type field equal to 4.

The 32-bit Number Of LSAs field carries the number of LSAs that the update contains.

The set of LSA fields are actually the complete LSAs that the update carries.

OSPF Link-State Acknowledgment PDU

The structure of OSPF link-state acknowledgment PDUs is shown in Figure 7.26.

The OSPF header of the link-state acknowledgment carries the Type field equal to 5.

The set of LSA Header fields carry the actual headers of the LSAs being acknowledged.

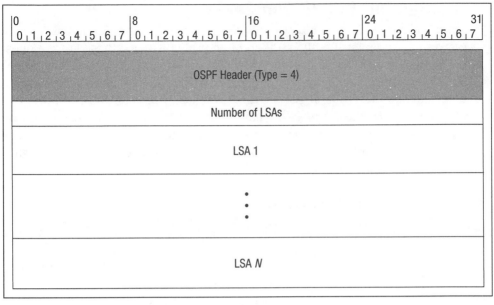

Figure 7.25 The format of OSPF link-state update PDUs.

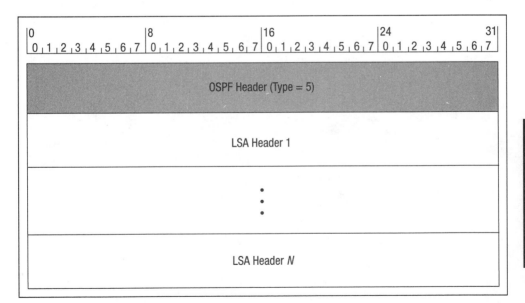

Figure 7.26 The format of OSPF link-state acknowledgment PDUs.

Architectural OSPF Constants

Some primary OSPF architectural constants are shown in Table 7.6. The shown constants are by far not all OSPF architectural constants; these are the ones that we came across in the above overview of the protocol. I'm mentioning these constants at all because, in my experience, I noticed that some people tend to think of these constants as tunable parameters, which they are not. Furthermore, I would like to emphasize the *architectural* nature of these constants—this essentially means that these constants have been theoretically and practically proven to produce the desired results and that any deviation from these constants would with high probability cause instable and/or inefficient OSPF operation.

Table 7.6   Architectural OSPF constants.

Constant	Value	Description
LSRefreshTime	30 min.	The maximum time between subsequent originations of the same LSA
MinLSInterval	5 sec.	The minimum time between subsequent originations of the same LSA
MinLSArrival	1 sec.	The minimum time that must elapse between receptions of instances of the same LSA during flooding
MaxAge	1 hr.	The maximum value that the age of the LSA can reach

Immediate Solutions

Performing Basic OSPF Configuration—Single Area

Because OSPF, by the conceptual framework it's based upon, is radically different from the distance-vector protocols such as RIP, IGRP, and EIGRP, its configuration is also different from their configurations.

We'll begin our tour through the configuration and operation of OSPF by examining how to configure OSPF for a single area.

The following guidelines should be used to perform a basic configuration of OSPF for a single area:

1. Create an OSPF ID by enabling a loopback interface and assigning it an IP address.

NOTE: *This step is optional, although very desirable. Unless your router runs IOS version 12.0 (which supports the **router-id** command, available under **router ospf** configuration, which we'll discuss later), the OSPF process looks at the IP addresses of the active interfaces and chooses the one with the highest value as the OSPF ID. If the interfaces on which this IP address is assigned later go down, the OSPF process uses the same procedure to choose the new ID among the IP addresses of the remaining active interfaces. Changing the router's OSPF ID is very undesirable, because it leads to the regeneration of all the LSAs that the router originates, which, in turn, introduces extra instability in the network.*

If, however, at least one loopback interface has an IP address assigned, the OSPF process won't consider the IP addresses of other active interfaces. It will, however, still choose the IP address with the highest value among the IP addresses of all loopback interfaces.

The loopback interface never goes down (unless administratively removed), so the OSPF process will never need to switch its OSPF ID.

If this step is performed after an OSPF configuration has already been entered, the OSPF process won't switch over its ID to the IP address of the loopback interface. To force it to switch over the ID, either the OSPF process must be restarted (by removing and then re-entering the OSPF configuration), or the interface whose IP address is used as the OSPF ID must be temporarily brought down and then back up.

---

2. Using the command **router ospf** *<process ID>*, create an OSPF process on the router. The parameter *<process ID>* is a number in the range 1 through 65535. Unlike IGRP and EIGRP, OSPF does not require this number to be identical on all routers in the autonomous system. This number merely allows multiple OSPF processes to be created on the same router.

TIP: For consistency, it makes sense to keep the <process ID> parameter the same on all routers in the autonomous system (or at least in the same area, in which case the process ID can coincide with the area ID).

3. Using the command **network** *<IP address> <wildcard mask>* **area 0** under **router ospf** configuration, enable processing of OSPF routing updates on the appropriate interfaces. The purpose of the pair of parameters *<IP address>* and *<wildcard mask>* is to specify the interfaces on which the OSPF process must run. Both parameters are written in dotted decimal notation.

   The OSPF process will run only on the interfaces whose IP addresses are matched by the *<IP address> <wildcard mask>* parameters. The cleared bits of the *<wildcard mask>* parameter denote the bits in the interface's IP address and the *<IP address>* parameter that must be compared. These bits, as we know, are called significant bits. The match occurs only if every significant bit of the IP address coincides with the significant bit of the *<IP address>* parameter at the same position.

   The meaning of the *<wildcard mask>* parameter is very similar to that of the parameter of the same name used in the access lists. The *<wildcard mask>* parameter of the OSPF **network** command does not have to be contiguous, just as the *<wildcard mask>* parameter used in the access lists doesn't, either.

Let's examine how the routers in the network shown in Figure 7.27 should be configured for single-area OSPF routing using the described guidelines. Although this network is very similar to the one that we used in basic EIGRP configuration, they do differ. Notice segments 1 and 6, whose callouts are circled with a dashed line. The length of the network prefix of segment 1 is 23, which is smaller than the length of classful network prefix 192.168.2.0/24. Segment 6 makes the network discontiguous from the classful perspective, because its network prefix (172.16.0.8/32) separates network prefix 10.0.8.0/24 of segment 8 from the other network prefixes belonging to the same classful network prefix—10.0.0.0/8. Sure enough, these two circumstances should not be obstacles for a true classless routing protocol. However, semi-true classless EIGRP stumbles at them, especially on the first one (unless you're using the new version of the **network** command and the **no auto-summary** command).

In addition, router R5 and segment 7 were added, making router R5 become R6 and segment 7 become 8.

Listings 7.1 through 7.6 show the configuration of all six routers. The shaded lines in some router configurations correspond to the circled callouts in Figure 7.27.

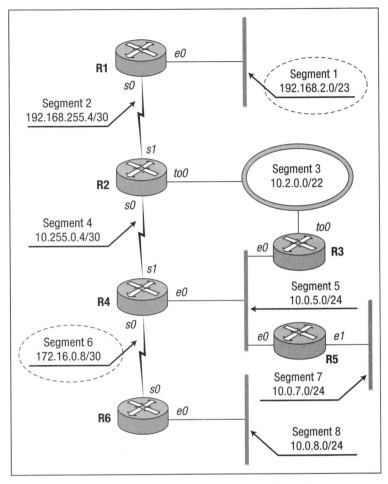

Figure 7.27 The routers in the network are configured for OSPF. The whole network lies in a single OSPF area.

Listing 7.1 Router R1's configuration.

```
interface Ethernet0
 ip address 192.168.2.1 255.255.254.0

interface Serial0
 ip address 192.168.255.5 255.255.255.252

router ospf 10
 network 192.0.0.0 0.255.255.255 area 0

ip classless
```

Listing 7.2   Router R2's configuration.

```
interface Loopback0
 ip address 10.0.0.2 255.255.255.255

interface Serial0
 ip address 10.255.0.5 255.255.255.252

interface Serial1
 ip address 192.168.255.6 255.255.255.252

interface TokenRing0
 ip address 10.2.0.1 255.255.252.0
 ring-speed 16

router ospf 1
 network 10.0.0.2 0.0.0.0 area 0
 network 10.2.0.1 0.0.0.0 area 0
 network 10.255.0.5 0.0.0.0 area 0
 network 192.168.255.6 0.0.0.0 area 0

ip classless
```

Listing 7.3   Router R3's configuration.

```
interface Loopback0
 ip address 10.0.0.3 255.255.255.255

interface Ethernet0
 ip address 10.0.5.1 255.255.255.0

interface TokenRing0
 ip address 10.2.0.1 255.255.252.0
 ring-speed 16

router ospf 1
 network 10.0.0.0 0.255.255.255 area 0

ip classless
```

Listing 7.4   Router R4's configuration.

```
interface Loopback0
 ip address 10.0.0.4 255.255.255.255

interface Ethernet0
 ip address 10.0.5.2 255.255.255.0
```

```
interface Serial0
  ip address 172.16.0.9 255.255.255.252

interface Serial1
  ip address 10.255.0.6 255.255.255.252

router ospf 1
  network 10.0.0.0 0.255.255.255 area 0
  network 172.16.0.0 0.0.255.255 area 0

ip classless
```

Listing 7.5   Router R5's configuration.

```
interface Loopback0
  ip address 10.0.0.5 255.255.255.255

interface Ethernet0
  ip address 10.0.5.3 255.255.255.0

interface Ethernet1
  ip address 10.0.7.1 255.255.255.0

router ospf 1
  network 10.0.0.0 0.255.255.255 area 0

ip classless
```

Listing 7.6   Router R6's configuration.

```
interface Loopback0
  ip address 10.0.0.6 255.255.255.255

interface Ethernet0
  ip address 10.0.8.1 255.255.255.0

interface Serial0
  ip address 172.16.0.10 255.255.255.252

router ospf 1
  network 0.0.0.0 255.255.255.255 area 0

ip classless
```

Before we discuss individual features of the network topology and router configurations, let's also see the routing table of router R3 (Listing 7.7). (Notice that OSPF routes begin with the letter O.)

Listing 7.7   The output of the show ip route command issued on router R3.

```
R3#show ip route
...
     10.0.0.0/8 is variably subnetted, 10 subnets, 4 masks
O       10.0.8.0/24 [110/84] via 10.0.5.2, 00:00:09, Ethernet0
O       10.0.0.2/32 [110/7] via 10.2.0.1, 00:00:09, TokenRing0
C       10.2.0.0/22 is directly connected, TokenRing0
C       10.0.0.3/32 is directly connected, Loopback0
O       10.0.0.6/32 [110/75] via 10.0.5.2, 00:00:09, Ethernet0
O       10.0.7.0/24 [110/20] via 10.0.5.3, 00:00:09, Ethernet0
O       10.0.0.4/32 [110/11] via 10.0.5.2, 00:00:09, Ethernet0
O       10.0.0.5/32 [110/11] via 10.0.5.3, 00:00:09, Ethernet0
C       10.0.5.0/24 is directly connected, Ethernet0
O       10.255.0.4/30 [110/70] via 10.2.0.1, 00:00:10, TokenRing0
     192.168.255.0/30 is subnetted, 1 subnets
O       192.168.255.4 [110/70] via 10.2.0.1, 00:00:10, TokenRing0
     172.16.0.0/30 is subnetted, 1 subnets
O       172.16.0.8 [110/74] via 10.0.5.2, 00:00:12, Ethernet0
O    192.168.2.0/23 [110/80] via 10.2.0.1, 00:00:12, TokenRing0
```

Several interesting observations can be made with regard to the router configurations and operation of OSPF in this network:

- Although the length of segment 1's network prefix is shorter than that of a similar classful network prefix, OSPF operates on router R1's interface connected to the segment and properly conveys the addressing information. Evidence of this is seen in Listing 7.7, in which the shaded line at the bottom shows the route for network prefix 192.168.2.0/23.

- Although segment 6 makes "classful" network prefix 10.0.0.0/8 noncontiguous, this does not affect routing in the network. Evidence of the correct routing again can be seen in Listing 7.7, in which the first shaded line shows the route for network prefix 10.0.8.0/24, which is behind segment 6.

- Another piece of evidence of OSPF's totally classful behavior is the presence of routes for "subnets" of classful network prefixes 172.16.0.0/16 and 192.168.255.0/24 in the routing table of router R3, none of whose interfaces is addressed within these classful network prefixes. These routes are shown as italicized lines at the bottom of Listing 7.7. This essentially means that OSPF, as a true classless routing protocol, does not perform any kind of automatic summarization.

NOTE: *The classful nature of the term "subnet" makes the term itself rather inappropriate in OSPF-related subjects. Notice, that the "subnetted" network prefixes in Listing 7.7 do not have typical classful network prefix lengths. For example, the line "172.16.0.0/30 is subnetted, 1 subnets" does not refer to 172.16.0.0/16.*

Another set of observations can be made with regard to specific oddities in the shown router configurations:

- The router configurations feature different methods of assigning interfaces into the OSPF process. For example, router R6's configuration uses the command **network 0.0.0.0 255.255.255.255 area 0**, which matches any IP address, thereby effectively enabling OSPF on every active interface that was assigned an IP address. On the contrary, router R3's configuration uses **network** commands, which specify exactly on which interfaces OSPF must run by making all bits of the *<IP address>* parameter significant.

- Different process IDs on router R1 and the rest of the routers do not prevent the routers from establishing OSPF routing in the network. The OSPF process IDs are not communicated among the routers.

Although these inconsistencies do not cause any problems in the example network, they should be avoided in production networks because they increase the administrative overhead associated with network maintenance. A single strategy should be developed for deciding what OSPF process IDs should be used and, even more importantly, for assigning individual interfaces into the OSPF process on the routers.

Using the Command **router-id** to Change the OSPF Router ID

Beginning with version 12.0, Cisco IOS provides a neat method for assigning an OSPF ID that doesn't suffer the restrictions of IP addressing and the inconveniences of creating a loopback interface and then assigning it the IP address equal to the desirable OSPF ID. The new method consists of using the command **router-id** *<OSPF ID>*, which is available under **router ospf** configuration. The *<OSPF ID>* parameter signifies the desired OSPF router ID, which must be formatted in dotted-decimal notation. The parameter is not subject to IP addressing restrictions, however. Every octet of the parameter can take any integer value in the range 0 through 255. The only exception is the value **0.0.0.0**, which, if used, actually removes any previously assigned OSPF ID and forces the OSPF process to resort to the old method of choosing an OSPF ID.

This old method is still available, which means that, if you upgrade IOS on the routers to version 12.0, the existing configurations will work as expected. However, if the **router-id** command is used, it supersedes the old method.

The **router-id** command, if used after the router became adjacent with any other routers, won't take effect unless you reload the router (or remove and then re-enter the **ospf** configuration) or use another new command, which was made available in IOS version 12.0: **clear ip ospf** [<*OSPF process-ID*>] **process**. The optional parameter <*OSPF process ID*> allows you to specify the OSPF process ID, in case you run multiple OSPF processes on a single router. If omitted, the command restarts all of the OSPF processes that are currently running on the router.

After you enter the **clear ip ospf process** command, the router will not restart the OSPF process(es) immediately; instead, it will prompt you if you really want to restart the processes. The router restarts the process(es) only if you type in "yes."

There is a difference between reloading the router (or removing and then re-entering the OSPF configuration) and using the **clear ip ospf process** command. The **clear ip ospf process** command is much more graceful, because it first flushes the LSA that the router originates from the OSPF routing domain and only then restarts the routing process. Flushing the LSAs is done by prematurely aging them.

NOTE: Oddly enough, the current release of the Cisco documentation doesn't mention either the **router-id** or **clear ip ospf process** command.

Understanding the **show ip ospf interface** Command

The **show ip ospf interface** command shows the interfaces on which OSPF operates. Listing 7.8. shows an example of this command entered on router R4.

Listing 7.8   The output of the show ip ospf interface command entered on router R4.

```
R4#show ip ospf interface
Ethernet0 is up, line protocol is up
  Internet Address 10.0.5.2/24, Area 0
  Process ID 1, Router ID 10.0.0.4, Network Type BROADCAST, Cost: 10
  Transmit Delay is 1 sec, State DR, Priority 1
  Designated Router (ID) 10.0.0.4, Interface address 10.0.5.2
  Backup Designated router (ID) 10.0.0.3, Interface address 10.0.5.1
  Timer intervals configured, Hello 10, Dead 40, Wait 40, Retransmit 5
    Hello due in 00:00:07
  Neighbor Count is 2, Adjacent neighbor count is 2
    Adjacent with neighbor 10.0.0.5
    Adjacent with neighbor 10.0.0.3  (Backup Designated Router)
  Suppress hello for 0 neighbor(s)
Loopback0 is up, line protocol is up
  Internet Address 10.0.0.4/32, Area 0
  Process ID 1, Router ID 10.0.0.4, Network Type LOOPBACK, Cost: 1
```

```
  Loopback interface is treated as a stub Host
Serial0 is up, line protocol is up
  Internet Address 172.16.0.9/30, Area 0
  Process ID 1, Router ID 10.0.0.4, Network Type POINT_TO_POINT, Cost: 64
  Transmit Delay is 1 sec, State POINT_TO_POINT,
  Timer intervals configured, Hello 10, Dead 40, Wait 40, Retransmit 5
    Hello due in 00:00:05
  Neighbor Count is 1, Adjacent neighbor count is 1
    Adjacent with neighbor 10.0.0.6
  Suppress hello for 0 neighbor(s)
Serial1 is up, line protocol is up
  Internet Address 10.255.0.6/30, Area 0
  Process ID 1, Router ID 10.0.0.4, Network Type POINT_TO_POINT, Cost: 64
  Transmit Delay is 1 sec, State POINT_TO_POINT,
  Timer intervals configured, Hello 10, Dead 40, Wait 40, Retransmit 5
    Hello due in 00:00:04
  Neighbor Count is 1, Adjacent neighbor count is 1
    Adjacent with neighbor 10.0.0.2
  Suppress hello for 0 neighbor(s)
```

This command typically produces output that is rather long; luckily, it's fairly self-explanatory. It shows parameters associated with the interface that are essential from the perspective of the OSPF operation, such as the hello interval and the RouterDeadInterval (shown as "Dead") of the interface. It also shows the IP address of the interface, to which area the interface is attached, how many OSPF neighbors are available through the interface, and so on.

Understanding the **show ip ospf neighbor** Command

The **show ip ospf neighbor** command shows the OSPF neighbors that the router knows about.

Listings 7.9 and 7.10 show the output of this command entered on routers R4 and R3, respectively. The first column, Neighbor ID, shows the OSPF ID of the neighbor, and the next column, Pri, shows the priority of the neighbor. The State column shows the neighbor state followed by a slash and the state of the neighbor's corresponding interface. The neighbor states correspond to those shown in the neighbor state machine depicted in Figure 7.18. On broadcast networks and NBMA networks configured as broadcast networks, the interface states can be either DR, BDR, or DROther, each of which corresponds to the states of the interface state machine with the same names (Figure 7.17). On all other types of networks, the neighbor's interface state is not shown (indicated by the dash sign). The Dead Time column shows the time elapsed since a hello was last seen from the neighbor. The Address column shows the IP address of the neighbor's interface attached to the segment. The last column, Interface, shows the router's own interface through which the neighbor is accessible.

Listing 7.9   The output of the show ip ospf neighbor command entered on router R4.

```
R4#show ip ospf neighbor

Neighbor ID     Pri   State          Dead Time   Address        Interface
10.0.0.5          1   FULL/DROTHER   00:00:37    10.0.5.3       Ethernet0
10.0.0.3          1   FULL/BDR       00:00:38    10.0.5.1       Ethernet0
10.0.0.6          1   FULL/  -       00:00:30    172.16.0.10    Serial0
10.0.0.2          1   FULL/  -       00:00:32    10.255.0.5     Serial1
```

Listing 7.10   The output of the show ip ospf neighbor command entered on router R3.

```
R3#show ip ospf neighbor

Neighbor ID     Pri   State          Dead Time   Address        Interface
10.0.0.5          1   FULL/DROTHER   00:00:30    10.0.5.3       Ethernet0
10.0.0.4          1   FULL/DR        00:00:39    10.0.5.2       Ethernet0
10.0.0.2          1   FULL/BDR       00:00:35    10.2.0.1       TokenRing0
```

Displaying the OSPF Link-State Database

Enter the **show ip ospf database** command without parameters to see the contents of all the router's link-state databases.

The output of this command entered on router R3 is shown in Listing 7.11.

Listing 7.11   The output of the show ip ospf database command on router R3.

```
R3#show ip ospf database

        OSPF Router with ID (10.0.0.3) (Process ID 1)

            Router Link States (Area 0)

Link ID         ADV Router      Age      Seq#        Checksum Link count
10.0.0.2        10.0.0.2        280      0x80000005 0x86A5    6
10.0.0.3        10.0.0.3        279      0x80000005 0xB7E3    3
10.0.0.4        10.0.0.4        305      0x8000000A 0xA522    6
10.0.0.5        10.0.0.5        173      0x80000003 0xD1E9    3
10.0.0.6        10.0.0.6        311      0x80000002 0x419E    4
192.168.255.5   192.168.255.5   323      0x80000002 0x8C55    2
```

```
        Net Link States (Area 0)

Link ID          ADV Router      Age      Seq#        Checksum
10.0.5.2         10.0.0.4        173      0x80000002 0x5596
10.2.0.2         10.0.0.3        280      0x80000001 0x64A4
```

The output of the command is divided into several parts. Each part corresponds to a single link-state database, which the router has; the parts showing the link-state databases with lower numbers appear first. Each part, in turn, consists of several sections, with each showing the LSAs of a single type. The sections corresponding to the LSAs with a lower type number appear first. For example, the section that describes router LSAs (type 1) appear first and is followed by the section describing network LSAs (type 2), and so on.

The command does not show the details of the LSAs; instead, it shows the most important fields of LSA headers—the Link State ID (the first column), the Advertising Router (the second column), the LSA age (the third column), the LSA sequence number (the fourth column), and the Link State Checksum (the fifth column). The sixth column, which is present in router LSAs, only shows the number of links that the LSA describes.

To see the details of LSAs, you should use the command **show ip ospf database** *<LSA Type>* [*<Link State ID>*]. The *<Link State type>* parameter specifies the desired link state type. The values it can take are **router**, **network**, **summary**, **asbr-summary**, **external**, and **nssa-external**, each of which corresponds to the respective link state type. The optional *<Link State ID>* parameter specifies the Link State ID of the LSA whose details are to be examined. If the last parameter is omitted, the router displays all LSAs of the specified type contained in all link-state databases.

Listing 7.12 is an example of the output of the **show ip ospf database router 10.0.0.4** command entered on router R3.

Listing 7.12   The output of the show ip ospf database router 10.0.0.4 command entered on router R3.

```
R3#show ip ospf database router 10.0.0.4

       OSPF Router with ID (10.0.0.3) (Process ID 1)

            Router Link States (Area 0)

  LS age: 428
  Options: (No TOS-capability, DC)
  LS Type: Router Links
  Link State ID: 10.0.0.4
```

```
Advertising Router: 10.0.0.4
LS Seq Number: 8000000A
Checksum: 0xA522
Length: 96
 Number of Links: 6

  Link connected to: another Router (point-to-point)
   (Link ID) Neighboring Router ID: 10.0.0.6
   (Link Data) Router Interface address: 172.16.0.9
    Number of TOS metrics: 0
     TOS 0 Metrics: 64

  Link connected to: a Stub Network
   (Link ID) Network/subnet number: 172.16.0.8
   (Link Data) Network Mask: 255.255.255.252
    Number of TOS metrics: 0
     TOS 0 Metrics: 64

...
  Link connected to: a Transit Network
   (Link ID) Designated Router address: 10.0.5.2
   (Link Data) Router Interface address: 10.0.5.2
    Number of TOS metrics: 0
     TOS 0 Metrics: 10
```

Although this listing appears to be long, it can be very useful because its content corresponds exactly to the structure of the examined LSA type. For example, the displayed LSA is of the router LSA type, so it consists of the header followed by the descriptions of the router links. The output shows the links of three types: point-to-point, stub network, and transit network.

Listing 7.13 shows how the command displays the content of a network LSA.

Listing 7.13   The output of the show ip ospf database network 10.2.0.2 command entered on router R3.

```
R3#show ip ospf database network 10.2.0.2

        OSPF Router with ID (10.0.0.3) (Process ID 1)

                Net Link States (Area 0)

  Routing Bit Set on this LSA
  LS age: 469
  Options: (No TOS-capability, DC)
  LS Type: Network Links
  Link State ID: 10.2.0.2 (address of Designated Router)
  Advertising Router: 10.0.0.3
```

```
LS Seq Number: 80000001
Checksum: 0x64A4
Length: 32
Network Mask: /22
      Attached Router: 10.0.0.3
      Attached Router: 10.0.0.2
```

As we might expect, the LSA consists of the header and a list of routers attached to the described transit network.

We'll see LSAs of the other types in the output of the **show ip ospf database** command as we progress through this and chapter and Chapters 8 and 9.

It was mentioned in the first section of "Immediate Solutions" that changing the OSPF ID is a bad idea. Let's see now just how bad it is by examining the contents of the link-state database after we change the OSPF router ID on router R1. However, we won't use the **clear ip ospf process** command, because we know that the OSPF process would prematurely age the old LSAs before changing the OSPF ID. Instead, we'll remove the OSPF process on router R1 by means of the **no router ospf 10** command and then re-enter the configuration, adding the **router-id 0.0.0.1** command.

If, after we've performed the described steps, we display the OSPF database on router R3, we'll see the following results:

```
R3#show ip ospf database
...
Link ID         ADV Router      Age      Seq#        Checksum Link count
0.0.0.1         0.0.0.1         27       0x80000002 0x4DEA    3
...
192.168.255.5   192.168.255.5   586      0x80000002 0xD50     3
...
```

Pay attention to the second shaded line because it describes the LSA that router R1 used to originate when its OSPF ID was equal to the IP address of the router's Serial0 interface. Right now, router R1's OSPF ID is equal to 0.0.0.1; hence, all the LSAs it originates must reference this number as the advertising router ID. Router R1 can originate only one LSA: its own router LSA, which is described by the first shaded line in the output.

Having examined this output, we can conclude only that the old LSA still lingers in the routers' link-state databases. Eventually, the routers will age it out. Until then, however, the LSA will sit in their memories. Whereas the presence of this LSA does not create a serious problem (because the routers won't use this LSA in calculating the routes), the LSA still occupies some space in each router's memory, and it slows the router down when it performs link-state database lookup. Hence, we must avoid restarting the router or removing and then re-entering its OSPF configuration as a method of changing the router's OSPF ID because this procedure tends to artificially introduce "dead" LSAs.

Finally, if we try to examine the contents of the "dead" LSA in more detail by using the **show ip ospf database router** command, we'll see the following output:

```
R3#show ip ospf database router 192.168.255.5
...
 Adv Router is not-reachable
  LS age: 659
  Options: (No TOS-capability, DC)
  LS Type: Router Links
  Link State ID: 192.168.255.5
  Advertising Router: 192.168.255.5
  LS Seq Number: 80000002
  Checksum: 0xD50
  Length: 60
   Number of Links: 3
...
```

The shaded line indicates that the router that originates the LSA is not reachable. The router comes to this conclusion by noticing that none of the LSAs pointed to by the links referenced in the "dead" LSA has any links pointing back to the "dead" LSA.

Reloading the router or removing and re-entering the OSPF configuration such that the OSPF ID remains the same won't create the above problem. However, this may not be so obvious at first glance. Once the OSPF process starts on the router, the router will create the router LSA with the same Link State ID, advertising router IDs, and Link State Type as its old router LSA. (Essentially, the two LSAs are instances of the same LSA.) However, the sequence number of the new LSA is going to be equal to InitialSequenceNumber, which is the smallest possible sequence number. At best, the sequence number of the old LSA is also equal to InitialSequenceNumber; however, it's more likely that it has a higher value. In accordance with the rules for comparing LSA instances, the instance with the higher sequence number is considered more recent, which essentially means that the new LSA is going to look "older" than the old LSA to the rest of the routers in the network. In fact, the new LSA is going to look older than the old LSA to even the router itself after it completes the database exchange processes in the course of bringing up adjacencies with the eligible neighbors. So, what's the router going to do?

The answer to this question is simple however. The router is going to install its own old LSA into the link-state database and discard the new one. Then the router will check if the states of the actual links are in agreement with the link states as described in the LSA. If they are, then there is no problem—the old LSA correctly describes the router's links and therefore the router will do nothing else. Otherwise, the router is going to regenerate the LSA using the standard procedure. As we remember, the sequence number of the new LSA instance will be by one higher than the sequence number of the previous instance. In other words, the router is going to create a new instance of the old LSA, which, because of the higher sequence number, will flush out the old LSA from the link state databases of the other routers.

Modifying OSPF Interface Costs

The OSPF cost of the interface can be modified in two ways. The first method is to use the **bandwidth** command. After the command is entered, the OSPF process recalculates the cost of the interface using the formula

$$C = \frac{10^5}{BW}$$

where C is the calculated cost of the interface and BW is the bandwidth of the interface in kilobits per second (Kbps), just as it appears in the output of the **show ip interfaces** command. OSPF costs are whole integer values, so the obtained value is rounded down to the closest whole integer.

For example, in the network in Figure 7.27, segment 6 has the physical bandwidth of 64Kbps. Right now, its logical bandwidth is at its default value, which, as suggested by the following partial output of the **show ip interfaces Serial 0** command entered on router R4, is 1544Kbps:

```
R4#show interfaces Serial 0
Serial0 is up, line protocol is up
...
   MTU 1500 bytes, BW 1544 Kbit, ...
```

The above formula translates the bandwidth to an OSPF cost of 64:

$$C = \frac{10^5}{1544} = 64.7668...=64$$

The evidence of this is seen in Listing 7.12, where the cost of the point-to-point link described in the LSA is revealed.

Let's change the logical bandwidth of the interface using the **bandwidth 64** command on router R4 in configuration mode of the interface Serial0. Using the formula, we can calculate what the resulting OSPF interface cost must be:

$$C_{new} = \frac{10^5}{64} = 1562.5 = 1562$$

The output of the **show ip ospf database router 10.0.0.4** command entered on router R3 confirms our calculations:

```
R3#show ip ospf database router 10.0.0.4
...
    Link connected to: another Router (point-to-point)
    (Link ID) Neighboring Router ID: 10.0.0.6
    (Link Data) Router Interface address: 172.16.0.9
     Number of TOS metrics: 0
       TOS 0 Metrics: 1562
```

Another method of changing the OSPF cost of an interface is to use the command **ip ospf cost** *<cost>*, which is available in interface configuration mode. The *<cost>* parameter is numeric and ranges from 1 through 65535. This command supersedes the **bandwidth** command.

Right now, we have configured only router R4's interface Serial0 with the correct cost. The other end of segment 6 is attached to router R6. So, to make the OSPF cost assignment on segment 6 consistent, we should also change the default cost of router R6's interface Serial0. Let's do that using the **ip ospf cost 1562** command. The partial output of the **show ip ospf database router 10.0.0.6** command shown below confirms the result of the command:

```
R3#show ip ospf database router 10.0.0.6
...
    (Link ID) Neighboring Router ID: 10.0.0.4
    (Link Data) Router Interface address: 172.16.0.10
     Number of TOS metrics: 0
       TOS 0 Metrics: 1562
```

Using OSPF Router Priorities

From the "In Depth" section, we know that multiple routers connected to a broadcast transit network must elect a designated and backup designated router with which the remaining routers become adjacent. When two or more routers detect each other, the one with the highest priority becomes the designated router. If the priorities are equal, the router with the highest OSPF ID becomes the designated router. A similar process governs the election of the backup designated router: Among the remaining routers, the one with the highest priority becomes the backup designated router. If the priorities are equal, then the one with the highest OSPF ID value wins.

The Cisco IOS command that allows changing OSPF router priority on an interface is **ip ospf priority** *<priority>*, where the *<priority>* parameter denotes the desired OSPF router priority for that interface. The values that the *<priority>* parameter can take range from 0 through 255. If 0 is specified, the router loses its eligibility to be the designated router and backup designated router on the segment even if it already has one of these statuses. If this is the case, re-election occurs among the remaining routers whose priorities are not equal to 0. Changing a priority to a non-0 value does not cause re-election. The existing designated and backup designated routers remain the same even if they have smaller priorities than one or more other routers on the segment. Likewise, connecting a router to a segment on which the designated and backup designated routers already exist does not cause re-election, regardless of the priority of the new router.

In the network that we have used so far (Figure 7.27), routers R3, R4, and R5 reside on only one segment (segment 5). Right now, no priorities have been assigned. Looking at either Listing 7.9 or 7.10, we can tell that router R4 is the designated router and that router R3 is the backup designated router.

Let's first change the priority of router R5 to 100 and then change the priority of router R4 to 0. To see the results of what happens, let's use the **show ip ospf neighbor** command on router R3. The part of the command's output that we're interested in follows:

```
R3#show ip ospf neighbor
...
10.0.0.5          100   FULL/BDR        00:00:33    10.0.5.3         Ethernet0
10.0.0.4            0   FULL/DROTHER    00:00:33    10.0.5.2         Ethernet0
```

Notice that router R3 becomes the new designated router although router R5 has a higher priority. We conclude this has happened because we do not see any neighbor labeled as DR; hence, the only choice is that router R3 itself is the designated router. Router R5 succeeds only in becoming the backup designated router.

The explanation of this is simple: If the designated router disappears, the existing backup designated router becomes the new designated router, the other routers' priorities notwithstanding. In our case, router R3 was originally the backup designated router, and so, when router R4 resigned as the designated router, router R3 replaced it in this role. This left router R3 only one option: to become the new backup designated router.

Understanding How OSPF Handles IP Unnumbered

As per the OSPF specification, Cisco's implementation of OSPF supports unnumbered interfaces.

To make OSPF run on an unnumbered interface, you have to make sure the IP address of the interface to which the **ip unnumbered** command points belongs to one of the **network** statements under **router ospf** configuration.

Let's consider the example shown in Figure 7.28.

The link between the two routers must be configured as IP unnumbered. The configurations of the two routers are shown in Listings 7.14 and 7.15.

Listing 7.14   Router R1's configuration.

```
ip subnet-zero

interface Loopback0
 ip address 10.0.0.1 255.255.255.255

interface Ethernet0
 ip address 10.0.1.1 255.255.255.0

interface Serial0
 ip unnumbered Loopback0

router ospf 1
 network 10.0.0.0 0.255.255.255 area 0

ip classless
```

7. Open Shortest Path First (OSPF) Protocol

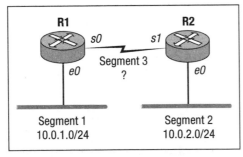

Figure 7.28   The link between routers R1 and R2 is configured as IP unnumbered.

Listing 7.15   Router R2's configuration.

```
ip subnet-zero

interface Loopback0
 ip address 10.0.0.2 255.255.255.255

interface Ethernet0
 ip address 10.0.2.1 255.255.255.0

interface Serial1
 ip unnumbered Loopback0

router ospf 1
 network 10.0.0.0 0.255.255.255 area 0

ip classless
```

Below is the OSPF part of router R1's routing table, which confirms that OSPF is able to learn of the network prefixes available off router R2:

```
R1#show ip route ospf
     10.0.0.0/8 is variably subnetted, 4 subnets, 2 masks
O       10.0.2.0/24 [110/74] via 10.0.0.2, 00:05:15, Serial0
O       10.0.0.2/32 [110/65] via 10.0.0.2, 00:05:15, Serial0
```

NOTE: *In Chapter 4, we considered an example in which only one of the routers was configured with the **ip unnumbered** command on its interface. We saw that RIP had no issue establishing correct routing across this type of unnumbered connection. In fact, RIP, IGRP, EIGRP, and OSPF handle both types of unnumbered connections without any issues.*

Understanding the **neighbor** Command

Sometimes, the underlying network layer technology does not support sending broadcast and multicast packets, which OSPF uses in the majority of cases to discover and maintain adjacency relationships among the routers.

To address such situations, the OSPF specification allows OSPF PDUs, such as hellos, to be sent directly to the IP address of the neighbor. The Cisco IOS, in turn, provides the command **neighbor** *<IP address>* under **router ospf** configuration to specify the IP addresses of the potential OSPF neighbors. The *<IP address>* parameter is the IP address of the neighbor (not the OSPF ID of the neighbor).

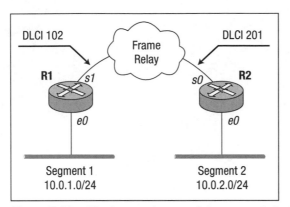

Figure 7.29   The two routers are interconnected with a frame relay PVC; the routers use the **neighbor** command to establish adjacency.

To see how the command works, let's consider the network shown in Figure 7.29.

The configurations of both routers are shown in Listings 7.16 and 7.17.

Listing 7.16   Router R1's configuration.

```
ip subnet-zero
no ip domain-lookup

interface Loopback0
 ip address 10.0.0.1 255.255.255.255

interface Ethernet0
 ip address 10.0.1.1 255.255.255.0

interface Serial1
 ip address 10.1.0.1 255.255.255.252
 encapsulation frame-relay
 frame-relay map ip 10.1.0.2 102

router ospf 1
 network 10.0.0.0 0.255.255.255 area 0
 neighbor 10.1.0.2 priority 1

ip classless
```

Listing 7.17   Router R2's configuration.

```
ip subnet-zero

interface Loopback0
 ip address 10.0.0.2 255.255.255.255
 !
```

```
interface Ethernet0
 ip address 10.0.2.1 255.255.255.0

interface Serial0
 ip address 10.1.0.2 255.255.255.252
 encapsulation frame-relay
 frame-relay map ip 10.1.0.1 201

router ospf 1
 network 10.0.0.0 0.255.255.255 area 0
 neighbor 10.1.0.1 priority 1

ip classless
```

Notice the shaded lines. They show the neighbor commands that allow the routers to establish adjacency over the Frame Relay permanent virtual circuit (PVC).

NOTE: When the **neighbor** command is used, the manual Frame Relay **map** statements do not have to contain the **broadcast** keyword.

Performing Equal-Cost Load Balancing with OSPF

OSPF, like all other routing protocols available on Cisco routers, can install multiple routes for the same network prefix provided they all have the same metric. This feature effectively enables load balancing of the traffic destined for the network prefix. By default, the maximum number of such parallel routes is four. The command **maximum paths** *<# of paths>* (which is available under **router ospf** configuration) allows the maximum number of paths to be changed. The *<# of paths>* parameter denotes the desired maximum number of paths, and its values can range from 1 through 6. If 1 is used, no load balancing is enabled.

Configuring OSPF with Multiple Areas

The guidelines for configuring OSPF for multiple areas essentially remain the same as those set forth for a single area. The only exception is the command **network** *<IP address> <wildcard mask>* **area** *<area ID>*, which, as you may notice, now features one extra parameter: *<area ID>*. (To be exact, this is not a new parameter per se; this parameter was present in the configuration guidelines for a single area, although its value was always 0.) This parameter specifies the area to which the interfaces matched by the command must belong. The parameter accepts integer values from 0 through 4294967295. (Alternatively, the area ID can be specified using dotted decimal notation.)

For each pair of *<IP address> <wildcard mask>* parameters, there can be only one **network** command; if a subsequent command with the same *<IP address> <wildcard mask>* parameters but different *<area ID>* parameter is entered, it overwrites the previously entered command. Multiple **network** commands can exist simultaneously, providing each has a unique combination of the significant bits of the *<IP address>* parameter and the *<wildcard mask>* parameter. For example, if the **network 10.0.1.0 0.0.0.255 area 5** and **network 10.0.1.0 0.0.0.192 area 10** commands are entered, they can coexist because their *<IP address> <wildcard mask>* parameters are unique. Hence, both these commands will appear in the router's configuration. If the **network 10.0.1.128 0.0.0.192 area 20** command is entered after these two commands, it will overwrite the **network 10.0.1.0 0.0.0.192 area 10** command because the *<IP address>* and *<wildcard mask>* parameters of the two commands are actually equal—the last octet of the *<wildcard mask>* parameter (192) actually masks out the last octet of the *<IP address>* parameter of the new command (128). After the last command is entered, the router's configuration will contain only **network 10.0.1.0 0.0.0.255 area 5** and **network 10.0.1.0 0.0.0.192 area 20** commands.

If the IP address of an interface is matched by multiple **network** commands with different *<area ID>* parameters, only the first command assigns the area ID to the interface.

NOTE: *Using **network** commands whose <IP address> and <wildcard mask> parameters define overlapping ranges is not a recommended practice. For example, the <IP address> and <wildcard mask> parameters of the commands **network 10.1.0.0 0.0.255.255 area 5** and **10.1.0.0 0.0.0.255 area 10** define overlapping ranges.*

Optionally, although very much desirable, the ABRs must also be configured with one or several area summary network prefixes. The command to configure area summary network prefixes is **area** *<area ID>* **range** *<IP address> <subnet mask>* [**not-advertise**]. The *<area ID>* parameter specifies the area for which summarization must be performed. The pair of parameters *<IP address>* and *<subnet mask>* specify the configured summary network prefix. Unlike the *<wildcard mask>* parameter of the **network** command, the *<subnet mask>* parameter specifies a subnet mask. The optional parameter **not-advertise** instructs the router to originate type 3 LSAs for neither the summary network prefix, nor for any network prefix that the summary network prefix matches. This parameter is useful if it is necessary to make certain network prefixes inaccessible from the other areas.

Once one or more summary network prefixes are configured on an ABR, the ABR originates a type 3 summary LSA for every configured summary network prefix, providing it has a route for at least one network prefix matched by the summary network prefix and providing the optional parameter **not-advertise** is not used. In addition, the router originates type 3 summary network prefixes for every network prefix for which it does not have a matching summary network prefix. Type 3 summary LSAs are originated into all areas to which the ABR is attached except for the area whose network prefixes they summarize.

Let's see how the routers in the network from Figure 7.30 should be configured to sustain the shown area assignment.

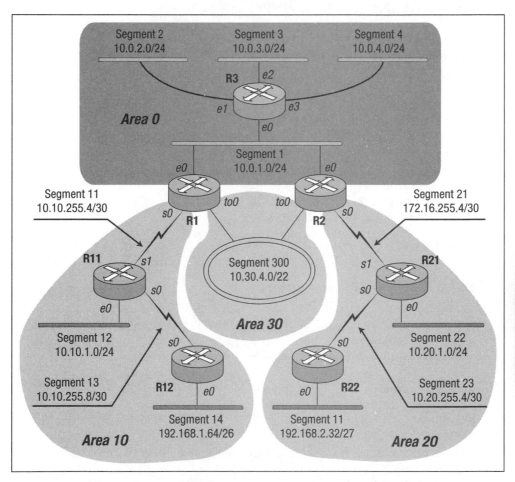

Figure 7.30   An example of an OSPF autonomous system with multiple areas.

Listings 7.18 through 7.24 show the configurations of all seven routers.

Listing 7.18   Router R1's configuration.

```
ip subnet-zero

interface Loopback0
 ip address 10.0.0.1 255.255.255.255

interface Ethernet0
 ip address 10.0.1.1 255.255.255.0

interface Serial0
 ip address 10.10.255.5 255.255.255.252

interface TokenRing0
 ip address 10.30.4.1 255.255.252.0
 ring-speed 16

router ospf 1
 network 10.0.0.0 0.0.255.255 area 0
 network 10.10.0.0 0.0.255.255 area 10
 network 10.30.0.0 0.0.255.255 area 30
 area 0 range 10.0.0.0 255.255.0.0
 area 10 range 10.10.0.0 255.255.0.0
 area 10 range 172.20.0.0 255.255.0.0
 area 30 range 10.30.0.0 255.255.0.0

ip classless
```

Listing 7.19   Router R2's configuration.

```
ip subnet-zero

interface Loopback0
 ip address 10.0.0.2 255.255.255.255

interface Ethernet0
 ip address 10.0.1.2 255.255.255.0

interface Serial0
 ip address 172.16.255.5 255.255.255.252

interface TokenRing0
 ip address 10.30.4.2 255.255.252.0
 ring-speed 16
```

The initial state for each neighbor is Down. After the router receives an OSPF hello from the neighbor, it transitions the neighbor to the Init state. After the router detects its own OSPF ID in the neighbor's hello, it transitions the neighbor into one of two states—2-Way or ExStart.

The 2-Way state means that the router will not establish adjacency with the neighbor. This happens only when the state of both routers' interfaces attached to the segment is DROther. In other words, none of the routers is a designated or backup designated router for the segment.

The other state is ExStart, which is the initial state of the formed adjacency between the two routers. The rest of the neighbor-state machine deals with bringing the state of adjacency between the two routers to Full. Before the ExStart state, the routers were not adjacent.

The ExStart stage also inaugurates the *link-state database synchronization process*. The database synchronization process consists of two stages. During the first stage, which is called the *database exchange*, the routers exchange database description PDUs in order to find out which parts of their link-state databases are not identical and/or outdated.

To perform the database exchange, the two routers form a master/slave relationship. The router whose OSPF router ID is higher becomes the master, and the other becomes the slave. Once the routers have decided which one of them is the master and which is the slave, the neighbor state machine transitions to the Exchange state and the actual database exchange begins.

The database description PDUs contain the headers of the LSAs residing in the sending router's corresponding link-state database (remember, the routers can have multiple link-state databases). The maximum size of each database description PDU depends on the type of interface through which the PDU is sent. Hence, it is possible that a single database description PDU may not be enough to accommodate the headers of all LSAs the router's database may contain. To indicate that there will be additional database description PDUs transmitted, a special bit called *M-bit* (for More) must be set in the header of the database description PDU.

Each database description PDU also contains a sequence number that is used to acknowledge receipt of the PDU by the receiving router. The master is responsible for generating the initial sequence number, which it places into its first database description PDU. After that, the master increases the sequence number each time it sends out its next database description PDU. Before sending a new database description PDU, the master must receive an acknowledgment from the slave in the form of the slave's database description PDU carrying the sequence number of the last master's database description PDU. If the master receives no acknowledgment within RxmtInterval, it retransmits the last sent database description PDU. (Only the master is allowed to request a retransmission.)

```
router ospf 1
 network 10.0.0.0 0.0.255.255 area 0
 network 10.30.0.0 0.0.255.255 area 30
 network 172.16.255.5 0.0.0.0 area 20
 area 0 range 10.0.0.0 255.255.0.0
 area 20 range 10.20.0.0 255.255.0.0
 area 20 range 172.16.0.0 255.240.0.0
 area 20 range 192.168.2.0 255.255.254.0

ip classless
```

Listing 7.20   Router R3's configuration.

```
ip subnet-zero

interface Loopback0
 ip address 10.0.0.3 255.255.255.255

interface Ethernet0
 ip address 10.0.1.3 255.255.255.0

interface Ethernet1
 ip address 10.0.2.1 255.255.255.0

interface Ethernet2
 ip address 10.0.3.1 255.255.255.0

interface Ethernet3
 ip address 10.0.4.1 255.255.255.0

router ospf 1
 network 10.0.0.0 0.255.255.255 area 0

ip classless
```

Listing 7.21   Router R11's configuration.

```
ip subnet-zero

interface Loopback0
 ip address 10.0.0.11 255.255.255.255
!
interface Ethernet0
 ip address 10.10.1.1 255.255.255.0

interface Serial0
 ip address 10.10.255.9 255.255.255.252
```

```
interface Serial1
 ip address 10.10.255.6 255.255.255.252

router ospf 1
 network 10.10.0.0 0.0.255.255 area 10

ip classless
```

Listing 7.22   Router R12's configuration.

```
ip subnet-zero

interface Loopback0
 ip address 10.0.0.12 255.255.255.255

interface Ethernet0
 ip address 192.168.1.65 255.255.255.192

interface Serial0
 ip address 10.10.255.10 255.255.255.252

router ospf 1
 network 10.10.0.0 0.0.255.255 area 10
 network 192.168.0.0 0.0.255.255 area 10

ip classless
```

Listing 7.23   Router R21's configuration.

```
ip subnet-zero

interface Loopback0
 ip address 10.0.0.21 255.255.255.255

interface Ethernet0
 ip address 10.20.1.1 255.255.255.0

interface Serial0
 ip address 10.20.255.5 255.255.255.252

interface Serial1
 ip address 172.16.255.6 255.255.255.252

router ospf 1
 network 10.20.0.0 0.0.255.255 area 20
 network 172.16.0.0 0.0.255.255 area 20

ip classless
```

Listing 7.24   Router R22's configuration.

```
ip subnet-zero

interface Loopback0
 ip address 10.0.0.22 255.255.255.255

interface Ethernet0
 ip address 192.168.2.33 255.255.255.224

interface Serial0
 ip address 10.20.255.6 255.255.255.252

router ospf 1
 network 10.20.0.0 0.0.255.255 area 20
 network 192.168.0.0 0.0.255.255 area 20

ip classless
```

The network has two ABRs, which are routers R1 and R2. Table 7.7 shows, in a brief form, the configured summary network prefixes for different areas on both routers.

Notice the few inconsistencies. First, router R2 does not have any summary configured for Area 30. Second, router R1 is configured with summary network prefix 172.20.0.0/16 for Area 10, whereas no network prefix in Area 10 is matched by this summary address. Finally, the network prefix of segment 14—192.168.1.64/26—is not matched by any summary network prefix configured in Area 10's ABR (router R1).

Let's examine the results of the configured summarization and its inconsistencies. Listing 7.25 shows the routing table of router R3.

Table 7.7   Summary network prefixes configured on the ABRs.

Area #	ABR	Configured Summary Network Prefix
0 (Backbone)	R1	10.0.0.0/16
0	R2	10.0.0.0/16
10	R1	10.10.0.0/16, 172.20.0.0/16 (?)
20	R2	10.20.0.0/16, 172.16.0.0/16, 192.168.2.0/23
30	R1	10.30.0.0/16
30	R2	None

Listing 7.25   The output of the show ip route ospf command entered on router R3.

```
R3#show ip route ospf
     10.0.0.0 is variably subnetted, 11 subnets, 4 masks
O IA    10.10.0.0/16 [110/74] via 10.0.1.1, 00:26:19, Ethernet0
O       10.0.0.2/32 [110/11] via 10.0.1.2, 00:26:19, Ethernet0
O       10.0.0.1/32 [110/11] via 10.0.1.1, 00:26:19, Ethernet0
O IA    10.30.4.0/22 [110/16] via 10.0.1.2, 00:26:19, Ethernet0
O IA    10.30.0.0/16 [110/16] via 10.0.1.1, 00:26:19, Ethernet0
O IA    10.20.0.0/16 [110/84] via 10.0.1.2, 00:26:19, Ethernet0
     192.168.1.0/26 is subnetted, 1 subnets
O IA    192.168.1.64 [110/148] via 10.0.1.1, 00:00:43, Ethernet0
O IA 192.168.2.0/23 [110/148] via 10.0.1.2, 00:26:19, Ethernet0
O IA 172.16.0.0/12 [110/74] via 10.0.1.2, 00:26:19, Ethernet0
```

First of all, the lines labeled by the letter O followed by the letters IA denote inter-area routes. In other words, the network prefixes in these routes reside in the areas to which the router is not attached. Apparently, such routes were created from type 3 summary LSAs. As we remember, type 4 summary LSAs result in router routing table entries, which are used internally by OSPF in calculating routes for network prefixes located outside the OSPF autonomous system (that is, external network prefixes).

Pay attention to the first two shaded lines because these represent routes for two summary network prefixes for Area 30. Remembering that router R1 was configured with only one summary network prefix, why are there two such routes? The problem is in router R2, which wasn't configured with any summary network prefix for Area 30. Hence, it created type 3 summary LSAs for every network prefix available inside Area 30. Because Area 30 contains only one network prefix—that of segment 300 (10.30.4.0/22)—router R2 created only one type 3 summary LSA for this network prefix. This resulted in the route in the first shaded line. The second shaded line shows the route for the summary network prefix of Area 30 configured on router R1.

The last two shaded lines actually represent a single inter-area route for network prefix 192.168.1.0/26, the one for which Area 10's only ABR router R1 does not have a matching summary network prefix. As the result, it "squeezed loose" through the summarization at router R1.

Finally, the routing table of router R3 does not show a route for summary network prefix 172.20.0.0/16. Because Area 10 has no network prefixes that this summary network prefix can match, it makes no sense to originate a type 3 summary LSA for it.

If we examine the output of the **show ip ospf database** command entered on router R3 (Listing 7.26), we'll see an additional section titled "Summary Net Link States." This section shows the type 3 summary LSA contained in router R3's topology database.

Listing 7.26   The output of the show ip ospf database command entered on router R3.

```
R3#show ip ospf database
...
                Summary Net Link States (Area 0)

Link ID            ADV Router        Age    Seq#        Checksum
10.10.0.0          10.0.0.1          27     0x80000002  0xAE2E
10.20.0.0          10.0.0.2          6      0x80000002  0x9433
10.30.0.0          10.0.0.1          27     0x80000002  0x778B
10.30.4.0          10.0.0.2          6      0x80000004  0x32CC
172.16.0.0         10.0.0.2          6      0x80000002  0xE160
192.168.1.64       10.0.0.1          28     0x80000002  0xD565
192.168.2.0        10.0.0.2          8      0x80000002  0xBD7D
```

The **show ip ospf database summary** command displays the contents of the type 3 summary LSAs that the router has in all of its link-state databases. This command can be optionally followed by the *<Link State ID>* parameter, which specifies the Link State ID of an existing type 3 summary LSA. This form of the command will show the content of only the specified LSA.

Listing 7.27 shows an example of the output of this command.

Listing 7.27   The output of the show ip ospf database summary command entered on router R3.

```
R3#show ip ospf database summary
    OSPF Router with ID (10.0.0.3) (Process ID 1)
                Summary Net Link States (Area 0)
...
  Routing Bit Set on this LSA
  LS age: 245
  Options: (No TOS-capability)
  LS Type: Summary Links(Network)
  Link State ID: 10.20.0.0 (summary Network Number)
  Advertising Router: 10.0.0.2
  LS Seq Number: 80000002
  Checksum: 0x9433
  Length: 28
  Network Mask: /16      TOS: 0  Metric: 74
...
```

As we remember, a type 3 summary LSA carries the metric of the summary network prefix that it advertises. If the summary network prefix is one of the configured summary network prefixes on the ABR that originates the LSA, the procedure prescribes to use the largest among the metrics of the routes that the ABR has for network prefixes that the configured summary network

7. Open Shortest Path First (OSPF) Protocol

prefix matches. Let's see if Cisco routers adhere to this rule when calculating the metrics of summary network prefixes.

The last element of the shaded line in Listing 7.27 shows the value router R2, the ABR originating the LSA, assigned to the Metric field of the LSA. Let's examine the partial output of the **show ip route ospf** command entered on router R2, which shows all routes for the network prefixes matched by the summary network prefix in the LSA. Quite opposite to what the procedure prescribes, the router uses the *smallest* metric as opposed to the *largest* when calculating the value of the Metric field in type 3 summary LSAs. Here is the partial output:

```
R2#show ip route
...
O       10.20.1.0/24 [110/74] via 172.16.255.6, 00:35:17, Serial0
O       10.20.255.4/30 [110/128] via 172.16.255.6, 00:35:17, Serial0
...
```

Configuring OSPF to Originate the Default Gateway Route

Similarly to RIP, OSPF on the Cisco routers can be configured to advertise a default network prefix (that is, 0.0.0.0/0). The default network prefix is advertised in a type 5 external LSA.

The **default-information originate** command issued under **router ospf** configuration makes the router advertise the default network prefix, proving it has a gateway of last resort. (For details on how to establish a gateway of last resort, please see Chapter 5.)

Let's see how this all works. We'll make router R22 advertise the default network prefix by using the **default-information originate** command under **router ospf** configuration and add the **ip route 0.0.0.0 0.0.0.0 Null0** command into router R22's configuration. The latter command creates a gateway of last resort.

If we examine the routing table of router R3, we'll now see an additional routing table entry, as follows:

```
R3#show ip route
...
O*E2 0.0.0.0/0 [110/1] via 10.0.1.2, 00:00:08, Ethernet0
```

Notice that this additional line is labeled with the letter O followed by E2, for external type 2 information. For now, we'll note only that the routing entry is an OSPF external type 2 route.

External LSAs are covered in Chapter 8, so we won't consider the details behind them and the related commands until then.

Understanding the **show ip ospf border-routers** Command

The **show ip ospf border-routers** command displays the auxiliary router routing table entries that OSPF creates for ABRs and ASBRs.

Right now, in the network from Figure 7.30, we should have two ABRs (routers R1 and R2) and one ASBR (router R22). Hence, we should be able to see these routers referenced in the output of the **show ip ospf border-routers** command.

Listing 7.28 shows the output of this command entered on router R3.

Listing 7.28   The output of the show ip ospf border-routers command entered on router R3.

```
R3#show ip ospf border-routers

OSPF Process 1 internal Routing Table

Codes: i - Intra-area route, I - Inter-area route

i 10.0.0.2 [10] via 10.0.1.2, Ethernet0, ABR, Area 0, SPF 3
i 10.0.0.1 [10] via 10.0.1.1, Ethernet0, ABR, Area 0, SPF 3
I 10.0.0.22 [138] via 10.0.1.2, Ethernet0, ASBR, Area 0, SPF 3
```

This output is similar to that of the **show ip route** command. The letter with which each line of the output begins denotes whether the router route entry is intra-area, denoted *i*, or inter-area, denoted *I*. ABRs R1 and R2 reside in the backbone in which router R3 also resides, so the route entries corresponding to them are labeled as intra-area. On the contrary, router R22 resides in Area 20, to which router R3 is not attached; hence, the router routing table for router R22 is labeled as inter-area.

The next field in the output is the OSPF ID of the router for which the router routing entry is created. It is followed by the OSPF metric in square brackets. The next field is the IP address of the next-hop router through which the router is

7. Open Shortest Path First (OSPF) Protocol

available. The IP address of the next-hop router is followed by the output interface. The next field denotes whether the router is ABR or ASBR. The following field is the area for which the router routing table entries were created. In our case, router R3 is connected to only Area 0, so we won't see references to any other areas in the output of the **show ip ospf border-routers** command. The last field is the internal number of Dijkstra's shortest-path algorithm iteration, which produced this router routing table entry.

Configuring OSPF Stub Areas

A stub area is configured on a router by issuing the **area** *<area ID>* **stub** command under **router ospf** configuration. The *<area ID>* parameter denotes the OSPF area that is made stub.

All routers within a stub area must be configured with the **area** *<area ID>* **stub** command. If a router attached to a stub area is not configured with this command, it won't be able to establish adjacency with any router within the stub area that is configured with this command. This happens because the OSPF hello PDUs sent out of the router interfaces attached to the stub area convey the E-bit of the Options field cleared. Two routers will refuse to establish adjacency if there is a mismatch in their E-bits of the Options field in the hello PDUs that they exchange.

Let's see what happens to the network from Figure 7.30 if all routers attached to Area 10 are configured with the **area 10 stub** command.

Once Area 10 is made stub, the routing tables of the routers in Area 10 won't contain the OSPF external route that we saw in the previous section in the routing table of router R3. Listing 7.29 shows the routing table of router R12 as an example.

Listing 7.29   The part of router R12's routing table populated with the OSPF routes.

```
R12#show ip route ospf
     10.0.0.0/8 is variably subnetted, 7 subnets, 4 masks
O       10.10.1.0/24 [110/74] via 10.10.255.9, 00:00:02, Serial0
O IA    10.0.0.0/16 [110/129] via 10.10.255.9, 00:00:02, Serial0
O IA    10.30.0.0/16 [110/134] via 10.10.255.9, 00:00:02, Serial0
O IA    10.20.0.0/16 [110/212] via 10.10.255.9, 00:00:02, Serial0
O       10.10.255.4/30 [110/128] via 10.10.255.9, 00:00:02, Serial0
O*IA 0.0.0.0/0 [110/129] via 10.10.255.9, 00:00:02, Serial0
O IA 172.16.0.0/12 [110/202] via 10.10.255.9, 00:00:02, Serial0
O IA 192.168.2.0/23 [110/276] via 10.10.255.9, 00:00:02, Serial0
```

Notice that instead of the OSPF external type 2 route for the default network prefix, router R12's routing table contains an inter-area route for the default network prefix. The type 3 summary LSA from which this route results was originated by Area 10's ABR, router R1.

It's possible to configure a Cisco router acting as an ABR so that it doesn't inject summary LSAs into an OSPF stub area but instead injects a single type 3 summary LSA for the default network prefix. In Cisco terminology, such stub areas are called *totally stubby*. The command that configures the area as totally stubby is **area** *<area ID>* **stub no-summary**. This command does not have to be present in the configurations of all routers that are attached to the area, only in the configurations of the ABRs of the area. The other routers must still be configured with the **area** *<area ID>* **stub** command.

If we use the **area 10 stub no-summary** command instead of the **area 10 stub** command on router R1, the routing table of router R12 will look as follows:

```
R12#show ip route ospf
     10.0.0.0/8 is variably subnetted, 4 subnets, 3 masks
O       10.10.1.0/24 [110/74] via 10.10.255.9, 00:00:12, Serial0
O       10.10.255.4/30 [110/128] via 10.10.255.9, 00:00:12, Serial0
O*IA 0.0.0.0/0 [110/129] via 10.10.255.9, 00:00:12, Serial0
```

Notice that a single inter-area route for the default network prefix (0.0.0.0/0) now also replaced all previously existing inter-area routes for the summary network prefixes of the other areas.

The OSPF link-state database of router R12 will contain only a single summary LSA, as shown in Listing 7.30.

Listing 7.30   The output of the **show ip ospf database summary** command issued on router R12.

```
R21#show ip ospf database summary

        OSPF Router with ID (10.0.0.12) (Process ID 1)

             Summary Net Link States (Area 10)

   Routing Bit Set on this LSA
   LS age: 150
   Options: (No TOS-capability, DC)
   LS Type: Summary Links(Network)
   Link State ID: 0.0.0.0 (summary Network Number)
   Advertising Router: 10.0.0.1
   LS Seq Number: 80000004
```

```
        Checksum: 0x4BE4
        Length: 28
        Network Mask: /0
              TOS: 0   Metric: 1
```

The shaded lines show the network prefix and its length advertised by the LSA.

Understanding How OSPF Handles Secondary IP Addresses

OSPF on Cisco routers represents secondary IP addresses as a stub network regardless of the type of interface on which they are assigned. The only requirement for the secondary IP addresses is that they have to belong to the same area to which the primary IP address belongs.

Listing 7.31 shows the partial output of the **show ip ospf database** command that displays the router LSA of a router whose Ethernet interface links are shown, is assigned IP address 172.16.100.1 as primary and 10.1.1.1 as secondary. Notice that the first link is shown as connected to a transit network, whereas the second link is connected to a stub network. This happens although both IP addresses are assigned on the same interface connected to a broadcast transit network.

Listing 7.31   A router LSA whose second link is for a secondary IP address assigned on the router interface.

```
R1#show ip ospf database router

        OSPF Router with ID (0.0.0.1) (Process ID 1)

              Router Link States (Area 0)

    LS age: 12
    Options: (No TOS-capability, DC)
    LS Type: Router Links
    Link State ID: 0.0.0.1
    Advertising Router: 0.0.0.1
    LS Seq Number: 80000003
    Checksum: 0x18ED
    Length: 48
     Number of Links: 2

      Link connected to: a Transit Network
       (Link ID) Designated Router address: 172.16.100.2
       (Link Data) Router Interface address: 172.16.100.1
```

```
      Number of TOS metrics: 0
       TOS 0 Metrics: 100

    Link connected to: a Stub Network
     (Link ID) Network/subnet number: 10.1.1.0
     (Link Data) Network Mask: 255.255.255.0
      Number of TOS metrics: 0
       TOS 0 Metrics: 100
```

Using Virtual Links to Connect Remote Areas

Virtual links are established on a point-to-point basis between two routers that are connected to a common area, one of which must also be connected to OSPF Area 0. Each router must have the command **area** *<area>* **virtual-link** *<router ID>* under **router ospf** configuration. The parameter *<area>* specifies the common (transit) area to which both routers are connected and through which the virtual link is established. Naturally, the *<area>* parameter must be the same on both routers. The specified area cannot be a stub area, however. The *<router ID>* parameter specifies the OSPF ID of the counterpart router. In other words, if a virtual link is established between routers A and B, the **area** *<area>* **virtual-link** command issued on router A must specify the OSPF ID of router B. Likewise, the counterpart command on router B must specify the OSPF ID of router A.

To see how the guidelines work, let's consider the network shown in Figure 7.31.

Notice that Areas 100 and 200 do not have any routers that are directly connected to the OSPF backbone, but that the only router in each area is also connected to Area 10. Hence, each of these routers (R5 and R6) can be configured with a virtual link going to one of the backbone routers (R1 and R2).

In this network, a single virtual link was created between routers R1 and R5 and between routers R2 and R6. Listings 7.32 through 7.37 show the configurations of all six routers.

Listing 7.32   Router R1's configuration.

```
ip subnet-zero

interface Loopback0
 ip address 10.0.0.1 255.255.255.255

interface Ethernet0
 ip address 10.0.1.1 255.255.255.0

interface Serial0
```

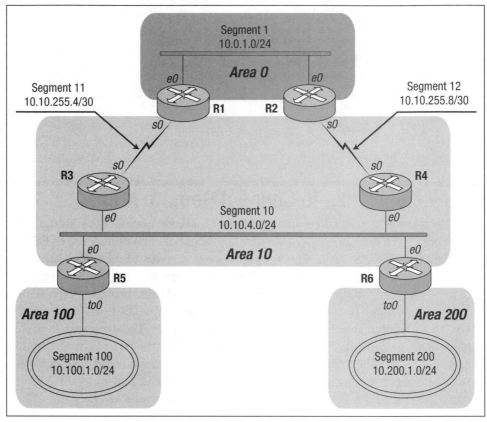

Figure 7.31 Routers R5 and R6 must use virtual links to ensure complete routing in the network.

```
ip address 10.10.255.5 255.255.255.252
bandwidth 64

router ospf 1
 network 10.0.0.0 0.0.255.255 area 0
 network 10.10.0.0 0.0.255.255 area 10
 area 0 range 10.0.0.0 255.255.0.0
 area 10 range 10.10.0.0 255.255.0.0
 area 10 virtual-link 10.0.0.5
ip classless
```

Listing 7.33 Router R2's configuration.

```
ip subnet-zero

interface Loopback0
 ip address 10.0.0.2 255.255.255.255

interface Ethernet0
 ip address 10.0.1.2 255.255.255.0
```

```
interface Serial0
 ip address 10.10.255.9 255.255.255.252
 bandwidth 64

router ospf 1
 network 10.0.0.0 0.0.255.255 area 0
 network 10.10.0.0 0.0.255.255 area 10
 area 0 range 10.0.0.0 255.255.0.0
 area 10 range 10.10.0.0 255.255.0.0
 area 10 virtual-link 10.0.0.6

ip classless
```

Listing 7.34   Router R3's configuration.

```
ip subnet-zero

interface Loopback0
 ip address 10.10.0.3 255.255.255.255

interface Ethernet0
 ip address 10.10.4.3 255.255.252.0

interface Serial0
 ip address 10.10.255.6 255.255.255.252
 bandwidth 64

router ospf 1
 network 10.10.0.0 0.0.255.255 area 10

ip classless
```

Listing 7.35   Router R4's configuration.

```
ip subnet-zero

interface Loopback0
 ip address 10.0.0.4 255.255.255.255

interface Ethernet0
 ip address 10.10.4.4 255.255.252.0

interface Serial0
 ip address 10.10.255.10 255.255.255.252
 bandwidth 64

router ospf 1
 network 10.10.0.0 0.0.255.255 area 10

ip classless
```

Listing 7.36   Router R5's configuration.

```
ip subnet-zero

interface Loopback0
  ip address 10.0.0.5 255.255.255.255

interface Ethernet0
  ip address 10.10.4.1 255.255.252.0

interface TokenRing0
  ip address 10.100.1.1 255.255.255.0
  ring-speed 16

router ospf 1
  network 10.100.0.0 0.0.255.255 area 100
  network 10.10.0.0 0.0.255.255 area 10
  network 10.0.0.0 0.0.255.255 area 0
  area 0 range 10.0.0.0 255.255.0.0
  area 10 range 10.10.0.0 255.255.0.0
  area 10 virtual-link 10.0.0.1
  area 100 range 10.100.0.0 255.255.0.0

ip classless
```

Listing 7.37   Router R6's configuration.

```
ip subnet-zero

interface Loopback0
  ip address 10.0.0.6 255.255.255.255

interface Ethernet0
  ip address 10.10.4.2 255.255.252.0

interface TokenRing0
  ip address 10.200.1.1 255.255.255.0
  ring-speed 16

router ospf 1
  network 10.0.0.0 0.0.255.255 area 0
  network 10.10.0.0 0.0.255.255 area 10
  network 10.200.0.0 0.0.255.255 area 200
  area 0 range 10.0.0.0 255.255.0.0
  area 10 range 10.10.0.0 255.255.0.0
  area 10 virtual-link 10.0.0.2
  area 200 range 10.200.0.0 255.255.0.0

ip classless
```

The shaded lines show the configuration commands of the virtual link.

The **show ip ospf virtual-links** command displays the status of all the virtual links configured on the routers. The output of this command issued on router R5 is shown in Listing 7.38.

Listing 7.38   The output of the **show ip ospf virtual-links** command issued on router R5.

```
R5#show ip ospf virtual-links
Virtual Link OSPF_VL0 to router 10.0.0.1 is up
  Run as demand circuit
  DoNotAge LSA not allowed (Number of DCbitless LSA is 1).
  Transit area 10, via interface Ethernet0, Cost of using 1572
  Transmit Delay is 1 sec, State POINT_TO_POINT,
  Timer intervals configured, Hello 10, Dead 40, Wait 40, Retransmit 5
    Hello due in 00:00:02
    Adjacency State FULL (Hello suppressed)
```

The first line shows the status of the virtual link. In our case, it's "up", which indicates that the routers can exchange OSPF PDUs over the virtual link.

The next line tells us that the link is established as a demand circuit. This essentially means that the OSPF routers do not exchange regular OSPF hellos; the ability to do so was originally indicated by setting the DC bit in the OSPF hellos that the routers exchanged when establishing the virtual link. Not all virtual links are established as a demand circuit. For example, in IOS versions prior to 11.2, the virtual links were established as on a regular basis, whereby the routers kept exchanging OSPF hellos after all becoming fully adjacent over the virtual link.

The next line indicates that, although the virtual link is established as a demand circuit, the router LSA describing the link is a DoNotAge LSA (bit #0 in the Link State Age field of the LSA header shown in Figure 7.9).

The third line shows the area through which the virtual link is established, followed by the output interface of the virtual link (through which the router sends OSPF PDUs destined for the router on the other end of the virtual link) and the cost of the link. The cost of the link is, as we know, the metric of the route to the router on the other end of the link.

The remaining lines shows the usual OSPF link-related parameters, such as the type of the link and the timers associated with the link.

In addition, you can look up the virtual link in both routers' router LSAs using the **show ip ospf database router** command. For example, Listing 7.39 shows the partial output of this command entered on router R5. The shaded part denotes the lines describing the virtual link.

Listing 7.39   Router R5's router LSA entry for the virtual link.

```
R5#show ip ospf database router
...
                  Router Link States (Area 0)
...
  LS age: 937
  Options: (No TOS-capability, DC)
  LS Type: Router Links
  Link State ID: 10.0.0.5
  Advertising Router: 10.0.0.5
  LS Seq Number: 80000003
  Checksum: 0xEEB3
  Length: 48
  Area Border Router
   Number of Links: 2

    Link connected to: a Virtual Link
      (Link ID) Neighboring Router ID: 10.0.0.1
      (Link Data) Router Interface address: 10.10.4.1
       Number of TOS metrics: 0
        TOS 0 Metrics: 1572
```

It was mentioned in the "In Depth" section that the OSPF implementation in Cisco IOS does not fully support transit areas (that is, areas through which at least one virtual link is established). In other words, the OSPF process on Cisco routers does not try to find better routes through available transit areas for the already calculated inter- and intra-area routes in the backbone.

For example, in the network in Figure 7.31, Area 10 is a transit area because two virtual links are established through that area. Therefore, routers R5 and R6 should be able to discover shorter alternative routes for the traffic going between Areas 100 and 200 through segment 10. Nevertheless, this doesn't happen, which can be seen by examining the routing table of router R5 (Listing 7.40).

Listing 7.40   The routing table of router R5.

```
R5#show ip route
...
     10.0.0.0/8 is variably subnetted, 11 subnets, 5 masks
O       10.10.0.3/32 [110/11] via 10.10.4.3, 00:13:17, Ethernet0
C       10.10.4.0/22 is directly connected, Ethernet0
O       10.0.0.2/32 [110/1583] via 10.10.4.3, 00:12:57, Ethernet0
O       10.0.1.0/24 [110/1582] via 10.10.4.3, 00:12:57, Ethernet0
O       10.0.0.1/32 [110/1573] via 10.10.4.3, 00:12:57, Ethernet0
O       10.0.0.6/32 [110/3155] via 10.10.4.3, 00:12:57, Ethernet0
C       10.0.0.5/32 is directly connected, Loopback0
C       10.100.1.0/24 is directly connected, TokenRing0
```

```
O IA    10.200.0.0/16 [110/3160] via 10.10.4.3, 00:12:57, Ethernet0
O       10.10.255.8/30 [110/1572] via 10.10.4.4, 00:13:18, Ethernet0
O       10.10.255.4/30 [110/1572] via 10.10.4.3, 00:13:18, Ethernet0
```

The shaded line shows the inter-area route for the summary network prefix of Area 200. Notice that the route points to the IP address of router R3 as opposed to that of router R6. If Cisco's implementation of OSPF supported transit areas, router R5 would discover the direct route for the summary network prefix of Area 200 through router R6. Instead, router R5 treats the virtual link almost as a regular interface and simply uses the next-hop router en route to the router on the other end of the virtual link (router R1) as the next-hop router for all destinations that appear to be available through the virtual link.

Router R3, however, is not aware of router R5's intentions to deliver the traffic destined for Area 200 to router R1. Router R3 simply uses its best local route to deliver the traffic to Area 200, whereby it sends the traffic back to segment 10 (although, unlike router R5, it forwards the traffic to the correct next-hop router—router R6).

If we try to use the **traceroute** command on router R5 for a destination inside Area 200, we'll see output similar to the following:

```
R5#traceroute 10.200.1.1
...
  1 10.10.4.3 4 msec 4 msec 4 msec
  2 10.10.4.2 8 msec *  8 msec
```

NOTE: *You can observe even more obvious evidence of the lack of transit area support in the current versions of Cisco IOS if you try to implement the network example from Figure 17 of RFC 2328 (page 172). Once interconnected and configured as suggested, the routers create a routing loop instead of the behavior described in RFC 2328.*

Nevertheless, don't get upset about this incompatibility because the benefits of employing the transit area feature are questionable, plus Cisco has slated to add support for transit areas in upcoming releases of IOS.

Using Virtual Links to Restore a Partitioned Backbone

As we know from the "In Depth" section, OSPF specification allows the backbone area to consist of parts that are separated by other areas, provided that the parts are interconnected by virtual links. As in the case with remote areas, virtual links can be placed through only those areas to which the two routers, which the virtual link interconnects, are attached.

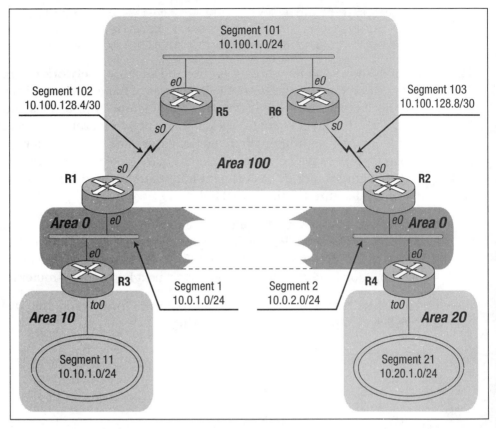

Figure 7.32   A virtual link must be used to restore the partitioned backbone (Area 0).

Figure 7.32 shows an example of a network in which a backbone consists of two partitions. The OSPF backbone is shown in the middle of the figure as the darker area torn apart. Because the backbone comprises only two segments—1 and 2—and because no router is connected to both segments, the backbone is partitioned. Thus, a virtual link must be established between at least two routers out of the four connected to the backbone—R1, R2, R3, and R4.

To see the effect of a partitioned backbone, let's see what happens if the routers are configured without a virtual link. The configurations of all four routers are shown in Listings 7.41 through 7.46.

Listing 7.41   Router R1's configuration.

```
interface Loopback0
 ip address 10.0.0.1 255.255.255.255

interface Ethernet0
 ip address 10.0.1.1 255.255.255.0
```

```
interface Serial0
 ip address 10.100.128.5 255.255.255.252

router ospf 1
 network 10.0.0.0 0.0.255.255 area 0
 network 10.100.0.0 0.0.255.255 area 100
 area 100 range 10.100.0.0 255.255.0.0
```

Listing 7.42   Router R2's configuration.

```
interface Loopback0
 ip address 10.0.0.2 255.255.255.255

interface Ethernet0
 ip address 10.0.2.1 255.255.255.0

interface Serial0
 ip address 10.100.128.9 255.255.255.252

router ospf 1
 network 10.0.0.0 0.0.255.255 area 0
 network 10.100.0.0 0.0.255.255 area 100
 area 100 range 10.100.0.0 255.255.0.0
```

Listing 7.43   Router R3's configuration.

```
interface Loopback0
 ip address 10.0.0.3 255.255.255.255

interface Ethernet0
 ip address 10.0.1.2 255.255.255.0

interface TokenRing0
 ip address 10.10.1.1 255.255.255.0
 ring-speed 16

router ospf 1
 network 10.0.0.0 0.0.255.255 area 0
 network 10.10.0.0 0.0.255.255 area 10
 area 0 range 10.0.0.0 255.255.0.0
 area 10 range 10.10.0.0 255.255.0.0
```

Listing 7.44   Router R4's configuration.

```
interface Loopback0
 ip address 10.0.0.4 255.255.255.255

interface Ethernet0
 ip address 10.0.2.2 255.255.255.0
```

```
interface TokenRing0
 ip address 10.20.1.1 255.255.255.0
 ring-speed 16

router ospf 1
 network 10.0.0.0 0.0.255.255 area 0
 network 10.20.0.0 0.0.255.255 area 20
 area 0 range 10.0.0.0 255.255.0.0
 area 20 range 10.20.0.0 255.255.0.0
```

Listing 7.45   Router R5's configuration.

```
interface Loopback0
 ip address 10.100.0.5 255.255.255.255

interface Ethernet0
 ip address 10.100.1.1 255.255.255.0

interface Serial0
 ip address 10.100.128.6 255.255.255.252

router ospf 1
 network 10.0.0.0 0.255.255.255 area 100
```

Listing 7.46   Router R6's configuration.

```
interface Loopback0
 ip address 10.100.0.6 255.255.255.255

interface Ethernet0
 ip address 10.100.1.2 255.255.255.0

interface Serial0
 ip address 10.100.128.10 255.255.255.252

router ospf 1
 network 10.0.0.0 0.255.255.255 area 100
```

So far, no virtual link has been set up, so we can't expect the routing to function properly. The consequences of the partitioned backbone become evident if we examine the routing table of router R3, which is shown in Listing 7.47.

Listing 7.47   The routing table of router R3.

```
R3#show ip route
...
   10.0.0.0/8 is variably subnetted, 5 subnets, 3 masks
C    10.10.1.0/24 is directly connected, TokenRing0
C    10.0.0.3/32 is directly connected, Loopback0
```

```
O    10.0.0.1/32 [110/11] via 10.0.1.1, 00:14:18, Ethernet0
C    10.0.1.0/24 is directly connected, Ethernet0
O IA 10.100.0.0/16 [110/74] via 10.0.1.1, 00:14:18, Ethernet0
```

Notice that router R3 has only one inter-area route—for the summary address of Area 100 (10.100.0.0/16). It does not have a route for the summary address of Area 20 (10.20.0.0/16). Also missing is a route for the network prefix of segment 2 (10.0.2.0/24), although segment 2 is a part of the backbone to which router R3 is connected.

Let's restore the backbone by adding the **area 100 virtual-link** command under **router ospf 1** configurations of routers R1 and R2. Listings 7.48 and 7.49 show the new configurations of routers R1 and R2.

Listing 7.48   Router R1's configuration featuring a virtual link.

```
interface Loopback0
 ip address 10.0.0.1 255.255.255.255

interface Ethernet0
 ip address 10.0.1.1 255.255.255.0

interface Serial0
 ip address 10.100.128.5 255.255.255.252

router ospf 1
 network 10.0.0.0 0.0.255.255 area 0
 network 10.100.0.0 0.0.255.255 area 100
 area 100 range 10.100.0.0 255.255.0.0
 area 100 virtual-link 10.0.0.2
```

Listing 7.49   Router R2's configuration featuring a virtual link.

```
interface Loopback0
 ip address 10.0.0.2 255.255.255.255

interface Ethernet0
 ip address 10.0.2.1 255.255.255.0

interface Serial0
 ip address 10.100.128.9 255.255.255.252

router ospf 1
 network 10.0.0.0 0.0.255.255 area 0
 network 10.100.0.0 0.0.255.255 area 100
 area 100 range 10.100.0.0 255.255.0.0
 area 100 virtual-link 10.0.0.1
```

7. Open Shortest Path First (OSPF) Protocol

Let's now take a look at the routing table of router R3 (Listing 7.50).

Listing 7.50   The routing table of router R3 after the virtual links have been configured on routers R1 and R2.

```
R3#show ip route
...
   10.0.0.0/8 is variably subnetted, 9 subnets, 3 masks
C     10.10.1.0/24 is directly connected, TokenRing0
O     10.0.0.2/32 [110/149] via 10.0.1.1, 01:55:46, Ethernet0
O     10.0.2.0/24 [110/158] via 10.0.1.1, 01:55:46, Ethernet0
C     10.0.0.3/32 is directly connected, Loopback0
O     10.0.0.1/32 [110/11] via 10.0.1.1, 01:55:46, Ethernet0
C     10.0.1.0/24 is directly connected, Ethernet0
O     10.0.0.4/32 [110/159] via 10.0.1.1, 01:55:46, Ethernet0
O IA 10.20.0.0/16 [110/164] via 10.0.1.1, 01:55:46, Ethernet0
O IA 10.100.0.0/16 [110/74] via 10.0.1.1, 01:55:46, Ethernet0
```

Bingo! An inter-area route for missing Area 20 as well as routes for the previously missing backbone's network prefixes are finally in the routing table of router R3 (the shaded lines).

NOTE: *Notice that we did not do any summarization of the backbone network prefixes into the transit area (Area 100). This is in total agreement with the OSPF specification. In fact, if we did perform summarization of the backbone's network prefixes into the transit area, a routing loop would be created such that no communication would be possible between the partitions of the backbone.*

Configuring OSPF over NBMA Networks

Configuring OSPF over NBMA networks, such as Frame Relay, on Cisco routers has always been fun. Hence, in the remaining sections, I'll try to give a recipe for configuring Cisco routers for OSPF over NBMA networks for most situations. Obviously, I'm not going to try all possible combinations, such as point-to-point PVCs versus multipoint PVCs, Frame Relay versus X.25, point-to-point subinterfaces versus multipoint subinterfaces versus pure interfaces, multiple areas versus single areas, and a mix-and-match of these and possibly some other options. Instead, I'll review the conceptually separate configurations, which includes the following:

- OSPF over a fully meshed NBMA network represented as a broadcast transit network

- OSPF over a non-fully meshed NBMA network in the point-to-multipoint mode as per the OSPF specification

- OSPF over a non-fully meshed NBMA network manually forced into being represented as a broadcast transit network

All of the three cases will be considered using three routers interconnected over a Frame Relay network, with all the routers residing in a single OSPF area. The Frame Relay configuration will always be done on serial interfaces, which are the functional equivalent of multipoint subinterfaces.

These three cases do not include the easiest way to configure OSPF over an NBMA network: representing each circuit (a PVC in the case of Frame Relay) as a pair of subinterfaces on the routers that the circuit interconnects. The primary reason this method is not considered in this section is that it is an instance of multiple point-to-point connections, which represents nothing particular. In addition, although this method is the easiest, it may not be the best from the point of view of OSPF routing if the network is fully meshed. Each individual point-to-point connection creates a more complex graph than the one created as the result of representing a fully meshed NBMA network as a broadcast transit network.

Configuring OSPF over Fully Meshed NBMA Networks

In this section, we'll consider how to configure Cisco routers to treat a fully meshed Frame Relay network as a broadcast transit network.

As an example, we'll use the network shown in Figure 7.33.

By default, a serial interface with Frame Relay encapsulation is treated as a point-to-point interface by OSPF. To make the interface be treated as broadcast, the **ip ospf network broadcast** command must be entered in interface configuration mode. In addition, if Frame Relay **map** statements are used to map the counterpart routers to the Frame Relay PVC, the statements must include the **broadcast** keyword, which enables sending IP datagrams destined for the broadcast and multicast addresses over the PVC. (InverseARP does it automatically.)

Listings 7.51 through 7.53 show the configurations of all three routers.

Listing 7.51   Router R1's configuration.

```
ip subnet-zero

interface Loopback0
 ip address 10.0.0.1 255.255.255.255

interface Ethernet0
 ip address 10.0.1.1 255.255.255.0

interface Serial1
 ip address 10.255.0.1 255.255.255.248
 encapsulation frame-relay
 ip ospf network broadcast
 frame-relay map ip 10.255.0.2 102 broadcast
 frame-relay map ip 10.255.0.3 103 broadcast
```

```
router ospf 1
 network 10.0.0.0 0.255.255.255 area 0

ip classless
```

Listing 7.52   Router R2's configuration.

```
ip subnet-zero

interface Loopback0
 ip address 10.0.0.2 255.255.255.255

interface Ethernet0
 ip address 10.0.2.1 255.255.255.0

interface Serial0
 ip address 10.255.0.2 255.255.255.248
 encapsulation frame-relay
 ip ospf network broadcast
 frame-relay map ip 10.255.0.1 201 broadcast
 frame-relay map ip 10.255.0.3 203 broadcast

router ospf 1
 network 10.0.0.0 0.255.255.255 area 0

ip classless
```

Listing 7.53   Router R3's configuration.

```
ip subnet-zero

interface Loopback0
 ip address 10.0.0.3 255.255.255.255

interface Ethernet0
 ip address 10.0.3.1 255.255.255.0

interface Serial0
 ip address 10.255.0.3 255.255.255.248
 encapsulation frame-relay
 ip ospf network broadcast
 frame-relay map ip 10.255.0.1 301 broadcast
 frame-relay map ip 10.255.0.2 302 broadcast

router ospf 1
 network 10.0.0.0 0.255.255.255 area 0

ip classless
```

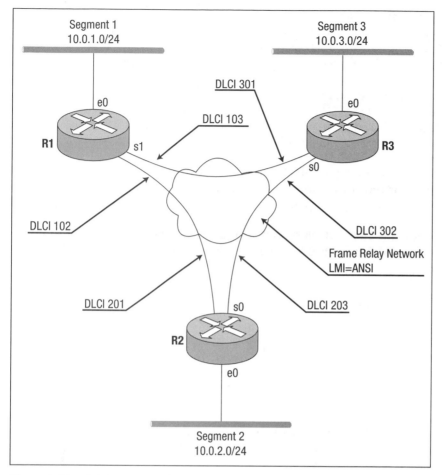

Segment 1
10.0.1.0/24

Segment 3
10.0.3.0/24

DLCI 301

e0

DLCI 103

e0

R1 s1

R3

s0

DLCI 102

DLCI 302

Frame Relay Network
LMI=ANSI

DLCI 201 s0

DLCI 203

R2

e0

Segment 2
10.0.2.0/24

Figure 7.33 A fully meshed Frame Relay network.

The **ip ospf network broadcast** commands are shown as shaded lines. In addition, the **broadcast** keywords are italicized to emphasize their importance.

Because the network is of the broadcast transit type, the routers must elect the designated and backup designated routers to establish adjacencies between each other. Listing 7.54 shows the output of the **show ip ospf neighbor** command entered on each of the three routers, which shows that router R2 was elected the designated router and router R3 the backup designated router for the network.

Listing 7.54 The output of the **show ip ospf neighbor** command entered on all three routers.

```
R1#show ip ospf neighbor
Neighbor ID     Pri   State        Dead Time    Address         Interface
10.0.0.2          1   FULL/DR      00:00:32     10.255.0.2      Serial1
10.0.0.3          1   FULL/BDR     00:00:31     10.255.0.3      Serial1
```

7. Open Shortest Path First (OSPF) Protocol

```
R2#show ip ospf neighbor
Neighbor ID     Pri   State          Dead Time   Address       Interface
10.0.0.1         1    FULL/DROTHER   00:00:30    10.255.0.1    Serial0
10.0.0.3         1    FULL/BDR       00:00:36    10.255.0.3    Serial0

R3#show ip ospf neighbor
Neighbor ID     Pri   State          Dead Time   Address       Interface
10.0.0.1         1    FULL/DROTHER   00:00:35    10.255.0.1    Serial0
10.0.0.2         1    FULL/DR        00:00:32    10.255.0.2    Serial0
```

Listing 7.55 shows the partial output of the **show ip ospf database** command and
show ip ospf database network command entered on router R1. The two outputs show that router R2 originated a network LSA for the Frame Relay network.

**Listing 7.55   The output of the show ip ospf database command and show ip ospf
database network command entered on router R1.**

```
R1#show ip ospf database
...
               Net Link States (Area 0)

Link ID          ADV Router       Age        Seq#       Checksum
10.255.0.3       10.0.0.3         103        0x80000002 0xAF3


R1#show ip ospf database network
...
               Net Link States (Area 0)

   Routing Bit Set on this LSA
   LS age: 129
   Options: (No TOS-capability, DC)
   LS Type: Network Links
   Link State ID: 10.255.0.3 (address of Designated Router)
   Advertising Router: 10.0.0.3
   LS Seq Number: 80000002
   Checksum: 0xAF3
   Length: 36
   Network Mask: /29
         Attached Router: 10.0.0.3
         Attached Router: 10.0.0.1
         Attached Router: 10.0.0.2
```

Configuring OSPF over Non-Fully Meshed NBMA Networks

In this section, we'll consider two ways to configure OSPF over non-fully meshed
Frame Relay networks.

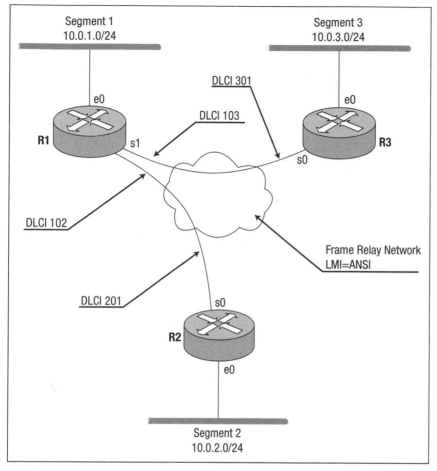

Figure 7.34   A non-fully meshed Frame Relay (NBMA) network.

We'll use the network shown in Figure 7.34 as an example.

Using the *ip ospf network point-to-multipoint* Command

When you enter the **ip ospf network point-to-multipoint** command in interface configuration mode, the OSPF process on the router treats the interface as connected to an NBMA network in point-to-multipoint mode. Such a network is modeled using the graph shown in Figure 7.7(b).

The command still assumes that the router can send IP datagrams destined for the broadcast and multicast addresses over the interface. This essentially means that, if the Frame Relay **map** statements are used, they must include the **broadcast** keyword.

Listings 7.56 through 7.58 show the configurations of all three routers.

Listing 7.56   Router R1's configuration.

```
ip subnet-zero

interface Loopback0
 ip address 10.0.0.1 255.255.255.255

interface Ethernet0
 ip address 10.0.1.1 255.255.255.0

interface Serial1
 ip address 10.255.0.1 255.255.255.248
 encapsulation frame-relay
 ip ospf network point-to-multipoint
 frame-relay map ip 10.255.0.2 102 broadcast
 frame-relay map ip 10.255.0.3 103 broadcast

router ospf 1
 network 10.0.0.0 0.255.255.255 area 0

ip classless
```

Listing 7.57   Router R2's configuration.

```
ip subnet-zero

interface Loopback0
 ip address 10.0.0.2 255.255.255.255

interface Ethernet0
 ip address 10.0.2.1 255.255.255.0

interface Serial0
 ip address 10.255.0.2 255.255.255.248
 encapsulation frame-relay
 ip ospf network point-to-multipoint
 frame-relay map ip 10.255.0.1 201 broadcast

router ospf 1
 network 10.0.0.0 0.255.255.255 area 0

ip classless
```

Listing 7.58   Router R3's configuration.

```
ip subnet-zero

interface Loopback0
 ip address 10.0.0.3 255.255.255.255
```

```
interface Ethernet0
 ip address 10.0.3.1 255.255.255.0

interface Serial0
 ip address 10.255.0.3 255.255.255.248
 encapsulation frame-relay
 ip ospf network point-to-multipoint
 frame-relay map ip 10.255.0.1 301 broadcast

router ospf 1
 network 10.0.0.0 0.255.255.255 area 0

ip classless
```

Let's examine the output of the **show ip ospf database router** command, which is shown in Listing 7.59.

Listing 7.59   The output of the show ip ospf database router command.

```
R3#show ip ospf database router

        OSPF Router with ID (10.0.0.3) (Process ID 1)

                Router Link States (Area 0)

   LS age: 425
   Options: (No TOS-capability, DC)
   LS Type: Router Links
   Link State ID: 10.0.0.1
   Advertising Router: 10.0.0.1
   LS Seq Number: 80000004
   Checksum: 0x827F
   Length: 84
    Number of Links: 5

     Link connected to: another Router (point-to-point)
      (Link ID) Neighboring Router ID: 10.0.0.2
      (Link Data) Router Interface address: 10.255.0.1
       Number of TOS metrics: 0
        TOS 0 Metrics: 64

     Link connected to: another Router (point-to-point)
      (Link ID) Neighboring Router ID: 10.0.0.3
      (Link Data) Router Interface address: 10.255.0.1
       Number of TOS metrics: 0
        TOS 0 Metrics: 64
```

```
    Link connected to: a Stub Network
     (Link ID) Network/subnet number: 10.255.0.1
     (Link Data) Network Mask: 255.255.255.255
      Number of TOS metrics: 0
       TOS 0 Metrics: 0
...
```

The first two links (point-to-point) represent the two edges going to the other routers. The third link represents the router's own interface modeled as a stub network. Notice that the length of the interface's network prefix is equal to /32 (255.255.255.255).

If we examine the routing table of router R3 (Listing 7.60), we'll notice two unusual routing table entries (shown as shaded lines). These are routes for the two other routers' interfaces connected to the Frame Relay network. They were modeled as stub networks, so the router created routes for them.

Listing 7.60   The output of the show ip route ospf command issued on router R3.

```
R3#show ip route ospf
     10.0.0.0/8 is variably subnetted, 9 subnets, 3 masks
O       10.0.2.0/24 [110/138] via 10.255.0.1, 00:09:04, Serial0
O       10.0.0.2/32 [110/129] via 10.255.0.1, 00:09:04, Serial0
O       10.0.1.0/24 [110/74] via 10.255.0.1, 00:09:04, Serial0
O       10.0.0.1/32 [110/65] via 10.255.0.1, 00:09:04, Serial0
O       10.255.0.1/32 [110/64] via 10.255.0.1, 00:09:04, Serial0
O       10.255.0.2/32 [110/128] via 10.255.0.1, 00:09:04, Serial0
```

Using OSPF Router Priorities

Finally, a non-fully meshed network that consists of a single router to which all other routers are connected through individual PVCs can be also modeled as a broadcast transit network.

If this model is to be used, however, the hub router must become the designated router for the network. The other routers are allowed to become neither the designated nor the backup designated routers.

These two conditions are easy to sustain if the interfaces that are connected to the Frame Relay network of all the routers except for the hub router are configured with the OSPF priority equal to 0. The priority equal to 0 guarantees that the router can become neither the designated nor backup designated router.

Listings 7.61 through 7.63 show the configurations of all three routers.

Listing 7.61   Router R1's configuration.

```
ip subnet-zero

interface Loopback0
 ip address 10.0.0.1 255.255.255.255
```

```
interface Ethernet0
 ip address 10.0.1.1 255.255.255.0

interface Serial1
 ip address 10.255.0.1 255.255.255.248
 encapsulation frame-relay
 ip ospf network broadcast
 frame-relay map ip 10.255.0.2 102 broadcast
 frame-relay map ip 10.255.0.3 103 broadcast

router ospf 1
 network 10.0.0.0 0.255.255.255 area 0

ip classless
```

Listing 7.62   Router R2's configuration.

```
ip subnet-zero

interface Loopback0
 ip address 10.0.0.2 255.255.255.255

interface Ethernet0
 ip address 10.0.2.1 255.255.255.0

interface Serial0
 ip address 10.255.0.2 255.255.255.248
 encapsulation frame-relay
 ip ospf network broadcast
 ip ospf priority 0
 frame-relay map ip 10.255.0.1 201 broadcast
 frame-relay map ip 10.255.0.3 201

router ospf 1
 network 10.0.0.0 0.255.255.255 area 0

ip classless
```

Listing 7.63   Router R3's configuration.

```
ip subnet-zero

interface Loopback0
 ip address 10.0.0.3 255.255.255.255

interface Ethernet0
 ip address 10.0.3.1 255.255.255.0
```

```
interface Serial0
 ip address 10.255.0.3 255.255.255.248
 encapsulation frame-relay
 ip ospf network broadcast
 ip ospf priority 0
 frame-relay map ip 10.255.0.1 301 broadcast
 frame-relay map ip 10.255.0.2 301

router ospf 1
 network 10.0.0.0 0.255.255.255 area 0

ip classless
```

As before, the serial interfaces of all three routers are configured as if they were connected to a broadcast network (**ip ospf network broadcast**). In addition, routers R2 and R3 feature the **ip ospf priority 0** command, which makes them ineligible to be elected as the designated or backup designated router for the segment.

If we check the output of the **show ip ospf neighbor** command entered on all three routers (Listing 7.64), we'll see that there is only a designated router, router R1.

Listing 7.64   The output of the show ip ospf neighbor command issued on all three routers.

```
R1#show ip ospf neighbor
Neighbor ID     Pri   State         Dead Time   Address       Interface
10.0.0.2          0   FULL/DROTHER  00:00:34    10.255.0.2    Serial1
10.0.0.3          0   FULL/DROTHER  00:00:34    10.255.0.3    Serial1

R2#show ip ospf neighbor
Neighbor ID     Pri   State         Dead Time   Address       Interface
10.0.0.1          1   FULL/DR       00:00:32    10.255.0.1    Serial0

R3#show ip ospf neighbor
Neighbor ID     Pri   State         Dead Time   Address       Interface
10.0.0.1          1   FULL/DR       00:00:39    10.255.0.1    Serial0
```

Finally, you must be wondering what the additional Frame Relay **map** statements without the keyword **broadcast** are for in the configurations of routers R2 and R3. (These are shown as the last shaded line in Listings 7.62 and 7.63.) The answer becomes obvious when we look at the resulting routing table of router R3 (Listing 7.65). The two shaded lines are the routes for the network prefixes behind router R2. Notice that both routes point to router R2, which is not accessible through the Frame Relay network. The only way to deliver the traffic to it is by sending the traffic through a PVC going to router R1 and then expecting router R1 to forward it further to router R2.

EIGRP

As I promised in Chapter 6, we'll now consider external IP route TLV entries. The format of an external IP route TLV entry is shown in Figure 6.9.

The first two fields—Protocol ID and Type Code—carry values 0x01 and 0x03, respectively.

The 16-bit Length field contains the lengths of the TLV entry. Because the network prefix described in the TLV entry can occupy a variable number of octets (from 1 through 4), the Length field can take values varying from 46 through 49.

The 32-bit Next Hop Router IP Address field carries the IP address of the next-hop router, which should forward traffic destined for the described network prefix from the segment onto which the EIGRP protocol data unit (PDU) carrying the TVL entry was transmitted. If this field carries the value of 0, the transmitting router itself is the next-hop router.

The 32-bit Originating Router IP Address field carries the IP address of the router that redistributed the network prefix described in the TLV entry into the EIGRP process.

The 32-bit Originating Autonomous System field carries the number of the autonomous system in which the network prefix resides. Apparently, not every source of routing information has an autonomous system number. For example, static and connected routes don't. Certain other sources of routing information such as Border Gateway Protocol (BGP) can report more than one autonomous system number. Table 7.1 shows what values the Originating Autonomous System field takes depending on the redistributed source of routing information.

The 32-bit Tag field carries an administratively assigned Tag value. This value can be assigned during redistribution by the router that performs redistribution as well as carried over from the redistributed source of routing information (providing the latter supports tags). For example, if a certain network prefix is originated and advertised with a certain tag by RIP version 2, this tag will be carried over into the EIGRP process on the redistributing router even if no tag is configured for redistribution. By default, the Tag field is equal to 0 except in one case: When EIGRP is configured to redistribute routing information from BGP or EGP, it uses the number of the autonomous system from which the network prefix was learned as the tag (the autonomous system number of the BGP or EGP process is used as the originating autonomous system). Both the default and carried-over tag values can be overwritten by explicitly specifying a tag for redistribution from the source of routing information.

NOTE: *Network administrators can assign values to the Tag field at their discretion.*

Listing 7.65   The routing table of router R3.

```
R3#show ip route ospf
     10.0.0.0/8 is variably subnetted, 7 subnets, 3 masks
O        10.0.2.0/24 [110/74] via 10.255.0.2, 00:11:19, Serial0
O        10.0.0.2/32 [110/65] via 10.255.0.2, 00:11:19, Serial0
O        10.0.1.0/24 [110/74] via 10.255.0.1, 00:11:19, Serial0
O        10.0.0.1/32 [110/65] via 10.255.0.1, 00:11:19, Serial0
```

Chapter 8

Controlling Routing Information

If you need an immediate solution to:	*See page:*
Understanding the Interoperation of Routing Protocols without Redistribution	556
Understanding and Using Redistribution of Routing Information	563
Filtering Routing Information	607
Understanding Routing Loops	623

In Depth

In this chapter, we'll consider two ways of interoperating routing protocols: redistributing and filtering routing information. In addition, we'll consider routing loops, which is the most common adverse effect of redistribution.

Redistribution

Multiple routing protocols can be run on a single router for several different reasons. Among the most typical are:

- Two networks are merged, and the routing in each is maintained by different routing protocols. Unless one of these networks is completely migrated to the routing protocol that is used in the other network before the merge, both routing protocols need to coexist at least on some routers. To ensure connectivity between the merged networks, these routers will have to handle the conversion of the routing information between the two routing protocols.

- A network is migrated from one routing protocol to another. Unless the migration is performed on all routers simultaneously (or the procedure allows a complete removal of the first routing protocol prior to implementing the new one), the routing protocols need to coexist on certain routers for some time. Again, in order to ensure connectivity between the part of the network that is already migrated to the new protocol and the one that is yet to be migrated, these routers must not only allow coexistence of the protocols but also perform conversion of the routing information between the protocols.

- Some "smart" hosts (that is, hosts that are capable of running a routing protocol) want to "silently" participate in dynamic routing, but the routing protocol of the network is not implemented on the hosts. (The word *silently* pertains to the fact that hosts do not advertise any routing information.) An example of such a situation can be that Unix or Windows NT machines run Routing Information Protocol (RIP) but the network is implemented with Cisco routers running Internet Gateway Routing Protocol (IGRP). Hence, the routers connected to the segments to which the smart hosts connected must convert IGRP to RIP specifically for these hosts.

Undoubtedly, we can think of many more cases that appear to warrant running multiple routing protocols on a single router. Disregarding the details behind each of these cases, it's clear that they all impose one common requirement: besides mere coexistence, the routing protocols must also exchange the routing information.

Simply running multiple routing protocols on the same router is not sufficient for the exchange of routing information among these protocols. Generally, the routers do not automatically pass the routing information of one routing protocol to another unless they are specifically instructed to do so. The reason for this is that multiple routing protocols—even being present on a single router—can yet serve different purposes. Therefore, it may be undesirable to have them exchange routing information.

Another reason that multiple routing protocols on a single router do not automatically exchange routing information is that different routing protocols typically calculate route metrics by different means, and these calculation methods are usually incompatible with each other. For example, RIP uses the simple hop-count as the metric, whereas IGRP and Enhanced Interior Gateway Routing Protocol (EIGRP) calculate the metric as the sum of the logical delays of the segments that constitute the path plus the inversed smallest bandwidth en route to the destination network prefix. The metrics are important, however; for example, one of the main functions of the metrics in distance-vector routing protocols is to prevent routing loops. Because the metrics are incompatible, there is no simple way to adequately convert the metrics of routes that are installed by different routing protocols. Inadequate conversion, however, can potentially lead to routing loops. Therefore, to avoid making a pernicious mistake, the routers do not "guess" how metrics must be converted. As a result, they do not automatically pass the routing information from one routing protocol to another.

The process of converting routing information among different sources of routing information is called *routing information redistribution*, or simply *redistribution*. The routing information that is passed from one source of routing information into another is said to be *redistributed*. Likewise, the routing information that is redistributed into some source of routing information is said to be redistributed into that source of routing information.

The sources of routing information are not limited to dynamic routing protocols: They also include static and connected routes. However, the static and connected routes can be redistributed into only dynamic routing protocols. For obvious reasons, there is no redistribution into static or connected routes.

Enabling redistribution on a router usually involves specifying the following three components:

- The source of the routing information to be redistributed
- The routing protocol into which the routing information must be redistributed

8. Controlling Routing Information

- The metrics that the routing protocol must use when advertising the redistributed routing information

The last component most typically comes down to specifying one or several fixed metrics that should be used by the routing protocol when advertising the redistributed routing information. If only one metric is specified, the routing protocol uses it for all redistributed network prefixes; if several metrics are specified, the routing protocol uses each of them for an individual set of redistributed network prefixes in accordance with separately provided rules.

One case of redistribution is specific to Cisco routers in which the last component is omitted: redistribution between EIGRP and IGRP, or between two IGRP or EIGRP processes on the same router. Because the metrics used by these two routing protocols are produced using the same formula times a different constant, they can be easily converted into each other.

Redistribution does not necessarily have to be two-way; that is, if one routing protocol is redistributed into another, then the second routing protocol does not have to be redistributed into the first one. It is possible—and sometimes desirable—to redistribute routing information from only one protocol to another, but not vice versa. For example, if hosts (such as Unix) that are capable of receiving routing information are present on a network whose routing protocol is not available on the hosts, the routing information can be provided to these hosts by redistributing the routing protocol of the network into the routing protocol that is implemented on the hosts. On the other hand, redistributing the routing protocol of the hosts into the routing protocol of the network is not necessary, because the hosts only receive routing information. Furthermore, it may even be desirable to prohibit such redistribution as a security measure in case a host becomes misconfigured and begins advertising bogus routing information. Such misconfiguration becomes even more of an issue on the hosts with multiple network interface cards (NICs) that may act as routers (which is sometimes the default and often overlooked). Most hosts, however, are not intended to be routers, and their routing performance is usually rather poor compared to that of the dedicated routers (such as Cisco routers). Nevertheless, a host with multiple NICs can learn of some routing information through one NIC and advertise this information through the other. The presence of the host acting as a router may create a topological shortcut such that some network prefixes may appear to certain routers to be better reachable through the host than through the real routers. If this happens, these routers begin forwarding the traffic that is destined for the affected network prefixes to the host. This, in turn, has two negative effects. First, it deteriorates the network performance, because the host can't forward network traffic as fast as the dedicated routers can. Second, it adversely affects the main function of the host, which is not routing.

Let's now discuss some side effects of redistribution.

As has already been mentioned, different routing protocols use different algorithms to calculate metrics. For example, RIP uses a simple hop-count as the metric; Open Shortest Path First (OSPF) calculates the metric as the sum of the costs of the individual segments that constitute the path to the destination; and EIGRP and IGRP not only summarize the costs (logical delays) of the segments but also track the smallest bandwidth en route to the destination network prefix in such a way that, should it decrease at some point, the resulting metric gets extra an increase. Regardless of the exact algorithm for the metric calculation, the metrics of all routing protocols (at least those that we considered) share a common feature: The metrics increase with the number of hops from the destination.

NOTE: Formally, the cumulative nature of metrics can be expressed using the following statement: For any d and d', such that $d' > d$, $M(d') > M(d)$, where d and d' are numbers of hops in the same path, and $M(x)$ is the metric function.

Given this common feature of the routing protocols' metrics, let's define the *metric domain* of a routing protocol as the part of the network in which the metrics of the routing protocol reflect the distances to the destinations. By the "part of the network," we assume a number of routers and segments; when we say "reflect the distances to the destination," we assume that the metrics increase with the number of hops from the destination (as per the above note). What's more, the metrics are calculated in accordance with the algorithm that the protocol prescribes for calculating metrics. In other words, any router within the metric domain of the routing protocol calculates the metric for the network prefix of any segment that resides within the metric domain in accordance with the algorithm that the routing protocol prescribes to calculate metrics. If a router uses any different algorithm to calculate the metric for a network prefix inside the metric domain, this router is located outside this metric domain. (This router may still reside inside some other metric domain, however.)

An example of a RIP version 1 metric domain is a contiguous group of segments whose network prefixes (subnets) belong to the same classful network prefix (classful network address). The boundary of this RIP metric domain lies through the routers, some interfaces of which are also connected to segments whose network prefixes do not belong to the aforementioned classful network prefix. As we know, when forming RIP routing updates that must be sent out of such interfaces, these routers replace the individual network prefixes with the classful network prefix whose metric they set to 1, thereby effectively discarding the accumulated metrics of the individual network prefixes. Apparently, any router without an interface assigned an Internet protocol (IP) address belonging to this classful network prefix can receive only these routing updates but no routing updates carrying individual network prefixes available within our RIP metric domain. (This constitutes the process that we previously called *classful summarization.*) These routers will have only routes for the classful network prefix itself; consequently, these routers will perceive any destination within the metric domain with a single metric—the one that they have for the classful network prefix. In other words, these routers no longer calculate metrics for the destinations within the RIP metric domain in accordance with the RIP-prescribed algorithm; hence, these routers reside outside the RIP metric domain. (As these routers use RIP, they belong to one or more other RIP metric domains.) Another example of a metric domain is an OSPF area whose ABRs are configured to perform summarization. (If the ABRs are not configured to summarize the area's network prefixes, the metric domain extends into the backbone and the other areas to which the ABRs are connected.)

The above examples all present natural metric domain boundaries, which are caused by summarization of longer network prefixes into aggregates, or summary network prefixes that hide individual (longer) network prefixes.

A metric domain boundary is also created on routers that perform the type of redistribution that replaces accumulated metrics with one or several fixed metrics. Depending on the routing protocol, redistribution may or may not be accompanied by summarization of the network prefixes. If it is, the produced metric domain boundary is not different from the natural metric domain boundary; otherwise, the metric domain boundary has a purely artificial nature: The individual network prefixes cross the boundary intact, but their metrics are reset to a fixed value.

The artificial network boundaries often negatively affect the network by inducing routing loops.

Routing Loops

Routing loops are paths in the network that bring the traffic to the same router more than once. Needless to say, routing loops are very undesirable because the traffic goes farther only to arrive at the same router. This, in turn, delays the traffic, if not completely preventing it from arriving at its destination. Routing loops subject the network to superfluous loads and cause enormous amounts of processing on the involved routers—both these events essentially decrease the effective throughput of the network.

Routing loops are deemed to be either *short-lived* or *long-lived*. As the terms suggest, short-lived routing loops do not subsist for long, and they typically disappear in a matter of seconds. In the worst case, they may exist for one or two minutes. Long-lived routing loops exist for much longer, anywhere from several minutes to forever. Most typically, long-lived routing loops won't go away unless special preventive measures are taken. Long-lived routing loops can be either *permanent* or *oscillating*. Permanent routing loops exist at all times, whereas oscillating routing loops go through cycles in which they disappear and reappear.

How do routing loops emerge? Short-lived routing loops usually emerge during convergence of dynamic routing protocols, although routing protocol convergence is not always accompanied by routing loops. Once the routing protocol converges, the routing loops disappear. Long-lived routing loops can be induced by multiple factors, all of which, however, originate from administrative intervention at some point (providing, of course, the network hardware and software function correctly).

Indeed, routing protocols are made self-stabilizing. Whereas temporary instability that is caused by network changes and often accompanied by short-lived routing loops may often be unavoidable, routing protocols eventually overcome the instability and establish loop-free routing. From that point on, the loop-free routing is sustained until another network change happens. No network protocol is designed to allow long-lived routing loops to occur at any moment of its operation.

All routing protocols are based on mathematical models that are proven not to induce long-lived routing loops. Most of these mathematical models enforce loop-free operation by requiring the metrics associated with destinations to grow with every hop away from the destinations. Formally, if router R_1 chooses a route for destination D through router R_2, then $M_1 > M_2$, where M_1 and M_2 are the metrics for destination D of routers R_1 and R_2, respectively. In other words, the farther the destination, the larger the metric. If this premise is sustained, a routing loop cannot emerge.

The proof of this is rather simple. Suppose that, in network N, all routers choose routes for destinations based on the aforementioned premise. Suppose, however, that a loop exists, and that there is router R_1, which established a route for destination D through router R_2, which in turn established its route for destination D through router R_3, and so on, up to router R_n, which established its route for destination D through router R_1. This situation is shown in Figure 8.1. As we presumed, the premise is sustained, so the metrics of all routers along the route must conform to the following:

$$\mathbf{M_1} > M_2 > M_3 > ... > M_{n-2} > M_{n-1} > M_n > \mathbf{M_1} ...$$

which essentially boils down to $M_1 > M_1$. Hence, our original assumption—that a loop can exist even if all routers sustain the premise—is incorrect.

Hence, routing loops won't emerge in a network in which routing is maintained by a single routing protocol, as long as the routing protocol restrictions (such as

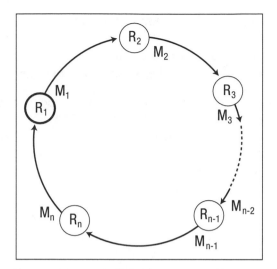

Figure 8.1   If router R1 chooses a route that eventually brings the traffic back to it, the metric must decrease at some step.

the maximum number of hops) are not violated and the network hardware and software function correctly.

However, once a network becomes maintained by more than one routing protocol or by a mix of static and dynamic routing, there is a potential for routing loops to emerge. This potential is increased by redistribution, because redistribution adjoins otherwise separate routing protocol domains while keeping the metric domains separate. In other words, destinations that reside within one routing protocol domain become reachable from the other routing protocol domain with an equal metric. How this facilitates routing loops to emerge is considered in the next two subsections.

Case 1: A Single Redistribution Point

Figure 8.2 shows a network in which a single point of redistribution can be a potential cause of routing loops.

Router R1 advertises network prefixes available in network N1 using routing protocol RP1 to router R2, which then redistributes these network prefixes into routing protocol RP2, by which it advertises them to its neighbors located in network N2. The administrative distance of routing protocol RP1 is equal to A1, and the administrative distance of routing protocol RP2 is equal to A2. The administrative distances are such that A2 < A1.

The large arrows with text inside show a flow of routing updates that, if it takes place, creates routing loops for all network prefixes located inside network N2.

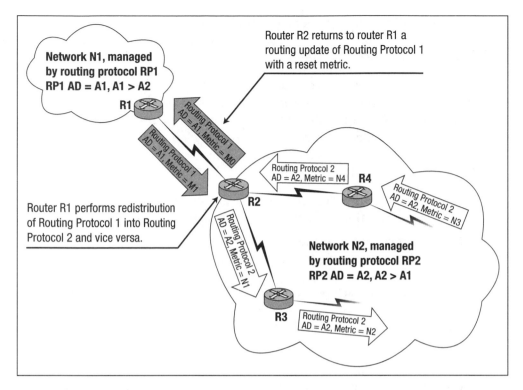

Figure 8.2   An oscillating routing loop emerges if router R2 receives a routing protocol
RP2 update that carries network prefixes located inside network N1.

The gray arrows denote the routing updates of routing protocol RP1, and the
white ones denote the updates of routing protocol RP2.

Let's first discuss the scenario that leads to routing loops, and then what can
facilitate the scenario to arise.

Router R1 sends a routing update that carries network prefixes located inside
network N1 to router R2. Router R2 picks up the routing update, establishes the
routes for the advertised network prefixes, and redistributes the network prefixes into routing protocol RP2 by which it then advertises the network prefixes to its neighbors. Suppose now that neighbor R3 receives router R2's routing
update and establishes its routes for the advertised network prefixes, after which
it itself begins to advertise the network prefixes to its neighbors. Eventually, a
routing update carrying the network prefixes located in network N2 arrives at
router R4, which—upon establishing the routes for the network prefixes—begins advertising them via routing protocol RP2 to router R2. At that point, router
R2 must replace its existing routes for the network prefixes pointing to router
R1 with new routes that point to router R4, because router R1 advertises the

network prefixes via routing protocol RP1, whereas router R4 advertises them via routing protocol RP2, whose administrative distance is smaller than that of routing protocol RP1.

However, this scenario has one tiny flaw: Router R2 would advertise the network prefixes it learned from router R1 to all of its neighbors almost simultaneously. That is, router R4 should most likely receive the first routing update that carries the network prefixes from router R2, after which it would establish its routes through router R2. From that point on, it should reject all other routing updates if they carry a higher metric than the metric of the routes through router R2.

Despite this flaw, the scenario is realistic and can happen, especially when facilitated by some additional events and circumstances:

- Router R2 may not send the routing update to all of its neighbors simultaneously. It may schedule to send the update first to router R3 and, only after that, to router R4. If the gap between transmitting the routing updates to routers R3 and R4 is large enough, router R4 may receive a routing update from another neighbor (as the scenario suggests), in which case it will advertise the network prefixes to router R2, thus causing it to establish bogus routes.

- The cost of the segment between router R2 and R4 is so large that router R4 would switch to the other route even if it previously installed a route through router R2. If this happens, router R4 will advertise the network prefixes located in network N1 to router R2, again causing router R2 to establish bogus routes for them.

- If router R4's interface (connecting it to the segment on which router R2 resides temporarily) goes down, router R4 would reestablish the routes for the network prefixes located in network N1 through another neighbor. After the interface comes back up, router R4 will advertise the network prefixes to router R2, which should cause router R2 to remove the correct routes and establish the bogus ones instead.

These are the most likely circumstances that help routing loops to emerge. Of course, some other circumstances could result in forcing router R2 to turn the routes for network prefixes located inside network N1 towards network N2.

Whatever circumstance made router R2 switch its routes, the events further evolve, as follows:

1. After router R2 changes the direction of its routes for the network prefixes located in network N1, it stops using the configured redistribution metric to advertise the network prefixes and instead begins using the metric it learned from router R4. This metric is obviously higher than the redistribution

metric, because it is essentially the original redistribution metric updated by the cost of the segments en route from router R3 to router R4.

2. Once router R3 notices the increase in the metric advertised by router R2, it puts its routes into holddown and begins advertising the network prefixes with the metric of infinity.

3. From this point on, the events can evolve in several different ways, with each resulting in routers R4 and R2 placing the bogus routes into holddown.

4. Once the holddown at router R2 expires, router R2 can reestablish the correct routes pointing to router R1, which shortly after that may be superseded by the bogus routes again. If the correct routes do get superseded, then another iteration of the described sequence of the events erupts, and the whole process will most probably repeat endlessly.

There is a certain probability that the process stops itself at some point, after which it never begins again (unless triggered by some event). The process can stop either after the first iteration or after a number of iterations.

The end result is that the described network configuration is very susceptible to routing loops. The following factors worsen the impact of the described routing loops:

- The loops may not emerge immediately. Instead, they can be triggered by some event. This can apparently happen at the least suitable time, such as during peak network use.

- The loops may oscillate either indefinitely or a limited number of times. Diagnosing oscillating routing loops in either case is more difficult than diagnosing permanent loops.

NOTE: *The section "Understanding Routing Loops Emerging from a Single Redistribution Point" later in this chapter presents an example of the described network configuration demonstrating a routing loop.*

Case 2: Multiple Redistribution Points

Unlike a single point of redistribution (which leads to oscillating routing loops), multiple points of redistribution usually lead to permanent routing loops. To better understand the problem, let's examine the network shown in Figure 8.3. The network is very similar to the one shown in Figure 8.2, except two routers—routers R2 and R5—now perform the redistribution between routing protocols RP1 and RP2. Everything else, including denotations, remains unchanged.

This time, the scenario is quite different. Suppose router R1 sends a routing update that carries the network prefixes located in network N1 to router R2. Just as before, router R2 receives the update, establishes routes for the network prefixes

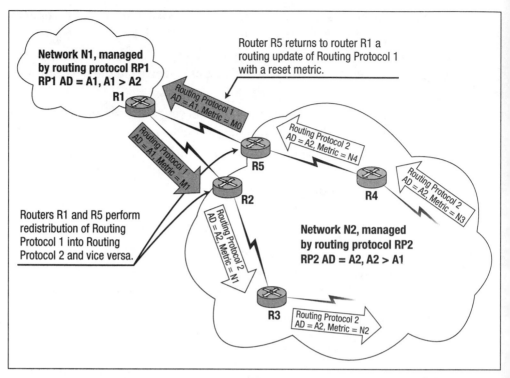

Figure 8.3   A permanent routing loop emerges if router R5 receives a routing protocol RP2 update carrying network prefixes located inside network N1, that were originally advertised by router R2 as the result of redistribution.

pointing to router R1, redistributes the network prefixes into routing protocol RP2, and begins advertising them to its neighbors. Router R2's neighbors also install the routes for the network prefixes and begin advertising them to their neighbors. Eventually, a routing update with the network prefixes arrives at router R4, which, after installing routes for them, begins advertising the network prefixes to router R5. Router R5 installs the routes for the network prefixes, redistributes the network prefixes back to routing protocol RP1, and starts advertising the network prefixes back into network N1. In our case, these routing updates hit router R1. If the redistribution metric with which router R5 advertises the network prefixes is smaller than the metric with which router R1 originally learned of the network prefixes, router R1 will dismiss the correct routes and install bogus routes pointing to router R5.

How likely is it that events would evolve as described? The answer is *very*. Unlike the scenario with a single redistribution point, the scenario with multiple redistribution points lacks the previously mentioned flaw, whereby router R2 would most probably advertise the redistributed network prefixes to all of its neighbors simultaneously, which would result in relatively stable loop-free routing. Although it's still possible that router R1 would advertise the network prefixes located in network N1 to both redistribution points (routers R2 and R5) simultaneously, this would require both that it be connected to the two routers and that the connections on both their ends be fully configured (the IP addresses assigned) and operational before even router R1 starts routing protocol R1 operation on its corresponding interfaces. A much more plausible situation is that the connections from router R1 to routers R2 and R5 are brought up one by one, which is exactly what's necessary for the described sequence of events to occur.

The subsequent events are completely different from those in the scenario with a single redistribution point. After router R1 establishes the bogus routes for the network prefixes located in network N2 through router R5, it changes the metrics with which it advertises the affected network prefixes. Most likely, the new metrics are going to be smaller than the correct ones (at least for some remote network prefixes in network N1). Thus, router R2 this time begins receiving routing updates from router R1 with *smaller* metrics (remember in the previous scenario, the metrics in router R1's routing updates *increased*), which essentially changes almost nothing. Router R2 simply corrects the metrics of the routes for the affected network prefixes of network N1, but as it redistributes the network prefixes into routing protocol RP2, it still keeps advertising them into network N2 with the configured fixed redistribution metric. This behavior of router R2 sustains the metrics at all routers along the path from router R2 to router R5. Router R5 redistributes the network prefixes into routing protocol RP1, via which router R5 advertises the network prefixes back to network N1 with the fixed redistribution metric, thereby completing the self-stabilizing cycle of mutual deception among the involved routers.

Figure 8.4 shows a more generic network diagram that is affected by a routing loop caused by two redistribution points. The routers are denoted by circles with router labels inside, the installed routes by thin arrows interconnecting routers, and the route metrics by indexed letters. The exchanged routing updates are shown as large white arrows containing indexed letters, and these letters denote the metrics with which the routers advertise the affected network prefix.

The metrics of routing protocols RP1 and RP2 use different metric systems; hence, the metrics are denoted using two different capital letters—M and N. The redistribution points—routers RX_1 and RX_2—advertise the affected network prefix with fixed redistribution metrics N^* and M^*, respectively. The routers installed their routes for the network prefix with the metrics M_0 and N_0, respectively. Notice that routers RX_1 and RX_2 advertise the network prefixes into one routing domain, whereas their routes for the network prefix point to the other. The routers in each domain have installed routes for the network prefix, which point towards

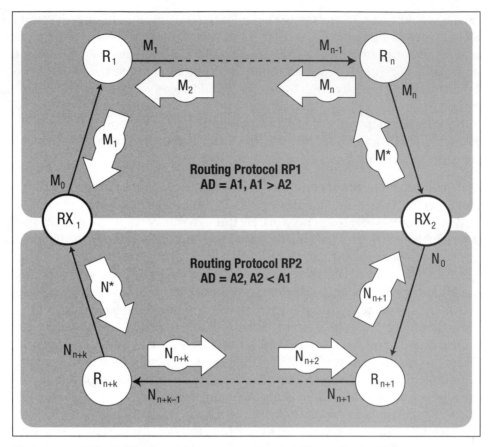

Figure 8.4 As redistribution points, routers RP_1 and RP_2 proliferate routing loops in the two routing domains.

the respective redistribution point—either router RX_1 or router RX_2. In the domain of routing protocol RP_1, router R_n installed a route for the network prefix through router RX_2 with metric M_n. This router advertises the network prefix to router R_{n-1} (not shown) with metric M_n as well. Router R_{n-1} installed the route for the network prefix through router R_n with metric R_{n-1}, with which it advertises the network prefix to router R_{n-2}.

This process continues until it reaches router R_1, which installed its route for the network prefix with metric M_1. Router R_1 also uses this metric when advertising the network prefix to router RX_1, which—upon updating the metric with the cost of the corresponding interface—installs the route pointing to router R_1 with metric M_0. At that point, router RX_1 redistributes the network prefix into routing protocol RP_2, via which it advertises the network prefix to router R_{n+k} with the fixed redistribution metric N^*, thereby effectively discarding the accumulated distance information. The routers along the path from router RX_1 to router RX_2 update their metrics in a similar way, so that router RX_2 installs its route for the network prefix with metric N_0. After this, it, like router RX_1, redistributes the network prefix into routing protocol RP_1 and discards the accumulated metric of routing protocol RP2.

NOTE: *The described scenarios (in this and the previous subsections) assume that split horizon is enabled on the interfaces of the involved routers, which is normally the case. If split horizon is turned off, the routing loops would still emerge, but their behavior might be different than described here.*

Other Causes Leading to Routing Loops

The previous two subsections described the two most common causes of routing loops, both of which share the same condition: The domain of the routing protocol with a lower administrative distance has redundant connections, which can potentially return the routing information originated by the routing protocol with the higher administrative distance. This causes routing loops because the new routes supersede the old ones (because they have a smaller administrative distance).

Routing loops can be caused during redistribution by other factors, as well. (One of these factors is demonstrated in the section "Understanding Routing Loops Emerging from Redistribution and the Disabled Split-Horizon Rule" later in this chapter.) However, all of these causes are rarer than the two we just examined.

Some other situations can cause routing loops. For example, if a partitioned OSPF backbone is interconnected via a transit area and the ABRs of the transit area perform summarization of the network prefixes located in the partitions of the backbone, the routes from one area to the other become looped at the routers within the transit area.

What Routing Protocols Are Affected

The above scenarios of how routing loops can emerge are described from the perspective of pure distance-vector protocols. Nevertheless, with minor changes, the scenarios apply for all kinds routing protocols, including link-state protocols. Even though routers running link-state protocols know the complete topology of the area in which they operate, they do not possess any topological knowledge of the inter-area and external destinations. Instead, the routers still handle these destinations in a fashion very much like that of distance-vector protocols, and therefore are susceptible to establishing the described routing loops.

Routing Protocol-Specific Aspects of Redistribution

EIGRP and OSPF are covered in the next two sections.

The 32-bit External Protocol Metric carries the metric of the route created by the redistributed source of routing information at the redistributing router.

The 16-bit Reserved field is reserved and typically should carry the value of 0.

The 8-bit External Protocol ID field carries the ID of the redistributed source of routing information. The possible values this field can take are shown in Table 8.1.

The 8-bit Exterior Flags field has the same meaning and structure as the Exterior Flags field of the internal IP route TLV entry (Figure 6.8 in Chapter 6).

The remaining fields (Delay, Bandwidth, MTU, Hop Count, Reliability, Load, Network Prefix Length and Network Prefix) are the same as the fields of the same name, in the internal IP route TLV entry. The 16-bit Reserved field is reserved and should typically carry the value of 0.

OSPF

Figure 7.16 of Chapter 7 shows the structure of type 5 and 7 link state advertisements (LSAs). As we remember, type 5 LSAs are used to convey network prefixes that appear outside of the autonomous system. Examples are network prefixes that reside in the Internet and other autonomous systems. Type 7 LSAs are used to convey network prefixes that reside in the autonomous system but are *not* originated by OSPF. Examples are network prefixes of another (relatively small) network that was merged into the autonomous system and whose routing was sustained by a routing protocol other than OSPF. There is one caveat, however—

Table 8.1   *The values of the External Protocol ID field and the routing information source they signify.*

Value	Routing Information Source	Originating Autonomous System	Default Tag
0x01	IGRP	IGRP AS number	0
0x02	EIGRP	EIGRP AS number	0
0x03	Static route	0	0
0x04	RIP	0	0
0x06	OSPF	Redistributing router's OSPF ID process	0
0x07	IS-IS	0	0
0x08	EGP	EGP AS number	The number of AS from which the network prefix was learned
0x09	BGP	Redistributing router's BGP AS number	The number of AS from which the network prefix was learned
0x0B	Connected route	0	0

this network is too small to handle all of the external routing information that exists in the autonomous system (as we remember, this routing information is propagated in the form of type 5 LSAs, which are flooded throughout the autonomous system except stub areas), and therefore it can't be made a part of a regular area. Yet, because the routing of the network is not sustained by OSPF, it can't be made a part of an OSPF stub area. The solution is to make the area to which the network is attached a *not-so-stubby area (NSSA)*. The behavior of ABRs of an NSSA is similar to that of ABRs of a stub area—instead of injecting all of the type 5 LSAs that exist in the autonomous system, NSSA ABRs inject only a single LSA conveying the default network prefix (0.0.0.0/0). The difference is that the ABRs of a regular stub area inject a type 3 LSA to convey the default network prefix, whereas the NSSA ABRs inject a type 7 LSA. In addition, NSSA ABRs are not required to inject the default network prefix (it's a configurable option).

Type 5 and 7 LSAs are originated by *autonomous system boundary routers (ASBRs)*. If an ASBR is located in a regular area, it originates type 5 LSAs; if an ASBR is located in an NSSA, it originates type 7 LSAs. The NSSA ABRs must convert type 7 LSAs to type 5 LSAs before flooding them into the rest of the network. Optionally, NSSA ABRs can be configured to perform summarization of network prefixes conveyed in type 7 LSAs before conversion to type 5 LSAs. If such a summarization is configured, the ABR will originate a single LSA for the summary network prefix in lieu of all individual network prefixes contained in type 7 LSAs and matched by the summary network prefix.

The section "Understanding the Specifics of Redistribution into OSPF" later in this chapter demonstrates how to inject external routing information into an OSPF autonomous system and how to configure NSSAs.

The structure of type 5 and 7 LSA is shown in Figure 7.16. The only difference between the two types of LSAs is in the Link State Type field of the LSA header, which carries either 5 or 7, depending on the LSA type.

Each type 5 and 7 LSA carries a single network prefix. All of the 32 bits of the network prefix are specified in the Link State ID field of the LSA header. The very first field of the LSA, the 32-bit Network Mask field, carries the subnet mask of the network prefix.

The next two fields—the 1-bit E field and 24-bit Metric field—specify the type of metric and the metric itself, respectively. If the E field carries the value of 0, the metric type is 1; otherwise it's 2. Type 1 metrics are "compatible" with OSPF metrics, which essentially means that the OSPF routers will calculate the actual metric for the network prefix as the sum of the metric carried in the LSA and the metric of the router routing table entry for the ASBR originating the LSA. Type 2 metrics are incompatible with OSPF metrics; hence, the OSPF routers simply use the value of the Metric field to create a route. If an OSPF router has two type 5 or 7 LSAs for the same network prefix, but one has metric type 1 and the other one metric type 2, the one with metric type 1 is used to create a route for the network prefix.

The 32-bit Forwarding IP Address field carries the IP address that should forward the traffic to the external network prefix. If this field carries the value of 0, the forwarding router is the ASBR that originates the LSA.

Finally, the 32-bit External Route Tag field carries the tag associated with the external network prefix. The meaning of this field and the considerations for its use are the same as those of the field of the same name for RIP version 2 route entries and EIGRP external IP route TLV entries.

Optionally, type 5 and 7 LSAs can carry up to four ToS entries. Each ToS entry specifies the metric, metric type, forwarding router, and tag for the corresponding ToS value (ToS values were discussed in Chapter 1). As ToS is hardly used, the ToS fields are kept in the OSPF version 2 specification primarily for the reasons of compatibility with OSPF version 1.

Filtering Routing Information

It's often necessary to propagate routing information in a controlled fashion. For example, in Figure 8.5, it might be desirable to prevent router R1 from advertising all of the network prefixes that are available in network 1 to router R2 because of lack of trust between the networks. Likewise, it may be a good idea to make router R1 learn from router R2 only the network prefixes that are needed in network 1, and make router R1 filter out all other network prefixes.

These and certain other similar tasks are frequently referred to by a generic term: *filtering of routing information.*

Filtering Routing Information Exchanged between Routers

One way to filter routing information is by checking the advertised network prefixes contained in routing updates against a certain condition. If a network prefix meets the condition, the network prefix in the routing update is processed; otherwise, it's discarded. The actual meaning of the word *processed* depends on whether the routing update is being received or sent. If the routing update is sent by the router itself, then it should contain only those network prefixes that successfully passed the specified condition. The network prefixes that did not pass the condition are removed from the routing update. The condition that is applied to the network prefixes that the router itself advertises is called an *outbound filter.* If

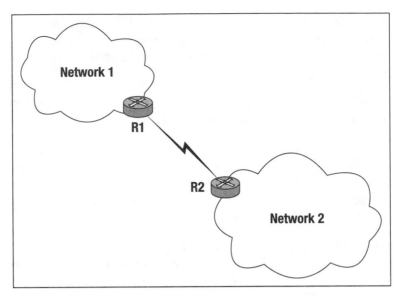

Figure 8.5   If lack of trust between the networks is an issue, routers R1 and R2 may not advertise all network prefixes available in the networks behind them. In addition, they can filter the routing information that they learn from each other.

the router receives the routing update, it considers (for updating the routing table) only those network prefixes that passed the condition. Again, those that did not pass the condition are discarded. The condition that the router applies to the network prefixes contained in the received routing updates is called an *inbound filter*.

Both inbound and outbound filters are most typically applied on a per-interface basis. The outbound filters can be used with only distance-vector routing protocols. They cannot be used with link-state routing protocols because link-state routing protocols operate on the premise that all routers are aware of the exact network topology (at least in the area to which they are attached). Outbound filtering prevents some routers from knowing the parts of the network topology that do not meet the condition of the outbound filter.

Although inbound filters can be used with both types of routing protocols, their effect differs depending upon whether the routing protocol is link state or distance vector. In both cases, the main function of an inbound filter is to prevent the router from establishing routes for the network prefixes that do not pass the filter through the interface on which the filter is applied. As we know, if a distance-vector routing protocol fails to install a route for a network prefix, it can't advertise the network prefix. Thus, a routing filter that filters out some network prefixes also prevents the router from advertising them. Unlike distance-vector protocols, link-state protocols do not rely on a routing database when propagating routing information. Instead, link-state protocols rely on their link-state databases, which are not affected by routing filters. Therefore, even if some network prefix becomes filtered out (and, thus, a route for it does not get installed in the router's routing table), the router still advertises it (if it runs a link-state protocol).

Filtering Routing Information during Redistribution

Alternatively, filtering can be done during redistribution between the redistributed routing information source and the routing protocol into which the routing information is redistributed. The routing information is passed from the redistributed routing information source into the routing protocol only if it successfully passes the specified condition. Otherwise, the routing information is not passed, which essentially results in the routing protocol not being advertised.

8. Controlling Routing Information

Immediate Solutions

Understanding the Interoperation of Routing Protocols without Redistribution

Obviously, nothing prevents you from configuring two or more routing protocols on a router without redistribution. In some cases, it may even be a good idea. For example, when considering a migration from one routing protocol to another, you might want to enable the new routing protocol in a "shadow mode," whereby you'd set the administrative distance of the new routing protocol to a higher value than that of the existing one and disable redistribution between the protocols. Then, you would check if the new routing protocol performs as expected by examining the protocol-specific data structures on the routers. After that, you'd start planning the actual migration.

Although the idea seems okay, it doesn't appear to be viable if the new routing protocol is of the distance-vector type. Indeed, the distance-vector routing protocols will advertise only those network prefixes for which they successfully installed routes into the routing table. In the described scenario, however, we deliberately make sure that the new routing protocol won't install any routes into the routing table by setting its administrative distance to a higher value than the administrative distance of the existing routing protocol.

However, it may seem that EIGRP would not abide by the described limitation, because—unlike the regular distance-vector routing protocols such as RIP and IGRP—EIGRP does not rely on the routing table only. It also uses its own data structure, the topology table, which contains enough information to re-create the routing table entries that EIGRP would install if its administrative distance allowed doing so.

Let's see if EIGRP's behavior is much different from that of the other distance-vector routing protocols in the proposed scenario. To do so, we'll use the network shown in Figure 8.6. In the network, two protocols are enabled: routing protocol 1 and routing protocol 2. The administrative distance of routing protocol 1 is smaller than that of routing protocol 2.

In our first experiment with the network, routing protocol 1 will be IGRP and routing protocol 2 will be EIGRP. Because the administrative distance of EIGRP is smaller than that of IGRP by default, we'll change the administrative distance

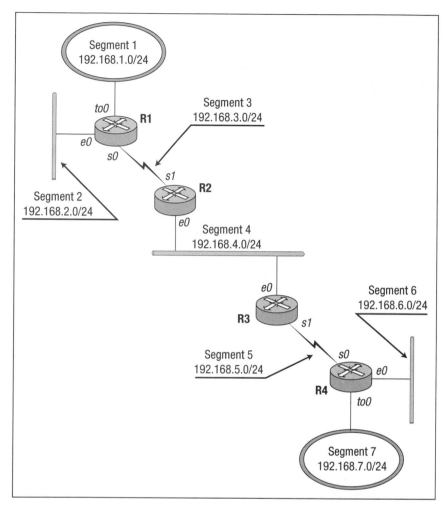

Figure 8.6 The routers are configured with two routing protocols without redistribution.

of the internal EIGRP routes to 130 using the **distance eigrp 130 170** command under the **router eigrp** configuration. (The **distance eigrp** command will be explained in the "Using the **distance eigrp** Command" section later in this chapter.) In addition, to avoid automatic redistribution, we'll configure IGRP and EIGRP processes on the routers with different autonomous system numbers.

Listings 8.1 through 8.4 show the configurations of all four routers.

Listing 8.1   Router R1's configuration.

```
interface Ethernet0
 ip address 192.168.2.1 255.255.255.0
```

8. Controlling Routing Information

```
interface Serial0
 ip address 192.168.3.1 255.255.255.0

interface TokenRing0
 ip address 192.168.1.1 255.255.255.0
 ring-speed 16

router eigrp 10
 network 192.168.1.0
 network 192.168.2.0
 network 192.168.3.0
 distance eigrp 130 170

router igrp 1
 network 192.168.1.0
 network 192.168.2.0
 network 192.168.3.0
```

Listing 8.2   Router R2's configuration.

```
interface Ethernet0
 ip address 192.168.4.1 255.255.255.0

interface Serial1
 ip address 192.168.3.2 255.255.255.0

router eigrp 10
 network 192.168.3.0
 network 192.168.4.0
 distance eigrp 130 170

router igrp 1
 network 192.168.3.0
 network 192.168.4.0
```

Listing 8.3   Router R3's configuration.

```
interface Ethernet0
 ip address 192.168.4.2 255.255.255.0

interface Serial1
 ip address 192.168.5.1 255.255.255.0

router eigrp 10
 network 192.168.5.0
 network 192.168.4.0
 distance eigrp 130 170
```

```
router igrp 1
 network 192.168.5.0
 network 192.168.4.0
```

Listing 8.4   Router R4's configuration.

```
interface Ethernet0
 ip address 192.168.6.1 255.255.255.0

interface Serial0
 ip address 192.168.5.2 255.255.255.0

interface TokenRing0
 ip address 192.168.7.1 255.255.255.0
 ring-speed 16

router eigrp 10
 network 192.168.5.0
 network 192.168.6.0
 network 192.168.7.0
 distance eigrp 130 170

router igrp 1
 network 192.168.5.0
 network 192.168.6.0
 network 192.168.7.0
```

Let's first take a look at the routing table of router R1, which is shown in Listing 8.5. As we might expect, the routing table shows no presence of EIGRP routes.

Listing 8.5   The routing table of router R1.

```
R1#show ip route
...
I    192.168.4.0/24 [100/8576] via 192.168.3.2, 00:01:26, Serial0
I    192.168.5.0/24 [100/10576] via 192.168.3.2, 00:01:26, Serial0
I    192.168.6.0/24 [100/10676] via 192.168.3.2, 00:01:26, Serial0
I    192.168.7.0/24 [100/10639] via 192.168.3.2, 00:01:26, Serial0
C    192.168.1.0/24 is directly connected, TokenRing0
C    192.168.2.0/24 is directly connected, Ethernet0
C    192.168.3.0/24 is directly connected, Serial0
```

Let's now take a look at the EIGRP topology table of router R1 (Listing 8.6). It contains only four network prefix records: three for the network prefixes to which router R1 is directly attached, and the fourth one, shown as two shaded lines, for the network prefix of segment 4. No records exist for the other network prefixes. As indicated by the router subrecord of the fourth network prefix record, it is

8. Controlling Routing Information

learned from router R2, which advertises it with the metric that is *not* equal to infinity. However, router R1 labels the network prefix record as inaccessible (actually, router R1 sets the feasible and reported distances to infinity), because the EIGRP process fails to install a route for the network prefix. An IGRP route with the smaller administrative distance already exists for this network prefix.

Listing 8.6   The topology table of router R1.

```
R1#show ip eigrp topology
...
P 192.168.1.0/24, 1 successors, FD is 176128
        via Connected, TokenRing0
P 192.168.2.0/24, 1 successors, FD is 281600
        via Connected, Ethernet0
P 192.168.3.0/24, 1 successors, FD is 2169856
        via Connected, Serial0
P 192.168.4.0/24, 0 successors, FD is Inaccessible
        via 192.168.3.2 (2195456/281600), Serial0
```

The EIGRP processes on the other routers do the same thing. They label as inaccessible all of the network prefixes that are learned from the neighbors' routing updates. As the network prefixes are inaccessible, the routers won't advertise them to their neighbors.

This example confirms that, regardless of EIGRP's topology table, the distance-vector nature of the protocol still prevails. If EIGRP cannot install a route into the routing table, it won't advertise it.

Let's now remove the **distance eigrp 130 170** command from router R1's configuration. Doing so should restore the default administrative distance of EIGRP, which is equal to 90. The default administrative distance of IGRP is 100, which is greater than 90; hence, EIGRP now must be able to install its routes into the routing table. Let's see if it happens. Listing 8.7 shows the output of the **show ip route** command after the default administrative distance of EIGRP has been restored on router R1.

Listing 8.7   The routing table of router R1 after the default administrative distance of EIGRP has been restored on router R1.

```
R1#show ip route
...
D    192.168.4.0/24 [90/2195456] via 192.168.3.2, 00:00:01, Serial0
I    192.168.5.0/24 [100/10576] via 192.168.3.2, 00:00:02, Serial0
I    192.168.6.0/24 [100/10676] via 192.168.3.2, 00:00:02, Serial0
I    192.168.7.0/24 [100/10639] via 192.168.3.2, 00:00:02, Serial0
C    192.168.1.0/24 is directly connected, TokenRing0
C    192.168.2.0/24 is directly connected, Ethernet0
C    192.168.3.0/24 is directly connected, Serial0
```

Notice the shaded line, which indicates the EIGRP route. This EIGRP route is for the only network prefix that appeared in the topology table of router R1 (Listing 8.6). An interesting feature of this network prefix is that it is located exactly one hop away from router R1. However, no EIGRP routes exist for network prefixes located farther than one hop away. This is not surprising because the EIGRP process on router R2 still has a higher administrative distance than IGRP. Thus, router R2 advertises via EIGRP only the network prefixes of the directly connected segments, which are at best located one hop away from router R1.

If we examine the topology table of router R1 now, we'll see that the network prefix record for segment 4's network prefix is no longer labeled as inaccessible:

```
R1#show ip eigrp topology
...
P 192.168.4.0/24, 1 successors, FD is 2195456
         via 192.168.3.2 (2195456/281600), Serial0
```

As EIGRP now has a lower administrative distance than IGRP and therefore can install its routes into the routing table, it no longer labels the learned network prefixes as inaccessible in the topology table.

We can conclude from this experiment that, although the idea of running EIGRP in shadow mode is attractive, it does not produce desirable results, which is the general rule for distance-vector routing protocols.

Let's now make routing protocol 2 OSPF. To do that, we'll remove the EIGRP configuration on each router by using the **no router eigrp 10** command and add the following OSPF configuration:

```
router ospf 1
 router-id 0.0.0.<router #>
 network 192.168.0.0 0.0.255.255 area 0
```

The *<router #>* parameter denotes the number of the router on which the configuration is added.

By default, OSPF has an administrative distance of 110, which is greater than the administrative distance of IGRP; hence, OSPF won't be able to install its routes into the routing table, which in turn means that the routing tables of the routers will still contain only IGRP routes. (For example, the routing table of router R1 will remain as shown in Listing 8.5.) But will the higher administrative distance prevent the routers from successfully exchanging the OSPF topology information among themselves? It won't, which is confirmed by the output of the **show ip ospf database** command entered on router R1 (Listing 8.8).

Listing 8.8   The output of the show ip ospf database command entered on router R1.

```
R1#show ip ospf database

         OSPF Router with ID (0.0.0.1) (Process ID 1)

                 Router Link States (Area 0)

Link ID          ADV Router       Age       Seq#        Checksum Link count
0.0.0.1          0.0.0.1          50        0x80000002 0xC5F9    4
0.0.0.2          0.0.0.2          1         0x80000003 0x6E5D    3
0.0.0.3          0.0.0.3          22        0x80000002 0xCA69    3
0.0.0.4          0.0.0.4          18        0x80000002 0x2584    4

                 Net Link States (Area 0)

Link ID          ADV Router       Age       Seq#        Checksum
192.168.4.2      0.0.0.3          2         0x80000001 0xD5EC
```

Notice that the link-state database contains the router LSAs of all four routers. This unequivocally confirms that, despite the nonfavorable administrative distance of OSPF, the routers exchange complete OSPF topology information without problems.

Let's make the administrative distance of OSPF on router R1 equal to 70 (using the **distance 70** command under **router ospf 1** configuration). After that, let's examine the output of the **show ip route** command on router R1 (Listing 8.9).

Listing 8.9   The routing table of router R1 after the administrative distance of OSPF was set to 70.

```
R1#show ip route
...
O    192.168.4.0/24 [70/74] via 192.168.3.2, 00:00:07, Serial0
O    192.168.5.0/24 [70/138] via 192.168.3.2, 00:00:08, Serial0
O    192.168.6.0/24 [70/148] via 192.168.3.2, 00:00:08, Serial0
O    192.168.7.0/24 [70/144] via 192.168.3.2, 00:00:08, Serial0
C    192.168.1.0/24 is directly connected, TokenRing0
C    192.168.2.0/24 is directly connected, Ethernet0
C    192.168.3.0/24 is directly connected, Serial0
```

Notice that OSPF routes have completely replaced the IGRP routes. This happens because OSPF has the complete topology information from which it can calculate all routes. Because it can calculate all the routes, it installs them into the routing table, thereby replacing all of the IGRP routes. This is quite a departure from the EIGRP versus IGRP scenario, in which EIGRP is able to install the routes for only those network prefixes that are located one hop away.

NOTE: *The other link-state protocol available on Cisco routers—IS-IS—behaves in the same manner as OSPF.*

After this experiment, our conclusion is that running link-state protocols in shadow mode does produce the desirable results and is thus worth being considered as a preliminary step in routing protocol migration projects.

WARNING! **Be extremely careful with the described scenario if OSPF must replace a distance-vector routing protocol (such as IGRP or RIP). Although OSPF is not affected by its inability to install routes into the routing table, once it gets the low administrative distance and replaces the other routing protocol's routes with its own, the other routing protocol won't be able to advertise the respective network prefixes.**

Understanding and Using Redistribution of Routing Information

Redistribution of routing information is covered in this section.

Configuring Basic Redistribution

Redistribution is enabled using the command **redistribute** *<source>* [metric *<fixed metric>*] available under each routing protocol configuration (for example, under **router rip** configuration). The *<source>* parameter indicates the source of routing information to be redistributed into the routing protocol. Table 8.2 shows some of the most typical values that this parameter can take.

Table 8.2   The most common values accepted by the <source> parameter of the redistribute command.

Keyword	Meaning
Connected	Connected
static	Static routes
rip	Routing Information Protocol (RIP)
igrp	Interior Gateway Routing Protocol (IGRP)
eigrp	Enhanced Interior Gateway Routing Protocol (EIGRP)
ospf	Open Shortest Path First (OSPF)
isis	ISO IS-IS
bgp	Border Gateway Protocol (BGP)

8. Controlling Routing Information

The optional part of the command, consisting of the **metric** keyword followed by the *<fixed metric>* parameter, denotes the protocol-specific metric with which the routing protocol advertises the network prefixes that it learns in the course of redistribution. Hereafter, we'll call this metric the *redistribution metric*. For example, in the case of RIP and OSPF, the *<fixed metric>* parameter takes integer values in the range from 1 through 4294967295. Obviously, in the case of RIP, specifying any value greater than 15 prevents RIP from advertising the redistributed routing information. In the case of IGRP and EIGRP, the *<fixed metric>* parameter consists of a set of values: *<B>*, *<D>*, *<R>*, *<L>* and *<MTU>*. These values correspond to the logical bandwidth, logical delay, reliability, load, and smallest maximum transmission unit (MTU) size, respectively, with which all network prefixes resulting from the redistribution must be advertised. The *<B>* parameter is measured in kilobits per second (Kbps) and accepts integer values from 1 through 4294967295. The *<D>* parameter is measured in tens of seconds and accepts integer values from 0 through 4294967295. The *<R>* parameter is measured on the scale from 0 through 255, with 255 denoting a totally reliable path. The *<L>* parameter is measured on the scale from 1 through 255, with 255 indicating a completely saturated path. Finally, the *<MTU>* parameter is measured in octets (8-bit bytes) and accepts integer values from 1 through 4294967295.

NOTE: *In the case of IGRP, specifying values greater than 16777215 for the <B> and <D> parameters does not make sense, because the Bandwidth and Delay fields in the IGRP route entries are only 3 octets long. The MTU field of the IGRP route entry is only 2 octets long; therefore, specifying values greater than 65535 for the <MTU> parameter also doesn't make sense (which makes perfect sense anyway because in reality, the biggest MTU size does not exceed 5,000 octets). In addition, the MTU field in the EIGRP IP internal and external TLV entries is 3 octets long, so specifying values greater than 16777215 does not make sense, either.*

To see how the command works, we'll use the network example shown in Figure 8.7.

Routers R1 and R2 run IGRP; routers R4 and R5 run just RIP; router 3 runs and also performs mutual redistribution of them. Listings 8.10 through 8.14 show the configuration of all five routers.

Listing 8.10   Router R1's configuration.

```
interface Ethernet0
 ip address 10.0.1.1 255.255.255.0

interface Serial0
 ip address 10.0.2.1 255.255.255.0

router igrp 1
 network 10.0.0.0
```

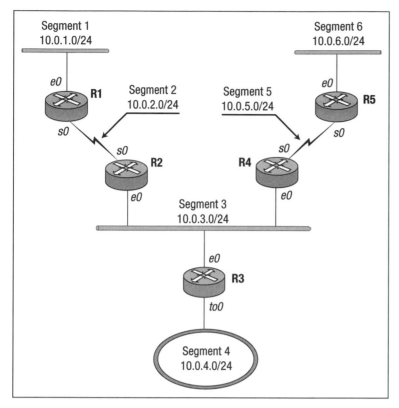

Figure 8.7   Routers R1 and R2 (IGRP), router R3 IGRP and RIP, (mutually redistributed) and routes R4 and R5 (RIP).

Listing 8.11   Router R2's configuration.

```
interface Ethernet0
 ip address 10.0.3.1 255.255.255.0

interface Serial0
 ip address 10.0.2.2 255.255.255.0

router igrp 1
 network 10.0.0.0
```

Listing 8.12   Router R3's configuration.

```
interface Ethernet0
 ip address 10.0.3.3 255.255.255.0
 no ip split-horizon

interface TokenRing0
 ip address 10.0.4.1 255.255.255.0
```

8. Controlling Routing Information

```
router rip
  redistribute igrp 1 metric 5
  network 10.0.0.0

router igrp 1
  redistribute rip metric 10000 10 255 1 1500
  network 10.0.0.0
```

Listing 8.13   Router R4's configuration.

```
interface Ethernet0
  ip address 10.0.3.2 255.255.255.0

interface Serial0
  ip address 10.0.5.1 255.255.255.0

router rip
  network 10.0.0.0
```

Listing 8.14   Router R5's configuration.

```
interface Ethernet0
  ip address 10.0.6.1 255.255.255.0

interface Serial0
  ip address 10.0.5.2 255.255.255.0

router rip
  network 10.0.0.0
```

The two shaded lines in Listing 8.12 show the redistribution configuration commands. Pay attention to the italicized line in Listing 8.12 (**no ip split-horizon**). Why is it needed? The reason why this command appears in router R3's configuration is simple: RIP and IGRP apply the split-horizon rule to all network prefixes, regardless of whether they were learned in the course of redistribution or from routing updates. Routers R2, R3, and R4 are interconnected only through segment 3. Router R2 advertises the network prefixes that it can reach via IGRP, whereas router R4 does so via RIP. Router R3 runs both routing protocols and so must re-advertise via RIP the network prefixes it learns via IGRP, and vice versa. Furthermore, router R3 must re-advertise the network prefixes through the same interface through which it learns of them: the Ethernet0 interface. Hence, unless the split-horizon rule is turned off on the Ethernet0 interface, router R3 won't be able to re-advertise the network prefixes as required. This, in turn, would result in the inability of routers R1 and R2 to learn of the network prefixes that routers R4 and R5 advertise, and vice versa.

Not all distance-vector routing protocols obey the split-horizon rule when deciding whether to advertise network prefixes learned via redistribution through a particular interface, nor in all situations do they. In general, the following rules apply with regard to performing the split-horizon rule for the redistributed network prefixes:

- RIP and IGRP obey the split-horizon rule when advertising the network prefixes learned via redistribution from distance-vector routing protocols. For example, if IGRP learns of a network prefix via redistribution from EIGRP, IGRP won't advertise the network prefix through the output interface of the route installed by EIGRP.

  If necessary, split-horizon can be turned off on the interface basis using the **no ip split-horizon** command.

- RIP and IGRP obey the split-horizon rule when advertising the network prefixes acquired via redistribution from static routes. For example, if RIP learns of a network prefix via redistribution of a static route, RIP won't advertise the network prefix through the output interface of the static route.

- RIP and IGRP do not obey the split-horizon rule when advertising routing information that is learned via redistribution from link-state routing protocols. For example, if RIP learns of a network prefix via redistribution from IS-IS, RIP advertises the network prefix through the output interface of the corresponding IS-IS route.

- EIGRP does not obey the split-horizon rule when advertising the routing information learned via redistribution. This applies to all sources from which the routing information is redistributed into EIGRP. In other words, EIGRP always advertises the network prefixes that it learns about through redistribution out of the output interfaces of the corresponding routes. This behavior of EIGRP does not depend on the **ip split-horizon eigrp** command.

Let's examine the routing table of router R1, which is shown in Listing 8.15.

Listing 8.15   The routing table of router R1.

```
R1#show ip route
...
     10.0.0.0/24 is subnetted, 6 subnets
C       10.0.2.0 is directly connected, Serial0
I       10.0.3.0 [100/8576] via 10.0.2.2, 00:00:06, Serial0
C       10.0.1.0 is directly connected, Ethernet0
I       10.0.6.0 [100/8586] via 10.0.2.2, 00:00:06, Serial0
I       10.0.4.0 [100/8639] via 10.0.2.2, 00:00:06, Serial0
I       10.0.5.0 [100/8586] via 10.0.2.2, 00:00:06, Serial0
```

The two shaded lines indicate the routes for the network prefixes of segments 6 and 5, respectively, which were originally advertised by routers R4 and R5 through RIP. Notice that, despite different physical distances for router R1 to segments 5 and 6, the metrics of the routes for the network prefixes are the same. This happens because router R3 discards the original RIP metrics and replaces them with the configured fixed redistribution metric.

Understanding Summarization when Redistributing into RIP and IGRP

Classful routing protocols—that is, IGRP and RIP version 1—perform classful summarization of the network prefixes that are learned through redistribution in the same manner that they perform classful summarization of the network prefixes they originate. In other words, classful routing protocols replace a set of network prefixes belonging to the same classful network address with the classful network address itself in the routing updates that are sent over interfaces whose IP addresses do not belong to the classful network address. This happens regardless of whether the summarized network prefixes were learned from other routers' routing updates or through redistribution.

Let's see how this rule works in the network shown in Figure 8.8. Router R1 runs IGRP, router R2 runs IGRP and RIP mutually redistributed, and router R3 runs just RIP. In addition, routers R1 and R3 have a number of static and connected routes redistributed into their respective routing protocols. Our goal is to see how the described rule applies in the different redistribution cases.

Listings 8.16 through 8.18 show the configurations of all three routers.

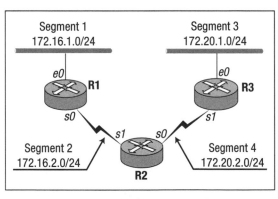

Figure 8.8   Router R2 performs summarization of redistributed network prefixes.

```
router rip
 redistribute connected metric 10
 redistribute static metric 5
 network 172.20.0.0

ip route 172.20.100.0 255.255.255.0 Null0
ip route 172.31.100.0 255.255.255.0 Null0
```

The IP addresses of the Serial0 and Ethernet0 interfaces of routers R1 and R3 belong to the classful network address specified in the **network** statement under the respective routing protocol configuration. In addition, routers R1 and R3 have two static routes: one for the network prefix belonging to that classful network address, and the other for network prefixes that belong to a different classful network address. Both routers are also configured with the Loopback0 interface, whose IP address does not belong to the classful network address specified in the **network** statement. Both routers are configured to redistribute static and connected routes into their respective routing protocols. Let's see how the routing protocols advertise these network prefixes.

Let's first take a look at the IGRP and RIP parts of the routing table of router R2, which are shown in Listing 8.19.

Listing 8.19   The IGRP and RIP parts of router R2's routing table.

```
R2#show ip route igrp
     172.16.0.0/24 is subnetted, 3 subnets
I       172.16.1.0 [100/8476] via 172.16.2.1, 00:00:34, Serial1
I       172.16.100.0 [100/8476] via 172.16.2.1, 00:00:34, Serial1
I       172.21.0.0/16 [100/8476] via 172.16.2.1, 00:00:34, Serial1
I       192.168.1.0/24 [100/8976] via 172.16.2.1, 00:00:34, Serial1

R2#show ip route rip
     172.20.0.0/24 is subnetted, 3 subnets
R       172.20.1.0 [120/1] via 172.20.2.1, 00:00:20, Serial0
R       172.20.100.0 [120/1] via 172.20.2.1, 00:00:20, Serial0
R       172.31.0.0/16 [120/5] via 172.20.2.1, 00:00:20, Serial0
R       192.168.2.0/24 [120/10] via 172.20.2.1, 00:00:20, Serial0
```

The shaded lines indicate the routes for the network prefixes that were redistributed into IGRP and RIP on routers R1 and R3. Network prefixes 172.16.100.0/24 and 172.20.100.0/24 were not summarized because they belong to the same classful network prefixes to which the IP addresses of the routers' interfaces belong. On the contrary, network prefixes 172.21.100.0/24 and 172.31.200.0/24 were replaced with classful network prefixes 172.21.0.0/16 and 172.31.0.0/24, because they belong to the classful network prefixes to which none of the routers' IP addresses belong.

The IP addresses of the routers' Loopback0 interfaces—192.168.1.1/32 and 192.168.2.1/32—were summarized as well.

If we look at the routing table of router R1 or router R3, we'll see further signs of summarization. For example, Listing 8.20 shows the RIP part of router R3's routing table, which does not contain individual routes for two network prefixes 172.16.1.0/24 and 172.16.100.0/24. Instead, it contains a single RIP route for summary network address 172.16.0.0/16 (the italicized line).

Listing 8.20   The RIP part of router R3's routing table.

```
R3#show ip route rip
R     172.16.0.0/16 [120/1] via 172.20.2.2, 00:00:24, Serial1
R     172.21.0.0/16 [120/1] via 172.20.2.2, 00:00:24, Serial1
R     192.168.1.0/24 [120/1] via 172.20.2.2, 00:00:24, Serial1
```

What happens if we replace classful RIP version 1 on routers R2 and R3 with classless RIP version 2? Will routers R2 and R3 still perform summarization, or will they pass the redistributed network prefixes intact?

Simply changing the version of RIP to 2 won't change the contents of the routing tables of routers R2 and R3. In other words, the routers will still perform the described and observed summarization. If RIP version 2 on routers R2 and R3 is configured with the **no auto-summary** statement, the routers will stop summarizing the network prefixes. Evidence of this can be seen in the output of the **show ip route rip** command issued on routers R2 and R3 after the **version 2** and **no auto-summary** statements were added under **router rip** configuration of both routers. The outputs of the command issued on routers R2 and R3 are shown in Listings 8.21 and 8.22.

Listing 8.21   The RIP part of router R2's routing table.

```
R2#show ip route rip
      172.20.0.0/24 is subnetted, 3 subnets
R        172.20.1.0 [120/1] via 172.20.2.1, 00:00:16, Serial0
R        172.20.100.0 [120/1] via 172.20.2.1, 00:00:16, Serial0
      172.31.0.0/24 is subnetted, 1 subnets
R        172.31.100.0 [120/5] via 172.20.2.1, 00:00:16, Serial0
      192.168.2.0/32 is subnetted, 1 subnets
R        192.168.2.1 [120/10] via 172.20.2.1, 00:00:16, Serial0
```

Listing 8.22   The RIP part of router R3's routing table.

```
R3#show ip route rip
      172.16.0.0/24 is subnetted, 3 subnets
R        172.16.1.0 [120/1] via 172.20.2.2, 00:00:24, Serial1
R        172.16.2.0 [120/1] via 172.20.2.2, 00:00:24, Serial1
R        172.16.100.0 [120/1] via 172.20.2.2, 00:00:24, Serial1
```

```
R    172.21.0.0/16 [120/1] via 172.20.2.2, 00:00:24, Serial1
R    192.168.1.0/24 [120/1] via 172.20.2.2, 00:00:24, Serial1
```

The shaded lines in both listings show the routes for the network prefixes that were previously summarized by RIP.

Understanding and Configuring Redistribution Metrics

In the previous section, we learned that the redistribution metric is an optional parameter. Instead, a default redistribution metric can be specified using the **default-metric** *<fixed metric>* command, which is available in each routing protocol configuration mode. The format of the *<fixed metric>* parameter is the same as that of the *<fixed metric>* parameter of the **redistribute** command.

If the **default-metric** command is present, and no explicit redistribution metric is defined in the **redistribute** command, the redistributed routing information receives the metric specified with the **default-metric** command. On the other hand, if the redistribution metric is explicitly defined in the **redistribute** command, it takes precedence over the metric specified in the **default-metric** command.

But what happens if neither the explicit nor default redistribution metric is specified at all? The answer depends on what routing information source is redistributed into which routing protocol. Table 8.3 shows the metrics that the redistributed routing information receives if neither metric is defined.

The columns of the table denote the routing information sources from which the routing information is redistributed, and the rows denote the routing protocols into which the routing information is redistributed. The keyword *translated* applies only to redistribution between IGRP and EIGRP, or between two IGRP or EIGRP processes. The keyword *translated* means that the accumulated metrics are converted using the equation $M_{EIGRP} = 256 * M_{IGRP}$, in which M_{EIGRP} and M_{IGRP} are the EIGRP and IGRP metrics, respectively. This process induces no loss of

Table 8.3   The metrics that different protocols use for the redistributed routing information if no default-metric command is specified and no explicit redistribution metric is assigned.

To/From	IGRP	RIP	EIGRP	OSPF	Static	Connected
IGRP	translated	infinity	translated	infinity	computed	computed
RIP	infinity	N/A	infinity	infinity	1	1
EIGRP	translated	infinity	translated	infinity	computed	computed
OSPF	20	20	20	20	20	20

accumulated distance information when the routing information is passed from one routing process to another. Likewise, the word *computed* applies only to the case of redistributing static and connected routes into IGRP and EIGRP. Here, *computed* means that the metric for the redistributed network prefix is calculated using the logical bandwidth and delay of the output interface of the corresponding static or connected route. The meaning of the keyword *infinity* depends upon the routing protocol: RIP and IGRP advertise the redistributed network prefixes with the metric of infinity, whereas EIGRP does not advertise the redistributed network prefixes at all. (Those network prefixes do not even appear in the EIGRP topology table.)

In addition, the following two metric-related rules apply for redistribution between IGRP and EIGRP, IGRP and IGRP, and EIGRP and EIGRP:

- IGRP always translates the metrics of routing information redistributed from another IGRP or EIGRP process, regardless of whether the **default-metric** command is present and/or an explicit redistribution metric is specified.

- EIGRP also translates the metrics of routing information that are redistributed from another IGRP or EIGRP process, unless the version of IOS is 12.0 or higher and the **default-metric** command is present and/or an explicit redistribution metric is specified. Commencing with IOS version 12.0, EIGRP uses the specified fixed default or explicit redistribution metric when advertising redistributed routing information. (In all prior versions of IOS, EIGRP ignored configured default and redistribution metrics.)

Finally, when IGRP and EIGRP are configured with the **default-metric** command, they apply it to redistributed static routes in lieu of the computed metrics used when no **default-metric** command and explicit redistribution metric are present. They do not apply it to redistributed connected routes, however. In other words, IGRP and EIGRP always calculate the metrics for the redistributed connected routes.

NOTE: *Redistribution between IS-IS and the other routing protocols is very similar to redistribution between OSPF and the other routing protocols.*

Using and Understanding One-Way Redistribution

As pointed out in the "In Depth" section of this chapter, it sometimes appears beneficial to supply exact routing information to the hosts. If, however, the routing protocol used throughout the network is not implemented on the hosts, redistribution into the routing protocol that is implemented on the hosts appears to be warranted. An example of such a situation is a network in which the routing is maintained by EIGRP. If this network contains Unix or Windows NT machines capable of running RIP version 2, the routers of the network need to redistribute EIGRP into RIP version 2 to allow the hosts to learn of the exact routing information.

Whereas the idea of redistribution seems to be good, it makes sense to first understand why the hosts might need the exact routing information and then if that goal can really be achieved through redistribution. If a host has a single NIC, it obviously can use the default route to access the network. In other words, running a routing protocol on a host with a single NIC does not add any value in most cases. If, however, a host has multiple NICs, running a routing protocol on the host may help achieve better routing. For example, in the network shown in Figure 8.9, host H1 can establish optimal routes for segments 1 and 8 if it runs a dynamic routing protocol.

The idea is attractive and even viable if the network and the host use the same routing protocol, but redistribution renders it useless. As we remember, redistribution does not preserve accumulated metrics: All network prefixes acquired via redistribution are advertised with an identical metric. This, in turn, means that all

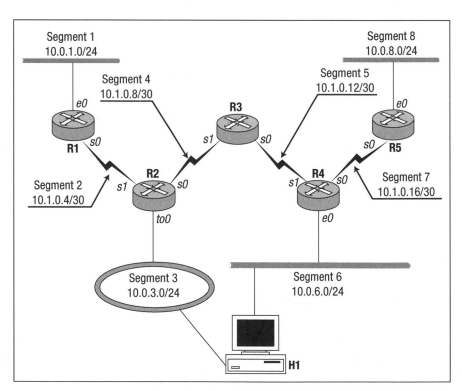

Figure 8.9   Host H1 may seem to be able to learn optimal routes.

the advertisements that the host receives through the same interface carry the same metric. Although the advertisements that the hosts receives through the other interface may carry a different metric, this metric is the same in all advertisements received through this interface. Hence, running a dynamic routing protocol notwithstanding, the host will still utilize the same NIC for all network prefixes that were redistributed into this routing protocol on the routers.

Let's see how this happens in reality. In our network, the host with multiple NICs is a Windows NT server running the routing and remote access service, which supports RIP version 2. The purpose of running RIP on the host is to achieve optimum access for segments 1 and 8. Although it can be achieved by setting up static routes on the host, with each pointing to the NIC that is closer to the respective segment, we also want redundancy such that, should one of the NICs fail, the host automatically switches over to the remaining functional NIC. Because this feature is not available with static routes, we expect RIP to provide it.

All routers in the network run EIGRP as the primary routing protocol. In addition, routers R2 and R4 run RIP version 2 and perform one-way redistribution of EIGRP into RIP. We are interested in only the configurations of routers R2 and R4, which are shown in Listings 8.23 and 8.24 respectively.

Listing 8.23   Router R2's configuration.

```
interface Serial0
 ip address 10.1.0.9 255.255.255.252

interface Serial1
 ip address 10.1.0.6 255.255.255.252

interface TokenRing0
 ip address 10.0.3.1 255.255.255.0
 ring-speed 16

router eigrp 1
 network 10.0.0.0

router rip
 version 2
 redistribute eigrp 1 metric 4
 passive-interface Serial0
 passive-interface Serial1
 network 10.0.0.0
 distance 255
```

8. Controlling Routing Information

Listing 8.24   Router R4's configuration.

```
interface Ethernet0
 ip address 10.0.6.1 255.255.255.0

interface Serial0
 ip address 10.1.0.17 255.255.255.252

interface Serial1
 ip address 10.1.0.14 255.255.255.252

router eigrp 1
 network 10.0.0.0

router rip
 version 2
 redistribute eigrp 1 metric 1
 passive-interface Serial0
 passive-interface Serial1
 network 10.0.0.0
 distance 255
```

The **distance 255** command ensures that the routers won't learn of any routes that host H1 may advertise via RIP. Also, notice that the **router eigrp 1** configuration on both routers does not contain any **redistribute** commands; this ensures one-way redistribution of EIGRP into RIP. Finally, we do not want unnecessary RIP routing updates on any interfaces except for the ones on which host H1 resides. So, to prevent RIP from sending routing updates over the other interfaces, the **router rip** configuration contains the two **passive-interface** commands.

Notice that RIP on router R4 is configured to advertise the network prefixes that are acquired through redistribution with the metric of 1, whereas it's 4 on RIP on router R2. Therefore, host H1 should establish routes for the network prefixes learned via RIP through router R4 (something that we actually do not want).

Let's now examine the routing table of host H1, which is shown in Listing 8.25.

Listing 8.25   The part of host H1's routing table that shows the routes for the network prefixes it learned from routers R2 and R4.

```
C:\>route print 10*
...
Active Routes:
Network Destination        Netmask          Gateway       Interface  Metric
        10.0.1.0     255.255.255.0        10.0.6.1       10.0.6.15        2
        10.0.8.0     255.255.255.0        10.0.6.1       10.0.6.15        2
```

10.1.0.4	255.255.255.252	10.0.3.1	10.0.3.15	2
10.1.0.8	255.255.255.252	10.0.3.1	10.0.3.15	2
10.1.0.12	255.255.255.252	10.0.6.1	10.0.6.15	2
10.1.0.16	255.255.255.252	10.0.6.1	10.0.6.15	2

The two shaded lines indicate the routes that point to router R2. These are the routes for the network prefixes of segments 2 and 4. Although RIP on router R2 is passive on the router's interfaces attached to these segments, RIP still advertises them over segment 3. As these network prefixes are not acquired through redistribution, the redistribution metric does not apply to them; instead, RIP uses the metric of 1, the natural default RIP metric for directly attached network prefixes.

The original goals were to establish optimum routing for segments 1 and 8 and to achieve redundancy in case one of the host's NICs fails. Whereas the redundancy is achieved, the first goal is obviously not. The host's routes for the network prefixes 1 and 8 (italicized lines in Listing 8.25) point to the same next-hop router IP address (router R4's). Furthermore, tracing the host's routes for the network prefixes of segments 1 and 8 reveals that the routes have different lengths (as indicated in Listing 8.26). Apparently, if the optimum routing were achieved, the routes would have the equal lengths of two hops.

Listing 8.26   **The output of the tracert -d 10.0.1.1 and tracert -d 10.0.8.1 commands entered on host H1.**

```
C:\>tracert -d 10.0.1.1

Tracing route to 10.0.1.1 over a maximum of 30 hops

  1    10 ms   <10 ms   <10 ms   10.0.6.1
  2    30 ms    30 ms    21 ms   10.1.0.13
  3    40 ms    50 ms    40 ms   10.1.0.9
  4   100 ms    80 ms    80 ms   10.0.1.1

Trace complete.

C:\>tracert -d 10.0.8.1

Tracing route to 10.0.8.1 over a maximum of 30 hops

  1    10 ms   <10 ms   <10 ms   10.0.6.1
  2    30 ms    20 ms    30 ms   10.0.8.1

Trace complete.
```

8. Controlling Routing Information

NOTE: *The last hop in the above traces appears to be missing. This happens because the traceroute's destinations are the IP address of the router. When the router detects that the traceroute PDUs are addressed to itself, it does not report itself as the last hop.*

Understanding the Automatic Redistribution of Pseudo-Connected Routes into IGRP and RIP

In Chapter 3, we defined pseudo-connected routes as static routes that point to an interface as opposed to the IP address of a next-hop router.

The pseudo-connected routes have an interesting feature: They are automatically redistributed into IGRP and RIP processes. However, not all pseudo-connected routes are automatically redistributed into RIP and IGRP; only those whose destination network prefix is matched by one or more **network** statements under **router igrp** or **router rip** configuration are.

To see how this rule works, we'll use the simple network shown in Figure 8.10.

The configurations of the two routers are shown in Listings 8.27 and 8.28 respectively.

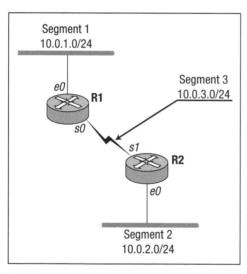

Figure 8.10   **The test network, in which router R1 advertises a network prefix of a pseudo-connected route.**

Listing 8.27   Router R1's configuration.

```
interface Ethernet0
 ip address 10.0.1.1 255.255.255.0

interface Serial0
 ip address 10.0.3.1 255.255.255.0

router igrp 1
 network 10.0.0.0

ip route 10.1.1.0 255.255.255.0 Null0
ip route 10.2.0.0 255.255.0.0 Null0
ip route 10.3.1.1 255.255.255.255 Null0
ip route 192.168.1.0 255.255.255.0 Null0
ip route 10.1.2.0 255.255.255.0 10.0.1.2
```

Listing 8.28   Router R2's configuration.

```
interface Ethernet0
 ip address 10.0.2.1 255.255.255.0

interface Serial1
 ip address 10.0.3.2 255.255.255.0

router igrp 1
 network 10.0.0.0
```

The four shaded lines in Listing 8.27 reveal the static routes configured on router R1. The first four static routes are pseudo-connected because they point to the Null0 interface. Notice, however, that only the first of the leading three routes is for a network prefix whose length coincides with the length of the network prefixes (/24) assigned on the segments of the network. The fourth pseudo-connected route is for network prefix 192.168.1.0/24, which is not matched by the **network 10.0.0.0** statement. The fifth static route is a regular static route. The latter two static routes appear in router R1's configuration because we want to see the following:

- Although the fourth static route is connected, it won't be automatically redistributed into RIP and IGRP because it is not matched by any **network** statement.

- Although the regular static route is for network prefix 10.1.2.0/24, which is matched by the **network 10.0.0.0** statement, it is not automatically redistributed into either IGRP or RIP.

Below is the output of the **show ip route igrp** command entered on router R2. It shows only two IGRP routes: one for the network prefix of the first pseudo-connected route of router R1, and the other for the network prefix of router R1's Ethernet0 interface:

8. Controlling Routing Information

```
R2#show ip route igrp
     10.0.0.0/24 is subnetted, 4 subnets
I       10.1.1.0 [100/8476] via 10.0.3.1, 00:00:41, Serial1
I       10.0.1.0 [100/8576] via 10.0.3.1, 00:00:41, Serial1
```

The routes for the network prefixes of the other two pseudo-connected routes are not present because IGRP is a classful routing protocol, and so it passes neither network prefix lengths nor subnet masks in its routing updates. Therefore, it can't correctly advertise network prefix 10.2.0.0/16, because its length is different from the length of the network prefix of interface Serial0, which is the output interface for the IGRP routing updates that are destined for router R2. IGRP also cannot advertise network prefix 10.3.1.1/32, because, as we know, IGRP, by its design, cannot advertise network prefixes whose lengths are /32.

As we expected, the network prefixes of the last two static routes of router R1 do not show up in router R2's routing table.

If we replace IGRP with RIP version 1 on both routers, the RIP part of router R2's routing table will look as shown below:

```
R2#show ip route rip
     10.0.0.0/8 is variably subnetted, 5 subnets, 2 masks
R       10.3.1.1/32 [120/1] via 10.0.3.1, 00:00:01, Serial1
R       10.1.1.0/24 [120/1] via 10.0.3.1, 00:00:01, Serial1
R       10.0.1.0/24 [120/1] via 10.0.3.1, 00:00:01, Serial1
```

Notice the presence of the RIP route for network prefix 10.3.1.1/32. As we know, RIP can advertise network prefixes whose length is /32. However, there is no RIP route for network prefix 10.2.0.0/16. RIP version 1 is a classful routing protocol, so it won't advertise this network prefix for the same reason IGRP didn't.

Finally, if we change the version of RIP from 1 to 2, the output of the **show ip route rip** command changes, as shown below:

```
R2#show ip route rip
     10.0.0.0/8 is variably subnetted, 6 subnets, 3 masks
R       10.2.0.0/16 [120/1] via 10.0.3.1, 00:00:06, Serial1
R       10.3.1.1/32 [120/1] via 10.0.3.1, 00:00:06, Serial1
R       10.1.1.0/24 [120/1] via 10.0.3.1, 00:00:06, Serial1
R       10.0.1.0/24 [120/1] via 10.0.3.1, 00:00:06, Serial1
```

This time, notice that there are RIP routes for all network prefixes of the pseudo-connected routes of router R1. Because RIP version 2 is a classless routing protocol, different lengths of network prefixes present no obstacle for it.

NOTE: Pseudo-connected routes are not automatically redistributed into EIGRP, OSPF, and IS-IS.

Understanding Redistribution into EIGRP

It is important to understand redistribution using the distance **eigrp command** and EIGRP external routes.

Using the *distance eigrp* Command

As we know, EIGRP uses IP external TLV entries to advertise network prefixes that are obtained through redistribution. Doing so allows the routers that receive EIGRP routing updates containing IP external TLV entries to recognize the network prefixes in them as being obtained through redistribution as opposed to being originated by EIGRP.

EIGRP installs so-called *EIGRP external routes* for network prefixes received in IP external TLV entries. Similarly, regular EIGRP routes, or routes for network prefixes received in IP internal TLV entries, are sometimes called *EIGRP internal routes*. The default administrative distances of EIGRP internal and external routes are 90 and 170, respectively.

Cisco IOS provides a command that allows you to change the administrative distances of EIGRP internal and external routes: **distance eigrp** *<internal>* *<external>*.

Understanding EIGRP External Routes

From the "Understanding Summarization when Redistributing into RIP and IGRP" section earlier in this chapter, we know that network prefixes are redistributed into RIP version 2 without summarization if the **router rip** configuration contains the **no auto-summary** statement. In the case of EIGRP, the redistributed network prefixes are not summarized, regardless of the presence of the **no auto-summary** command. When redistributing the EIGRP external routes into other routing protocols, routers follow the regular summarization rules.

This feature has a justification, however. It helps implement migration from other routing protocols to EIGRP. Usually, it's recommended that migration begin at the core of the network and then be propagated to the perimeter. If, however, routers summarized the network prefixes before injecting them into the EIGRP domain, the EIGRP core could, in some cases, break the network into noncontiguous areas. This, in turn, can potentially make it impossible for the old routing protocol to correctly maintain the routing.

Figure 8.11 shows an example of a partially migrated network. The EIGRP core is shown as the white area in the middle of the picture. The parts of the network routing that have yet to be migrated to EIGRP are shown as the shaded areas. By not summarizing the network prefixes that are learned via redistribution from the old routing protocol, EIGRP allows every nonmigrated area to receive the exact routing information just as it happened before the core was migrated to EIGRP.

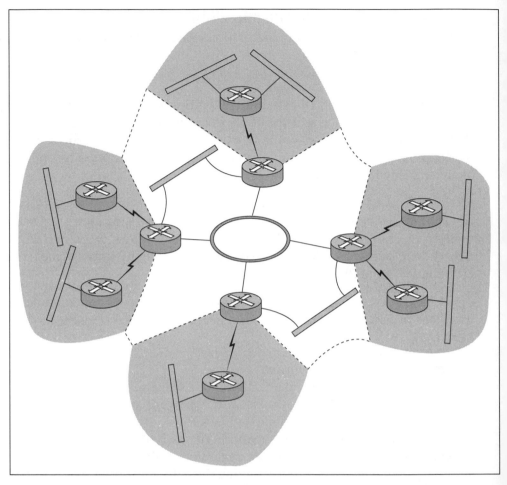

Figure 8.11   The white part of the network has already been migrated to EIGRP, and the shaded one has not. Nevertheless, routing works correctly because EIGRP passes external network prefixes intact among the nonmigrated parts of the network.

Let's see how the described EIGRP feature works in the network shown in Figure 8.12.

The network consists of three routing domains: RIP, EIGRP, and IGRP. The majority of the network prefixes in the RIP and IGRP routing domains belong to the same classful network prefix (172.16.0.0/16). The RIP domain has only one segment, segment 2, whose network prefix (172.17.1.0/24) belongs to a different classful network (172.17.0.0/16). The only network prefix in the EIGRP domain, 172.20.4.0/22, belongs to a different classful network prefix (172.20.0.0/16), which

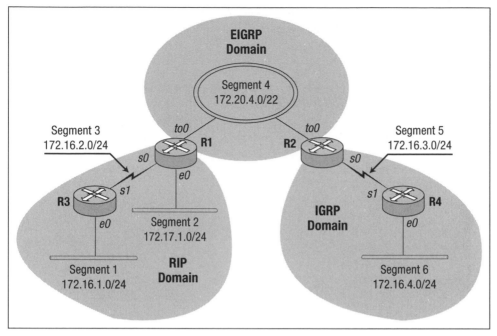

Figure 8.12   The EIGRP domain separates the RIP and IGRP domains, which share
classful network prefix 172.16.0.0/16. Yet the routing works correctly
because EIGRP does not summarize redistributed network prefixes and
therefore passes them intact between the RIP and IGRP domains.

essentially means that classful network prefix 172.16.0.0/16 is noncontiguous. As
we know, classful routing protocols such as RIP and IGRP are unable to operate
in noncontiguously addressed networks. Let's see if EIGRP changes anything.

The configurations of all four routers are shown in Listings 8.29 through 8.32.

Listing 8.29   Router R1's configuration.

```
interface Ethernet0
 ip address 172.17.1.1 255.255.255.0

interface Serial0
 ip address 172.16.2.1 255.255.255.0

interface TokenRing0
 ip address 172.20.4.1 255.255.252.0
 ring-speed 16

router eigrp 1
 redistribute rip metric 1500 1 255 1 1500
 network 172.20.0.0
```

```
router rip
 redistribute eigrp 1 metric 1
 network 172.16.0.0
 network 172.17.0.0
```

Listing 8.30   Router R2's configuration.

```
interface Serial0
 ip address 172.16.3.1 255.255.255.0

interface TokenRing0
 ip address 172.20.4.2 255.255.252.0
 ring-speed 16

router eigrp 1
 redistribute static
 redistribute igrp 10
 network 172.20.0.0

router igrp 10
 redistribute eigrp 1
 network 172.16.0.0

ip route 10.1.1.0 255.255.255.0 Null0
```

Listing 8.31   Router R3's configuration.

```
interface Ethernet0
 ip address 172.16.1.1 255.255.255.0

interface Serial1
 ip address 172.16.2.2 255.255.255.0

router rip
 network 172.16.0.0
```

Listing 8.32   Router R4's configuration.

```
interface Ethernet0
 ip address 172.16.4.1 255.255.255.0

interface Serial1
 ip address 172.16.3.2 255.255.255.0

router igrp 10
 network 172.16.0.0
```

Let's first examine the EIGRP routes in the routing tables of routers R1 and R2, which are shown in Listings 8.33 and 8.34.

Listing 8.33   The EIGRP part of the routing table of router R1.

```
R1#show ip route eigrp
        172.16.0.0/24 is subnetted, 4 subnets
D EX    172.16.4.0 [170/2211584] via 172.20.4.2, 00:14:12, TokenRing0
D EX    172.16.3.0 [170/2185984] via 172.20.4.2, 00:14:12, TokenRing0
        10.0.0.0/24 is subnetted, 1 subnets
D EX    10.1.1.0 [170/176128] via 172.20.4.2, 00:14:12, TokenRing0
```

Listing 8.34   The EIGRP part of the routing table of router R2.

```
R2#show ip route eigrp
        172.17.0.0/24 is subnetted, 1 subnets
D EX    172.17.1.0 [170/1722880] via 172.20.4.1, 00:14:23, TokenRing0
        172.16.0.0/24 is subnetted, 4 subnets
D EX    172.16.1.0 [170/1722880] via 172.20.4.1, 00:14:23, TokenRing0
D EX    172.16.2.0 [170/1722880] via 172.20.4.1, 00:14:23, TokenRing0
```

As we should expect, the EIGRP processes on both routers installed EIGRP external routes for the exact network prefixes, as opposed to their summaries.

Listings 8.35 and 8.36 show the RIP and IGRP parts of the routing tables of routers R3 and R4, respectively. The italicized lines indicate the routes for the network prefixes that were passed through the EIGRP core. Notice that the network prefixes are not summarized. The shaded lines show the routes for the summary network addresses. Those were created by the redistributing routers in accordance with the classful summarization rule (described in the "Understanding Summarization when Redistributing into RIP and IGRP" section earlier in this chapter).

Listing 8.35   The RIP part of router R3's routing table.

```
R3#show ip route rip
R       172.17.0.0/16 [120/1] via 172.16.2.1, 00:00:23, Serial1
        172.16.0.0/24 is subnetted, 4 subnets
R         172.16.4.0 [120/1] via 172.16.2.1, 00:00:23, Serial1
R         172.16.3.0 [120/1] via 172.16.2.1, 00:00:23, Serial1
R       172.20.0.0/16 [120/1] via 172.16.2.1, 00:00:23, Serial1
R       10.0.0.0/8 [120/1] via 172.16.2.1, 00:00:23, Serial1
```

Listing 8.36   The IGRP part of router R4's routing table.

```
R4#show ip route igrp
I       172.17.0.0/16 [100/8730] via 172.16.3.1, 00:00:28, Serial1
        172.16.0.0/24 is subnetted, 4 subnets
I         172.16.1.0 [100/8730] via 172.16.3.1, 00:00:28, Serial1
```

Listing 8.16   Router R1's configuration.

```
interface Loopback0
 ip address 192.168.1.1 255.255.255.255

interface Ethernet0
 ip address 172.16.1.1 255.255.255.0
 no ip directed-broadcast

interface Serial0
 ip address 172.16.2.1 255.255.255.0

router igrp 1
 redistribute connected metric 10000 0 255 1 1500
 redistribute static metric 10000 0 255 1 1500
 network 172.16.0.0

ip route 172.16.100.0 255.255.255.0 Null0
ip route 172.21.100.0 255.255.255.0 Null0
```

Listing 8.17   Router R2's configuration.

```
interface Serial0
 ip address 172.20.2.2 255.255.255.0

interface Serial1
 ip address 172.16.2.2 255.255.255.0

router rip
 redistribute igrp 1 metric 1
 network 172.20.0.0

router igrp 1
 redistribute rip metric 64 1 255 1 1500
 network 172.16.0.0
```

Listing 8.18   Router R3's configuration.

```
interface Loopback0
 ip address 192.168.2.1 255.255.255.255

interface Ethernet0
 ip address 172.20.1.1 255.255.255.0

interface Serial1
 ip address 172.20.2.1 255.255.255.0
```

```
I          172.16.2.0 [100/8730] via 172.16.3.1, 00:00:28, Serial1
I       172.20.0.0/16 [100/8539] via 172.16.3.1, 00:00:28, Serial1
```

NOTE: *The actual reason why RIP version 2 performs summarization of the redistributed network prefix if the* **no auto-summary** *command is not present in the router's configuration is because, unlike EIGRP, RIP version 2 does not keep track of which network prefixes are external and which are internal. As EIGRP does know the difference, it does not try to apply classful summarization to the network prefixes of unknown origin.*

Although the explanation appears to be justified, it's sometimes desirable to make redistributing routers summarize redistributed network prefixes, especially in the cases of migration from IGRP to EIGRP.

Understanding and Using Redistribution between EIGRP and IGRP

If an EIGRP process and an IGRP process share the same autonomous system number when both are enabled on a single router, automatic redistribution takes place between the routing processes.

This automatic redistribution has two important features:

- The metrics accumulated by the two protocols are translated between the routing processes using the equation $M_{EIGRP} = 256 * M_{IGRP}$, in which M_{EIGRP} and M_{IGRP} are the EIGRP and IGRP metrics, respectively. For example, if IGRP learns of network prefix 10.1.1.0/24 with the metric of 1000, the EIGRP process will advertise it with the metric of 256000.

NOTE: *Commencing with IOS version 12.0, EIGRP, if configured with a default or explicit redistribution metric, will use it in lieu of the translated metrics. This change does not affect IGPR, which always ignores the configured redistribution metric when advertising the network prefixes learned from EIGRP.*

- The router disregards the lower administrative distance of IGRP when resolving the ambiguity that results in an attempt to establish an IGRP route and an EIGRP external route for the same network prefix. Under normal circumstances, IGRP would get installed into the routing table, because its default administrative distance is equal to 100, whereas the default administrative distance of EIGRP external routes is 170. Nevertheless, the router disregards IGRP's smaller administrative distance and instead uses the routes' metrics to resolve the ambiguity. If the EIGRP external route metric is smaller or equal to the IGRP metric multiplied by 256, the EIGRP external route gets installed; otherwise, the IGRP route is installed.

NOTE: *Formally, if $M_{EIGRP} \leq M_{IGRP} * 256$ is true, the EIGRP route gets installed; otherwise, the IGRP route gets installed. M_{EIGRP} and M_{IGRP} are the metrics of the EIGRP and IGRP routes, respectively.*

To see how the rules apply, let's use the network shown in Figure 8.13.

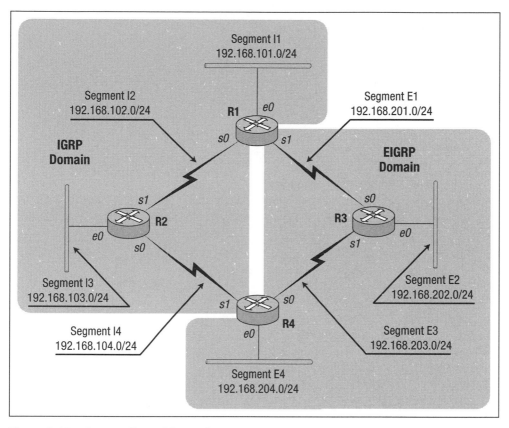

Figure 8.13   Routers R1 and R4 perform mutual redistribution between IGRP and EIGRP.

The network is divided into two parts (shown as shaded areas). The segments falling into the shaded area on the left are a part of the IGRP domain; the segments falling into the shaded area on the right are a part of the EIGRP domain. Notice that the names of the segments in the IGRP domain begin with the letter "I", and the names of the segments in the EIGRP domain begin with the letter "E". IGRP and EIGRP on all routers are configured with the same autonomous system number (equal to 1). Hence, routers R1 and R4 perform automatic mutual redistribution between EIGRP and IGRP.

The configurations of all four routers are shown in Listings 8.37 through 8.40.

Listing 8.37   Router R1's configuration.

```
interface Ethernet0
 ip address 192.168.101.1 255.255.255.0

interface Serial0
 ip address 192.168.102.1 255.255.255.0
```

8. Controlling Routing Information

```
interface Serial1
 ip address 192.168.201.1 255.255.255.0

router eigrp 1
 network 192.168.201.0

router igrp 1
 network 192.168.102.0
 network 192.168.101.0
```

Listing 8.38   Router R2's configuration.

```
interface Ethernet0
 ip address 192.168.103.1 255.255.255.0

interface Serial0
 ip address 192.168.104.1 255.255.255.0

interface Serial1
 ip address 192.168.102.2 255.255.255.0

router igrp 1
 network 192.168.102.0
 network 192.168.103.0
 network 192.168.104.0
```

Listing 8.39   Router R3's configuration.

```
interface Ethernet0
 ip address 192.168.202.1 255.255.255.0

interface Serial0
 ip address 192.168.201.2 255.255.255.0

interface Serial1
 ip address 192.168.203.1 255.255.255.0

router eigrp 1
 network 192.168.201.0
 network 192.168.202.0
 network 192.168.203.0
```

Listing 8.40   Router R4's configuration.

```
interface Ethernet0
 ip address 192.168.204.1 255.255.255.0
```

```
interface Serial0
 ip address 192.168.203.2 255.255.255.0

interface Serial1
 ip address 192.168.104.2 255.255.255.0

router eigrp 1
 network 192.168.203.0
 network 192.168.204.0

router igrp 1
 network 192.168.104.0
```

Let's examine the routing table of router R4, which is shown in Listing 8.41.

Listing 8.41   The routing table of router R4.

```
R4#show ip route
...
C     192.168.104.0/24 is directly connected, Serial1
D     192.168.201.0/24 [90/2681856] via 192.168.203.1, 00:00:02, Serial0
D     192.168.202.0/24 [90/2195456] via 192.168.203.1, 00:00:02, Serial0
C     192.168.203.0/24 is directly connected, Serial0
C     192.168.204.0/24 is directly connected, Ethernet0
I     192.168.102.0/24 [100/10476] via 192.168.104.1, 00:00:02, Serial1
I     192.168.103.0/24 [100/8576] via 192.168.104.1, 00:00:02, Serial1
D EX 192.168.101.0/24 [170/2707456] via 192.168.203.1, 00:00:02, Serial0
```

The shaded line indicates the EIGRP external route for network prefix of segment I1. Interestingly enough, segment I1 belongs to the IGRP domain, so we might expect to see an IGRP route for the network prefix as opposed to the EIGRP external route. If we look closer at Figure 8.13, however, we'll see that segment I1 is accessible through two equal paths: One goes through the IGRP domain and the other through the EIGRP domain. Because of automatic redistribution between EIGRP and IGRP on router R1, the network prefix of segment I1 is advertised by both IGRP and EIGRP. Hence, router R4 receives two advertisements for the network prefix of segment I1: one through IGRP and the other through EIGRP. Because router R4 runs the two routing protocols with automatic redistribution, it disregards IGRP's smaller administrative distance when deciding which route to install in the routing table. Apparently, the EIGRP metric should be precisely 256 times greater than the IGRP one, which, from the comparison point of view, represents equal metrics. Therefore, the EIGRP route gets installed and the IGRP one gets dropped.

8. Controlling Routing Information

The EIGRP metric is indeed precisely 256 times greater than the IGRP one, which is evidenced in the output of the **debug ip igrp transactions** command entered on router R4. The partial output of the command is shown below:

```
R4#debug ip igrp transactions
IGRP protocol debugging is on
...
IGRP: received update from 192.168.104.1 on Serial1
...
      network 192.168.101.0, metric 10576 (neighbor 8576)
...
```

The shaded line shows the metric with which router R2 advertises the network prefix of segment I4, 10576. (When this number is multiplied by 256, you get 2707456, which is precisely equal to the metric of the EIGRP external route for the network prefix (the shaded line in Listing 8.41).

To see more evidence of automatic redistribution, let's examine the output of the **show ip route igrp** and **show ip route eigrp** commands entered on routers R2 and R3, respectively. The outputs are shown in Listings 8.42 and 8.43.

Listing 8.42   The output of the **show ip route igrp** command entered on router R2.

```
R2#show ip route igrp
I    192.168.201.0/24 [100/10476] via 192.168.102.1, 00:00:58, Serial1
I    192.168.202.0/24 [100/10576] via 192.168.102.1, 00:00:58, Serial1
                       [100/10576] via 192.168.104.2, 00:00:00, Serial0
I    192.168.203.0/24 [100/10476] via 192.168.104.2, 00:00:00, Serial0
I    192.168.204.0/24 [100/8576] via 192.168.104.2, 00:00:00, Serial0
I    192.168.101.0/24 [100/8576] via 192.168.102.1, 00:00:58, Serial1
```

Listing 8.43   The output of the **show ip route eigrp** command entered on router R3.

```
R3#show ip route eigrp
D EX 192.168.104.0/24 [170/2681856] via 192.168.203.2, 00:04:23, Serial1
D    192.168.204.0/24 [90/2195456] via 192.168.203.2, 00:04:22, Serial1
D EX 192.168.102.0/24 [170/2681856] via 192.168.201.1, 00:02:45, Serial0
D EX 192.168.103.0/24 [170/2707456] via 192.168.201.1, 00:02:45, Serial0
                      [170/2707456] via 192.168.203.2, 00:02:45, Serial1
D EX 192.168.101.0/24 [170/2195456] via 192.168.201.1, 00:04:22, Serial0
```

Listing 8.42, showing the IGRP part of router R2's routing table, exhibits all network prefixes belonging to the EIGRP domain; similarly, Listing 8.43, showing the EIGRP part of router R3's routing table, exhibits all network prefixes from the IGRP domain.

Finally, you can disable automatic redistribution by entering the **no redistribute** command followed by the routing process name and the autonomous system number. For example, to get rid of automatic redistribution between IGRP and EIGRP on router R1, its configuration should include the commands shown as the shaded lines in Listing 8.44.

Listing 8.44   The part of router R1's configuration showing how to turn off the automatic redistribution between IGRP and EIGRP.

```
...
router eigrp 1
 no redistribute igrp 1
 network 192.168.201.0

router igrp 1
 no redistribute eigrp 1
 network 192.168.101.0
 network 192.168.102.0
...
```

Understanding and Using Nonautomatic Redistribution between EIGRP and IGRP
If EIGRP and IGRP processes are present on a single router but are configured with different autonomous system numbers, the automatic redistribution described in the previous section does not occur. If required, nonautomatic redistribution can be configured in the regular way—that is, by using the **redistribute** command under **router igrp** and/or **router eigrp** configuration mode.

Although it must be explicitly enabled, nonautomatic redistribution is not different from automatic distribution. Nonautomatic redistribution also has the two features described in the beginning of the previous section.

Understanding the Specifics of Redistribution into OSPF
Redistribution into OSPF is covered in this section.

Configuring ASBRs
Once an OSPF router is configured to redistribute routing information into an OSPF process, it automatically becomes an ASBR. As we know from Chapter 7, ASBRs cannot be placed in stub areas. From the "In Depth" section of this chapter, we also know that regular ASBRs cannot be placed into an NSSA.

The **redistribute** command issued under **router ospf** configuration accomplishes the basic configuration of an ASBR. However, the **redistribute** command has one important parameter to use under **router ospf** configuration. If used, the **subnets** parameter makes OSPF redistribute the exact network prefixes from the specified routing information source; otherwise, OSPF will accept only classful network prefixes.

Understanding and Using Type 1 and Type 2 External Metrics

As we know from the "In Depth" section, ASBRs can place two types of metrics into the type 5 LSAs they originate: type 1 and type 2. By default, OSPF uses the type 2 metric; alternatively, type 1 can be specified in the **redistribute** command using the optional pair of parameters **metric-type 1**. (You can also specify **metric-type 2**. However, because external metric type 2 is the default, the parameters won't appear in the router's configuration.)

Let's see how the metric type can be used in the network shown in Figure 8.14.

Routers R4 and R5 are ASBRs connected to routers ER1 and ER2, respectively, through serial links. Router ER1 is connected to a network routing that is maintained

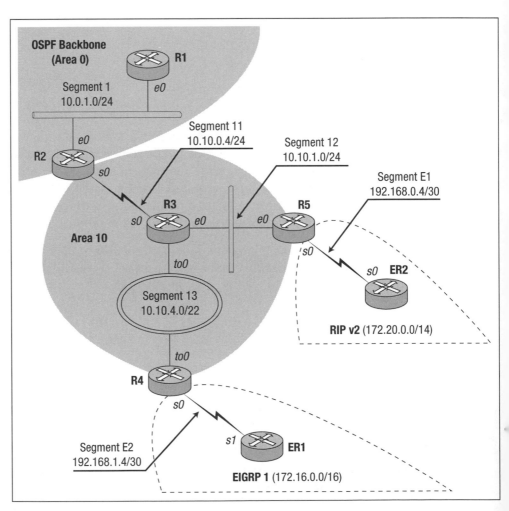

Figure 8.14   Routers R4 and R5 are ASBRs.

with EIGRP; router ER2 is connected to a network routing that is maintained by RIP version 2. Let's require that router R4 redistribute the EIGRP routes into OSPF as external type 1 routes, and that router R5 redistribute the RIP version 2 routes as external type 2 routes.

Listings 8.45 through 8.49 show the configurations of the OSPF routers (R1 through R5).

Listing 8.45   Router R1's configuration.

```
interface Ethernet0
 ip address 10.0.1.1 255.255.255.0

router ospf 1
 router-id 0.0.0.1
 network 10.0.0.0 0.0.255.255 area 0
```

Listing 8.46   Router R2's configuration.

```
interface Ethernet0
 ip address 10.0.1.2 255.255.255.0

interface Serial0
 ip address 10.10.0.5 255.255.255.252

router ospf 1
 router-id 0.0.0.2
 area 0 range 10.0.0.0 255.255.0.0
 area 10 range 10.10.0.0 255.255.0.0
 network 10.0.0.0 0.0.255.255 area 0
 network 10.10.0.0 0.0.255.255 area 10
```

Listing 8.47   Router R3's configuration.

```
interface Ethernet0
 ip address 10.10.1.1 255.255.255.0

interface Serial0
 ip address 10.10.0.6 255.255.255.252

interface TokenRing0
 ip address 10.10.4.1 255.255.252.0
 ring-speed 16

router ospf 1
 router-id 0.0.0.3
 network 10.10.0.0 0.0.255.255 area 10
```

8. Controlling Routing Information

Listing 8.48   Router R4's configuration.

```
interface Serial0
 ip address 192.168.1.5 255.255.255.252

interface TokenRing0
 ip address 10.10.4.2 255.255.252.0
 ring-speed 16

router eigrp 1
 redistribute ospf 1 metric 10000 1 255 1 1500
 network 192.168.1.0

router ospf 1
 router-id 0.0.0.4
 redistribute eigrp 1 metric 2000 metric-type 1 subnets
```

Listing 8.49   Router R5's configuration.

```
interface Ethernet0
 ip address 10.10.1.2 255.255.255.0

interface Serial0
 ip address 192.168.0.5 255.255.255.252

router ospf 1
 router-id 0.0.0.5
 redistribute rip metric 1000 subnets
 network 10.10.0.0 0.0.255.255 area 10

router rip
 version 2
 redistribute ospf 1 metric 1
 network 192.168.0.0
 no auto-summary
```

The shaded lines in Listings 8.48 and 8.49 reveal the OSPF **redistribute** commands. Notice that both commands have the **subnets** keyword. Also notice the use of the **metric-type 1** parameter in the **redistribute** command in router R4's configuration (Listing 8.48).

Let's examine the OSPF part of the routing table of router R1 (Listing 8.50). It shows a number of OSPF external type 1 and 2 routes. If we look closer, we'll see that the OSPF external type 1 routes are for the network prefixes learned by router R4 via EIGRP, and type 2 routes are for the network prefixes learned by router R5 via RIP version 2.

Listing 8.50   The OSPF part of the routing table of router R1.

```
R1#show ip route ospf
     172.16.0.0/16 is variably subnetted, 5 subnets, 2 masks
O E1    172.16.255.4/30 [110/2080] via 10.0.1.2, 00:02:06, Ethernet0
O E1    172.16.255.8/30 [110/2080] via 10.0.1.2, 00:02:06, Ethernet0
O E1    172.16.1.0/24 [110/2080] via 10.0.1.2, 00:02:06, Ethernet0
O E1    172.16.2.0/24 [110/2080] via 10.0.1.2, 00:02:06, Ethernet0
O E1    172.16.3.0/24 [110/2080] via 10.0.1.2, 00:02:06, Ethernet0
     172.21.0.0/22 is subnetted, 2 subnets
O E2    172.21.8.0 [110/1000] via 10.0.1.2, 00:02:06, Ethernet0
O E2    172.21.4.0 [110/1000] via 10.0.1.2, 00:02:07, Ethernet0
     172.20.0.0/16 is variably subnetted, 4 subnets, 2 masks
O E2    172.20.128.0/22 [110/1000] via 10.0.1.2, 00:02:07, Ethernet0
O E2    172.20.1.0/24 [110/1000] via 10.0.1.2, 00:02:07, Ethernet0
O E2    172.20.2.0/24 [110/1000] via 10.0.1.2, 00:02:07, Ethernet0
O E2    172.20.3.0/24 [110/1000] via 10.0.1.2, 00:02:07, Ethernet0
     172.22.0.0/24 is subnetted, 1 subnets
O E2    172.22.1.0 [110/1000] via 10.0.1.2, 00:02:07, Ethernet0
     10.0.0.0/8 is variably subnetted, 2 subnets, 2 masks
O IA    10.10.0.0/16 [110/84] via 10.0.1.2, 00:02:07, Ethernet0
     192.168.0.0/30 is subnetted, 1 subnets
O E2    192.168.0.4 [110/1000] via 10.0.1.2, 00:02:07, Ethernet0
     192.168.1.0/30 is subnetted, 1 subnets
O E1    192.168.1.4 [110/2080] via 10.0.1.2, 00:02:07, Ethernet0
```

Router R5 redistributes RIP version 2 routes into OSPF with the redistribution metric of 1000. Because the metric type is 2, the metric is not compatible with the OSPF metric; hence, all routers in the OSPF domain that receive the corresponding type 5 LSAs will establish routes for advertised network prefixes with the same metric (1000).

Router R4 redistributes EIGRP routes into OSPF with the redistribution metric of 2000. This time, however, the metric type is 1, which makes the metric "compatible" with the OSPF internal metrics. Hence, the routers must update the metric before installing the routes for the network prefixes contained in the corresponding type 5 LSAs.

Most frequently, the updated metric is equal to the sum of the metric in the OSPF router routing table for the ASBR and the type 1 metric contained in the type 5 LSA. For example, the metric of the OSPF external type 1 route for network prefix 172.16.1.0/24 is equal to 2080. If we examine router R1's OSPF router routing table entry for router R4, the ASBR that originates the type 5 LSA carrying network prefix 172.16.1.0/24, we'll see that the metric contained in it is equal to 80 (the shaded line in Listing 8.51). As mentioned, the redistribution metric on router R4 is equal to 2000, which, when summarized with 80, produces 2080, which we see in the routing table of router R1.

Listing 8.51   The output of the show ip ospf border-routers command issued on router R1.

```
R1#show ip ospf border-routers

OSPF Process 1 internal Routing Table

Codes: i - Intra-area route, I - Inter-area route

i 0.0.0.2 [10] via 10.0.1.2, Ethernet0, ABR, Area 0, SPF 3
I 0.0.0.4 [80] via 10.0.1.2, Ethernet0, ASBR, Area 0, SPF 3
I 0.0.0.5 [84] via 10.0.1.2, Ethernet0, ASBR, Area 0, SPF 3
```

Router R1's link-state database apparently contains all type 5 LSAs that are origi-nated by routers R4 and R5. Evidence of this can be seen in the part of the output of the **show ip ospf database** command describing the type 5 LSAs (Listing 8.52).

Listing 8.52   The part of the show ip ospf database command issued on router R1 describing the type 5 LSAs.

```
R1#show ip ospf database
...
            Type-5 AS External Link States
```

Link ID	ADV Router	Age	Seq#	Checksum	Tag
172.16.1.0	0.0.0.4	280	0x80000001	0x5A41	0
172.16.2.0	0.0.0.4	280	0x80000001	0x4F4B	0
172.16.3.0	0.0.0.4	280	0x80000001	0x4455	0
172.16.255.4	0.0.0.4	280	0x80000001	0x2B70	0
172.16.255.8	0.0.0.4	280	0x80000001	0x394	0
172.20.1.0	0.0.0.5	235	0x80000001	0x748D	0
172.20.2.0	0.0.0.5	235	0x80000001	0x6997	0
172.20.3.0	0.0.0.5	235	0x80000001	0x5EA1	0
172.20.128.0	0.0.0.5	235	0x80000001	0xEA9A	0
172.21.4.0	0.0.0.5	235	0x80000001	0x38C8	0
172.21.8.0	0.0.0.5	235	0x80000001	0xCF0	0
172.22.1.0	0.0.0.5	235	0x80000001	0x5CA3	0
192.168.0.0	0.0.0.4	281	0x80000001	0x39B6	0
192.168.0.0	0.0.0.5	235	0x80000001	0x83D6	0

Let's examine a single type 5 LSA originated by routers R4 and R5. To do that, we'll use the **show ip ospf database external** command followed by the link-state IDs of the type 5 LSA, which we want to examine. Listing 8.53 shows the outputs of the two instances of the command issued on router R1. The first in-stance was entered with link-state ID 172.16.1.0; the second with 172.20.1.0. (As we remember, the link-state ID of a type 5 LSA is equal to the 32-bit advertised network prefix, the network prefix not adjusted for its length.)

Listing 8.53 The outputs of the **show ip ospf database external 172.16.1.0** and **show ip ospf database external 172.20.1.0** commands on router R1.

```
R1#show ip ospf database external 172.16.1.0

        OSPF Router with ID (0.0.0.1) (Process ID 1)


                Type-5 AS External Link States

   Routing Bit Set on this LSA
   LS age: 411
   Options: (No TOS-capability, DC)
   LS Type: AS External Link
   Link State ID: 172.16.1.0 (External Network Number )
   Advertising Router: 0.0.0.4
   LS Seq Number: 80000001
   Checksum: 0x5A41
   Length: 36
   Network Mask: /24
         Metric Type: 1 (Comparable directly to link state metric)
         TOS: 0
         Metric: 2000
         Forward Address: 0.0.0.0
         External Route Tag: 0

R1#show ip ospf database external 172.20.1.0

        OSPF Router with ID (0.0.0.1) (Process ID 1)


                Type-5 AS External Link States

   Routing Bit Set on this LSA
   LS age: 423
   Options: (No TOS-capability, DC)
   LS Type: AS External Link
   Link State ID: 172.20.1.0 (External Network Number )
   Advertising Router: 0.0.0.5
   LS Seq Number: 80000006
   Checksum: 0x6A92
   Length: 36
   Network Mask: /24
         Metric Type: 2 (Larger than any link state path)
         TOS: 0
```

```
Metric: 1000
Forward Address: 0.0.0.0
External Route Tag: 0
```

The output of the command essentially follows the type 5 LSA structure, shown in Figure 7.16 of Chapter 7.

Understanding and Using the *summary-address* Command

The command **summary-address** *<IP address> <subnet mask>* **[not-advertise]** provides the means to summarize the network prefixes that OSPF learns from the redistributed source of routing information. The pair of parameters, *<IP address> <subnet mask>*, specifies the network prefix, which replaces all redistributed network prefixes that it matches. The format of each of the parameters is dotted decimal notation.

An ASBR being configured with a **summary-address** *<IP address> <subnet mask>* command, instead of originating a separate type 5 LSA for every network prefix matched by the parameters *<IP address> <subnet mask>*, originates a single type 5 LSA that carries the network prefix that the pair of parameters defines. The command does not affect the redistributed network prefixes that the pair of parameters does not match. In other words, the ASBR still originates a single type 5 LSA for every redistributed network prefix for which there is no **summary-address** command with the matching pair of parameters *<IP address> <subnet mask>*.

If the optional **not-advertise** parameter is used, the ASBR does not originate any type 5 LSAs for all redistributed network prefixes that the command's parameters match.

NOTE: *The command operation is similar to that of the **area** <area ID> **range** command. The difference is that the **area** <area ID> **range** command is used on ABRs to summarize inter-area network prefixes, whereas the **summary-address** command is used on ASBRs to summarize the external network prefixes.*

Let's apply this command on routers R4 and R5 from Figure 8.14. The number of OSPF external type 1 and type 2 routes in router R1's routing table (Listing 8.50) is quite large, yet the network prefixes of most of them are matched by network prefixes 172.20.0.0/14 and 172.16.0.0/16. In fact, these two network prefixes do not match only the network prefixes of serial links E1 and E2. So, let's use these two network prefixes to summarize the external network prefixes that they match as well as get rid of the route for the network prefixes of serial links E1 and E2.

Instead of network prefix 172.20.0.0/14, we'll first try network prefix 172.20.0.0/16, which does not summarize all of the network prefixes advertised by router

ER2. We're interested in what happens to the network prefixes that are not matched by network prefix 172.20.0.0/16, used as the **summary-address** command's parameter.

The revised configurations of routers R4 and R5 are shown in Listings 8.54 and 8.55, respectively.

Listing 8.54 Router R4's configuration.

```
interface Serial0
 ip address 192.168.1.5 255.255.255.252

interface TokenRing0
 ip address 10.10.4.2 255.255.252.0
 ring-speed 16

router eigrp 1
 redistribute ospf 1 metric 10000 1 255 1 1500
 network 192.168.1.0

router ospf 1
 router-id 0.0.0.4
 summary-address 172.16.0.0 255.255.0.0
 summary-address 172.17.0.0 255.255.0.0
 summary-address 192.168.0.0 255.255.0.0 not-advertise
 redistribute eigrp 1 metric 2000 metric-type 1 subnets
```

Listing 8.55 Router R5's configuration.

```
interface Ethernet0
 ip address 10.10.1.2 255.255.255.0

interface Serial0
 ip address 192.168.0.5 255.255.255.252

router ospf 1
 router-id 0.0.0.5
 summary-address 192.168.0.0 255.255.0.0 not-advertise
 summary-address 172.20.0.0 255.255.0.0
 redistribute rip metric 1000 subnets
 network 10.10.0.0 0.0.255.255 area 10

router rip
 version 2
 redistribute ospf 1 metric 1
 network 192.168.0.0
 no auto-summary
```

8. Controlling Routing Information

The **summary-address** commands are shown as shaded lines. In Listing 8.54, pay attention to the second shaded line: Its parameters do not match any network prefix router advertised by ER1. We're interested to see if router R4 will originate a type 5 LSA for it.

The OSPF part of router R1's routing table, shown in Listing 8.56, now looks much slimmer. It contains only one OSPF external type 1 route, for network prefix 172.16.0.0/16, which matched and replaced all of the network prefixes advertised by router ER1. As we should expect, the routing table does not contain routes for network prefixes of serial links ER1 and ER2; these were filtered out by the **summary-address 192.168.0.0 255.255.0.0 not-advertise** commands of both routers. Naturally, the routing table does not have a route for network prefix 172.17.0.0/16, as it does not match any redistributed network prefixes on router R4.

Listing 8.56   The OSPF part of router R1's routing table.

```
R1#show ip route ospf
O E1 172.16.0.0/16 [110/2080] via 10.0.1.2, 00:27:39, Ethernet0
     172.21.0.0/22 is subnetted, 2 subnets
O E2    172.21.8.0 [110/1000] via 10.0.1.2, 00:27:39, Ethernet0
O E2    172.21.4.0 [110/1000] via 10.0.1.2, 00:27:39, Ethernet0
O E2 172.20.0.0/16 [110/1000] via 10.0.1.2, 00:27:39, Ethernet0
     172.22.0.0/24 is subnetted, 1 subnets
O E2    172.22.1.0 [110/1000] via 10.0.1.2, 00:27:39, Ethernet0
     10.0.0.0/8 is variably subnetted, 2 subnets, 2 masks
O IA    10.10.0.0/16 [110/84] via 10.0.1.2, 00:27:39, Ethernet0
```

What's a bit disturbing, however, is that the routing table is still full of the OSPF external type 2 routes. Apparently, network prefix 172.20.0.0/16 did not match all of the network prefixes advertised by router ER2, and the unmatched prefixes manifested themselves in the form of type 5 LSAs originated by router R5, which made all routers in the OSPF autonomous system install an equal amount of the OSPF external type 2 routes. Those that were matched, however, were indeed replaced by single network prefix 172.20.0.0/16, for which we can see a route in the routing table.

Let's now go one step further and replace the **summary-address 172.20.0.0 255.255.0.0** command with the **summary-address 172.20.0.0 255.252.0.0** command. After that, router R1's routing table will look as shown below:

```
R1#show ip route ospf
O E1 172.16.0.0/16 [110/2080] via 10.0.1.2, 00:40:42, Ethernet0
     10.0.0.0/8 is variably subnetted, 2 subnets, 2 masks
O IA    10.10.0.0/16 [110/84] via 10.0.1.2, 00:40:42, Ethernet0
O E2 172.20.0.0/14 [110/1000] via 10.0.1.2, 00:00:27, Ethernet0
```

The link-state database of router R1 also greatly diminished in size. It now contains only two type 5 LSAs, as shown below:

```
R1#show ip ospf database
...
            Type-5 AS External Link States

Link ID         ADV Router      Age      Seq#       Checksum Tag
172.16.0.0      0.0.0.4         1279     0x80000004 0x5F3A   0
172.20.0.0      0.0.0.5         69       0x80000001 0x7392   0
```

Configuring NSSA

Making an area NSSA is very similar to making an area stub. All routers residing in the area must be configured with the **area** *<area ID>* **nssa** command. Unlike the **area** *<area ID>* **stub** command, however, the **area** *<area ID>* **nssa** command does not automatically make the ABRs inject the default network prefix (0.0.0.0/0) into the NSSA. To make the NSSA ABRs inject the default network prefix, the command must be followed by the optional parameter **default-information-originate**.

Another optional parameter—**no-redistribution**—prevents the router from performing redistribution to inject the redistributed network prefixes into the NSSA.

Similar to the **area** *<area ID>* **stub** command, the **area** *<area ID>* **nssa** command can be followed by the **no-summary** parameter, which prevents the ABR from injecting type 3 and 4 summary LSAs into the NSSA. (The area becomes a "totally not-so-stubby area," similar to a "totally stubby area".)

Obviously, an NSSA cannot be a transit area (that is, no virtual links can be placed through it).

The ASBR configuration does not change in NSSA. All the commands remain the same, including the ones used for summarization, which can and should be done whenever possible.

Let's convert Area 10 in the network from Figure 8.14 to an NSSA. Previously, external routers ER1 and ER2 become a part of NSSA 10 (of which they are not even aware because no changes on the routers are necessary). Routers R4 and R5 still perform summarization of the network prefixes that they learn from routers ER1 and ER2, as defined in the previous section (see Figure 8.15).

Router R1 underwent an additional change: It is now Area 0's ASBR because it redistributes the network prefix defined on its own Loopback0 interface.

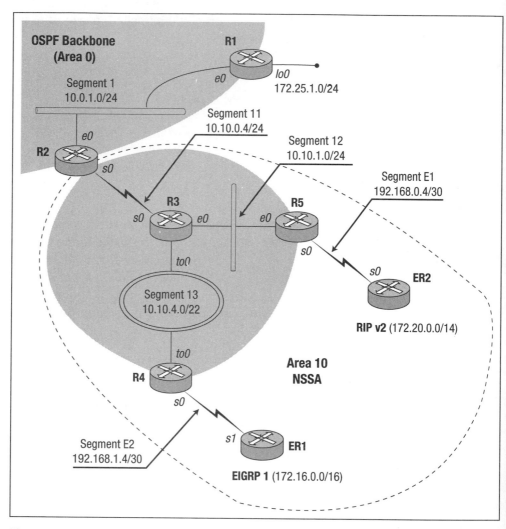

Figure 8.15   The routers that previously resided in Area 10 and the two external routers now constitute NSSA 10.

Listings 8.57 through 8.61 show the configurations of all five OSPF routers (R1 through R5).

Listing 8.57   Router R1's configuration.

```
interface Loopback0
 ip address 172.25.1.1 255.255.255.0

interface Ethernet0
 ip address 10.0.1.1 255.255.255.0

router ospf 1
```

```
router-id 0.0.0.1
redistribute connected metric 500 metric-type 1 subnets
network 10.0.0.0 0.0.255.255 area 0
```

Listing 8.58   Router R2's configuration.

```
interface Ethernet0
 ip address 10.0.1.2 255.255.255.0

interface Serial0
 ip address 10.10.0.5 255.255.255.252

router ospf 1
 router-id 0.0.0.2
 area 0 range 10.0.0.0 255.255.0.0
 area 10 nssa default-information-originate
 area 10 range 10.10.0.0 255.255.0.0
 network 10.0.0.0 0.0.255.255 area 0
 network 10.10.0.0 0.0.255.255 area 10
```

Listing 8.59   Router R3's configuration.

```
interface Ethernet0
 ip address 10.10.1.1 255.255.255.0

interface Serial0
 ip address 10.10.0.6 255.255.255.252

interface TokenRing0
 ip address 10.10.4.1 255.255.252.0
 ring-speed 16

router ospf 1
 router-id 0.0.0.3
 area 10 nssa
 network 10.10.0.0 0.0.255.255 area 10
```

Listing 8.60   Router R4's configuration.

```
interface Serial0
 ip address 192.168.1.5 255.255.255.252

interface TokenRing0
 ip address 10.10.4.2 255.255.252.0
 ring-speed 16
```

8. Controlling Routing Information

```
router eigrp 1
 redistribute ospf 1 metric 10000 1 255 1 1500
 network 192.168.1.0

router ospf 1
 router-id 0.0.0.4
 area 10 nssa
 network 10.10.0.0 0.0.255.255 area 10
 summary-address 172.16.0.0 255.255.0.0
 summary-address 192.168.0.0 255.255.0.0 not-advertise
 redistribute eigrp 1 metric 2000 metric-type 1 subnets
```

Listing 8.61   Router R5's configuration.

```
interface Ethernet0
 ip address 10.10.1.2 255.255.255.0

interface Serial0
 ip address 192.168.0.5 255.255.255.252

router ospf 1
 router-id 0.0.0.5
 area 10 nssa
 summary-address 192.168.0.0 255.255.0.0 not-advertise
 summary-address 172.20.0.0 255.252.0.0
 redistribute rip metric 1000 subnets
 network 10.10.0.0 0.0.255.255 area 10

router rip
 version 2
 redistribute ospf 1 metric 1
 network 192.168.0.0
 no auto-summary
```

If we examine the OSPF part of the routing table of router R2 (Listing 8.62), we'll see that the routes that previously appeared as OSPF external type 1 and 2 routes are now OSPF NSSA external type 1 and 2 routes, which is designated by the labels N1 and N2 following the letter "O" in the output of the **show ip route** command.

Listing 8.62   The OSPF part of router R2's routing table.

```
R2#show ip route ospf
O N1 172.16.0.0/16 [110/2070] via 10.10.0.6, 00:08:18, Serial0
     172.25.0.0/24 is subnetted, 1 subnets
O E1    172.25.1.0 [110/510] via 10.0.1.1, 00:08:18, Ethernet0
```

```
       10.0.0.0/8 is variably subnetted, 4 subnets, 3 masks
O         10.10.1.0/24 [110/74] via 10.10.0.6, 00:09:17, Serial0
O         10.10.4.0/22 [110/70] via 10.10.0.6, 00:09:17, Serial0
O N2 172.20.0.0/14 [110/1000] via 10.10.0.6, 00:08:18, Serial0
```

NOTE: *The OSPF external type 1 route appearing in Listing 8.62 is for the network prefix of router R1's Loopback0 interface, which is redistributed into the OSPF process on router R1.*

However, if we check the OSPF part of router R1's routing table (shown below), we won't see any OSPF NSSA external routes. Instead, we'll see the same OSPF external routes that we saw before. It happens because router R2, being an ABR of NSSA 10, converts type 7 LSAs that are originated by routers R4 and R5 into type 5 LSAs that carry the same network prefixes and the same metrics.

```
R1#show ip route ospf
O E1 172.16.0.0/16 [110/2084] via 10.0.1.2, 00:11:52, Ethernet0
       10.0.0.0/8 is variably subnetted, 2 subnets, 2 masks
O IA    10.10.0.0/16 [110/84] via 10.0.1.2, 00:11:52, Ethernet0
O E2 172.20.0.0/14 [110/1000] via 10.0.1.2, 00:11:52, Ethernet0
```

Unlike router R2's routing table, the routing tables of the routers that reside within NSSA 10 won't show the OSPF external route for network prefix 172.25.1.0/24 (the italicized line in Listing 8.62). Instead, as the output of the **show ip route ospf** command issued on router R3 (shown below) suggests, there is an OSPF NSSA external type 2 route for the default network prefix (0.0.0.0/0), which is originated by router R2 because it is configured with the optional parameter **default-information-originate** of the **area 10 nssa** command.

```
R3#show ip route ospf
O N1 172.16.0.0/16 [110/2006] via 10.10.4.2, 00:18:06, TokenRing0
       10.0.0.0/8 is variably subnetted, 4 subnets, 4 masks
O IA    10.0.0.0/16 [110/74] via 10.10.0.5, 00:18:07, Serial0
O*N2 0.0.0.0/0 [110/1] via 10.10.0.5, 00:18:07, Serial0
O N2 172.20.0.0/14 [110/1000] via 10.10.1.2, 00:18:07, Ethernet0
```

Let's conclude our experimenting with NSSAs by surveying the link-state database of router R2. First, let's examine the output of the **show ip ospf database** command, which is shown in Listing 8.63.

Listing 8.63   **The output of the show ip ospf database command entered on router R2.**

```
R2#show ip ospf database

...
```

8. Controlling Routing Information

```
                        Type-7 AS External Link States (Area 10)

    Link ID             ADV Router        Age         Seq#         Checksum Tag
    0.0.0.0             0.0.0.2           1992        0x80000002 0xFEAF    0
    172.16.0.0          0.0.0.4           1420        0x80000003 0x472     0
    172.20.0.0          0.0.0.5           1491        0x80000003 0xEAF7    0

                        Type-5 AS External Link States

    Link ID             ADV Router        Age         Seq#         Checksum Tag
    10.0.1.0            0.0.0.1           1523        0x80000001 0xA290    0
    172.16.0.0          0.0.0.2           1577        0x80000001 0xA8DB    0
    172.20.0.0          0.0.0.2           1577        0x80000001 0x955C    0
    172.25.1.0          0.0.0.1           1524        0x80000001 0x3344    0
```

Notice that a whole new section is dedicated for type 7 LSAs. In our case, it shows three type 7 LSAs: The first one was originated by router R2 itself for the default network prefix, and the other two were originated by routers R4 and R5. Notice also that, unlike the section showing type 5 LSAs, the section showing type 7 LSAs is labeled as being a part of Area 10, which it is.

The section dedicated to type 5 LSAs shows the duplicate type 5 LSAs for the type 7 LSAs that are originated by routers R4 and R5. These duplicate type 5 LSAs, however, are originated by router R2, the NSSA ABR that performs the conversion of type 7 LSAs to type 5 LSAs.

Also pay attention to an interesting outcome of redistributing the connected routes into OSPF on router R1. The first LSA shown in the section dedicated to type 5 LSAs exhibits the link-state ID equal to 10.0.1.0, the network prefix of the Ethernet0 interface of router R1. As we redistributed all of the connected routes at router R1, it created a type 5 LSA for each of them, including the network prefix of the Ethernet0 interface. Because router R2 installed an intra-area route for that network prefix, we don't see an OSPF external route for the network prefix in router R2's routing table. (Remember, intra-area routes take precedence over all other OSPF routes for the same network prefixes.) Nor do we see an OSPF external route for this network prefix in the routing tables of any other routers because all of them are located in NSSA 10 and hence do not receive any type 5 LSA. If, however, there were another area that wasn't an NSSA or stub, and its ABR would summarize Area 0's network prefixes just as router R2 does, we would see an OSPF external route for the network prefix in the routing tables of the routers in that area. This would happen because the ABRs of the area would inject a single type 3 LSA into the new area, which would advertise Area 0's summary network prefix (10.0.0.0/16). Therefore, the routers wouldn't have any intra- and inter-area routes for network prefix 10.0.1.0/24. As type 5 LSAs are flooded unchanged throughout the OSPF autonomous system (excluding the stub areas and NSSAs), the type 5 LSA for network prefix 10.0.1.0/24 would produce OSPF external routes on the routers in the new area. The bottom line in this situation is that redistribution into OSPF should be done carefully, because it may inadvertently produce undesirable OSPF external routes.

Finally, NSSA ABRs can perform summarization when converting type 7 LSAs to type 5 LSAs. This is achieved by using the **summary-address** command under the **router ospf** configuration of the NSSA ABRs. In our example, router R2 is the only NSSA ABR; hence, if we enter the **summary-address 172.0.0.0 255.0.0.0** command under **router ospf 1**, router R1 should no longer have a separate OSPF external type 1 route for network prefix 172.16.0.0/16 and a separate OSPF external type 2 route for network prefix 172.20.0.0/14. Instead, it should now have a single OSPF external type 1 route for network prefix 172.0.0.0/8, which is confirmed by the output of the **show ip route ospf** command, shown below:

```
R1#show ip route ospf
        10.0.0.0/8 is variably subnetted, 2 subnets, 2 masks
O IA    10.10.0.0/16 [110/45] via 10.0.1.2, 00:09:50, Ethernet0
O E1 172.0.0.0/8 [110/2010] via 10.0.1.2, 00:09:50, Ethernet0
```

Filtering Routing Information

You can filter routing updates using access and prefix lists and also during redistribution.

Filtering Routing Updates Using Access Lists

The easiest way to filter network prefixes that are sent and received in the routing updates is to use a standard IP access list, which is then applied as the routing information filter.

The procedure is as follows:

1. Define a standard IP access list as explained in the "Using Standard Access Lists" section of Chapter 1. Use the **permit** clauses to allow the matched network prefixes and the **deny** clauses to filter out the matched network prefixes.

Warning! *The wildcard mask does not allow matching the network prefix lengths! For example, the access list clause access-list 1 deny host 10.1.0.0 matches network prefixes 10.1.0.0/24 and 10.1.0.0/24.*

2. Apply the access list as the routing update filter using the command **distribute-list** *<ACL #>* {**out**|**in**} *<interface>* *<#>* in the corresponding routing protocol configuration mode (for example, under **router eigrp 1**

configuration). The **{out|in}** parameter specifies whether the access list
must be applied for the routing updates received or sent out of the interface. The pair of parameters *<interface> <#>* specifies the interface on
which the routing updates must be filtered.

Let's see how the guidelines work using the network shown in Figure 8.16.

In our first experiment, all routers run EIGRP, and router R2 has the configuration shown in Listing 8.64.

Listing 8.64   Router R2's configuration.

```
interface Serial0/0
 ip address 172.16.255.6 255.255.255.252

interface Serial0/1
 ip address 172.16.255.9 255.255.255.252

router eigrp 1
 network 172.16.0.0
 distribute-list RtFilterIn in Serial0/0
 distribute-list 1 out Serial0/1

ip access-list standard RtFilterIn
 permit 172.16.1.0
 deny   172.16.100.0
 deny   172.16.1.0 0.0.0.255
 permit any
```

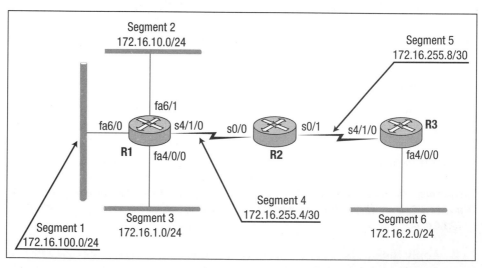

Figure 8.16   Router R2 performs filtering of network prefixes advertised by router R1.

```
access-list 1 deny    172.16.10.0
access-list 1 permit 172.16.10.0 0.0.0.255
```

The two shaded lines indicate the applied routing filter. The first routing filter is inbound and defined as the named access list **RtFilterIn**; the second routing filter is outbound and is defined as standard access list 1.

Notice that the first **permit** clause matches 172.16.1.0 precisely, whereas the following **deny** clause matches 172.16.1.X, where the X can be any number from 0 through 255. The idea is to see which clause catches the network prefix of segment 3 (172.16.1.0/24). Although both match all bits, the **deny** clause also tries to match the network prefix length. (Wildcard mask 0.0.0.255 can be thought of as the inverted subnet mask 255.255.255.0, which corresponds to the network prefix length.)

Following is the EIGRP part of router R2's routing table:

```
R2#show ip route eigrp
     172.16.0.0/16 is variably subnetted, 5 subnets, 2 masks
D       172.16.10.0/24 [90/2172416] via 172.16.255.5, 00:01:41, Serial0/0
D       172.16.1.0/24 [90/2172416] via 172.16.255.5, 00:31:25, Serial0/0
D       172.16.2.0/24 [90/2172416] via 172.16.255.10, 00:04:37, Serial0/1
```

Apparently, the **permit** clause matched the network prefix, which caused the router to install the route for it (the shaded line). The second **deny** clause filtered out the network prefix of segment 1 (172.16.100.0/24).

Let's now take a look at the routing table of router R3, which is shown below:

```
R3#show ip route
...
     172.16.0.0/16 is variably subnetted, 2 subnets, 2 masks
C       172.16.255.8/30 is directly connected, Serial4/1/0
C       172.16.2.0/24 is directly connected, FastEthernet4/0/0
```

Why doesn't this contain any EIGRP routes? The reason lies in a common mistake: forgetting that every existing access list contains an implicit **deny any** at the end. (Undefined access lists are treated as single **permit any** clauses.) This **deny any** clause filtered out all network prefixes that have not been matched by the two explicitly defined clauses. We have only one network prefix that is matched by both explicit clauses: 172.16.10.0/24. As the network prefix is matched by both clauses and the first clause is **deny**, no network prefixes survived the access list. Hence, router R3's routing table contains no EIGRP routes.

Let's add **permit any** at the end of the access list. Now the routing table of router R3 looks as follows:

```
R3#show ip route
...
     172.16.0.0/16 is variably subnetted, 4 subnets, 2 masks
D       172.16.255.4/30 [90/2681856] via 172.16.255.9, 00:00:09, Serial4/1/0
C       172.16.255.8/30 is directly connected, Serial4/1/0
D       172.16.1.0/24 [90/2684416] via 172.16.255.9, 00:00:09, Serial4/1/0
C       172.16.2.0/24 is directly connected, FastEthernet4/0/0
```

The shaded lines show the routes for the network prefixes that survived the updated access list.

Finally, let's examine how the inbound and outbound filters affect the propagation of EIGRP queries. First, let's fail the FastEthernet6/0 interface on router R1, which should cause router R1 to begin querying its EIGRP neighbors (which consist of only router R2) for a route for the interface's network prefix (172.16.100.0/24). The network prefix, however, is filtered by the inbound routing filter on router R2, which originally prevented router R2 from installing an EIGRP route for it. Listing 8.65 shows the output of the **debug eigrp fsm** command issued on router R2. As we might expect, the behavior of router R2 corresponds to the behavior of an EIGRP router that receives a query for a network prefix for which it does not have an EIGRP route: It responds with a reply carrying the metric of infinity without becoming active for the network prefix.

Listing 8.65   The output of the debug eigrp fsm command issued on router R2 when router R1's interface FastEthernet6/0 failed.

```
R2#debug eigrp fsm
EIGRP FSM Events/Actions debugging is on
R2#
DUAL: dest(172.16.100.0/24) not active
DUAL: dual_rcvquery():172.16.100.0/24 via 172.16.255.5
      metric 4294967295/4294967295, RD is 4294967295
DUAL: Send reply about 172.16.100.0/24 to 172.16.255.5
DUAL: Removing dest 172.16.100.0/24, nexthop 172.16.255.5
DUAL: No routes.  Flushing dest 172.16.100.0/24
```

Let's now fail router R1's interface FastEthernet6/1, whose network prefix is filtered out by the outbound filter of router R2. As router R1 becomes active for the network prefix, it sends a query to its neighbor, router R2. Router R2 previously had a route for the network prefix; moreover, the route pointed to router R1. Hence, router R2 received a query from the network prefix's successor, which makes it become active for the network prefix. Thus, it must begin querying its neighbors if they know a route for it, and so router R2 sends a query to router R3, which has never had a route for the network prefix. Router R3's reaction is similar to the reaction of router R2 in our previous experiment: respond with a reply carrying the metric of infinity. This is demonstrated in Listing 8.66, which shows the output of the **debug eigrp fsm** command issued on router R3.

Listing 8.66   The output of the **debug eigrp fsm** command issued on router R3 when router R1's interface FastEthernet6/1 failed.

```
R3#debug eigrp fsm
EIGRP FSM Events/Actions debugging is on
R3#
DUAL: dest(172.16.10.0/24) not active
DUAL: dual_rcvquery():172.16.10.0/24 via 172.16.255.9
     metric 4294967295/4294967295, RD is 4294967295
DUAL: Send reply about 172.16.10.0/24 to 172.16.255.9
DUAL: Removing dest 172.16.10.0/24, nexthop 172.16.255.9
DUAL: No routes.  Flushing dest 172.16.10.0/24
```

Let's now examine how OSPF and routing information filtering interoperate. Although the network remains as shown in Figure 8.16, all routers are now configured with OSPF. In particular, router R2 has the configuration shown in Listing 8.67.

Listing 8.67   Router R2's configuration.

```
interface Serial0/0
 ip address 172.16.255.6 255.255.255.252

interface Serial0/1
 ip address 172.16.255.9 255.255.255.252

router ospf 1
 router-id 0.0.0.2
 network 172.16.0.0 0.0.255.255 area 0
 distribute-list RtFilterIn in Serial0/0

ip access-list standard RtFilterIn
 deny    172.16.10.0
 deny    172.16.100.0
 permit any
```

The shaded line indicates the **distribute-list** command whose argument is the named access list **RtFilterIn** defined at the end of the listing. If we, out of curiosity, tried to apply the access list as an outbound routing filter, the result would be:

```
R2(config-router)#distribute-list RtFilterIn out s0/1
% Interface not allowed with OUT for OSPF
```

After the access list is applied as the inbound routing filter, the OSPF part of the routing table of router R2 looks as shown below:

```
R2#show ip route ospf
     172.16.0.0/16 is variably subnetted, 4 subnets, 2 masks
O       172.16.1.0/24 [110/65] via 172.16.255.5, 00:02:55, Serial0/0
O       172.16.2.0/24 [110/65] via 172.16.255.10, 00:02:55, Serial0/1
```

Notice that the routing table does not contain any routes for network prefixes 172.16.10.0/24 and 172.16.100.0/24, because these routes were prevented from being installed by the filter.

Nevertheless, the routing table of router R3 does contain routes for those network prefixes, which is confirmed by the following output of the **show ip route ospf** command entered on router R3:

```
R3#show ip route ospf
     172.16.0.0/16 is variably subnetted, 6 subnets, 2 masks
O       172.16.255.4/30 [110/128] via 172.16.255.9, 00:07:49, Serial4/1/0
O       172.16.10.0/24 [110/129] via 172.16.255.9, 00:07:49, Serial4/1/0
O       172.16.1.0/24 [110/129] via 172.16.255.9, 00:07:49, Serial4/1/0
O       172.16.100.0/24 [110/129] via 172.16.255.9, 00:07:49, Serial4/1/0
```

As we know, this happens because routing filters do not affect the link-state databases of the routers, only their routing tables. As router R3 does not have any routing filters defined, it does not filter any network prefixes during the process of building the OSPF part of the routing table. Hence, the routing table contains the routes for the network prefixes.

Filtering Routing Updates Using Prefix Lists

The length of a network prefix is an important component of the network prefix. Sometimes, the only difference between two network prefixes is their lengths, and so the ability to match network prefix lengths should be an important feature of routing information filters.

As we discussed in the previous section, regular IP access lists that are applied as routing filters do not allow matching of the lengths of network prefixes. Therefore, there must be some other means to match the lengths.

The IP prefix lists were implemented in certain releases of IOS version 11.1 and 11.3, and were implemented on a permanent basis in IOS version 12.0.

IP prefix lists are logical expressions that can match specified leading sets of bits in IP network prefixes and the lengths of the network prefixes. Similarly to access lists, IP prefix lists consist of one or several clauses, each of which defines a match criterion. Like access list clauses, prefix list clauses return **permit** or **deny**. However, unlike access list clauses, prefix list clauses have sequence numbers, which allow for the removal of individual prefix list clauses without affecting the whole prefix list. (As we remember, the clauses of numbered IP access lists cannot be removed individually; however, the clauses of named access lists can.)

IP prefix lists can be used only as routing filters.

IP prefix list clauses have the following format:

ip prefix-list *<PL name>* [**seq** *<PL #>*] **{permit|deny}** *<NP>*/*<NP length>* [**ge** *<GE value>*] [**le** *<LE value>*]

The *<PL name>* parameter defines the name of the prefix list. It has the same functionality as that of the name of a named access list: providing a means for referencing the prefix list in the commands that apply it as the filter.

The optional pair of parameters **seq** *<PL #>* specifies the sequence number of the prefix list clause. If this is omitted, the router automatically generates this number by adding five to the maximum among the sequence numbers of the existing prefix list clauses with the same *<PL name>* parameter. If no clauses with the *<PL name>* parameter exist, the generated number is equal to five.

The pair of parameters *<NP>*/*<NP length>* specifies the leading bits that will be compared with the corresponding leading bits in the network prefixes. The format of this pair of parameters is bit count, such as 10.0.0.0/8.

The pair of parameters **ge** *<GE value>* specifies the maximum length that the matching network prefixes can have. Likewise the pair of parameters **le** *<LE value>* specifies the minimum length of the matching network prefixes. Each of the parameters is optional. If used, *<GE value>* and *<LE value>* must satisfy the following criteria:

If both are used:

$NP\ length > GE\ value > LE\ value \geq 32$

If only *<GE value>* is used:

$NP\ length > GE\ value \geq 32$

If only *<LE value>* is used:

$NP\ length > LE\ value \geq 32$

NOTE: *The angle brackets surrounding the parameter names are omitted in the above equations to avoid confusion with the "greater than" mathematical symbol.*

The rules that the router uses when comparing network prefixes against an IP prefix list are:

• The router treats the IP prefix list as an ordered list. That is, the router compares the network prefixes against the clauses with the smaller numbers before the ones with the higher numbers. The first comparison is done against the clause with the smallest number.

- The router looks only for the first match. After the match is found, prefix list lookup is terminated. Then, the result (**permit** or **deny**) that is specified in the clause that produced the match is returned as the result of comparing the network prefix against the prefix list.

- When comparing a network prefix against a clause, the router first checks if the length of the network prefix—let's call it L—is greater than or equal to the value of the *<NP length>* parameters (that is, $L \geq NP\ lengths$). If so, the router then compares the leading *<NP length>* bits of the network prefix against the leading *<NP length>* bits of the *<NP>* parameter. If all bits are equal, then the following applies:

  If neither **ge** *<GE value>* nor **le** *<LE value>* are specified, the clause produces a match only if the network prefix lengths are equal to the *<NP length>* parameters (that is, $L = NP\ lengths$). Otherwise, the clause produces a match only if the network prefix length satisfies one of the following conditions:

  $L \geq GE\ value$, if only **ge** *<GE value>* is specified;

  $L \leq LE\ value$, if only **le** *<LE value>* is specified; or

  $LE\ value \geq L \geq GE\ value$, if both are specified.

  In all other cases, the clause and the network prefix do not produce a match.

- At the end of every defined prefix list is an implicit **deny 0.0.0.0/0 le 32** clause, which matches any network prefix that hasn't been matched by any of the explicit clauses.

Following are some examples of prefix list clauses:

- **ip prefix-list TestPL permit 172.0.0.0/8 ge 16**—This clause permits any network prefix whose first octet is equal to 172 and whose network prefix length is greater than or equal to 16. For example, network prefixes 172.16.0.0/16 and 172.20.4.0/22 are matched, although 172.24.0.0/14 is not.

- **ip prefix-list TestPL deny 192.168.1.0/24 le 31**—This clause denies all network prefixes whose first 3 octets are equal to 192.168.1 and whose lengths are smaller than 31 (but greater than 24). For example, 192.168.1.0/24 and 192.168.1.4/30 are matched, although 192.168.1.1/32 is not.

- **ip prefix-list TestPL permit 0.0.0.0/0 ge 32**—This clause permits any network prefixes whose length is equal to 32. We previously called these network prefixes host addresses. (They are still network prefixes.) For example, the clause matches 10.1.0.1/32, 192.168.255.255/32, and so on.

- **ip prefix-list TestPL deny 0.0.0.0/0 ge 16 le 24**—This clause denies any network prefix whose length is in the range from 16 through 24. For example, the clause denies 172.16.0.0/16, 192.168.192.0/18, and 192.168.1.0/24.

To apply an IP prefix list as an outbound routing filter, use the **distribute-list prefix** <*PL name*> **out** <*interface*> command. The <*PL name*> parameter specifies the name of a previously defined prefix list, and the <*interface*> parameter specifies the output interface. To apply an IP prefix list as an inbound routing filter, use the command **distribute-list prefix** <*PL name*> [**gateway** <*GW-PL name*>] **in** <*interface*>. The additional optional parameter <*GW-PL name*> specifies the prefix list, which should be used to match the IP addresses of the advertising routers. If the <*GW-PL name*> parameter is used, the <*PL name*> prefix list is applied only against the network prefix that is advertised by a router whose IP address passes the <*GW-PL name*> prefix list.

NOTE: The **ge** and **le** parameters are irrelevant in the case of <GW-PL name> parameter.

To see how the prefix lists can be used to filter routing updates, let's use the network shown in Figure 8.17.

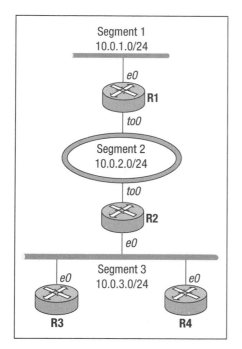

Figure 8.17   Router R2 filters the routing updates that it receives from its neighbors using prefix lists.

Before any filtering on router R2 is done, its routing table looks as shown in Listing 8.68.

Listing 8.68   The EIGRP part of router R2's routing table.

```
R2#show ip route eigrp
     172.23.0.0/16 is variably subnetted, 4 subnets, 3 masks
D       172.23.128.0/18 [90/409600] via 10.0.3.129, 00:00:12, Ethernet0
D       172.23.2.0/24 [90/409600] via 10.0.3.129, 00:00:12, Ethernet0
D       172.23.1.0/24 [90/409600] via 10.0.3.129, 00:00:12, Ethernet0
D       172.23.0.4/30 [90/409600] via 10.0.3.129, 00:00:12, Ethernet0
     172.24.0.0/16 is variably subnetted, 4 subnets, 3 masks
D       172.24.128.0/18 [90/409600] via 10.0.3.130, 00:00:12, Ethernet0
D       172.24.0.4/30 [90/409600] via 10.0.3.130, 00:00:12, Ethernet0
D       172.24.1.0/24 [90/409600] via 10.0.3.130, 00:00:12, Ethernet0
D       172.24.2.0/24 [90/409600] via 10.0.3.130, 00:00:12, Ethernet0
     10.0.0.0/8 is variably subnetted, 6 subnets, 2 masks
D       10.0.0.3/32 [90/409600] via 10.0.3.129, 00:00:12, Ethernet0
D       10.0.1.0/24 [90/297728] via 10.0.2.1, 00:00:12, TokenRing0
D       10.0.0.1/32 [90/304128] via 10.0.2.1, 00:00:12, TokenRing0
D       10.0.0.4/32 [90/409600] via 10.0.3.130, 00:00:12, Ethernet0
D*EX 0.0.0.0/0 [170/176128] via 10.0.2.1, 00:00:12, TokenRing0
```

Our task is to devise a prefix list that would keep only those network prefixes whose lengths are either /24 or /32. Listing 8.69 shows an example of router R2's configuration that solves this task.

Listing 8.69   An example of router R2's configuration that allows EIGRP to install routes only for those network prefixes whose lengths are either /24 or /32.

```
router eigrp 1
 network 10.0.0.0
 distribute-list prefix ClassfulAndHosts in

ip prefix-list ClassfulAndHosts seq 5 permit 0.0.0.0/0 ge 32
ip prefix-list ClassfulAndHosts seq 10 permit 0.0.0.0/0 ge 24 le 24
```

After the configuration is entered on router R2, the EIGRP part of its routing table becomes as shown in Listing 8.70. Notice that the only EIGRP routes are for network prefixes whose lengths are either /24 or /32.

Listing 8.70   The EIGRP part of router R2's routing table after the filtering was applied.

```
R2#show ip route eigrp
     172.23.0.0/24 is subnetted, 2 subnets
D       172.23.2.0 [90/409600] via 10.0.3.129, 00:00:13, Ethernet0
D       172.23.1.0 [90/409600] via 10.0.3.129, 00:00:13, Ethernet0
     172.24.0.0/24 is subnetted, 2 subnets
```

```
D        172.24.1.0 [90/409600] via 10.0.3.130, 00:00:13, Ethernet0
D        172.24.2.0 [90/409600] via 10.0.3.130, 00:00:13, Ethernet0
     10.0.0.0/8 is variably subnetted, 6 subnets, 2 masks
D        10.0.0.3/32 [90/409600] via 10.0.3.129, 00:00:13, Ethernet0
D        10.0.0.1/32 [90/304128] via 10.0.2.1, 00:00:13, TokenRing0
D        10.0.1.0/24 [90/297728] via 10.0.2.1, 00:00:13, TokenRing0
D        10.0.0.4/32 [90/409600] via 10.0.3.130, 00:00:13, Ethernet0
```

Filtering Routing Information during Redistribution

The command **distribute-list** {*<AL name>*|*<AL number>*|**prefix** *<PL name>*} **out** *<source>* allows the filtering of routing information during redistribution. The *<AL name>* and *<AL number>* parameters specify either the name or the number of a standard access list. Alternatively, the pair of **prefix** *<PL name>* parameters can be used to specify the name of a prefix list. The *<source>* parameter specifies the source of routing information from which the network prefixes are redistributed into the routing protocol. The routing protocol into which redistribution is performed accepts only the network prefixes that pass the specified access or prefix list.

To see how redistributed routing information is filtered, let's consider the network shown in Figure 8.18.

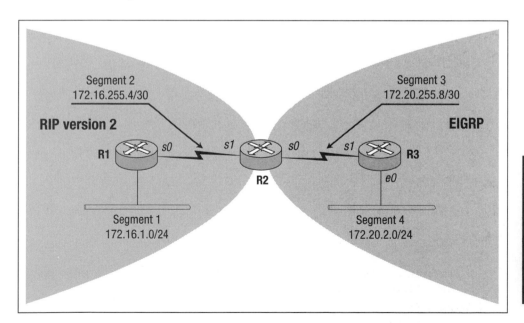

Figure 8.18   Router R2 performs filtering of redistributed routing information.

Right now, router R2 performs pure redistribution of RIP and EIGRP without any filtering.

The RIP part of router R1's routing table looks as shown below:

```
R1#show ip route rip
     172.20.0.0/16 is variably subnetted, 2 subnets, 2 masks
R       172.20.255.8/30 [120/1] via 172.16.255.6, 00:00:06, Serial0
R       172.20.2.0/24 [120/1] via 172.16.255.6, 00:00:06, Serial0
```

The EIGRP part of router R3's routing table looks as shown below:

```
R3#show ip route eigrp
     172.16.0.0/16 is variably subnetted, 2 subnets, 2 masks
D EX    172.16.255.4/30 [170/40512256] via 172.20.255.9, 00:00:32, Serial1
D EX    172.16.1.0/24 [170/40512256] via 172.20.255.9, 00:00:32, Serial1
```

Let's configure router R2 so that it redistributes only those network prefixes whose lengths are shorter than or equal to /24 into RIP version 2, and network prefixes that begin with 172.16.1 into EIGRP.

Listing 8.71 shows the router R2 configuration that accomplishes the task.

Listing 8.71   Router R2's configuration.

```
...
router eigrp 1
 redistribute rip metric 64 1 255 1 1500
 network 172.20.0.0
 distribute-list Only_172.16.1 out rip

router rip
 version 2
 redistribute eigrp 1 metric 1
 network 172.16.0.0
 distribute-list prefix PrefLenghLE24 out eigrp 1
 no auto-summary

ip prefix-list PrefLenghLE24 seq 5 permit 0.0.0.0/0 le 24

ip access-list standard Only_172.16.1
 permit 172.16.1.0 0.0.0.255
...
```

After the suggested configuration is entered on router R2, router R1's RIP part of the routing table becomes:

```
R1#show ip route rip
     172.20.0.0/24 is subnetted, 1 subnets
R       172.20.2.0 [120/1] via 172.16.255.6, 00:00:02, Serial0
```

The EIGRP part of the routing table of router R3 becomes:

```
R3#show ip route eigrp
     172.16.0.0/24 is subnetted, 1 subnets
D EX    172.16.1.0 [170/40512256] via 172.20.255.9, 00:02:02, Serial1
```

Filtering Routing Information during Redistribution Using Route Maps

Another way to filter the routing information during redistribution is to use special logical expressions called *route maps*.

A route map is a logical expression that consists of one or several clauses, each of which can contain a zero; one or several match conditions; and zero, one, or several set actions. Like the clauses of an IP prefix list, the route map clauses are numbered. When redistributing a network prefix into a routing protocol, the router checks the network prefix against the match conditions of the clauses of the specified route map in the ascending order of clause sequence numbers. The router detects a match of a network prefix and a route map clause only if all of the clause's match conditions are satisfied. If a match is detected, the router redistributes the network prefix in accordance with the set actions specified in the clause. If no clause produces a match, the network prefix is not redistributed.

Similar to the clauses for IP prefix and access lists, route map clauses can return **permit** or **deny**. If a network prefix matches a **deny** route map clause, the network prefix is not redistributed, regardless of the set actions. No further route map lookup is performed for the network prefix.

A route map clause that contains no match conditions matches all routes.

To configure route map-based filtering of routing information during redistribution, follow these steps:

1. Create a route map clause header using the command **route-map** *<RM name>* [{**permit**|**deny**}] *<sequence #>*.

2. Add match conditions using the statement **match** followed by specific parameters. Some of the most popular match conditions are:

   To match a network prefix against an access list, use the **match ip address** {*<AL number>*|*<AL name>*} clause, where the {*<AL number>*|*<AL name>*} parameter is either an access list number or an access list name.

Nevertheless, let's try to use route maps to improve the usability of one-way redistribution such as the one that we tried in the network illustrated in Figure 8.9. Although the improvement is not universal but on the contrary rather dependent on individual network topology, it's worth considering.

The major problem with one-way redistribution performed by routers R2 and R4 in Figure 8.9 was that each of the routers advertised all network prefixes that were acquired via redistribution with the same fixed metric. Whereas it is possible to tweak the metrics for individual network prefixes using the **offset-list** command in such a way that router R2 would advertise network prefix 10.0.1.0/24 with a smaller metric than router R4, and router R4 would advertise network prefix 10.0.8.0/24 with a smaller metric than router R2, this tweaking is of a static nature. In other words, if routers R1 and R5 begin advertising new network prefixes, routers R2 and R4 won't adopt the tweaked metrics for them and instead will advertise them to host H1 with the fixed redistribution metrics.

The use of route maps, however, can make routers R2 and R4 a little more dynamic. As we know, route maps allow the matching of not only the redistributed network prefixes against access or prefix lists, but also some parameters of the routes that the original source installed for the redistributed network prefixes. One of these parameters is the output interfaces of such routes. In our situation, we can create a route map on router R2 that matches all network prefixes for which the routes are established through the Serial1 interface and sets the metric with which these network prefixes must be advertised to 1. For all other network prefixes, the route map sets the metric to 6. A similar route map should be created on router R4, but, in the case of router R4, the route map should set the metric to 1 for network prefixes that are accessible through the Serial0 interface.

Listings 8.72 and 8.73 show the revised configurations of routers R2 and R4 from Figure 8.9.

Listing 8.72   Router R2's revised configuration.

```
interface Serial0
 ip address 10.1.0.9 255.255.255.252

interface Serial1
 ip address 10.1.0.6 255.255.255.252

interface TokenRing0
 ip address 10.0.3.1 255.255.255.0
 ring-speed 16

router eigrp 1
 network 10.0.0.0
```

```
router rip
 version 2
 redistribute eigrp 1 route-map TweakRIP
 passive-interface Serial0
 passive-interface Serial1
 network 10.0.0.0
 distance 255

ip access-list standard Net10
 permit 10.0.0.0 0.255.255.255

route-map TweakRIP permit 10
 match interface Serial1
 set metric 1

route-map TweakRIP permit 20
 match ip address Net10
 set metric 6
```

Listing 8.73   Router R4's revised configuration.

```
interface Ethernet0
 ip address 10.0.6.1 255.255.255.0

interface Serial0
 ip address 10.1.0.17 255.255.255.252

interface Serial1
 ip address 10.1.0.14 255.255.255.252

router eigrp 1
 network 10.0.0.0

router rip
 version 2
 redistribute eigrp 1 route-map TweakRIP
 passive-interface Serial0
 passive-interface Serial1
 network 10.0.0.0
 distance 255

ip access-list standard Net10
 permit 10.0.0.0 0.255.255.255
```

```
route-map TweakRIP permit 10
 match interface Serial0
 set metric 1

route-map TweakRIP permit 20
 match ip address Net10
 set metric 6
```

If we trace routes for network prefixes 10.0.1.0/24 and 10.0.8.0/24 now, we'll see that host H1 uses the optimum next-hop routers (Listing 8.74).

Listing 8.74   The output of the tracert -d 10.0.1.1 and tracert -d 10.0.8.1 commands entered on host H1.

```
C:\>tracert -d 10.0.1.1

Tracing route to 10.0.1.1 over a maximum of 30 hops

  1     10 ms    <10 ms    10 ms   10.0.3.1
  2     30 ms     30 ms    40 ms   10.0.1.1

Trace complete.

C:\>tracert -d 10.0.8.1

Tracing route to 10.0.8.1 over a maximum of 30 hops

  1    <10 ms    <10 ms    <10 ms   10.0.6.1
  2     30 ms     20 ms     30 ms   10.0.8.1

Trace complete.
```

Understanding Routing Loops

It is important to understand where routing loops can emerge from.

Understanding Routing Loops Emerging from a Single Redistribution Point

This section presents an example of how routing loops can emerge from a single point of redistribution.

The test network used in this section is shown in Figure 8.19.

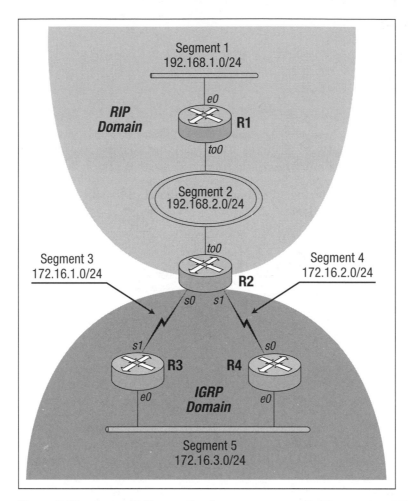

Figure 8.19   An oscillating routing loop can emerge if either segment 3 or segment 4 goes down temporarily.

Router R2 performs mutual redistribution between IGRP and RIP. The only network prefix that router R2 can learn via RIP is 192.168.1.0/24. Hence, our further experiments concentrate only on routing for that network prefix.

The configurations of all four routers are shown in Listings 8.75 through 8.78.

Listing 8.75   Router R1's configuration.

```
interface Ethernet0
 ip address 192.168.1.1 255.255.255.0

interface TokenRing0
 ip address 192.168.2.1 255.255.255.0
 ring-speed 16
```

```
router rip
 network 192.168.1.0
 network 192.168.2.0
```

Listing 8.76   Router R2's configuration.

```
interface Serial0
 ip address 172.16.1.1 255.255.255.0

interface Serial1
 ip address 172.16.2.1 255.255.255.0

interface TokenRing0
 ip address 192.168.2.2 255.255.255.0
 ring-speed 16

router rip
 network 192.168.2.0
 redistribute igrp 1 metric 1

router igrp 1
 redistribute rip metric 16000 1 255 1 1500
 network 172.16.0.0
```

Listing 8.77   Router R3's configuration.

```
interface Ethernet0
 ip address 172.16.3.1 255.255.255.0

interface Serial1
 ip address 172.16.1.2 255.255.255.0

router igrp 1
 network 172.16.0.0
```

Listing 8.78   Router R4's configuration.

```
interface Ethernet0
 ip address 172.16.3.2 255.255.255.0

interface Serial0
 ip address 172.16.2.2 255.255.255.0

router igrp 1
 network 172.16.0.0
```

8. Controlling Routing Information

If we're lucky, after all routers are configured and all involved interfaces on them enabled, no loop is created and the routers' routes for network prefix 192.168.1.0/24 look as shown in Listing 8.79.

Listing 8.79   The routes that routers R2, R3, and R4 have for network prefix 192.168.1.0/24.

```
R2#show ip route
...
R    192.168.1.0/24 [120/1] via 192.168.2.1, 00:00:23, TokenRing0
...

R3#show ip route
...
I    192.168.1.0/24 [100/8477] via 172.16.1.1, 00:00:08, Serial1
...

R4#show ip route
...
I    192.168.1.0/24 [100/8577] via 172.16.3.1, 00:00:08, Ethernet0
...
```

If, however, the serial connection between routers R2 and R4 goes down temporarily, router R4 would have no choice but to establish another route for the network prefix through router R3. After the serial connection is fully restored, the routing table will look as shown in Listing 8.80.

Listing 8.80   The routes that routers R2, R3, and R4 have for network prefix 192.168.1.0/24 after the routing loop emerged.

```
R2#show ip route
...
I    192.168.1.0/24 [100/10577] via 172.16.2.2, 00:00:34, Serial1
...

R3#show ip route
...
I    192.168.1.0/24 is possibly down, routing via 172.16.1.1, Serial1

R4#show ip route
...
I    192.168.1.0/24 [100/8477] via 172.16.2.1, 00:00:44, Serial0
```

Notice that, although router R3's route is correct, it's labeled as "possibly down", and that router R2's route points to router R4, whereas router R4's route points to router R2—which is obviously a routing loop.

Why is this happening? The answer can be easily found if we look at certain fragments of the output of the **debug ip routing** and **debug ip igrp transactions** commands issued on routers R2 and R3. First, let's take a look at the output of the commands issued on router R3, which is shown in Listing 8.81.

Listing 8.81 The output of the debug ip routing and debug ip igrp transactions commands issued on router R3.

```
IGRP: received update from 172.16.1.1 on Serial1
...
     network 192.168.1.0, metric 8477 (neighbor 626)
...
IGRP: sending update to 255.255.255.255 via Ethernet0 (172.16.3.1)
...
     network 192.168.1.0, metric=8477
...
IGRP: Update contains 1 interior, 2 system, and 0 exterior routes.
...
IGRP: received update from 172.16.1.1 on Serial1
...
     network 192.168.1.0, metric 12577 (neighbor 10577)
RT: delete route to 192.168.1.0 via 172.16.1.1, igrp metric [100/8477]
RT: no routes to 192.168.1.0, entering holddown
...
IGRP: sending update to 255.255.255.255 via Ethernet0 (172.16.3.1)
...
     network 192.168.1.0, metric=4294967295
...
```

The first shaded line indicates the metric with which router R2 originally advertised network prefix 192.168.1.0/24 (626). The next shaded line shows that router R2 increased the metric from 626 to 10577, which caused router R3 to place its own route into holddown and begin advertising the network prefix with the metric of infinity. This explains the "possibly down" status of router R3's route for the network prefix.

Let's now take a look at the output of the **debug ip routing** and **debug ip igrp transactions** commands issued on router R2 (Listing 8.82).

Listing 8.82 The output of the debug ip routing and debug ip igrp transactions commands issued on router R2.

```
%LINK-3-UPDOWN: Interface Serial1, changed state to up
...
IGRP: sending update to 255.255.255.255 via Serial1 (172.16.2.1)
...
     network 192.168.1.0, metric=626
...
IGRP: received update from 172.16.2.2 on Serial1
...
```

```
      network 192.168.1.0, metric 10577 (neighbor 8577)
RT: closer admin distance for 192.168.1.0, flushing 1 routes
RT: add 192.168.1.0/24 via 172.16.2.2, igrp metric [100/10577]
...
IGRP: sending update to 255.255.255.255 via Serial0 (172.16.1.1)
...
      network 192.168.1.0, metric=10577
...
```

The first shaded line reveals the metric with which router R2 advertises network prefix 192.168.1.0/24 right after the interface becomes functional (the first line). Although router R4 has received this routing update, it has already scheduled its own update advertising the network prefix. Its own update, however, still contains the metric of router R4's route for the network prefix through router R3, which is equal to 8577. Once router R4 sends the update, router R2 picks it up, and, because it's an IGRP update and IGRP has a smaller administrative distance than RIP does, router R2 discards the RIP route and establishes a bogus IGRP route instead. This is demonstrated by the group of the three shaded lines in Listing 8.82. Following that, router R2 sends an update to router R3 carrying the new metric of 10577, which (as we learned from Listing 8.81) makes router R3 place its own route into holddown.

From this point on, the situation stabilizes for several minutes. Router R2 has established a route for network prefix 192.168.1.0/24 through router R4, and router R4 has established its route for the network prefix through router R2. Because split horizon is enabled on all interfaces of all routers, routers R2 and R4 do not send each other routing updates. Instead, they bombard router R3 with routing updates, which router R3 ignores because it placed its own route for the network prefix into holddown. Eventually, the timeout timers that routers R2 and R4 maintain for their routes for the network prefix expire (because the routers no longer receive the updates from each other for the network prefix), and they themselves place their routes into holddown and label them "possibly down". After the holddowns expire, the routers keep the routes in the routing table until the flush timer expires, after which they remove the routes.

Once router R2 removes the bogus IGRP route, it immediately restores the RIP route for the network prefix, redistributes the network prefix into IGRP, and advertises it to routers R3 and R4 again. At that point, the possibility for the routing loop to reemerge depends on whether router R3's routing update makes it to router R4 fast enough for router R4 to schedule its own advertisement to router R2 before it receives router R2's new routing update.

In the lab where this experiment was conducted, router R4 had time to advertise network prefix 192.168.1.0/24 to R2 before R2 sent R4 its own update. Thus, router

R2 went through the same cycle indefinitely, which is demonstrated by the output of the **debug ip routing** command issued on router R2 (Listing 8.83). The shaded lines show how router R2 first restores the RIP route and then replaces it with the IGRP route.

Listing 8.83 The output of the **debug ip routing** command issued on router R2.

```
...
07:30:25: RT: add 192.168.1.0/24 via 192.168.2.1, rip metric [120/1]
07:31:29: RT: closer admin distance for 192.168.1.0, flushing 1 routes
07:31:29: RT: add 192.168.1.0/24 via 172.16.2.2, igrp metric [100/10577]
07:36:22: RT: delete route to 192.168.1.0 via 172.16.2.2, igrp metric [100/
10577]
07:36:22: RT: no routes to 192.168.1.0, entering holddown
07:41:36: RT: 192.168.1.0 came out of holddown
07:42:22: RT: garbage collecting entry for 192.168.1.0
07:42:28: RT: add 192.168.1.0/24 via 192.168.2.1, rip metric [120/1]
07:43:43: RT: closer admin distance for 192.168.1.0, flushing 1 routes
07:43:43: RT: add 192.168.1.0/24 via 172.16.2.2, igrp metric [100/10577]
07:48:26: RT: delete route to 192.168.1.0 via 172.16.2.2, igrp metric [100/
10577]
07:48:26: RT: no routes to 192.168.1.0, entering holddown
07:53:46: RT: 192.168.1.0 came out of holddown
07:54:38: RT: garbage collecting entry for 192.168.1.0
07:54:57: RT: add 192.168.1.0/24 via 192.168.2.1, rip metric [120/1]
07:55:51: RT: closer admin distance for 192.168.1.0, flushing 1 routes
07:55:51: RT: add 192.168.1.0/24 via 172.16.2.2, igrp metric [100/10577]
...
```

Understanding Routing Loops Emerging from Multiple Redistribution Points

As explained in the "In Depth" section, multiple points are unlike single points of redistribution in that they typically result in permanent routing loops—that is, loops that do not go through the cycles of disappearing and reappearing but instead remain unchanged at all times.

To demonstrate the emergence of a routing loop, we'll use the network illustrated in Figure 8.20. In this network, routers RR1 and RR2 redistribute the routing information that is learned via EIGRP into RIP, and vice versa. Hence, they are two points of redistribution.

In addition, router BR1 is a "border router" between the IGRP domain on the top and the EIGRP domain in the middle. Hence, the network prefixes in the IGRP domain are reachable from the EIGRP domain through EIGRP external routes,

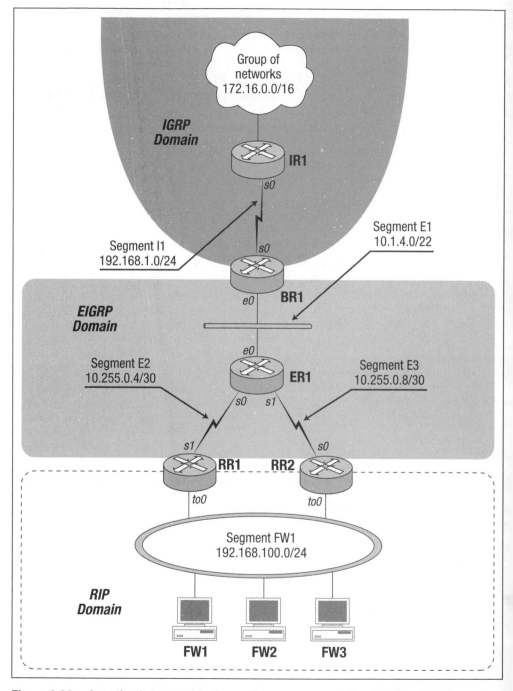

Figure 8.20   A routing loop emerges immediately upon activating the TokenRing0 interfaces of routers RR1 and RR2.

whose administrative distance is 170 by default. This is important because regular EIGRP routes have the default administrative distance of 90, which is lower than RIP's (120). Thus, RIP won't be able to affect the EIGRP routes.

The configurations of routers RR1, RR2, ER1, and BR1 are shown in Listings 8.84 through 8.87, respectively.

Listing 8.84   Router RR1's configuration.

```
interface Serial1
 ip address 10.255.0.6 255.255.255.252

interface TokenRing0
 ip address 192.168.100.1 255.255.255.0
 ring-speed 16

router eigrp 1
 redistribute rip metric 10000 1 255 1 1500
 network 10.0.0.0

router rip
 redistribute eigrp 1 metric 1
 network 192.168.100.0
```

Listing 8.85   Router RR2's configuration.

```
interface Serial0
 ip address 10.255.0.10 255.255.255.252

interface TokenRing0
 ! ip address 192.168.100.2 255.255.255.0
 ring-speed 16

router eigrp 1
 redistribute rip metric 10000 1 255 1 1500
 network 10.0.0.0

router rip
 redistribute eigrp 1 metric 1
 network 192.168.100.0
```

Listing 8.86   Router ER1's configuration.

```
interface Ethernet0
 ip address 10.1.4.1 255.255.252.0

interface Serial0
 ip address 10.255.0.5 255.255.255.252
```

8. Controlling Routing
Information

```
interface Serial1
 ip address 10.255.0.9 255.255.255.252

router eigrp 1
 network 10.0.0.0
```

Listing 8.87   Router BR1's configuration.

```
interface Ethernet0
 ip address 10.1.4.2 255.255.252.0

interface Serial0
 ip address 192.168.1.1 255.255.255.0
 bandwidth 64
 delay 400

router eigrp 1
 network 10.0.0.0

router igrp 1
 network 192.168.1.0
```

The shaded line in Listing 8.85 indicates that the IP address has not been entered yet on router RR2's TokenRing0 interface. (In the listing, it's indicated by the exclamation point which is treated as a comment by Cisco IOS.) Hence, router RR2 is not yet connected to the RIP domain.

We are interested in what should happen to the routes that the routers have for network prefix 172.16.0.0/16, which resides in the IGRP domain. For example, until the IP address is entered on router RR2's TokenRing0 interface, the route for the network prefix of router BR3 looks as shown below:

```
BR1#show ip route
...
I    172.16.0.0/16 [100/156750] via 192.168.1.2, 00:00:37, Serial0
...
```

After we enter the IP address on router RR2's TokenRing0 interface, the route changes as follows:

```
BR1#show ip route
...
D EX 172.16.0.0/16 [170/2195712] via 10.1.4.1, 00:00:02, Ethernet0
...
```

The route no longer points to the IGRP domain and instead points into the EIGRP domain towards the RIP domain. This is indicative of a routing loop.

To further see the signs of the routing loop, let's examine the routes that routers RR1, RR2, and ER1 have for the network prefix (Listing 8.88).

Listing 8.88   **The routes that routers RR1, RR2, and ER1 have for the network prefix after the routing loop emerges.**

```
RR1#show ip route
...
R    172.16.0.0/16 [120/1] via 192.168.100.2, 00:00:19, TokenRing0
...

ER1#show ip route
...
D EX 172.16.0.0/16 [170/2170112] via 10.255.0.6, 00:06:11, Serial0
...

RR2#show ip route
...
D EX 172.16.0.0/16 [170/2682112] via 10.255.0.9, 00:07:12, Serial0
...
```

Router RR1 has a RIP route pointing to router RR2; router RR2 has an EIGRP external route pointing to router ER1; and router ER1 has an EIGRP external route pointing to router RR1.

Warning!   The case of a network with three routing protocols—one of which is RIP mutually redistributed—is quite typical. At the same time, it almost always results in routing loops at some point unless special measures, such as filtering, are taken. Usually, two routing protocols, none of which is RIP, coexist when one of these protocols is migrated to the other. The most common justification for having RIP in addition to the two other protocols is a requirement to provide the exact routing information to hosts with multiple NICs, which appear to be able to use optimum next-hop routers should they know the exact routing information. If that's the case, I suggest examining the sections "Using and Understanding One-Way Redistribution" and "Filtering Routing Information during Redistribution Using Route Maps" earlier in this chapter. And then reassessing whether the requirement is really sustained by RIP. (Most probably, it's not.)

Understanding Routing Loops Emerging from Redistribution and Disabled Split-Horizon Rule

The mix of redistribution and disabled split horizon often results in a routing loop. If a router learns of a network prefix via a routing protocol with a higher administrative distance and then redistributes the network prefix into a routing protocol with a lower administrative distance, it can potentially hear of the network prefix from the neighbors running the routing protocol with the lower administrative distance if they do not adhere to the split-horizon rule.

Although such a situation seems unlikely, it happens quite naturally in one case. This case involves redistribution between IGRP, which is enabled on a router interface connected to an NBMA network, and another protocol whose administrative distance is lower than that of IGRP. By default, the split-horizon rule is turned off for IGRP on multipoint NBMA interfaces.

An example of the described network is shown in Figure 8.21. Router R1 performs the redistribution between OSPF and IGRP. OSPF is enabled on router R1's Ethernet0 interface and Serial1.2 subinterface, which connects router R1 to router R2 through the Frame Relay network. IGRP is enabled on only router R1's subinterface Serial1.3, which connects router R1 to router R3 through the same Frame Relay network.

The configurations of all three routers are shown in Listings 8.89 through 8.91.

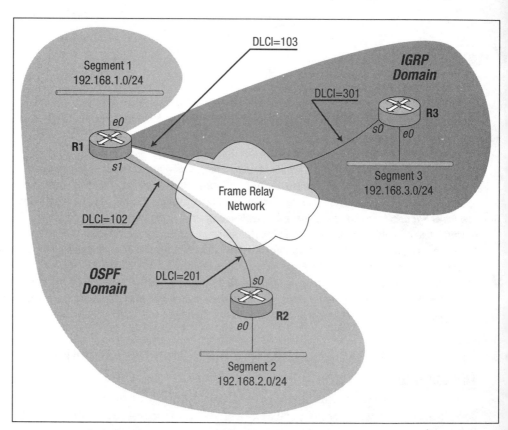

Figure 8.21   Router R1 performs redistribution between OSPF and IGRP, which results in a routing loop because router R3 sends the network prefixes it learns from router R1 via IGRP back to router R1.

Listing 8.89   Router R1's configuration.

```
interface Ethernet0
 ip address 192.168.1.1 255.255.255.0

interface Serial1
 no ip address
 encapsulation frame-relay

interface Serial1.2 multipoint
 ip address 192.168.102.1 255.255.255.0
 ip ospf network broadcast
 frame-relay map ip 192.168.102.2 102 broadcast

interface Serial1.3 multipoint
 ip address 192.168.103.1 255.255.255.0
 frame-relay map ip 192.168.103.2 103 broadcast

router ospf 1
 router-id 0.0.0.1
 redistribute igrp 1 metric 400 subnets
 network 192.168.1.0 0.0.0.255 area 0
 network 192.168.102.0 0.0.0.255 area 0

router igrp 1
 redistribute ospf 1 metric 64 1 255 1 1500
 network 192.168.103.0
```

Listing 8.90   Router R2's configuration.

```
interface Ethernet0
 ip address 192.168.2.1 255.255.255.0

interface Serial0
 ip address 192.168.102.2 255.255.255.0
 encapsulation frame-relay
 ip ospf network broadcast
 frame-relay map ip 192.168.102.1 201 broadcast

router ospf 1
 router-id 0.0.0.2
 network 0.0.0.0 255.255.255.255 area 0
```

Listing 8.91   Router R3's configuration.

```
interface Ethernet0
 ip address 192.168.3.1 255.255.255.0
```

```
interface Serial0
 ip address 192.168.103.2 255.255.255.0
 encapsulation frame-relay
 frame-relay map ip 192.168.103.1 301 broadcast

router igrp 1
 network 192.168.3.0
 network 192.168.103.0
```

Before router R3 is connected to the Frame Relay network, the routing table of router R1 looks as follows:

```
R1#show ip route
...
C    192.168.102.0/24 is directly connected, Serial1.2
C    192.168.1.0/24 is directly connected, Ethernet0
C    192.168.103.0/24 is directly connected, Serial1.3
O    192.168.2.0/24 [110/74] via 192.168.102.2, 00:00:02, Serial1.2
```

Soon after router R3 is connected to the Frame Relay network, the routing table of router R1 changes to the following:

```
R1#show ip route
...
C    192.168.102.0/24 is directly connected, Serial1.2
C    192.168.1.0/24 is directly connected, Ethernet0
C    192.168.103.0/24 is directly connected, Serial1.3
I    192.168.2.0/24 [100/160251] via 192.168.103.2, 00:00:03, Serial1.3
I    192.168.3.0/24 [100/8576] via 192.168.103.2, 00:00:03, Serial1.3
...
```

The shaded line indicates the route that must clearly be installed by OSPF; yet it's an IGRP route, because, as soon as router R3 learned of the route's network prefix, it immediately advertised it back to router R1, which installed it in lieu of the OSPF route.

From that point on, different scenarios can evolve depending on the combination of enabled and disabled split horizons on the routers' interfaces. In our case, split horizon is enabled on router R1's subinterface; hence, once router R1 installs the IGRP route, it will no longer advertise network prefix 192.168.2.0/24 to router R3. This causes router R3 to eventually time out its route for the network prefix, after which it places the route into holddown and sends a poisoned-reverse update to router R1. The latter event makes router R1 place its route into holddown. Once this holddown expires, router R1 installs the OSPF route again, which will soon be wiped off by the IGRP route and the whole process will repeat. Both routers will cycle through the process endlessly.

This form of match condition matches routes whose network prefixes are matched by the access list.

To match a redistributed network prefix against an IP prefix list, use the **match ip address prefix-list** *<PL name>* clause. The *<PL name>* parameter is the name of a prefix list.

To match the network prefixes for which the original source of routing information installed routes through a certain next-hop router, use the **match ip next-hop** {*<AL name>*|*<AL number>*|**prefix-list** *<PL name>*} clause. The parameters *<AL name>* and *<AL number>* specify either the name or the number of a standard access list. Alternatively, the pair of parameters **prefix-list** *<PL name>* can be used to specify the name of the prefix list. The clause matches only those network prefixes for which the original source of routing information installed routes through next-hop routers whose IP addresses satisfy the specified access or prefix list.

To match the network prefixes for which the original source of routing information installed routes pointing to a particular router interface, use the **match interface** *<interface>* clause. The *<interface>* parameter references one of the router's interfaces. The route map clause matches only those network prefixes whose routes point to the specified interface.

NOTE: For information on the other available parameters of the **match** statement, see the Cisco documentation.

---

3. Add set actions using the **set** statement followed by specific parameters. The most typical **set** action is **set metric** *<metric>*, where the *<metric>* parameter specifies the metric of the routing protocol into which the routing information is redistributed. The routing protocol will advertise the redistributed network prefixes that matched this clause with the metric equal to the *<metric>* parameter.

NOTE: For information on available parameters, see the Cisco documentation.

---

4. If the route map consists of multiple clauses, repeat the sequence of Steps 1 through 3 until all clauses are entered. Each time, use the same *<RM name>* parameter but different *<sequence #>* parameters. Don't forget that the clauses with the smaller *<sequence #>* parameters are tested first.

5. Apply the route map as a routing filter using the parameter **route-map** *<RM name>* of the **redistribute** command.

Route maps have numerous applications, and it would be too big a task to try to provide examples for even a moderate set of common route map applications.

If split horizon were turned off on router R1's subinterface as well, the stage preceding placing the routes on both routers into holddown would be much faster. The routers would exchange a series of triggered updates, each bringing the metric to a lower value, which, sure enough, would be followed by placing both routes into holddown.

Whatever the scenario, the outcome is the same: The routing does not work properly because of the oscillating routing loop.

This particular network is easy to cure: All it takes is to enable turned-off split horizon on router R3's Serial0 interface. However, this solution may not always be applicable, and it works only on NBMA networks whose topology is hub-spoke. Apparently, split horizon can be safely enabled on the spoke routers, which would prevent the described type of routing loop. If, however, the NBMA network is more densely meshed than hub-spoke, the routers connected to more than one permanent virtual circuit (PVC) may not be good candidates for enabling split horizon.

The best approach to avoiding the described type of routing loops is probably to configure all PVCs on the routers as point-to-point subinterfaces and make sure split horizon is enabled on them. (It should be enabled on the subinterface by default.) An even better solution would be to entirely avoid redistribution in such environments.

Chapter 9

Special Cases of Routing

If you need an immediate solution to:	See page:
Configuring Policy-Based Routing	657
Configuring NAT	672
Configuring HSRP	696

In Depth

In this chapter, we'll discuss those special cases of Internet Protocol (IP) routing that do not conform to the IP routing model that has been presented thus far. These special cases of routing are policy-based routing, Network Address Translation (NAT), and Hot Standby Router Protocol (HSRP).

Policy-Based Routing

Policy-based routing is a form of routing in which IP datagrams are routed based on administratively defined rules that can take into consideration the characteristics of the datagrams other than the destination address when drawing routing decisions.

NOTE: *Although this type of routing is referenced in the Cisco documentation as policy routing, I have chosen to use the term* policy-based routing *because it is more widely used.*

Policy-based routing is implemented on a per-interface basis. When certain characteristics of arriving traffic match administratively defined policy conditions, the traffic is forwarded in accordance with the policy that prescribes which next-hop router or output interface (or both) must be used to forward the traffic to the next hop. Traffic that is not matched by the policy match conditions is forwarded in accordance with the routing algorithm.

For example, in Figure 9.1, router R1 may be configured to always forward to router R2 the traffic that host H1 originates, regardless of the traffic's actual destination. At the same time, router R1 still uses the routing algorithm to decide to which next-hop router to forward the traffic originated by the other hosts on segment 1.

Policy-based routing is similar to static routing in that it cannot adapt to changes in the network topology (like dynamic routing protocols do). Hence, policy-based routing inherits the shortcomings of static routing that we discussed in Chapter 3. If not properly planned and implemented, it can adversely affect existing dynamic routing. What makes policy-based routing even more perilous is that dynamic routing protocols are totally unaware of it. (Static routing is a bit better because it affects only the routing table and because static routes can be redistributed into a dynamic routing protocol, thereby improving the "awareness" of

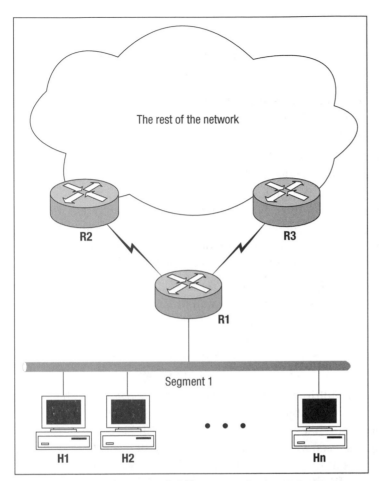

Figure 9.1   Router R1 is configured with a policy that dictates the forwarding of host
H1's traffic to router R2, regardless of the traffic's destination. The policy
does not affect the traffic originated by the other hosts on segment 1.

the dynamic routing protocol of the static routing.) For example, a router can be
configured for policy-based routing, which will forward certain traffic to another
router. This router itself happens to have a route for the destination pointing back
to the router that performed the policy-based routing. (Such a route could be
installed by a dynamic routing protocol.) Hence, when policy-based routing makes
the first router forward the traffic to the second router, the second router bounces
the traffic back to the first one. What happens further depends on how policy-
based routing is implemented; however this situation, at best, leads to superfluous router hops in the path that the traffic takes to reach the destination. (At
worst, it leads to routing loops.)

NAT

NAT is a procedure whereby a router replaces the original source or destination IP address in the datagrams with a different IP address.

The question that naturally arises from the definition of NAT is: What's the purpose of replacing the original source or destination IP addresses? The purpose is to solve the following three problems:

- *The depletion of global IP network address space*—New IP addresses are becoming more difficult to allocate because the global IP address space is approaching its capacity. NAT helps solve this problem by reusing some addresses at multiple locations. For example, it is possible to use private IP addresses—described in Request for Comments (RFC)— 1918, "Address Allocation for Private Internets") on networks that are not supposed to be directly accessed from the Internet, such as corporate intranets.

- *A merger of networks that use overlapping IP address space*—If two companies use private IP addresses—or if one company uses IP addresses that officially belong to another company—and these two companies merge, it may be too costly to readdress the hosts whose IP addresses overlap. In such situations, NAT can be used to perform IP address translation in the traffic that is exchanged by the hosts with overlapping IP addresses.

- *Load balancing*—If multiple servers run an identical service, such as a Web server, NAT can be used to balance among all servers the traffic destined for this service. The hosts that access the service will still perceive these multiple servers as a single server with a single IP address. When the first datagram of a connection arrives at the router performing NAT, the destination IP address is replaced with the IP address of one of the servers, and all subsequent datagrams of this connection are sent to this server.

NAT is the Internet standard procedure and is documented in RFC 1631, "The IP Network Address Translator (NAT)." NAT for load balancing is documented in RFC 2391, "Load Sharing Using IP Network Address Translation (LSNAT)." Finally, NAT terminology and considerations are set forth in RFC 2663, "IP Network Address Translator (NAT) Terminology and Considerations." The latter RFC is a very useful read—it summarizes a number of modern approaches to implementing and employing NAT; most of these approaches evolved in the course of specific practical requirements and subsequent implementations by various vendors, including Cisco, striving to meet the requirements.

NAT Terminology

When viewed from the perspective of NAT, all networks fall into two categories: *inside networks* and *outside networks*. The inside networks are networks whose IP addresses are not legitimate and hence must be translated. Similarly, the outside networks are networks whose IP addresses are legitimate.

NOTE: *Legitimate in the context of NAT does not necessarily mean that the IP addresses are officially assigned. For example, two networks can be configured with private overlapping IP address ranges; if they merge and NAT is chosen as the way to resolve the addressing ambiguities, one of the networks must become an inside network and the other one an outside network. In that case, the IP addresses of the first network are not legitimate.*

The following terms are commonly used to describe the types of IP addresses specific to NAT:

- *Inside local addresses*—IP addresses of hosts and routers residing on inside networks. The inside local addresses may not be known in the outside network address space, which essentially means that the routers connected to the outside networks may not have routes for the inside local addresses.

  For example, in Figure 9.2, the two clouds denote the inside and outside networks. Router NR1 performs NAT over the traffic between the outside and inside networks. Host OH1 and routers OR1 and OR2 reside on the outside network; likewise, hosts IH1 and IH2 and routers IR1 and IR2 reside on the inside network. The IP addresses of hosts IH1 and IH2—as well as those of routers IR1 and IR2—are inside local addresses. The IP addresses assigned on the interfaces of router NR1, which are connected to the segments belonging to the inside network, are also inside local addresses.

- *Inside global addresses*—IP addresses into which the inside local addresses are translated. Inside global addresses are legitimate and, therefore, must be known in the outside address space. (This assumes that the routers connected to the outside networks must have routes for the inside global addresses.)

  For example, if, in Figure 9.2, host IH1 communicates with host OH1, router NR1 must replace the IP address of host IH1, an inside local address, with an inside global address. Routers OR1 and OR2 should have a route for the network prefix to which this inside global address belongs. Most typically, router NR1 would advertise this network prefix.

- *Outside local addresses*—IP addresses through which the hosts residing on the inside networks can access the hosts residing on the outside networks. These addresses are actually part of the inside address space; therefore, they do not have to be legitimate, and the routers of the outside networks do not have to have routes for them. However, the routers of the inside networks must have routes for the outside local addresses.

9. Special Cases of Routing

For example, in Figure 9.2, host IH2 might communicate with host OH1 not by host OH1's actual IP address but through an outside local address. This outside local address can be a part of the inside address space. Routers IR1 and IR2 should have routes for the network prefix to which the outside local address belongs. This network prefix is most typically advertised by router NR1.

- *Outside global addresses*—IP addresses of the hosts residing on outside networks. These addresses must be legitimate, and the router of the outside networks must have routes for them.

For example, in Figure 9.2, the IP addresses of host OH1 and routers OR1 and OR2 are outside global addresses as are the IP addresses of router NR1's interfaces connected to the segments belonging to the outside networks.

NOTE: *The routers performing NAT reside on both inside and outside networks. In addition, the IP addresses assigned on the interfaces of a router performing NAT do not necessarily have to be inside or outside global addresses.*

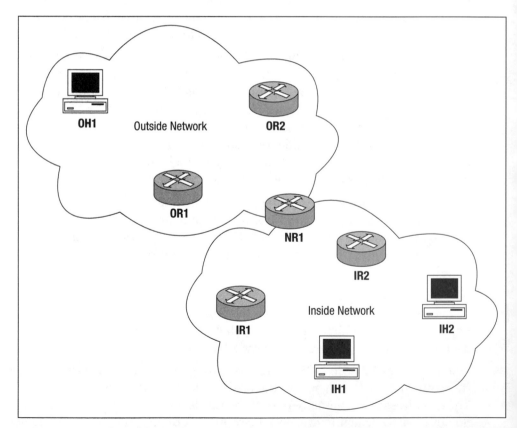

Figure 9.2   The inside and outside networks interconnected with a router performing NAT.

The described types of NAT IP addresses serve different purposes; therefore, it's unlikely to find all four types in a single NAT configuration. For example, if, in Figure 9.2 the addresses of the inside network belonged to a private IP address range (such as 172.16.0.0/12) and the outside network were a part of the Internet (and hence had only officially assigned IP addresses), router NR1 would perform NAT, whereby the local inside addresses of the inside network would be translated into global inside addresses, which would be a part of the outside network's address space. Obviously, no local outside addresses would be present in this NAT configuration.

A router performing NAT maintains a special data structure called the *NAT table*, which consists of one or more entries of the same structure. Every NAT table entry comprises five fields:

1. Protocol
2. Inside local IP address
3. Inside global IP address
4. Outside local IP address
5. Outside global IP address

The functional role of the latter four fields is to store the corresponding IP addresses. The first field denotes the IP protocol whose connections must be translated using the IP addresses that are contained in the entry. Depending on the NAT application, all of these fields may or may not be used.

The NAT table can be populated with entries in two ways, the first of which is called *static NAT*. In static NAT, the NAT table entries are created administratively. After the entries are created, they immediately appear in the NAT table. The second way to populate the NAT table is called *dynamic NAT*. In dynamic NAT, the entries in the NAT table are created dynamically when the router receives IP datagrams whose characteristics satisfy administratively configured NAT rules.

HSRP

HSRP is a Cisco-proprietary protocol used to provide a redundant "default router" for those hosts that are unable to discover routers dynamically.

NOTE: It is recommended that HSRP not be used if the hosts can dynamically discover routers. Nevertheless, the popularity of HSRP is such that it is often preferred to the dynamic methods, such as ICMP Router Discovery Protocol (IRDP).

HSRP is documented in RFC 2281, "Cisco Hot Standby Router Protocol (HSRP)." The status of this document is "informational," which means that HSRP is not an Internet standard protocol.

NOTE: *RFC 2338, "Virtual Router Redundancy Protocol," defines the Virtual Router Redundancy Protocol (VRRP), whose functionality is very similar to that of HSRP. No IOS version currently supports VRRP; however, future releases of IOS are slated to support it.*

The idea behind HSRP is simple: Create a redundant default gateway IP address for the hosts residing on a local area network (LAN) segment by utilizing multiple routers attached to that segment. Only one of the routers actually serves as the default gateway for the hosts; however, if it fails one of the remaining routers picks up where the failed router left off by inheriting the IP and media access control (MAC) addresses of the failed router's interface attached to the segment. Because the replacement router accepts LAN frames destined for the MAC address of the failed router, no established session is interrupted—even if the first router failed right in the middle of it.

The HSRP router that is currently acting as the default router is called the *active router*, and the IP address that the hosts use as the default router is called the *virtual IP address*. The virtual IP address is different from the IP address configured on the active router's interface attached to the segment. The MAC address corresponding to the virtual IP address is called the *virtual MAC address*. Unlike the virtual IP address, the virtual MAC address may or may not coincide with the MAC address of the interface, depending on the router interface hardware. (The details behind virtual MAC addresses are set forth in the "Virtual MAC Address" section later in the chapter.)

In addition to the active router, HSRP defines a standby router as the router that takes over the virtual MAC and IP addresses if the currently active router fails. In this case, the standby router becomes the active router. A segment can have only one active and one standby router.

HSRP Process

The HSRP entity is called an *HSRP process*, and every router interface on which HSRP is enabled has a separate HSRP process. Furthermore, multiple HSRP processes can run on a single interface, if it is necessary to provide multiple virtual IP addresses on that interface. (An example demonstrating why you may need multiple virtual IP addresses on a single router interface can be found in the "Using MHSRP for Load Balancing" section at the end of this chapter.)

A set of parameters is associated with every HSRP process running on a router, and the following sections detail them.

Group

The group denotes the HSRP group, which the HSRP process serves. HSRP processes with different groups do not interoperate; only HSRP processes whose groups are equal interoperate. A one-to-one relationship exists between the HSRP group and the virtual MAC address used for the group. This relation is explained in the "Virtual MAC Address" section later in this chapter.

Virtual IP Address

This parameter denotes the virtual IP address that the HSRP process serves. The HSRP process may be configured without the virtual IP address, in which case it is supposed to learn the virtual IP address from the active router.

Priority

The priority is used to make the desired routers be elected as active or standby. Typically, the router whose HSRP process has the highest priority becomes the active router, and the router whose HSRP process has the highest priority among the remaining routers becomes the standby. (The exact process of the active and standby routers, election is described in the "HSRP State Machine" section later in this chapter.)

Preempt Capability

The preempt capability allows a router whose HSRP process has a priority higher than that of the active router's HSRP process to replace the active router. If the preempt capability is not set, the router may not replace the active router—even if its HSRP process has the highest priority.

Active and Standby Hold Times

These parameters are used to monitor the active and standby routers. The exact usage of these parameters is explained in the "HSRP Timers" section later in this chapter.

Hello Time

The Hello Time is used to generate certain HSRP protocol data units (PDUs) at regular intervals. The exact usage of the Hello Time is explained in the "HSRP Timers" section later in this chapter.

HSRP PDU Format

HSRP PDUs are encapsulated into User Datagram Protocol (UDP) datagrams destined for multicast IP address 224.0.0.2 and UDP port 1985. The Time-to-Live (TTL) field of the IP datagrams carrying those UDP datagrams is set to 1, which prevents HSRP PDUs from being forwarded between segments if some routers are not configured with HSRP but instead perform multicast routing.

The format of HSRP PDUs is shown in Figure 9.3.

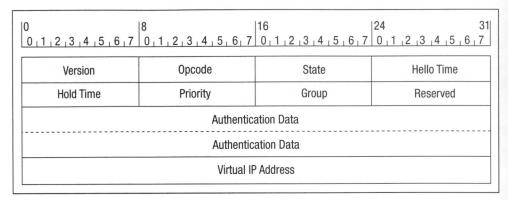

Figure 9.3   The format of HSRP Hello PDUs.

Table 9.1   The values that the Opcode field of the HSRP PDU can carry.

Value	Meaning	Descriptions
0	Hello	The router's interface is configured for HSRP, and the router can become the active or standby router.
1	Coup	The router is trying to become the active router.
2	Resign	The active router indicates that it ceases to be the active router.

The 8-bit Version field denotes the current HSRP version. This field must carry the value of 4.

The 8-bit Opcode field denotes the purpose of the HSRP PDU. Table 9.1 shows the possible values for this field and the descriptions of the purposes that the corresponding HSRP PDUs serve.

The 8-bit State field denotes the current state of the interface's HSRP state machine. The possible values that this field can carry are shown in Table 9.2. The HSRP state machine is described in the next section.

Table 9.2   The values that the State field of the HSRP PDU can carry.

Value	State
0	Initial
1	Learn
2	Listen
4	Speak
8	Standby
16	Active

The 8-bit Hello Time field carries the value of the configured time (in seconds) that the router waits before sending a subsequent Hello PDU (Opcode=0). This field is meaningful in only the Hello PDUs.

This field is present in a Hello PDU to allow the routers that were not configured with a hello time to learn it from the Hello PDUs of the active routes.

The 8-bit Holdtime field carries the value of the configured hold time (in seconds). Every router maintains a separate hold timer for active and standby routers. If the timer reaches the hold time, the corresponding router (active or standby) is considered to be no longer available, and a new router is elected as a replacement. The hold timer is reset each time the router receives a Hello PDU from the corresponding router (active or standby).

This field is present in a Hello PDU to allow the routers that were not configured with the hold time to learn it from the Hello PDUs of the active router. Like the Hello Time field, the Holdtime field is meaningful in only Hello PDUs.

The 8-bit Priority field carries the value of the HSRP process's priority. When the HSRP process receives an HSRP PDU and has to compare the priority of the PDU's sender with its own priority, it first compares the value of the Priority field of the PDU with its own priority. The higher value denotes the higher priority. If these values are equal, then the router compares the value of the interface's IP address with the source IP address of the IP datagram that carries the UDP datagram in which the received HSRP PDU was encapsulated. The IP address with the higher value denotes the higher priority.

The 8-bit Group field carries the value of the HSRP group. Each HSRP process has a group number, which can range from 0 through 255. The function of the group number is very similar to that of a Transmission Control Protocol (TCP) or UDP port—it identifies the HSRP process to which the HSRP PDU is destined. This identification is needed to allow multiple HSRP processes to be run on a single interface, each with its own virtual IP and MAC addresses. (Possible uses of multiple HSRP processes on a single interface are demonstrated in the "Using MHSRP for Load Balancing" section later in this chapter.) When generating an HSRP PDU, the HSRP process places its group number into the Group field of the PDU. When another router receives the PDU, it first checks if it has an HSRP process running on the interface on which the PDU has been received and whose group number is equal to the Group field of the PDU. If such a process exists the router delivers the HSRP PDU to the HSRP process; otherwise, the router discards the PDU.

The Reserved field is not currently used for anything.

The 64-bit Authentication Data field carries a clear-text password, which, if used, must be the same in all HSRP PDUs with the same group number. The routers are required to drop HSRP PDUs whose Authentication Data field carries a value that is different from what the router's interface is configured for this HSRP group. If no authentication is needed, it is recommended that this field carry the value of 0x636973636F000000, which, if converted to ASCII code, produces "cisco." (The last three octets are 0 characters that have no humanly readable interpretation and carry no language information.)

The last field is the 32-bit Virtual IP Address field, which carries the virtual IP address configured for the group. The presence of the Virtual IP Address field allows the routers that were not configured with the virtual IP address to learn it from the active router.

HSRP Timers

An HSRP process maintains three timers: *active*, *standby*, and *hello*.

The active timer is used to monitor the active router. The active timer is reset each time the HSRP process receives a Hello PDU from the active router. The active timer expires if it reaches the Active Hold Time value, which can be either configured or learned from one of the Hello PDUs previously received from the active router.

The standby timer is used to monitor the standby router. The standby timer is reset each time the HSRP process receives a Hello PDU from the standby router. The standby timer expires if it reaches the Standby Hold Time value, which also can be either configured or learned from one of the Hello PDUs previously received from the standby router.

The HSRP process uses the hello timer in the Speak, Active, and Standby states to regularly generate Hello PDUs. When the hello timer is started, it is set to the Hello Time. When the hello timer reaches 0, the router restarts the hello timer and generates a Hello PDU. The Hello Time can be either configured or learned from the one of the Hello PDUs previously received from the active router.

NOTE: Each time the hello timer is restarted, the Hello Time must be modified by adding or subtracting a random jitter value. The jitter value must be significantly smaller than the Hello Time itself. (RFC 2281 does not specify the exact boundaries for the jitter value.)

The HSRP State Machine

The HSRP process implements the HSRP state machine, which describes the rules of how the HSRP process should transition among the states and which actions it should take when performing transitions and/or processing events. The schematic representation of the HSRP state machine is shown in Figure 9.4.

9. Special Cases of Routing

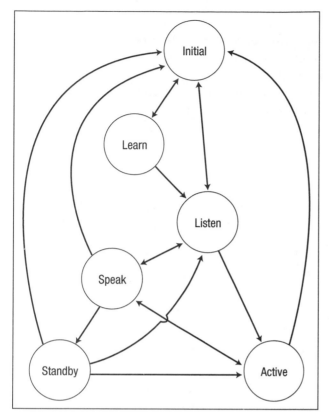

Figure 9.4 The HSRP state machine.

The states are shown as vertices, and the transitions are shown as edges inter-connecting the vertices. The arrows at the ends of the edges denote the direction in which the transition between the two vertices can happen. Some edges allow transitions in both directions, whereas the others allow transitions only in one direction.

The following sections provide a description of each of the states, the events that make the HSRP process change the states, and the actions that accompany the events.

Initial

Initial is the state from which the operation of the HSRP state machine begins. In the Initial state, no HSRP process is yet operating on an interface.

Once an HSRP process is configured on a physically and logically operational interface, it immediately transitions into either the Learn or Listen state. If no virtual IP address is assigned to the HSRP process, the HSRP process transitions to the Learn state. Otherwise, the HSRP process starts the active and standby timers, after which it transitions to the Listen state.

Learn

The HSRP process remains in the Learn state until it receives a Hello from the active router. Upon receipt of the active router's Hello PDU, the HSRP process sets the virtual IP address and the Active Hold Time to the values of the Virtual IP Address and Hold Time fields contained in the Hello PDU. Optionally, the HSRP process can also set the Hello Time to the value of the Hello Time field. After that, the HSRP process starts the active and standby timers and transitions to the Listen state.

Listen

The HSRP process knows the virtual IP address and monitors the active and standby routers. The router can remain in the Listen state indefinitely if its HSRP priority is lower than the priorities of the active and standby routers.

The following events cause the router to transition into the Speak state:

- *The expiration of the active timer*—After the active timer expires, the HSRP process restarts the active and standby timers and transitions to the Speak state.

- *The expiration of the standby timer*—After the standby timer expires, the HSRP process restarts the standby timer and transitions to the Speak state.

- *The receipt of a Resign message from the active router*—Following the receipt of a Resign message from the active router, the HSRP process restarts the active and standby timers and transitions to the Speak state.

- *The receipt of a Hello PDU from the standby router whose priority is lower than that of the HSRP process*—Following this event, the HSRP process restarts the standby timer and transitions to the Speak state.

If the HSRP process is configured with the preempt capability, the receipt of a Hello PDU from the active router whose priority is lower than that of the HSRP process makes the HSRP process transition to the Active state. Before the transition, the HSRP process must reset the standby timer, send Coup and Hello messages, and broadcast a *gratuitous* Address Resolution Protocol (ARP) PDU. A gratuitous ARP PDU is an ARP response PDU that carries the virtual IP and MAC addresses.

Speak

The Speak state is a temporary state in which the HSRP process participates in the election of the active and/or standby router. The HSRP process generates periodic Hello messages and waits for an event that will transition it to the Listen, Standby, or Active state.

The following events cause the HSRP process to transition into the Standby state:

- *The expiration of the standby timer*—Following this event, the HSRP process stops the standby timer and transitions to the Standby state.

- *The receipt of a Hello PDU from the standby router whose Priority field's value is lower than the configured priority of the HSRP process*—Following this event, the HSRP process stops the standby timer and transitions to the Standby state.

If the HSRP process receives a Hello PDU whose State field is either Speak or Standby (4 or 8) and whose sender's priority is higher than that of the HSRP process, the HSRP process restarts the standby timer and transitions to the Listen state.

If the HSRP process is configured with the preempt capability and receives a Hello PDU from the active router whose priority is lower than that of the HSRP process, the HSRP process transitions to the Active state. Before the transition, the HSRP process must reset the standby timer, send Coup and Hello messages, and broadcast a gratuitous ARP PDU.

Standby

The HSRP process in the Standby state is ready to replace the active router if the active router fails. The HSRP process generates periodic Hello PDUs. The router whose HSRP process is in the Standby state is referred to as a standby router. Under stable conditions, each HSRP group must not have more than one standby router.

The following events cause the HSRP process to transition to the Active state:

- *The expiration of the active timer*—Following this event, the HSRP process stops the active timer, sends a Hello PDU, and broadcasts a gratuitous ARP PDU.

- *The receipt of a Resign PDU from the active router*—Following this event, the HSRP process stops the active timer, sends a Hello PDU, and broadcasts a gratuitous ARP PDU.

- *The receipt of a Hello PDU from the active router whose priority is lower than that of the HSRP process*—The HSRP process transitions to the Active state only if it is configured with the preempt capability. Before the transition, the HSRP process must start the standby timer, send Coup and Hello messages, and broadcast a gratuitous ARP PDU.

If the HSRP process receives a Hello PDU whose State field is either Speak or Standby and whose sender's priority is higher than that of the HSRP process, the HSRP process starts the standby timer and transitions to the Listen state.

9. Special Cases of Routing

Active

A router whose HSRP process is in the Active state forwards IP datagrams encapsulated into MAC frames sent to the virtual MAC address. Such a router is referred to as the *active router*. The HSRP process in the Active state generates periodic Hello PDUs.

The following events cause the HSRP process to transition from the Active state to the Speak state:

- *The receipt of a Hello PDU whose State field is set to Active (16) and whose Priority field's value is higher than the HSRP process's priority*—Following this event, the HSRP process starts active and standby timers and transitions to the Speak state.

- *The receipt of a Coup PDU whose sender's priority is higher than that of the HSRP process*—Following this event, the HSRP process starts active and standby timers, sends a Resign PDU, and transitions to the Speak state.

If the HSRP process in the Active state receives a Hello PDU whose State field is equal to Active but whose sender's priority is lower than that of the HSRP process, the HSRP process must respond by sending a Coup PDU.

Finally, if in any state the HSRP process becomes administratively disabled, it stops the active and standby timers and transitions to the Initial state. If the HSRP process becomes administratively disabled in the Active state, it must also send a Resign PDU.

Virtual MAC Address

Depending on the media type of the interface configured for HSRP, a different MAC address is used as the virtual MAC address. In the case of token ring interfaces, the HSRP virtual MAC address can be one of the three functional token ring addresses: C000.0001.0000, C000.0002.0000, and C000.0004.0000, which correspond to groups 0, 1, and 2, respectively. This also limits the number of HSRP groups on the token ring interfaces to three.

On other media, the virtual MAC addresses must be 0000.0C07.ACXX, where XX corresponds to the HSRP group number. The active router must use the virtual MAC address as the source MAC address in the data link layer frames that carry UDP-encapsulated HSRP packets. Neither the standby nor any other HSRP router can use the virtual MAC address as the source address in any frames. This is necessary because HSRP may not otherwise work in the presence of transparent bridges.

The HSRP MAC addresses described in the previous paragraph are unicast MAC addresses. Certain types of router interface hardware do not allow multiple unicast MAC addresses to be assigned on a single interface. Therefore, if such an interface is configured for HSRP, the router must change the interface's MAC address to the virtual MAC address. Then, from that point on, the router must respond with the virtual MAC address for the ARP requests for the interface's actual IP address and the virtual IP address.

Example

Figure 9.5 shows an example of an HSRP configuration with three routers. All routers have identical priorities. Hence, router R4 becomes the active router, because

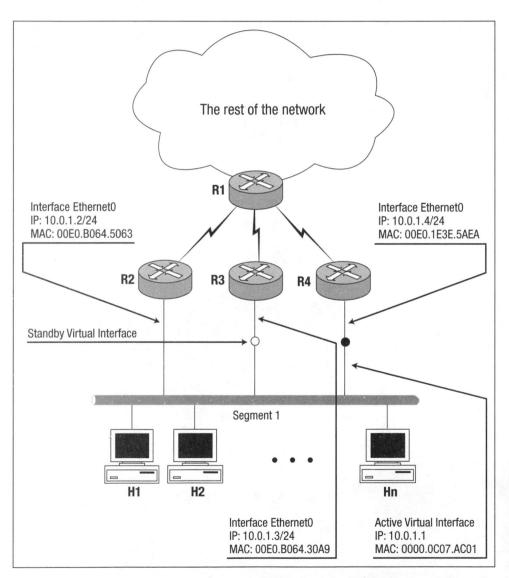

Figure 9.5   Router R4 has become the active HSRP router, and router R3 has become the standby HSRP router.

its IP address (10.0.1.4) has the highest value; router R3 becomes the standby router, because its IP address (10.0.1.3) has a value higher than that of router R2 (10.0.1.2).

In addition, Figure 9.5 shows the virtual IP and MAC addresses. The virtual MAC address is equal to 0000.0C07.AC01, which means that the HSRP processes on the routers are configured with HSRP group 1.

Immediate Solutions

Configuring Policy-Based Routing

Configuring policy-based routing on Cisco routers is based on route maps, which are applied as routing policies on the routers' interfaces. Thus, the route map clauses are applied not to the routing updates (as described in Chapter 8) but to the datagrams that are received on the interface.

To configure policy-based routing, follow these steps:

1. Create a route map whose clauses contain the match statement **match ip address** {*<AL number>*|*<AL name>*}, and the actions **set interface** *<interface>* and **set ip next-hop** *<IP address>* or **set default interface** *<interface>* and **set ip default next-hop** *<IP address>*. Use the route map syntax described in "Using Route Maps to Filter Routing Updates During Redistribution" (Chapter 6).

   The {*<AL number>*|*<AL name>*} parameter is the number or name of an access list that defines which datagrams must be policy-routed. If the access list returns **permit**, the **set** actions are applied; otherwise, the datagram's characteristics are compared against the match conditions of the next clause.

   The router uses the actions **set interface** *<interface>* and **set ip next-hop** *<IP address>* to route the datagrams whose characteristics are matched by the match conditions. These datagrams are routed via the interface *<interface>* and through the next-hop router whose IP address is *<IP address>*. The set actions contain the keyword **default**, and only those datagrams that are destined for the IP addresses that do not have a route in the routing table are routed in accordance with the **set** actions.

   WARNING! *Although you can omit either the set interface <interface> or set ip next-hop <IP address> action, I advise you to use both of them. If either is omitted, the router replaces the missing element with the corresponding information from the routing table. For example, if you omit the* **set ip next-hop <IP address>** *action, the router retrieves from the routing table the IP address of the next-hop router. However, this IP address may not be available via the interface that is specified in the* **set interface <interface>** *action. In this case, the policy-routed datagrams are not picked up by any router, and the connection won't be established.*

2. Apply the route map on the appropriate interface using the command **ip policy route map** *<RM name>*, in which the parameter *<RM name>* is the name of the route map. The datagrams received on this interface are checked against the route map. If any route map clause returns **permit**, the datagram is policy-routed as just described. Otherwise, the datagram is routed in accordance with the routing table.

NOTE: *Unlike access lists, route maps that are applied as routing policies can be inbound only.*

Policy-based routing has numerous applications that—unlike applications that are based on most other network technologies—lack generic similarity. Thus, even an attempt to cover some of the situations that might be resolved by policy-based routing is too great a task for a single section of a chapter of a book on general IP routing. Furthermore, using policy-based routing is somewhat of an art: It might be entirely impossible to compose generic guidelines that explain how and when to apply policy-based routing. In addition, we should not forget that policy-based routing is a considerable deviation from normal IP routing (normal IP routing is only destination driven, whereas policy-based routing is often done based on the traffic characteristics other than only the destination). Therefore, applying policy-based routing must be considered only as a last resort, after having exhausted all other means that do not require changes to normal IP routing.

Therefore, we'll discuss only three situations that potentially can be best resolved via policy-based routing. Although the number of examples is limited, they still demonstrate the broadness of when and how policy-based routing can come in handy. (Still, it is wise to think twice about using possible alternatives before getting too creative with policy-based routing and rushing to implement it.)

The first two situations are based on the network shown in Figure 9.6. The network consists of the headquarters with its own network (the shaded area labeled "HQ") and multiple branches, of which only two are shown in Figure 9.6 (the shaded areas labeled "Br.1" and "Br.2"). This topology is commonly referred to as *hub and spoke*, because all of the branch networks (the spokes) are interconnected via the central network (the hub).

Nevertheless, two branches have established a sort of "backdoor link" (labeled "segment 7" in Figure 9.6), whose conditions of use will be defined for each example separately.

Using Policy-Based Routing for Routing over a Dedicated Link

Suppose that branches Br.1 and Br.2 have some users who have complained that the performance of their computers was unacceptable during periods of heavy

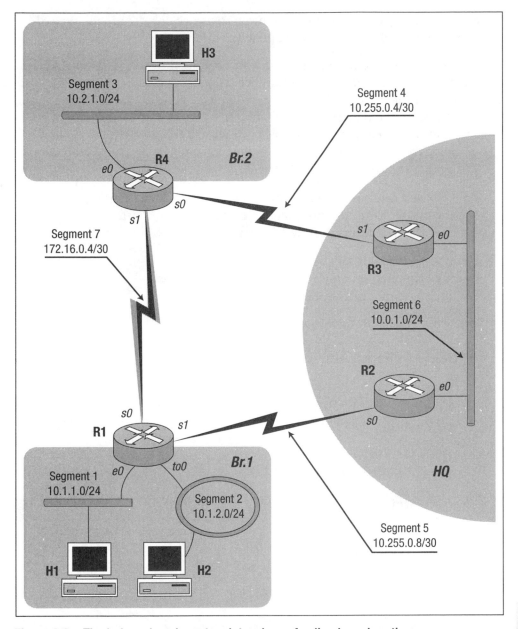

Figure 9.6   The hub-and-spoke network topology of policy-based routing.

traffic at the headquarters. Suppose also that these users are located in both branches and that they must communicate with each other. The branches have decided that they will establish a dedicated link between the branches' networks (segment 7) specifically for these users.

Suppose that the users who are allowed to use segment 7 are all located on segment 1 at branch Br.1 and on segment 3 at branch Br.2.

At first, it may seem that this task can be solved by using only static routing. However, if we think more carefully, we'll realize that static routing is indiscriminate about the source address of the routed datagrams. Thus, static routing will equally route the datagrams originating from segments 1 and 2 and destined for segment 3 via segment 7. However, we want to allow only the datagrams that originate from segment 1 and are destined for segment 3 to be routed via segment 7. All other traffic must be routed according to the routing table.

Policy-based routing can easily solve this task. The idea is to define policy-based routing on the Ethernet interfaces of routers R1 and R4 using a route map that matches the datagrams destined for segments 1 and 3.

Listings 9.1 through 9.4 show the configurations of all four routers. Policy-based routing is applied on only routers R1 and R4; the shaded lines show the specific configuration of policy-based routing.

Listing 9.1   Router R1's configuration.

```
interface Loopback0
 ip address 10.0.0.1 255.255.255.255

interface Ethernet0
 ip address 10.1.1.1 255.255.255.0
 ip policy route-map Seg1-Seg6

interface Serial0
 ip address 172.16.0.5 255.255.255.252

interface Serial1
 ip address 10.255.0.10 255.255.255.252

interface TokenRing0
 ip address 10.1.2.1 255.255.255.0
 ring-speed 16

router eigrp 10
 network 10.0.0.0

access-list 100 permit ip any 10.2.1.0 0.0.0.255

route-map Seg1-Seg6 permit 10
 match ip address 100
 set interface Serial0
 set ip next-hop 172.16.0.6
```

Listing 9.2   Router R2's configuration.

```
interface Loopback0
 ip address 10.0.0.2 255.255.255.255

interface Ethernet0
 ip address 10.0.1.1 255.255.255.0

interface Serial0
 ip address 10.255.0.9 255.255.255.252

router eigrp 10
 network 10.0.0.0
```

Listing 9.3   Router R3's configuration.

```
interface Loopback0
 ip address 10.0.0.3 255.255.255.255

interface Ethernet0
 ip address 10.0.1.2 255.255.255.0

interface Serial1
 ip address 10.255.0.5 255.255.255.252

router eigrp 10
 network 10.0.0.0
```

Listing 9.4   Router R4's configuration.

```
interface Loopback0
 ip address 10.0.0.4 255.255.255.255

interface Ethernet0
 ip address 10.2.1.1 255.255.255.0
 ip policy route-map Seg6-Seg1

interface Serial0
 ip address 10.255.0.6 255.255.255.252

interface Serial1
 ip address 172.16.0.6 255.255.255.252

router eigrp 10
 network 10.0.0.0

access-list 100 permit ip any 10.1.1.0 0.0.0.255

route-map Seg6-Seg1 permit 10
```

```
match ip address 100
set interface Serial1
set ip next-hop 172.16.0.5
```

Although we are interested in applying policy-based routing to the datagrams with specific source addresses, notice that we do not specify these addresses in the access list (access list 100 on both routers). We don't specify the address because policy-based routing is applied on a per-interface basis. In our case, policy-based routing must be applied to the datagrams that originate from all hosts on the segments connected via the interfaces that are configured for policy-based routing and destined for a specific address. Therefore, we can match all of the datagrams that specify only the destination address pattern in the access list. If, however, we want to allow only some hosts on, let's say, segment 1 to send traffic to the hosts located on segment 3 via segment 7, we must specify their IP addresses explicitly. That is, instead of the keyword **any**, the access list must contain a specific IP address pattern.

> **WARNING!** Although you can use standard access lists in route maps applied as routing policies, you should remember that standard access lists allow matching only the source addresses, not the destination ones.

Policy-based routing does not affect the routing table of the routers. Listing 9.5 shows the routing table of router R1.

Listing 9.5   The routing table of router R1.

```
R1#show ip route
...
 172.16.0.0/30 is subnetted, 1 subnets
C   172.16.0.4 is directly connected, Serial0
 10.0.0.0/8 is variably subnetted, 10 subnets, 3 masks
D   10.0.0.2/32 [90/2297856] via 10.255.0.9, 06:46:53, Serial1
C   10.1.2.0/24 is directly connected, TokenRing0
D   10.2.1.0/24 [90/2733056] via 10.255.0.9, 06:46:53, Serial1
D   10.0.0.3/32 [90/2323456] via 10.255.0.9, 06:46:53, Serial1
C   10.1.1.0/24 is directly connected, Ethernet0
D   10.0.1.0/24 [90/2195456] via 10.255.0.9, 06:46:53, Serial1
C   10.0.0.1/32 is directly connected, Loopback0
D   10.0.0.4/32 [90/2835456] via 10.255.0.9, 06:46:53, Serial1
D   10.255.0.4/30 [90/2707456] via 10.255.0.9,06:46:53,Serial1
C   10.255.0.8/30 is directly connected, Serial1
```

To verify that policy-based routing works, let's use the **traceroute** command on host H1 for different destinations. (In our example, all hosts are Windows NT workstations, and the version of the **traceroute** command is called **tracert**.)

Listing 9.6 shows the output of the command **tracert -d 10.2.1.120**, where 10.2.1.120 is the IP address of host H3. The command confirms that the traffic destined for a host located on segment 3 from a host located on segment 1 does go through segment 7. (Notice the shaded line in Listing 9.6.)

Listing 9.6   The output of the command tracert -d 10.2.1.120 entered on host H1.

```
C:\>tracert -d 10.2.1.120

Tracing route to 10.2.1.120 over a maximum of 30 hops

    1    20 ms    10 ms    10 ms  10.1.1.1
    2    31 ms    20 ms    20 ms  172.16.0.6
    3    40 ms    40 ms    40 ms  10.2.1.120

Trace complete.
```

Listing 9.7 shows the output of the command **tracert -d 10.0.1.2**, where 10.0.1.2 is the IP address of router R3's Ethernet0 interface. This time, the traffic is not sent over segment 7, because it is not destined for segment 3.

Listing 9.7   The output of the command tracert -d 10.0.1.2 entered on host H1.

```
C:\>tracert -d 10.0.1.2

Tracing route to 10.0.1.2 over a maximum of 30 hops

    1    10 ms    10 ms    10 ms  10.1.1.1
    2    10 ms    10 ms    10 ms  10.255.0.9
    3    10 ms    10 ms    10 ms  10.0.1.2

Trace complete.
```

Finally, Listing 9.8 shows the output of the command **tracert -d 10.2.1.120** (the IP address of host H3). This time, the command was entered on host H2, which is located on segment 2. As the output of the command confirms, policy-based routing does not apply to the traffic that is not originated from segment 1, even if it's destined for segment 3.

Listing 9.8   The output of the command tracert -d 10.2.1.120 entered on host H2.

```
C:\>tracert -d 10.2.1.120

Tracing route to 10.2.1.120 over a maximum of 30 hops

    1   <10 ms   <10 ms   <10 ms  10.1.2.1
    2   <10 ms    10 ms   <10 ms  10.255.0.9
    3   <10 ms    10 ms   <10 ms  10.0.1.2
    4   <10 ms    10 ms   <10 ms  10.255.0.6
    5   <10 ms    11 ms   <10 ms  10.2.1.120

Trace complete.
```

9. Special Cases of Routing

Using Application-Sensitive Policy-Based Routing

Suppose now that branches Br.1 and Br.2 have some applications (such as real-time databases) that are sensitive to network congestion and that may not work properly during periods of heavy traffic at the headquarters. This time, the branches decided that they would use segment 7 only for the traffic generated by these applications. As before, the applications are located on segment 1 at branch Br.1 and segment 3 at branch Br.2.

For our experiment, Telnet is the application that is sensitive to network congestion. Thus, our task is to allow only the Telnet traffic that was initiated by the hosts located on segment 1 and destined for the hosts on segment 3 to traverse segment 7. The returning Telnet traffic must also use segment 7. However, the Telnet traffic that is initiated by the hosts on segment 3 and destined for the hosts located on segment 1 must not be policy-routed.

A Telnet connection at the Telnet client end uses an arbitrary, unused TCP port. The value of this TCP port is placed into the Source TCP Port field of the TCP segments generated by the host running the Telnet client. These segments are destined for TCP port 23, which is where the Telnet server typically resides. Similarly, the source and destination TCP ports of the TCP segments generated by the host that is running the Telnet server are equal to 23 and the TCP port number assigned to the client (which the Telnet server learns from the first TCP segment that it receives from the client).

Thus, we have to modify the access lists on routers R1 and R2 as follows:

- The access list on router R1 must match the datagrams carrying the TCP segments that are destined for TCP port 23.

- The access list on router R4 must match the datagrams carrying the TCP segments with source TCP port 23.

Listings 9.9 and 9.10 show the revised configurations of routers R1 and R4. The configurations of routers R2 and R3 remain unchanged.

Listing 9.9   Router R1's configuration.

```
interface Loopback0
 ip address 10.0.0.1 255.255.255.255

interface Ethernet0
 ip address 10.1.1.1 255.255.255.0
 ip policy route-map Seg1-Seg6

interface Serial0
 ip address 172.16.0.5 255.255.255.252
```

```
interface Serial1
 ip address 10.255.0.10 255.255.255.252

interface TokenRing0
 ip address 10.1.2.1 255.255.255.0
 ring-speed 16

router eigrp 10
 network 10.0.0.0

ip access-list extended telnet172
 permit tcp any 10.2.1.0 0.0.0.255 eq telnet

route-map Seg1-Seg6 permit 10
 match ip address telnet172
 set interface Serial0
 set ip next-hop 172.16.0.6
```

Listing 9.10   Router R4's configuration.

```
interface Loopback0
 ip address 10.0.0.4 255.255.255.255

interface Ethernet0
 ip address 10.2.1.1 255.255.255.0
 ip policy route-map Seg6-Seg1

interface Serial0
 ip address 10.255.0.6 255.255.255.252

interface Serial1
 ip address 172.16.0.6 255.255.255.252

router eigrp 10
 network 10.0.0.0

ip access-list extended telnet172
 permit tcp any eq telnet 10.1.1.0 0.0.0.255

route-map Seg6-Seg1 permit 10
 match ip address telnet172
 set interface Serial1
 set ip next-hop 172.16.0.5
```

Notice, this time, that named access lists are used instead of regular extended access lists.

9. Special Cases of Routing

To verify that the policy routing worked, we can no longer use the **traceroute** command, which sends UDP traffic destined for a nonexistent UDP port. Instead, we can use the **debug ip policy** command to see how the router actually performs policy routing.

Listings 9.11 and 9.12 show the output of the **debug ip policy** command on routers R1 and R4, respectively, after the **ping 10.2.1.120** command is entered on host H1. Because the **ping** traffic is not matched by the access lists on both routers, it is not policy-routed. (Notice the shaded lines *policy rejected — normal forwarding.*)

Listing 9.11 The output of the debug ip policy command on router R1 after the ping 10.2.1.120 command is entered on host H1.

```
R1#debug ip policy
Policy routing debugging is on
R1#
IP: s=10.1.1.10 (Ethernet0), d=10.2.1.120 (Serial1), len 100,
 policy rejected -- normal forwarding
IP: s=10.1.1.10 (Ethernet0), d=10.2.1.120 (Serial1), len 100,
 policy rejected -- normal forwarding
IP: s=10.1.1.10 (Ethernet0), d=10.2.1.120 (Serial1), len 100,
 ...
```

Listing 9.12 The output of the debug ip policy command on router R4 after the ping 10.2.1.120 command is entered on host H1.

```
R4#debug ip policy
Policy routing debugging is on
R4#
IP: s=10.2.1.120 (Ethernet0), d=10.1.1.10 (Serial0), len 100,
 policy rejected -- normal forwarding
IP: s=10.2.1.120 (Ethernet0), d=10.1.1.10 (Serial0), len 100,
 policy rejected -- normal forwarding
 ...
```

If, however, we try to Telnet from host H1 to host H3, the output of the **debug ip policy** command on both routers shows that the Telnet traffic is policy-routed (Listings 9.13 and 9.14).

Listing 9.13 The output of the debug ip policy command on router R1 after the telnet 10.2.1.120 command is entered on host H1.

```
R1#debug ip policy
Policy routing debugging is on
R1#
IP: s=10.1.1.10 (Ethernet0), d=10.2.1.120, len 44, policy match
```

```
IP: route map Seg1-Seg6, item 10, permit
IP: s=10.1.1.10 (Ethernet0), d=10.2.1.120 (Serial0), len 44, policy routed
IP: Ethernet0 to Serial0 172.16.0.6
IP: s=10.1.1.10 (Ethernet0), d=10.2.1.120, len 40, policy match
IP: route map Seg1-Seg6, item 10, permit
IP: s=10.1.1.10 (Ethernet0), d=10.2.1.120 (Serial0), len 40, policy routed
IP: Ethernet0 to Serial0 172.16.0.6
...
```

Listing 9.14 The output of the **debug ip policy** command on router R4 after the **telnet 10.2.1.120** command is entered on host H1.

```
R4#debug ip policy
Policy routing debugging is on
R4#
IP: s=10.2.1.120 (Ethernet0), d=10.1.1.10, len 44, policy match
IP: route map Seg6-Seg1, item 10, permit
IP: s=10.2.1.120 (Ethernet0), d=10.1.1.10 (Serial1), len 44, policy routed
IP: Ethernet0 to Serial1 172.16.0.5
IP: s=10.2.1.120 (Ethernet0), d=10.1.1.10, len 40, policy match
IP: route map Seg6-Seg1, item 10, permit
IP: s=10.2.1.120 (Ethernet0), d=10.1.1.10 (Serial1), len 40, policy routed
IP: Ethernet0 to Serial1 172.16.0.5
...
```

Another helpful command is **show route-map**, which not only shows the route map clauses but also the policy-based routing utilization (provided the route map is applied as the routing policy). The last line of the command output shows how many matches have been encountered and how many traffic bytes were policy-routed.

Sample output of the **show route-map** command is shown in Listing 9.15.

Listing 9.15 The output of the **show route-map** command entered on router R4.

```
R4#show route-map
route-map Seg6-Seg1, permit, sequence 10
  Match clauses:
    ip address (access-lists): telnet172
  Set clauses:
    interface Serial1
    ip next-hop 172.16.0.5
  Policy routing matches: 241 packets, 19386 bytes
```

Using Policy-Based Routing in Migration Scenarios

One more potential application for policy-based routing is migration of a number of servers from one LAN segment to another, so that:

1. The server IP addresses cannot be changed.

2. The LAN segments are of incompatible types, such as token ring and Ethernet.

3. The number of servers is such that all of the servers cannot be migrated at once but instead must be migrated in several steps.

At first, the above conditions—especially the first one—might seem artificial. The immediate question most people have is: Why can't the IP addresses of the servers be changed? If they could, a much better migration path would be to give the new LAN segment a new network prefix and then migrate the servers one by one by moving them to the new segment and giving them the new IP addresses. Whereas this migration path might sound better, the reality sometimes dictates circumstances that render it unfeasible. One of the most common reasons given for not readdressing the segments is that the software of the workstations accessing the server is poorly written: It uses the hard-coded IP addresses, which cannot be changed. Therefore, the servers cannot be readdressed.

However warranted the circumstances may or may not be, let's consider what can be done to solve the task—besides readdressing, that is.

An example of this situation is shown in Figure 9.7. Segments 1 and 2 are the new and old segments on which the non-readdressable servers reside. Figure 9.7 shows that servers S1, S3, and S5 have already been migrated to segment 1, whereas servers S2, S4, and S6 have not. Obviously, the network prefixes of segments 1 and 2 are identical: 10.0.1.0/24. Host H1 represents a workstation that runs the homegrown software, which features hard-coded server IP addresses. Our task is to configure routers in the network so that host H1 has equal access to the servers on segments 1 and 2.

One of the ways we can resolve the ambiguous addressing of segments 1 and 2 is by configuring policy-based routing on router PR (<u>P</u>olicy <u>R</u>outer). The idea is to implement a policy such that, if it matches the IP addresses of the servers remaining on segment 2 in the traffic received on router PR's interface Ethernet8, it will direct the traffic towards segment 2. All other traffic, however, must not be affected by the policy.

The only trouble with this solution is that it is impossible to assign the same network prefix to two interfaces of the same router. Moreover, it is impossible to assign two different but overlapping network prefixes on two interfaces of the same router. (*Overlapping* means that there is at least one address that belongs to both network prefixes. For example, IP address 10.0.1.10 belongs to 10.0.0.0/16 and 10.0.1.0/24. Hence, the network prefixes are overlapping.) This issue, however, can be resolved by introducing an additional router, one interface of which

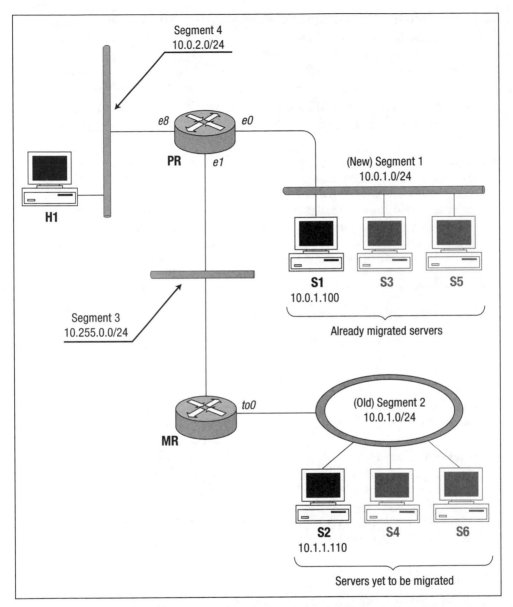

Figure 9.7 Router PR is configured with policy-based routing, which (depending on the server to which the traffic is destined) directs it to either segment 1 or 2.

is to be connected to a segment to which one of router PR's interfaces is connected, and another interface to be connected to the old segment. The network prefix of the segment common to both routers should have a legitimate network prefix, whereas the old segment obviously has the same network prefix as that of segment 1. This router will have a very simple configuration: two interfaces, a static route for the default network prefix (0.0.0.0/0) pointing to router PR, and the **ip classless** command (to allow the servers to communicate with the rest of 10.0.0.0/8). Let's call this router MR (Migration Router). The policy at router PR now can direct the traffic destined for the yet-to-be-migrated servers to router MR, which will forward it directly to the servers. Nothing should change at the servers, because router MR's interface connected to segment 2 is assigned the same address as that of router PR's interface connected to segment 1.

NOTE: *In the previous paragraph, I said that it is impossible to assign the same IP address to two different interfaces on the same router. This is not exactly true, because, as we know, the command **ip unnumbered** <interface> makes the router "borrow" the IP address of the referenced interface for the unnumbered interface, which is essentially equal to assigning the same IP address to two different interfaces. Although this might seem an alluring alternative to the described solution, it is (unfortunately) not a viable one, because the **ip unnumbered** command is available on only non-multi-access interfaces, such as Serial and Tunnel interfaces. I must say, however, that, if it were an option, the described solution could be implemented without using the extra router, MR.*

The configurations of routers PR and MR are shown in Listings 9.16 and 9.17.

Listing 9.16   Router PR's configuration.

```
interface Ethernet0
 ip address 10.0.1.1 255.255.255.0

interface Ethernet1
 ip address 10.255.0.1 255.255.255.0

interface Ethernet8
 ip address 10.0.2.1 255.255.255.0
 ip policy route-map MigrateTR

access-list 100 permit ip any host 10.0.1.110
access-list 100 permit ip any host 10.0.1.115
access-list 100 permit ip any host 10.0.1.120

route-map MigrateTR permit 10
 match ip address 100
 set interface Ethernet1
 set ip next-hop 10.255.0.2
```

Listing 9.17   Router MR's configuration.

```
interface Ethernet0
 ip address 10.255.0.2 255.255.255.0

interface TokenRing0
 ip address 10.0.1.1 255.255.255.0
```

```
ring-speed 16
```

ip classless

```
ip route 0.0.0.0 0.0.0.0 10.255.0.1
```

The shaded line in router PR's configuration shows how the policy is applied. The policy itself comprises access list 100 and route map MigrateTR, consisting of a single clause with sequence number 10. Access list 100 matches three host addresses: 10.0.1.110, 10.0.1.115, and 10.0.1.120 (the IP addresses of the servers remaining on segment 2). Access list 100 is further used in the only clause of route map MigrateTR as the **match** condition. The **set** action forces the router to forward the traffic to router MR's IP address 10.255.0.2 through router PR's Ethernet1 interface.

If we try to Telnet to either server S1 or S2 from host H1, Telnet will succeed, which is demonstrated in Listing 9.18.

Listing 9.18   The results of the commands telnet 10.0.1.100 and telnet 10.0.1.110 issued on host H1.

```
H1#telnet 10.0.1.100
Trying 10.0.1.100 ... Open

Welcome to server S1
User Access Verification

Username:
...
H1#telnet 10.0.1.110
Trying 10.0.1.110 ... Open

Welcome to server S2
User Access Verification

Username:
```

A little more research through the use of the **traceroute** command demonstrates that—despite the same destination network prefix—the traffic does traverse along two different routes. The outputs of the commands **traceroute 10.0.1.100** and **traceroute 10.0.1.110** are shown in Listing 9.19.

Listing 9.19   The output of the commands traceroute 10.0.1.100 and traceroute 10.0.1.110 issued on host H1.

```
H1#traceroute 10.0.1.100

Type escape sequence to abort.
```

9. Special Cases of Routing

```
Tracing the route to 10.0.1.100

   1 10.0.2.1 0 msec 4 msec 4 msec
   2 10.0.1.100 4 msec *  4 msec

H1#traceroute 10.0.1.110

Type escape sequence to abort.
Tracing the route to 10.0.1.110

   1 10.0.2.1 0 msec 4 msec 4 msec
   2 10.255.0.2 8 msec 4 msec 4 msec
   3 10.0.1.110 4 msec *  4 msec
```

The shaded line shows the extra hop that the traffic has to take if it is destined for yet-to-be-migrated server S2.

> **WARNING!**   The solution presented in this section may not be viable for all migration scenarios with the described requirements. For example, if the migrated and yet-to-be-migrated servers must communicate with each other, this solution won't suffice.

Configuring NAT

Configuring NAT is discussed in the sections below.

Configuring Static Translation of Inside IP Addresses

The static translation of inside IP addresses is only one of several static NAT configurations. (The others are performed using the steps defined in this section.)

With the static translation of inside IP addresses, you can configure a router to translate individual local inside IP addresses to global inside IP addresses. The router compares the source IP addresses of the datagrams that are destined for the global outside IP addresses and received on the interfaces labeled "inside" against the Inside Local Address field of the NAT table entries. If the source IP address matches an entry in the NAT table, it is replaced with the corresponding inside global IP address.

To configure static translation of inside IP addresses, follow these steps:

1. Create NAT mapping between the inside local address and the inside global address using the command **ip nat inside source** <*local IP address*> <*global IP address*>. The parameter <*local IP address*> is the inside local

IP address that is translated into the inside global IP address, which is passed in the *<global IP address>* parameter.

2. Apply NAT on the interfaces connected to the segments with the local inside addresses using the **ip nat inside** command in interface configuration mode.

3. Apply NAT on the interfaces connected to the segments with the global outside addresses using the **ip nat outside** command in interface configuration mode.

NOTE: *The global inside address must be known in the global address space. Moreover, the other routers in the network should perceive the global inside address as available via the router performing NAT. This can be achieved either by static routing or by making the router performing NAT advertise this address via a dynamic routing protocol.*

Figure 9.8 shows an example of a network in which router R3 is connected to segment 3, whose network address is not legitimate from the perspective of the rest of the network. Thus, router R3 must perform NAT to allow host H1 (located on segment 3) to communicate with the rest of the network.

Listings 9.20 through 9.22 show the configurations of all three routers. Notice that only router R3 is configured to perform NAT. The NAT-related commands are shown as the shaded lines.

Listing 9.20   Router R1's configuration.

```
interface Ethernet0
 ip address 10.1.0.1 255.255.255.0

interface Serial1
 no ip address
 encapsulation frame-relay
 frame-relay lmi-type ansi

interface Serial1.2 point-to-point
 ip address 10.255.0.5 255.255.255.252
 frame-relay interface-dlci 102

interface Serial1.3 point-to-point
 ip address 10.255.0.9 255.255.255.252
 frame-relay interface-dlci 103

router eigrp 10
 network 10.0.0.0
```

```
encapsulation frame-relay
frame-relay lmi-type ansi

interface Serial0.1 point-to-point
 ip address 10.255.0.6 255.255.255.252
 frame-relay interface-dlci 201

router eigrp 10
 network 10.0.0.0
```

Listing 9.22 Router R3's configuration.

```
interface Loopback0
 ip address 10.100.0.1 255.255.255.0

interface Ethernet0
 ip address 172.16.1.1 255.255.255.0
 ip nat inside

interface Serial0
 no ip address
 encapsulation frame-relay
 frame-relay lmi-type ansi

interface Serial0.1 point-to-point
 ip address 10.255.0.10 255.255.255.252
 ip nat outside
 frame-relay interface-dlci 301

router eigrp 10
 network 10.0.0.0

ip nat inside source static 172.16.1.111 10.100.0.111
```

Listing 9.23 shows that a Telnet session started on host H1 to host H2 is successful.

Listing 9.23 The Telnet session started from host H1 to host H2 is successful.

```
C:\>telnet 10.2.0.120

Welcome to the Telnet Service on H2

Username:
```

As expected, the output of the **netstat -n** command entered on host H2 (shown in Listing 9.24) indicates that the Telnet connection is between host H2's IP address and the inside global IP address (10.100.0.111) that we used in static NAT configuration.

Listing 9.24   The output of the netstat -n command entered on host H2 shows that host H2 has an active Telnet connection with the global inside address 10.100.0.111.

```
C:\WINDOWS\system32>netstat -n

Active Connections

Proto  Local Address        Foreign Address       State
TCP    10.2.0.120:23        10.100.0.111:1052     ESTABLISHED
TCP    127.0.0.1:1027       127.0.0.1:1028        ESTABLISHED
TCP    127.0.0.1:1028       127.0.0.1:1027        ESTABLISHED
```

A Telnet connection started from host H2 to host H1 also succeeds, as shown in Listing 9.25.

Listing 9.25   The Telnet session to host H1 initiated from host H2 also succeeds.

```
C:\>telnet 10.100.0.111

Welcome to the Telnet Service on H1

Username:
```

The output of the **netstat -n** command entered on host H1 (shown in Listing 9.26) indicates that the Telnet connection is between host H1's IP address, which is the inside local IP address, and host H2's IP address, which is the outside global IP address.

Listing 9.26   The output of the netstat -n command confirms that the router translates the global inside address into the local inside address.

```
C:\>netstat -n

Active Connections

Proto  Local Address        Foreign Address       State
TCP    127.0.0.1:1026       127.0.0.1:1027        ESTABLISHED
TCP    127.0.0.1:1027       127.0.0.1:1026        ESTABLISHED
TCP    172.16.1.111:23      10.2.0.120:1111       ESTABLISHED
```

However, the output of the command **netstat -n** entered on host H2 (shown in Listing 9.27) also shows that the active Telnet connection is between host H2's IP address and the global inside IP address 10.100.0.111.

Listing 9.27   The output of the command netstat -n on host H2 shows that the active connection was made to the global inside address.

```
C:\>netstat -n
Active Connections
```

```
Proto   Local Address        Foreign Address      State
TCP     10.2.0.120:1111      10.100.0.111:23      ESTABLISHED
TCP     127.0.0.1:1027       127.0.0.1:1028       ESTABLISHED
TCP     127.0.0.1:1028       127.0.0.1:1027       ESTABLISHED
```

Configuring Dynamic Translation of Inside IP Addresses

Dynamic translation of inside IP addresses is one of several dynamic NAT configurations. (The others are performed using the steps defined in this section.)

The operation of dynamic translation of inside IP addresses differs from that of static translation of inside IP addresses only in how the NAT table is populated. In the static version, the NAT table is populated by administratively entering pairs of IP addresses. In the dynamic version, the router itself populates the NAT table when an IP datagram arrives on an interface labeled "inside" and the datagram's characteristics match certain criteria. The subsequent datagrams arriving on the router's interfaces labeled "inside" and whose source IP address matches an existing entry in the NAT table are processed in the same way as in the static version.

The criteria that are used to verify a datagram's eligibility to create an entry in the NAT table are expressed using an access list. The datagram should match an entry in the access list with the **permit** result to be eligible to create an entry in the NAT table.

Finally, when creating entries in the NAT table, the router uses an administratively configured pool of inside global addresses. For every new entry, the router picks the next available IP address from the pool in ascending order. If the pool no longer contains any IP addresses, the corresponding entry is not created.

To configure dynamic NAT, follow these steps:

1. Define a pool of global inside IP addresses using the command **ip nat pool** *<name> <start IP address> <end IP address>* {**netmask** *<subnet mask>*|**prefix-length** *<prefix length>*} in global configuration mode. The *<name>* parameter is used to identify the address pool. The *<start IP address>* and *<end IP address>* parameters identify the range of global inside IP addresses that the router will use when translating the local inside IP addresses. The parameters **netmask** *<subnet mask>* and **prefix-length** *<prefix length>* are two different ways to specify the length of the network prefix to which the defined global inside address space belongs. The format of the *<subnet mask>* parameter is dotted decimal; because this parameter actually specifies the network prefix length, it must be contiguous (unlike an access list wildcard mask). The *<prefix length>* parameter is an integer value ranging from 0 through 32.

The described procedure allows you to define a contiguous pool of NAT addresses. If you would like to configure a noncontiguous pool, you must omit the *<start IP address>* and *<end IP address>* parameters in the described command. In this case, you enter NAT pool configuration mode and define multiple IP address ranges using the following syntax: **address** *<start IP address> <end IP address>*.

2. Define an access list that specifies which traffic arriving on the interfaces labeled "inside" is eligible to create entries in the NAT table.

NOTE: You can use extended access lists in this step. Remember, however, that the access list is used only if the NAT table does not contain an inside local address coinciding with the source IP address of the datagram. If the NAT table already contains such an address, the access list is no longer used. In this case, the source address of the datagram is translated even though the other characteristics of the datagram may not satisfy the access list.

---

3. Establish an association between the eligible local inside addresses and the pool of global inside addresses using the command **ip nat inside source list {***<ACL number>***|***<ACL name>***} pool** *<pool name>*. The *<ACL number>* parameter is the number of the access list defined in Step 2. This parameter must be used if the access list is numbered. If the access list defined in Step 2 is named, the *<ACL name>* parameter must be used instead; this parameter denotes the name of the access list. The *<pool name>* parameter is the name of the global inside addresses pool defined in Step 1.

4. Apply NAT on the interfaces connected to the segments with the local inside addresses using the **ip nat inside** command in interface configuration mode.

5. Apply NAT on the interfaces connected to the segments with the global outside addresses using the **ip nat outside** command in interface configuration mode.

To see how the configuration guidelines work, let's modify the task we performed to configure static NAT for a single host H1 (see the previous section) to configure dynamic NAT for hosts whose addresses are in the range 172.16.1.0/25. The global address space will range from 10.100.0.50 to 10.100.0.100. In addition, let's require that only a TCP connection to a host on segment 2 can create a translation entry.

Listing 9.28 shows the revised configuration of router R3. The other routes retain their configurations from the previous section.

Listing 9.28   Router R3's configuration.

```
ip nat pool pool172 10.100.0.50 10.100.0.100 prefix-length 24
ip nat inside source list TCP172 pool pool172
```

```
interface Loopback0
 ip address 10.100.0.1 255.255.255.0

interface Ethernet0
 ip address 172.16.1.1 255.255.255.0
 ip nat inside

interface Serial0
 no ip address
 encapsulation frame-relay
 frame-relay lmi-type ansi

interface Serial0.1 point-to-point
 ip address 10.255.0.10 255.255.255.252
 ip nat outside
 frame-relay interface-dlci 301

router eigrp 10
 network 10.0.0.0

ip access-list extended TCP172
 permit tcp 172.16.1.0 0.0.0.127 10.2.0.0 0.0.0.255
```

A useful command for monitoring NAT is **show ip nat translations**, which displays the contents of the NAT table. If, however, the router is configured just for dynamic NAT, the NAT table may not contain any entries, and the **show ip nat translations** command produces no output.

To create entries in the NAT table, a router must first receive traffic that matches the access list used in the NAT configuration. If the access list is standard, any traffic whose source IP address matches the access list will create an entry in the NAT table. If, however, the access list is extended (as in our case), the other characteristics of the traffic must also be matched by the access list. In our case, the traffic eligible for NAT must not only be originated from a local inside address (that is, an IP address from the range 172.16.1.0/25) but also must be TCP and destined for a host on segment 2.

If we simply try to ping a host whose IP address belongs to the global outside address space, we won't succeed, because the **ping** command produces Internet Control Message Protocol (ICMP) traffic. Listing 9.29 shows the results of attempts to ping the Ethernet interface of host H2 and router R1.

9. Special Cases of Routing

Listing 9.29 The results of pinging host H2 and router R1's Ethernet0 interface from host H1 before the NAT table of router R3 contains an entry for host H1's IP address.

```
C:\>ping 10.2.0.120

Pinging 10.2.0.120 with 32 bytes of data:

Request timed out.
Request timed out.
Request timed out.
Request timed out.

C:\>ping 10.1.0.1

Pinging 10.1.0.1 with 32 bytes of data:

Request timed out.
Request timed out.
Request timed out.
Request timed out.
```

Trying to Telnet to router R1 using the IP address configured on its Ethernet0 interface will also be unsuccessful.

However, a Telnet session from host H1 to host H2 is successful (as shown below):

```
C:\>telnet 10.2.0.120

Welcome to the Telnet Service on H2

Username:
```

After that, the NAT table of router R3 contains an entry for host H1's IP address (172.16.1.111). The output of the **show ip nat translations** command is shown below:

```
R3#show ip nat translations
Pro Inside global  Inside local  Outside local Outside global
-- 10.100.0.50    172.16.1.111  --            --
```

After the entry is created, all connections from host H1 to the rest of the network are successful. (Listing 9.30 shows that previously unsuccessful attempts to ping host H1 and router R1 now succeed.) The connection is successful because the NAT table contains only pairs of local and global IP addresses, unlike the access list that was used to verify if the outgoing traffic is eligible to create an entry in the NAT table.

Listing 9.30   After an entry for host H1's IP address is added to the NAT table, all connections from host H1 to the rest of the network are successful.

```
C:\>ping 10.2.0.120

Pinging 10.2.0.120 with 32 bytes of data:

Reply from 10.2.0.120: bytes=32 time=91ms TTL=125
Reply from 10.2.0.120: bytes=32 time=80ms TTL=125
Reply from 10.2.0.120: bytes=32 time=81ms TTL=125
Reply from 10.2.0.120: bytes=32 time=80ms TTL=125


C:\>ping 10.1.0.1

Pinging 10.1.0.1 with 32 bytes of data:

Reply from 10.1.0.1: bytes=32 time=60ms TTL=254
Reply from 10.1.0.1: bytes=32 time=50ms TTL=254
Reply from 10.1.0.1: bytes=32 time=50ms TTL=254
Reply from 10.1.0.1: bytes=32 time=50ms TTL=254
```

After a Telnet session to host H2 was established from host H1, the output of the **netstat -n** command entered on host H2 (shown in Listing 9.31) shows the inside global address that was used to replace the original IP address of host H1.

Listing 9.31   The output of the netstat -n command entered on host H2.

```
C:\>netstat -n

Active Connections

  Proto  Local Address          Foreign Address        State
  TCP    10.2.0.120:23          10.100.0.50:1047       ESTABLISHED
  TCP    127.0.0.1:1027         127.0.0.1:1028         ESTABLISHED
  TCP    127.0.0.1:1028         127.0.0.1:1027         ESTABLISHED
```

TIP: *You can use the command **clear ip nat translation *** to remove all of the NAT table entries. In lieu of the asterisk, other parameters can be used to perform more-specific removals.*

Using NAT in the Presence of Open Shortest Path First (OSPF) Routing

Configuring NAT in conjunction with OSPF routing may present a little surprise. This surprise does not pertain to the interoperation between NAT and OSPF per se, but it is related to how OSPF changes the auxiliary configuration that we introduced for NAT—namely, how OSPF represents the network prefix configured on a loopback interface.

9. Special Cases of Routing

In the previous section, we defined the range of global inside addresses using the interface Loopback0 on router R3. We relied on Enhanced Interior Gateway Routing Protocol (EIGRP) to establish dynamic routing in the network and to advertise this global inside address space to the rest of the network. However, if we replace EIGRP on routers R1 through R3 with OSPF, we'll find out that NAT does not work anymore.

Listings 9.32 through 9.34 show the configurations of all three routers in which EIGRP is replaced with OSPF. No other changes were made.

Listing 9.32   Router R1's configuration.

```
interface Loopback0
 ip address 10.0.0.1 255.255.255.255

interface Ethernet0
 ip address 10.1.0.1 255.255.255.0

interface Serial1
 no ip address
 encapsulation frame-relay
 frame-relay lmi-type ansi

interface Serial1.2 point-to-point
 ip address 10.255.0.5 255.255.255.252
 frame-relay interface-dlci 102

interface Serial1.3 point-to-point
 ip address 10.255.0.9 255.255.255.252
 frame-relay interface-dlci 103

router ospf 10
 network 10.0.0.0 0.255.255.255 area 0

ip classless
```

Listing 9.33   Router R2's configuration.

```
interface Loopback0
 ip address 10.0.0.2 255.255.255.255

interface Ethernet0
 ip address 10.2.0.1 255.255.255.0

interface Serial0
 no ip address
 encapsulation frame-relay
 frame-relay lmi-type ansi
```

```
interface Serial0.1 point-to-point
 ip address 10.255.0.6 255.255.255.252
 frame-relay interface-dlci 201

router ospf 10
 network 10.0.0.0 0.255.255.255 area 0

ip classless
```

Listing 9.34   Router R3's configuration.

```
ip nat pool pool172 10.100.0.50 10.100.0.100 prefix-length 24
ip nat inside source list TCP172 pool pool172

interface Loopback0
 ip address 10.100.0.1 255.255.255.0

interface Ethernet0
 ip address 172.16.1.1 255.255.255.0
 ip nat inside

interface Serial0
 no ip address
 encapsulation frame-relay
 frame-relay lmi-type ansi

interface Serial0.1 point-to-point
 ip address 10.255.0.10 255.255.255.252
 ip nat outside
 frame-relay interface-dlci 301

router ospf 10
 network 10.0.0.0 0.255.255.255 area 0

ip classless

ip access-list extended TCP172
 permit tcp 172.16.1.0 0.0.0.127 10.2.0.0 0.0.0.255
```

After the changes, the **telnet 10.2.0.120** command issued on host H1 no longer works. Interestingly enough, NAT isn't to blame. The Telnet command no longer works because the global inside address range defined on the Loopback0 interface of router R3 is no longer advertised as such. Instead, the network prefix of the Loopback0 interface is advertised as 10.100.0.1/32. Listing 9.35, which shows the routing table of router R2, demonstrates this.

Listing 9.35   The routing table of router R2.

```
R2#show ip route
...
 10.0.0.0/8 is variably subnetted, 7 subnets, 3 masks
C   10.0.0.2/32 is directly connected, Loopback0
C   10.2.0.0/24 is directly connected, Ethernet0
O   10.1.0.0/24 [110/74] via 10.255.0.5, 00:12:40, Serial0.1
O   10.0.0.1/32 [110/65] via 10.255.0.5, 00:12:40, Serial0.1
O   10.100.0.1/32 [110/129] via 10.255.0.5, 00:12:40,Serial0.1
C   10.255.0.4/30 is directly connected, Serial0.1
O   10.255.0.8/30 [110/128] via 10.255.0.5, 00:12:40,Serial0.1
```

If we enter the command **show ip ospf interface Loopback 0** on router R3 shown in Listing 9.36, we'll see that the last line of the command output indicates that the loopback interfaces are treated (and therefore advertised) as stub hosts.

Listing 9.36   The output of the show ip ospf interface Loopback 0 command on router R3.

```
R3#show ip ospf interface Loopback 0
Loopback0 is up, line protocol is up
  Internet Address 10.100.0.1/24, Area 0
  Process ID 10, Router ID 10.100.0.1, Network Type LOOPBACK,
 Cost: 1
  Loopback interface is treated as a stub Host
```

In addition, because the Loopback0 interface in our example has an IP address with a number higher than any global outside IP address, it is used as the OSPF router ID. It is inconsistent with the OSPF IDs of the other router.

The straightforward solution is to define a static route for the global inside address space pointing to the Null0 interface and to give the Loopback0 interface a consistent OSPF router ID. The static route then needs to be redistributed into the OSPF process.

Another solution is to give the Loopback0 interface a consistent IP address (in our example, it is 10.0.0.3/32) and then define a Tunnel0 interface whose source and destination addresses are equal to the new IP address of the Loopback0 interface. As with loopback interfaces, tunnel interfaces are logical. However, unlike loopback interfaces, tunnel interfaces are not treated by OSPF as stub. Thus, if the global IP address is defined using a tunnel interface, it is advertised by OSPF exactly as we expect it to be advertised. This solution also eliminates the need to redistribute static routes into the OSPF process of router R3 (which in turn creates type 5 LSAs, which may not be desirable or even suitable for the area).

Listing 9.37 shows the updated configuration of router R3.

Listing 9.37 Router R3's configuration.
```
ip nat pool pool172 10.100.0.50 10.100.0.100 prefix-length 24
ip nat inside source list TCP172 pool pool172

interface Loopback0
 ip address 10.0.0.3 255.255.255.255

interface Tunnel0
 ip address 10.100.0.1 255.255.255.0
 tunnel source 10.0.0.3
 tunnel destination 10.0.0.3

interface Ethernet0
 ip address 172.16.1.1 255.255.255.0
 ip nat inside

interface Serial0
 no ip address
 encapsulation frame-relay
 frame-relay lmi-type ansi

interface Serial0.1 point-to-point
 ip address 10.255.0.10 255.255.255.252
 ip nat outside
 frame-relay interface-dlci 301

router ospf 10
 network 10.0.0.0 0.255.255.255 area 0

ip classless

ip access-list extended TCP172
 permit tcp 172.16.1.0 0.0.0.127 10.2.0.0 0.0.0.255
```

The routing table of router R2 (shown in Listing 9.38) now contains the route for the global inside address space.

Listing 9.38 The routing table of router R2 after the Tunnel0 interface was added on router R3.
```
R2#show ip route
...
 10.0.0.0/8 is variably subnetted, 8 subnets, 3 masks
C   10.0.0.2/32 is directly connected, Loopback0
C   10.2.0.0/24 is directly connected, Ethernet0
```

```
O   10.0.0.3/32 [110/129] via 10.255.0.5, 00:00:11, Serial0.1
O   10.1.0.0/24 [110/74] via 10.255.0.5, 00:00:11, Serial0.1
O   10.0.0.1/32 [110/65] via 10.255.0.5, 00:00:11, Serial0.1
O   10.100.0.0/24 [110/11239]via 10.255.0.5,00:00:11,Serial0.1
C   10.255.0.4/30 is directly connected, Serial0.1
O   10.255.0.8/30 [110/128] via 10.255.0.5, 00:00:11,Serial0.1
```

NAT now functions properly.

Using the **type match-host** Parameter of the **ip nat pool** Command

As mentioned in the previous section, the router allocates the inside global IP address from the pool in ascending order. Sometimes, however, you may want to preserve the host IDs when translating the network IDs. Specifically for this purpose, the optional **type match-host** parameter can be used at the end of the **ip nat pool** command.

If this parameter is used, the router calculates the inside global IP addresses using the following formula:

$$IP_{inside,global} = IP_{pool} + (IP_{inside,local} \: NP_{inside,local})$$

where $IP_{inside,global}$ is the resulting inside global IP address, IP_{pool} is the first IP address in the pool to which the pool's subnet mask was applied, $IP_{inside,local}$ is the inside local IP address (that is, the address to be translated), and $NP_{inside,local}$ is the network prefix to which the inside local IP address belongs.

The pool's subnet mask is defined either by the **prefix-length** *<length>* parameter or by the **netmask** *<subnet mask>* parameter. All parameters must be treated as 32-bit numbers.

> **WARNING!** *The calculated inside global IP address must remain within the ranges of IP addresses defined by the pool. Otherwise, the translation is not performed.*

Let's replace the pool of inside global IP addresses that we used in the previous section with a new one accompanied by the **type match-host** parameter. The new configuration of router R3 is shown in Listing 9.39.

Listing 9.39   Router R3's configuration.

```
ip nat pool pool172 10.100.0.96 10.100.0.127 prefix-length 24 type match-
host

ip nat inside source list 1 pool pool172

interface Loopback0
 ip address 10.100.0.1 255.255.255.0
```

```
interface Ethernet0
 ip address 172.16.1.1 255.255.255.0
 ip nat inside

interface Serial0
 no ip address
 encapsulation frame-relay
 frame-relay lmi-type ansi

interface Serial0.1 point-to-point
 ip address 10.255.0.10 255.255.255.252
 ip nat outside
 frame-relay interface-dlci 301

router eigrp 10
 network 10.0.0.0


access-list 1 permit 172.16.1.0 0.0.0.127
```

The new NAT table looks as shown below.

```
R3#show ip nat translations
Pro Inside global  Inside local  Outside local Outside global
-- 10.100.0.111    172.16.1.111  --            --
```

> **NOTE:**   The outside hosts cannot reach the inside hosts via the corresponding global inside addresses until the NAT table contains the corresponding entries. In the case of dynamic NAT, the entry in the NAT table is created only after traffic that satisfies the access list is routed to an outside network by the router performing NAT. In the case of static NAT, the entry is always present in the NAT table.

Configuring NAT with Overloading Global Inside IP Addresses

Sometimes, it isn't possible to define a large enough pool of global inside addresses. One such example is a network with private IP addresses that must be connected to the Internet. If the network is large—and therefore uses a broad range of private IP addresses, such as 10.0.0.0/8—it may be impossible to get an equal-sized pool of inside global IP addresses. (On the other hand, if it were possible to get such a big pool, then why bother using private IP addresses?)

A NAT solution is available specifically for such situations. It is referenced in the RFCs as *Network Address Port Translation* (*NAPT*) and in the Cisco documentation as *Port Address Translation* (*PAT*). NAPT allows multiple hosts that are located on the inside networks to access hosts that are located on outside networks using either a single inside global address or a limited number of those.

9. Special Cases of Routing

This is made possible by translating transport layer identifiers—namely, TCP/UDP ports and ICMP query identifiers—that are created by the hosts on the inside networks into transport identifiers associated with a single (or only a few) inside global addresses. The router performing NAPT has to keep track of transport layer identifiers and the corresponding inside local IP addresses.

To configure NAPT, you can use the procedure described in "Configuring Dynamic Translation of Inside IP Addresses" earlier in this chapter—except in Step 3 you must append the **overload** parameter to the **ip nat inside source** command.

Alternatively, you can use the following version of the command: **ip nat inside source list** {*<AL number>*|*<AL name>*} **interface** *<interface>*. In this instance, the router replaces the inside local IP addresses with the single IP address configured on the corresponding interface.

Listing 9.40 shows the configuration of router R3, which now performs the translation of the inside local IP address into the IP address configured on subinterface Serial0.1.

Listing 9.40   Router R3's configuration.

```
ip nat inside source list 1 interface Serial0.1 overload

interface Loopback0
 ip address 10.100.0.1 255.255.255.0

interface Ethernet0
 ip address 172.16.1.1 255.255.255.0
 ip nat inside

interface Serial0
 no ip address
 encapsulation frame-relay
 frame-relay lmi-type ansi

interface Serial0.1 point-to-point
 ip address 10.255.0.10 255.255.255.252
 ip nat outside
 frame-relay interface-dlci 301

router eigrp 10
 network 10.0.0.0

access-list 1 permit 172.16.1.0 0.0.0.127
```

The new NAT table of router R3 is shown below; notice that the NAT table now has all fields filled out:

```
R3#show ip nat translations
Pro Inside global      Inside local        Outside local   Outside global
tcp 10.255.0.10:1054   172.16.1.111:1054   10.2.0.120:23   10.2.0.120:23
```

NOTE: *Because of the format limitations of this book, the lines of output shown in Listing 7.40 were broken in the middle. Ellipses indicate the breaks. Lines 1 and 2 are continued at lines 3 and 4, respectively.*

Configuring NAT to Translate between Overlapping Address Spaces

If two networks using the same IP addresses are merged and one of these networks is a stub network, it's possible to use NAT to perform the IP address translation of the overlapped IP addresses.

This NAT solution is based on using Domain Name System (DNS) by the hosts on the stub network (an inside network) to resolve the IP addresses of the hosts that are located on the outside network. The router configured for NAT intercepts the DNS replies. If the returned IP address overlaps with an IP address in the stub network, the router translates it to a nonambiguous IP address routable in the stub network.

To configure NAT to translate between overlapping address spaces, follow these steps:

1. Using the **ip nat pool** command, define a pool of outside local addresses into which the IP addresses in the DNS replies will be translated. These addresses must be routable inside the stub network. The syntax of the **ip nat pool** command is the same as before.

2. Define an access list that specifies which traffic arriving on the interfaces labeled "outside" is eligible to create entries in the NAT table.

3. Establish an association between the eligible outside global addresses and the pool of outside local addresses using the command **ip nat outside source list {**<AL number>|<AL name>**} pool** <name>.

4. Apply NAT on the interfaces that are connected to the segments with the local inside addresses using the **ip nat inside** command in interface configuration mode.

5. Apply NAT on the interfaces that are connected to the segments with the global outside addresses using the **ip nat outside** command in interface configuration mode.

NOTE: *The IP addresses that constitute the pool of outside local addresses to the router performing NAT must appear to be routable exactly as the outside global IP addresses that they will replace. Because the routers on the outside networks don't know anything about the outside local addresses, they can't advertise these addresses to the router performing NAT. Thus, it is possible that static routing is the only way to establish the necessary routing for the outside local address.*

---

9. Special Cases of Routing

TIP: *Translation of the outside addresses makes sense only if it is performed in conjunction with the inside address translation.*

Figure 9.9 shows an example of two merged networks, one of which (the shaded area) uses the IP address from the other. Luckily, the first network is not large, and it is a stub network from the second network's perspective. Thus, NAT can be used to translate the overlapping IP addresses.

The configurations of all three routers are shown in Listings 9.41 through 9.43.

Listing 9.41   Router R1's configuration.

```
interface Ethernet0
 ip address 10.1.0.1 255.255.255.0

interface Serial1
 no ip address
 encapsulation frame-relay
 frame-relay lmi-type ansi

interface Serial1.2 point-to-point
 ip address 10.255.0.5 255.255.255.252
 frame-relay interface-dlci 102

interface Serial1.3 point-to-point
 ip address 10.255.0.9 255.255.255.252
 frame-relay interface-dlci 103

router eigrp 10
 network 10.0.0.0
```

Listing 9.42   Router R2's configuration.

```
interface Ethernet0
 ip address 172.16.1.1 255.255.255.0

interface Serial0
 no ip address
 encapsulation frame-relay
 frame-relay lmi-type ansi

interface Serial0.1 point-to-point
 ip address 10.255.0.6 255.255.255.252
 frame-relay interface-dlci 201

router eigrp 10
 network 10.0.0.0
 network 172.16.0.0
```

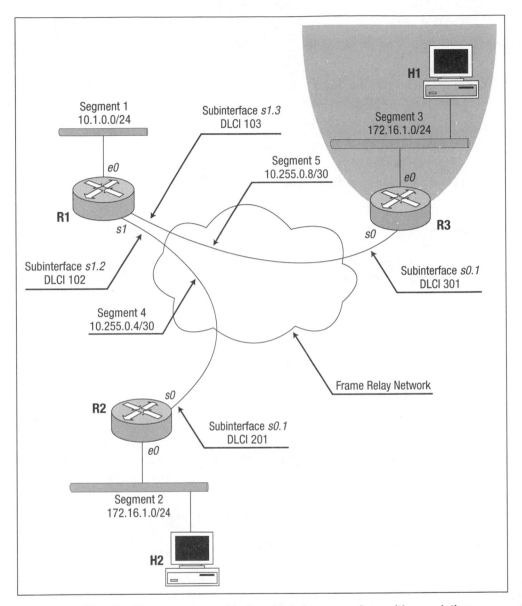

Figure 9.9   The IP address space used in the shaded area overlaps with an existing
IP address space (segment 2).

Listing 9.43   Router R3's configuration.

```
interface Loopback0
 ip address 10.100.0.1 255.255.255.0

interface Ethernet0
 ip address 172.16.1.1 255.255.255.0
```

```
 ip nat inside

interface Serial0
 no ip address
 encapsulation frame-relay
 frame-relay lmi-type ansi

interface Serial0.1 point-to-point
 ip address 10.255.0.10 255.255.255.252
 ip nat outside
 frame-relay interface-dlci 301

router eigrp 10
 network 10.0.0.0

ip nat pool ext172 10.200.0.30 10.200.0.80 prefix-length 24
ip nat pool int172 10.100.0.50 10.100.0.100 prefix-length 24
ip nat inside source list 1 pool int172
ip nat outside source list 1 pool ext172

ip route 10.200.0.0 255.255.255.0 10.255.0.9

access-list 1 permit 172.16.1.0 0.0.0.255
```

NOTE: *Although two different NAT pools are used to translate outside global addresses and inside local addresses, the access list to match the IP datagrams that establish the NAT table entries remains the same for the inside and outside networks. This happens because the translated IP address spaces are overlapped and therefore can be matched using the same access list. However, a single access list in this NAT configuration is not a requirement.*

The NAT table of router R3 is shown in Listing 9.44.

Listing 9.44   The NAT table of router R3.

```
R3#show ip nat translations
Pro Inside global  Inside local  Outside local Outside global
-- 10.100.0.50     172.16.1.111  --            --
-- --              --            10.200.0.31   172.16.1.1
-- --              --            10.200.0.30   172.16.1.120
-- 10.100.0.50     172.16.1.111  10.200.0.30   172.16.1.120
```

Configuring NAT for TCP Load Balancing

As explained in the "In Brief" section in this chapter, it is possible to use NAT for load balancing. This version of NAT is called *Load Sharing Using IP Network Address Translation (LSNAT)*. This NAT technology is documented in RFC 2391.

If you have multiple servers that run the same service that is accessible via the network (such as a Web or File Transfer Protocol—FTP—server), you can use LSNAT to allow network access to the service via a single IP address—called a *virtual server IP address*—still using all of the servers. A router performing LSNAT redistributes the connections incoming on that IP address to this service via all of the servers by translating the virtual server IP address into the real servers' IP addresses. Once such a connection is established, all subsequent packets of that connection are forwarded to only the same server that was originally chosen.

The first packet of those connections is used to establish a corresponding entry in the NAT table of the router. The segments on which the real servers reside are inside networks, and the segments on which the hosts accessing the service via the virtual server IP address reside are outside networks.

To configure LSNAT, follow these steps:

1. Define the pool of IP addresses into which the virtual server IP address will be translated. All of the addresses that the pool defines must be the IP addresses of existing servers. If the IP addresses of the existing servers are not contiguous, you have to define a noncontiguous pool.

   Define the pool using the same command syntax as described in "Configuring Dynamic Translation of Inside IP Addresses" earlier in this chapter with the keywords **type rotary** appended at the end.

2. Create an access list that matches the virtual server IP address with the **permit** result.

3. Establish an association between the virtual server IP address and the pool using the command **ip nat inside destination list {**<*AL number*>|<*AL name*>**} pool** <*pool name*>.

4. Apply NAT on the interfaces connected to the segments on which the real servers reside using the **ip nat inside** command in interface configuration mode.

5. Apply NAT on the interfaces connected to the segments with the global outside addresses using the **ip nat outside** command in interface configuration mode.

NOTE: *The virtual server IP address must appear to be accessible via the router performing NAT.*

Figure 9.10 shows an example of a network that is suitable for deploying LSNAT. Servers S1 and S2 run the Telnet service, which is supposed to be accessible by hosts H1 and H2 via a single IP address.

9. Special Cases of Routing

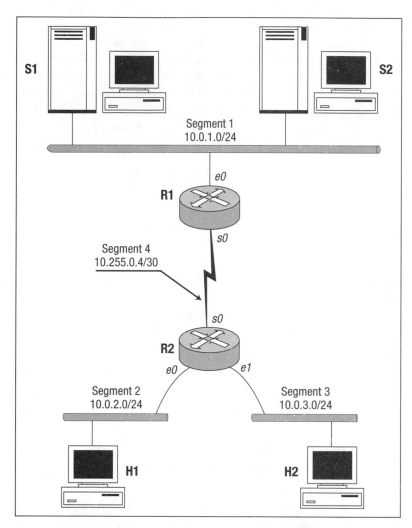

Figure 9.10   Router R1 performs load balancing of TCP sessions to servers S1 and S2.

Listings 9.45 and 9.46 show the configurations of routers R1 and R2. Notice that—because the servers' IP addresses (10.0.1.111 and 10.0.1.222) collectively constitute a noncontiguous address space—we are forced to use a noncontiguous NAT pool.

Listing 9.45   Router R1's configuration.

```
interface Ethernet0
 ip address 10.0.1.1 255.255.255.0
 ip nat inside

interface Serial0
 ip address 10.255.0.5 255.255.255.252
 ip nat outside
```

```
router eigrp 10
 network 10.0.0.0

ip nat pool Servers prefix-length 24 type rotary
 address 10.0.1.111 10.0.1.111
 address 10.0.1.222 10.0.1.222

ip nat inside destination list 1 pool Servers

access-list 1 permit 10.0.1.100
```

Listing 9.46   Router R2's configuration.

```
interface Ethernet0
 ip address 10.0.2.1 255.255.255.0

interface Ethernet1
 ip address 10.0.3.1 255.255.255.0

interface Serial0
 ip address 10.255.0.6 255.255.255.252

router eigrp 10
 network 10.0.0.0
```

Listing 9.47 shows the results of telnetting from hosts H1 and H2 to the virtual server IP address. The output clearly indicates that, although the same destination IP address is used, the Telnet sessions are connected to the two different servers. (The shaded lines show servers S1 and S2.)

Listing 9.47   The results of telnetting the virtual server IP address from hosts H1 and H2.

```
H1# telnet 10.0.1.100

Welcome to the Telnet Service on S1

Username:

H2# telnet 10.0.1.100

Welcome to the Telnet Service on S2

Username:
```

Listings 9.48 and 9.49 show the outputs of the **netstat -n** command entered on servers S1 and S2, respectively. The outputs show the server's local IP addresses with which router R1 replaces the virtual server IP address.

9. Special Cases of Routing

Listing 9.48 The output of the **netstat -n** command entered on server S1.

```
C:\WINDOWS\system32>netstat -n

Active Connections

  Proto  Local Address        Foreign Address      State
  TCP    10.0.1.111:23        10.0.2.120:11004     ESTABLISHED
  TCP    127.0.0.1:1025       127.0.0.1:1026       ESTABLISHED
  TCP    127.0.0.1:1026       127.0.0.1:1025       ESTABLISHED
```

Listing 9.49 The output of the **netstat -n** command entered on server S2.

```
C:\WINDOWS\system32>netstat -n

Active Connections

  Proto  Local Address        Foreign Address      State
  TCP    10.0.1.222:23        10.0.3.120:11005     ESTABLISHED
  TCP    127.0.0.1:1025       127.0.0.1:1026       ESTABLISHED
  TCP    127.0.0.1:1026       127.0.0.1:1025       ESTABLISHED
```

The NAT table of router R1 is shown below:

```
R1#show ip nat translations
Pro Inside global   Inside local    Outside local       Outside global
tcp 10.0.1.100:23   10.0.1.222:23   10.0.3.120:11005    10.0.3.120:11005
tcp 10.0.1.100:23   10.0.1.111:23   10.0.2.120:11004    10.0.2.120:11004
```

Configuring HSRP

Configuring basic HSRP, using Multigroup HSRP for load balancing, and using HSRP in backup scenarios are covered in this section.

Configuring Basic HSRP

Two or more Cisco routers can be configured for HSRP on their interfaces connected to the same LAN segment. To perform basic HSRP configuration, perform the following steps in interface configuration mode:

1. Use the command **standby** [*<group #>*] **ip** [*<IP address>*] to enable an HSRP process on an interface. The optional *<group #>* parameter is the standby group number; the parameter is numeric and ranges from 0 through 3 for token ring interfaces and from 0 through 255 for all other LAN interfaces. If omitted, the parameter defaults to 0. The optional *<IP address>* parameter specifies the virtual IP address (the IP address, which the hosts residing on the segment must use as the default gateway); if this

parameter is omitted, the router will wait until it receives a Hello PDU from the active router, from which it will learn the virtual IP address. The *<IP address>* parameter is specified in dotted decimal notation.

NOTE: *The remaining steps are optional.*

---

2. The command **standby** *<group #>* **priority** *<priority>* can be used to assign an HSRP router priority. The *<priority>* parameter specifies the HSRP priority of the router for HSRP group *<group #>*. The parameter is numeric and ranges from 0 through 255. The highest priority must be assigned to the router that must become the active router for the HSRP group. If this command is not entered, the router uses the default HSRP priority of 100.

3. The command **standby** *<group #>* **preempt** permits the router to supersede the current active or standby router, if its HSRP priority is ever higher than that of the active or standby router. The presence of this command on the active or standby router ensures that, if it temporarily loses its state (standby or active) because its priority decreased or it went down, it will regain the state once it recovers.

4. The command **standby** *<group #>* **track** *<interface>* [*<priority decrease>*] makes the router decrease its HSRP priority if the interface *<interface>* goes down (logically or physically). The *<priority decrease>* parameter, if used, specifies the amount by which the router's priority must be decreased; if omitted, it defaults to 10.

Let's consider the network example shown in Figure 9.11. Routers R1 and R2 can be configured for HSRP to provide a redundant default router for the hosts connected on segment 1.

Listings 9.50 through 9.52 show the configurations of all three routers.

Listing 9.50   Router R1's configuration.

```
interface Ethernet0
 ip address 10.1.0.2 255.255.255.0
 no ip redirects
 standby 10 priority 100
 standby 10 preempt
 standby 10 ip 10.1.0.1
 standby 10 track Serial0 50

interface Serial0
 ip address 10.3.0.1 255.255.255.0

router eigrp 1
 network 10.0.0.0
```

9. Special Cases of Routing

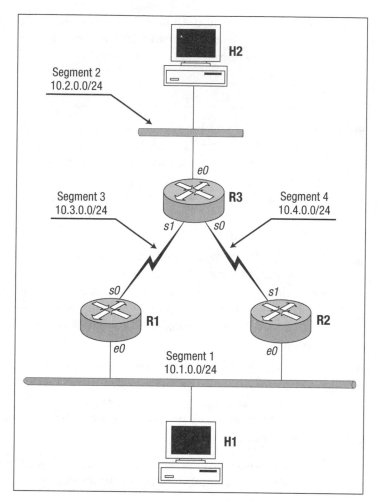

Figure 9.11   Routers R1 and R2 are configured with HSRP to back each other up in case either one of them (or one of their interfaces) fails.

Listing 9.51   Router R2's configuration.

```
interface Ethernet0
 ip address 10.1.0.3 255.255.255.0
 no ip redirects
 standby 10 priority 80
 standby 10 preempt
 standby 10 ip 10.1.0.1

interface Serial1
 ip address 10.4.0.1 255.255.255.0

router eigrp 1
 network 10.0.0.0
```

Listing 9.52   Router R3's configuration.

```
interface Ethernet0
  ip address 10.2.0.1 255.255.255.0

interface Serial0
  ip address 10.4.0.2 255.255.255.0

interface Serial1
  ip address 10.3.0.2 255.255.255.0

router eigrp 1
  network 10.0.0.0
```

NOTE: *The **no redirects** command is added automatically by the router itself when an HSRP process becomes enabled on the interface. This command prevents the router from generating ICMP redirect messages if it is requested to forward a datagram whose destination is best reachable through another router.*

The command that can be used to verify the status of HSRP is **show standby** [*<interface>* [*<group>*]]. The optional parameters *<interface>* and *<group>* allow the output of the command to be limited to the desired interface and the HSRP group on that interface. An alternative format of the command is **show standby brief**, which displays the HSRP-related information in a compact form.

Listings 9.53 and 9.54 show the output of the **show standby** command entered on routers R1 and R2. As you can see, the output of the commands displays the HSRP parameters and internal states in an easily readable form.

Listing 9.53   The output of the **show standby** command entered on router R1.

```
R1#show standby
Ethernet0 - Group 10
  Local state is Active, priority 100, may preempt
  Hellotime 3 holdtime 10
  Next hello sent in 00:00:01.056
  Hot standby IP address is 10.1.0.1 configured
  Active router is local
  Standby router is 10.1.0.3 expired
  Standby virtual mac address is 0000.0c07.ac0a
  Tracking interface states for 1 interface, 1 up:
    Up   Serial0 Priority decrement: 50
```

Listing 9.54   The output of the **show standby** command entered on router R2.

```
R2#show standby
Ethernet0 - Group 10
  Local state is Standby, priority 80, may preempt
```

```
Hellotime 3 holdtime 10
Next hello sent in 00:00:01.546
Hot standby IP address is 10.1.0.1 configured
Active router is 10.1.0.2 expires in 00:00:09
Standby router is local
Standby virtual mac address is 0000.0c07.ac0a
```

As mentioned in the "In Depth" section, depending on the interface hardware type, the virtual MAC address may or may not be the same as the MAC address of the active router's interface on which HSRP is enabled. Routers R1's Ethernet0 interface is an example of hardware that forces the router to use the same MAC address as the interface MAC address and the virtual MAC address. Hence, the router changes the MAC address of the interface to the value of the virtual MAC address.

Below are the first two lines of the output of the **show interfaces Ethernet0** command entered on router R1:

```
R1#show interfaces Ethernet0
Ethernet0 is up, line protocol is up
  Hardware is Lance, address is 0000.0c07.ac0a (bia 00e0.b064.5063)
...
```

The first italicized text element in the output shows the current MAC address of the interface Ethernet0; the second one shows the original "burned-in" MAC address of the interface (labeled *bia* for b̲urned-i̲n a̲ddress).

Nevertheless, router R2 still uses the original MAC address as the interface MAC address (as the first two lines of the output—shown below—of the **show interfaces Ethernet0** command suggest):

```
R2#show interfaces Ethernet 0
Ethernet0 is up, line protocol is up
  Hardware is Lance, address is 00e0.b064.30a9 (bia 00e0.b064.30a9)
...
```

However, if router R1 fails and router R2 becomes the active router, router R2 changes the interface MAC address to the value of the virtual MAC address, unless its interface hardware allows different interface and virtual MAC addresses.

Remember from the "In Depth" section that a segment can have only one active and one standby router. If more than two routers are attached to a segment, the remaining routers must be in the Listen state during stable HSRP operation. Thus, if we connect another HSRP router to segment 1 whose interface Ethernet0 configuration is as shown in Listing 9.55, its state should be Listen. (The router is called R4 in Listing 9.56; this router is not shown in Figure 9.11.)

Listing 9.55   The configuration of interface Ethernet0 of router R4.

```
interface Ethernet0
 ip address 10.1.0.4 255.255.255.0
 no ip redirects
 standby 1 priority 50
 standby 1 preempt
 standby 1 ip 10.1.0.1
```

Listing 9.56, which shows the output of the **show standby** command entered on router R4, confirms that the state of the HSRP process on the Ethernet0 interface of this router is Listen.

Listing 9.56   The output of the show standby command entered on router R4.

```
R4#show standby
Ethernet0 - Group 10
  Local state is Listen, priority 50, may preempt
  Hellotime 3 holdtime 10
  Hot standby IP address is 10.1.0.1 configured
  Active router is 10.1.0.2 expires in 00:00:08
  Standby router is 10.1.0.3 expires in 00:00:07
```

Let's now see what happens if router R1 becomes temporarily unavailable on segment 1. The message shown below soon appears on the console of router R2; it serves as a notification that router R2 is now the active router:

```
R2#
%STANDBY-6-STATECHANGE: Standby: 10: Ethernet0 state Standby -> Active
```

Let's now examine how long it takes the routers to switch over the virtual MAC and IP addresses to the new active router. To do this, I used a simple **perl** script that ran the **ping** command with the specified IP address—10.2.0.120, host H2's IP address—every second and displayed its output. (The **perl** script itself can be found in Appendix D.)

Listing 9.57 shows the output of the **perl** script as it appears on host H1.

Listing 9.57   The output of the ping 10.2.0.120 command executed on host H1 from within the perl script, which also printed the time when the command was executed.

```
C:\>perl tping.pl 10.2.0.120
[41:25] Reply from 10.2.0.120: bytes=32 time=10ms TTL=126
[41:26] Reply from 10.2.0.120: bytes=32 time=10ms TTL=126
[41:27] Reply from 10.2.0.120: bytes=32 time=10ms TTL=126
[41:28] Reply from 10.2.0.120: bytes=32 time=10ms TTL=126
```

9. Special Cases of Routing

```
[41:30] Request timed out.
[41:32] Request timed out.
[41:34] Request timed out.
[41:36] Request timed out.
[41:37] Reply from 10.2.0.120: bytes=32 time=10ms TTL=126
[41:38] Reply from 10.2.0.120: bytes=32 time=10ms TTL=126
[41:39] Reply from 10.2.0.120: bytes=32 time=10ms TTL=126
[41:40] Reply from 10.2.0.120: bytes=32 time=10ms TTL=126
[41:41] Reply from 10.2.0.120: bytes=32 time=10ms TTL=126
```

As the output shows, the default router was unavailable for only 4 seconds.

NOTE: *The timeout can also depend upon the routing protocol convergence time. Even if the standby router has already taken over the virtual MAC and IP addresses, the routing protocol can still be converging.*

If we restore router R1, we may not see any timeout (shown in Listing 9.58), because the previous active router supersedes the current active router. Therefore, one of these routers is available all the time.

Listing 9.58 **The perl script executing the ping 10.2.0.120 command was started, and router R1 was then made available. As the output shows, no timeout was detected when router R1 became the active router.**

```
C:\>perl tping.pl 10.2.0.120
[46:03] Reply from 10.2.0.120: bytes=32 time=20ms TTL=126
[46:04] Reply from 10.2.0.120: bytes=32 time=10ms TTL=126
[46:05] Reply from 10.2.0.120: bytes=32 time=10ms TTL=126
[46:06] Reply from 10.2.0.120: bytes=32 time=11ms TTL=126
[46:07] Reply from 10.2.0.120: bytes=32 time=10ms TTL=126
[46:08] Reply from 10.2.0.120: bytes=32 time=10ms TTL=126
[46:09] Reply from 10.2.0.120: bytes=32 time=10ms TTL=126
[46:10] Reply from 10.2.0.120: bytes=32 time=10ms TTL=126
[46:11] Reply from 10.2.0.120: bytes=32 time=10ms TTL=126
[46:12] Reply from 10.2.0.120: bytes=32 time=10ms TTL=126
[46:13] Reply from 10.2.0.120: bytes=32 time=10ms TTL=126
[46:14] Reply from 10.2.0.120: bytes=32 time=10ms TTL=126
[46:15] Reply from 10.2.0.120: bytes=32 time=10ms TTL=126
[46:16] Reply from 10.2.0.120: bytes=32 time=10ms TTL=126
```

Using MHSRP for Load Balancing

Using two routers just to back up each other is a waste of routing resources. However, using the same two routers to also share the load of traffic requested by the local hosts is an efficient utilization of resources.

This sharing of resources can be addressed by modifying the basic HSRP configuration (sometimes called MHSRP). The idea behind MHSRP is simple. If two routes are configured with two standby groups on the same interfaces, the first router can be active for the first group, and the second router can be active for the second group. Obviously, the two groups can be used only to back up two IP addresses. Therefore, the local hosts should be divided into two groups: The first group must use the first IP address—the second group, the second IP address. Thus, the first group of hosts sends all outbound traffic to the first router, and the second group sends all outbound traffic to the second router.

The steps that must be taken to configure MHSRP on a router remain the same as those for the basic HSRP configuration. The only difference is that these steps must be taken for each standby group configured on the same interface.

Let's see how the routers from Figure 9.12 should be configured for MHSRP to provide two redundant default routers for hosts H1 and H2. Host H1 uses the first "redundant" IP address—host H2, the second IP address.

Listings 9.59 and 9.60 show the configurations of routers R1 and R2. The configuration of router R3 remains exactly the same as in the previous section.

Listing 9.59   Router R1's configuration.

```
interface Serial0
 ip address 10.3.0.1 255.255.255.0

interface TokenRing0
 ip address 10.1.0.3 255.255.255.0
 no ip redirects
 ring-speed 16
 standby 1 priority 100
 standby 1 preempt
 standby 1 ip 10.1.0.1
 standby 1 track Serial0 50
 standby 2 priority 80
 standby 2 preempt
 standby 2 ip 10.1.0.2

router eigrp 1
 network 10.0.0.0
```

Listing 9.60   Router R2's configuration.

```
interface Serial1
 ip address 10.4.0.1 255.255.255.0

interface TokenRing0
 ip address 10.1.0.4 255.255.255.0
 no ip redirects
 ring-speed 16
```

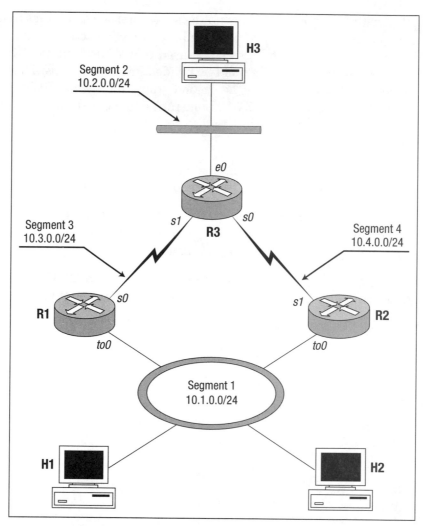

Figure 9.12   Routers R1 and R2 perform load balancing by being configured for two standby groups. Router R1 is the primary router in the first group, and router R2 is the primary router in the second group.

```
standby 1 priority 80
standby 1 preempt
standby 1 ip 10.1.0.1
standby 2 priority 100
standby 2 preempt
standby 2 ip 10.1.0.2
standby 2 track Serial1 50

router eigrp 1
 network 10.0.0.0
```

Listings 9.61 and 9.62 show the outputs of the **show standby** command entered on routers R1 and R2. Notice that the **show standby** command now displays two standby groups for each router. Router R1 is the active router for group 1 and the standby router for group 2, whereas router R2 is the active router for group 2 and the standby router for group 1.

Listing 9.61   The output of the show standby command entered on router R1.

```
R1#show standby
TokenRing0 - Group 1
  Local state is Active, priority 100, may preempt
  Hellotime 3 holdtime 10
  Next hello sent in 00:00:00.000
  Hot standby IP address is 10.1.0.1 configured
  Active router is local
  Standby router is 10.1.0.4 expired
  Standby virtual mac address is c000.0002.0000
  Tracking interface states for 1 interface, 1 up:
    Up   Serial0 Priority decrement: 50
TokenRing0 - Group 2
  Local state is Standby, priority 80, may preempt
  Hellotime 3 holdtime 10
  Next hello sent in 00:00:02.486
  Hot standby IP address is 10.1.0.2 configured
  Active router is 10.1.0.4 expires in 00:00:08
  Standby router is local
  Standby virtual mac address is c000.0004.0000
```

Listing 9.62   The output of the show standby command entered on router R2.

```
R2#show standby
TokenRing0 - Group 1
  Local state is Standby, priority 80, may preempt
  Hellotime 3 holdtime 10
  Next hello sent in 00:00:01.268
  Hot standby IP address is 10.1.0.1 configured
  Active router is 10.1.0.3 expires in 00:00:09
  Standby router is local
  Standby virtual mac address is c000.0002.0000
TokenRing0 - Group 2
  Local state is Active, priority 100, may preempt
  Hellotime 3 holdtime 10
  Next hello sent in 00:00:00.496
  Hot standby IP address is 10.1.0.2 configured
  Active router is local
  Standby router is 10.1.0.3 expired
  Standby virtual mac address is c000.0004.0000
  Tracking interface states for 1 interface, 1 up:
    Up   Serial1 Priority decrement: 50
```

Listing 9.63 shows the output of the **show interfaces TokenRing0** command entered on routers R1 and R2. Notice how the interface hardware now allows the routers to use different virtual and interface MAC addresses.

Listing 9.63   The output of the show interfaces TokenRing 0 command entered on routers R1 and R2.

```
R1#show interfaces TokenRing 0
TokenRing0 is up, line protocol is up
  Hardware is TMS380, address is 0007.0d26.0a46 (bia 0007.0d26.0a46)
...


R2#show interfaces TokenRing 0
TokenRing0 is up, line protocol is up
  Hardware is TMS380, address is 0007.0d26.0c15 (bia 0007.0d26.0c15)
...
```

NOTE: As mentioned before, some interface hardware does not support different virtual and interface MAC addresses. The reason is that this hardware does not allow assigning multiple unicast MAC addresses on the same interface. Subsequently, MHSRP cannot be implemented on such hardware, because different standby groups require different virtual MAC addresses.

Using HSRP in Backup Scenarios

One more network scenario can benefit from HSRP. Unlike the examples in the previous two sections, which were quite generic, the scenario presented in this section is somewhat specific. It pertains primarily to remote branches whose network consists of a few segments interconnected with two routers, which also provide connectivity of the branch's network to the central site. Furthermore, one of the routers is connected to the central site with a high-capacity link, whereas the other router is separately connected to the central site with a smaller-capacity link. The routers also implement HSRP on the branch's LAN segments.

An example of this network scenario is shown in Figure 9.13. Routers R1 and R2 are the branch routers, and the branch has only a single token ring segment, on which the routers implement HSRP. Router R1 is interconnected with the central site's router R3 with a high-capacity Frame Relay permanent virtual circuit (PVC); router R2 is interconnected with the central site's router R4 with a dial-up serial connection.

Notice segment 2. At first, it may seem unusual: Its network prefix allows only two hosts to reside on it. These two hosts are routers R1 and R2. Why is this segment even needed?

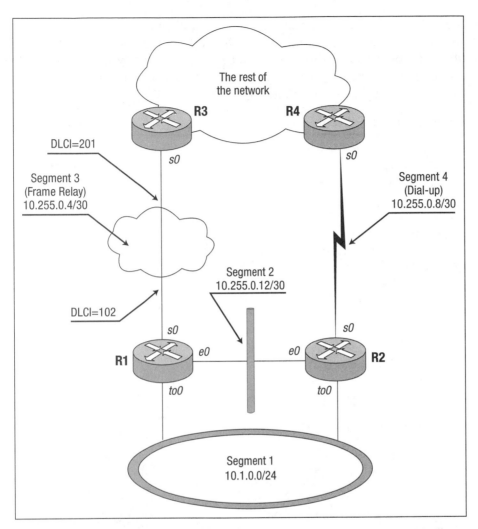

Figure 9.13   Routers R1 and R2 implement HSRP for segment 1; segment 2 allows
router R2 to utilize high-capacity Frame Relay segment 3 if router R1's
TokenRing0 interface fails.

To answer this question, let's consider what happens if different components of
the network fail. If the Serial0 interface of router R1, or the Frame Relay PVC
between routers R1 and R3 fails, the HSRP process on router R1 should obviously
detect it and thus lower its priority to let router R2 become the active router.
After that, all traffic addressed to the destinations that are reachable through the
central site will flow through router R2 and the link between it and router R4.

If the TokenRing0 interface of router R2 fails, router R2 will eventually detect it
and become the active router for segment 1. Notice, however, that the failure of

router R1's TokenRing0 interface does not impair in any way the Frame Relay connection between routers R1 and R3. But, if there were no Ethernet segment 2, router R2 would route all traffic through the low-capacity link between it and router R4. Therefore, the presence of segment 2 addresses the situation that arises from the failure of the TokenRing0 interface of router R1.

The configurations of routers R1 and R2 are shown in Listings 9.64 and 9.65.

Listing 9.64 Router R1's configuration.

```
interface Ethernet0
 ip address 10.255.0.13 255.255.255.252

interface Serial0
 encapsulation frame-relay

interface Serial0.1 multipoint
 bandwidth 4000
 ip address 10.255.0.5 255.255.255.252
 frame-relay map ip 10.255.0.6 102 broadcast

interface TokenRing0
 ip address 10.0.1.2 255.255.255.0
 ring-speed 16
 standby 1 priority 110 preempt
 standby 1 ip 10.0.1.1
 standby 1 track Serial0.1 50

router eigrp 10
 network 10.0.0.0
```

Listing 9.65 Router R2's configuration.

```
interface Ethernet0
 ip address 10.255.0.14 255.255.255.252

interface Serial0
 bandwidth 64
 ip address 10.255.0.9 255.255.255.252

interface TokenRing0
 ip address 10.0.1.3 255.255.255.0
 ring-speed 16
 standby 1 priority 80
 standby 1 preempt
 standby 1 ip 10.0.1.1
```

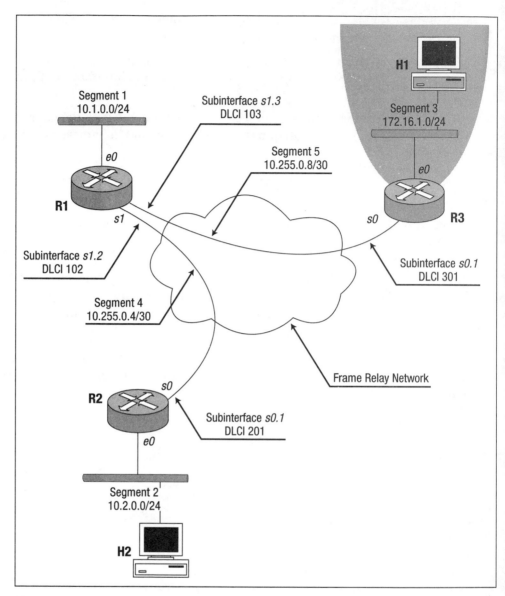

Figure 9.8   The shaded area denotes an illegal address space from the perspective of the rest of the network.

Listing 9.21   Router R2's configuration.

```
interface Ethernet0
 ip address 10.2.0.1 255.255.255.0

interface Serial0
 no ip address
```

```
router eigrp 10
 network 10.0.0.0
```

The shaded lines show the bandwidth statements that reflect the actual band-width of the corresponding segments. These statements are necessary for EIGRP to prefer segment 3 to segment 4, if segment 3 is available.

Below is the output of the **traceroute 10.100.0.1** command entered on a host residing on segment 1 when no network component failed (the host is now shown in Figure 9.13; IP address 10.100.0.1 is available through routers R3 and R4):

```
C:\>tracert -d 10.100.0.1

Tracing route to 10.100.0.1 over a maximum of 30 hops

  1    <10 ms    <10 ms    <10 ms   10.0.1.2
  2     10 ms    <10 ms     10 ms   10.100.0.1

Trace complete.
```

If the Frame Relay PVC fails, router R1 detects it and lowers its HSRP priority so that router R2 becomes the active router. After this happens, the output of the **traceroute 10.100.0.1** command changes as follows:

```
C:\>tracert -d 10.100.0.1

Tracing route to 10.100.0.1 over a maximum of 30 hops

  1    <10 ms    <10 ms     10 ms   10.0.1.3
  2     20 ms     20 ms     30 ms   10.255.0.10
  3     20 ms     30 ms     30 ms   10.100.0.1

Trace complete.
```

The shaded line shows that the second hop of the route is router R4, which con-firms that the traffic goes through the dial-up link between routers R2 and R4.

Finally, if the TokenRing0 interface of router R1 fails, router R2 eventually de-tects this and becomes the active router for segment 1. Still, router R2 perceives the destinations shown as "The rest of the network" cloud in Figure 9.13 as best reachable through segment 2, which connects router R2 to router R1. Evidence of this can be seen in the output of the **traceroute 10.100.0.1** command shown below (the command was entered on the host after router R2 becomes the active router following the failure of router R1's TokenRing0 interface):

9. Special Cases of Routing

```
C:\>tracert -d 10.100.0.1

Tracing route to 10.100.0.1 over a maximum of 30 hops

  1    10 ms    <10 ms    <10 ms   10.0.1.3
  2    <10 ms   <10 ms     10 ms   10.255.0.13
  3    10 ms    <10 ms     10 ms   10.100.0.1

Trace complete.
```

The shaded line shows that the second hop of the route for the destination is router R1.

Appendix A

Connecting Two Cisco Routers
Back-to-Back

For testing purposes, you'll find it sometimes necessary to connect two Cisco routers back-to-back through their serial interfaces. (For instance, many of the examples used in this book were devised in a lab in which routers were connected this way.)

A normal serial line involves two types of communication equipment: data terminal equipment (DTE) and data communication equipment (DCE). Because the DTE is physically interconnected by the serial connection, it resides at the ends of the serial connection. Routers and hosts are typical examples of DTE. The other type of equipment, DCE, provides the logical interface between the physical line and the DTE. A typical example of serial line DCE is DSU/CSU. DTE must always be connected to DCE, and two DCE devices are interconnected via the physical line.

When two routers are interconnected back-to-back via their serial interfaces, one of them must be DTE and the other DCE. Although this configuration does not represent a true serial connection—which typically consists of the chain DTE to DCE to another DCE to DTE—it's still legitimate because DTE is connected to DCE.

However, the connectors of the serial interfaces on the Cisco routers are neither DTE nor DCE. Furthermore, the connectors are proprietary. The most typical of them is a 60-pin, high-density connector, but there are other types of connectors (primarily on the older models of routers).

A serial interface of a Cisco router "becomes" either DCE or DTE depending on the cable that is attached to the interface connector. In addition, the cable makes the interface of the standard type, such as X.21, V.35, and so on. Once the cable is attached, the router immediately detects the cable type and whether it is DTE or DCE. After this detection procedure, the router sets up the appropriate parameters on the interface.

The attached cable's type and whether it is DCE or DTE can be verified by examining the second line of the output of the command **show controllers Serial** <*interface #*>. (A space must be present between the **Serial** and <*interface #*> parameters, or the command produces an error.) Sample output of this command is shown below:

```
R1#show controllers Serial 0
HD unit 0, idb = 0x10D474, driver structure at 0x1148D8
buffer size 1524  HD unit 0, V.35 DCE cable
cpb = 0xE4, eda = 0xC140, cda = 0xC000
...
```

We're interested in the shaded line. Notice the type of cable—V.35 DCE cable—at the end of the shaded line. The same command issued for the Serial1 interface (to which a DTE cable is attached) is shown below:

```
R1#show controllers Serial 1
HD unit 1, idb = 0x119B60, driver structure at 0x120FC8
buffer size 1524  HD unit 1, V.35 DTE cable
cpb = 0xE5, eda = 0xA940, cda = 0xA800
...
```

The serial interfaces on most models of Cisco routers are synchronous and therefore require a source of clocking. In real life, clocking is typically supplied by the serial line DCE, such as CSUs/DSUs. However, in the case of routers connected back-to-back, no such equipment exists. So, one of the routers must provide clocking. The router that can physically provide clocking is the one to which the DCE cable is attached. The command that enables clocking on a serial interface is **clock rate** *<value>*. The *<value>* parameter specifies the speed of the connection and is measured in bits per second (bps). Depending on the version of the IOS, the router may or may not be able to display the available values using the syntax **clock rate ?**. In general, the values shown in Table A.1 should work with most versions of IOS. Values available for use with the **clock rate** command are as follows:

- 1200
- 2400
- 4800
- 9600
- 19200
- 38400
- 56000
- 64000
- 72000
- 125000
- 148000
- 250000

- 500000
- 800000
- 1000000
- 1300000
- 2000000
- 4000000

Alternatively, the **clock rate** command can be entered as a single word (e.g., **clockrate** *<value>*). However, contrary to intuition, **clockrate ?** won't work.

Appendix B

Configuring Cisco Routers for Frame Relay Switching

The following guidelines explain how to configure a Cisco router to perform Frame Relay switching:

1. Enable Frame Relay switching by entering the **Frame Relay switching** command in the global configuration mode.

2. Configure Frame Relay encapsulation using the **encapsulation Frame Relay** command in configuration mode of the serial interfaces on which Frame Relay switching is to be performed.

3. Using the command **Frame Relay intf-type dce**, configure the serial interfaces as Frame Relay DCE interfaces. This command actually makes the router behave as a Frame Relay switch on the corresponding interfaces. By default, interfaces configured with Frame Relay encapsulation are Frame Relay DTE interfaces.

NOTE: *The interfaces that you configure for Frame Relay DCE do not have to be physical DCE interfaces. In other words, an interface can still be configured as Frame Relay DCE even if it has a DTE cable attached to it. Similarly, an interface can be configured as Frame Relay DTE even if it has a DCE cable attached.*

---

4. Establish the desired Frame Relay PVC switching using the command **Frame Relay route** *<input DLCI>* **interface** *<interface> <output DLCI>* in the interface configuration mode of the interfaces that are involved in Frame Relay switching. The *<input DLCI>* parameter is the DLCI of the PVC that this interface must service. The *<interface>* parameter specifies the interface to which the PVC must be switched. This parameter does not necessarily have to be a serial interface, just any interface that supports the transmission of Frame Relay traffic. Possible choices include (but are not limited to) Serial, HSSI, and Tunnel interfaces. Finally, the *<output DLCI>* parameter defines the DLCI of the PVC on the output interface.

NOTE: Whether the Tunnel interface supports transmission of Frame Relay traffic or not depends on the feature set of IOS. If the keyword **Tunnel** is not available in the **Frame Relay route** command, try switching to a higher feature set of the IOS.

5. Optionally, you can configure a desired LMI type using the command **frame-relay lmi-type {ansi|cisco|q933a}** under the configuration of the interfaces involved in Frame Relay switching. By default, the LMI type is **cisco**.

Let's examine the configurations of the routers from Figure B.1.

Figure B.1 demonstrates a very economical way to implement Frame Relay switching in a lab if your routers have a maximum of only two serial interfaces. This solution also employs normally forgotten AUX lines of the routers as Async (asynchronous) interfaces, thus allowing you to use the remaining interfaces possibly at some other locations of the network.

NOTE: The auxiliary interface is intended as an alternative console port. Unlike the console port, however, the auxiliary port has the complete RS-232 pinouts and therefore can be used to connect a router to a modem. Alternatively, the auxiliary port can be used as an asynchronous interface, as described in this section.

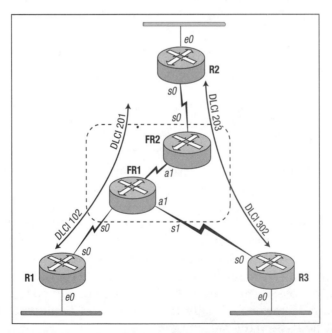

Figure B.1   Routers FR1 and FR2 are configured for Frame Relay switching.

Listings B.1 through B.5 show the configuration of all five routers. Only routers FR1 and FR2 implement Frame Relay switching.

Listing B.1   Router FR1's configuration.

```
username FR2 password 0 cisco
frame-relay switching

interface Tunnel0
 tunnel source 1.0.0.1
 tunnel destination 1.0.0.2

interface Ethernet0
 ip address 169.124.84.34 255.255.255.0

interface Serial0
 encapsulation frame-relay
 clockrate 64000
 frame-relay lmi-type ansi
 frame-relay intf-type dce
 frame-relay route 102 interface Tunnel0 421

interface Serial1
 encapsulation frame-relay
 frame-relay lmi-type ansi
 frame-relay intf-type dce
 frame-relay route 302 interface Tunnel0 423

interface Async1
 ip address 1.0.0.1 255.255.255.0
 encapsulation ppp
 async default routing
 async mode dedicated
 ppp authentication chap

line aux 0
 rxspeed 38400
 txspeed 38400
```

Listing B.2   Router FR2's configuration.

```
username FR1 password 0 cisco
frame-relay switching

interface Tunnel0
 tunnel source 1.0.0.2
 tunnel destination 1.0.0.1
```

Appendix B Configuring Cisco Routers for Frame Relay Switching

```
interface Ethernet0
 ip address 169.124.84.36 255.255.255.0

interface Serial0
 encapsulation frame-relay
 frame-relay lmi-type ansi
 frame-relay intf-type dce
 frame-relay route 201 interface Tunnel0 421
 frame-relay route 203 interface Tunnel0 423

interface Async1
 ip address 1.0.0.2 255.255.255.0
 encapsulation ppp
 async default routing
 async mode dedicated
 ppp authentication chap

line aux 0
 rxspeed 38400
 txspeed 38400
```

Listing B.3   Router R1's configuration.

```
interface Ethernet0
 ip address 10.1.0.1 255.255.255.0

interface Serial0
 encapsulation frame-relay
 frame-relay lmi-type ansi

interface Serial0.1 point-to-point
 ip address 10.255.0.10 255.255.255.248
 frame-relay interface-dlci 102
```

Listing B.4   Router R2's configuration.

```
interface Ethernet0
 ip address 10.2.0.1 255.255.255.0

interface Serial0
 ip address 10.255.0.9 255.255.255.248
 encapsulation frame-relay
 clockrate 64000
 frame-relay map ip 10.255.0.10 201 broadcast
 frame-relay map ip 10.255.0.11 203 broadcast
 frame-relay lmi-type ansi
```

Listing B.5   Router R3's configuration.

```
interface Ethernet0
 ip address 10.3.0.1 255.255.255.0

interface Serial0
 encapsulation frame-relay
 clockrate 64000
 frame-relay lmi-type ansi

interface Serial0.1 multipoint
 ip address 10.255.0.11 255.255.255.248
 frame-relay map ip 10.255.0.9 302 broadcast
```

The shaded lines in the configurations of routers FR1 and FR2 (Listings B.1 and B.2) indicate the commands that are essential to Frame Relay switching. The italicized lines indicate the commands that define Async and Tunnel interfaces.

If you decide to use the AUX line as an Async interface, prepare to be patient. You may need to try several different versions of Cisco IOS before you'll be able to stabilize the connection between two Async interfaces. If PPP used in the above example does not work, try SLIP, which is the other encapsulation available for asynchronous interfaces.

TIP: *If you have spare LAN interfaces on the routers performing Frame Relay switching, don't bother with the Async interfaces: Just configure the tunnel to run through a LAN segment to which the LAN interfaces of both routers doing Frame Relay switching are connected.*

The **show frame-relay route** command allows you to verify if Frame Relay switching is working. Listings B.6 and B.7 show the output of this command entered on routers FR1 and FR2, respectively.

Listing B.6   The output of the **show frame-relay route** command on router FR1.

```
FR1#show frame-relay route
Input Intf    Input Dlci    Output Intf    Output Dlci    Status
Serial0       102           Tunnel0        421            active
Serial1       302           Tunnel0        423            active
Tunnel0       421           Serial0        102            active
Tunnel0       423           Serial1        302            active
```

Listing B.7   The output of the **show frame-relay route** command on router FR2.

```
FR2#show frame-relay route
Input Intf    Input Dlci    Output Intf    Output Dlci    Status
Serial0       201           Tunnel0        421            active
Serial0       203           Tunnel0        423            active
```

```
Tunnel0      421       Serial0      201       active
Tunnel0      423       Serial0      203       active
```

The output of this command is very informative. The first column, labeled "Input Intf", displays the Frame Relay input interface. The next column, "Input Dlci", shows the PVC's DLCI on the input interface. The next two columns—"Output Intf" and "Output Dlci"—show the Frame Relay output interface and the PVC's DLCI on that interface, respectively. The last column, "Status", shows the status of the PVC, for which the possible values are "active" and "inactive".

Each PVC is represented by two lines in the output of the **show frame-relay route** command. Each line represents one direction in which traffic can traverse the PVC, and the two lines of a fully functional PVC must both have "active" status.

Appendix C

Using RSH and RCP with Cisco Routers

In this appendix, we'll discuss accessing Cisco routers via the RCP and RSH protocols. Cisco IOS provides the implementation of both the client and server sides of these two protocols. Therefore, not only it is possible to run RCP and RSH commands from a Cisco router, but you can use these commands to access the router itself from the external systems, such as Unix and Windows 2000.

Configuring RCP and RSH Servers

By default, however, RCP and RSH servers are not enabled on the routers. The following guidelines explain how to enable and configure RSH and RCP servers on the Cisco routers:

- To enable an RSH server on a router, use the **ip rcmd rsh-enable** command in global configuration mode.

- To enable an RCP server on a router, use the **ip rcmd rcp-enable** command.

- On most systems (including Cisco routers), RCP and RSH servers require a certain level of authentication. Normally r-style authentication is achieved by specifying which user on which system can communicate with RSH and RCP servers under which local user name. To configure r-style authentication on a Cisco router, use the command **ip rcmd remote-host** *<local username>* {*<remote IP address>*I*<remote system name>*} *<remote username>* [**enable**]. The *<local username>* parameter specifies the name configured on the router using the command **username** *<local username>*. (In some versions of IOS, the **username** command is not necessary; in other words, the **ip rcmd remote-host** command alone may suffice.) The {*<remote IP address>*I*<remote system name>*} parameter specifies either the IP address or the DNS name of the remote system that is allowed to access the router via RSH and RCP.

> **NOTE:**   *If a DNS name is used, the router must have a valid DNS configuration. However, if you do not use DNS on your routers, it makes sense to completely turn off DNS lookup by issuing the **no ip domain-lookup** command in global configuration mode. This command can also save you a lot of time if you experiment with the routers in a lab (where you normally do not use DNS), because a typo in the command line typically makes the router try to connect to a host whose DNS name is equal to the mistyped command. As the DNS server is unavailable, the router waits until the DNS request times out—which can be quite an annoying process even if you manage to stop it by entering the break keystroke (typically ^^6). If, however, the **no ip domain-lookup** command is present in the router's configuration, the router never tries to resort to DNS, and instead immediately returns an error.*

The *<remote username>* parameter specifies the name under which the remote user must be logged in on the remote system to be eligible to execute commands on the router. The RCP and RSH protocols pass this name in their PDUs (along with the other parameters) when establishing the connection.

> **NOTE:**   *The* <local username> *and* <remote username> *parameters do not have to coincide.*

The optional *<enable>* parameter specifies that authenticated remote users can issue privileged commands using RSH and manipulate the vital IOS files (such as the router's running and stored configurations and IOS images) via RCP.

Listing C.1 shows a sample router configuration that enables RSH and RCP servers.

Listing C.1   Router R1's configuration.

```
username Admin1

ip rcmd rcp-enable
ip rcmd rsh-enable
ip rcmd remote-host Admin1 10.6.0.15 Administrator enable

interface TokenRing0
 ip address 10.6.0.1 255.255.255.0
 ring-speed 16
```

Listing C.2 shows how the **rsh** command can be used on a Windows 2000 machine to execute commands on the router.

Listing C.2   The **rsh** command is used from a Windows 2000 computer to execute commands remotely on router R1.

```
C:\>rsh 10.6.0.1 -l Admin1 -n show ip route

Codes: C-connected, S-static, I-IGRP, R-RIP, M-mobile, B-BGP
  D-EIGRP, EX-EIGRP external, O-OSPF, IA-OSPF inter area
  N1-OSPF NSSA external type 1, N2-OSPF NSSA external type 2
```

```
E1-OSPF external type 1, E2-OSPF external type 2, E-EGP
i-IS-IS, L1-IS-IS level-1, L2-IS-IS level-2, *-candidate
default
 U-per-user static route, o-ODR
 T-traffic engineered route

Gateway of last resort is not set

     10.0.0.0/24 is subnetted, 1 subnets
C       10.6.0.0 is directly connected, TokenRing0
```

Notice that you have to specify the name under which you want to execute the commands on the router. In the Windows 2000 and Windows NT implementation of RSH, you'll do this by using the parameter **-l** *<remote username>*. In our case, it was **Admin1**, which is equal to the name specified on the router in the **ip rcmd remote-host** and **username** commands.

If you omit this parameter, however, the host will most probably use the name under which you've logged in on it in lieu of the *<remote username>* parameter. ("Probably" implies that the name the host will use if no name is explicitly specified in the command line depends on the operating system of the host; most operating systems use the login name.) For example, if you logged in to a Windows NT system as "Administrator", the RSH would try to log in to the remote system as "Administrator".

The output below shows that the **rsh** command fails if it is entered without the **-l** parameter.

```
C:\>rsh 10.6.0.1 -n show ip route
10.6.0.1: Permission denied.
rsh: can't establish connection
```

In some situations, it may be difficult to understand why the RSH and RCP commands won't work. An easy way to discover the reason for the failure is to use the **debug ip tcp rcmd** command.

NOTE: Although the **debug ip tcp rcmd** command is not processing intensive and therefore should not lead to high CPU utilization on the router, I advise against using it—as well as any other **debug** command—in a production environment. If you happen to have a production issue with the RCP and/or RSH authentication, try to implement the same configuration in the lab, where you can safely use the command.

For example, if the **debug ip tcp rcmd** command had been entered before the failed **rsh** command, we would see the output shown in Listing C.3.

Listing C.3   The output of the debug ip tcp rcmd command on router R1.

```
R1#debug ip tcp rcmd
RCMD transactions debugging is on
R1#
RCMD: [514 <- 10.6.0.15:1018] recv 1017\0
RCMD: [514 <- 10.6.0.15:1018] recv
 Administrator\0Administrator\0show ip route\0
RCMD: [514 <- 10.6.0.15:1018] recv —
 Administrator 10.6.0.15 Administrator not in trusted hosts database
RCMD: [514 -> 10.6.0.15:1018] send <BAD,Permission denied.>\n
```

Despite being a bit fuzzy, the output allows us to easily see why the **rsh** command failed. The second of the two shaded lines (in reality it's one line, only a bit too long) reads "**Administrator 10.6.0.15 Administrator not in trusted hosts database**". This must be interpreted as the user from host **10.6.0.15** on which he or she is logged on as **Administrator** tried to execute a command under the local name **Administrator**. The next line—containing the words "**BAD, Permission denied**"—essentially tells us that the router does not have a corresponding authentication entry for this RSH request. In other words, the router's configuration does not contain the **ip rcmd remote-host Administrator 10.6.0.15 Administrator** command.

Using RSH Clients

A client version of RSH is also available on Cisco routers. If you need to execute some command remotely using RSH, you have to use the command **rsh** {*<remote IP address>*|*<remote system name>*} [**/user** *<remote username>*] *<router command>*. The parameter **rsh** {*<remote IP address>*|*<remote system name>*} specifies the IP address or the DNS name of the remote system (such as another router). The two optional parameters, **/user** and *<remote username>*, to specify under which name you want to execute the command on the remote system.

Finally, the last parameter is the command that you want to execute.

NOTE: *If you do not log in to a router under a specific username (which can be defined using the **username** command or via some authentication mechanism such as RADIUS, TACACS+, and the like), the router will use its own name (specified in the **hostname** command) in lieu of the local login name in the RSH and RCP communication. Notice that the local username is not overwritten by the **/user <remote username>** parameter.*

To demonstrate how this note applies, let's examine what happens if we try to use the **rsh** command on a router to which we connected without specifying a username. Suppose there is another router, R2, on the same token ring segment to which router R1 (configured as shown in Listing C.1) is connected. The following output shows the result of the **rsh** command entered on router R2:

```
R2#rsh 10.6.0.1 /user Admin1 show ip route
%Permission denied.
```

If we use the **debug ip tcp rcmd** command, we'll see the reason for the failure. Listing C.4 shows the output of the **debug ip tcp rcmd** command on router R1.

Listing C.4 The output of the **debug ip tcp rcmd** command on router R1 shows that the RSH connection is made using the router name (R2) as the remote login name.

```
R1#debug ip tcp rcmd
RCMD transactions debugging is on
R1#
01:48:07: %SYS-5-CONFIG_I: Configured from console by console
01:48:37: RCMD: [514 <- 10.6.0.2:1016] recv \0
01:48:37: RCMD: [514 <- 10.6.0.2:1016] recv R2\0Admin1\0show
 ip route\0
01:48:37: RCMD: [514 <- 10.6.0.2:1016] recv —
 Admin1 10.6.0.2 R2 not in trusted hosts database
01:48:37: RCMD: [514 -> 10.6.0.2:1016] send
 <BAD,Permission denied.>\n
```

To fix the problem, the **ip rcmd remote-host Admin1 10.6.0.2 R2** command should be entered in global configuration mode of router R1.

NOTE: *As a router usually has multiple IP addresses, it is necessary to find out which one it is going to use for RCP/RSH communication before issuing **ip rcmd remote-host** commands on the remote router. If the router is configured for dynamic routing, the source IP address that it will use for RCP/RSH can change if a network change occurs. In addition, in some versions of IOS, the router won't use the secondary IP address as the source IP address in the communication that it initiates.*

Using RCP Clients

RCP is very useful if you need to download a new Cisco IOS image to a router when an RCP server is available. It is much faster and more reliable than regular TFTP, and is therefore preferable to TFTP.

You can specify the keyword **rcp** instead of **tftp** in the **copy** commands. For example, if you would like to copy an IOS image from an RCP server, you can use the **copy rcp flash** command, the output of which is shown in Listing C.5.

Listing C.5   The output of the copy rcp flash command entered on router R2.

```
R2#copy rcp flash
                    ****  NOTICE  ****
Flash load helper v1.0
This process will accept the copy options and then terminate
the current system image to use the ROM based image for the
copy. Routing functionality will not be available during
that time. If you are logged in via telnet, this connection
will terminate. Users with console access can see the results
of the copy operation.
                    ―― ******** ――

Proceed? [confirm]
Address or name of remote host []?10.6.0.1
Source username [R2]? Admin1
Source filename []? c2500-d-l.120-2a.bin
Destination filename [c2500-d-l.120-2a.bin]?
The returned username is R2(8CF68)
```

TIP: *It's a good idea to switch to the ROM version of IOS on the routers that do not support multiple images on a single flash module before downloading a new IOS image. The command that you use to switch to the ROM version of IOS depends on the router platform and the version of IOS currently running on the router. Nevertheless, all versions of the command begin with the keywords **boot system**, which are followed by version-dependent parameters. For example, in Cisco IOS version 11.1 on 2500 series routers, this command is **boot system rom**. The command must be entered in global configuration mode, after which the configuration needs to be saved in the router's NVRAM (**copy running-config startup-config** or the old-fashioned **write**), and the router itself must be rebooted.*

*If you use the ROM version of Cisco IOS, you can download a new image without reloading the router. Remember, however, that the ROM version of Cisco IOS does not support routing. You have to use the command **ip default-gateway** <IP address>, in which the <IP address> parameter is the IP address of another router that can serve as the default gateway.*

The combination of the ROM version of IOS and RCP can be very helpful if you need to upgrade the IOS image on a router at a remote location connected to your site via some type of WAN, such as Frame Relay.

The proposed solution, however, has a couple of caveats. First, the ROM version of IOS does not support authentication, such as TACACS+, so if that's in use, it must be turned off before you can save the router's configuration and reloading the router itself. Second, some old versions of ROM IOS do not support RCP. This situation has no cure other than upgrading the ROM.

Alternatively, the **rcp** command can be used on a remote host to download or upload configuration files and IOS images to and from a router. Host implementations of **rcp** typically require you to explicitly specify the names of the source and destination files. When you copy files between regular hosts (such as Unix or Windows), those names are obvious. The same isn't true, however, if you copy a file to or from a Cisco router. Table C.1 shows the names of the files on Cisco routers.

Table C.1 The names of files on Cisco routers.

File	File Name
Running configuration	running-config
Configuration stored in NVRAM	startup-config
IOS Image	*<device><filename>*

The last row requires some clarification because the file name consists of two parameters. The *<device>* parameter is the name of the router storage device on which the IOS image resides or should be placed in to. The device names are router-platform dependent. For example, on 25XX-series routers, this parameter is equal to **flash:**. On the RSMs, it can be equal to **slot0:**, **slot1:**, or **bootflash:**. The *<filename>* parameter is the name of the IOS image file—for example, **c2500-js-l.112-22.bin**.

Let's see how **rcp** can be used to manage files on the routers. Suppose the configuration of router R1 now looks as shown in Listing C.6.

Listing C.6 The RCP part of router R1's configuration.

```
R1#show run
Building configuration...

Current configuration:
!
version 12.1
no service timestamps debug uptime
no service timestamps log uptime
service password-encryption
!
hostname R1
!
enable secret 5 $1$xDmI$BV50cOxmIhblNFVG8hnCz1
!
username admin
!
!
ip subnet-zero
ip rcmd rcp-enable
ip rcmd rsh-enable
ip rcmd remote-host admin 172.16.1.201 Administrator enable
no ip domain-lookup

...
```

We'll use the **rcp** command that is available on Windows 2000/Windows NT machines. The format of the command is **rcp -b** [*<source host>*][.*<user1>*:]*<source file>* [*<destination host>*][.*<user2>*:]*<destination file>*. The **-b** parameter instructs RCP to use binary transfer mode. (The default is ASCII, in which case RCP translates every line-feed character to a pair of line-feed, carriage-return characters, thereby corrupting IOS images.) The *<source host>* and *<user1>* parameters denote, respectively, the host from which the file must be copied and with which username RCP should communicate with the host. Likewise, the *<destination host>* and *<user2>* parameters denote the host onto which the file must be copied and with which name RCP should communicate with this host, respectively. The *<source file>* and *<destination>* parameters denote the names of the source and destination files, respectively.

First, let's copy the IOS image from router R1 (whose configuration is shown in Listing C.6) to the host. To do that, we'll use the following command:

```
C:\>rcp -b 192.168.4.1.admin:flash:/c2500-p-l.121-3.bin iosimg.bin
```

> **NOTE:**   *The IOS image name shown here contains a slash (/), which is, in fact, a part of the image name. Certain recent versions of IOS automatically add a slash character when storing IOS images onto the flash memory.*

Now let's save the router's running configuration to the host. To do that, we'll use the following command:

```
C:\>rcp -b 192.168.4.1.admin:running-config R1.cfg
```

Let's first modify the saved configuration by adding the line "! Router R1's configuration uploaded via RCP" in the very beginning, and then copying it to the router's NVRAM by using the following command:

```
C:\>rcp -b R1.cfg 192.168.4.1.admin:startup-config
```

If we now examine the router's startup configuration, it will look as shown in Listing C.7.

Listing C.7   The output of the show startup-config command confirms that the configuration upload via RCP was successful.

```
R1#show startup-config
Using 908 out of 32762 bytes
! Router R1's configuration uploaded via RCP
!
version 12.1
no service timestamps debug uptime
no service timestamps log uptime
```

```
service password-encryption
!
hostname R1
!
enable secret 5 $1$xDmI$BV50cOxmIhblNFVG8hnCz1
!
username admin
!
!
...
```

> **WARNING!** *Exercise extreme caution when uploading IOS images to the router flash memory and configuration files into the router's running or startup configuration. Uploading incorrect or corrupted images (the latter can be caused by transferring a file in ASCII mode) can prevent the router from booting. When you copy a configuration file into the router's running configuration, you actually merge the commands in the file with the commands in the running configuration. However, if you copy a configuration file to the router's NVRAM, you overwrite the stored configuration commands.*

Appendix D

Using ping with Timestamps

Most implementations of the **ping** command do not produce output with timestamps. A timestamp feature, however, would be quite useful in situations when you need to know how long it takes some resource to become available, or the amount of time that a resource is unavailable during network recovery caused by network component failures.

When testing HSRP in Chapter 9, we needed to see how quickly HSRP handles different types of failures. Especially for that chapter, I wrote a short perl script that actually runs the **ping** command once every second and time stamps the output. Because I thought that some of you would find the script useful, I put it in this Appendix. The text of the script is shown in Listing D.1.

Listing D.1 Perl script that runs the **ping** command and time stamps its output.

```
# This procedure creates a stamp on the moment it's invoked.
sub tstamp
{
    local($sec,$min,$hour) = localtime;
    return sprintf( "%02i:%02i", $min, $sec );
}


# This variable will be used to invoke the NT ping command
# to ping the remote destination only once. In other
# operating systems the option "-n 1" must be replaced
# with the option that makes ping send only a single
# ICMP packet.
$OS_SPING = 'ping -n 1 ';

# The destination IP address is passed as the first and the
# only command line argument. I do not perform any command
# line syntax checking, so it's important to pass the
# correct IP address.
$IP_ADDR = $ARGV[0];
```

```
$T_PREV = '';

while (1)
{
    # Wait until one second expires
    while( $T_PREV eq &tstamp ) {}

    # Parse ping output
    ( $tmp1,$tmp2, $tmp3, $P_RES ) =
        split( "\n", `$OS_SPING $IP_ADDR` );

    # Print time stamp
    print "[". &tstamp ."] ";

    # Print the fourth line of ping output
    print $P_RES . "\n";

    # Refresh the time stamp
    $T_PREV = &tstamp;
}
```

As you may have noticed, the script runs indefinitely. To stop it, use the Ctrl+Break keystroke.

Appendix E

Performing Summarization in RIP Version 2 by Means of Prefix Lists

As we know so far, Routing Information Protocol (RIP) version 2 is a classless routing protocol, which means that it passes network prefixes as well as their lengths in its routing updates. Yet, unlike the other classless routing protocols such as Enhanced Interior Gateway Routing Protocol (EIGRP) and Opent Shortest Path First (OSPF)—RIP version 2 lacks certain classless features. One of the most important of these features is the ability to perform nonclassless summarization. For example, no RIP-specific commands are available to advertise network prefix 172.16.0.0/14 in lieu of all the network prefixes belonging to this range but whose lengths are greater than /14. (EIGRP, for example, has the **ip summary-address eigrp** command that performs such summarization.)

Of course, it is still possible to manually perform the described summarization by redistributing appropriate static routes into RIP version 2 and filtering out all individual network prefixes by distribute lists. Until the advent of prefix lists, however, the implementation of such summarization was rather cumbersome. In addition, it prohibited the use of "subnet-zero-like" network prefixes, which include all network prefixes whose lengths are greater than that of the summary network prefix and whose bits residing after the summary bits are equal to 0. For instance, if 172.16.0.0/14 is a summary network prefix, then 172.16.0.0/16 and 172.16.0.0/26 are examples of such network prefixes.

After prefix lists became available, summarization with RIP version 2 became much simpler to implement, and—although it's still not as simple as summarizing with EIGRP and OSPF—it's available.

Let's recall how EIGRP and OSPF perform summarization. Once the summary network prefixes are defined, the router ceases to advertise the network prefixes that are matched by them. Instead, the router advertises the summary network prefixes. The router still advertises intact all of the network prefixes that are not matched by any of the summary network prefixes.

To perform the same type of summarization with RIP, we should inject the summary network prefixes into RIP through a redistribution of appropriate static routes that point to the Null0 interface. After that, we should use distribute lists to filter out all of the individual network prefixes that belong to the summary network prefixes.

The distribute lists, however, are no longer based on access lists; instead, they are based on prefix lists. The big advantage that prefix lists has over access lists is that prefix lists can match lengths of network prefixes—a crucial ability to perform summarization correctly.

In addition, the syntax of prefix lists—unlike the syntax of access lists—fits naturally for the job of summarization. When summarizing, we tend to think of the summary network prefix as the network prefix whose length is shorter than that of any summarized network prefix. In prefix lists, we specify exactly that: the length of the network prefix, which we make smaller than that of any network prefix we wish to summarize. On the contrary, in access lists, we specify a wildcard mask, which—aside from being unable to match the lengths of network prefixes—does not provide a natural (from the human point of view) image of the significant bits we want to match. In other words, with wildcard masks, we do not think of the *leading bits*; we think of the bits that correspond to the cleared bits of the wildcard mask.

To perform summarization with RIP version 2, follow these steps:

1. For each of the summary network prefixes, define a static route that points to the Null0 interface.

NOTE: *Some sources indicate that static routes pointing to the Loopback interface work faster.*

---

2. Create an "outbound" prefix list consisting of the following entries:

    For each of the summary network prefixes, create two prefix list clauses as follows:

    ip prefix-list *<SumPL>* **seq** *<s1>* **permit** *<summary>/<len>*

    ip prefix-list *<SumPL>* **seq** *<s2>* **deny** *<summary>/<len>* **ge** *<len+1>*

    where the *<SumPL>* parameter is the name of the prefix list, the *<s1>* and *<s2>* parameters are sequence numbers such that *s1 < s2*; and the *<summary>* and *<len>* parameters are the summary network prefix and its length, respectively. The value of the *<len+1>* parameter is 1 greater than that of *<len>*. As you can see, these two prefix clauses permit the summary network prefix and deny all of the network prefixes it summarizes.

Conclude the prefix list with the following clause:

ip prefix-list *<SumPL>* **seq** *<s>* **permit 0.0.0.0/0 le 32**

The clause's sequence number, represented by the *<s>* parameter, must be greater than that of any other previously defined clause. The purpose of this clause is to permit all of the network prefixes that were not matched by the above pairs of clauses. These network prefixes are those that do not belong in any of the summary network prefixes.

3. Using the **distribute-list prefix** command, apply the outbound prefix list (*<SumPL>*) as the outbound routing-update filter for all interfaces through which the summarization must be performed.

4. Optionally, create an "inbound" prefix list as follows:

   For every summary network prefix, create the following clause:

   ip prefix-list *<NoSumPL>* **seq** *<s1>* **deny** *<summary>*/*<len>*

   where the *<summary>* and *<len>* parameters represent the summary network prefix. (These parameters are identical to those of the same name from Step 2.)

   Conclude the prefix list with the following clause:

   ip prefix-list *<NoSumPL>* **seq** *<s>* **permit 0.0.0.0/0 le 32**

   The idea of this step is to create a prefix list that filters out the summary network prefixes and keeps everything else.

5. If optional Step 4 is performed, use the **distribute-list** command to apply the prefix list (*<NoSumPL>*) as an outbound routing-update filter on all other interfaces. This prevents the router from advertising the summary network prefixes back to the network whose network prefixes are summarized.

6. Using the **redistribute static** command, redistribute the static routes into the RIP process.

NOTE: *The redistribution metric must be specified either explicitly through the use of the parameters* **metric** *<value> of the* **redistribute static** *command or implicitly by defining the default redistribution metric (the* **default-metric** *statement in* **router rip** *configuration). If it is necessary to filter redistributed static routes, apply the appropriate redistribution filter.*

To see how the guidelines work, let's consider the network example shown in Figure E.1.

Router R4 is connected to two networks. One network comprises the segments residing in the shaded area, and the other comprises segment 6 and a number of undefined segments shown as the cloud below router R5.

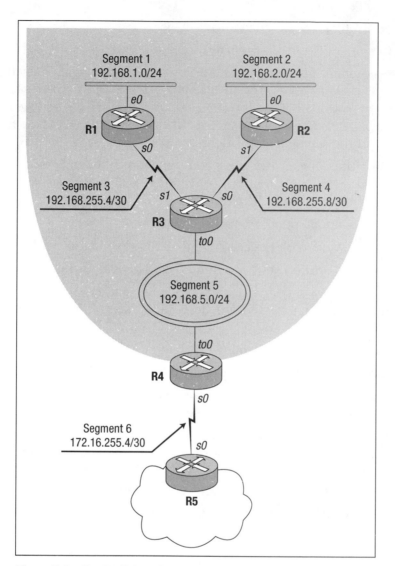

Figure E.1   Router R4 performs summarization by advertising network prefix 192.168.0.0/16 in lieu of all of the network prefixes defined on the segments residing in the shaded area.

The network prefixes of all segments residing in the shaded area begin with 192.168. Among these network prefixes are network prefixes 192.168.100.X/32 defined on the Loopback0 interface of each router; the X is the number of the router on which the network prefix is defined. In addition, router R2 has a Loopback1 interface whose network prefix is 192.168.0.0/24. (This is a "subnet-zero-like" network prefix.)

Nevertheless, all these network prefixes can be summarized by summary network prefix 192.168.0.0/16, and our task, therefore, is to configure router R4 to perform this summarization.

The configuration of router R4 is shown in Listing E.1.

Listing E.1   Router R4's configuration.

```
interface Loopback0
 ip address 192.168.100.4 255.255.255.255

interface Serial0
 ip address 172.16.255.5 255.255.255.252

interface TokenRing0
 ip address 192.168.5.2 255.255.255.0
 ring-speed 16

router rip
 version 2
 redistribute static metric 4
 network 172.16.0.0
 network 192.168.5.0
 network 192.168.100.0
 distribute-list prefix 192.168_Summmary out Serial0
 distribute-list prefix 192.168_NoSum out TokenRing0
 no auto-summary

ip classless

ip route 192.168.0.0 255.255.0.0 Null0

ip prefix-list 192.168_NoSum seq 10 deny 192.168.0.0/16
ip prefix-list 192.168_NoSum seq 15 permit 0.0.0.0/0 le 32

ip prefix-list 192.168_Summmary seq 10 permit 192.168.0.0/16
ip prefix-list 192.168_Summmary seq 15 deny 192.168.0.0/16 ge 17
ip prefix-list 192.168_Summmary seq 20 permit 0.0.0.0/0 le 32
```

The shaded lines indicate the commands that result from this above-described procedure.

Before we examine the routing tables of the other routers, let's take a look at router R4's routing table (Listing E.2).

Listing E.2   The routing table of router R4.

```
R4#show ip route
...
        172.16.0.0/30 is subnetted, 1 subnets
C       172.16.255.4 is directly connected, Serial0
C     192.168.5.0/24 is directly connected, TokenRing0
      192.168.255.0/30 is subnetted, 2 subnets
R       192.168.255.4 [120/1] via 192.168.5.1, 00:00:13, TokenRing0
R       192.168.255.8 [120/1] via 192.168.5.1, 00:00:13, TokenRing0
R     192.168.0.0/24 [120/2] via 192.168.5.1, 00:00:13, TokenRing0
R     192.168.1.0/24 [120/2] via 192.168.5.1, 00:00:13, TokenRing0
R     192.168.2.0/24 [120/2] via 192.168.5.1, 00:00:14, TokenRing0
      192.168.100.0/32 is subnetted, 4 subnets
C       192.168.100.4 is directly connected, Loopback0
R       192.168.100.1 [120/2] via 192.168.5.1, 00:00:14, TokenRing0
R       192.168.100.2 [120/2] via 192.168.5.1, 00:00:14, TokenRing0
R       192.168.100.3 [120/1] via 192.168.5.1, 00:00:15, TokenRing0
S     192.168.0.0/16 is directly connected, Null0
```

The first shaded line reveals a route for 192.168.0.0/24 (the previously mentioned "subnet-zero-like" network prefix); the second shows the static route for the summary network prefix. As you may remember, OSPF and EIGRP also create routes for summary network prefixes; furthermore, these routes point to the Null0 interface. The only difference between OSPF and EIGRP summary routes and the ones that we define here is that the former are automatically created, whereas the latter must be created manually.

After this configuration is implemented on router R4, the RIP part of router R5's routing table should look as shown below:

```
R5#show ip route rip
R     192.168.0.0/16 [120/4] via 172.16.255.5, 00:00:13, Serial0
```

Notice that router R5 has only a single RIP route for summary network prefix 192.168.0.0/16.

Because we performed optional Steps 4 and 5, we should not see routes for the summary network prefix in the routing tables of routers R1, R2, and R3. Listing E.3 shows the routing table of router R1. Notice that there is no route for summary network prefix 192.168.0.0/16.

Listing E.3   The routing table of router R1.

```
R1#show ip route
...
     172.16.0.0/30 is subnetted, 1 subnets
R       172.16.255.4 [120/2] via 192.168.255.6, 00:00:25, Serial0
R     192.168.5.0/24 [120/1] via 192.168.255.6, 00:00:25, Serial0
     192.168.255.0/30 is subnetted, 2 subnets
C       192.168.255.4 is directly connected, Serial0
R       192.168.255.8 [120/1] via 192.168.255.6, 00:00:25, Serial0
R     192.168.0.0/24 [120/2] via 192.168.255.6, 00:00:25, Serial0
C     192.168.1.0/24 is directly connected, Ethernet0
R     192.168.2.0/24 [120/2] via 192.168.255.6, 00:00:25, Serial0
     192.168.100.0/32 is subnetted, 4 subnets
R       192.168.100.4 [120/2] via 192.168.255.6, 00:00:26, Serial0
C       192.168.100.1 is directly connected, Loopback0
R       192.168.100.2 [120/2] via 192.168.255.6, 00:00:26, Serial0
R       192.168.100.3 [120/1] via 192.168.255.6, 00:00:26, Serial0
```

Appendix F

Configuring IS-IS

Intermediate System to Intermediate System is a link-state routing protocol that was originally developed for CLNP (Connectionless Network Protocol). CLNP is a part of the ISO protocol stack, whose functionality is similar to that of the TCP/IP protocols.

NOTE: RFC 1195, "Use of OSI IS-IS for Routing in TCP/IP and Dual Environments," describes the modifications to IS-IS that provide support for IP routing. In addition to reading the RFC, I recommend the oft-mentioned book, Interconnections, *written by Radia Perlman. Although Perlman is one of the authors of IS-IS, she actually began to work on the protocol much earlier when she was the network architect at DEC.*

IS-IS was later expanded to provide routing for IP as well. Nevertheless, IS-IS does not use IP as transport; instead, IS-IS PDUs are encapsulated directly into data link layer frames. (To be exact, IS-IS uses the OSI encapsulation.)

NOTE: A single IS-IS PDU can carry topology information for CLNP and IP; this is why IS-IS is sometimes called integrated IS-IS. IS-IS is the only protocol that uses the same PDUs to maintain routing of two distinct routed protocols. Unlike IS-IS, the versions of EIGRP for IP, IPX, and AppleTalk use the PDUs of the respective routed protocols to propagate routing information; therefore, the versions of EIGRP are essentially different routing protocols, although they are based on the same concept and algorithm.

OSI Addressing Overview

Although IS-IS can be used purely for IP, it still requires each router running an IS-IS process to have an OSI identity in the form of a *network entity title (NET)*. An NET is essentially a combination of an OSI address and what is known as a *selector*. The function of the selector is similar to that of the TCP or UDP port. In the NET, however, the selector is always equal to 0 (which essentially denotes that this is an NET—otherwise, the selector must have a non-zero value, which denotes a specific service on an OSI node).

The OSI address consists of two parts: the area ID and the node ID. The area ID's function is similar to that of the IP network prefix, whereas the node ID's function is similar to that of the host ID of the IP address. However, the area ID is unlike the IP network prefix in that the area ID in the OSI address does not identify a segment, but rather an area similar to an OSPF area. The node ID uniquely identifies the node on which it is assigned, which means that, even if a node has multiple NICs (an example of such a node is a router), it nevertheless does not require multiple node IDs. Even with multiple NICs, one node ID per node is sufficient.

The OSI addresses can have variable lengths. Unlike the sizes of the network prefix and the host ID of an IP address, the sizes of the area and the node ID of an OSI address are not interdependent. The total size of an OSI address can be as large as 20 octets, and the size of the node ID can vary from 0 to 8 octets. Any number of the remaining octets can be occupied by the area ID.

Despite the potential variety in the sizes of the OSI addresses, the sizes of the area and node ID usually remain the same within the boundaries of a single network. Furthermore, the most typical size of an OSI node ID is 6 octets, which is equal to the size of the MAC address of most LAN technologies (such as Ethernet). This feature facilitates automatic discovery of node IDs, as the OSI node can simply take the node ID from its own NIC (which is guaranteed to be globally unique). It makes sense to keep the size of the area ID identical to facilitate faster routing-table lookup.

To maintain the described addressing model, OSI defines two types of routing: level-1 and level-2 routing. Level-1 routing serves routing within an area and thereby provides the nodes with knowledge of which destinations are reachable through which output interface and next-hop router. Level-2 routing works between the areas, allowing the routers to know which destinations in the other areas are accessible through which routers.

Regular nodes, such as hosts, have access to only level-1 routing information. When they need to reach destinations in other areas, they won't know the exact routing information. Instead, they'll know of the closest router, which performs level-2 routing, and it is this router that knows how to reach the remote destinations.

Brief IS-IS Operation Overview

IS-IS provides level-1 and level-2 routing. As mentioned, level-1 routing is routing within an area, and level-2 routing is routing between areas.

Being a link-state routing protocol, IS-IS requires the routers to possess the knowledge of the exact topology of areas to which they are attached. For each area, a router running IS-IS has a separate link-state database. In addition, the IS-IS routers that are configured for level-2 routing have a separate level-2 link-state database.

IS-IS uses three types of PDUs:

- *IS-to-IS Hello*—whose function is similar to that of OSPF Hello PDUs.

- *LSP (link-state packet)*—whose function is similar to that of OSPF router and network LSAs (type 1 and 2 LSAs): carrying information about directly reachable neighbors. If multiple routers are connected to a broadcast segment, then one of the routers issues an LSP on behalf of the segment. (As in OSPF, this router is called a *designated router*.) A segment represented by a designated router is called *pseudonode*.

  Unlike OSPF LSAs, LSPs are actually IS-IS PDUs. (As we remember in OSPF, LSAs are conveyed inside OSPF update PDUs.)

  LSPs are of two types: level-1 and level-2.

- *SNP (sequence number packet)*—which performs multiple functions, such as acknowledging the receipt of LSPs, requesting LSPs, and ensuring identity of link-state databases among neighbors.

Unlike OSPF, IS-IS does not require that the border routers of areas be connected to a single area similar to the OSPF backbone. The areas can be interconnected in any desirable way.

Unlike OSPF, IS-IS uses a rather narrow range of metrics: Its metrics are only 6 bits long, which means that the largest metric equals 63.

NOTE: *Whereas such a small range of metric values might suffice for the OSI addressing model, it's not practically sufficient for IP. To address this issue, the IETF proposed extended metrics (of 4 octets) specifically for IP to be incorporated into IS-IS. The "Using Extended IS-IS Metrics" section later in this appendix explains how to configure a Cisco router to use these extended metrics.*

IS-IS uses the following rules to advertise IP network prefixes:

- IS-IS routers use level-1 LSPs to encode individual links to neighbors that are directly reachable. The links contain the network prefixes assigned on them.

- IS-IS routers place all the network prefixes they know of into level-2 LSPs. The network prefixes can and should be summarized, and this summarization is handled in a manner similar to how it's done in OSPF—by configuring the routers participating in level-1 and level-2 routing with the summary network prefixes (or ranges) that must replace all individual network prefixes they match. The routers performing level-1 and level-2 routing are therefore similar to OSPF ABRs; unlike OSPF ABRs, IS-IS level-1 and 2 routers do not have to reside on the "border" of the areas. In other words, in order to produce level-2 LSPs, IS-IS level-1 and level-2 routers in one area do not have to be connected to level-2 only and/or level-1 and level-2 routers in another area.

Performing Basic IS-IS Configuration for IP

Use the following guidelines to perform IS-IS configuration for a single area:

1. Create an IS-IS routing process on a router using the command **router isis** [<*tag*>]. The optional <*tag*> parameter defines a name for the routing process; it does not provide any functionality if IS-IS is used for IP only.

2. Define an NET for the routing process using the **net** <*OSI address*>.**00** command in the router **isis** configuration mode. The <*OSI address*> parameter is the OSI address component of the NET, written as several groups of four hexadecimal digits. The last three groups of four hexadecimal digits represent the node ID; any groups of hexadecimal digits in front of these are treated as the area ID. If the area ID does not require four digits, it can be represented by only two hexadecimal digits. An example of NET is 01.0000.0000.0001.00, where 01 is the area ID and 0000.0000.0001 is the node ID.

   If the routers are configured for the same area, the area ID must be the same on all of them. The node ID must be unique on every router.

3. Use the command **ip router isis** [<*tag*>] in interface configuration mode to assign interfaces into the IS-IS process. The optional <*tag*> parameter must be used only if the IS-IS process was defined with the same <*tag*> parameter. IS-IS will advertise the network prefixes that are assigned on the functional interfaces whose configurations contain this command.

Let's see how routers in the network from Figure F.1 have to be configured to maintain IP routing using IS-IS.

Listings F.1 through F.6 show the configurations of all six routers.

Listing F.1   Router R1's configuration.

```
clns routing

interface Ethernet0
 ip address 192.168.1.1 255.255.255.0
 ip router isis

interface TokenRing0
 ip address 192.168.4.1 255.255.252.0
```

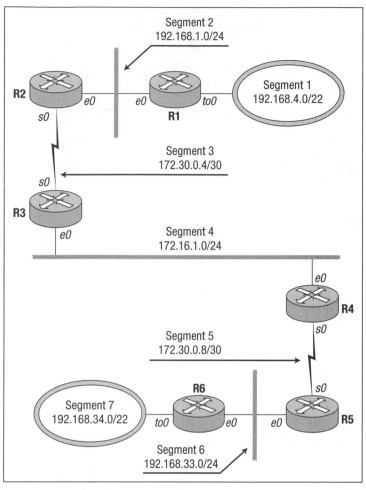

Figure F.1 The routers are configured for IS-IS to sustain IP routing in the network.

```
ip router isis
ring-speed 16

router isis
 net 01.0000.0000.0001.00

ip classless
```

Listing F.2   Router R2's configuration.

```
clns routing

ip address 192.168.1.2 255.255.255.0
 no ip directed-broadcast
 ip router isis
```

```
interface Serial0
 ip address 172.30.0.6 255.255.255.252
 ip router isis

router isis
 net 01.0000.0000.0002.00

ip classless
```

Listing F.3   Router R3's configuration.

```
clns routing

interface Ethernet0
 ip address 172.16.1.1 255.255.255.0
 ip router isis

interface Serial0
 ip address 172.30.0.5 255.255.255.252
 ip router isis

router isis
 net 01.0000.0000.0003.00

ip classless
```

Listing F.4   Router R4's configuration.

```
clns routing

interface Ethernet0
 ip address 172.16.1.2 255.255.255.0
 ip router isis

interface Serial0
 ip address 172.30.0.9 255.255.255.252
 ip router isis

router isis
 net 01.0000.0000.0004.00

ip classless
```

Listing F.5   Router R5's configuration.

```
clns routing

interface Ethernet0
 ip address 192.168.33.2 255.255.255.0
```

```
 ip router isis

interface Serial0
 ip address 172.30.0.10 255.255.255.252
 ip router isis

router isis
 net 01.0000.0000.0005.00

ip classless
```

Listing F.6   Router R6's configuration.

```
clns routing

interface Ethernet0
 ip address 192.168.33.1 255.255.255.0
 ip router isis

interface TokenRing0
 ip address 192.168.36.1 255.255.252.0
 ip router isis
 ring-speed 16

router isis
 net 01.0000.0000.0006.00

ip classless
```

Notice the italicized line at the beginning of every listing: *clns routing*. This command is required for IS-IS to operate. C*onnectionless network service (CLNS)* is essentially the same term as CLNP. However, you do not have to enter it manually. Once you enter the **router isis** command, the router will automatically generate *clns routing*.

Let's examine the routing table of router R1 (Listing F.7).

Listing F.7   The routing table of router R1.

```
R1#show ip route
...
     172.16.0.0/24 is subnetted, 1 subnets
i L1     172.16.1.0 [115/30] via 192.168.1.2, Ethernet0
     172.30.0.0/30 is subnetted, 2 subnets
i L1     172.30.0.4 [115/20] via 192.168.1.2, Ethernet0
i L1     172.30.0.8 [115/40] via 192.168.1.2, Ethernet0
C    192.168.1.0/24 is directly connected, Ethernet0
i L1 192.168.33.0/24 [115/50] via 192.168.1.2, Ethernet0
```

```
C    192.168.4.0/22 is directly connected, TokenRing0
i L1 192.168.36.0/22 [115/60] via 192.168.1.2, Ethernet0
```

The shaded lines show the routes created by IS-IS. Each line begins with a lower-case *i*, which denotes IS-IS. Right after the lowercase *i* appears a label that denotes the type of IS-IS route. Two types of labels exist: L1 and L2 (for level-1 and level-2 routes, respectively). Because all routers in our network are configured with the same area ID, all routes are therefore level-1. The remaining part of the line is not different from that of the other routing protocols.

Configuring IS-IS Routing with Multiple Areas

To configure IS-IS routing with multiple areas, you need to assign different area IDs on different routers. Typically, multiple areas are accompanied by the summarization of network prefixes defined with areas. The command **summary-address** *<IP address> <subnet mask>* [{**level-1**|**level-1-2**|**level-2**}] allows you to perform summarization. The *<IP address>* and *<summary address>* parameters define the summary network prefix, and the optional parameter {**level-1**|**level-1-2**|**level-2**} tells the router how it should summarize network prefixes:

- **level-1** tells the router to summarize network prefixes when placing them into level-1 LSP.

- **level-1-2** tells the router to summarize network prefixes when placing them into both level-1 and level-2 LSPs.

- **level-2** tells the router to summarize network prefixes when placing them into level-2 LSPs.

If this parameter is omitted, the command defaults to level-2 only.

NOTE: *Level-1 summarization is practically useful only when summarizing network prefixes that are redistributed from another routing protocol.*

It's easy to notice that the IP addressing in the network shown in Figure F.1 allows you to easily divide the network into three areas, each of which has its own single summary network prefix. The areas and their respective summary addresses are shown in Figure F.2.

The modified configurations of all six routers are shown in Listings F.8 through F.13.

NOTE: *The **clns routing** commands that were present in the previous set of listings are omitted in this and subsequent listings.*

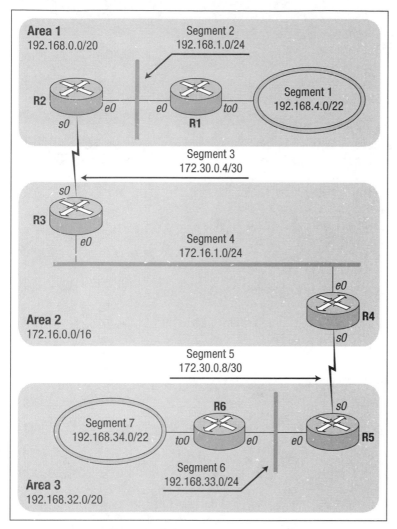

Figure F.2 The network from Figure F.1 can be divided into three areas, with each having its own single summary network prefix.

Listing F.8 Router R1's configuration.

```
interface Ethernet0
 ip address 192.168.1.1 255.255.255.0
 ip router isis

interface TokenRing0
 ip address 192.168.4.1 255.255.252.0
 ip router isis
 ring-speed 16
```

```
router isis
 summary-address 192.168.0.0 255.255.240.0
 net 01.0000.0000.0001.00

ip classless
```

Listing F.9   Router R2's configuration.

```
interface Ethernet0
 ip address 192.168.1.2 255.255.255.0
 ip router isis

interface Serial0
 ip address 172.30.0.6 255.255.255.252
 ip router isis

router isis
 summary-address 192.168.0.0 255.255.240.0
 net 01.0000.0000.0002.00

ip classless
```

Listing F.10   Router R3's configuration.

```
interface Ethernet0
 ip address 172.16.1.1 255.255.255.0
 ip router isis

interface Serial0
 ip address 172.30.0.5 255.255.255.252
 ip router isis

router isis
 summary-address 172.16.0.0 255.255.0.0
 net 02.0000.0000.0003.00

ip classless
```

Listing F.11   Router R4's configuration.

```
interface Ethernet0
 ip address 172.16.1.2 255.255.255.0
 ip router isis

interface Serial0
 ip address 172.30.0.9 255.255.255.252
 ip router isis
```

```
router isis
 summary-address 172.16.0.0 255.255.0.0
 net 02.0000.0000.0004.00

ip classless
```

Listing F.12   Router R5's configuration.

```
interface Ethernet0
 ip address 192.168.33.2 255.255.255.0
 ip router isis

interface Serial0
 ip address 172.30.0.10 255.255.255.252
 ip router isis

router isis
 summary-address 192.168.32.0 255.255.240.0
 net 03.0000.0000.0005.00

ip classless
```

ssListing F.13   Router R6's configuration.

```
interface Ethernet0
 ip address 192.168.33.1 255.255.255.0
 ip router isis

interface TokenRing0
 ip address 192.168.36.1 255.255.252.0
 ip router isis
 ring-speed 16

router isis
 summary-address 192.168.32.0 255.255.240.0
 net 03.0000.0000.0006.00

ip classless
```

First notice that the NETs of the routers now feature three different area IDs: Routers R1 and R2 are configured with area ID 01, routers R3 and R4 with area ID 04, and routers R5 and R6 with area ID 03.

Also, notice the **summary-address** commands in the configurations of all routers. If we examine the routing table of router R1 again, it will look as shown in Listing F.14.

Listing F.14   The routing table of router R1.

```
R1#show ip route
...
i L2 172.16.0.0/16 [115/30] via 192.168.1.2, Ethernet0
     172.30.0.0/30 is subnetted, 2 subnets
i L1    172.30.0.4 [115/20] via 192.168.1.2, Ethernet0
i L2    172.30.0.8 [115/40] via 192.168.1.2, Ethernet0
C    192.168.1.0/24 is directly connected, Ethernet0
C    192.168.4.0/22 is directly connected, TokenRing0
i su 192.168.0.0/20 [115/10] via 0.0.0.0, Null0
i L2 192.168.32.0/20 [115/50] via 192.168.1.2, Ethernet0
```

The shaded lines indicate the level-2 routes, which we have for network prefixes 172.16.0.0/16 and 192.168.32.0/20 (the summary network prefixes of areas 2 and 3, respectively). Because no router was configured with any summarization for network prefixes assigned on the serial links (segments 3 and 5), they remained unsummarized.

The italicized line shows a route that IS-IS created for the summary network prefix of area 1 (in which router R1 resides). The route is labeled *su* for summary. Only IOS version 12.1 (or higher) creates explicit IS-IS summary routes; prior versions did not create the summary routes. (Despite being visually less clean from the IP routing paradigm perspective, the absence of explicit IS-IS routes for summary network prefixes had no impact on the operation of summarization.)

Although it is understandable why the **summary-address** commands are needed on the routers that reside on the borders of the areas (routers R2 through R5), it may not be so obvious why these commands are also necessary on the routers that reside within the areas (routers R1 and R6). If we remember, however, how IS-IS forms level-2 LSPs, we'll see the reason. When a router creates a level-2 LSP, it places into it all of the network prefixes that it knows of, unless the router is explicitly configured to perform summarization. Because IS-IS is a link-state protocol, the LSP created by the router will get into the level-2 link-state databases of all other level-2 routers unchanged. When these routers start to build routing tables, they will create routes for all of the network prefixes that are contained in the LSP.

All routers in our network are level-1 and level-2 routers. Therefore, if we do not configure summarization on inner routers R1 and R6, summarization won't work as expected. For example, let's remove the **summary-address 192.168.32.0 255.255.240.0** command from router R6's configuration and see how the routing table of router R1 changes. The new routing table of router R1 is shown in Listing F.15.

Listing F.15   The routing table of router R1.

```
R1#show ip route
...
i L2 172.16.0.0/16 [115/30] via 192.168.1.2, Ethernet0
     172.30.0.0/30 is subnetted, 2 subnets
i L1    172.30.0.4 [115/20] via 192.168.1.2, Ethernet0
i L2    172.30.0.8 [115/40] via 192.168.1.2, Ethernet0
C    192.168.1.0/24 is directly connected, Ethernet0
i L2 192.168.33.0/24 [115/60] via 192.168.1.2, Ethernet0
C    192.168.4.0/22 is directly connected, TokenRing0
i L2 192.168.36.0/22 [115/60] via 192.168.1.2, Ethernet0
i su 192.168.0.0/20 [115/10] via 0.0.0.0, Null0
i L2 192.168.32.0/20 [115/50] via 192.168.1.2, Ethernet0
```

The two shaded lines indicate the routes for the unsummarized network prefixes 192.168.33.0/24 and 192.168.36.0/22, which were created from the level-2 LSP of router R6. To see evidence of this, we can use the **show isis database detail** command, which is similar to the **show ip ospf database router** command. Listing F.16 shows the output of the command entered on router R1.

Listing F.16   The output of the show isis database detail command entered on router R1.

```
R1#show isis database detail

IS-IS Level-1 Link State Database:
LSPID                LSP Seq Num  LSP Checksum  LSP Holdtime      ATT/P/OL
R1.00-00             * 0x00000012  0x5C0B        806               1/0/0
   Area Address: 01
   NLPID:       0xCC
   Hostname: R1
   IP Address:   192.168.4.1
   Metric: 10        IP 192.168.1.0 255.255.255.0
   Metric: 10        IP 192.168.4.0 255.255.252.0
   Metric: 10        IS R1.01
...
IS-IS Level-2 Link State Database:
LSPID                LSP Seq Num  LSP Checksum  LSP Holdtime      ATT/P/OL
...
R5.00-00             0x00000030   0x17B4        989               0/0/0
   Area Address: 03
   NLPID:       0xCC
   Hostname: R5
   IP Address:   172.30.0.10
   Metric: 10        IS R6.01
   Metric: 10        IS R4.00
   Metric: 10        IP 172.30.0.8 255.255.255.252
```

```
    Metric: 10           IP 192.168.32.0 255.255.240.0
R6.00-00                 0x00000031   0x1B52      1009                0/0/0
  Area Address: 03
  NLPID:        0xCC
  Hostname: R6
  IP Address:   192.168.36.1
  Metric: 10        IS R6.01
  Metric: 20        IP 172.30.0.8 255.255.255.252
  Metric: 10        IP 192.168.33.0 255.255.255.0
  Metric: 10        IP 192.168.36.0 255.255.252.0
...
```

Because the command's output is rather long, I skipped the uninteresting parts. The output begins with the contents of the router's level-1 link-state database (or multiple level-1 databases, if the router is attached to multiple areas). The beginning of the level-1 link-state database contents is shown as the first shaded line. (I kept only the LSP that corresponds to router R1.) Notice the italicized part of the LSP, because it shows the network prefixes that are assigned on router R1's interfaces. Right after the contents of the level-1 link-state database are the contents of the level-2 link-state database, the beginning of which is shown as the second shaded line in Listing F.16.

Router R5 created the first LSP in the level-2 link-state database. The italicized lines show the network prefixes contained in the LSP, and these include only area 3 summary network prefix 192.168.32.0/20 and nonsummarized network prefix 172.30.0.8/30 of segment 5. Right after router R5's level-2 LSP is router R6's level-2 LSP. The italicized lines show the network prefixes 172.30.0.8/30, 192.168.33.0/24, and 192.168.36.0/22. The last two network prefixes are nonsummarized network prefixes of area 3. Their presence in router R6's level-2 LSP explains why routes for them appear in router R1's routing table (as well as in the routing table of every other router in the network).

Examining IS-IS Neighbors

The **show clns is-neighbors** command displays known IS-IS neighbors. (The functionality of this command is similar to that of the **show ip ospf neighbor** command.) Entering this command on router R2 produces the following result:

```
R2#show clns is-neighbors

System Id      Interface    State  Type Priority  Circuit Id          Format
```

```
0000.0000.0001 Et0          Up      L1L2 64/64      0000.0000.0001.0Phase V
0000.0000.0003 Se0          Up      L2   0          00              Phase V
```

The first column shows the neighbor's node ID, and the next shows over which interface the neighbor appears. After that is the neighbor's state. The next column shows what kind of adjacency is established with the neighbor. The next column shows the priority of the neighbor, and the last two columns are of no significance for IP.

The first shaded line of the above output corresponds to router R1. Notice that router R2 established level-1 and level-2 adjacencies with router R1. This is the default behavior of routers of IS-IS neighbors residing in the same area. The second shaded line corresponds to router R3. Router R2 was able to establish only level-2 adjacency with router R3 because router R3 resides in a different area.

Modifying Interface Costs

The **isis metric** [{**level-1**|**level-2**}] command (available in interface configuration mode) allows you to modify the IS-IS cost of the interfaces. The optional {**level-1**|**level-2**} parameter specifies on what routing level the cost should be modified. If this parameter is omitted, the command defaults to **level-1**.

By default, all interfaces have the IS-IS cost of 10.

Let's make the level-1 cost of the Serial0 interface of router R2 equal to 3. To do that, we need to issue the **isis metric 3** command under **interface Serial0** configuration of router R3. After that, the IS-IS part of router R1's routing table will look as shown in Listing F.17.

Listing F.17   The output of the **show ip route isis** command confirms the modification of the IS-IS cost of router R2's interface Serial0.

```
R1#show ip route isis
i L2 172.16.0.0/16 [115/30] via 192.168.1.2, Ethernet0
     172.28.0.0/24 is subnetted, 1 subnets
i L2    172.28.3.0 [115/30] via 192.168.1.2, Ethernet0
     172.30.0.0/30 is subnetted, 2 subnets
i L1    172.30.0.4 [115/13] via 192.168.1.2, Ethernet0
i L2    172.30.0.8 [115/40] via 192.168.1.2, Ethernet0
i su 192.168.0.0/20 [115/10] via 0.0.0.0, Null0
i L2 192.168.32.0/20 [115/50] via 192.168.1.2, Ethernet0
```

The shaded line reflects the new metric for network prefix 172.30.0.4/30 of segment 3.

Using Extended IS-IS Metrics

Commencing with version 12.1, IOS supports extended 4-octet metrics, which are enabled by the **metric-style wide** [{**level-1**|**level-1-2**|**level-2**}] command under **router isis** configuration.

Performing Redistribution into IS-IS in Conjunction with Filtering and Summarization

The **redistribute** *<source>* command allows you to redistribute into IS-IS the routing information produced by the source of routing information that is specified with the *<source>* parameter. Unlike EIGRP and OSPF, however, IS-IS does not have a concept of external routes. IS-IS instead allows redistributed routing information to be presented as level-1, level-2, or level-1 and level-2 simultaneously—which is achieved by specifying an optional parameter: **level-1**, **level-2** or **level-1-2**, respectively.

> **NOTE:**   *The IS-IS version of the **redistribute** command has most parameters available with the **redistribute** command of the other routing protocols. Listing F.18 demonstrates how to use the **route-map** parameter.*

The **distribute-list** command is available and performs the same function—allows you to filter network prefixes redistributed into IS-IS and for which the router installs IS-IS routes. Because IS-IS is a link-state routing protocol, the **distribute-list** command does not allow the outbound filtering of routing information, but inbound filtering is available (just as in OSPF). If inbound filtering is performed, the router does not modify the LSPs. Instead, it performs filtering of the network prefixes for which it creates IS-IS routes: The router will install routes only for those network prefixes that passed the condition specified in the **distribute-list** command. The condition can be specified via access or prefix lists.

Let's modify the configuration of router R6 as shown in Listing F.18.

Listing F.18   The new configuration of router R6.

```
interface Loopback0
 ip address 172.25.1.1 255.255.255.252

interface Loopback1
 ip address 172.25.1.5 255.255.255.252
```

```
interface Loopback2
 ip address 172.25.1.9 255.255.255.252

interface Loopback3
 ip address 192.25.1.129 255.255.255.255

interface Ethernet0
 ip address 192.168.33.1 255.255.255.0
 ip router isis

interface TokenRing0
 ip address 192.168.36.1 255.255.252.0
 ip router isis
 ring-speed 16

router isis
 summary-address 192.168.32.0 255.255.240.0
 redistribute connected route-map Con2ISIS level-1
 net 03.0000.0000.0006.00

ip classless

ip prefix-list LBacks30 seq 5 permit 172.25.1.0/24 ge 30 le 30

route-map Con2ISIS permit 10
 match ip address prefix-list LBacks30
 set metric 4
```

The shaded lines in the beginning of Listing F.18 show four Loopback interfaces. The IP addresses of the first three Loopback interfaces belong to network prefixes whose length are equal to /30. The IP address of the Loopback3 interface belongs to the network prefix with the length of /32.

The **redistribute** command under **router isis** configuration instructs the router to redistribute the network prefixes that reside on the operational interfaces and only those that pass route map **Con2ISIS**. Route map **Con2ISIS** consists of a single clause whose **match** condition is specified by the prefix list **Lbacks30**; the **set** action makes the router advertise the redistributed network prefixes with the metric of 4. The prefix list **Lbacks30** matches the network prefixes that begin with 172.25.1.X and whose lengths are equal to /30. In other words, the prefix list matches only those network prefixes that are defined on interfaces Loopback0 through Loopback2. Finally, the remaining **level-1** parameter of the **redistribute** command instructs the router to advertise the redistributed network prefixes using level-1 routing.

Let's examine the routing table of router R5, which is shown in Listing F.19.

Listing F.19   The routing table of router R5.

```
R5#show ip route isis
i L2 172.16.0.0/16 [115/20] via 172.30.0.9, Serial0
     172.25.0.0/30 is subnetted, 3 subnets
i L1    172.25.1.4 [115/14] via 192.168.33.1, Ethernet0
i L1    172.25.1.0 [115/14] via 192.168.33.1, Ethernet0
i L1    172.25.1.8 [115/14] via 192.168.33.1, Ethernet0
     172.28.0.0/24 is subnetted, 1 subnets
i L2    172.28.3.0 [115/30] via 172.30.0.9, Serial0
     172.30.0.0/30 is subnetted, 2 subnets
i L2    172.30.0.4 [115/30] via 172.30.0.9, Serial0
i L1 192.168.36.0/22 [115/20] via 192.168.33.1, Ethernet0
i L2 192.168.0.0/20 [115/40] via 172.30.0.9, Serial0
i su 192.168.32.0/20 [115/10] via 0.0.0.0, Null0
```

The three shaded lines show the level-1 routes that are produced as the result of the redistribution that was performed at router R6.

Let's now perform summarization of the redistributed network prefixes by issuing the **summary-address 172.25.1.0 255.255.255.0 level-1** command on router R6. The **level-1** parameter instructs the router to perform summarization of redistributed network prefixes, which will be advertised using level-1 routing.

Listing F.20 shows the new routing table of router R5.

Listing F.20   The new routing table of router R5.

```
R5#show ip route isis
i L2 172.16.0.0/16 [115/20] via 172.30.0.9, Serial0
     172.25.0.0/24 is subnetted, 1 subnets
i L1    172.25.1.0 [115/14] via 192.168.33.1, Ethernet0
     172.28.0.0/24 is subnetted, 1 subnets
i L2    172.28.3.0 [115/30] via 172.30.0.9, Serial0
     172.30.0.0/30 is subnetted, 2 subnets
i L2    172.30.0.4 [115/30] via 172.30.0.9, Serial0
i L1 192.168.36.0/22 [115/20] via 192.168.33.1, Ethernet0
i L2 192.168.0.0/20 [115/40] via 172.30.0.9, Serial0
i su 192.168.32.0/20 [115/10] via 0.0.0.0, Null0
```

The single level-1 route shown as the shaded line replaced the three level-1 routes from Listing F.19.

Glossary

adjacency—A special relationship between two routers that are running a link-state protocol—such as Open Shortest Path First (OSPF) or IS-IS. Topologically, the adjacency corresponds to the two directed edges that interconnect the two vertices representing the routers in the graph model. If the routers are interconnected by a point-to-point link, they always form an adjacency. If the routers are interconnected by a broadcast network segment, the routers elect a single router—called the *designated router*—that represents the segment. After that, the routers form adjacencies with the designated router.

all-routes explorer (also called *all-routes broadcast*)—A token ring frame that allows the host that created it to find a route to the destination in a source-route bridged network. The all-routes explorer is destined for a broadcast media access control (MAC) address (FFFF-FFFF-FFFF). The difference between the all-routes explorer and any other token ring frame is the presence of the Routing Information field (see *RIF*) whose first 3 bits are equal to 100 (binary). The operation of the all-routes explorer allows the host that issued it to discover multiple paths to the destination. Although the host is free to choose any one of these paths, most hosts typically pick the first discovered route and discard all the other. See also *route source-route bridging (RSRB), source-route bridging (SRB),* and *spanning explorer.*

Automatic Spanning Tree (AST)—A version of the standard Institute of Electrical and Electronics Engineers (IEEE) 802.1D bridging protocol that is adapted for selecting ports (interfaces) of source-route bridges to forward spanning explorers. (See also *spanning explorer* and *SRB.*) See also *route source-route bridging (RSRB), source-route bridging (SRB),* and *spanning explorer.*

autonomous system—1) A group of network segments under a single administrative authority, such as corporate networks and the networks of Internet Service Providers (ISPs). 2) A group of networks (typically under the same administrative authority) that's connected to the Internet and represented as a whole by the routers running an exterior gateway protocol (EGP) typically BGP (border gateway protocol). Each autonomous system in the Internet is identified by the autonomous system number.

bit count notation—A notation used to denote Internet Protocol (IP) network prefixes by specifying the IP address in dotted decimal notation followed by a slash (/) and the network prefix length in decimal notation, such as 10.0.1.0/24.

bridge—A packet switch that interconnects segments on the data link layer. The bridge receives the frames on its ports and forwards them through its ports against which the frames' destinations appear. Bridges are mostly used to interconnect LAN segments. See also *local area network (LAN)*, *Layer-2 Switch*, and *switch*.)

Bridge Protocol Data Unit (BPDU)—A protocol data unit (PDU) of the Institute of Electrical and Electronic Engineers (IEEE) 802.1D bridging protocol.

classful network address (also called *major network address* and *major network number*)—Any network prefix whose length is equal to the default network prefix length of the Internet Protocol (IP) network class to which the network prefix belongs. The three IP network classes are A, B, and C. Class A comprises network prefixes from 1.0.0.0/8 to 127.0.0.0/8, and its default network prefix length is /8. Class B comprises network prefixes from 129.0.0.0/16 to 191.255.0.0/16, and its default network prefix length is /16. Class C comprises network prefixes from 192.0.0.0/24 to 223.255.255.0/24, and its default network prefix length is /24.

Data Communication Equipment (DCE)—Supplementary equipment whose purpose is to provide a standardized interface to data terminal equipment (DTE). Examples of DCE are modems and Channel Service Units/Data Service Units (CSUs/DSUs). See *Data terminal equipment (DTE)*.

Data Terminal Equipment (DTE)—Equipment residing on the ends of a physical connection, such as hosts and routers.

Diffusing Updates Algorithm (DUAL)—One of the algorithms whose goal is to discover the shortest path between two vertices of an arbitrarily interconnected graph. DUAL requires every vertex to know its neighbors and the destinations that these neighbors can reach. Based on that information, the vertex calculates its own list of the destinations that it can reach. If the graph changes, the vertex applies the feasibility condition to see if it still has correct reachability information or if it has to request updated reachability information from its neighbors. The algorithm was formulated by J. J. Garcia-Luna-Aceves. Cisco uses DUAL in its proprietary routing protocol, Enhanced Interior Gateway Routing Protocol (EIGRP).

distance-vector algorithm (also called Bellman-ford algorithm and Ford-Fulkerson algorithm)—One of the algorithms whose goal is to discover the shortest path between two vertices of an arbitrarily interconnected graph. The distance-vector algorithm is characterized by a total lack of topological information at the vertices during the algorithm operation and upon its completion. A version of the distance-vector algorithm is used in the network routing protocol to maintain routing in the network. Routing Information Protocol (RIP) and Internet Gateway Routing Protocol (IGRP) are two examples of routing protocols that are based on the distance-vector algorithm.

dotted decimal notation—The notation in which Internet Protocol (IP) addresses are represented as four decimal numbers separated by periods. Each decimal number represents 8 bits of an IP address. The first number represents bits 0 through 7, the second bits 8 through 16, and so on. For example: 10.1.13.10.

Enhanced Interior Gateway Routing Protocol (EIGRP)—Cisco's proprietary distance-vector routing protocol, which is based on Diffusing Updates Algorithm (DUAL).

Exterior Gateway Protocol (EGP)—A cumulative name for the group of dynamic routing protocols that are used to propagate reachability information among autonomous systems in the Internet. BGP (border gateway protocol) is an example of an EGP.

feasible successor—A router's neighbor meeting the feasibility condition that the succeeding router discovers a failure of its route for some destination. See also *Diffusing Updates Algorithm (DUAL)* and *feasibility condition*.

feasibility condition—The condition used in Diffusing Updates Algorithm (DUAL) to verify that the router has enough information to reestablish a failed route without querying its neighbors for updated reachability information. See also *Diffusing Updates Algorithm (DUAL)* and *feasible successor*.

Interior Gateway Protocol (IGP)—Any routing protocol that is suited for maintaining routing within the boundaries of an autonomous system. Examples of IGPs are Enhanced Interior Gateway Routing Protocol (EIGRP), Interior Gateway Routing Protocol (IGRP), Intermediate System-to Intermediate System (IS-IS), Open Shortest Path First (OSPF), and Routing Information Protocol (RIP).

Interior Gateway Routing Protocol (IGRP)—Cisco's distance-vector Internet Protocol (IP) routing protocol.

Internet Control Message Protocol (ICMP)—A supplementary protocol that Internet Protocol (IP) uses to report errors and communicate control messages.

Glossary

Internet Protocol (IP)—The only Internet layer protocol of the IP suite. IP is characterized as a best-effort, nonreliable, connectionless delivery service.

layer-2 switch—A bridge. Layer 2 is the data link layer of Open Systems Interconnection Reference Model (OSI/RM). A packet switch operating on the data link layer is called a *bridge.*

layer-3 switch—A router. Layer 3 is the network layer of Open Systems Interconnection Reference Model (OSI/RM). A packet switch operating on the network layer is called a *router.*

Link-State Advertisement (LSA)—An Open Shortest Path First (OSPF) data unit whose goal is to describe a piece of topological information. An LSA corresponds to a vertex in the graph that represents the network.

Link-State Packet (LSP)—An IS-IS protocol data unit (PDU) carrying topological information.

Link-state database—The data structure of a link-state routing protocol such as Open Shortest Path First (OSPF) and IS-IS containing the topological information of the network.

network prefix—The part of the Internet Protocol (IP) address that indicates the ID of the segment that is connected to the host's interface on which the IP address is assigned. In classful IP terminology, the network prefix is often referred to as a *subnet.*

Nonbroadcast Multiple Access (NBMA)—A type of network that can interconnect multiple hosts but that does not provide a means to address a single packet (frame) to all of the hosts that it interconnects. Examples of NBMA networks are Frame Relay and X.25.

Open Shortest Path First (OSPF)—The standard-based, link-state Internet Protocol (IP) routing protocol.

Open Systems Interconnection Reference Model (OSI/RM)—This International Organization for Standardization (ISO) standard multilayer communication model comprising seven layers—application, presentation, session, transport, network, data link, and physical.

protocol data unit (PDU)—A chunk of data formed in accordance with the communication protocol to which it belongs.

route source-route bridging (RSRB)—A modification of regular token ring source-route bridging (SRB), which allows a source-route bridge to conduct SRB over non-token ring media.

router—A packet switch that accepts Internet Protocol (IP) datagrams on its input interfaces and forwards them towards the destination via its output interfaces. The distinction between the input and output interfaces is made mostly for the purposes of the definition. Although a router interface can be only input or only output, the same interface can typically serve as both input and output. See also *layer-3 switch*.

spanning explorer (also called *single route explorer* or *single route broadcast*)—A token ring frame that allows the host that created it to find a route to the destination in a source-route bridged network. The spanning explorer is destined for a broadcast media access control (MAC) address (FFFF-FFFF-FFFF). What makes the spanning explorer different from any other token ring frame is the presence of the routing information field (see *RIF*) whose first three bits are equal to 110 (binary). The operation of the spanning explorer allows the host that issued it to discover a single path to the destination. The operation of the spanning explorer requires the source-route bridges to be configured in such a way that exactly one path exists between any two hosts that the spanning explorer can traverse. See also *route source-route bridging (RSRB)* and *source-route bridging (SRB)*.

spanning-tree algorithm—The algorithm whose purpose is to create a spanning-tree topology in an arbitrarily interconnected bridged network. The spanning-tree topology is a loop-free topology, which yet provides paths between any two segments of the network. The topology is enforced by placing certain ports (interfaces) on the bridges into a so-called *blocking state*. A bridge port in a blocking state is prohibited from receiving and transmitting traffic.

SPF algorithm—Dijkstra's shortest-path algorithm, whose purpose is to find the shortest path between two vertices of an arbitrarily interconnected graph. The shortest-path algorithm is used in link-state routing algorithms to calculate the routing table from the topology information.

source-route bridging (SRB)—Differs from transparent bridging in that it requires the hosts to actively participate in bridging. See also *route source-route bridging (RSRB)*, and *spanning explorer*.

spanning tree protocol (STP)—It is often used to refer to the Institute of Electrical and Electronics Engineers (IEEE) 802.1D bridging protocol or (rarely) to the Digital Equipment Corporation (DEC) bridging protocol, both of which are based on the spanning-tree algorithm. See also *Automatic Spanning Tree (AST)*.

successor—A next-hop router. This term is primarily used in the Diffusing Updates Algorithm (DUAL) terminology.

Glossary

switch—1) A bridge. A marketing term primarily used to describe a fast bridge with multiple ports. The Institute of Electrical and Electronics Engineers (IEEE) 802.1D bridging standard does not pose any limitation on the number of ports (interfaces) that a bridge can have and does not limit in any way the speed and capacity of the bridges. 2) A packet switch; a device capable of receiving packets on its input ports (or interfaces) and transmitting them through its output ports (interfaces) towards the destination. Examples of switches are routers, Frame Relay switches, bridges, and so on. The term *switch* is now rarely used to describe a packet switch.

Type of Service (ToS)—A field in the Internet Protocol (IP) datagram header whose goal is to provide routers a "hint" about the characteristics of the path that the datagrams should preferably traverse. The characteristics include low delay, high bandwidth, high reliability, and low monetary cost. (These characteristics are mutually exclusive.)

Index

A

ABRs (area border routers), 442, 457–460, 463, 499, 507, 540
access-list *<AL number>* **permit|deny** *<source IP address><wildcard mask>* command, 81
Access lists, 81–88
   extended access lists, 84–87
   filtering routing updates using, 607–612
   named access lists, 87–88
   standard access lists, 81–84
Acknowledgment, 451–452
Active router, 646, 652, 654
Active state, 366, 378, 654
Active time, 378, 422
Active timer, 650, 652, 653
Address, 12
Address field, 96
Addressing, 12
Address resolution, 55
Address Resolution Protocol. *See* ARP.
Adjacencies, 439–441, 464–469
Administrative distance, 57
   connected routes, 182
   EIGRP, 384
   metrics different from, 224
   RIP, 257, 287–294
   static routes, 180, 186–191
Aging time, 96, 108
All routes broadcast, 117–119
All routes explorer, 117–119
Application layer
   internet communication model, 19
   Internet Protocol suite, 21
   OSI/RM, 17
Application-sensitive policy-based routing, 664–667
Architectural constants, OSPF, 476

B

Backup designated router, 440
BackupSeen event, 465
bandwidth command, 492

area 10 stub command, 508
area 10 stub no-summary command, 509
area 100 virtual-link command, 521
area *<area>* **virtual-link** *<router ID>* command, 511
area *<area ID>* **nssa** command, 601
area *<area ID>* **range** *<IP address><subnet mask>* **[not-advertise]** command, 498
area *<area ID>* **range** command, 598
area *<area ID>* **stub** command, 508
area *<area ID>* **stub no-summary** command, 509
Area border routers. *See* ABRs.
ARP (Address Resolution Protocol), 66
   IP unnumbered, 277
   source-route bridging and, 121–122
ARPANET, 17
ARPANET reference model, 17
ASBRs (autonomous system boundary routers), 442, 446, 457, 462, 507, 552, 591–592
AST (Automatic Spanning Tree), configuring spanning explorers using, 168–175
Authentication, RIP version, 2, 236
Automatic redistribution, pseudo-connected routes, 578–580
Automatic Spanning Tree. *See* AST.
Autonomous system, 59, 442, 499
Autonomous system boundary routers. *See* ASBRs.
Auto-summarization
   EIGRP, 384
   RIP, 259–261, 305–312

bandwidth 64 command, 492
bandwidth *<new bandwidth>*
command, 341
Basic Match
classful routing algorithm, 52, 53–54
classless routing algorithm, 49, 50
BDR state, 465, 466
Bellman-Ford algorithm. *See* Distance-vector
algorithm.
Best local routes, 326
Big-endian order, 26
Bit order, internet protocol, 26
Blocking state, 99, 107–108
Bookstrap Protocol. *See* BOOTP.
BOOTP (Bookstrap Protocol), 19
BPDUs (bridge protocol data units), 99–112
configuration BPDUs, 99, 100, 110–112
topology change notification BPDUs,
99, 112
BPDU type field
configuration BPDU, 111
topology change notification BPDU, 112
bridge *<bridge group>* **protocol iee/dec**
command, 139
bridge *<bridge group #>* **priority**
<priority> command, 169
bridge *<bridge group #>* **protocol**
<bridging protocol> command, 127, 129, 134
bridge *<bridge group #>* **protocol ibm**
command, 169
bridge crb command, 137, 139
Bridged LANs, 91
blocking state, 99, 107–108
BPDUs, 100–107
forwarding state, 99, 107–108
learning, 107
listening, 107
message age timer, 106–107
spanning tree algorithm, 99, 100
topology change notification, 108–109
transition from blocking to forwarding,
107–108
bridge-group *<group number>* command,
127, 129, 134
bridge *<group number>* **path-cost 100**
command, 147
bridge *<group number>* **priority** *<new
priority>* command, 145

bridge *<group number>* **protocol**
<protocol> command, 134
bridge *<group number>* **route ip** command,
139, 140
Bridge groups, 126
Bridge ID, 99, 109
Bridge identifier field, configuration
BPDU, 111
bridge irb command, 139
Bridge priority, 109
Bridge protocol data units *See* BPDUs.
Bridges, 90–92
Bridge virtual interface. *See* BVI interface.
Bridging, 90–92
concurrent routing and bridging
(CRB), 126
configuring over HDLC, 132–133
configuring over source-route bridging,
147–175
configuring over transparent bridging,
125–147
integrated routing and bridging (IRB), 126
source-route bridging, 91–92, 112–125
source-route translational bridging,
176–178
transparent bridging, 91, 96–112
Bridging loop, 98
Bridging protocol, 99
Broadcast, 92
Broadcast bits, RIF, 114, 115, 116
Broadcast indicators, 114
Broadcast networks, 65, 66
Broadcast segment, 216
BVI interface (bridge virtual interface), 139

C

Candidate default routes, 243–245
Candidate routes, 326
Checksum field, ICMP control message, 61
CIDR (Classless Inter-Domain Routing), 59
Cisco, LMI, 71
Cisco IOS 12.0(X)T
extended **network** command, 394–399
transit area support, 516, 517
Cisco routers
bridging, 92, 132–137

candidate default routes, 244–245
concurrent routing and bridging
  (CRB), 126
configuring, 126–131, 137–140, 147–149,
  151–167
direct encapsulation available, 154
DLSw+, 124
EIGRP, 34
fast-switching modes, 206
gateway of last resort, 242–248
HSRP, 21
IGRP, 33
IGRP timers, 356
integrated routing and bridging (IRB), 126
metrics, 232
OSPF, 516
ping command, 279
proxyARP, 80
RIP, 232, 233–234
RIP timers, 232–234, 299
routing updates, 232
spanning tree parameters, tuning, 140–147
tunnel interface, 77
Classful network addresses, 40, 226
Classful routers, 227
Classful routing algorithms, 52–55, 198–200
Classful routing protocols, 225–228, 320,
  540, 568
Classful summarization, 540, 568
Classless Inter-Domain Routing. *See* CIDR.
Classless IP addressing, 41–44, 59
Classless routing, 195–198
Classless routing algorithms, 49–52, 198–200
Classless routing protocols, 225
Class X IP address, 38
clear ip ospf process command, 484, 489
Code field, ICMP control message, 61
Communication model, 2–4. *See also*
  Multilayer communication model.
Concurrent routing and bridging. *See* CRB.
Configuration BPDUs, 99, 100, 110–112
Configuring
  ASBRs, 591–592
  CRB, 137–138
  EIGRP, 384, 385–399
  Frame Relay interface, 70–75
  HSRP, 696–710
  IGRP, 328–331, 348–355

IP addressing, on an interface, 70
IP unnumbered, 79
IRB, 139–140
loopback interface, 76–77
LSNAT, 693
mixed-media transparent bridging, 131
multiple bridge groups, 129–131
NAT, 672–696
NSSA, 601–607
OSPF, 477–510, 522–533
policy-based routing, 657–672
proxyARP, 80
redistribution, 563–568
redistribution metrics, 572–573
RIP, 249–252, 264–265, 303–305
route summarization with EIGRP, 416–422
RSRB, 151–167
source-route bridging, 147–175
source-route translational bridging,
  176–178
standard access lists, 81–84
static routing, 183–186, 195–198, 200–211
transparent bridging, 126–147
tunnel interface, 77–78
Connectionless communication, 16
Connection-oriented communication, 16–17
Contiguous subnet masks, 39, 41
Convergence, 219
Convergence time, 219
Counting to infinity, 219–221
CRB (concurrent routing and bridging),
  126, 137–138
CRC (cyclic redundancy check), 19
Cyclic redundancy check. *See* CRC.

D

Database description PDUs, 467, 472–473
Database exchange, 467–468
Data communication equipment. *See* DCE.
Datagrams, 22, 25
  fragmentation, 30–32
  IP routers. *See* IP routers.
Data link circuit identifiers. *See* DLCIs.
Data link layer, OSI/RM, 16, 18, 20
Data link switching. *See* DLSw.
Data terminal equipment. *See* DTE.

DCE (data communication equipment), 70

debug arp command, 195, 277, 279

debug command, 278

debug eigrp fsm command, 403–408, 610

debug eigrp packet update reply query command, 403–408

debug ip command, 238

debug ip igrp transactions command, 238, 331–335, 340, 355, 590, 626–629

debug ip packet command, 201, 206–207, 211

debug ip packet detail command, 277, 278, 279

debug ip packet detail 100 command, 285

debug ip policy command, 666–667

debug ip rip command, 252–257, 271, 285

debug ip routing command, 403–408, 626–629

debug source bridge command, 157

Default addresses, 226

Default gateway, 60, 242

default-information originate command, 264, 506

default-metric command, 572, 573

default-metric *<fixed metric>* command, 572

Default route, 60, 264
IGRP, 348–355
OSPF, 506–507
static routing, 200–202

Default subnet masks, 40

delay command, 399

Delayed acknowledgment, 451

delay *<new delay>* command, 341

Demultiplexing, 7, 11

Demultiplexing key, 12

Designated bridge, 100

Designated port, 100

Designated router, 439

Destination address, IP header, 34

Destination-based routing, 46

Destination Unreachable message, 63, 84

DF bit, 30

Diffusing computation, 366

Diffusing update algorithm. *See* DUAL.

Digital Equipment Corp. (DEC), bridging protocol, 99

Digraph, 428

Dijkstra's shortest-path algorithm, 426–427, 428–431, 457, 460, 461, 463

Direct acknowledgment, 451

Directed broadcast address, 36, 42

Direct encapsulation, configuring RSRB with, 152–160

Direction field, RIF, 115, 116

Directly connected route, 56

Discontiguous subnetting, 307

distance command, 288–294

distance 70 command, 562

distance 150 192.168.6.2 0.0.0.0 1 command, 292–293

distance 255 command, 576

distance eigrp command, 581

distance eigrp 130 170 command, 557

distance *<new AD>* [*<IP address><wildcard mask[<standard access-list #>]]* command, 287

Distance-vector algorithm, 214–224, 359, 424–426
counting to infinity, 219–221
defined, 215
holddowns, 222, 223, 234
IP-specific, 216–218
network changes, 219
poisoned-reverse updates, 222–223
split-horizon rule, 221–222
triggered updates, 223–224

Distance-vector protocols, 216

distribute-list *<ACL #>* **out|in** *<interface><#>* command, 607–608

distribute-list *<AL name>|<AL number>|***prefix** *<PL name>* **out** *<source>* command, 617

distribute-list command, 611

distribute-list prefix *<PL name>* [**gateway** *<GW-PL name>* **in** *<interface>* command, 615

distribute-list prefix *<PL name>* **out** *<interface>* command, 615

DLCIs (data link circuit identifiers), 71

DLSw (data link switching), 123–125

DLSw+, 124

DNS (Domain Name System), 19

Domain Name System. *See* DNS.

Dotted decimal notation, IP addressing, 35, 41

Down state, 465
DROther state, 465, 466
DR state, 465, 466
DTE (data terminal equipment), 70
DUAL (diffusing update algorithm), 358–367
    EIGRP, 399–408
    feasibility condition (FC), 364–367
    feasible distance (FD), 364
    IP EIGRP, 369
    topology table, 362–364
Dynamic entries, filtering database, 96
Dynamic NAT, 645
Dynamic routes, 56
Dynamic routing protocols, 207
    distance-vector algorithm, 216
    timers, 299
Dynamic translation, of inside IP addresses,
    configuring, 677–687

E

EBP (EIGRP bandwidth percentage), 378
Echo message, 63
Echo Reply message, 63
Edges, 216, 428
EGPs (exterior gateway protocols), 59
EIGRP (Extended Interior Gateway
  Routing Protocol), 358, 384, 426
    active time, 422
    administrative distance, 384
    auto-summarization, 384
    comparison with RIP and IGRP, 384
    configuring, 384, 385–399, 416–422
    disabling an interface, 412
    DUAL, 358–367, 399–408
    external routes, 581–586
    hello protocol, 369–370, 373–374
    incremental updates, 368
    internal routes, 581–586
    IP EIGRP, 358, 369
    IP unnumbered, 384
    metrics, 368, 384, 537, 539, 572, 573
    NBMA networks, 412–416
    PDUs, 370–374
    protocol number, 34
    query processing rules, 369–370, 382–383
    redistribution, 550–551, 581–591

redistribution metrics, 572, 573
reliable transport protocol (RTP), 369–370,
    375–378
    routing updates, 368
    secondary IP addresses, 408–412
    stability features, 379
    timing out, 368
    topology table, 391–392
EIGRP bandwidth percentage. *See* EBP.
EIGRP external routes, 581–586
EIGRP internal routes, 581–586
Encapsulation, 9, 77
encapsulation frame-relay command,
    71, 73, 134
End node, 14
End system, 6, 14
End-to-end connectivity, 16
Entity, 5
Equal-cost load balancing
    configuring with static routing, 203–208
    EIGRP, 384
    IGRP, 344–349
    OSPF, 497
    RIP, 294–296
Error messages, ICMP control messages,
    61–65
Ethernet
    MAC addresses, 92–93
    MTU size, 20
ExStart state, 467
Extended access lists, 84–87
Extended Interior Gateway Routing
    Protocol. *See* EIGRP.
Extended **network** command, 394–399
Extended offset-lists, 297
Exterior gateway protocols. *See* EGPs.
Exterior network prefixes, 321
Exterior networks, 321
External LSAs, 448, 461, 463

F

Failures, spanning tree algorithm, 105–107
Fast switching
    configuring RSRB over fast-switched
    TCP connection, 165
    defined, 205–206

FC (feasibility condition), 364–367
FD (feasible distance), 364
FDDI, MTU size, 20
Feasibility condition. *See* FC.
Feasible distance. *See* FD.
Feasible successor, 365, 367
File Transfer Access and Management. *See* FTAM.
File Transfer Protocol. *See* FTP.
Filtering, 60, 553–555
   access lists for, 81–88
   during redistribution, 555, 617–623
   inbound filter, 554
   outbound filter, 553
   routing updates, 607–617
Filtering database, 96–99
Flags field
   configuration BPDU, 111
   IP header, 30
Floating routes, 188
Flooding, 438, 451
Flows in Networks (Ford and Fulkerson), 214
Flush time, 234, 327
Ford-Fulkerson algorithm. *See* Distance-vector algorithm.
Forward delay, 107
Forward delay field, configuration BPDU, 111
Forwarding state, 99, 107–108
Fragmentation, 25–26, 30–32
Fragment Offset field, IP header, 30
Fragments, 25
Frame, 16
Frame Relay, 70–71
   configuring on an interface, 71–73
   configuring bridging over, 134–136
   configuring on a subinterface, 73–75
   EIGRP, 412–416
Frame Relay encapsulation, configuring RSRB with, 160–163
Frame Relay interface, configuring, 70–75
frame-relay interface-dlci *<DLCI>* command, 74
frame-relay inverse-arp ip *<DLCI>*, 72
frame-relay lmi-type *<lmi-type>* command, 71, 73, 134
frame-relay map bridge *<DLCI>* **broadcast** command, 134

frame-relay map ip command, 302
frame-relay map ip *<IP address>* *<DLCI>*[broadcast] command, 72, 73
frame-relay map ip *<remote IP address>* *<DLCI>* command, 74
frame-relay map rsrb *<DLCI>* **broadcast** command, 161
Frame Relay network, 72, 74, 85
   OSPF in, 522–533
   RIP in, 300–302
FST encapsulation, configuring RSRB with, 165–167
FTAM (File Transfer Access and Management), 17
FTP (File Transfer Protocol), 18, 19
Fully adjacent, 457
Functional MAC address, 94

G

Garbage-collection timer, 233, 234, 257
Gateway, 22
Gateway of last resort, 242–248
General Routing Encapsulation. *See* GRE.
Generic multilayer communication model, 4, 5–15
   addressing, 12–13
   benefits, 14–15
   components, 5–6
   PDUs, 5, 6–12
Global inside IP addresses, configuring NAT with overloading global inside IP addresses, 687–689
GRE (General Routing Encapsulation), 34, 77, 78
Group/individual bit, 93, 114

H

Half bridges, 123
HDLC, bridging over, 132–133
Header
   cyclic redundancy check, 19
   datagram, 25
   IP datagram, 25, 26–34
   token ring frames, 113

Header Checksum field, IP router, 34
Hello message, 368, 379
Hello PDUs
    HSRP, 652–653
    OSPF, 472–473
Hello protocol
    EIGRP, 369–370, 373–374
    OSPF, 441
Hello time, 105
Hello time field, configuration BPDU, 111
Hello timer, 650
Holddowns, 222, 223, 234
Hold time, 368
Hop count, 232
Hop-to-hop communication, 16, 18
Host ID, 35, 38, 41
Hosts, 22, 60–61
    default gateway, 242
    fragmentation, 32
    IP hosts, 60–61
HSRP (Hot Standby Router Protocol), 21,
645–656
    backup scenarios, 706–710
    configuring, 696–710
    HSRP process, 646–647
    HSRP state machine, 650–654
    HSRP timers, 650
    multigroup HSRP (MHSRP), 702–706
    PDU format, 647–650
    virtual MAC address, 646, 654–655
HSRP process, 646–647
HSRP state machine, 650–654
HSRP timers, 650
HTTP (Hypertext Transfer Protocol), 19
Hub and spoke topology, 658, 659

I

ICMP (Internet Control Message Protocol),
33, 61
ICMP control messages, 61–65
ICMP Destination Unreachable message,
63, 84
ICMP Echo message, 63
ICMP Echo Reply message, 63
ICMP Redirect message, 64
ICMP Source Quench message, 64

ICMP Time Exceeded message, 65
Identification field, IP header, 30
IEEE 802.1D standard, 94, 99, 111, 112
IEEE 802.3 frames, 112
IGPs (interior gateway protocols), 59
IGRP (Interior Gateway Routing Protocol),
244, 316, 328
    comparison with EIGRP and RIP, 384
    comparison with RIP, 328
    configuring, 328–331, 348–355
    metrics, 322–326, 341–344, 537, 539,
      572, 573
    metric weights, 356
    network prefixes, 320–322
    protocol number, 33
    redistribution, 568–572, 586–591
    redistribution metrics, 572, 573
    route entries, 318–320
    routing updates, 316–320, 331–335
    secondary IP addresses, 335–341
    stability features, 316
    unequal-cost load balancing, 325–326
IGRP routers, metrics, 322–326
IGRP timers, 326–327, 356
IHL (IP Header Length) field, 26
InactivityTimer event, 468
Inbound filter, 554
Incremental updates
    EIGRP, 368
    OSPF, 463
Individual host addresses, 43, 226, 261–264
InfTransDelay, 446
InitialSequenceNumber, 449
Initial state, HSRP state machine, 651
Input interface, 47
Inside global addresses, 643
Inside IP addresses
    configuring NAT with overloading global
      inside IP addresses, 687–689
    configuring static translation of, 672–677
Inside local addresses, 643
Inside networks, 643
Integrated routing and bridging. *See* IRB.
Interconnections (Perlman), 112, 427–428
interface BVI <*bridge group*>
    command, 139
InterfaceDown event, 465

interface Loopback <*Interface #*>
command, 76
interface loopback <*number*>
command, 262
interface Serial <*Interface #*>.
<*Subinterface #*> **multipoint** command, 73
interface Serial <*Interface #*>.
<*Subinterface #*> **point-to-point**
command, 73
Interface states, OSPF, 464–466
interface tunnel <*Interface #*>
command, 78
Interior gateway protocols. *See* IGPs.
Interior Gateway Routing Protocol.
See IGRP.
Intermediate node, 14
Intermediate System to Intermediate
System. *See* IS-IS.
Internet communication model, 4, 17–19
Internet Control Message Protocol.
See ICMP.
Internet layer
internet communication model, 18, 90
Internet Protocol suite, 21
Internet protocol
bit and octet order in, 26
datagrams, 22, 25
distance-vector algorithm, 216–218
DUAL and, 369
fragmentation, 25–26, 30–32
hosts, 22
routers, 22–24
source-route bridging and, 121–122
Internet protocol suite, 20, 21
Interoperability, multilayer communication
model, 14
Intra-area routes, 462–463
Invalid time, 234, 327
Inverse ARP (Inverse Address Resolution
Protocol), 67, 72
ip access-group <*AL number*> **in|out**
command, 82
IP addressing, 34–35
classful, 34–41, 45
classful routing protocols, 226
classless, 41–44, 59
Classless Inter-Domain Routing (CIDR), 59
configuring, 70

destination address, 34
dotted decimal notation, 35, 41
inside IP addresses, 672–687
IP unnumbered, 79
multicast, 35
NAT, 643–645
network classes, 36–41, 45
notation, 35, 41, 45
primary IP addresses, 44
private IP addresses, 45
rules of comparison, 49
secondary IP addresses, 44–45, 195
significant bit, 49
source address, 34
unicast, 35
ip address <*IP address*>
255.255.255.255 command, 262
ip address <*IP address*><*subnet mask*>
command, 70, 72, 74, 129
ip classless command, 195–198, 200, 670
IP datagrams, 25, 26–34
ip default-network command, 381
ip default-network <*IP address*>
command, 244, 349
IP EIGRP, 358, 369
IP header
destination address, 34
Flags field, 30
Fragment Offset field, 30
Identification field, 30
length, 26
MBZ field, 28, 29
Options field, 26, 34
Padding field, 34
Precedence field, 27, 28
Protocol field, 33–34
source address, 34
Time to Live (TTL) field, 32–33
ToS octet, 27–29
Total Length Field, 29
Type of Service field, 27, 28
Version field, 26
IP Header Length field. *See* IHL field.
IP hosts, 60–61
ip maximum paths command, 294
ip nat inside command, 673, 678, 689, 693
ip nat inside destination list
<*AL number*>|<*AL name*> **pool** <*pool
name*> command, 693

ip nat inside source list <*AL number*>| <*AL name*> **interface** <*interface*> command, 688

ip nat inside source <*local IP address*> <*global IP address*> command, 672–673

ip nat outside command, 673, 678, 689, 693

ip nat outside source list <*AL number*>|<*AL name*> **pool** <*name*> command, 689

ip nat pool command, 686

ip nat pool <*name*><*start IP address*> <*end IP address*> **netmask** <*subnet mask*>|**prefix-length** <*prefix length*> command, 677

ip netmask-format bit-count|decimal|hexadecimal command, 241

IP network classes, 36–37

IP networks, DUAL in, 369

ip ospf cost 1562 command, 492

ip ospf cost <*cost*> command, 492

ip ospf network broadcast command, 523, 525

ip ospf network point-to-multipoint command, 527–530

ip ospf priority 0 command, 532

ip ospf priority <*priority*> command, 493

ip policy route map <*RM name*> command, 658

ip prefix-list <*PL name*> [**seq** <*PL #*>] **permit|deny** <*NP*>/<*NP length*> [**ge**<*GE value*>] [**le**<*LE value*>], 613

ip proxy-arp command, 80

ip rip receive version 1|2 command, 312

ip rip send version 1|2 command, 312

ip route 0.0.0.0 0.0.0.0 <*next-hop router*> command, 200

ip route 0.0.0 0.0.0 Null0 command, 506

ip route-cache command, 206

ip route <*IP address*> **255.255.255.255** <*next-hop router*> command, 202

ip route <*remote network address*><*subnet mask*><*next-hop router*> command, 183

ip route <*remote network address*><*subnet mask*><*next-hop router*><*distance*> command, 186

ip route <*remote network address*> <*subnet mask*><*output interface*> command, 191

IP routers, 22–24, 47
   components, 47–48
   defined, 47
   Header Checksum field, 34

IP routing
   Classless Inter-Domain Routing (CIDR), 59
   destination-based, 46
   filtering, 60
   Hot Standby Router Protocol (HSRP), 645–656
   load balancing, 55
   multicast, 46
   Network Address Translation (NAT), 642–645
   policy-based routing, 640–641, 657–672
   prefix-based, 46
   routing algorithms, 48–55
   routing protocols, 58–59
   routing tables, 47–48, 55–58
   unicast, 46–61

ip routing command, 127, 166, 181

IP routing protocols, 59

ip split-horizon eigrp <*AS #*> command, 415, 416

ip subnet-zero command, 196, 415

ip summary-address eigrp <*AS #*> command, 417, 418

ip summary-address eigrp <*AS #*><*IP address*><*subnet mask*> command, 416

IP unnumbered
   ARP, 277
   configuring, 79
   EIGRP, 384
   OSPF, 494–495
   RIP, 272–280

ip unnumbered command, 494

ip unnumbered <*interface*> command, 79, 670

ip unnumbered TokenRing0 command, 280

ipx routing command, 127

IRB (integrated routing and bridging), 126, 139–140

IS-IS (Intermediate System to Intermediate System), 426

ISO/IEC 10038, 94

J

Jitter time, 327

K

Kann, Steve, 209
KillNeighbor event, 468

L

LAN frames, 92
LANs, 66
    bridged. *See* Bridged LANs.
    source-route bridged LAN. *See* Source-
        route bridged LANs.
LAN segment, 91
Largest frame field, RIF, 115, 116
Layers, 4, 5
Layer stack, 4
Layer two switches, 91
Layer two switching, 91
Learning, port state, 107
Learning process, filtering database, 96
Learn state, HSRP state machine, 652
Length field, RIF, 114–115
Link layer
    internet communication model, 18
    Internet Protocol suite, 21
Link layer addressing, 65–66
Link-state acknowledgment PDU, 474, 475
Link-state database, 437
Link-state database synchronization
    process, 467
Link-state dynamic routing protocol, 424
Link-state protocol, IS-IS, 426
Link-state request PDU, 473–474
Link-state update PDU, 474, 475
Listening, port state, 107
Listen state, HSRP state machine, 652
Little-endian order, 26
LLDown event, 468
LMI (local management interface), 71
Load balancing, 55, 207
    EIGRP, 384
    equal-cost load balancing. *See* Equal-
        cost load balancing.

IGRP, 325–326, 344–349
MHSRP for, 702–706
NAT, 642
OSPF, 497
per-packet load balancing, 55, 206
RIP, 294–296
static routing, 203–211
TCP load balancing, configuring NAT
    for, 692–696
unequal-cost load balancing. *See* Un-
    equal-cost load balancing.
Load Sharing Using IP Network Address
    Translation. *See* LSNAT.
Local broadcast address, 36, 42
Local management interface. *See* LMI.
Longest Match
    classful routing algorithm, 52, 54
    classless routing algorithm, 50
Longest match concept, 198–200
Long-lived routing loops, 540–541
Loopback address, 37, 42
Loopback interface, configuring, 76–77
Loop-digraph, 428
*Loop-Free Routing Using Diffusing
    Computations* (Garcia-Luna-Aceves), 358
Loop-free topology, 98, 99
LSA header, 446–450
LSAs, 437–441, 443, 446–463
    acknowledgment, 451–452
    external LSAs, 448, 461
    flooding, 438, 451
    header, 446–450
    network LSAs, 448, 456–457
    NSSA external LSAs, 448, 461
    premature aging procedure, 451
    reliable flooding, 439, 451
    router LSAs, 448, 453–456, 504
    summary LSAs, 448, 457–460, 504, 505
LSNAT (Load Sharing Using IP Network
    Address Translation), 692–693
LSRefreshTime value, 450

M

MAC (Media Access Control) address, 66,
    92–94
    changing, 147
    filtering database, 96–99

functional, 94
multicast, 93, 94
nonfunctional, 94
source-bridge remote-peer command, 159
unicast, 93
virtual MAC address, 646, 654–655
mac-address *<new MAC address>* command, 147
MAC frames, 92
match ip address *<AL number>*| *<AL name>* command, 657
MaxAge, 446, 450
Maximum age, 106
Maximum age field, configuration BPDU, 111
maximum-paths *<# of paths>* command, 497
maximum-paths *<# of routes>* command, 203–204, 344
Maximum transfer unit. *See* MTU.
MaxSequenceNumber, 449
MBZ field, IP header, 28, 29
Media Access Control address. *See* MAC address.
Meshed NBMA networks, configuring OSPF over, 523–526
Message age, 106
Message age increment, 107
Message age timer, 106–107
Message field, configuration BPDU, 111
Metric domain boundary, 540
Metric domains, 539
Metrics, 217, 224
Cisco routers, 232
cumulative nature of, 539
different from administrative distance, 224
EIGRP, 368, 384, 537, 539
IGRP, 322–326, 341–344, 537, 539
OSPF, 539
RIP, 224, 232, 233, 297–298, 537, 539
Metric weights, IGRP, 356
metric weights 0 0 0 1 0 0 command, 400
metric weights 0 <k1> <k2> <k3> <k4> <k5> command, 356
MF bit, 30
MHSRP (Multigroup HSRP), 702–706
MinLSInterval, 451
Mixed-media transparent bridging, configuring, 131

Modularity, multilayer communication mode, 14
MTU (maximum transfer unit), 20, 25, 32, 159–160, 163
mtu 4464 command, 163
Multicast groups, 36
Multicast IP routing, 46
Multicast MAC addresses, 93
Multilayer communication model, 4, 5
addressing, 12–13
benefits, 14–15
components, 5–6
generic, 4, 5–15
internet communication model, 4, 17–19
OSI/RM, 4, 15–17
PDUs, 5, 6–12
Multiplexing, 7, 11
Multiplier, 326
Multipoint subinterface, 71, 73
Multiport source-route bridges, 121, 122, 123
Multiring ip command, 150

N

Named access lists, 87–88
NAPT (Network Address Port Translation), 687–688
NAT (Network Address Translation), 642–645
configuring, 677–696
dynamic translation of inside IP addresses, 677–687
OSPF and, 681–687
overloading global inside IP addresses, 687–689
RFCs, 642
static translation of inside IP addresses, 672–677
for TCP load balancing, 692–696
to translate between overlapping address spaces, 689–692
NBMA networks (Non-Broadcast Multiple Access networks), 65, 67
configuring RIP in, 300–302
EIGRP, 412–416
OSPF, 436, 439, 440, 522–533
NBMA segment, 216
neighbor 192.168.5.1 command, 284
neighbor 192.168.5.2 command, 282

neighbor 192.168.6.2 command, 284
NeighborChange event, 465
neighbor command, 495–497
neighbor *<IP address>* command, 282, 495–497
Neighbors, 437
NetBIOS, 148
netstat -n command, 675–676, 681, 695–696
network 0.0.0.0 255.255.255.255 area 0 command, 483
network 10.0.0.0 command, 579
network 172.16.0.0 command, 311
network 192.168.135.0 command, 387
Network adapter, 2–3
Network address, 37, 41, 45
Network Address Port Translation.
   See NAPT.
Network Address Translation. *See* NAT.
Network Associates Web site, 428
Network classes, 36–41, 45
network *<classful IP address>* command, 262
network command, 249, 385, 394
Network component, 2
Network ID, 35, 36, 41
network *<IP address>* command, 249, 385
network *<IP address><wildcard mask>* **area 0** command, 478
network *<IP address><wildcard mask>* **area** *<area ID>* command, 497
network *<IP address><wildcard mask>* command, 394
Network layer, OSI/RM, 16, 18, 90
Network LSAs, 448, 456–457, 463
Network prefix, 41, 42, 45
   format, modifying, 240–241
   IGRP, 320–322
   length, 41
   notation, 41, 45
   RIP, 231–232
   routing updates, 217
   rules of comparison, 49, 50
   significant bit, 49
Next-hop router, 48
no auto-summary command, 306–312, 384, 571
no interface Loopback *<Interface #>* command, 77

no ip classless command, 201
no ip proxy-arp command, 80
no ip route-cache command, 206
no ip routing command, 127, 129, 134, 137, 148, 152, 160, 163, 181
no ip split-horizon command, 566, 567
no ip split-horizon eigrp 1 command, 415, 416
Nonautomatic redistribution, between EIGRP and IGRP, 591
Non-Broadcast Multiple Access networks.
   See NBMA networks.
Noncontiguous subnet masks, 39–40
Non-fully meshed NBMA networks, configuring OSPF over, 526–533
Nonfunctional MAC address, 94
no redirects command, 699
no redistribute command, 591
No reverse forwarding, 95
no router eigrp 10 command, 561
no router ospf 10 command, 489
Not-so-stubby areas. *See* NSSA.
NSSA (not-so-stubby areas), 444–445, 552, 601
NSSA ABRs, 552
NSSA external LSAs, 448, 461, 463

O

Octet order, Internet Protocol, 26
offset-list *<access-list>* **in|out** *<offset>* [*<interface>*] command, 297
offset-list command, 297–298, 621
One-way redistribution, 573–578, 621
Open Shortest Path First. *See* OSPF.
Open System Interconnection Reference Model. *See* OSI/RM.
Options field, IP header, 26, 34
Oscillating routing loops, 541
OSI/RM (Open System Interconnection Reference Model), 4, 15
   bridging, 90
   layers, 15–17, 18, 20, 90
OSPF (Open Shortest Path First), 424–428
   adjacencies, 439–441, 464–469
   architectural constants, 476
   autonomous system, 499

configuring, 477–483, 497–506, 508–510, 522–533

Dijkstra's shortest-path algorithm, 426–427, 428–431, 457, 460, 461, 462

incremental updates, 463

interface costs, 491–492

interface states, 464–466

IP unnumbered, 494–495

link-state database, displaying, 486–491

LSAs, 437–441, 443, 446–463

metrics, 539, 572

NAT with, 681–687

NBMA networks, 436, 439, 440, 522–533

network topology, 431–437

NSSA, 444–445

operation, 437–446

PDUs, 469–475

protocol number, 34

redistribution, 551–553, 591–607

redistribution metrics, 572

reliable flooding, 439

router ID, changing, 483–484

router priorities, 492–493, 530–533

routing hierarchy, 441–445

secondary IP addresses, 510–511

stub areas, 444

summarization, 441

virtual links, 445–446, 511–517

OSPF backbone, 441–442, 444, 445, 446

OSPF network, traffic flow, 446

OSPF routers, 437

OSPF: Anatomy of an Internet Routing Protocol (Moy), 428

Outbound filter, 553

Output interface, 47

Outside global addresses, 644

Outside local addresses, 643–644

Outside networks, 643

Overlapping, 668

P

Pacing interval, 377

Pacing packets, 378

Packet, 5

Padding field, IP header, 34

Partitioned backbone, OSPF, restoring, 517–522

passive-interface *<interface>* command, 412

passive-interface *<interface>* *<interface #>* command, 280

Passive interfaces, RIP, 280–282

passive-interface TokenRing0 command, 283

Passive state, 366

PAT (Port Address Translation), 687

Payload, 9, 14

PDUs (protocol data units), 5–6

components, 9

database description PDUs, 467, 472–473

EIGRP, 370–372

hello PDUs, 472–473

HSRP, 647–650

ICMP, 61

link-state acknowledgment PDU, 474, 475

link-state request PDUs, 473–474

link-state update PDUs, 474, 475

maximum size, 19–20

OSPF, 469–475

Peer entity, 5, 6, 13

Peer relation, 151

Peers, 151

Per-destination load balancing, 55

Perlman, Radia, 99, 112, 427

Permanent routing loops, 541

Permanent virtual circuits. *See* PVCs.

Per-packet load balancing, 55, 206

Physical layer, OSI/RM, 15, 18, 20

ping, 63, 84–85

ping command, 159, 185, 195, 279, 679

Pointing, 48

Point-to-multipoint model, 436

Point-to-point networks, 65, 66

Point-to-point segment, 216

Point-to-point state. *See* P-to-P state.

Point-to-point subinterface, 71, 74, 135

Poisoned-reverse updates, 222–223

Poison reverse, 221

Policy-based routing, 640–641

application-sensitive, 664–667

configuring, 657–672

in migration scenarios, 667–672

over a dedicated link, 658–663

Policy routing, 640

Port Address Translation. *See* PAT.

Port field, 96
Port ID, 99, 109
Port identifier field, configuration
  BPDU, 111
Port priority, 109
Ports, 91, 96
  blocking state, 99
  forwarding state, 99
Precedence field, IP header, 27, 28
Prefix-based routing, 46
Prefix lists, filtering routing updates using,
  612–617
Premature aging procedure, 451
Premature aging process, 449
Presentation layer, OSI/RM, 17
Primary IP addresses, 44
Private IP addresses, 45
Protocol data units. *See* PDUs.
Protocol field, IP header, 33–34
Protocol identifier field, configuration
  BPDU, 111
Protocols, 5, 14, 19
Protocol version identifier field, configura-
  tion BPDU, 111
ProxyARP, 80, 192–193
Pseudo-connected routes, 192, 195, 578–580
P-to-P state (Point-to-point state), 465, 466
Pure classful IP addressing, 38
PVCs (permanent virtual circuits), 71, 412

R

Redirect message, 64
redistribute command, 572, 591–607
redistribute *<source>* [metric *<fixed
  metric>*] command, 563
Redistribution, 536–540
  between EIGRP and IGRP, 586–591
  configuring, 563–568
  effects of, 539–540
  EIGRP, 550–551, 581–586
  enabling, 537–538
  filtering during, 555, 617–623
  IGRP, summarization, 568–572
  multiple redistribution points, 545–549
  one-way redistribution, 573–578, 621
  OSPF, 551–553, 591–607

pseudo-connected routes, 578–580
  redistribution metrics, 564, 572–573
  RIP, summarization, 568–572
  routing loops, 540–549
  single redistribution point, 542–545
Redistribution metrics, 564, 572–573
Regular routing updates, 219
Reliable flooding, 439, 451
Reliable transport protocol. *See* RTP.
Remote source-route bridging. *See* RSRP.
Reported distances, 362
Requests for Comments. *See* RFCs.
Retransmission timeout. *See* RTO.
RFCs (Requests for Comments), 17, 20
  RFC 791, 21, 22
  RFC 792, 63
  RFC 871, 17
  RFC 1042, 122
  RFC 1122, 61
  RFC 1518, 59
  RFC 1519, 59
  RFC 1631, 642
  RFC 1700, 63
  RFC 1795, 124
  RFC 1812, 59, 61
  RFC 1918, 45
  RFC 2178, 428
  RFC 2281, 21, 646
  RFC 2328, 427
  RFC 2391, 642, 692
  RFC 2453, 228, 232, 237
  RFC 2663, 642
RIF (routing information field), 114–116
RII (routing information indicator), 111
RIP (Routing Information Protocol), 214,
  228, 259
  administrative distance, 257, 287–294
  auto-summarization, 259–261, 305–312
  comparison with EIGRP and IGRP, 384
  comparison with IGRP, 328
  configuring, 249–252, 264–265
  distance-vector algorithm, 214–224
  equal-cost load balancing, 294–296
  individual host addresses, 261–264
  IP unnumbered, 272–280
  metric domain, 539–540
  metrics, 224, 232, 233, 297–298, 537,
    539, 572

NBMA networks, 300–302
network prefixes, 231–232
passive interfaces, 280–282
redistribution, summarization, 568–572
redistribution metrics, 572
routing table, 257–258
routing updates, 228–231, 235, 252–258, 282–287
secondary IP addresses, 265–272
stability features, 232
timers, 232–234
unicast routing updates, 282–287
version 1, 214, 237, 312–313, 539–540
version 2, 214, 228, 234–236, 237, 303–313
RIP timers, 232–234, 297
Root bridge, 99
Root identifier field, configuration BPDU, 111
Root path cost field, configuration BPDU, 111
Root port, 100
Route, 48
Route designator field, RIF, 116
routed program, 228
Route entries, IGRP, 318–320
route-map <*RM name*> [**permit|deny**] <*sequence #*> command, 619
Route maps, filtering during redistribution with, 619–622
Router commands, notation, 67
RouterDeadInterval parameter, 468
router eigrp <*AS #*> command, 385
router-id command, 477, 483–484
router id 0.0.0.1 command, 489
router igrp <*AS #*> command, 328
Router LSAs, 448, 453–456, 463, 510
router ospf <*process ID*> command, 477
Router priorities, OSPF, 492–493, 530–533
router rip command, 249
Router routing table entries, 462
Routers, 22–24
  active state, 366
  defined, 47
  diffusing computation, 366
  fragmentation, 30–32
  gateway of last resort, 242–248
  passive state, 366
  RTP, 369–370, 375–378

stuck in active condition, 378
topology table, 362–364
ToS octet, 27–29
updates, 379–382
Route summarization, configuring with EIGRP, 416–422
Routing, 16, 46
  connected interfaces, 181–182
  distance-vector protocol based, 216–218
  multicast IP routing, 46
  unicast IP routing, 46–61
Routing algorithms
  classful, 52–55
  classless, 49–52
  IP routing, 48–55
"Routing by rumors," 218
Routing domain, 59
Routing engine, 47, 48
Routing information field. *See* RIF.
Routing information indicator. *See* RII.
Routing Information Protocol. *See* RIP.
Routing information redistribution. *See* Redistribution.
Routing loops, 540–549, 623–637
  causes of, 549
  multiple redistribution points, 545–549, 629–633
  redistribution and disabled split horizon, 633–637
  single redistribution point, 542–545, 623–629
Routing protocols, 58–59
  exterior gateway protocols (EGPs), 59
  interior gateway protocols (IGPs), 59
  interoperation without redistribution, 556–563
  metric domains, 539
  multiple routing protocols on single router, 537
Routing table, 47–48
  maintenance rules, 224–225
  OSPF, calculation, 461–463
  populating, 55–58
  RIP, 257–258
  static routing, 180–211
Routing table entries, 48
  administrative distance, 57
  classful routing algorithm, 52–55, 56
  classless routing, 49–52, 56

Routing updates, 217, 379
  Cisco routers, 232
  EIGRP, 368
  filtering, 607–617
  IGRP, 316–320, 331–335
  learning, 217
  RIP, 228–231, 235, 252–258, 282–287
RSRB (remote source-route bridging), 123,
  124, 151–167
RTO (retransmission timeout), 377
RTP (reliable transport protocol), 369–370,
  375–378
RxmInterval time, 451

S

SAP (service(s) access point), 6
Secondary IP addresses, 44–45, 195
  EIGRP, 408–412
  IGRP, 335–341
  OSPF, 510–511
  RIP, 265–272
Segments, 217
SeqNumberMismatch event, 468
Serial interface, configured for Frame
  Relay, 71–75
Services, 6
Service(s) access point. *See* SAP.
service timestamps debug command, 253
service timestamps debug datetime
  command, 253
Session layer, OSI/RM, 17
set default interface *<interface>*
  command, 657
set interface *<interface>* command, 657
set ip default next-hop *<IP address>*
  command, 657
set ip next-hop *<IP address>*
  command, 657
Shortest-path algorithm. *See* Dijkstra's
  shortest-path algorithm.
Short-lived routing loops, 540, 541
show arp command, 278
show bridge command, 131, 133, 136–137
show bridge *<group number>* command,
  128–129
show interfaces command, 159

show interfaces Ethernet0 command,
  341, 700
show interfaces *<Interface
  ID><Interface #>* command, 76
show interfaces *<interface><interface #>*
  command, 341
show interfaces TokenRing0 command,
  156, 706
show ip eigrp interfaces command, 393
show ip eigrp neighbors command,
  392–393, 397–398
show ip eigrp topology all-links command, 392, 403
show ip eigrp topology command, 391–392,
  398, 399, 403, 419, 420
show ip interfaces command, 342, 491
show ip interfaces *<interface ID>
  <interface #>* command, 181
show ip interfaces Serial 0 command, 491
show ip nat translations command,
  679, 680
show ip ospf border-routers command,
  507–508, 596
show ip ospf database command, 486,
  489, 504, 510, 526, 561–562, 596, 605–606
show ip ospf database external
  command, 596
**show ip ospf database external
  172.16.1.0** command, 597
**show ip ospf database external
  172.20.1.0** command, 597
show ip ospf database network
  command, 526
**show ip ospf database network
  10.2.0.2** command, 488
show ip ospf database router
  command, 490, 529
show ip ospf database router 10.0.0.4
  command, 487, 492
show ip ospf database router 10.0.0.6
  command, 492
show ip ospf database summary
  command, 505, 509
show ip ospf interface command, 484–485
show ip ospf interface Loopback 0
  command, 684
show ip ospf neighbor command, 485–486,
  493, 525, 532

show ip ospf virtual-links command, 515

show ip route command, 181–182, 238–240, 241, 251, 343, 420, 482, 560, 562

show ip route eigrp command, 402, 590

show ip route igrp command, 579, 590

show ip route ospf command, 504, 530, 605, 612

show ip route rip command, 571, 580

show route-map command, 667

show source-bridge command, 156

show spanning command, 173

show spanning 60 command, 173–175

show spanning-tree [*<bridge group number>*] command, 142–147

show standby brief command, 699

show standby command, 701, 705

show standby [*<interface>* [*<group>*]] command, 699

SIA (stuck in active), 378

Simple Mail Transfer Protocol. *See* STMP.

Single route broadcast, 119–121

Smoothed roundtrip time. *See* SRTT.

SMTP (Simple Mail Transfer Protocol), 19

SNA, 148

Sniffer (Network Associates), 428

SnifferPro (Network Associates), 428

Source address, IP header, 34

source-bridge fst-peername *<local IP address>* command, 166

source-bridge *<local ring#><bridge #>* *<virtual ring #>* command, 149

source-bridge remote-peer commands, 154, 159, 161

source-bridge remote-peer *<virtual ring #>* command, 152, 163

source-bridge remote-peer *<virtual ring #>* **frame relay interface** *<interface ID><interface #><DLCI>* command, 160

source-bridge remote-peer *<virtual ring #>* **fst** *<remote IP address>* command, 166

source-bridge remote-peer *<virtual ring #>* **interface** *<interface ID>* *<interface #>* command, 153

source-bridge remote-peer *<virtual ring #>* **tcp** *<local IP address>* command, 163

source-bridge remote-peer *<virtual ring #>* **tcp** *<remote IP address>* command, 163

source-bridge ring-group *<virtual ring #>* command, 149, 152, 160, 163, 166

source-bridge spanning *<bridge group #>* **[path-cost** *<path-cost>*] command, 170

source-bridge spanning command, 167

source-bridge *<this ring #><bridge #>* *<other ring #>* command, 147–148

source-bridge *<this ring #><bridge #>* *<virtual ring #>* command, 154, 161

Source Quench message, 64

Source-route bridged LAN, 112–125, 150

Source-route bridging, 91–92, 112–125
    all routes broadcast, 117–119
    all routes explorer, 117–119
    alternatives to, 123–125
    ARP and, 121–122
    configuring, 147–175
    data link switching (DLSw), 123–125
    IP and, 121–122
    MTU size, 159–160
    multiport source-route bridges, 121, 122, 123
    remote source-route bridging (RSRB), 123, 124
    routes, 116–121
    routing information field (RIF), 114–116
    single route broadcast, 119–121
    spanning explorer, 119–121

Source-route translational bridging, 176–178

Spanning explorers, 119–121, 167–175

Spanning tree, 99

Spanning tree algorithm, 99–107

Spanning tree parameters, tuning, 140–147

Speak state, HSRP state machine, 652–653

Split-horizon with poison reverse, 221, 379

Split-horizon rule, 221–222, 379, 415

SRTT (smoothed roundtrip time), 377

Standard access lists, 81–84

standby [*<group #>*] **ip** [*<IP address>*] command, 696–697

standby [*<group #>*] **preempt** command, 697

standby [*<group #>*] **priority** [*<priority>*] command, 697

standby [<*group #*>] **track** <*interface*> [<*priority decrease*>] command, 697
Standby state, HSRP state machine, 653
Standby timer, 650, 652
Static entries, filtering database, 96
Static mapping, 74
Static NAT, 645
Static routes, 56
   administrative distance, 180, 186–191
   metric, 224
   with output interface, 191–195
Static routing
   configuring, 183–186, 195–198, 200–211
   floating routes, 188
   longest match concept, 198–200
   with output interface, 191–195
   routing table, 180–211
Static translation, of inside IP addresses, configuring, 672–677
Stub areas, configuring OSPF stub areas, 508–510
Stubs, 444
Stub segments, 434
Stuck in active. *See* SIA.
Subinterface, 71, 73–75
Subnet address, 41, 45
Subnet addresses, 226
Subnet ID, 38, 41
Subnet mask, 38, 43, 44
Subnetting, 38–41
Summarization, 441
   auto-summarization, 259–261, 305–312, 384
   classful summarization, 540, 568
   configuring with EIGRP, 416–422
   OSPF, 441
summary-address command, 598, 607
summary-address 172.0.0.0 255.0.0.0 command, 607
summary-address 172.20.0.0 255.252.0.0 command, 600
summary-address 172.20.0.0 255.255.0.0 command, 600
summary-address 192.168.0.0 255.255.0.0 not-advertise command, 600
summary-address <*IP address*><*subnet mask*> **[not-advertise]** command, 598

Summary LSAs, 448, 457–460, 504, 505
Supernets, 40, 41, 45
Support protocols, 19
SVCs (switched virtual circuits), 71
Switches, 91
Switching, 91

T

TCP (Transmission Control Protocol), 18
   configuring RSRB over, 163–165
   protocol number, 33
TCP/IP protocol stack, 20
TCP load balancing, configuring NAT for, 692–696
telnet 10.0.1.100 command, 671
telnet 10.0.1.110 command, 671
telnet 10.1.0.111 command, 199–200
telnet 10.2.0.120 command, 683
terminal ip netmask-format bit-count|decimal|hexadecimal command, 241
Termination Detection for Diffusing Computations (Dijkstra and Scholten), 358
TFTP (Trivial File Transfer Protocol), 19
Time Exceeded message, 65
Timeout, 219
Timeout timer, 233
Timers
   dynamic routing protocol, 299
   HSRP timers, 650
   IGRP timers, 326–327, 356
   RIP timers, 232–234, 297
timers active-time command, 422
timers active-time disabled command, 422
timers active-time <*minutes*>|**disabled** command, 422
timers basic <*update*><*invalid*><*holddown*><*flush*> [<*sleep time*>] command, 299, 356
Time to Live field. *See* TTL field.
Token ring frame, source-route bridging, 112–125
Token ring networks
   MAC addresses, 92–94
   source-route translational bridging, 176–178

Topology change acknowledgment flat, 108
Topology change flag, 109
Topology change notification, bridged
  LANs, 108–109
Topology change notification BPDUs, 99, 112
Topology change timer, 109
Topology table, EIGRP, 391–392
ToS octet, 27–29
ToS routing, 48
ToS value, classless routing algorithm, 50
Total Length Field, IP header, 29
Totally not-so-stubby area, 601
Totally stubby area, 509, 601
traceroute command, 517, 662
traceroute 10.0.1.100 command, 671
traceroute 10.0.1.110 command, 671
traceroute 10.1.0.1 command, 306–307
traceroute 10.100.0.1 command, 709
tracert -d 10.0.1.1 command, 577, 623
tracert -d 10.0.1.2 command, 663
tracert -d 10.0.8.1 command, 577, 623
tracert -d 10.2.1.120 command, 663
Traffic filtering. *See* Filtering.
Trailer
  CRC, 19
  data link protocols, 16
Transit area, 465
Translational bridging, 131
Transmission Control Protocol. *See* TCP.
Transparent bridging, 91
  blocking state, 99, 107–108
  bridging protocol, 99
  configuring, 126–147
  filtering database, 96–99
  forwarding state, 99, 107–108
  learning, 107
  listening, 107
  mixed-media transparent bridging, 131
  MTU size, 160
  no reverse forwarding, 95
  spanning tree algorithm, 99–105
  topology change notification, 108–109
  transition from blocking to forwarding,
    107–108
Transport layer
  internet communication model, 18
  Internet Protocol suite, 21
  OSI/RM, 16–17, 18

Triggered updates, 223–224
Trivial File Transfer Protocol. *See* TFTP.
TTL field (Time to Live field), IP header,
  32–33
tunnel destination <*IP address*>
  command, 78
Tunnel interface, 77–78
tunnel source <*Interface*> command, 78
tunnel source <*IP address*> command, 78
2-Way state, 467
Type 1 LSAs, 448, 453–456, 463
Type 2 LSAs, 448, 456–457, 463
Type 3 LSAs, 448, 457–460, 463, 504, 505
Type 4 LSAs, 448, 457–460, 463
Type 5 LSAs, 448, 461, 463, 552–553, 595,
  598, 605, 606, 684
Type 7 LSAs, 448, 461, 463, 552–553, 605, 606
Type field, ICMP control message, 61
Type of Service field, IP header, 27, 28

U

UDP (User Datagram Protocol), 18, 33
Unequal-cost load balancing, 224
  configuring with static routing, 208–211
  EIGRP, 384
  IGRP, 325–326, 344–349
Unicast IP address, 35
Unicast IP routing, 46–61
  filtering, 60–61
  IP routers, 47–48
  routing algorithms, 48–55
  routing protocols, 58–59
  routing tables, 55–58
Unicast MAC addresses, 93
User Datagram Protocol. *See* UDP.
User protocols, 19

V

variance <*multiplier*> command, 346
Version field, IP header, 26
Vertices, 428, 462
Virtual bridge, 126
Virtual IP address, 646
Virtual links, 445–446, 511–522
Virtual MAC address, 646, 654–655

Virtual rings, 121–123, 149–150
Virtual Router Redundancy Protocol.
  See VRRP.
Virtual server IP addresses, 693
Virtual Terminal (VT), 17
VRRP (Virtual Router Redundancy
  Protocol), 646
VT. *See* Virtual Terminal.

W

Waiting state, 465
Weak ToS, 50–52

lated Coriolis Technology Press Titles

Open Source Development with CVS

By Karl Fogel
ISBN: 1-57610-490-7
$39.99 US • $58.99 CAN
Media: None • Available Now

Learn the best practices of open source software development with CVS—a tool that allows several individuals to work simultaneously on the document. CVS is covered in detail, as is the ense, software design and development, tyles, documentation procedures, testing, of software, and troubleshooting.

HTML Black Book

By Steven Holzner
ISBN: 1-57610-617-9
Price: $59.99 US • $89.99 CAN
Media: CD-ROM • Available Now

Explores HTML programming thoroughly, from the essentials up through issues of security, providing step-by-step solutions to everyday challenges. This comprehensive guide discusses HTML in-depth, as well as covering XML, dynamic XML, JavaScript, Java, Perl, and CGI programming, to create a full Web site programming package.

Java Black Book

By Steven Holzner
ISBN: 1-57610-531-8
Price: $49.99 US • $74.99 CAN
Media: CD-ROM • Available Now

A comprehensive reference filled with examples, tips, and problem-solving solutions. Discusses the Java language, Abstract Windowing Toolkit, Swing, Java 2D, advanced ns, the Java Database Connectivity Package, internalization and security, streams and and more.

The Mac OS 9 Book

By Mark R. Bell
ISBN: 1-57610-776-0
Price: $39.99 US • $59.99 CAN
Media: MacAddict CD-ROM • Available Now

In-depth coverage of powerful new technologies—including improvements and bug fixes in 9.0.4—and over 50 new features available in Mac OS 9. Includes trouble-shooting tips to help beginners and intermediate users utilize important new features and leverage the Internet using this newer, more robust OS.

Game Architecture and Design

By Andrew Rollings and Dave Morris
ISBN: 1-57610-425-7
Price: $49.99 US • $74.99 CAN
Media: CD-ROM • Available Now

Teaches design principles, architecture, and project management, and provides real-life case studies of what works and what doesn't. bject-oriented design, core design, game-game balance. Written for PC, Mac, and tforms.

Windows® 2000 Professional Upgrade Little Black Book

By Nathan Wallace
ISBN: 1-57610-748-5
Price: $29.99 US • $44.99 CAN
Media: None • Available Now

This book includes complete guidance on newly introduced technologies to help administrators upgrade or migrate users of Windows 9x, NT 4, Unix and Macintosh. Covers advanced features of Windows 2000 Professional using a concise task-oriented approach for quickly accessing solutions.

IE CORIOLIS GROUP, LLC   Telephone: 800.410.0192 • www.coriolis.com
Coriolis books are also available at bookstores and computer stores nationwide.

Related Coriolis Technology Press Tit

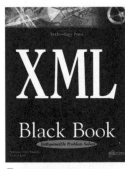
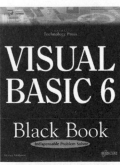

indows® 2000 Titles from Coriolis

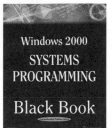

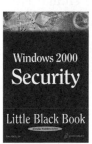
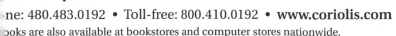

What's on the CD-ROM

The *Cisco Routers for IP Networking Black Book* companion CD-ROM contains Requests For Comments (RFCs) specifically selected to enhance the usefulness of this book.

System Requirements

Software

- Windows 95/98/NT or Macintosh System 8 or higher.

Hardware

- An Intel (or equivalent) Pentium 100MHz processor is the minimum platform required; an Intel (or equivalent) Pentium 133MHz processor is recommended.
- RAM: 32MB of RAM is the minimum requirement.